THE GUINNESS BOOK OF

NUMBER ONE HITS

Paul Gambaccini

Tim Rice and Jo Rice

Editorial Associates: Nick Todd and Tony Brown

GUINNESS BOOKS

ACKNOWLEDGEMENTS

The three authors would like to thank all those who have helped in the production of this book, in particular Justin Green, Graham Walker, Mark Shaoul, the BBC Hulton Picture Library and London Features International. Special thanks are also due to Eileen Heinink, Jan Rice, Fay Rawlinson, and Carol Hughes.

We also thank *Music Week* and *New Musical Express*. The first best-selling record chart was published in *New Musical Express* on 14 November 1952, consisting of a list of just 15 singles. The *NME* chart increased over the years to a top 30, but on 10 March 1960 the trade publication *Record Retailer* (now *Music Week*) published the first UK top 50 singles chart. The *Music Week* chart, compiled by Gallup and used by the BBC, is now accepted as the country's premier chart. This book uses the *NME* chart until 10 March 1960 (the first 96 number ones) and the *RR/MW* chart thereafter.

Editor: Honor Head   Design: David Roberts
Picture Editor: Alex Goldberg

Typeset in Rockwell by SX Composing Limited, Rayleig
Printed and bound in Great Britain by Adlard & Sons Ltd
worth
'Guinness' is a registered trade mark of Guinness Publish

British Library Cataloguing in Publication Dat

Gambaccini, Paul
The Guinness book of number one hits. — 2nd
1. Music, Popular (Songs, etc.) — Great Britain — Disco
I. Title   II. Rice, Tim   III. Rice, Jo
IV. The Guinness book of 500 number one hits
016.7899'1245   ML156.4.P6

ISBN 0-85112-893-9

CONTENTS

Acknowledgements

Introduction

PART ONE

The full story of each hit, listed chronologically, with artist details. Information includes song writer and producer, catalogue number, plus the date the record reached the top and the number of weeks at number one. **Page 7**

PART TWO

The number ones listed alphabetically by artist, with chronological title list showing the date a record reached number one, its label, catalogue number and the weeks spent on top of the chart. **Page 223**

PART THREE

The number ones listed alphabetically by record title, showing the name of the artist and the chronological reference number. **Page 239**

PART FOUR

The Statistics including Most Number One Hits, Most Weeks At Number One, Most Successful Producers, Most Successful Writers, Most Successful Record Labels, Most Successful Songs, and much more. **Page 249**

INTRODUCTION
INTRODUCTION
INTRODUCTION
INTRODUCTION
INTRODUCTION

Thirty five years ago, at the end of November 1952, when the Queen had been on the throne for scarcely nine months and Winston Churchill was still Prime Minister, a revolution occurred in the leisure industry. A British newspaper, the *New Musical Express*, published a chart listing fifteen best-selling records in Britain the previous week.

As prosperity very slowly returned to Britain after the war, people became more interested in buying records to play on their newly acquired gramophones rather than the sheet music of songs to play on their pianos at home or at school. This switch in the balance of power away from the music publishers and towards the record companies was given a further shove by the record charts which created interest in particular recordings of songs rather than in the songs themselves. Although in the first few years of the record charts there were frequently several different versions of the same song listed in the Top 20, the recording artist rather than the song became the factor in record sales.

The development of the record chart was a logical addition to the sheet music charts that already existed and to the American record charts which had, since the war, become the standard for the industry. However, it was two other revolutions, one social and one technical, that really turned the music business from a pastime into an industry. The social revolution was simply peace. A generation grew up that did not know what war was like and who, therefore, did not have the background of discipline and group consciousness that the generations that fought in two World Wars took for granted. The logical answer was rebellion against their parents, and the simplest form of rebellion was in their leisure interests. The form the rebellion took was rock and roll.

The technical revolution has taken many forms. The first major breakthrough was the development of the unbreakable 7 inch single, which displaced the 10 inch 78 in the latter half of the '50s. This gave the record industry a firm base, as the public did not begrudge spending 6s 8d (about 33p) for a single that would last, even if some fool sat on it. The technical revolution has been going on at a regular pace since then, spurred on by public demand for better sound (stereo, compact discs) and cheaper and longer lasting playing equipment (transistors, diamond styli). The revolution has also spread to the musical instruments themselves, so that in the '80s, almost every record that hits the charts (Flying Pickets excepted) features at least one synthesized sound, whether it is a rhythm section or a keyboard sound. It is ironic, then, that of the 100 hits that have topped the

INTRODUCTION
INTRODUCTION
INTRODUCTION
INTRODUCTION
INTRODUCTION

charts since our *500 Number One Hits* was published five years ago, two were recorded over 25 years ago and another pair were the first *a cappella* chart toppers in British chart history.

The revolution that the record charts have noted week by week has, if anything, speeded up over the past few years. Technology has turned the record companies into leisure industries, and videos, albums and every variation of 12 inch mix are essential ingredients in the success of the single. However, even after 35 years, the ultimate achievement in popular music is still a number one hit.

The Number One Hits brings the story up to the end of 1987, but just as in 1982, when Nicole chalked up the 500th chart-topping single, it is impossible to say that the charts follow any set pattern. The most recent 100 chart toppers have included the entire catalogue of number one hits of chart record-breakers like Madonna and Wham!, but they also include such totally unexpected hits as Jackie Wilson's 1957 disc *Reet Petite* and the novelties *Chicken Song* and *Star Trekkin'*. Where is the logical path of chart history if those are the stepping stones?

There is still no room for a solo hit by Elton John, even though we detail the greatest hits of both Rolf Harris and Nick Berry. Renée and Renato are here but U2 are not. Marvin Rainwater's contribution to our charts gets a mention, but Ricky Nelson, Billy Fury, Bruce Springsteen and Simple Minds all miss out. David Bowie manages three solo hits and two others in partnership firstly with Queen and then with Mick Jagger, but his total of five number ones is insignificant compared with the 17 achieved by the Beatles and Elvis Presley. Can that total ever be overtaken, unless a posthumous Elvis single adds to his tally, or an old Beatles track is re-issued with ultimate success? We doubt it, but then we never thought that Gerry and the Pacemakers' record of three number ones with their first three releases could be equalled, and Frankie Goes To Hollywood proved us wrong.

We very much hope we can continue the story, not only in our regular biennial publication *British Hit Singles*, but also in future editions of *The Number One Hits*. As long as people still want to buy singles, which remain the ultimate test of a performer's popularity, the story will be updated once a week with the publication of the singles chart.

PAUL GAMBACCINI · JO RICE · TIM RICE

THE AUTHORS

THE AUTHORS

THE AUTHORS

THE AUTHORS

PAUL GAMBACCINI figures that since *Who's Who* won't have him he might as well tell you about himself here.

Born in the Bronx, he graduated from Dartmouth College (New Hampshire) and University College (Oxford) and has lived in London since 1975. His life heroes are Carl Barks, Willie Mays, Artur Rubinstein and whoever is at number one next week.

TIM RICE celebrated his 100th week on the UK singles chart as a writer in 1987. He enjoys a number one hit single at intervals of exactly eight years. His third is therefore due in February 1993 and will be recorded by a female trio, continuing the long-established tradition that each Tim Rice chart-topper is sung by an act containing one more girl than the previous one. Before this remarkable display of consistency his links with number one singles were through his post as personal assistant to the late Norrie Paramor, producer of no less than 27 of them, a record equalled only by George Martin.

JO RICE was born under the sign of Aquarius, and like all typical Aquarians, he is tall, left-handed and lives by the English Channel. He was also born in the Year Of The Wild Boar, according to the Chinese zodiac, and therefore also displays all the characteristics of an Oriental pig. His collection of British number one hits is now almost complete, although if anybody has any Stargazers 78s they wish to part with, he might be interested.

THE AUTHORS

THE AUTHORS

THE AUTHORS

THE AUTHORS

PART 1

The Number Ones Listed Chronologically
The Facts and Stories

1

HERE IN MY HEART

AL MARTINO

14 November 1952, for nine weeks

●●●●●●●●●

Capitol CL 13779

Written by Pat Genaro, Lou Levinson and Bill Borelli. Produced by Voyle Gilmore.

Al Martino's career was at its height when the *New Musical Express* established the record sales chart on 14 November 1952. *Here In My Heart* was at the top for the first nine weeks of the new chart, setting a record for the longest continuous run at number one which even after 35 years has only been beaten twice. By staying at number one until 1953, Martino secured for himself for all time the record of being the only performer to have a number one hit in 1952. Needless to say, no subsequent act has ever dominated the top spot so entirely in any later year. All the same, Martino was not the top chart act of 1952 in terms of weeks on chart. That honour fell to Vera Lynn, who clocked up ten chart weeks in the seven final weeks of the year.

Al Martino, born Alfred Cini in Philadelphia on 7 October 1927, faded from the charts after his version of *The Man From Laramie* made the Top 20 late in 1955. His strong US comeback in the mid-'60s did not impress UK buyers, but they came around in the end. After Martino's strong performance as the Mafia-owned night club singer in *The Godfather* he had a Top 5 hit in 1973 with *Spanish Eyes*.

On 25 November 1952, 11 days after the British singles chart was instituted, another British cultural phenomenon began. *The Mousetrap* opened in London.

2

YOU BELONG TO ME

JO STAFFORD

16 January 1953, for one week

●

Columbia DB 3152

Written by PeeWee King, Red Stewart and Chilton Price. Produced by Paul Weston.

You Belong To Me came on the chart on 14 November 1952 and made number one in its tenth week on the chart. This is no longer the slowest climb to the top, that record currently belonging to Jennifer Rush (see no. 558), who took 16 weeks to climb through the Top 75 in 1985. But as the chart in 1952 and 1953 was only a Top 12, Miss Stafford certainly took her time to climb up the final few rungs of the ladder.

In her one week at the top, Jo Stafford claimed for herself for all time the title of first female performer at number one. Forty-six solo female vocalists and one female instrumentalist (Winifred Atwell, see nos. 26 and 45) have followed Miss Stafford to number one, not counting female members of goups such as Stargazers, Abba, Blondie and Pretenders. *You Belong To Me* was also an American number one and the biggest selling record of Jo Stafford's career.

Paul Weston, who produced the record and whose orchestra backed Jo on this and practically all her records from the time she left the Tommy Dorsey Orchestra in 1942, was also her husband. *You Belong To Me* became the first chart topping single whose singer and producer were husband and wife.

Make Love To Me, Jo Stafford's only other

Here In My Heart was **Al Martino's** *first hit in the US and a number one there, too.*

Top 10 hit in Britain, was also her final US chart-topper in 1954. Her last week on the British charts was from 3 February 1956, 14 weeks before Elvis Presley first hit the charts.

Jo Stafford

Kay Starr *signs autographs for disabled war veterans in London.*

3

COMES A-LONG
A-LOVE

KAY STARR

23 January 1953, for one week

●

Capitol CL 13876

Written by Al Sherman. Produced by Mitch Miller.

Kay Starr shares with Marvin Rainwater (see no. 70) the distinction of being the only full-blooded American Indian to have reached number one in Britain. Johnnie Ray and Cher also have Indian blood flowing in their veins, but not as many pints of it as Kay or Marvin.

Kay Starr was born Katherine Starks on 21 July 1922 on an Oklahoman Indian reservation and began her career in the 1940s singing with the Glenn Miller, Bob Crosby and Charlie Barnet big bands. She moved away from the big band sound towards a more countrified sound by recording a few titles with Tennessee Ernie Ford in the early '50s. One of their duets, *I'll Never Be Free*, reached number 3 on the US charts, but that was in 1950, before the British charts began. Her biggest American hit came in 1952 with the million-selling *Wheel Of Fortune*, a Stateside number one. By then her music had become more middle of the road. *Comes A-Long A-Love* only reached num-

ber 9 in her home country but it gave both Miss Starr and super-producer Mitch Miller their first number one on this side of the Atlantic. Before Kay Starr's final hit (see no. 44), her other British chart entries were two standards, *Side By Side* and *Changing Partners*, and a real country tune, *Am I A Toy Or A Treasure*.

4

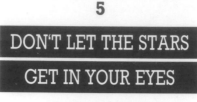

OUTSIDE OF HEAVEN

EDDIE FISHER

30 January 1953, for one week

●

HMV B 10362

Written by Sammy Gallop and Chester Conn. Produced by Hugo Winterhalter.

The chart was just getting into its stride as January moved to a close. After Al Martino's nine week run at the top Eddie Fisher's first number one was the third consecutive chart-topper to stay only one week at the top. This meant that for five consecutive weeks there was a different record at the top. This has never happened again.

Edwin Jack Fisher was born on 10 August 1928 in Philadelphia, and although he is better known in the 1980s as an ex-husband of Elizabeth Taylor, he was at the time of his first UK chart-topper married to Debbie Reynolds. Their daughter, Carrie Fisher, went on to star as Princess Leia in the Star Wars movies and marry Paul Simon (see no. 283).

Eddie Fisher first appeared on radio in 1940 as a member of the cast of *The Magic Lady Slipper Club* on station WFIL in Philadelphia. Eddie Cantor took him under his wing, and by the time he was 21 he had signed a recording contract with RCA Victor. His army call-up came only a short time later and he spent much of his army career entertaining the troops in Korea. He was still in the army when *Outside Of Heaven* hit the top, and he was not discharged until 10 April 1953. In June that year, he performed at the Savoy, where Princess Margaret sent a message backstage to request her favourite song of the time, *Outside Of Heaven*.

5

DON'T LET THE STARS GET IN YOUR EYES

PERRY COMO

6 February 1953, for five weeks

● ● ● ● ●

HMV B 10400

Written by Slim Willet. Produced by Eli Oberstein.

Born on 18 May 1912 in Canonsburg, Pennsylvania, 'The Singing Barber', as Perry Como became known, is one of the most long-lasting of all performers on the British charts. He began his singing career in the 1930s with the Freddie Carlone Band. His first major success was singing *Deep In The Heart Of Texas* with Ted Weems and his orchestra in 1942. After the war he began to come up with big hits, starting with *Till The End Of Time*, his first US number one, in 1945. *Don't Let The Stars Get In Your Eyes* had originally been a country hit for the composer Slim Willet in addition to Pat Boone's father-in-law, Red Foley, as well as Skeets McDonald and Ray Price. Gisele McKenzie and Eileen Barton also hit with the song on the pop charts in the States, as did Como and Foley.

Como hit a blank chart period in Britain for over a year after this first hit dropped off the charts in April 1953, but three more hits in the latter half of 1954 re-established him as a chart star. By the time of his second number one hit, *Magic Moments* (see no. 69), he had become the world's highest paid television star in succession to the man he took over from at the top of the British charts, Eddie Fisher.

6

SHE WEARS RED FEATHERS

GUY MITCHELL

13 March 1953, for four weeks

● ● ● ●

Columbia DB 3238

Written by Bob Merrill. Produced by Mitch Miller.

The inexhaustibly successful early 50s team of Bob Merrill, Mitch Miller and Guy Mitchell came up with an astonishing run of successes in the first years of the chart. *She Wears Red Feathers* was their first number one. Of Guy Mitchell's first eight hits in UK, six were written by Bob Merrill and all were produced by Mitch Miller and his team at Columbia (CBS) in America.

Guy Mitchell (real name Al Cernik) was born on 27 February 1927. His parents had emigrated from Yugoslavia. Mitchell made a name for himself as a child actor before the war. By the 1950s he had given up acting for singing, and was hugely popular all over the world. *She Wears Red Feathers* was his second success in the UK, following the number 2 hit *Feet Up (Pat Him On The Po-Po)*, which set the pattern of bouncy sentimentality for which Merrill, Miller and Mitchell became rich and famous. *She Wears Red Feathers* was a bizarre tale of an English banker's love for a hula-hula girl, a story line which may explain why the record did so much better in Britain than in the US, where it peaked at number 19. The formula was repeated with less success in a later song, *Chick-A-Boom*, which extolled the virtues of a rich Eskimo lady and which Mitchell took to number 4 early in 1954.

A fan is awestruck meeting **Lita Roza** in her dressing room. Lita's How Much Is That Doggie In The Window was the first of 23 number ones to contain a question in the title (see pg. 12).

7

BROKEN WINGS

THE STARGAZERS

10 April 1953, for one week

●

Decca F 10047

Written by John Jerome and Bernard Gunn.
Produced by Dick Rowe.

A British act hit the number one position for the first time 21 weeks after the chart was established. This period of British weakness does not compare with the dominance of American acts from July 1957 to November 1958, when only two weeks of Michael Holliday (see no. 68) interrupted 70 weeks of American number ones, but it was long enough to make the emergence of the first British number one an important day in chart history. The group in question was The Stargazers, in the early '50s Britain's most popular – indeed almost only – vocal group.

Three versions of *Broken Wings* made the charts in UK, although no version hit the pop charts in the song's homeland America. The Stargazers' version was the first cover version of any song to hit the top, but the original by Art and Dotty Todd, as well as another cover by Dickie Valentine, both hit the charts. A different song of the same title gave a big hit to the American band, Mr. Mister, in 1986.

Art and Dotty Todd suffered from cover versions as badly as Ray Peterson, the original recorder of both *Tell Laura I Love Her* and *The Wonder Of You*. Art and Dotty were first with *Broken Wings* and with another song that they took into the Top 20 charts in America, *Chanson D'Amour*. All four titles became British number ones by different artists.

(HOW MUCH IS) THAT DOGGIE IN THE WINDOW

LITA ROZA

17 April 1953, for one week

●

Decca F 10070

Written by Bob Merrill. Produced by Dick Rowe.

The first question to be asked from the number one spot was also probably the silliest. Twenty-two other questions have been asked over the years by number ones, deep philosophical questions like *Da Ya Think I'm Sexy?* and *Are 'Friends' Electric?* but nobody else has asked how much anything is. For an industry in which money is the Holy Grail, it is surprising how unsuccessful money songs have been. Abba and the Bay City Rollers both failed to hit number one with money songs when they were at the peaks of their careers, and apart from this burning question only a handful of songs, like *Can't Buy Me Love* and *Sixteen Tons*, have dealt with money in any way and still made it to the very top. There must be a moral there somewhere.

For Lita Roza, whose record was a cover of Patti Page's original, this was the peak of her recording career. Producer Dick Rowe became the first of eleven producers or production teams to achieve two consecutive number ones, and Bob Merrill became the first writer to come up with two number ones.

On 19 April, the first *New Musical Express* Poll Winners' Concert took place at the Royal Albert Hall. Lita Roza was there as Top Female Vocalist. Her employer Ted Heath was leader of the Dance Band of the Year.

Frankie Laine is welcomed to Battersea Park by his fan club presidents in 1953, while I Believe *was in the midst of its historic number one run.*

I BELIEVE

FRANKIE LAINE

24 April 1953, for nine weeks
3 July 1953, for six weeks
21 August 1953, for three weeks

● ● ● ● ● ● ● ● ●
● ● ● ● ● ● ● ● ●

Philips PB 117

Written by Erwin Drake, Irvin Graham, Jimmy Shirl and Al Stillman. Produced by Mitch Miller.

Frankie Laine's quasi-religious hit *I Believe* broke all number one longevity records and after 591 successors still holds the record for most weeks on top. Although two records subsequently stayed at number one for longer than nine consecutive weeks, no record has approached the 18 weeks in total for which this record was number one. During those weeks Queen Elizabeth was crowned, Mount Everest was climbed for the first time and the England cricket team won back the Ashes from Australia after 19 years.

No disc has matched the record of *I Believe* in having three separate runs at number one, although Guy Mitchell's *Singing The Blues* (see no. 53) almost did. No artist has matched Frankie Laine's 27 weeks at number one in 1953, a year in which his discs notched up a total of 66 weeks on the chart, more than any of his rivals. Laine's success was mainly responsible for a run from 24 April 1953 to 1 January 1954 during which time the Philips label retained the top spot for 34 out of 37 weeks, a domination by a single company that has never been equalled.

I Believe was revived by David Whitfield in 1960 and by the Bachelors in 1964 to give the tune a total of 54 weeks on the chart, the eleventh most successful song in British chart history.

*Everything looked just ducky when **Eddie Fisher** and fiancée Debbie Reynolds took a Thameside stroll in 1955 (see over).*

10

I'M WALKING BEHIND YOU

EDDIE FISHER

26 June 1953, for one week

●

HMV B 10489

Written by Billy Reid. Produced by Hugo Winterhalter.

Eddie Fisher became the first performer to achieve a second British number one when *I'm Walking Behind You* ousted *I Believe* for one week. Like *Outside Of Heaven*, the song dealt with lost love. In this lyric British-born Billy Reid pictured Mr Fisher walking behind his love down the aisle as she prepares to marry somebody else.

This was to be Eddie Fisher's last number one, although he had four more Top 10 entries stretching to early 1957, when *Cindy Oh Cindy* dropped off the charts. By that time Tommy Steele had reached the top with *Singing The Blues* (see no. 54) and British pop music was gradually changing irreversibly.

I'm Walking Behind You gave Dorothy Squires one week of chart glory with her cover version, but it was to be 16 years before she would reappear in the list as a solo act. Eddie Fisher's version also reached number one in the States, becoming his fifth million-selling single. He was at this time hosting the American TV show *Coke Time* and by his own admission making around $25,000 a week. He had a network of 65,000 fan clubs around the world, and for a time walked behind no one.

11

MOULIN ROUGE

MANTOVANI AND HIS ORCHESTRA

14 August 1953, for one week

●

Decca F 10094

Written by Georges Auric. Produced by Frank Lee.

The first instrumental to top the charts was the theme tune from the film *Moulin Rouge*

(subtitled *Where Is Your Heart?*) by the legendary British orchestra of Mantovani. Only 25 more instrumentals have reached the number one spot, less than one in twenty of all number ones.

Annunzio Paulo Mantovani was born in Venice, Italy on 15 November 1905 and moved to England with his parents in 1921. By the 1930s he had formed his own orchestra, which became known for its 'cascading strings'. In the 1940s he began recording with Decca. He immediately became immensely popular on record as he had long been on radio. In 1951 he recorded an album aimed at the American market. It was a huge hit, and a single from the LP, *Charmaine*, reached the US Top 10 and sold over one million copies.

Two years later, with no sign of his popularity fading, Mantovani recorded the theme from *Moulin Rouge*, the film which starred José Ferrer as the French painter Henri de Toulouse Lautrec. Percy Faith had the biggest hit version in the States, but Mantovani also hit their Top 10. Both versions sold over a million,. Mantovani, who also backed David Whitfield on virtually all of his recordings, died on 31 March 1981.

12

LOOK AT THAT GIRL

GUY MITCHELL

11 September 1953, for six weeks

●●●●●●

Philips PB 162

Written by Bob Merrill. Produced by Mitch Miller.

When Frankie Laine's *I Believe* finally relinquished the top spot it let in Guy Mitchell for his second number one. Mitchell's first four chart singles produced two number two hits and two number ones, and his chart career rolled on with fabulous success from 14 November 1952 until July 1957 when for the first time a Guy Mitchell single failed to make the Top 20. By then he had scored four number ones and seven other Top 10 hits, a track record almost as good as that of label mate Frankie Laine.

Annunzio Paolo **Mantovani***, the first orchestra leader to get a UK number one and the first musician to sell a million stereo albums.*

Once again it was the team of Merrill, Miller and Mitchell that created the record. It was their last chart topper together. Interestingly, the record failed to chart at all in the United States.

One girl at whom part of America was looking during the autumn of 1953 was Jacqueline Bouvier, who on 12 September became Mrs John Fitzgerald Kennedy.

13

HEY JOE

FRANKIE LAINE

23 October 1953, for two weeks

●●

Philips PB 172

Written by Boudleaux Bryant. Produced by Mitch Miller.

In direct contrast to his massively longlasting *I Believe*, Frankie Laine's second number one only stayed in the chart for eight weeks, having reached the number one position in its second week on the chart. That week Frankie Laine had three singles on the list, which was only a Top 12 at the time. *I Believe* was in its 31st week of chart action, *Where The Wind Blows* (a number two hit) was in its eighth week and *Hey Joe* was at the top of the heap. The next week, 30 October 1953, Frankie Laine's third number one *Answer Me* (see no. 15) entered the chart, and for the next three weeks Frankie Laine singles occupied four of the Top 12 chart positions, giving the Chicagoan one third of all the records on the chart, a feat that cannot be equalled in these days of a Top 75.

Hey Joe is not of course, the same song as the one that gave Jimi Hendrix his first hit in 1967. It is a country-tinged ditty in which the singer gives Joe due warning that he intends to steal his girlfriend away from him. It was also the first number one to be written by Boudleaux Bryant, whose main success was to come a few years later, when he started writing songs with his wife Felice, for the Everly Brothers.

14

ANSWER ME

DAVID WHITFIELD

6 November 1953, for one week
11 December 1953, top equal for one week

●●

Decca F 10192

Written by Gerhard Winkler and Fred Rauch, English lyrics by Carl Sigman. Produced by Bunny Lewis.

David Whitfield, the biggest-selling British vocalist of the mid-'50s, began his chart career at the beginning of October 1953 with a ballad called *Bridge Of Sighs*. Two weeks later his version of *Answer Me* hit the chart, two weeks ahead of Frankie Laine's recording, and within three weeks David Whitfield had his first number one. On 13 November, for the first but not the only time in chart history, one version of a song was knocked off the top by another version of the same song. Four weeks later, for the only time in British chart history, the two versions of the same song were at number one together. Eleven songs (*Answer Me, Cherry Pink and Apple Blossom White, Everything I Own, I Got You Babe, Living Doll, Mary's Boy Child, Singing The Blues, Spirit In The Sky, This Ole House, You'll Never Walk Alone, Young Love*) have made number one in two different versions. None of the other ten has been on the chart in as many as four versions. Ray Peterson, this time covering an original rather than vice versa, hit the UK chart for the only time in his career with *Answer Me* in 1960, and Barbara Dickson gave the song its third Top 10 outing in 1976.

15

ANSWER ME

FRANKIE LAINE

13 November 1953, for eight weeks
(11 December 1953, top equal)

●●●●●●●●

Philips PB 196

Written by Gerhard Winkler and Fred Rauch, English lyrics by Carl Sigman. Produced by Mitch Miller.

Frankie Laine rounded off an astonishing period of chart success by becoming the first act to have three number ones, the first act to hit number one with consecutive releases, and still the only man in chart history to have spent as many as 27 weeks of any calendar year in the top slot. Nobody else has ever managed more than 18 weeks at number one in a year. Elvis Presley achieved that in 1961.

Frankie Laine was born Frank Lovecchio in Chicago on 30 March 1913. Early publicity handouts talk of his holding the all time marathon dance record of 145 days, set in 1932. However, his hold on that record must have been much shorter than his strangle hold on the top of the British charts in 1953, because according to our sister publication the *Guinness Book Of Records* the marathon dancing record was set at 173 days on 30 November 1932, by two dancers, neither of whom was Frank Lovecchio. However, it may have been marathon dancing that ruined his clothes. On one trip to Britain a reviewer criticized his clothing, which led Laine to reply from the stage that 'they can criticize my voice, but not my tailor'.

Answer Me was known in its original German as *Mutterlein*. The feat of placing top equal with itself on the British charts is all the more amazing for the fact that the BBC banned the English language version because of its semi-religious lyric (a fate which had not befallen the equally semi-religious *I Believe*). Nat 'King' Cole brought out a version which changed the lyric from 'Answer me, oh my Lord', to 'Answer me, oh my love', and his version was much more successful than Laine's in the US. In Britain, Cole missed out altogether.

OH MEIN PAPA

EDDIE CALVERT

8 January 1954, for nine weeks

●●●●●●●●●

Columbia DB 3337

Written by Paul Burkhard, English lyrics by John Turner and Geoffrey Parsons. Produced by Norrie Paramor.

British trumpeter Eddie Calvert, 'The Man With The Golden Trumpet', scored his first and biggest hit with the sentimental Swiss tune *Oh Mein Papa*. Most of the lyrics had been excised. A female chorus wistfully sang the title from time to time behind Calvert's vigorous trumpet, but listeners who could not stomach the treacle of the lyrics in Eddie Fisher's vocal version could keep their emotions in check by buying the Calvert arrangement.

Eddie Fisher, who decided to record the song as soon as he heard the title, took the record to number one in the United States, where Calvert had to be content with climbing only as far as number 6. On this side of the Atlantic the positions were reversed, with Fisher reaching number 9 and Eddie Calvert touching the very top. The lyrics, originally in German for the Swiss musical film *Fireworks*, were described by Eddie Fisher as 'pure schmaltz, but somehow they touched everyone'. Since the Calvert version was almost lyricless we can only assume that the great British public preferred to be untouched.

The record has a further claim to fame as the first number one hit recorded at the most successful of all British studios, Abbey Road. At least 75 of the 600 number ones have been recorded there.

I SEE THE MOON

THE STARGAZERS

12 March 1954, for five weeks
23 April 1954, for one week

●●●●●●

Decca F 10213

Written by Meredith Wilson. Produced by Dick Rowe.

In taking *I See The Moon* to number one the Stargazers became the first of twelve acts in British chart history to reach number one with their first two chart hits. Like three others of those twelve (Tennessee Ernie Ford, Art Garfunkel and the man that the Stargazers displaced at the top, Eddie Calvert), the Stargazers' number ones were not with consecutive releases. All the singles between *Broken Wings* and *I See The Moon* missed the charts.

The Stargazers were led by Cliff Adams, the man who a few years later had a small hit with the tune from the Strand cigarettes TV advertisement, *The Lonely Man Theme*. At that time Cliff Adams became the top act alphabetically in chart history, taking over from Alfi and Harry, who had led the list for four years. Cliff Adams stayed at the head of the alphabetical list for 14 years until current champions Abba debuted with *Waterloo* (see no. 348). Cliff Adams is also famous for years of *Sing Something Simple* with his Cliff Adams Singers on BBC Radio. The other Stargazers were Marie Benson, Fred Datchler, Bob Brown and Dave Carey.

I See The Moon was at the top of the chart when on 31 March 1954, the Soviet Union made one of its more bizarre postwar attempts to reduce tension in Europe by offering to become a member of NATO. The offer was refused.

SECRET LOVE

DORIS DAY

16 April 1954, for one week
7 May 1954, for eight weeks

●●●●●●●●●

Philips PB 230

Written by Paul Francis Webster and Sammy Fain. Produced by Ray Heindorf.

Doris Day, born Doris Kappelhoff on 3 April 1922, was by far the most successful female vocalist of the early 1950s. Her two number ones (see also no. 49) remain two of the best-known songs of the pre-rock era, though some of her sillier songs from the Mitch Miller production line, like *Ooh Bang Jiggily Jang*, failed to prise open the purse strings of the record buying public.

Secret Love won the Oscar for Best Original Song of 1953 and came from the film *Calamity Jane*, starring Doris Day and Howard Keel. The film was an enormous box-office success, justifying Miss Day's belief that the producers of *Annie Get Your Gun* were wrong not to cast her in the title role. The success of the film owed much to Howard Keel, who was then one of the top Hollywood musical stars with hits like *Seven Brides For Seven Brothers* to his credit. In the 1980s he found further fame and fortune playing Miss Ellie's second husband, Clayton Farlowe, in the TV megasoap *Dallas*. Doris Day, who had first hit the American charts in the late '40s, continued a recording and film career throughout the '50s and early '60s. She earned the title of Top Box Office Star as a result of her light comedies with Rock Hudson. The theme song of one of those movies, *Move Over Darling*, was a Top 10 hit in 1964 and reappeared in the charts in 1987 as a result of being featured in a television commercial for tights.

There was 'such a night' for world athletics that week. On the evening of 6 May 1954, Roger Bannister completed four laps of the Iffley Road track at Oxford in 3 minues 59.4 seconds, becoming the first man to break the four minute mile.

20

CARA MIA

DAVID WHITFIELD
with chorus and
Mantovani and his
orchestra

2 July 1954, for ten weeks
●●●●●●●●●●
Decca F 10327

Written by Lee Lange and Tulio Tropani.
Produced by Bunny Lewis.

David Whitfield's second number one was one of the biggest selling British records of the pre-rock era, moving well over a million copies. Whitfield joined Dame Vera Lynn in the ranks of British stars who had achieved a Top 10 hit in America. At home the ten week run at the top was then the longest run of consecutive weeks at the top, and 580 hits later Whitfield still takes second place only to Slim Whitman (see no. 36).

The writers of *Cara Mia*, Lee Lange and Tulio Trapani, were actually David Whitfield's producer Bunny Lewis and his arranger Mantovani. On this record Mantovani's orchestra is given full label credit, and there is no doubt that the lush strings of the Mantovani sound were a major contribution to the phenomenal success of this record.

Although David Whitfield (born in Hull on 2 February 1926) never topped the charts again, his light operatic tenor tones were regular fixtures in the charts until the end of 1956, when he, like many others, was swept away by the tidal wave of rock and roll. He never managed to make the sort of money that his success would have brought him if it had happened ten years later, although it was said that his voice was insured for £18,000. When he died on 15 January 1980, he left only £3,000 but was accorded a four-column obituary in *The Times*.

David Whitfield *teaches a Blackpool crowd to sing* Cara Mia.

19

SUCH A NIGHT

JOHNNIE RAY

30 April 1954, for one week
●
Philips PB 244

Written by Lincoln Chase. Produced by Mitch Miller.

Johnnie Ray, born in Dallas, Oregon on 10 January 1927, was partially deafened in an accident at the age of nine. Like Beethoven before him, he did not allow hearing prob-lems to interfere with a musical career. At 15 he appeared on a child talent radio show in nearby Portland and at 17 worked his way south to Los Angeles where he became a soda fountain assistant and movie extra. He was among the millions who failed to be dis-covered and at the age of 24 in 1951 moved eastwards to Detroit to sing at the Flame Club. By the end of that year he had moved to Cleveland and made his first smash record, the classic double-sided hit *Cry* and *The Little White Cloud That Cried*. The Prince Of Wails was on his way.

Such A Night was not a major hit for Johnnie Ray in the US, partly because it was refused airplay on many radio stations there. The original version by the Drifters reached number 5 on the R&B chart in 1954. In 1964 the song was a hit for Elvis Presley both in the UK (no. 13) and the US (no. 16).

LITTLE THINGS MEAN A LOT

KITTY KALLEN

10 September 1954, for one week

●

Brunswick 05287

Written by Carl Stutz and Edith Lindemann. Produced by Milt Gabler, musical arrangement by Jack Pleis.

Kitty Kallen is the first of the one-hit wonders, the recording acts whose only chart hit has reached number one. Nobody would pretend that Kitty Kallen or the Floaters have made a greater contribution to British popular music than the Who or Billy Fury, but whereas neither of those acts has had a number one, Kitty Kallen has.

Kallen's career in her native America was not nearly so short-lived. She began as a big band singer with Jack Teagarden, Jimmy Dorsey and Harry James, with whom she hit the very top of the American charts in 1945 with *I'm Beginning To See The Light*. Her first solo hit was in 1949, and apart from *Little Things Mean A Lot*, her biggest hit on both sides of the Atlantic, she made sporadic chart entries in the States until early 1963, when her last hit, a Top 20 version of *My Coloring Book*, dropped off the charts. *Little Things Mean A Lot* was written by disc jockey Carl Stutz, from Richmond, Virginia, and the leisure editor of the *Richmond Times-Despatch*, Edith Lindemann. They are as much one-hit wonders as Kitty Kallen.

Frank Sinatra *sings at the 1955 opening of the new Ziegfeld Follies in Las Vegas. The woman in front of the stage overcome with emotion, Gladys Gardner, had appeared in the 1913 Follies in New York.*

THREE COINS IN THE FOUNTAIN

FRANK SINATRA

17 September 1954, for three weeks

●●●

Capitol CL 14120

Written by Sammy Cahn and Jule Styne. Produced by Voyle Gilmore, musical arrangement by Nelson Riddle.

The Academy Award-winning Best Original Song of 1954 was Frank Sinatra's first number one. Written by the prolific

team of Sammy Cahn and Jule Styne for a lightweight film of the same name, *Three Coins In The Fountain* was Sinatra's first major chart hit in Britain. It actually entered the charts one week after Sinatra's version of *Young At Heart* had given him his first hit, but that song lasted only one week and disappeared as *Three Coins In The Fountain* arrived.

Francis Albert Sinatra was born in Hoboken, New Jersey on 12 December 1915. By the early 1940s he was creating scenes of hysteria among the 'bobbysoxers' which would only be equalled with the rise of Elvis Presley in 1956 and the Beatles in 1963. In the 1980s, still performing and still selling records, Frank Sinatra is Ol' Blue Eyes to record company executives and his fans alike.

Twenty 'number' songs have reached the top, of which this was the first. Four of these songs have included the number three in the title (*Three Coins In The Fountain*, *Three Steps To Heaven*, *Knock Three Times* and *Three Times A Lady*), which is one more than the number two, which has hit three times (*Two Little Boys*, *Goody Two Shoes* and *Two Tribes*). Frank Sinatra, however, never had another hit record, in Britain or America, with a number in the title.

*Years after he rejected her as a singer with his band, Henry Hall affectionately acknowledges the success of **Vera Lynn**.*

23

HOLD MY HAND

DON CORNELL

8 October 1954, for 4 weeks

●●●●

Vogue Q 2013

Written by Jack Lawrence and Richard Myers. Produced by Bob Thiele.

Don Cornell, one of the least known number one hitmakers of the '50s as far as British audiences are concerned, had two coincidental links with rock music which overtook him and many other big band singers a year or two later. He recorded on the same label as Buddy Holly and the Crickets, who gave the label their only other British number one, and he also put out a single of the song *Mailman Bring Me No More Blues*, which Buddy Holly heard, liked and subsequently recorded.

Don Cornell was born in New York City and from the late 1930s worked as a singer-guitarist with a number of American bands. He served briefly in the Army but in 1946 came back to the Sammy Kaye band that he had left in 1942 and recorded a number of major chart hits. Beginning with *That's My Desire* in 1947, Cornell vocals took the Sammy Kaye Band into the American Top 10 eight times. They never climbed higher than number two, which they hit three times. In 1949 Cornell left Kaye and began his solo career, but did not hit the American Top 10 until 1952, when his first two records on the Coral label (Vogue in UK) brought Don firmly back into the spotlight. In that year he also charted with what is still the shortest title ever to hit the American or any charts, *I*. The song *Hold My Hand* was featured in the 1954 film *Susan Slept Here* starring Dick Powell and Debbie Reynolds. The musical accompaniment for this hit was by Jerry Carr's Orchestra. In Britain, Cornell's only other hit was his version of *Stranger In Paradise*. In America, he continued to hit the Hot Hundred until 1957, but his big days ended with *Hold My Hand*.

24

MY SON MY SON

VERA LYNN

5 November 1954, for two weeks

●●

Decca F 10372

Written by Bob Howard, Melville Farley and Eddie Calvert. Produced by Frank Lee.

Dame Vera Lynn, born Vera Walsh on 20 March 1919 in East Ham, had sung a certain amount with Joe Loss and the Ambrose Orchestra by the time she began her wartime radio series, *Sincerely Yours*. This quickly earned her such popularity that she became known as 'The Forces' Sweetheart'. She spent the remaining war years touring and entertaining the troops to become by the end of the war one of the most famous voices in Europe. Her popularity was not limited to Europe, because the American troops also liked her.

Most of us would have thrown up or made our excuses and left, but not Mr Hamblen. He sat down and wrote this song, which Rosemary Clooney (and later Shakin' Stevens, see no. 477) treated as a bouncy novelty number rather than the epitaph for a mountain man that it was meant to be.

Rosemary Clooney, born on 23 May 1928, began her music career in the late 1940s with her sister Betty, singing with the Tony Pastor band. Together they provided the vocals for one of Pastor's biggest hits, *A You're Adorable*. She married José Ferrer, star of the film *Moulin Rouge*, which gave Mantovani his chart-topping hit of the same name. Clooney's first number one in America was *Come On-A My House*, written by author William Saroyan and his cousin Ross Bagdasarian, but it preceded the British charts. Bagdasarian is the man who scored hits under the pseudonyms of David Seville, Alfi and Harry and the Chipmunks, making him the only man to hit the charts as a soloist, both halves of a duo and all three of a trio. Miss Clooney was possibly less versatile, but in chart terms far more successful.

26

LET'S HAVE ANOTHER PARTY

WINIFRED ATWELL

3 December 1954, for five weeks

●●●●●

Philips PB 268

Produced by Johnny Franz.
Medley of the following songs: *Another Little Drink Wouldn't Do Us Any Harm*, by Nat D. Ayer and Clifford Grey; *Broken Doll*, by James W. Tate; *Bye Bye Blackbird* by Ray Henderson and Mort Dixon; *Honeysuckle And The Bee*, by Albert Fitz and William Penn; *I Wonder Where My Baby Is Tonight*, by Gus Cahn and Walter Donaldson; *Lily Of Laguna*, by Leslie Stuart; *Nellie Dean*, by Harry Armstrong; *Sheik Of Araby*, by Ted Snyder; *Somebody Stole My Gal*, by Leo Wood; *When The Red Red Robin (Comes Bob Bob Bobbin' Along)*, by Harry Woods.

Despite the almost total blanketing of the upper reaches of the chart by medley discs

In one of the strangest charity stunts ever,
Winifred Atwell *plays in the lions' den of the Jack Hylton Circus to benefit the Variety Club of Great Britain.*

25

THIS OLE HOUSE

ROSEMARY CLOONEY

26 November 1954, for one week

●

Philips PB 336

Written by Stuart Hamblen. Produced by Mitch Miller.

Stuart Hamblen was apparently out on a hunting expedition when he and his fellow hunters came across a tumbledown hut in the mountains, many miles from civilisation. They went into the hut and there, lying amongst the rubbish and rubble of a crumbling building, was the body of an old man.

In 1952, her recording of *Auf Wiederseh'n Sweetheart* climbed to the very top of the American charts and stayed there throughout the summer months. She would, no doubt, have repeated the feat in Britain had there been a chart here at that time. In the event she had to wait until the ballad *My Son My Son* hit the number one spot over two years later. On the record, she sang with the Frank Weir Orchestra. Eddie Calvert, who co-wrote the song, joined Mantovani as the second number one hit recording star to write a number one hit for somebody else.

Through the 1980s, Dame Vera is still singing *The White Cliffs Of Dover* and *Auf Wiederseh'n Sweetheart*, and still to full houses of all ages. She remains one of popular music's most enduring and well-loved legends.

in the summer of 1981, Winifred Atwell's Christmas chart-topper of 1954 remains the only medley of over two songs to reach the number one slot. Winifred Atwell, the vast West Indian with the smile and the 'other piano', was the first black person to have a number one hit in Britain, and is still the only female instrumental soloist to hit the top. Her hit, the third instrumental number one, was the first piano piece to top the lists, and after thirty-five years only pianists Russ Conway, Floyd Cramer, B.Bumble and Lieutenant Pigeon have matched Miss Atwell's success.

This was Winifred's sixth single hit and her second medley. Its title refers to *Let's Have A Party*, a medley winner the previous Christmas. That record had climbed to number two, and in subsequent festive seasons Atwell treated us to *Let's Have A Ding Dong* (1955 – no. 3), *Make It A Party* (1956 – no. 7), *Let's Have A Ball* (1957 – no. 4) and *Piano Party* (1959 – no. 10). In 1958 it was Russ Conway's *More Party Pops* (a no. 10) that won the Christmas singalong race.

Rosemary Clooney *gives Italian lessons.*

27

FINGER OF SUSPICION

DICKIE VALENTINE

7 January 1955, for one week
21 January 1955, for two weeks

● ● ●

Decca F 10394

Written by Al Lewis and Paul Mann.
Produced by Dick Rowe.

Dickie Valentine, born Richard Bryce, was given his big break by Ted Heath in 1951 when he invited him to become vocalist with his Band, the most successful of all British big bands. By 1952, Valentine was voted Britain's Most Popular Singer, a title he retained for years beyond his chart heyday, which began early in 1953. His first number one came only two months after his marriage at Caxton Hall to Elizabeth Flynn, which caused scenes of crowd hysteria and was expected to sound the death knell to his chart career. In fact, 1955 was by far his best chart year, with two number ones and three other Top 10 hits.

But even when the hits stopped coming, Valentine kept working as hard as ever. There was a publicity story that reported Valentine had been a pageboy at the London Palladium, but had been sacked for some undisclosed misdemeanour. 'I'll be back,' vowed the determined young Master Bryce, 'I'll be back at the top of the bill.' And so he was, time and again throughout the Fifties.

28

MAMBO ITALIANO

ROSEMARY CLOONEY

14 January 1955, for one week
4 February 1955, for two weeks

● ● ●

Philips PB 382

Written by Bob Merrill. Produced by Mitch Miller.

Only twelve of the songs that have reached number one have had foreign language titles, and of these five were instrumentals. Rosemary Clooney's second consecutive number one was the fourth of the foreign language titles to reach the top. It was the last vocal chart-topper with a foreign title until Jane Birkin and Serge Gainsbourg's excessively vocal *Je T'Aime . . . Moi Non Plus* made the top 14 years 235 days and 249 number ones later. Miss Clooney was the first lady to hit the top of the British charts twice, a record that has been equalled many times but was not beaten until Sandie Shaw scored her third number one 12 years and 103 days later (see no. 232).

There is a story that around this time a visitor came to dinner at the home of José Ferrer and Rosemary Clooney. On seeing a child or two scattered about the furniture, the guest enquired how many children the Ferrers had. 'Seven', was the reply. 'And what are their ages?' asked the polite guest. 'Seven, six, five, four, three, two and one', said Miss Clooney. 'Oh, I do hope I'm not interrupting anything', replied the guest, tucking into his meal. Perhaps it was not surprising that her next Top 10 hit, in May 1955, was *Where Will The Baby's Dimple Be?*

In 1955, the year of her greatest success, **Ruby Murray** *performs on the programme* Quite Contrary.

29

SOFTLY SOFTLY

RUBY MURRAY

18 February 1955, for three weeks

● ● ●

Columbia DB 3558

Written by Mark Paul and Pierre Dudan,
English lyrics by Paddy Roberts. Produced
by Norrie Paramor.

The tenth female artist to top the charts was
Ruby Murray, the shy little 19-year-old from
Belfast, who was easily the most successful
singer on the British charts in 1955. Her total
of 80 weeks on the charts in that year stood
as the record for only one year, because Bill
Haley clocked up the as yet unmatched total
of 110 weeks in 1956. It was not until 1985 that
Madonna passed Miss Murray's 1955 record
for a female vocalist.

Ruby Murray's first chart entry had been on
3 February 1954 with the song *Heartbeat*,
which was destined to rise to number three.
At the end of January, her second hit *Softly
Softly* entered the hit parade and within a
month was number one. By the end of the
year Miss Murray had taken seven songs
into the British Top 10, including both sides
of her third hit single, *Happy Days And
Lonely Nights* (no. 6) backed by *Let Me Go
Lover* (no. 5). Yet just as suddenly as it had
begun, it all stopped. *I'll Come When You*

Call, her sixth Top 10 record, dropped off
the chart at the end of November 1955, and
no Ruby Murray record hit the chart after
that until the end of August 1956, when *You
Are My First Love* tottered up to number 16.
In 1957 she was hitless. Her last brief spell of
chart success came when *Real Love* hit the
Top 20 over Christmas 1958 and a few
months later *Goodbye Jimmy Goodbye*
gave Miss Murray her final Top 10 hit. Then
it was goodbye, Ruby, goodbye, at least as
far as the record buyers were concerned.

30

GIVE ME YOUR WORD

TENNESSEE ERNIE FORD

11 March 1955, for seven weeks

● ● ● ● ● ● ●

Capitol CL 14005

Written by George Wyle and Irving Taylor.
Produced by Lee Gillette

Ernest Jennings Ford was born on a farm
near Bristol, Tennessee on 13 February 1919,
a background not so different from the hero
of his final hit, Davy Crockett, who was 'born
on a mountain-top in Tennessee'. At school
he played the trombone, and on graduation
he joined the local radio station as an
announcer. Ford studied music in Cincin-
nati and by the end of 1941 was working for a
radio station in Knoxville, Tennessee. He
served in the US Air Force during the war
and in 1945 moved to Pasadena, California
with his wife Betty Ford (no relation to the
wife of President Ford). It was while he was
working on KXLA Pasadena that he was
heard singing along with a record by Capitol producer Lee Gillette, and in 1949 he was
signed to an exclusive recording contract.
Mule Train, a Top 10 hit in the States, followed at the very end of 1949.

Give Me Your Word was Ford's first hit on
this side of the Atlantic. He is now best
known here for his deep-voiced country-
tinged songs, including his own composition *Shotgun Boogie* and his biggest hit of
all, *Sixteen Tons* (see no. 41), but his biggest
selling album was a religious compilation
called *Hymns*. This arose because for
several years from the mid-'50s he was the
regular host of a television series in America
and he ended each show with a gospel
song.

CHERRY PINK AND APPLE BLOSSOM WHITE

PEREZ PRADO

29 April 1955, for two weeks

● ●

HMV B 10833

Written by Louiguy. Produced by Herman Diaz.

Originally a French tune (by a Spanish composer!), and therefore not surprisingly initially titled *Cerisier Rouge et Pommier Blanc*, *Cherry Pink and Apple Blossom White* was used as the theme tune for the 1955 film *Underwater*. This epic starred Jane Russell, the girl for whom Howard Hughes reinvented the bra. Perez Prado was born in Cuba on 23 November 1918 and began playing in those pre-Castro days in Havana with Orquestra Casino de la Playa. He first recorded *Cherry Pink* in 1951 but when the producers of *Underwater* decided to use the tune as their theme they asked the King Of The Mambo to re-record it. The new version spent ten weeks at the top of the American charts before being knocked off the top by Bill Haley and another film theme, *Rock Around The Clock*. In Britain, its success was less long-lived, but Prado helped to establish two very minor chart records. Firstly the title was the longest number one title at the time, equalling the record set by Lita Roza's *Doggie* two years earlier. Secondly, *Cherry Pink* joined *Answer Me* as the second song to hit number one in two different versions when Eddie Calvert's recording took over the top slot at the end of May. After 600 chart-toppers, it is still the only instrumental on that particular list.

English lyrics to the song were written by Mack David, but as not used in either version. Perez Prado, who died on 4 December 1983, a few days after his 65th birthday, hit number one again in America with *Patricia* in 1958, a record which climbed as high as number 8 in Britain. Prado was not the featured soloist on either hit – the lead trumpeter on *Cherry Pink* was Billy Regis.

STRANGER IN PARADISE

TONY BENNETT

13 May 1955, for two weeks

● ●

Philips PB 420

Written by Robert Wright and George Forrest, based on a theme by Aleksandr Borodin. Produced by Mitch Miller.

Anthony Dominick Benedetto was born on 13 August 1926 in Queens, New York City. His first public appearance was at the age of seven in a church minstrel show, but his climb from there to the top was interrupted by World War II, by the end of which Benedetto was an infantryman in Europe. After the war an appearance on Arthur Godfrey's Talent Show led to a concert engagement with Bob Hope. Bennett's career was under way. In 1951 he topped the American charts twice, first with *Because Of You* and then with the Hank Williams song *Cold Cold Heart*. In 1953 he recorded *Stranger in Paradise* with backing as usual by Percy Faith's Orchestra.

The show *Kismet* opened on Broadway in 1953. Its hit song, *Stranger in Paradise*, was based on a theme from the Polovetsian Dances in Borodin's 1888 opera, *Prince Igor*. The first recording of this theme had been by Sir Thomas Beecham in 1915, but its popularity was timeless. *Kismet* came to London in 1955, and in that year no fewer than six versions of *Stranger In Paradise* hit the British charts. In America in 1953 Bennett had stopped at number 2 with the song, but in Britain two years later he climbed one rung higher. It proved not only to be his only chart-topper, but also his only Top 10 hit in Britain.

In The Middle Of An Island in 1957 gave Bennett one more Top 10 hit in his home country, but his most famous recording, *I Left My Heart In San Francisco*, peaked at number 19 in America and at number 25 in Britain. Despite a comparative lack of chart success over the years, Bennett has been acknowledged as one of the great jazz balladeers of his time.

CHERRY PINK AND APPLE BLOSSOM WHITE

EDDIE CALVERT

27 May 1955, for four weeks

● ● ● ●

Columbia DB 3581

Written by Louiguy. Produced by Norrie Paramor.

The day after Winston Churchill's last General Election victory as leader of the Conservative Party, Eddie Calvert moved his version of *Cherry Pink* into the top position, giving him his second number one. He was the first instrumentalist to achieve this feat.

Eddie Calvert was born in Preston, Lancashire on 15 March 1922. His father was an amateur musician in a brass band, and it was he who taught Eddie Calvert to play the cornet. No wonder Eddie's first million-seller was *Oh Mein Papa*. During the war, Calvert was a dispatch rider and played part-time with various bands, graduating from Jimmy McMurray's Band at the Birmingham Casino and Billy Ternent's Band at BBC Wales. He toured Europe at the end of the war with Geraldo. By this time he was beginning to take centre stage during performances and playing his solos in a dramatic spotlight, while the rest of the orchestra accompanied him from a darkened stage.

His chart career, which had begun with two widely-spaced number one hits, *Oh Mein Papa*, number one in January 1954 and *Cherry Pink and Apple Blossom White* in May 1955, then faded. He reached the Top 20 with an instrumental version of the song he replaced at the top, *Stranger In Paradise*, also in 1955, and still had enough of a following in 1958 to score a Top 10 hit with *Mandy*. By mid-1958 his chart successes had finished, but his simple style had showed the way for later chartbound trumpeters such as Herb Alpert, Al Hirt and Nini Rosso. Calvert died in South Africa on 8 August 1978.

*In addition to her own number one, **Alma Cogan** charted with her version of three other number ones.*

UNCHAINED MELODY

JIMMY YOUNG

24 June 1955, for three weeks

● ● ●

Decca F 10502

Written by Alex North and Hy Zaret.
Produced by Dick Rowe.

A cheap and instantly forgettable American B-film called *Unchained* had one redeeming feature, its theme tune. Those who came to see the film could be forgiven for thinking that any film with a tune as strong as *Unchained Melody* behind the credits would be worth sitting through. In fact anybody who walked out of the cinema as soon as he had heard the tune missed nothing else of any merit. The original version was by the American singer Todd Duncan, but Dick Rowe at Decca decided it was right for a recently signed singer, whose career was then as far down as it had been up when his *Too Young* had been a major hit on the tiny Polygon label in pre-chart days.

So Jimmy Young got the song and the mighty Decca publicity machine was rolled out to support it. The American Al Hibbler's version took off first and seemed to be winning the race, but as more versions flooded on to the market it was the British singer who started picking up airplay and sales. By the end of June he was at number one, and Hibbler had to be content with taking his only British hit to number 2. Suddenly Jimmy Young was an overnight sensation again.

Unchained Melody is one of only two songs that have been a hit in seven different versions. Apart from Jimmy Young and Al Hibbler, Les Baxter and Liberace reached the charts in 1955. Jimmy Young re-recorded his hit in 1964 and took it back into the Top 50. The following year the Righteous Brothers made the sixth hit version of the song, and in 1986 Leo Sayer brought the song back into the lists after a 21 year absence. Only *White Christmas*, which has never hit the very top of the charts, can match these seven hit versions, and only *Rock Around The Clock* (see no. 39) among the 600 number ones can beat the total of 65 weeks that the different versions of *Unchained Melody* have spent on the British charts.

DREAMBOAT

ALMA COGAN

15 July 1955, for two weeks

● ●

HMV B 10872

Written by Al Hoffman. Produced by Walter Ridley.

Throughout the mid-'50s the most consistently successful singer in Britain, in chart terms, was Alma Cogan. From March 1954, when her first hit *Bell Bottom Blues* came on to the hit parade, until 1959, she was rarely out of the charts. She never achieved the huge record sales that Ruby Murray achieved in the same year that Alma had her only chart-topper, nor the volume that Shirley Bassey managed when she was enjoying simultaneous Top 10 hits in early 1959, but Miss Cogan's 18 hit records made a list longer than any other female star could boast by the time her last hit, *Cowboy Jimmy Joe*, dropped off the charts in May 1961.

Only four of the 18 singles she recorded reached the Top 10, but her versions of the big hits of the day always gave the original artists a run for their money. Apart from her own number one, she hit the charts with her versions of three previous number ones, *Little Things Mean A Lot* (no. 11), *Why Do Fools Fall In Love* (no. 22) and *The Story Of My Life* (no. 25).

Alma Cogan was known for her chuckle and her extravagant dresses which all seemed to feature yards of tulle petticoat. Yet her musical image was not just lightweight and happy-go-lucky. Shortly before her tragic death from cancer, she recorded a few titles with Andrew Loog Oldham, then the manager and producer of the Rolling Stones. The tracks were never released, but the mere fact that the Stones' mastermind wanted to record her shows that her range was far greater than bubbly songs like *Never Do A Tango With An Eskimo* or *Dreamboat*. *Dreamboat*, incidentally, provided an American Top 20 hit in 1961 for another major female star of the '50s, Connie Francis.

36

ROSE MARIE

SLIM WHITMAN

29 July 1955, for eleven weeks

●●●●●●●●●●●

London HL 8061

Written by Rudolf Friml, Otto Harbach and Oscar Hammerstein II. Produced by Lew Chudd.

The song that was number one when James Dean died was sung by Otis Dewey Whitman Jnr, who was born on 20 January 1924, the same year that the musical *Rose Marie* was first produced. Like other country singers before and since (Charley Pride is perhaps the best-known example) Slim Whitman was an excellent baseball player, and it was only the intervention of the war, which resulted in his enlistment in the US Navy, that turned him into a singer rather than a baseball player.

Whitman's recording career began to flourish at Imperial Records, one of America's fastest growing independent labels thanks largely to the success of Fats Domino. Whitman's career hit the very peak when he recorded a 30-year-old love song which broke all records for sustained chart success. None of the 564 records that have followed *Rose Marie* to the top have matched its record of eleven consecutive weeks at number one. It was actually the second song from the musical that Whitman had turned into a million-seller. In 1951, before the British charts were around to be dominated by Mr Whitman, he topped the American charts with *Indian Love Call*.

There were no more number ones for Slim Whitman after *Rose Marie*. Nevertheless, he came back so strongly in the mid-'70s that two of his albums topped the British charts and a single, *Happy Anniversary*, reached number 14 at the end of 1974, almost 20 years since the success of *Rose Marie*. Slim Whitman's other claim to fame is that of being the first left-handed guitarist to hit the top spot, many years before Paul McCartney or Jimi Hendrix joined that select band.

37

THE MAN FROM

LARAMIE

JIMMY YOUNG

14 October 1955, for four weeks

●●●●

Decca F 10597

Written by Lester Lee and Ned Washington. Produced by Dick Rowe.

On Harry Webb's fifteenth birthday, Jimmy Young established a new record which Cliff Richard was to equal but never beat – he became the first British solo star to put two consecutive single releases at number one. Once again, Jimmy Young relied on the combination of producer Dick Rowe, musical director Bob Sharples and a song from a Hollywood film. This song was the theme from a big budget western starring James Stewart. Six versions of *The Man From Laramie* were released in Britain. In reviewing the records the *Daily Mirror* wrote 'it might just as well be "The Man From The Coal Board" for all the fire some get into it.' Only two of the six versions hit the British charts, the Al Martino version, which climbed to number 19, and Jimmy Young's triumphant effort.

The main immediate result of the success of *The Man From Laramie* was that Jimmy Young won a starring role opposite Hylda Baker in the Christmas pantomime *Robinson Crusoe* at the Grand Theatre, Wolverhampton. Success does not come much bigger than that, but more was to follow for JY. The *New Musical Express* listed him as the second biggest selling artist of 1955 (after Ruby Murray, of course), and in the *NME Annual*, that latterday bible of pop orthodoxy, Young (born September 1927) was described as 'the success of the year. One name above all others deserves to shine forth in letters of gold. The name of course is Jimmy Young'. The *Record Mirror* agreed, and called him 'Mr Comeback 1955 – Jimmy Young, the man they said was finished, the man who hasn't had a hit for years'.

That was not the only comeback that JY has made during his long and ultimately highly successful showbiz career. Now, more than 30 years after his second and last chart-topping single, he is one of Britain's most famous radio voices, and with an OBE to boot. TTFN.

38

HERNANDO'S

HIDEAWAY

THE JOHNSTON BROTHERS

11 November 1955, for two weeks

●●

Decca F 10608

Written by Richard Adler and Jerry Ross. Produced by Hugh Mendl.

The musical *Pajama Game* was the source of this much recorded song. It provided the British Johnston Brothers with their only number one hit. Sadly, it reached number one in Britain on the day that one of the composers, Jerry Ross, died in New York. It was the second big hit from the musical; *Hey There* had been a Top 20 hit in no less than four versions – Rosemary Clooney (no. 4), Johnnie Ray (no. 5), Lita Roza (no. 17) and Sammy Davis Jr (no. 19). Johnnie Ray's version included *Hernando's Hideaway* on the B-side, and that track climbed to number 11. In America, Rosemary Clooney hit number one with *Hey There* but it was the Everly Brothers' mentor, Archie Bleyer, who had the biggest hit with *Hernando's Hideaway*. His version on his own Cadence label climbed to number 2, thanks to Maria Alba's castanet solo.

The Johnston Brothers were, like the Righteous Brothers, not brothers at all. They were Johnny Johnston, Miff King, Eddie Lester and Frank Holmes. Their vocal style was very much in the Stargazers mould. To complicate matters, the Johnston Brothers often included Jean Campbell in their line-up. They were then known as the Keynotes, although they never hit the charts under that name. Two of the Johnston Brothers' hits were vocal equivalents of Winifred Atwell's Christmas medleys – tracks called *Join In*

And Sing Again and *Join In And Sing No. 3.* The Brothers' ability to come up with hit versions of middle of the road tunes continued until May 1957, when their *Heart* lost the chart race to Max Bygraves (Brothers 23; Bygraves 14).

39

ROCK AROUND THE CLOCK

BILL HALEY AND HIS COMETS

25 November 1955, for three weeks
6 January 1956, for two weeks

● ● ● ● ●

Brunswick 05317

Written by Jimmy de Knight (James Myers) and Max C Freedman. Produced by Milt Gabler.

On 12 April 1954, a 28-year-old country and western band leader went into Decca's Pythian Table studios in New York to record as a favour to manager Jim Myers a song which had been part of his stage act for

almost one year but which his previous recording company, Essex, had been unwilling for him to record. When first released, the record was a small hit for Bill Haley (born William John Clifton Haley in Highland Park, Michigan on 6 July 1925) and his Comets, who for this session were Danny Cedrone, Billy Williamson, John Grande, Marshall Lytle and session man Billy Guesack on drums.

It was not until *Rock Around The Clock* was featured in a 1955 Glenn Ford movie called *Blackboard Jungle* that the record became perhaps the single most significant recording in popular music history. Nine months after the song had briefly entered the British charts it reappeared and within six weeks was at number one. Eventually it sold over a million copies in Britain alone and changed popular music for ever. Not bad for a little song co-written by a man (Max Freedman) born in 1893! In 1956 Bill Haley had more

chart success in one year than any other act before or since, but his tour of Britain early in 1957 marked the beginning of the end. In the flesh, the twice-married Haley was not every teenage girl's dream, and Elvis Presley took over and built on Haley's amazing success.

It is impossible to analyse the reasons for Haley's success with *Rock Around The Clock*. It reached the Top 20 in Britain twice more, in 1968 and 1974, and in chart longevity terms is the most successful number one of all time. Bill Haley died on 9 February 1981.

40

CHRISTMAS ALPHABET

DICKIE VALENTINE

16 December 1955, for three weeks

● ● ●

Decca F 10628

Written by Buddy Kaye and Jules Loman. Produced by Dick Rowe.

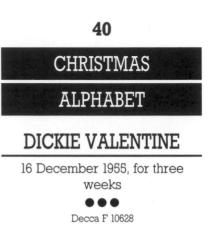

For three weeks at Christmas Dickie Valentine played King Canute to Bill Haley's incoming tide of rock and roll. More than that, this record marked the first time that a song created for the Christmas market had hit number one, showing that his astute management had learned from Winifred Atwell's singalong successes of previous Christmas seasons. *Christmas Alphabet* was the first of the big Christmas hits apart from *White Christmas* but its chart career was almost as brief as the season of goodwill itself. *Christmas Alphabet* spent only seven weeks on the chart in total, three of which were at number one, and it held the undisputed title of Shortest-Lived Number One Hit until Ferry Aid's *Let It Be* (see no. 589) equalled its seven week chart run in 1987.

(Left) It's 1957 and **Bill Haley** *is getting a clue why Johnnie Ray is having another number one and he isn't.*

Dickie Valentine was busy that Christmas not only with his hit record but also because he was playing the part of Wishee Washee in the pantomime *Aladdin*, and preparing for the birth of his first child, daughter Kim, who was born in January 1956.

Valentine's next and final Top 10 hit did not come until a year later with a song called *Christmas Island*, but even so he remained year in and year out Britain's 'Most Popular Male Vocalist' until Cliff Richard appeared on the scene. Dickie Valentine never lost his popularity, and was still playing to full houses when he died in a car crash in 1971.

The Ballad Of Davy Crockett, a record that had been a hit for him in America before *Sixteen Tons*, but which had been kept under wraps for the British market until the film starring Fess Parker was released. *Davy Crockett* made number 3 in the charts, but was kept off the top spot not only by Bill Hayes' original version of the song which peaked at number 2, but also by his own *Sixteen Tons* at number one. On 27 January 1956, Ford had two of the top three chart placings, a feat that 559 number ones later has been equalled only by Guy Mitchell, Frankie Laine, Elvis Presley, Shirley Bassey, the Beatles, John Lennon, Frankie Goes To Hollywood and Madonna.

Dickie Valentine *reacts to the news that his* Christmas Alphabet *has the shortest chart run of any number one.*

41

SIXTEEN TONS

TENNESSEE ERNIE FORD

20 January 1956, for four weeks

● ● ● ●

Capitol CL 14500

Written by Merle Travis. Produced by Lee Gillette.

Eleven days before Sex Pistol Johnny Rotten was born the song that ushered in rock and roll dropped off the top of the charts, to be replaced by Tennessee Ernie Ford's second number one hit. Country and Western star Merle Travis wrote the coal-mining song *Sixteen Tons* and recorded it in 1947. Travis' father was a coal miner in Beech Creek, Kentucky and the chorus was based on a saying of his father, 'another day older and deeper in debt'.

Sixteen Tons was the biggest hit of Ford's career. In America, it was one of the fastest selling records in pop history. It stayed at the top of the charts for seven weeks from late November 1955. The week before it climbed to number one in Britain, it was knocked from the top in America by the same record that was to topple it in Britain five weeks later, Dean Martin's *Memories Are Made Of This*.

Sixteen Tons was Tennessee Ernie Ford's second consecutive number one in Britain, although like Eddie Calvert and the Stargazers before him he had released records between number ones that had missed altogether. His follow-up to *Sixteen Tons* was

42

MEMORIES ARE MADE

OF THIS

DEAN MARTIN

17 February 1956, for four weeks

● ● ● ●

Capitol CL 14523

Written by Terry Gilkyson, Richard Dehr and Frank Miller. Produced by Lee Gillette.

Dean Martin, born Dino Paul Crocetti on 7 June 1917 in Steubenville, Ohio, had in true show business tradition been a petrol pump attendant, a steelworker, a dealer in a casino and even a prizefighter under the name Kid Crochet before he switched to singing in the mid-'40s. By 1946 he was vocalist with the Cleveland based Sammy Watkins Band. During a spell at a club in Atlantic City he met a young comedian called Jerry Lewis. Within a few months they had become one of the most popular comedy duos in the nation.

Dean Martin's biggest selling single of his career, a number one hit on both sides of the Atlantic, hit the top just a few months before the Martin/Lewis partnership broke up. *Memories Are Made Of This* was sung by Mario Lanza in the film *The Seven Hills Of Rome*. The backing voices, singing 'Sweet, sweet, the memories you gave to me' were the three co-writers of the song. Working under the name the Easyriders they went on

to have a Stateside Top 10 hit of their own, *Marianne*, as well as to feature on Frankie Laine's final American Top 10 hit, *Love Is A Golden Ring*, in 1957.

Dean Martin's chart career extended until 1969, when his last hit, *Gentle On My Mind*, became his fourth number 2. Even without Jerry Lewis his film and stage career has been continuously successful, with leading roles in such films as *Airport*, *Rio Bravo* and *Kiss Me, Stupid*. At 70 years of age Martin is still a star.

43

IT'S ALMOST

TOMORROW

THE DREAMWEAVERS

16 March 1956, for two weeks
6 April 1956, for one week

● ● ●

Brunswick 05515

Written by Wade Buff and Eugene Adkinson. Produced by Wade Buff, Eugene Adkinson and Milt Gabler.

Gene Adkinson and Wade Buff from Miami, Florida wrote *It's Almost Tomorrow* but could find nobody to record it. Being resourceful they formed a group and recorded the song themselves. Milt Gabler at American Decca picked it up for national distribution and in November 1955 the session group hit the Hot Hundred. It was a top 10 hit in their own country, but in Britain things went even better. By climbing to number one, the Dreamweavers established two rather minor chart records. Firstly, they became the first studio band to hit the top, to head a list that now includes the Archies, Edison Lighthouse, Spitting Image and others. Secondly, by having no more chart success at all, they joined the one-hit wonder club, which at the time only included Kitty Kallen (see no. 21). They remain the only one-hit wonders to climb back to number one after being ousted from the top.

In America, the Dreamweavers managed two more hit singles, both sides of which hit the chart. Only one of those tracks, *A Little Love Can Go A Long Long Way*, hit the Top 40. At the end of June 1956 the Dreamweavers simultaneously dropped off both the British and American charts, never to return. *It's Almost Tomorrow* returned, though. David Whitfield sang the song on *All Star Hit Parade*, which reached number 2 in July 1956, and Mark Wynter's version climbed to number 12 at the very end of 1963 to give him his penultimate hit.

number one with the phrase 'Rock And Roll' in the title, put her onto the list of female performers with two number ones. At that time it was a short list, with just Miss Starr and Rosemary Clooney on it, but two weeks later Winifred Atwell added her name to it, and by late 1987 the list was a long one, the latest addition being Whitney Houston. Only two solo female performers have ever managed more than two number ones, Madonna (five) and Sandie Shaw (three).

Kay Starr's other number one (see no. 3) had been her first British hit, so as she failed to hit the charts again after *Rock And Roll Waltz* she established a weird record, subsequently equalled only by the duo of John Travolta and Olivia Newton-John, of starting and finishing with a number one. Kay Starr had recorded for Capitol until 1955, when she switched to RCA (released on HMV in England). At her first recording session for RCA she was given *Rock And Roll Waltz*. To begin with she did not like it at all. However, her new producer, Joe Carlton, was insistent, and the song, which brilliantly combined modern music with the more conservative sound of the 1940s, reached the summit both in Britain and in the United States. In America, Kay Starr hit the charts several more times, but even a change back to Capitol in the early '60s could not bring her name back onto the charts in Britain. Her achievement of hitting number one on two different labels did not remain unique for long either. Winifred Atwell equalled that feat two weeks later.

'French' instrumental, after Mantovani's *Moulin Rouge*, to top the hit parade. Winifred Atwell, a qualified chemist, began playing for charity in Trinidad before going first to New York and then to London to study the piano. She hit the big time when she realised that boogie piano was more lucrative than classical piano, and by 1951 she had a recording contract. It was a happy birthday for her in 1956, for on that day, 27 April, she was at number one. The rest of the year proved to be a good one for her as well. She did not win on the Premium Bonds, which were introduced in that year's budget on 17 April, but she had big hits with two more French sounding tunes, *Port Au Prince* (which is the capital of French speaking island of Haiti) and *Left Bank* (of which there is one in Paris). And all this on that 'other piano' which reportedly cost Miss Atwell 50 shillings (£2.50) in a Battersea junk shop.

Poor People Of Paris was a genuine French tune, written by composer Marguerite Mannot with lyrics by Rene Rouzaud. It had been made popular in France by the legendary Edith Piaf. The original title was *La Goulante Du Pauvre Jean*, which can be translated as *The Ballad Of Poor John*. However, a mistake in a cable from Paris to Capitol Records in Hollywood meant that when Les Baxter recorded his instrumental version (a number one in America) he was told that the song was about Pauvres Gens (Poor People), not Pauvre Jean. His hit became *The Poor People Of Paris*, and so did Winifred Atwell's cover version. It is possible, perhaps, that the title may have been referring to those not super-rich or super-chic enough to be invited to the wedding of the year in Monte Carlo, where Prince Rainier married Grace Kelly on 19 April 1956.

44

ROCK AND ROLL
WALTZ

KAY STARR with the Hugo Winterhalter Orchestra

30 March 1956, for one week

●

HMV POP 168

Written by Dick Ware and Shorty Allen. Produced by Joe Carlton.

Kay Starr's *Rock And Roll Waltz*, the only

45

POOR PEOPLE OF
PARIS

WINIFRED ATWELL

13 April 1956, for three weeks

●●●

Decca F 10681

Written by Marguerite Mannot. Produced by Hugh Mendl.

The second chart topper for the girl from Tunapuna, Trinidad was the second

46

NO OTHER LOVE

RONNIE HILTON

4 May 1956, for six weeks

●●●●●●

HMV POP 198

Written by Richard Rogers and Oscar Hammerstein II. Produced by Walter Ridley.

Ronnie Hilton took the song *No Other Love*

from the comparatively unsuccessful Rodgers and Hammerstein musical *Me And Juliet* and scored his one and only number one. The song had already been a Top 10 hit in America for Jo Stafford in 1950 and a number one there three years later for Perry Como, but in 1956, Hilton's opposition came only from the Canadian born Edmund Hockridge and Britain's Johnston Brothers. No American versions of this song ever hit the British charts.

Ronnie Hilton's light operatic style, which first saw the professional light of day at the Hippodrome Theatre, Dudley, was being overtaken by major changes in public tastes by mid-1956. Elvis Presley's British chart career began in the second week of Ronnie Hilton's six week run at the top, when *Heartbreak Hotel* entered the *NME* Top 30. By the time *No Other Love* dropped off the charts, Elvis had also introduced *Blue Suede Shoes* and *I Want You I Need You I Love You* to the charts. 1956 was the year in which Bill Haley clocked up an all time record of 110 chart weeks, so the efforts of British stars like Hilton and Winifred Atwell, were entirely against the run of play. Nevertheless, Ronnie Hilton continued to hit the charts until 1965, and his total of 128 weeks on the chart places him equal with the likes of the Searchers and Jonathan King.

47

I'LL BE HOME

PAT BOONE

15 June 1956, for five weeks

● ● ● ● ●

London HLD 8253

Written by Ferdinand Washington and Stan Lewis. Produced by Randy Wood.

Charles Eugene 'Pat' Boone, born 1 June 1934, was the clean-cut All American Boy of popular music. A descendant of the American frontiersman Daniel Boone, Pat was raised in Tennessee. It was winning a talent contest in Nashville that drew him to the attention of Randy Wood at Dot Records. His first American hit was a song called *Two Hearts*, but the British record-buying public were introduced to him through his version of Fats Domino's *Ain't That A Shame*, which hit number 7 at the beginning of 1956. His follow-up was a version of another rhythm and

*Adrian Hill worked as a fitter in Leeds engineering works before finding disc stardom as **Ronnie Hilton**. After his last day at the factory he bought his first made-to-measure suit.*

blues hit, the Flamingos' *I'll Be Home*. It gave him his first chart-topping single on either side of the Atlantic and his only number one in Britain. The Flamingos also made the first US chart version of Art Garfunkel's number one *I Only Have Eyes For You* (see no. 379), but their only British chart entry was a minor skirmish with the lower reaches of the Top 40 late in 1969 with *Boogaloo Party*.

Pat Boone's chart career has been far more distinguished. Hits like *Friendly Persuasion, Don't Forbid Me, April Love* and his biggest world-wide hit, *Love Letters In The Sand*, established him as the acceptable alternative to the rebellious Elvis Presley. His

British chart career continued for seven years, until 1962, but 25 years later he still ranks as one of the 20 most successful chart acts of all time.

He is married to country star Red Foley's daughter, Shirley. The eldest of their four daughters, Debbie Boone, had the biggest hit of the 1970s in the United States with her multi-million selling smash *You Light Up My Life*.

48

WHY DO FOOLS FALL IN LOVE

THE TEENAGERS featuring FRANKIE LYMON

20 July 1956, for three weeks

● ● ●

Columbia DB 3772

Written by Frankie Lymon and George Goldner. Produced by Richard Barrett

Rarely has a star shone so brightly so soon and gone out more quickly than in the case of Frankie Lymon. Discovered singing gospel songs in the hallway of a New York apartment block, Lymon and the Teenagers had a hit with their very first attempt. *Why Do Fools Fall In Love* entered the US Top 100 in the first week of February 1956, ultimately reaching number 6. It got to the top of the rhythm and blues list in the first week of March, and remained there for five weeks. By summertime, the record had spread to the UK and began a three week run at the summit in July. It was the first R&B side to go to number one in Britain.

In the time-honoured tradition of overnight sensations, it was all so nearly very different. The song had been written as *Why Do The Birds Sing So Gay*, based on some love letters received by a friend of the group. The group was called the Premiers and the lead singer was one Herman Santiago. George Goldner, the head of Gee Records, persuaded the group to rework the lyrics. Before the session Herman Santiago fell ill, so 13-year-old Frankie Lymon stood in for him. The leader of the backing band on the session, Jimmy Wright, came up with the name The Teenagers, and the rest is history.

Lymon became the youngest act to top the bill at the London Palladium, when he was 14 in 1957. In that year the group scored three more chart hits, including the immortal *I'm Not A Juvenile Delinquent*, the Top 10 hit *Baby Baby* and the evergreen *Goody Goody*. Lymon's career went downhill from then on. Diana Ross took his song to the Top 10 a quarter of a century later, but Frankie

was not alive to see it. He died of a drug overdose on 28 February 1968, aged 25, one of the very first rock drug casualties.

49

WHATEVER WILL BE WILL BE

DORIS DAY

10 August 1956, for six weeks

● ● ● ● ● ●

Philips PB 586

Written by Ray Evans and Jay Livingston. Produced by Mitch Miller.

Whatever Will Be Will Be (Que Sera Sera) was the Oscar-winning song from the 1956 film, *The Man Who Knew Too Much* directed by Alfred Hitchcock and starring James Stewart and Doris Day, with a supporting cast of well known British actors like Bernard Miles, Richard Wattis and Brenda de Banzie. It was the second time within a year that a song from a James Stewart movie had hit number one in Britain, coming only ten months after Jimmy Young's *The Man From Laramie*. It was also the second time that Doris Day had taken an Oscar-winning song to number one in Britain, an achievement that is still unequalled. Irene Cara, who took the 1980 Oscar-winning song to number one (see no. 505) and the 1983 winner *Flashdance – What A Feeling*, to number 2, is the only person to get near to Doris Day's double.

Ray Evans and Jay Livingston wrote many movie songs and even featured as themselves in the film *Sunset Boulevard*. *Whatever Will Be Will Be* was inspired by the family motto of the character played by Rossano Brazzi in the 1954 film *The Barefoot Contessa*. The motto in the film was in Italian, 'Che Sera Sera', but Evans and Livingston switched it to the Spanish 'Que Sera Sera' on the sound principle that more people speak Spanish than Italian, espe-

cially in the world's biggest record-buying market, the United States. The song was not written particularly for Hitchcock's movie, but when the producers asked for a song that could be sung in the film by Miss Day to her young son the half-written *Que Sera Sera* seemed to fit the bill perfectly. The legal department at Paramount studios objected to the title *Que Sera Sera*, so the song became officially known as *Whatever Will Be Will Be*. Doris Day did not think at first that the song would become a hit, thus proving the lyrics of the song correct – the future's not ours to see.

50

LAY DOWN YOUR ARMS

ANNE SHELTON

21 September 1956, for four weeks

● ● ● ●

Philips PB 616

Written by Leon Land and Ake Gerhard, English lyrics by Paddy Roberts. Produced by Johnny Franz

Paddy Roberts, the humorist and songwriter who had put English lyrics to Ruby Murray's *Softly Softly* (see no. 29), found a Swedish song called *Ann-Caroline* and turned it into the saga of a returning soldier, *Lay Down Your Arms*. He showed it to the popular band vocalist, Anne Shelton, who liked it enough to record it. Miss Shelton had been vocalist with the Ambrose Orchestra since the age of 14 and was the only serious rival in popularity to Vera Lynn during the war years, so it was shrewd of Miss Shelton to record a song which harked back to her great years a decade earlier. Messrs Land and Gerhard thus became the only nationals of Sweden, a neutral country during World War II, to write a British number one until Andersson, Anderson and Ulvaeus almost twenty years later. Anne Shelton had previously had happy experiences of recording a European song with English lyrics when her version of Tommy Connor's adaptation of *Lilli Marlene* gave her a hit in 1946. In 1949, she recorded *The Wedding Of Lilli*

Marlene, and her version became the biggest-selling record of a song that topped the British sheet music charts for 7 weeks, from June to August that year.

In America, the Chordettes recorded *Lay Down Your Arms* in a reverse of the usual route for cover versions in the '50s, and took it to number 16 on the Top 100. Britain had its revenge when the Mudlarks covered their *Lollipop* and took it to number 2 in Britain, leaving the Chordettes a few places lower down at number 6.

51

A WOMAN IN LOVE

FRANKIE LAINE

19 October 1956, for four weeks

●●●●

Philips PB 617

Written by Frank Loesser. Produced by Mitch Miller.

A Woman In Love has been the title of two different songs that have reached number one. Frankie Laine's song and Barbra Streisand's song (see no. 468) have nothing in common except their title. The same can be said for the other titles used twice for chart-topping songs, *Forever And Ever* (no. 384 by Slik and no. 392 by Demis Roussos) and *The Power Of Love* (no. 542 by Frankie Goes To Hollywood and no. 558 by Jennifer Rush). Laine's *A Woman In Love* was written by Frank Loesser, composer of many popular songs in the '40s and '50s, including for example *Slow Boat To China*, which Emile Ford turned into a Top 10 hit in 1960.

This was Frankie Laine's fourth and, as it turned out, final number one. His total of four chart toppers established a record which was equalled just over six months later, on 17 May 1957, by Guy Mitchell. Laine and Mitchell then shared the lead until they were joined by Elvis Presley on 15 May 1959 and overtaken on 3 November 1960 when *It's Now Or Never* crashed into the charts at number one. By that time Laine had held or shared the record for most number ones since *Hey Joe* hit the top seven years and eleven days earlier.

During *A Woman In Love*'s run at the top,

many people had their minds on other things. The British Prime Minister Sir Anthony Eden stated that there were 'very grave issues at stake', and on 31 October 1956 the combined Anglo-French invasion of the Suez canal area began. This action was not supported by President Eisenhower of the United States, and for some time there was a rift in the special relationship between Britain and America which not even the lungs of Mr Laine could repair.

52

JUST WALKIN' IN THE

RAIN

JOHNNIE RAY

16 November 1956, for seven weeks

●●●●●●●

Philips PB 024

Written by Johnny Bragg and Robert S Riley. Produced by Mitch Miller.

Two and a half years after his previous number one, at a time when the gathering tide of rock and roll was preparing to swoop the crooners of the early '50s into obscurity, both Johnnie Ray and Guy Mitchell came back with a pair of number ones apiece. By this time, Johnnie Ray was already a show business institution, but many people considered him to be nothing more than a gimmick. The Sultan Of Sob, the Cry Guy, the Tearleader, the Prince Of Wails were all nicknames given by the cynical critics who recognized but scorned Ray's ability to play on the emotions of his audience. To that one can only reply in the words of the sleevenotes on one of his albums: 'Johnnie's tears were always real, induced by the sadness of the songs he sang, and did not originate in some carefully concealed artificial tear duct devised by some James Bondian genius of refined gadgetry. He didn't hide his feelings, which meant he was the centre of controversy around the world, particularly here in Britain, where our upper lips retain much of their traditional stiffness and we are often embarrassed by public displays of emotion.' We may have been embarrassed, but not enough to stop buying his records.

Guy Mitchell *holds a barbecue at the Savoy. Here he feeds fan Clory Smith of Fulham.*

Just Walkin' In The Rain was a song first recorded by The Prisonaires, inmates at Tennessee State Prison, in 1954. In America it gave Johnnie Ray his biggest hit since his only chart-topper *Cry*, by climbing up to number 2, stopped only by Elvis Presley's *Love Me Tender*.

53

SINGING THE BLUES

GUY MITCHELL

4 January 1957, for one week
18 January 1957, for one week
1 February 1957, for one week
(top equal)

●●●

Philips PB 650

Written by Melvin Endsley. Produced by Mitch Miller.

Guy Mitchell's third number one and the fourth song to hit number one in two

different versions was written in '54 by Melvin Endsley, who had been paralysed since contracting polio at the age of three in 1937. It was a number one in America for 10 consecutive weeks from early December 1956, beating the Marty Robbins original which peaked at 17. Mitchell repeated his success in Britain, although the local competition proved stronger than in the United States. The backing that the Ray Conniff Orchestra gave to Guy Mitchell's version of *Singing The Blues* made it a very different sound from the slap-happy skiffle-rock of the Steelmen, who may well have come closer to the sound Melvin Endsley was looking for than the men under Mr Conniff's baton.

Guy Mitchell's *Singing The Blues* all but equalled the record of *I Believe* by returning twice to the number one spot, but the second time it had to share the top ranking with Frankie Vaughan (see no. 55). Mitchell's stay of 22 weeks on the chart gave him the longest chart run of any of his 14 hits. When Dave Edmunds revived the song in 1980, he took it to number 28 and increased the total number of weeks the song has

spent on the chart to 45, making it one of the more successful songs in history.

54

SINGING THE BLUES

TOMMY STEELE AND THE STEELMEN

11 January 1957, for one week

●

Decca F 10819

Written by Melvin Endsley. Produced by Hugh Mendl.

The story of Tommy Hicks, the merchant seaman from Bermondsey who became Tommy Steele, Britain's answer to Elvis

Tommy Steele celebrates his number one with his family at home in Frean Street, Bermondsey.

Presley, is too well known to bear repetition here. Steele was never really a rock and roller, despite a first hit called *Rock With The Caveman*. All the same he hit number one six months and a day before Elvis himself hit the top of the British charts for the first time.

Tommy Steele at the time was managed by John Kennedy, who discovered him playing at the 2 I's coffee bar during a period of shore leave. At about this time Larry Parnes, the legendary promoter known as Mr Parnes Shillings and Pence, also took an interest. Despite Parnes' subsequent stableful of pop stars (Marty Wilde, Duffy Power, Georgie Fame, Vince Eager, Billy Fury etc.) Tommy Steele was his only act ever to achieve a number one. Marty Wilde, Billy Fury and Joe Brown all reached number 2, and Georgie Fame's number ones came only after he left the Larry Parnes fold. Incidentally, when Kim Wilde followed her father to number 2 in 1981, they became the only case of two generations of family reaching number 2 without making number one. Kim Wilde, did, however, reach the very top in America early in 1987 with her revival of the Supremes' *You Keep Me Hanging On*.

Lionel Bart was writing for Tommy Steele at this time, although both this song and the follow-up, *Knee Deep In The Blues*, were Guy Mitchell covers written by Melvin Endsley. Two and a half years later, Lionel Bart wrote his first number one hit, *Living Doll*, which like *Singing The Blues* went on to become a chart-topper in two different versions.

55

GARDEN OF EDEN

FRANKIE VAUGHAN

25 January 1957, for four weeks
(1 week top equal)

●●●●

Philips PB 660

Written by Denise Norwood. Produced by Johnny Franz.

Frankie Vaughan was the first Liverpool act to top the charts, but his style was far apart from his famous successors like the Beatles and Frankie Goes To Hollywood. Vaughan's was an extension of the music-hall tradition and his high-kicking top-hatted routine of 'Give me the moonlight, give me the girl and leave the rest to me' is still instantly recognizable thirty years on.

In the late '50s Frankie Vaughan was one of Britain's most popular male vocalists, and one of the main pillars of his success was his recording of *Garden Of Eden*. The original version of the song had been by the American Joe Valino, scoring his only chart success on either side of the Atlantic. It was covered for the British market by Dick James (later to achieve fame and fortune as music publisher for the Beatles and Elton John) Gary Miller and Frankie Vaughan. Vaughan won the chart battle easily and moved into a string of hits with cover versions of songs by acts as varied as Charlie Gracie, Jimmy Rodgers, Edith Piaf and Perry Como. Four and a half years later he topped the charts again (see no. 130).

Garden Of Eden featured lyrics including 'a voice in the Garden tells you she is forbidden', which attracted censure from various circles at the time and even gave rise to a partial broadcast ban on the song. There was no long term effect on Frankie Vaughan's reputation, however, and the singer went on to gain a thoroughly deserved OBE for his charity work.

56

YOUNG LOVE

TAB HUNTER

22 February 1957, for seven weeks

●●●●●●●

London HLD 8380

Written by Carole Joyner and Ric Cartey. Produced by Billy Vaughn.

Tab Hunter was born Arthur Kelm on 11 July 1931 in New York, but was known by his mother's maiden name, Gelien, until he was discovered working at a stable by talent scout Dick Clayton. The surname Hunter came naturally from the horses and legend has it that Hollywood agent Harry Wilson, who gave Rock Hudson his name, said, 'We have to tab you with something', and a star was born. Tab Hunter made his debut in the 1948 film *The Lawless*, and soon landed his first starring role opposite Linda Darnell in *Island Of Desire*.

Young Love was written by two close friends from Atlanta, Georgia. The first recorded version, by co-writer Ric Cartey, failed to set the charts alight. However, Sonny James was given the song to record, and in December 1956 his version began to break into the charts. Randy Wood, president of Pat Boone's label, Dot, had the idea of asking film idol Tab Hunter to record the song, and by early January 1957, Hunter's rival version was in the American record stores. In America, Hunter and James chased each other right to the top of the charts, with Hunter eventually edging out Sonny James, whose record peaked at number 2. In Britain, James only reached number 11, but none of the British cover versions made the charts at all.

Tab Hunter had one more hit on Dot, *99 Ways*, before Warner Brothers, to whom he was under contract for virtually everything, formed their own record label and signed Tab. The first Warner Brothers single to be released in Britain hit number one (see no. 101), but Tab Hunter never hit the charts again. He is still acting in films and on television, though, including a starring role with vocalist Divine in the western *Lust In The Dust*.

57

CUMBERLAND GAP

LONNIE DONEGAN

12 April 1957, for five weeks

●●●●●

Pye Nixa B 15087

A traditional song, arranged by Lonnie Donegan. Produced by Alan Freeman.

Lonnie Donegan, born Anthony Donegan in Glasgow on 29 April 1931, was the most successful British act up to the arrival of Cliff Richard. He was the King Of Skiffle, the craze that swept the world in the early '50s and which enabled anybody with a tea-chest, a broomhandle and a washboard to perform popular songs. After completing National Service in 1951 (note Donegan is only two and a half months older than teen idol Tab Hunter), Lonnie joined Ken Colyer's Jazzmen. He took the name 'Lonnie' after his hero Lonnie Johnson. He played guitar in Ken Colyer's skiffle group along with Chris Barber, and when Barber formed his own jazz band Lonnie Donegan went with him as banjoist.

In 1954 Barber's band recorded *Rock Island Line* as a skiffle record, with Lonnie Donegan on vocals. Included originally on an album, it was not released as a single until the beginning of 1956. It rose quickly into the British Top 10 and, more amazingly, up to number 8 in the American charts. Donegan left Barber, somewhat reluctantly, and the hits rolled out with a consistency that had never before been achieved, even by the likes of Frankie Laine and Guy Mitchell. *Cumberland Gap* was Donegan's fifth single. The previous four had all reached the Top 10. He was so popular in 1956 that an EP, *Skiffle Session*, and an album, *Lonnie Donegan Showcase*, also reached the singles Top 30.

58

ROCK-A-BILLY

GUY MITCHELL

17 May 1957, for one week

●

Philips PB 685

Written by Woody Harris and Eddie V Deane. Produced by Mitch Miller.

Mitch Miller's fifteenth number one production was also Guy Mitchell's fourth and final number one in Britain. It was as near as Mitch Miller would ever get to admitting the existence of rock and roll, skiffle or the blues. The title of the song became the name for a whole style of music, a cross between rock and hillbilly country music. The tempo of the song is much brisker than anything else Mitchell took into the charts, and despite the jangling piano, which sounds more like Winifred Atwell than Floyd Cramer, the mood is unlike any other Guy Mitchell or Mitch Miller hit. It also predates Rocky Burnette's claim that rockabilly was invented by his father, the late Johnny Burnette, and his uncle, Dorsey Burnette, and that they named their music after Rocky and his cousin, Dorsey's son Billy.

Rock-A-Billy just scraped into the American Top 10, and proved to be his last major hit for almost three years. During that time, rockers completed their conquest of world charts and left the disciples of Mitch Miller out in the cold. Mitchell's comeback hit, his last hit in Britain, was called *Heartaches By The Number*. It reached number one in America. In Britain it climbed as high as 5, making it the most successful of the comeback hits of the three 1950s superstars who were all briefly back on the charts at the same time at the end of 1959. Frankie Laine's TV theme tune *Rawhide* reached number 6 and Johnnie Ray's *I'll Never Fall In Love Again* made number 26 before the three cornerstones of Philips' success faded into the sunset.

59

BUTTERFLY

ANDY WILLIAMS

24 May 1957, for two weeks

●●

London HLA 8399

Written by Anthony September. Produced by Archie Bleyer.

Howard Andrew Williams was born on 3 December 1928 in the town of Wall Lake, Iowa. He was one of four brothers who sang in the local church choir, and a little later performed regularly, together with their parents, on their own radio show. The Williams Brothers made their first recording in 1944, when Andy was 15. That session was with Bing Crosby, and the record they made hit number one in the States for 9 weeks. It was *Swinging On A Star*, the song that was revived by Big Dee Irwin and Little Eva in 1963. In 1952, Andy Williams began his solo career in earnest, featuring regularly on Steve Allen's *Tonight* television show until 1955.

His first hit in the States was *Walk Hand In Hand* in April 1956. The song gave Tony Martin a Top 10 hit on both sides of the Atlantic. The next year, Andy Williams released the only record that has ever given him a number one, *Butterfly*. The song was written by Kal Mann and Bernie Lowe under the pseudonym Anthony September.

Mann and Lowe were the writers of Elvis Presley's *Teddy Bear* and founders of the Cameo-Parkway label which gave us Chubby Checker, Bobby Rydell and the Orlons. It also gave us Charlie Gracie, who recorded the original version of *Butterfly*, but who failed to beat the Andy Williams version despite hitting the Top 20 with his record both in Britain (no. 12) and America (no. 7).

Since that early success Andy Williams has established himself as one of the most popular of all American ballad singers, with an immensely successful and long-running television show of his own and a long list of Top 10 hits including *Can't Get Used To Losing You, Almost There, Where Do I Begin? (Love Story)* and *Can't Take My Eyes Off You.*

60

YES TONIGHT

JOSEPHINE

JOHNNIE RAY

7 June 1957, for three weeks

●●●

Philips PB 686

Written by Winfield Scott and Dorothy Goodman. Produced by Mitch Miller.

Johnnie Ray's third and final number one was one of the few happy songs he recorded. It was an up tempo number and, like stablemate Guy Mitchell's *Rock-A-Billy* (see no. 58), it involved producer Mitch Miller in something closer to rock and roll than his usual bouncy style. That is not to say that *Yes Tonight Josephine* was a rock song, as it was more in the tradition of *Dreamboat* and *Rock And Roll Waltz* than of *Hound Dog* or even *Why Do Fools Fall In Love*. The song was revived by producer Stuart Colman in 1981 for the Jets, but its pedigree ensured that it was not as successful as his revamping of *This Ole House* or *Green Door* with Shakin' Stevens.

On 14 June, the second week that *Yes Tonight Josephine* topped the charts, Elvis Presley's *All Shook Up* came in at number 24 and then dropped off the chart again. This false start for the first number one by The King was just a hiccup in the revolution that was to sweep all the big Columbia acts under Mitch Miller's control out of the world's number one positions for ever. From then on, it was the nostalgia market that guaranteed record sales for the early '50s balladeers, not the pop fans. For producer Mitch Miller it was the end of his British successes. Only one more of his productions was to make the top, and that was a song (see no. 72) recorded in 1956. Miller had fought against rock, he had condemned it and ignored it, but it hadn't gone away.

61

GAMBLIN' MAN/
PUTTING ON THE
STYLE

LONNIE DONEGAN

28 June 1957, for two weeks

●●

Pye Nixa N 15093

Written by (Gamblin' Man) Woody Guthrie and Lonnie Donegan, (Putting On The Style) traditional, arranged by Norman Cazden. Produced by Alan Freeman and Michael Barclay (recorded live at the London Palladium).

Lonnie Donegan's second consecutive number one, his sixth consecutive Top 10 hit, was also Britain's first live chart-topper and the first double-sided number one. Only 18 of Britain's number ones have been listed as double-sided hits (apart from the two number one EPs), and few have been so genuinely split in sales between the two sides as this classic skiffle single.

Gamblin' Man was a Woody Guthrie tune, adapted by Donegan, just as he later adapted Guthrie's *Grand Coolie Dam* for yet another Top 10 hit a year later. Guthrie, whose son Arlo has charted in America with songs like *Alice's Restaurant* and *Coming Into Los Angeles*, was the major influence on Bob Dylan and other folk artists of the early '60s. But by the time Lonnie Donegan was at number one with the only Woody Guthrie song that ever reached the very top, the writer had already given up performing as a result of his increasing disability caused by a rare nerve disease, Huntington's Chorea. He died on 3 October 1967.

Putting On The Style hit the charts twice more after its ultimate success in the summer of 1957. In August and September of that year, a version by Billy Cotton (father of BBC executive Bill Cotton) roamed around the lower reaches of the Top 20 as part of the *All Star Hit Parade No. 2* package. At Christmas in 1958, Lonnie Donegan brought it back into the charts as part of his medley single *Lonnie's Skiffle Party*, which peaked at number 23. Donegan thus is on the short list of those acts who have had hits with re-recorded versions of their own earlier number ones – along with Elvis Presley, Jimmy Young, Slade and Cliff Richard.

62

ALL SHOOK UP

ELVIS PRESLEY

12 July 1957, for seven weeks

●●●●●●●

HMV POP 359

Written by Otis Blackwell and Elvis Presley. Produced by Steve Sholes.

After two number 2 hits and seven other hits in the first year of his chart career, Elvis finally hit number one with his tenth British hit single, his only number one on the HMV label and the only one of his seventeen number ones on which he shares a writing credit.

Otis Blackwell had written the classic *Don't Be Cruel* (which was not issued as an A-side in UK until 1978, despite topping the US charts for 11 weeks in 1956) and was looking for a follow-up for Elvis. A publishing colleague, Al Stanton, suggested the title, and within a few days Blackwell came up with another classic. Elvis was not entirely satisfied with the song and so, with Blackwell's consent, rewrote some of the words. The rest is history.

Born in Tupelo, Mississippi on 8 June 1935, Elvis Aaron Presley was to prove to be the King, the man who defined rock'n'roll and was responsible for creating the demand for rock music on which a mammoth industry has been built. He once said, 'Rhythm is something you either have or you don't have, but when you have it, you have it all over.' He had it so much that when, as a publicity stunt, TV host Ed Sullivan announced he would only show Elvis from the waist up, it was front page news in the *New York Times*.

*The 21-year-old **Elvis Presley** faces his fans at a 1956 appearance in Texas.*

63

DIANA

PAUL ANKA

30 August 1957, for nine weeks

●●●●●●●●●

Columbia DB 3980

Written by Paul Anka. Produced by Don Costa.

Canadian-born Paul Anka was 16 years and 31 days old when his self-penned single reached the number one spot, and he was not much older by the time his paean to young love had become one of the biggest-selling records of all time. Its total sales of over eight million copies made it the biggest hit his American label ABC-Paramount ever had, and it made Anka a world star.

Diana was a real girl, Diana Ayoub, who used to baby-sit for Anka's younger brother and sister. She was 20, Paul was 15, and the heartache of the age-gap poured out in the song. In April 1957 Paul Anka borrowed $100 from his father, travelled to New York and in true show-business tradition persuaded ABC staff producer Don Costa to listen to his limited repertoire. Costa, one of the great producers of the rock era, knew a hit when he heard it and promptly flew Anka's father to New York to sign a contract on behalf of his 15-year-old son. The next day Diana was recorded – in one take.

Paul Anka never had another number one hit in Britain, although his chart career included six more Top 10 hits and lasted until 1974 when his US number one *(You're) Having My Baby* reached number 6 in Britain at the end of that year. He also wrote *It Doesn't Matter Anymore* for Buddy Holly and thus became the first person ever to write a British chart-topper for himself and for somebody else. His *Puppy Love*, a small hit for the composer in 1960, became a number one for Donny Osmond over a decade later, while his main claim to composing fame must now be his English lyrics to the only song that has been a hit for the Sex Pistols, Elvis Presley and Frank Sinatra – *My Way*.

Jerry Lee Lewis *in action in 1958, the year of his only number one.*

Paul Anka *thinking of* Diana.

64

THAT'LL BE THE DAY

THE CRICKETS

1 November 1957, for three weeks

● ● ●

Vogue Coral Q 72279

Written by Buddy Holly, Jerry Allison and Norman Petty. Produced by Norman Petty.

That'll Be The Day was the phrase used by John Wayne, playing the role of ex-Confederate soldier Ethan Edwards in the classic 1956 John Ford Western *The Searchers* (a film which also gave the *Needles and Pins* group their name). A group of high-school boys from Lubbock, Texas, led by Charles 'Buddy' Holley, saw the film and remembered the phrase. Holly (the 'e' disappeared for stage purposes) and his friend and drummer Jerry Allison turned it into a song and took it to Decca. The song was recorded but this first release by the Crickets flopped. Lead-singer Buddy Holly still had faith in the song, so the Crickets (Holly, Allison, Larry Welborn and Niki Sullivan) drove to Norman Petty's studios in Clovis, New Mexico and re-recorded it in a very different style.

The Crickets' contract at Decca meant they could not sell the recording elsewhere, but eventually Bob Thiele, A&R manager at the

Decca subsidiary Coral Records, decided he wanted to release the track, so Decca released them from their contract with Decca and bound them to another one with Coral.

The record was released in the States in June 1957, but moved very slowly at first. By the end of July it had broken out regionally in New England, and it crept onto the lower reaches of the national chart. From there on, it rose rapidly to the top and Buddy Holly and the Crickets had arrived.

65

MARY'S BOY CHILD

HARRY BELAFONTE

22 November 1957, for seven weeks

● ● ● ● ● ● ●

RCA 1022

Written by Jester Hairston. Produced by Rono Farnon.

Harry Belafonte, whose record label in the UK had changed from HMV to RCA when the American giant formed their own UK Sales subsidiary in the summer of 1957, gave his employers their first British number one with the most famous Christmas hit of all. It was the first record to sell a million copies in Britain alone, and it reached the top over a month before Christmas. Its seven week run at number one is the longest by a song with a Christmas theme, and it is the only Christmas song to reach number one in two versions, a feat accomplished when Boney M took it back to the top in 1978 (see no. 430).

Harold George Belafonte was born in New York on 1 March 1927. He spent three years in the US Navy and then enrolled at the American Negro Theatre Workshop. His singing came to the attention of manager Marty Kaye, and eventually a recording contract with RCA Victor followed. He starred in a series of films, such as *Carmen Jones, The World, The Flesh and The Devil* and *Island In The Sun*. It was this last film, together with his 1957 albums *Calypso* and *Belafonte Sings Of The Caribbean*, which gave him the nickname, 'King Of Calypso' and hits like the self-penned *Banana Boat Song, Scarlet Ribbons* and *Mary's Boy Child. Island In The Sun* was also the inspiration for the name Island Records.

Writer Jester Hairston was seen 10 years later acting in the Sidney Poitier/Rod Steiger film, 'In The Heat Of The Night' and Belafonte himself returned to number one 28 years later when he and one of his most ardent admirers of the late '50s, Bob Dylan, both participated in USA For Africa's *We Are The World* (see no. 548).

66

GREAT BALLS OF FIRE

JERRY LEE LEWIS

10 January 1958, for two weeks

● ●

London HLS 8529

Written by Otis Blackwell and Jack Hammer. Produced by Sam Phillips.

Jerry Lee Lewis, born in Ferriday, Louisiana on 29 September 1935, was, and is, one of the great originals of rock. Like Elvis Presley, Roy Orbison and Johnny Cash, he began his career at Sam Phillips' Sun label in Memphis, and he became the only white rock'n'-roller of real note to use a piano rather than a guitar as his main weapon.

Great Balls Of Fire, co-written by Otis Blackwell of *All Shook Up* fame and the aptly named Jack Hammer, is one of the wildest rock records ever to top the British charts. Jerry Lee lived as frantic a life as the music he played, and his first career came to an abrupt end when it was disclosed that he had married his 14-year-old cousin. Three years later he was back in the Top 10 with what is still the only version of the Ray Charles classic *What'd I Say* to reach the British charts. Then a move back to his country roots, coupled with further personal problems, pushed his career into obscurity as far as Britain was concerned.

In America, Jerry Lee had established himself by the early '70s as a major country star with a string of hits to his name. However, as far as the fans on this side of the Atlantic are concerned, his last hit has been with the Big Bopper's classic *Chantilly Lace*, which Lewis took to number 33 in 1972.

Happily, he survived serious illness in 1981 after hovering between life and death for several days, but ill health has continued to dog him throughout the '80s.

67

JAILHOUSE ROCK

ELVIS PRESLEY

24 January 1958, for three weeks

● ● ●

RCA 1028

Written by Jerry Lieber and Mike Stoller.
Produced by Steve Sholes.

For the first time since the chart began over five years earlier, a record entered the hit parade at number one. Needless to say, it was Elvis Presley who achieved this unthinkable feat with the title tune from his third film, *Jailhouse Rock*. Most Elvis fans would list *Jailhouse Rock* as his best movie; his four pre-Army films seem in hindsight to be in a completely different class from the increasingly insipid post-demobilization efforts.

Written by Jerry Lieber and Mike Stoller, whose hit songs for the Coasters and others had made them one of the most successful of rock writing teams, the title tune of *Jailhouse Rock* showed off Elvis' talents at their very best. Elvis cut over 20 Lieber/Stoller songs during his career, after he had come across their work through a lounge group's version of Willie Mae Thornton's original R&B hit

Michael Holliday.

Hound Dog, but this was the only UK chart-topper written solely by these two song-writing giants. They were two-thirds of the team that wrote Elvis' 12th number one *She's Not You*. The recording was made at MGM's studio in Culver City on 2 May 1957 with the following line-up: Elvis (vocals and guitar), Scotty Moore (guitar), Mike Stoller and Elvis Presley (piano), Bill Black (bass), D J Fontana (drums), and the Jordanaires (backing vocals).

For five weeks one of the records selling in opposition to *Jailhouse Rock* in Britain was an EP containing five songs from the movie, including *Jailhouse Rock* itself. No other number one A-side has ever appeared in the Top 20 twice in the same week, but many fans were presumably buying both single and EP, needing both to get all six songs from the movie, as the flip of the single, *Treat Me Nice* (another Lieber/Stoller song) was not on the EP.

68

THE STORY OF MY LIFE

MICHAEL HOLLIDAY

14 February 1958, for two weeks

● ●

Columbia DB 4058

Written by Burt Bacharach and Hal David.
Produced by Norrie Paramor.

The story of Michael Holliday's life was tragic. Born in Liverpool in the late 1920s, Michael Miller changed his name by deed poll to Michael Milne, but then used his mother's maiden name for his singing career. By the beginning of 1956 he was breaking through the ranks of British hopefuls and into the charts, basing his style on the casual phrasing and delivery of people like Perry Como and Bing Crosby. In 1956 he had three chart singles (the highest of which climbed to number 13) and was given his own TV show. However Holliday lacked self-confidence and was unable to cope with the success he found. All the same, his popularity continued beyond the end of the decade and in 1960 he scored his second chart-topper. Three years later he shot himself.

The Story Of My Life was the first of six Bacharach/David number one hits and had been first recorded by Marty Robbins. In Britain, Michael Holliday also faced competition from Alma Cogan, Dave King and Gary Miller, but Holliday's version won easily. This was the second time that Marty Robbins had missed out on the British market, because his first major American hit, *A White Sport Coat*, was covered by Terry Dene, who took his version to the British Top 20. Marty Robbins did not enter the British charts until 1960, when his four-minute single *El Paso* climbed to number 19. Robbins never hit number one in Britain, while even Michael Holliday proved much less successful than the writers of his first chart-topper, Burt Bacharach and Hal David.

69

MAGIC MOMENTS

PERRY COMO

28 February 1958, for eight weeks

● ● ● ● ● ● ● ●

RCA 1036

Written by Burt Bacharach and Hal David.
Produced by Joe Reisman.

For the first time in chart history, consecutive number ones were written by the same writers, a feat that was not to be repeated for over five years, when Bruce Welch co-wrote both *Summer Holiday* and *Foot Tapper* (nos. 148 and 149). Burt Bacharach and Hal David were never firmly linked with any particular act (although they wrote a lot for Dionne Warwick in the '60s), and their immense success is based entirely on the brilliance of their songs rather than the popularity of the performer.

Having said that, Perry Como in 1958 was a very popular singer. His 'Perry Como Show' was the most successful television variety show of the time in America, Britain and many other countries, and Como was the highest paid television performer of that time, a title he took over from Eddie Fisher. *Magic Moments* and the flip side *Catch A Falling Star* were both sung by Perry on his show early in January 1958, and both sides immediately took up separate chart positions on both sides of the Atlantic. In America it was *Catch A Falling Star* that climbed all the way to the top, while *Magic Moments* just scraped into the Top 30. In

Britain the roles were reversed: *Catch A Falling Star* climbed to number 9 but *Magic Moments* held on to the number one position for eight weeks.

During those eight weeks, a major moment in rock history occurred. Elvis Presley was drafted into the Army on 24 March 1958.

70

WHOLE LOTTA
WOMAN

MARVIN RAINWATER

25 April 1958, for three weeks

●●●

MGM 974

Written by Marvin Rainwater. Produced by Jim Vinneau.

With a name like Marvin Rainwater, you either had to succeed outrageously or else sink without trace. He actually did both, in that order. Born on 2 July 1925 in Wichita, Kansas, full blooded Cherokee Marvin Percy took his mother's maiden name to become a country singer.

He first scored on the national charts in America in the summer of 1957 with *Gonna Find Me A Bluebird*. That had reached number 3 on the American country charts, and number 22 on the pop charts, and the combination of Marvin Rainwater and the hot MGM label seemed certain to carry on succeeding. His follow-up was a duet with the girl destined to be MGM's hottest star of the late '50s, Connie Francis, which also sold a million. Then came *Whole Lotta Woman*, which for no apparent reason (it made only number 60 on the Billboard pop charts) was released in the UK and started picking up airplay action, what little of it there was in 1958. In a year which featured *Great Balls Of Fire*, *Jailhouse Rock* and *It's Only Make Believe* at the top of the British charts, *Whole Lotta Woman* stands comparison with those greats as a fine rock and roll record, typical of the era when country and rock were still blood brothers.

Marvin Rainwater's follow-up was a lesser hit, called *I Dig You Baby*. Thereafter, obscurity reclaimed him almost as quickly as he had found fame.

Marvin Rainwater was replaced at the top by the woman with whom he had earlier recorded a million-selling duet, Connie Francis.

71

WHO'S SORRY NOW?

CONNIE FRANCIS

16 May 1958, for six weeks

●●●●●●

MGM 975

Written by Ted Snyder, Bert Kalmar and Herman Ruby. Produced by Harry Myerson. Orchestra and chorus arranged by Joe Lippman.

For one last attempt at a hit before her recording contract at MGM lapsed, pint-sized Concetta Franconero revived the 1920s standard *Who's Sorry Now?* The answer – nobody except the acts she kept away from the top of the charts for six weeks in the early summer of 1958.

Born on 12 December 1938, Connie Francis left university in New York before graduation to concentrate on her musical career. At first the decision seemed mistaken. Apart from a duet with Marvin Rainwater, *Majesty Of Love* in 1957, all her recordings failed totally. Then she was given a song from 1923 to record, and with a very straightforward arrangement she took it to the top of the British charts. Contrary to popular legend, *Who's Sorry Now?* did not make number one in the States, peaking at number 4. Her other British number one, *Stupid Cupid* coupled with *Carolina Moon* (see no. 75), made only number 17 in America, while her three American number ones all failed to reach the very top in Britain. Generally speaking, her successful songs in Britain were the up-tempo numbers like *Stupid Cupid* and *Robot Man* and *Lipstick On Your Collar. Who's Sorry Now?* was the exception that launched her career.

72

ON THE STREET
WHERE YOU LIVE

VIC DAMONE

27 June 1958, for two weeks
(one week top equal)

●●

Philips PB 819

Written by Alan Jay Lerner and Frederick Loewe. Produced by Mitch Miller.

The musical *My Fair Lady* is probably the best known of all 1950s musicals. It launched the career of Julie Andrews, while Rex Harrison gave non-singers new career prospects in the musical with his expert and much imitated style of talking to music.

Vic Damone *had enjoyed an American number one,* You're Breaking My Heart, *in 1949.*

When the show opened on Broadway, the producers went to great lengths to ensure that the music was not exported, so that the show could open in markets like Britain in front of audiences to whom it would all be new. The formula worked.

Vic Damone was the lucky man with the British hit version of the hit song, *On The Street Where You Live.* Damone had the advantage of having already had an American Top 10 hit with the song, even though it had been two years earlier in the spring of 1956. Thus it was that Mitch Miller's final British number one production, his 17th, was actually recorded before his 16th, Johnnie Ray's *Yes Tonight Josephine* (see no. 60), not to mention the 15th, 14th, 13th, 12th and 11th (see nos. 58, 53, 52, 51 and 49). Such was the time lag in musicals between Broadway and London that by the time *On The Street Where You Live* reached number one in Britain, Damone's version of the title tune from Lerner and Loewe's next musical, *Gigi,* had been and gone from the American charts. Many years later, during a BBC Radio Two interview, Damone claimed that had this single, recorded while *My Fair Lady* was in an out-of-town preview, not been a hit, *On The Street Where You Live* would have been cut from the Broadway production.

Although it is close to 30 years since Vic Damone was in the British charts, he remains a popular performer in cabaret and on television on both sides of the Atlantic. In 1987 he married Diahann Carroll, the American singer and star of *Dynasty.*

73

ALL I HAVE TO DO IS
DREAM/CLAUDETTE

THE EVERLY BROTHERS

4 July 1958, for seven weeks
(one week top equal)

 ●●●●●●●

London HLA 8618

Written by *(All I Have To Do Is Dream)* Felice and Boudleaux Bryant, *(Claudette)* Roy Orbison. Produced by Archie Bleyer, arranged by Don Everly.

Four number ones out of thirteen top tens for the **Everly Brothers**.

Don (born 1 February 1937) and Phil (born 19 January 1939) Everly launched their careers as the most successful vocal group in pre-Beatles history with the classic *Bye Bye Love.* That was written for them by the husband and wife team of Boudleaux and Felice Bryant, so when a year later the same writers came up with *All I Have To Do Is Dream,* it was to the Everlys that they took their song.

Don and Phil hailed from Brownie, Kentucky, but soon moved to Shenandoah, Iowa, where their parents Ike and Margaret began hosting their own country radio show on the local station, KMA. When Phil was six and Don eight, they made their debuts on their parents' show, and from then on they kept on singing. *All I Have To Do Is Dream* was their fourth American single. The Bryants claim they wrote it in fifteen minutes. If so, it was one of the most profitable quarter-hours ever spent, because the song has become a standard, with hundreds of different recorded versions over the years. Bobbie Gentry and Glen Campbell took their version to number 3 in 1969, but nobody has ever quite matched the plaintive harmonies of the Everly Brothers, with whom the song will always be associated. At their Reunion Concerts at the Albert Hall in

1984, this was the song that drew the biggest applause.

The flip side, which was listed with the A-side for 20 of the record's 21 weeks of chart action, was written by the then unknown Roy Orbison as a rocking tribute to his wife Claudette. It was the first of two number ones for the Everlys with a girl's name in the title – *Cathy's Clown* (see no. 101) was to follow. All in all, Don and Phil charted with songs about Susie, Claudette, Mary, Jenny, Cathy, Lucille and Ebony Eyes, who were only seven of the millions of girls who worshipped the Everlys when they were at their peak.

74

WHEN

THE KALIN TWINS

22 August 1958, for five weeks

●●●●●

Brunswick 05751

Written by Jack Reardon and Paul Evans. Produced by Jack Pleis.

Harold and Herbie Kalin were born on 16 February 1939, making them one day older than John Leyton (see no. 124). They were discovered by Clint Ballard Jr, the writer of many hits including *Good Timin'* for Jimmy Jones and *I'm Alive* for the Hollies. Harold and Herbie were the first set of twins to reach number one in Britain, and remain the only set to make it on their own. Twins Robin and Maurice Gibb of the Bee Gees and Dervin and Lincoln Gordon of the Equals are probably the only other twins to reach number one.

The Kalin Twins proved to be one-hit wonders, the third on the list. The plea of their follow-up, *Forget Me Not*, was not heeded and the fans quickly forgot them. The song was longer lasting. Showaddywaddy revived it in 1977 as the follow-up to their only chart-topper, *Under The Moon Of Love* (see no. 397), and took it to number 3. It was to prove the second in a run of seven consecutive top ten hits for Showaddywaddy, but the first and last for the Kalin Twins.

75

CAROLINA MOON/

STUPID CUPID

CONNIE FRANCIS

26 September 1958, for six weeks

●●●●●●

MGM 985

Written by *(Carolina Moon)* Benny Davis and Joe Burke, *(Stupid Cupid)* Neil Sedaka and Howard Greenfield. Produced by Connie Francis and Leroy Holmes. Arranged and conducted by Leroy Holmes.

The combination of a revival of a Twenties American standard and a brand new teenybop rocker by Neil Sedaka and Howard Greenfield gave Connie Francis her second number one in three releases. It also meant that she spent 12 weeks of 1958 at the very top of the charts, a domination of the top spot beaten only six times in 35 years. At the end of 1958, she was second only to Frankie Laine's unbeatable total of 27 weeks at number one in 1953, but she has subsequently been overtaken by Elvis Presley (18 weeks at the top in 1961 and 15 weeks in 1962), the Beatles (16 weeks in 1963), John Travolta and Olivia Newton-John (16 weeks in 1978) and Frankie Goes to Hollywood (15 weeks in 1984).

Carolina Moon *was a number one in America for Gene Austin in 1929 and in Britain by* **Connie Francis** *in 1958*

After 1958, Connie Francis never hit number one again in the UK. Top 10 hits, eight more in all, continued until 1962, and she remains, behind Shirley Bassey and Diana Ross, the third most successful female vocalist in British chart history, despite having seen no chart action since 1966. Perhaps more surprisingly, *Stupid Cupid* is the only Neil Sedaka song ever to hit the top in the UK. Sedaka himself scored his first hit *I Go Ape*, some six months after *Stupid Cupid* dropped off the summit, but in a career spanning 190 chart weeks, seven Top 10 hits and 18 chart entries from 1959 to 1975, Neil Sedaka never climbed higher than number 3, a position claimed by both *Oh Carol* and *Happy Birthday Sweet Sixteen*.

76

IT'S ALL IN THE GAME

TOMMY EDWARDS

7 November 1958, for three weeks

● ● ●

MGM 989

Written by Charles Gates Dawes and Carl Sigman. Produced by Harry Myerson.

In 1951 Tommy Edwards (born 17 February 1922) hit the American charts with two singles *Morning Side Of The Mountain* and *It's All In The Game*. The latter tune had been written in 1912 by a Chicago banker who went on to become Vice-President of the United States from 1925 to 1929. He called the tune *Melody In A Major* and almost 40 years later Carl Sigman added the lyrics that turned the tune into a standard.

After Edwards' successes in 1951 he failed to chart again. MGM were about to release him from his contract when they decided to use him to re-record some of his early hits as a demonstration of the new technological breakthrough – stereo. To everybody's astonishment *It's All In The Game* became a massive hit, selling over three million copies worldwide and hitting number one in both Britain and the USA. Five years later Cliff Richard took it to number 2 in the UK and number 25 in the US, his biggest hit in America until the mid-'70s. The Four Tops version reached number 5 in Britain in 1970. By then Tommy Edwards was dead, having died at the age of 47 on 22 October 1969.

Conway Twitty *has tallied over thirty number ones in the US country music chart.*

77

HOOTS MON

LORD ROCKINGHAM'S XI

28 November 1958, for three weeks

● ● ●

Decca F 11059

Written by Harry Robinson. Produced by Harry Robinson.

The stomping party hit *Hoots Mon* was based upon a traditional Scottish folk song called *100 Pipers* and adapted by the XI's bandleader, Harry Robinson. The record owed its popularity to continual plugging on Jack Good's television show *Oh Boy*, on which Lord Rockingham's XI were the house band. The music featured the rasping tenor saxophone of Red Price, who retired from the music business a short while after the zenith of *Hoots Mon* (it is not known if the two events are connected) and spent the remainder of his days happily pulling pints in his own pub until his death in the mid-'70s. Ironically the band included author and critic Benny Green, a man who has vowed not to rest until rock and roll is slain.

The track was recorded at Decca's studios in West Hampstead and despite sales of over half-a-million the musicians were only

paid £6 each for their part in the only number one single to feature Roman numerals. The actual identity of Lord Rockingham himself remains uncertain. Some say it was Robinson, some Good, some even a combination of the two, but what is known is that *Hoots Mon* was the only major chart success for the shadowy peer. The follow up, *Wee Tom*, crept into the lower part of the Top 20.

78

IT'S ONLY MAKE BELIEVE

CONWAY TWITTY

19 December 1958, for five weeks

● ● ● ● ●

MGM 992

Written by Conway Twitty and Jack Nance. Produced by Jim Vinneau.

Conway Twitty, born Harold Jenkins in Mariana, Arkansas on 1 September 1933, is reputed to have chosen his stage name from the names of two towns he passed through on one of his early tours as a back-up musician in a country band. The name was certainly memorable, and it gave Peter Sellers the inspiration for his parody of a pop star of the late '50s, Twit Conway.

Even in 1956 and 1957 record companies knew that Elvis imitators could strike lucky. Twitty was signed to Mercury until 1957 making a stream of totally unsuccessful country singles and almost equally unsuccessful rock singles, based on his ability to sound like Elvis. It was his switch to MGM which changed everything. Perhaps it was knowing that any company which already had Marvin Rainwater on its roster would not find anything odd about the name Conway Twitty, but whatever the reason, Twitty came up with a massive worldwide hit with his first single for MGM.

It's Only Make Believe was number one in America, number one in Britain and has gone on to become the only song in history to reach the British Top 10 in four different versions. After Twitty's original success Billy Fury took the song to number 10 in 1964, Glen Campbell reached number four in 1970 and finally teenybop group Child made number 10 in 1978.

Since the early '70s, Conway Twitty has returned to country music, and by the 1980s had chalked up more number one country singles in America than any other performer.

79

THE DAY THE RAINS CAME

JANE MORGAN

23 January 1959, for one week

●

London HLR 8751

Written by Gilbert Becaud, English lyrics by Carl Sigman. Produced by Vic Schoen.

Jane Morgan, born Jane Currier in Boston, Massachusetts, was trained as a lyric soprano at the Julliard School of Music in New York. To work her way through school, she sang blues in the night clubs and was there noticed by French impresario Bernard Hilda, who offered her a contract to sing in Paris. What happened to her lyric soprano training is veiled in the mists of time, but within weeks of Miss Morgan's arrival in the French capital she had taken the city by storm. For the next few years she appeared all over Europe establishing a fine reputation and a growing following. In 1958, she recorded a song by Gilbert Becaud in French, called *Le Jour Où La Pluie Viendra* which she decided to record in English as well. It climbed only to number 21 in the States, but in Britain her European reputation helped to push this dramatic ballad to the very top. The French version, incidentally, was on the B-side of the British release.

She subsequently married Jerry Weintraub, the man who put Elvis back on the road in 1970, and who managed John Denver among others.

80

ONE NIGHT/I GOT STUNG

ELVIS PRESLEY

30 January 1959, for three weeks

● ● ●

RCA 1100

Written by *(One Night)* Dave Bartholomew and Pearl King, *(I Got Stung)* Aaron Schroeder and David Hill. Produced by Steve Sholes and Chet Atkins.

Elvis' third UK number one was his first to get there after he went into the US Army in March 1958, and was his first double-sided British chart-topper. *One Night* was written by Dave Bartholomew, responsible for many of Fats Domino's hits, and Pearl King, and was recorded without great commercial success by Smiley Lewis in 1956. Elvis got to grips with it in Radio Recorders Studio, in Hollywood in February 1957, his vocal and guitar being supported by Scotty Moore (guitar), Dudley Brooks (piano), Bill Black (bass), D J Fontana (drums) and the backing vocals of the Jordanaires. It thus remained unissued for two years, to become one of many tracks that kept Elvis' name in the chart while he was a guest of Uncle Sam in Germany and unable to make many new recordings.

I Got Stung was actually cut shortly after Elvis' induction into the Army, at RCA in Nashville in June 1958, his last sessions for nearly two years. It was written by Aaron Schroeder and David Hill. By this point in Elvis' career, his recording output was controlled by music publisher Freddy Bienstock who acted as a clearing house for all the enormous number of songs that were submitted for Elvis, together with Steve Sholes and Chet Atkins. Atkins played guitar on *I Got Stung*, the rest of the line-up being Floyd Cramer on piano, Bob Moore on bass, D J Fontana on drums, Murray Harmon bashing the bongoes, and the Jordanaires backing Elvis Presley's vocals.

81

AS I LOVE YOU

SHIRLEY BASSEY

20 February 1959, for four weeks

● ● ● ●

Philips PB 845

Written by Jay Livingston and Ray Evans. Produced by Johnny Franz.

The most successful female vocalist on the British charts has been Shirley Veronica Bassey, born in Cardiff on 8 January 1937, Elvis Presley's second birthday and, by coincidence, the 44th birthday of Max Freedman, co-writer of *Rock Around The Clock*. Shirley Bassey's chart career began a month after her 20th birthday, when her version of Harry Belafonte's *Banana Boat Song* entered the charts. Although outsold by the original version, she nevertheless secured her first of twelve Top 10 hits. Two more small hits followed, but 1956 was a blank year chartwise for the girl from Tiger Bay until TV exposure broke *As I Love You*.

As I Love You, written by the same American team that had come up with *Whatever Will Be Will Be* for Doris Day (see no. 49), reached number one nine weeks after its first chart placing, and at the same time her next single, *Kiss Me Honey Honey Kiss Me*, was racing into the Top 10 to peak at number 3. For one week, the two singles shared the number 3 position in the charts, making Miss Bassey one of only nine acts to have had two hits in the Top 3 in the same week.

After that Shirley Bassey's chart career just kept on rolling. No fewer than four of her hits have enjoyed runs of more than 20 weeks on the chart, the longest running of all being her 1960 recording of the hit song from Lionel Bart's *Oliver*, *As Long As He Needs Me*, which enjoyed 30 weeks of chart action but only climbed to number 2.

Jane Morgan *not dressed for the rain.*

*The hits of **Russ Conway** spent a total of 79 weeks on chart during 1959, the year's highest figure.*

Platters, and their first four singles bobbed in and out of the charts no fewer than 12 times between them. In 1958, the Platters switched to recording oldies, and this the fans loved. *Twilight Time* written in 1944, climbed to number 3, and the follow-up, *Smoke Gets In Your Eyes*, from the 1933 musical *Roberta*, hit the very top.

83

SIDE SADDLE

RUSS CONWAY

27 March 1959, for four weeks

● ● ● ●

Columbia DB 4256

Written by Trevor Stanford. Produced by Norman Newell.

Trevor Stanford was born in Bristol on 2 September 1927 and joined the Merchant Navy at the age of 15 in 1942. Two years later he joined the Royal Navy and almost immediately cut off the top of the third finger of his right hand in mortal combat with a bread slicer. It was not for this action that he won the Distinguished Service Medal, but by the time he left the Navy in 1955, he was Trevor Stanford DSM.

The transformation into Russ Conway was rapid. Stanford had taught himself piano during his sea-going years and on demobilization began playing in clubs. There he was heard by the dancer Irving Davies, who recommended him to Norman Newell.

Russ Conway's recording career began on the well-worn lines of Winifred Atwell, with a medley, *Party Pops*, at Christmas 1957 and *More Party Pops*, his first Top 10 hit, at Christmas 1958. Then he wrote and recorded *Side Saddle* which hit number one, sold a million and stayed on the chart for 30 consecutive weeks, a run which at the time was second only to Frankie Laine's *I Believe*.

Side Saddle remains the longest run by any instrumental to reach number one, but it pales into insignificance beside the 55 week run of Mr. Acker Bilk's *Stranger On The Shore*, which never climbed higher than number 2.

82

SMOKE GETS IN YOUR
EYES

THE PLATTERS

20 March 1959, for one week

●

Mercury AMT 1016

Written by Jerome Kern and Otto Harbach. Produced by Buck Ram.

The Platters were formed in 1953, and by the time *Smoke Gets In Your Eyes* hit number one, the line-up was Tony Williams, lead vocalist, David Lynch, Herb Reed, Paul Robi and Zola Taylor. But the brains behind the group was their manager and producer, Buck Ram. At the end of 1955, the Platters kicked off their American chart career with a Top 10 million-seller which has now hit the British chart in five versions, *Only You*. The follow-up in America was *The Great Pretender* which was a Stateside number one, but nothing was released in Britain until late 1956 shortly after the fourth Platters single in America had given them their second number one. Their first British single was possibly the greatest double-sided single ever released, at least until the Beatles' *Penny Lane/Strawberry Fields Forever*. It was *Only You/The Great Pretender*, which eventually climbed to number 5.

The British public was a little unsure of the

84

IT DOESN'T MATTER

ANYMORE

BUDDY HOLLY

24 April 1959, for three weeks

● ● ●

Coral Q 72360

Written by Paul Anka. Produced by Norman Petty, orchestra directed by Dick Jacobs.

The death of Buddy Holly in an air crash near Clear Lake, Iowa on 3 February 1959 is one of the major events of rock history. Buddy Holly, already established as a major force in pop music through his work with the Crickets, was beginning a solo career which, to judge from the tapes made just before he died, would have been even more spectacular than his time with the Crickets. Since his death it is possible that he has been the biggest single influence on the development of British pop music. The Beatles and the Rolling Stones recorded his songs, the Hollies named themselves after him, Adam Faith copied the pizzicato string section that featured so heavily in *It Doesn't Matter Anymore* and too many acts to mention have used the Holly 'hiccup' on their hits.

It Doesn't Matter Anymore was Holly's only solo number one, and it was the first of nine records that have hit number one after the performer's death. It was written by Paul Anka, who was on that fateful tour with Buddy Holly. While the rest of the musicians on the package tour took the bus to their next destination, Fargo, North Dakota, the three biggest stars, Holly, Ritchie Valens (writer of *La Bamba*, see no. 597) and the Big Bopper flew ahead to get their laundry done. Originally, one of Buddy's backing musicians, Waylon Jennings, was to be on the flight, but at the last minute he gave up his seat to the Big Bopper, who had a cold and who was finding the long bus journeys very uncomfortable.

The flip side of *It Doesn't Matter Anymore*, the classic *Raining In My Heart*, was written by Felice and Boudleaux Bryant. It was the only single up till then by either the Crickets or Buddy Holly on which Holly had no hand in the writing of either side.

Both A Fool Such As I *and* I Need Your Love Tonight *were recorded while* **Elvis Presley** *was in the US Army.*

85

A FOOL SUCH AS I/

I NEED YOUR LOVE

TONIGHT

ELVIS PRESLEY

15 May 1959, for five weeks

● ● ● ● ●

RCA 1113

Written by (*A Fool Such As I*) William Trader, (*I Need Your Love Tonight*) Sid Wayne and Bix Reichner. Produced by Steve Sholes and Chet Atkins.

Elvis' fourth number one in Britain not only put him level with Guy Mitchell and Frankie Laine in the list of most number one hits, but also provided him with his first instance of number ones with consecutive releases, this double-sider following on directly after *One Night/I Got Stung* (see no. 80). *A Fool Such As I* had been a favourite of Elvis' since 1953, when it had reached number four in the American country charts recorded by Hank Snow, an artist at one time handled by Colonel Tom Parker. The first number one ballad hit for Elvis, it had been written by Bill Trader in 1952 and also provided a fairsized pop hit in the States for Jo Stafford in 1953.

I Need Your Love Tonight was a new song written by Sid Wayne and Bix Reichner, and both titles were recorded in Nashville at the same sessions that produced *I Got Stung*. Almost certainly none of Elvis' number ones featured all the legendary musicians who regularly backed Elvis – Chet Atkins, Floyd Cramer, D J Fontana and Bill Black. These tracks featured the first three, but not Bill Black or even Scotty Moore, who had both been on *One Night*.

86

ROULETTE

RUSS CONWAY

19 June 1959, for two weeks

●●

Columbia DB 4298

Written by Trevor Stanford. Produced by Norman Newell.

The only solo instrumentalist ever to achieve consecutive number one hits is Russ Conway. He achieved this feat with ridiculous ease as his second self-penned composition glided up to the number one spot eight weeks after *Side Saddle* dropped off the top. *Roulette* was not as memorable a tune as *Side Saddle*, which is still earning Russ Conway a crust or two, but it was still good enough to beat all opposition for two weeks.

After *Roulette* Russ Conway never topped the charts again, but still racked up four

Russ Conway.

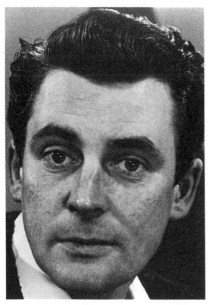

more Top 10 hits and a succession of smaller chart entries up to 1963. *More And More Party Pops* and *Even More Party Pops* gave Conway two more Christmas medley hits, bringing his total up to four, a good number but still a long way short of Winifred Atwell's seven medley hits, the most by any act ever.

The hits stopped in the mid-'60s, and although Russ Conway went on working almost as busily as ever, he subsequently suffered a nervous breakdown and went into retirement for several years. Now happily restored to health, the breezy smile and 9½ finger playing style of Russ Conway can once again be seen and heard on radio and television, even if your collection of Russ Conway 78s has long since been broken.

87

DREAM LOVER

BOBBY DARIN

3 July 1959, for four weeks

●●●●

London HLE 8867

Written by Bobby Darin. Produced by Ahmet Ertegun.

The first record produced on Atlantic Records new 8-track machine was cut on 19 May 1958. The producer was Ahmet Ertegun, the song was *Splish Splash* and the singer was Bobby Darin. *Splish Splash* was his first hit (covered by Charlie Drake in Britain), his second climbed to number 24 in Britain but his third was another self-penned song which reached number one on both sides of the Atlantic, *Dream Lover*. Walden Robert Cassotto (born 14 May 1936) had made it. It was his last teeny-bopping single, though, for his next release turned him into a major jazz-orientated star, and thus began the odyssey through different styles which proved that Bobby Darin was a great singer looking for a style. If he had settled in one style, he would have had a far greater following. But *Dream Lover, Mack The Knife, Multiplication, Things* and *If I Were A Carpenter*, five of Darin's hits, were in five completely different styles, so as Darin picked up one set of followers, he was continually losing others.

He suffered from heart problems for most of his career, which limited his output, and he

died from a heart attack at the age of 37 on 20 December 1973. Two number ones and seven other Top 10 hits is not the achievement of an unsuccessful performer, but he was vastly underrated, even at the peak of his popularity.

88

LIVING DOLL

CLIFF RICHARD AND THE DRIFTERS

31 July 1959, for six weeks

●●●●●●

Columbia DB 4306

Written by Lionel Bart. Produced by Norrie Paramor.

After Elvis Presley and the Beatles, Cliff Richard has had more number one singles in Britain that any other act. He has had six number ones backed by the Shadows, three as a soloist, one in conjunction with the Young Ones and one other with the Shadows when they were still known as the Drifters.

Cliff was born Harry Roger Webb in Lucknow, India on 14 October 1940, and with his sister and his parents moved back to England, their native country, in 1948.

After playing with various local groups in Cheshunt, Hertfordshire, he signed a long-term contract with Columbia on 9 August 1958, and made his television debut on ABC TV's *Oh Boy* just four weeks later. The beginning of 1959 saw Cliff with his first permanent backing group, who were still called the Drifters when they played on his first chart-topper *Living Doll*. The song was written by Lionel Bart for the film *Serious Charge*, starring Anthony Quayle; in which Cliff had a small part, and although initially conceived by the composer as an up-tempo rock'n'roll song, it was the Drifters' rhythm guitarist, Bruce Welch, who suggested the slower country feel which was eventually adopted. *Living Doll* won an Ivor Novello Award and became Cliff Richard's first million seller, earning him his first of many Gold Discs. In 1986 he re-recorded the song with the comedy quartet The Young Ones (see no. 567) in aid of Comic Relief, and once again climbed to the very top, almost 27 years on.

ONLY SIXTEEN

CRAIG DOUGLAS

11 September 1959, for four weeks

● ● ● ●

Top Rank JAR 159

Written by 'Barbara Campbell' (Lou Adler, Herb Alpert, Sam Cooke). Produced by Bunny Lewis.

Only Sixteen was Sam Cooke's eighth American hit, but like six of its seven predecessors, it peaked outside the Top 20. In Britain it gave Cooke his second of eight hits, four of which eventually reached the Top 10. *Only Sixteen* was not one of them, mainly because of the local competition from an Isle of Wight milkman called Terence Perkins. Perkins had transformed himself into Craig Douglas a few months earlier and first brushed the charts with his rendition of Dion and the Belmonts' immor-

tal piece of '50s punk, *Teenager In Love.* That song had taken Marty Wilde, father of Kim, to his highest ever chart placing at number 2, but Craig Douglas, who had stopped at number 13, was undaunted. Picking up another American hit, Craig Douglas and his cover version climbed to the summit and gazed down on Sam Cooke's and Al Saxon's versions far below.

Craig Douglas starred in the 1961 movie *It's Trad Dad* with Helen Shapiro, which did not really set up a permanent acting career for either of them. He also achieved the almost impossible feat of four consecutive number 9 hits, which included probably his best record, *Our Favourite Melodies.* Shortly after his final hit, *Town Crier,* lost its voice in March 1963, Douglas signed to do commercials for a well-known brand of detergent. This proved very lucrative for some years and Craig Douglas has never had to go back to his milk round.

HERE COMES SUMMER

JERRY KELLER

9 October 1959, for one week

●

London HLR 8890

Written by Jerry Keller. Produced by Richard Wolf.

Jerry Keller, born on 20 June 1937 in Arkansas, moved with his family to Tulsa at the age of 6. His first group, which went under the zippy name of The Lads Of Note was formed in Tulsa in the early '50s, and soon won a talent contest which led to a job with Jack Dalton's band in the mid-west. That was short-lived, and Keller then became a disc jockey back in Tulsa from mid-1955 for less than a year. In 1956, still only 19 years old, Keller went to New York to try to hit the big time as a singer.

Sometimes being good pays off, as it did

Craig Douglas and Nicole Gueden looking mighty friendly at a 1961 Savoy Hotel reception

with Jerry Keller. Another regular member of the congregation of Keller's church in New York was Pat Boone, and he gave Keller the introductions that led to his being signed by Kapp Records. His first single was *Here Comes Summer* which hit the British charts at the end of August. Either summer was even shorter than usual in 1959, or else Keller's timing was about as good as Wizzard's *Rock'n'Roll Winter*, released in April 1974. Not that it mattered, as *Here Comes Summer* became the ultimate high-school summer song and it soared to number one, his only hit in Britain and America.

That meant that three of the four one hit wonders of the 1950s had surnames beginning with K (Kallen, Kalin and Keller) and no K act really broke the jinx until the Kinks in 1965.

Bobby Darin.

91

MACK THE KNIFE

BOBBY DARIN

16 October 1959, for two weeks

● ●

London HLE 8939

Written by Bertolt Brecht and Kurt Weill, English lyrics by Marc Blitzstein. Produced by Ahmet Ertegun.

One of the biggest hits in history would never have been made had not the artist insisted. A teen rock and roll favourite, Bobby Darin longed to be a respectable mass audience artist. He recorded an album of adult-oriented material, including Brecht and Weill's *Moritat* from *The Threepenny Opera*, translated into English by Marc Blitzstein and called *Mack the Knife*. The inclusion of the song was not as odd as it may sound, since at one point in early 1956 there had been five versions in the American Top 40, the greatest cover battle in chart history. Even more confusingly, the competing artists included Dick Hyman and Richard Hayman.

It was Louis Armstrong's version that inspired Darin. The young rocker gave the song a hip, jazz-flavoured treatment. Bobby phoned the television disc jockey Dick Clark, a personal friend, and informed him he would debut the record on Clark's Satur-

day night ABC network show. The host told him he was crazy, and the programme's producer said 'If he wants to turn his career into chopped liver, so be it.' It was Darin who was right. *Mack the Knife* was his second consecutive number one, America's list leader for nine weeks, and Atlantic's best selling single to date. Bobby Darin had a new career and never returned to rock and roll.

92

TRAVELLIN' LIGHT

CLIFF RICHARD AND THE SHADOWS

30 October 1959, for five weeks

● ● ● ● ●

Columbia DB 4351

Written by Sid Tepper and Roy C Bennett. Produced by Norrie Paramor.

Living Doll was the only record that ever topped the chart for Cliff Richard and the Drifters as the name was changed to Cliff Richard and the Shadows for the follow-up, *Travellin' Light*. The change was to avoid confusion with the American Drifters, as

Cliff's singles began to be released in the States.

Cliff's first four singles had all been uptempo, all in the fashionable rock'n'roll vein, and all sung with a hint of surliness in the voice, but it wasn't until the easy paced *Living Doll* that he had actually topped the charts. The same winning format was used for his sixth single, *Travellin' Light*, which topped the singles chart for five weeks from October to December 1959, and re-appeared in December 1960 on *Cliff's Silver Discs* EP. The B-side *Dynamite* was so popular that it charted for four weeks in its own right, reaching number 16.

Travellin' Light was an aptly titled song to be at the top when the first sections of the M1 were opened. The motorway system has done at least as much for live gigs as the invention of the synthesiser.

93

WHAT DO YOU WANT

ADAM FAITH

4 December 1959, for three weeks (one week top equal)

● ● ●

Parlophone R 4591

Written by Les Vandyke. Produced by John Burgess, arranged by John Barry.

Few people watching BBC-TV's *Drumbeat* in the summer of 1959 would have expected the blond, moody Adam Faith to become one of Britain's most successful acts of the early '60s. His first singles, including a version of Thurston Harris' *Runk Bunk*, deservedly failed to sell, and it was Adam Faith's good fortune that composer/arranger Johnny Worth decided Adam was the person to put over his songs, songs written under the name Les Vandyke. He took his name Vandyke from his telephone exchange in London. (His real name was not Worth, it was Yani Skordalides.)

Adam Faith, born Terence Nelhams on 23 June 1940, was taken into the Parlophone studios and, despite his uninspiring track record, produced one of the pop classics of the pre-Beatles era. The last line, 'Wish you wanted my love bay-bee' gave Adam a catch phrase that lasted well beyond his first

hit. It was also the first ever number one for Parlophone, Adam Faith being at the time the only pop act recording on Parlophone. Before George Martin signed the Beatles to Parlophone and turned it into the most successful record label of all time, Faith's stable mates were acts like the Temperance Seven, Mike Sarne (both of whom subsequently reached number one) and Peter Sellers. Long on talent, short on rock and roll.

94

WHAT DO YOU WANT TO MAKE THOSE EYES AT ME FOR?

EMILE FORD AND THE CHECKMATES

18 December 1959, for six weeks
(one week top equal)

●●●●●●

Pye 7N 15225

Written by Joseph McCarthy, Howard Johnson and Jimmy Monaco. Produced by Michael Barclay.

Emile Ford was born Emile Sweetman in Nassau in the Bahamas on 16 October 1937, and as a young boy he moved to Britain with his family. His first single was a revival of a song which remains the longest question ever asked by a number one single. Ford was also the first black man living in Britain to have a major hit, although Winifred Atwell and Shirley Bassey, two black women in Britain, had already reached the top before him.

Emile owed his success to the arrangement and his gentle delivery of lyrics like 'I'll get you alone some night, and baby you'll find you're messing with dynamite'. It was a happy, friendly, singalong version of the old song, which made it perfect for the Christmas season.

His follow-up was Frank Loesser's *Slow Boat To China* which reached number 3 early in 1960, but apart from the upbeat *Counting Teardrops* at the end of that year there were no more Top 10 hits, and in March 1962 Ford

disappeared from the charts for the last time. He is remembered for his number one hit not only for the length of its title but also because on 18 December 1959, he shared the top slot with Adam Faith's *What Do You Want*, the last time that two songs were placed top equal on the British charts.

95

STARRY EYED

MICHAEL HOLLIDAY

29 January 1960, for one week

●

Columbia DB 4378

Written by Earl Shuman and Mort Garson. Produced by Norrie Paramor.

Michael Holliday had been out of the charts for 18 months since the last of three consecutive 'Love' hits (*In Love, Stairway of Love* and *I'll Always Be In Love With You*) disappeared in mid-July 1958. However, at the end of 1959 his producer Norrie Paramor found a song by American writers Mort Garson and Earl Shuman (neither related to Mort Shuman) which fitted Holliday's style perfectly. The American version, by a singer almost as unknown then as he is now by the name of Gary Stites, had stopped at number 77 on the *Billboard* charts, but the confidence of Holliday and Paramor paid of. On the first day of the new decade the single entered the charts and four weeks later it was at the very top.

The hit was not enough to give Michael Holliday's career a real boost. After *Starry Eyed* he enjoyed two more small hits, but neither of them would have featured on the charts had the chart not expanded from a Top 30 (courtesy of *New Musical Express*) to a Top 50 (published by *Record Retailer*) while *Starry Eyed* was still in the charts. His last, and aptly-titled, chart single was *Little Boy Lost* which achieved the minimum possible ranking of number 50 for one week in September that year.

Starry Eyed was one thing Michael Holliday never was about his life in show business. He was the first Liverpudlian to achieve two number ones, but by the time his record was broken, by the Liverpool group Gerry and the Pacemakers at the end of 1963, Holliday was dead.

96

WHY

ANTHONY NEWLEY

5 February 1960, for four weeks

●●●●

Decca F 11194

Written by Bob Marcucci and Peter de Angelis. Produced by Ray Horricks.

Like John Leyton and David Soul after him, Anthony Newley was an actor who fell into being a pop star almost by accident. He had appeared in such films as *Oliver Twist* in which he played the part of the Artful Dodger, and Peter Ustinov's *Vice Versa*, in which one of his co-stars was another child star turned pop singer, Petula Clark.

The film *Idle On Parade*, a quickly thrown together movie about a pop star called up for National Service inspired by the brief but highly publicised Army career of Terry Dene, gave Newley his first chance to be a pop star, and the EP of songs fom the film reached number 13 in mid-1959. A single from the film, *I've Waited So Long*, was also released, and despite the fact that the song was included on the *Idle On Parade* EP, it still climbed to number 3. The only man to do better than that was a man whose US Army career ended during *Why*'s weeks on top – Acting Sergeant US 53310761 Presley, Elvis – whose *Jailhouse Rock* single had been at number one while the EP from the film also made the Top 20 (see no. 67).

Why was a cover version of Frankie Avalon's American number one, and it became the seventh question to reach number one in England, the third in four chart-toppers. It was also at the time the shortest title ever to reach number one, a record it has subsequently surrendered to Telly Savalas' *If* (no. 367). At the end of its four week run on top, *Record Retailer* magazine launched a Top 50, at that time the largest and most accurate industry chart devised. From that time on we have used that chart (and its successors) as the basis of our chart statistics, which means incidentally that Anthony Newley's four week run at the top was in reality four weeks and six days, thanks to a different date base of the two charts.

*In May 1960, **Adam Faith** (right) was Best Man at the wedding of his pianist Les Reed to June Williams.*

97

POOR ME

ADAM FAITH

10 March 1960, for one week

●

Parlophone R 4623

Written by Les Vandyke. Produced by John Burgess, arranged by John Barry.

The first number one on the *Record Retailer* chart was Adam Faith's second consecutive chart-topper, written, produced and arranged by the same team that had been responsible for *What Do You Want* (see no. 93). A very similar construction, with pizzicato strings and hiccuping delivery of the lovelorn lyrics made it a formula number one. Adam Faith was close to a hat-trick but, like Cliff Richard a few weeks earlier, he failed in his attempt at a third chart-topper in a row when his follow-up *(Someone Else's Baby)* stopped at number 2. Unlike Cliff, Adam never had another number one, but when his final hit dropped off the chart six and a half years later, he had clocked up two number ones, nine other Top 10 hits and a total of 255 weeks on the chart. In 1988, this still makes him one of the 30 most successful chart acts of all time.

A rare example of a pop singer who can really act, Adam's subsequent career in films and television has won him even more praise than his long string of record smashes. He also played a big part in bringing the talents of Sandie Shaw and Leo Sayer to the public. Now known more as a successful businessman than a pop star, Adam Faith remains delightfully (and wrongly) modest about his days in music.

98

RUNNING BEAR

JOHNNY PRESTON

17 March 1960, for two weeks

● ●

Mercury AMT 1079

Written by J. P. Richardson.
Produced by J. P. Richardson.

John Preston Courville was born on 28 August 1939 in Port Arthur, Texas. He formed a high-school band called The Shades and became very popular within Southern Texas. Late in 1958 a local disc jockey from KTRM approached him during a gig and asked if he would like to record a few songs. The disc-jockey was J. P.

Richardson, better known as the Big Bopper.

The first few attempts at coming up with a single were unsuccessful, but one winter's morning in Houston they cut *Running Bear*, the Romeo and Juliet saga of the Indian brave and Little White Dove, whose warring tribes ensured their love could never be. Singing background vocals on the disc (ook-a-chunka, ook-a-chunka) are the Big Bopper himself and, among others, country star George Jones, erstwhile husband of Tammy Wynette (see no. 370). Shortly after the record was cut the Big Bopper died with Buddy Holly and Richie Valens in the plane crash in Iowa, and Mercury decided not to put the record out for almost a year. It was finally released in America in October 1959 and it climbed all the way to the top.

The ook-a-chunka vocal style was copied years later by Jonathan King with his inventive version of *Hooked On A Feeling*. That arrangement was in turn lifted in its entirety by a Swede called Bjorn Skifs, who called himself Blue Swede and took his version of *Hooked On A Feeling* to number one in America in 1974. In the 1980s Skifs took the role of the Arbiter in the Andersson/Ulvaeus/Rice musical *Chess*. Tim Rice had won an album from the pop newspaper *Disc* in 1960 by writing a letter headlined 'I Tip Johnny Preston For Number One Hat Trick'. It was to be a year and a week before anybody managed the elusive hat-trick, and it was not to be Johnny Preston but the rather more consistent Elvis Presley.

99

MY OLD MAN'S

A DUSTMAN

LONNIE DONEGAN

31 March 1960, for four weeks

● ● ● ●

Pye 7N 15256

A traditional song with new lyrics by Lonnie Donegan, Peter Buchanan and Beverly Thorn. Produced by Alan Freeman and Michael Barclay (recorded live at the Gaumont, Doncaster).

Lonnie Donegan's third number one, *My*

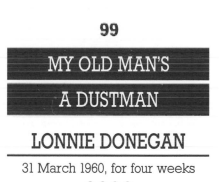

Old Man's A Dustman, is a record that is often quoted as having crashed into the chart at number one. It didn't: it reached the top in its second week on the chart, which is still pretty good going but not all that unusual. It made Donegan the third act, after Adam Faith and Michael Holliday, to have a number one in two decades, and it also affected his musical style for the rest of his career. Having had two number ones and eight Top 10 hits in his nasal bluesy style of skiffle, he switched his priorities away from the American tradition to the British music-hall type of skiffle, which had already provided him with one Top 10 hit, *Does Your Chewing Gum Lose Its Flavour?* a year earlier.

My Old Man's A Dustman, complete with dreadful jokes ('my dustbin's full of lilies' – 'How d'you know they're lilies?' – 'Lily's wearing them'), was a cleaned up version of the old pub song *What Do You Think About That?* and gave Lonnie Donegan his biggest hit of all.

In 1985 Lonnie underwent heart surgery, from which he happily recovered, but news of his illness had a surprising effect on the Japanese Stock Market. As the tickertapes announced the fact that Lonnie Donegan had undergone heart surgery, share prices plunged. The reason was not that Donegan was particularly well-known in Japan, in fact quite the opposite. The first Japanese interpreters of the news thought the patient was Ronnie Reagan, rather than Lonnie Donegan. The stock market recovered almost as quickly as the patient himself.

Lonnie Donegan is shown in 1955 playing with Chris Barber's band.

fame in the musical theatre, but for Newley it was his last touch of chart supremacy. After consecutive number ones with question songs, Newley's chart career faded gradually, although his personal fortune was assured by writing with Leslie Bricusse another question song, *What Kind Of Fool Am I?*, which became the hit of the show which he wrote and in which he starred, *Stop The World I Want To Get Off*. It is not often remembered that before the success of *Stop The World*, Newley played the title role in the unusual TV series, *The World Of Gurney Slade*. The theme tune of the series, by Max Harris, reached number eleven at the beginning of 1961.

For Lionel Bart, *Oliver* was imminent. By the end of 1960 it was the most successful British musical in history, and was well set on a run in London that would not be eclipsed until *Jesus Christ Superstar* broke all box-office records in the late '70s. But the biggest hit from *Oliver*, Shirley Bassey's version of *As Long As He Needs Me*, reached only number 2, despite a 30 week run on the charts. Bart's career has been down and up since *Oliver*, but nobody can deny his leading place among British popular composers of this century.

101

CATHY'S CLOWN

EVERLY BROTHERS

5 May 1960, for seven weeks

●●●●●●●

Warner Brothers WB 1

Written by Don and Phil Everly. Produced by Wesley Rose.

The day before Princess Margaret married Anthony Armstrong-Jones, Don and Phil

*After his chart dynasty and before her television one, **Anthony Newley** and wife Joan Collins arrive for the 1967 premiere of the film Dr Dolittle.*

100

DO YOU MIND

ANTHONY NEWLEY

28 April 1960, for one week

●

Decca F 11220

Written by Lionel Bart. Produced by Ray Horricks.

The 100th number one hit in British chart history was the second number one for both the singer Anthony Newley and the composer Lionel Bart. Both went on to greater

Everly took over the number one spot, which they held on to until well after the *Caribbean Honeymoon* (a no. 42 hit for the Frank Weir Orchestra) was over.

The Everly Brothers had recently signed a million-dollar contract with the newly-formed Warner Brothers label, but the industry felt that splitting Don and Phil from Cadence and its owner Archie Bleyer, as well as from writers Felice and Boudleaux Bryant, was a considerable risk. The Brothers replied with the biggest hit of their career as the first single on the Warner Brothers label. If Warner Brothers had been able to ship enough copies in the week of its release, it may well have entered the charts at number one. As it was, it enjoyed five weeks at the top of the American charts and seven weeks at the head of the British lists, a longer run at number one than any record since their own *All I Have To Do Is Dream*, which had spent seven weeks on top in July and August 1958.

Cathy's Clown remains one of the greatest of all pop records, capturing in less than three minutes all the excitement, harmonies and emotion of the Everlys at their best. They easily remain, almost 30 years later, the most successful duo in British chart history.

102

THREE STEPS TO HEAVEN

EDDIE COCHRAN

23 June 1960, for two weeks

● ●

London HLG 9115

Written by Bob and Eddie Cochran. Produced by Jerry Capehart and Eddie Cochran.

Eddie Cochran, born 3 October 1938, was killed in a car crash at Chippenham, Wiltshire on his way from Bristol to London airport on 17 April 1960, shortly after recording the prophetically titled *Three Steps To Heaven*. It became his only number one hit single and the second posthumous number one on the British charts. Since his death at the age of 21, Cochran has become a legend for his astonishing guitar work and the songs

he wrote, some of which can rank with the best of Chuck Berry and Buddy Holly as rock classics. *Three Steps To Heaven*, written with his brother Bob and revived with great success in the 1970s by Showaddy-waddy, was not his greatest composition. *C'mon Everybody* and *Summertime Blues* remain the songs for which he is best remembered. His great influence on the people that followed him was not his writing, but his guitar style. Listen to his playing on *Hallelujah I Love Her So* or *Don't Ever Let Me Go* and you will hear the roots of the styles of many of the great rock guitarists of the '60s and '70s.

103

GOOD TIMIN'

JIMMY JONES

7 July 1960, for three weeks

● ● ●

MGM 1078

Written by Fred Tobias and Clint Ballard Jr. Produced by Otis Blackwell.

Jimmy Jones, born on 2 June 1937, began his career with an all-time classic single that failed to make number one. That song was *Handy Man*, a number 3 hit which introduced rock falsetto to the British charts, and subsequently gave hits to Del Shannon and James Taylor. Following that up ought to have been impossible, but Jones came up with a song as different as possible from *Handy Man* and reached the very top. *Good Timin'*, a simply structured verse/chorus/verse/chorus song about what Carl Jung called synchronicity was really nowhere as good as the free-running *Handy Man*. But it was *Good Timin'* that hit the top.

There it stopped. Jones' follow-up was the underrated *I Just Go For You/That's When I Cried*, which like Jones' next two singles hit the charts but failed to make the Top 30. *Good Timin'* was also the last record at the top in a long while for MGM. After four number ones on the yellow label in 1958, *Good Timin'* was their only chart-topper until the Osmonds between them gave MGM five more number ones and 18 more weeks at the top between 1972 and 1974.

In 1982, *Good Timin'* was revived by who

else but Showaddywaddy, proving it is still remembered by the rock fans.

104

PLEASE DON'T TEASE

CLIFF RICHARD AND THE SHADOWS

28 July 1960, for one week
11 August 1960, for two weeks

● ● ●

Columbia DB 4479

Written by Pete Chester and Bruce Welch. Produced by Norrie Paramor.

Cliff's third chart-topper held the unique distinction of having been chosen by members of the public.

A cross-section of people were played a selection of songs and over tea and biscuits were asked to choose their favourite. The majority went for a song written by the Shadows' rhythm guitarist Bruce Welch and Pete Chester, son of Charlie Chester the comedian. The song was *Please Don't Tease*, which Cliff re-recorded in a slower vein in 1978. It was subsequently released on the B-side of *Please Remember Me* in July of that year.

After two consecutive number two hits, it was no doubt a great pleasure for Cliff to be back on top. Cliff Richard has never achieved a hat-trick of number one hits, despite the fact that all 19 single releases between *Living Doll* and *Don't Talk To Him* at the end of 1963 reached the top four. In that period, he had seven number ones, six numbers 2s, four number 3s and two number 4 hits, but never more than two consecutive number ones. Twice he issued five consecutive singles which gave him three number ones and two number 2s.

105

SHAKIN' ALL OVER

JOHNNY KIDD AND THE PIRATES

4 August 1960, for one week

●

HMV POP 753

Written by Frederick Heath and Gus Robinson. Produced by Walter Ridley.

Johnny Kidd was born Frederick Heath in Willesden, London on 23 November 1939. He learned to play both the guitar and banjo, forming the group Freddie Heath and the Nutters in 1958. The group was rechristened Johnny Kidd and the Pirates in 1959 and appearances on BBC Radio's *Saturday Club* led to a recording contract with HMV.

The Pirates, appropriately dressed in the garb of swashbucklers, released their first single *Please Don't Touch* in May 1959. Both

Johnny Kidd *marries Jean Heath in 1966 and isn't shaking at all.*

this and their cover version of Marv Johnson's US hit, *You Got What It Takes,* struggled to number 25 in the charts. Then came their fourth release, *Shakin' All Over*, which Kidd wrote with Pirates' manager Gus Robinson and which ranks with Cliff Richard's *Move It* as one of the few original rock and roll sounds to be produced by a British group.

The Pirates on this single were guitarist Alan Caddy, bassist Brian Gregg and drummer Clem Cattini, although the distinctive guitar riff was not played by a Pirate at all but by session man Joe Moretti. Two lesser hits followed until Caddy, Gregg and Cattini left the Pirates to join the Tornados (see no. 141) at the end of 1961. New Pirates were taken on board and Johnny Kidd set sail again, scoring another Top 10 hit in 1963 with *I'll Never Get Over You*, a song with a definite Merseybeat flavour. Kidd was returning from a gig on 7 October 1966 when he was killed in a car accident outside Bury, Lancashire. The Pirates continued to perform into the '70s as a tribute to the perhaps underrated Kidd who was a true pioneer of British rock.

106

APACHE

THE SHADOWS

25 August 1960, for five weeks

● ● ● ● ●

Columbia DB 4484

Written by Jerry Lordan. Produced by Norrie Paramor.

In 1960 the Shadows were Hank B Marvin on lead guitar, Bruce Welch on rhythm guitar, Jet Harris on bass and Tony Meehan on drums. As well as backing Cliff Richard, they had issued three records in their own right before the success of *Apache*. Two of these discs were issued under the name The Drifters, a name which they changed after the American Drifters (*Save The Last Dance For Me* etc.) issued an injunction over the name duplication.

The group first heard *Apache* while they were on tour around Britain, when a fellow artiste on the bill, singer Jerry Lordan, played them the tune on his ukelele. Bert Weedon had already recorded the song,

Ricky Valance *indicates the peak position of* Tell Laura I Love Her.

but seemingly had no plans to release it. The Shadows recorded the tune, released it and soon had knocked their boss (see no. 104) off the top. In America they were beaten out by a cover version by the Danish guitarist Jorgen Ingmann, who three years later won the Eurovision Song Contest with his sister Grethe.

The Shadows won many accolades in the polls of 1960, including being voted Britain's top instrumental group of the year and *Apache* being voted Top Record of 1960 in the prestigious *New Musical Express* Readers' Poll.

107

TELL LAURA I

LOVE HER

RICKY VALANCE

29 September 1960, for three weeks

● ● ●

Columbia DB 4493

Written by Jeff Barry and Ben Raleigh. Produced by Norrie Paramor.

In the 1950s and early 1960s the BBC was the only national source of broadcast music in Britain, and almost invariably it refused to play any song that mentioned death in any way. This unusual 'moral' attitude meant that several American hit records were not even released by record companies in Britain, or else that the hits sank without trace, a fate that befell Mark Dinning's massive American smash, *Teen Angel*. Most of these songs were tasteless (*Tell Laura I Love Her* most certainly is), but they were not immoral nor likely to exert a bad influence on the listener. After all, who would go out and kill himself in a stock car race as a result of listening to the sad story of Laura and Tommy?

Because of its restrictive pop music 'needle-time' agreements with the Musicians Union, the BBC Light Programme was scarcely more important to the pop fans of Britain than Radio Luxembourg, which never banned records just because they featured a grisly death or two. So when RCA decided not even to release Ray Peterson's original version of *Tell Laura I Love Her* in England, EMI decided to go ahead with a cover by a Welsh singer called David Spencer, who had nothing to lose.

Spencer changed his name to Ricky Valance, and the great Norrie Paramor produced the record. The BBC banned it, Radio Luxembourg did not, and it climbed quickly to the top of the charts. Ricky Valance, however, could not find the right follow-up, and after 16 weeks of chart action, became another name on the list of one-hit wonders. He has not left the business, however, and still performs regularly today, although he has not yet found his way back into the charts.

108

ROY ORBISON

20 October 1960, for two weeks

● ●

London HLU 9149

Written by Roy Orbison. Produced by Fred Foster.

The first song that six-year-old Roy Kelton Orbison (born Vernon, Texas, 23 April 1936) learned to pick out on his guitar was *You Are My Sunshine*. By the age of 13 he'd put together a band, the Wink Westerners, and

by the time his education had progressed to the North Texas State College, where he was a contemporary of Pat Boone, he had formed his third group, the Teen Kings.

In 1956 Orbison cut his first single, *Ooby Dooby*, with his own money. This became a minor US hit when rerecorded by the singer on Sun Records in Memphis. He was signed to that legendary label for only a brief period before moving on to Nashville and Fred Foster's Monument Records.

As a songwriter Orbison was never comfortable with rock and roll. His forte was the rock ballad. Jerry Lee Lewis and Buddy Holly recorded his material and the Everly Brothers had taken his song *Claudette* to the top in 1958 (see no. 73). In 1960 he set out from his Texas home to record his third single for Monument. Having already released two flops Orbison decided to try to sell his new song to an established star. Stopping off in Memphis he called in on Elvis Presley to see if he was interested, but the King was asleep. Getting back in his car he continued to Nashville and played his song to the Everly Brothers. They liked it but had just recorded their latest single and didn't need a new song so Orbison was forced to record it himself. Released on London in the UK, the single became the first of 28 hits for The Big O, reaching the summit 12 weeks after it had first appeared on the chart. In the US it peaked at number 2.

109

ELVIS PRESLEY

3 November 1960, for eight weeks

● ● ● ● ● ● ● ●

RCA 1207

Written by Eduardo di Capua, Aaron Schroeder and Wally Gold. Produced by Steve Sholes and Chet Atkins.

As soon as Elvis left the Army in March 1960, he rushed back to the recording studios at RCA in Nashville. Sessions there in March and April produced some of Presley's most famous and successful sides, including the entire *Elvis Is Back* album, *It's Now Or Never* and *Are You Lonesome Tonight?*. *It's Now Or Never* was Elvis' fifth single to reach number one in Britain, but for quite some

time it seemed possible that it would never be issued over here at all. Instead of being Elvis' second post-Army single (*Stuck on You*, which reached number 3, was the first), it was delayed by copyright problems arising from the fact that the song was an adaptation of the 1901 Italian song, *O Sole Mio*. The song had been popularized by Elvis' favourite Italian tenor, Mario Lanza, and Presley's music publisher Freddie Bienstock had asked the American writers Aaron Schroeder and Wally Gold to put new words to Eduardo di Capua's tune.

No copyright problems existed in America, where the single became the biggest hit of Elvis Presley's career during the summer of 1960. To keep his British fans happy, RCA released the American B-side, *A Mess Of Blues*, as an A-side, and even that made number 2 thanks in part to the enormously popular song put onto the British flip, *The Girl Of My Best Friend*. When *It's Now Or Never* was finally cleared for UK release in November, interest had built up to such a level that a second straight-in-at-number-one single for Elvis was a foregone conclusion. Recorded on 3/4 April 1960, *It's Now Or Never* gave Presley a new adult audience to add to his millions of younger fans. It featured Scotty Moore (guitar), Hank Garland (guitar), Floyd Cramer (piano), Bob Moore (bass), Murray Harmon (drums) and the Jordanaires (backing vocals). No other Elvis single spent as many as eight weeks at the top of the UK charts.

O Sole Mio had been a major American pop hit in 1949 for singer Tony Martin, under the title *There's No Tomorrow*. It is more widely known today as the tune for the 'Just One Cornetto' advertisement.

110

CLIFF RICHARD AND THE SHADOWS

29 December 1960, for two weeks

● ●

Columbia DB 4547

Written by Bruce Welch. Produced by Norrie Paramor.

Cliff's fourth number one reverted to the

easy-paced style of his first two chart-toppers, *Living Doll* and *Travellin' Light*. For the first time Cliff took over from Elvis at number one, a feat that was to be repeated exactly three years later when *Return To Sender* was displaced by Cliff's *The Next Time/Bachelor Boy* (see nos. 143 and 144). Elvis only displaced Cliff at the top once, when his double-sided hit *Rock-A-Hula Baby/Can't Help Falling In Love* moved Cliff's biggest British hit *The Young Ones* (see nos. 132 and 133) out of the top slot. Written by Bruce Welch, *I Love You* stayed in pole position for a fortnight over New Year 1961.

It was now apparent that Cliff and his group were fast becoming a self-contained unit thanks to the songwriting talents of Shadows Hank Marvin and Bruce Welch. *I Love You* was Cliff's eleventh single in just over two years, and only one of those, his third single *Livin' Lovin' Doll*, had failed to reach the Top 10. Cliff's 26 consecutive Top 10 hits, of which *I Love You* was the eighth, constitute a record that will probably remain unbeaten.

I Love You must be the most unimaginative title of all the number ones. Nevertheless, it was the first song of that title to enter the British charts, and it was not until 1977 that a second song called *I Love You*, this time by Donna Summer, hit the UK charts. In 1983 the Swiss band Yello used the title for their chart debut single, but three songs of this name are nothing compared to the nine different songs called *Tonight* which have become British hit singles.

Johnny Tillotson.

son's biggest UK hit was written by two New Yorkers who gave it to Cadence chief Archie Bleyer. Bleyer recorded Tillotson twice with the song, once in New York where the result was not quite right and once in Nashville, where Tillotson's performance was enough to make the record a number one hit in many countries around the world. Johnny Tillotson's other singles were more countrified, which may explain their relative lack of success in Britain, but in America he is still as well known for songs like *It Keeps Right On A-Hurting* and *Talk Back Trembling Lips* as for his British number one.

When the Everly Brothers moved from Cadence to Warner Brothers in 1960, it was not long before Archie Bleyer wound up his record company, incidentally selling most of his masters to Andy Williams. Tillotson moved to MGM, where the country hits continued in the States for many years. Johnny Tillotson is still an active country singer, even though the hits in Britain have long since dried up.

111

POETRY IN MOTION

JOHNNY TILLOTSON

12 January 1961, for two weeks

●●

London HLA 9231

Written by Paul Kauffman and Mike Anthony. Produced by Archie Bleyer.

Johnny Tillotson was born on 20 April 1939 in Jacksonville, Florida, and before the age of 20 had been signed to Cadence Records, the label that built the careers of the Everly Brothers, the Chordettes and Andy Williams. Basically a country singer, Tillot-

112

ARE YOU LONESOME TONIGHT?

ELVIS PRESLEY

26 January 1961, for four weeks

●●●●

RCA 1216

Written by Roy Turk and Lou Handman. Produced by Steve Sholes and Chet Atkins.

For his sixth number one hit, Elvis

revamped a song from 1926 and shot to number one mainly on the basis of a long spoken passage beginning with the immortal line based loosely on Jaques' speech in Act II Scene VII of Shakespeare's *As You Like It* – 'You know, someone said that all the world's a stage'. He hardly ever seemed to be able to remember this long recitation or to want to recite it accurately at his concerts in the '70s. RCA even released a live version of *Are You Lonesome Tonight?* in the UK in 1982 in which Elvis sings incorrect (and unfunny) lyrics and laughs all the way through the spoken word section of the number. Not a worthy release. The 1960 version, however was deservedly one of Elvis' most popular recordings of all. Recorded in Nashville at the *It's Now Or Never* sessions of April 1960 (see no. 109) the track did nearly as well as its predecessor on both sides of the Atlantic. By the beginning of 1961, Elvis was at his peak of popularity with the record-buying public. *Are You Lonesome Tonight?* was the second of a run of a dozen successive Presley single releases in the UK, of which ten made number one. From now until the emergence of the Beatles, Elvis had no challenger to his position as the most popular singer in the world.

113

SAILOR

PETULA CLARK

23 February 1961, for one week

●

Pye 7N 15324

Written by Fini Busch, Werner Scharfenburger, English lyrics by David West. Produced by Alan Freeman.

Petula Clark first came to public notice immediately after the war in a radio series called *Meet The Huggetts* in which she played Jack Warner's daughter. She was born in Epsom on 15 November 1933, and was only in her mid-teens when stardom struck. By the mid-'50s, she was well established not only as an actress but also a bouncy singer, a British derivation of the all conquering Mitch Miller style, and she managed four Top 10 hits before 1958. Her first

number one was a song written by two Austrians, Fini Busch and Werner Scharfenburger, and titled *Seemann*. A German girl called Lolita turned it into a monster European smash. English lyrics were then added by EMI producer Norman Newell, under the pen-name David West, and Lolita re-recorded the song in English. So did Petula Clark. Lolita's English version then took off in the States, where it reached number 5 in the Billboard charts, but on home ground Petula Clark not only annihilated Lolita, who failed to make the top 50, but also beat Anne Shelton (see No. 50) who was hoping for a second number one with a European song but had to be content with a Top 10 hit.

114

WALK RIGHT BACK

THE EVERLY BROTHERS

2 March 1961, for three weeks

● ● ●

Warner Brothers WB 33

Written by Sonny Curtis. Produced by Wesley Rose.

The Everly Brothers' third number one hit, and their second for the new Warner Brothers label, was a double-sided number one in all but chart listing. There have been 19 double-sided number ones altogether, including four by Elvis and two by the Beatles, but only one officially by the Everly Brothers.

The most played side was written by Sonny Curtis of the Crickets. The other side was called *Ebony Eyes*, and was less played because it was a death song, a classic to rank with *Tell Laura I Love Her* and *Leader Of The Pack*. The writer, John D. Loudermilk, has over the years come up with a wide range of highly original songs, but *Ebony Eyes* is probably his best known. Songs like *Indian Reservation* for Don Fardon, *Tobacco Road* for the Nashville Teens and *Language Of Love* which he performed himself, are all Loudermilk compositions and all Top 20 hits in Britain.

The sad saga of Flight 1203 ('And then came the announcement over the loudspeaker: Will all those having relatives and friends on Flight 1203 please report to the chapel across the street') made *Ebony Eyes* one of the most parodied songs in pop history.

115

WOODEN HEART

ELVIS PRESLEY

23 March 1961, for six weeks

● ● ● ● ● ●

RCA 1226

Written by Bert Kaempfert, Kay Twomey, Fred Wise and Ben Weisman. Produced by Steve Sholes.

Elvis' seventh UK number one was unique in that it was not released as a single in the US at the time of its enormous success in Britain and Europe. The most popular song from Elvis' first post-Army movie, *GI Blues*, it made Elvis the first artist to score three number one hits with consecutive British releases (see also nos 109 and 112). It was an adaptation of a German folk song, *Muss I Denn*, by Fred Wise, Kay Twomey, Ben Weisman and Bert Kaempfert, the latter being the German bandleader who recorded the Beatles in Hamburg in 1961 and had his own US number one that year with *Wonderland By Night*, which knocked Presley's *Are You Lonesome Tonight?* off the top! Bert Kaempfert also wrote *Strangers In The Night* for Frank Sinatra, and thus has close connections with three of the top four chart acts of all time.

RCA's baffling decision not to release *Wooden Heart* as an American single allowed unknown singer Joe Dowell to take his version to number one in America in the summer of 1961. The 27 weeks that Elvis Presley's *Wooden Heart* spent in the UK Top 50 was the longest consecutive run by any of Presley's 100-plus singles.

116

BLUE MOON

THE MARCELS

4 May 1961, for two weeks

● ●

Pye International 7N 25073

Written by Richard Rodgers and Lorenz Hart. Produced by Stu Phillips.

One of the only songs that Rodgers and Hart wrote outside a musical, *Blue Moon* was published in 1934 as a 'slow foxtrot ballad'. It had survived most recorded versions over the next 27 years (including a straight version by Elvis Presley), but the Marcels brought a new meaning to the song with their astonishing arrangement, featuring vocals not in the original version, ending each chorus with the unanswerable 'dang-a-dang-dang, ding-a-dong-ding Blue Moon'.

There was a record issued in 1957 called *Zoom Zoom Zoom* by the Collegians on the obscure Wimley label. It failed to do anything on any chart, but it has been mentioned as an inspiration for the Marcels' *Blue Moon*. Listening to the two records clarifies the issue – *Blue Moon* was not so much inspired by *Zoom Zoom Zoom*, it was virtually a direct copy of the arrangement.

There is some confusion as to who the Marcels were on the record. The probable line-up of the lads from Philadelphia is Cornelius Hart (lead vocals), Ronald Mundy, Fred Johnson, Dick Knauss and Gene Bricker. Anyway five Marcels appeared in the Chubby Checker movie *Twist Around The Clock* which still holds the world record as the quickest-made feature film of all time – 28 days from the day producer Sam Katzman got the idea to release of the film. Not much shorter than the Marcels' career.

117

ON THE REBOUND

FLOYD CRAMER

18 May 1961, for one week

●

RCA 1231

Written by Floyd Cramer. Produced by Chet Atkins.

Floyd Cramer, born in Shreveport, Louisiana on 27 November 1933, was Elvis Presley's pianist on many of the early RCA hits. The Nashville sound of the late '50s and early '60s was built around the guitar style of Chet Atkins and Les Paul, the bass of Bill Black, the drums of D J Fontana and the piano of Floyd Cramer. Elvis was never a pure country singer, even though he regularly used many of these musicians on his sessions, but just as he influenced a thousand pure country singers, so his musicians were more versatile than the country styles their imitators created.

Floyd Cramer's biggest hit, a number 2 in America, demonstrates this perfectly. It was called *Last Date* and failed to register in Britain, but it was more than just country piano. It had traces of jazz, rock and rhythm and blues which crop up again in the records of people as diverse as Alan Price, Roger Williams and Elton John. If *Last Date* was Floyd Cramer's masterpiece, *On The Rebound* was not far behind. It climbed to number 4 in America as the follow up to *Last Date*, and in Britain it gave Cramer the first of three hits over the next 18 months.

118

YOU'RE DRIVING ME CRAZY

THE TEMPERANCE SEVEN

25 May 1961, for one week

●

Parlophone R 4757

Written by Walter Donaldson. Produced by George Martin.

The Temperance Seven was formed, so their publicity said, in 1906 for a season at the Pasadena Cocoa Rooms in the Balls Pond Road. The personnel were Captain Cephas Howard (trumpet and euphonium), leader of the gang, Sheikh Haroun Wadi el John R T Davies (trombone and alto sax), Frank Paverty (sousaphone), Mr Philip 'Fingers' Harrison (alto and baritone sax), Alan Swainston-Cooper (clarinet, soprano sax, phonofiddle, swanee whistle and pedal clarinet), Canon Colin Bowles (piano and harmonium), Brian Innes (drums), Dr John Gieves-Watson (banjo), with vocal refrain by Whispering Paul McDowell. *You're Driving Me Crazy* was written in 1930 by Walter Donaldson, whose *I Wonder Where My Baby Is Tonight* was one of the tunes on *Let's Have Another Party* (see no. 26). Perhaps The Temperance Seven's most important contribution to pop music history is the fact that *You're Driving Me Crazy* was producer George Martin's first number one hit single.

The Temperance Seven, so named because they are always one over the eight, were a dance band rather than a jazz band in the style of Kenny Ball or Acker Bilk, and their brief spell of glory inspired acts like the Bonzo Dog Doo Dah Band and the New Vaudeville Band in the years that followed. They broke up not long after their hits ended less than a year later, although in the early 1970s Ted Wood, brother of Face and Stone Ron Wood, briefly reformed the band. Little success ensued.

119

SURRENDER

ELVIS PRESLEY

1 June 1961, for four weeks

●●●●

RCA 1227

Written by Ernesto de Curtis, B.G. de Curtis, English lyrics by Doc Pomus and Mort Shuman. Produced by Steve Sholes.

For his eighth British number one, Elvis revamped another old Italian song using the *It's Now Or Never* formula with almost equal success. This time it was *Torna A Sorrento* (Return to Sorrento), written in 1911 by Ernesto and B.G. de Curtis, who sound no more Italian than Doc Pomus and Mort Shuman, who provided the English lyrics. The song gave Elvis his fifth US number one with successive releases and his fourth on the trot in the UK.

Surrender was recorded in Nashville on 30 and 31 October 1960, the only non-spiritual song laid down at those sessions. Elvis recorded *His Hand In Mine*, his highly successful gospel album, as well as *Crying In The Chapel*, which was not on the album but which was to hit number one in Britain four years later.

The Jordanaires sing on the single but there is no accurate record of the musicians who played on the tracks, which were all produced as usual by Steve Sholes.

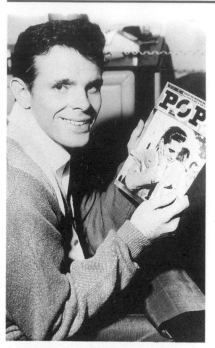

Del Shannon *contemplates the face of the man he replaced at number one.*

120

RUNAWAY

DEL SHANNON

29 June 1961, for three weeks

●●●

London HLX 9317

Written by Del Shannon, Max Crook. Produced by Harry Balk and Irving Micahnik.

Del Shannon, born Charles Westover in Cooperville, Michigan on 30 December 1939, began his recording career with one of the most influential records in pop history, a disc that used the organ for the first time in a really commercial way. The organ (or more correctly, the 'musitron') was played by Max Crook, who co-wrote the song with Del Shannon, and his solo in the middle of the record has become one of the best known instrumental breaks of all time.

Del Shannon built a successful four-year chart career on the strength of *Runaway*. He had no other number ones, but his seven other Top 10 hits included two number 2 hits,

Hey Little Girl and *Swiss Maid*, a song written by the then unknown Roger Miller. Shannon also recorded *From Me To You* for the American market in 1963 when the Beatles were unheard of in the States, and with that record became the first man to take a Lennon/McCartney song into the US Hot Hundred. He also wrote Peter and Gordon's big American hit *I Go To Pieces* and produced Brian Hyland's 1970s comeback hit *Gypsy Woman*, which also featured Max Crook on organ. Del Shannon is still active, but even if he were to give up tomorrow his reputation as a rock innovator is secure.

121

TEMPTATION

THE EVERLY BROTHERS

20 July 1961, for two weeks

●●

Warner Brothers WB 42

Written by Nacio Herb Brown and Arthur Freed. Produced by Wesley Rose.

The Everly Brothers' fourth and final chart-topper was a drum-dominated reworking of *Temptation*, a song originally performed by Bing Crosby in the 1933 film *Going Hollywood*. Twenty-one records reached number one in 1961, of which five were old songs (*Are You Lonesome Tonight, Blue Moon, You're Driving Me Crazy, Temptation* and *Michael*) and a further two (*Wooden Heart* and *Surrender*) were old tunes with new lyrics. There has never been before or since such a dominance of the top of the charts by old songs, even at the peak of charity-disc mania in the mid-'80s. With hindsight it is clear that the pop world was ready for something new, something which would fill the void in musical imagination which was in 1961 being filled by reworkings of old songs. A little over a year later, the something new emerged when *Love Me Do* entered the charts.

The Beatles were destined to take over the Everly Brothers' title as the world's top vocal group, but the decline in Don and Phil's popularity was not connected with the Beatles' rise. It may have been their stint in the US Marines from mid-1962 which kept the brothers out of the limelight at a crucial time which contributed to their fall from the top of the charts.

In 1984 their reunion gave them more chart action. Sixteen years and 96 days after their previous chart hit, the Everly Brothers came back into the British Top 50 with a song written by ex-Beatle Paul McCartney, *On The Wings Of A Nightingale*.

122

WELL I ASK YOU

EDEN KANE

3 August 1961, for one week

●

Decca F 11353

Written by Les Vandyke. Produced by Bunny Lewis.

Almost two years after Johnny Worth (alias Les Vandyke) wrote *What Do You Want?* and *Poor Me* for Adam Faith, he came up with his third and final chart-topping song for another newcomer with a name taken from Genesis, Chapter One, Eden Kane. Eden Kane began life on 29 March 1942 as Richard Sarstedt. Like Cliff Richard and Engelbert Humperdinck, he was born in India and came to Britain as a child. He first created interest with an advertising jingle for Cadbury's called *Hot Chocolate Crazy*, which was played almost as often as Horace Batchelor's football pools advertisement on Radio Luxembourg. *Well I Ask You* followed, and then further Top 10 hits, *Get Lost, Forget Me Not* and *I Don't Know Why*.

A couple of flops, financial problems and a change in labels finished Eden Kane's chart career. One comeback hit, *Boys Cry* on Fontana in 1964, did not re-establish him permanently in the charts, and he was left with a list of five hits to his name, all of which made the Top 10. Of all the other 4000 or so chart acts over 35 years, only one – The Specials – has had more than Eden Kane's five chart hits, all of which were Top 10 hits. The Specials hit the Top 10 seven times with only seven chart entries, but everybody else either failed to reach the Top 10 at least once or else had fewer hits in total than Eden Kane.

In 1969 Kane's brother, Peter Sarstedt, hit number one (see no. 267), and in 1976 brother Clive, who for some reason called himself Robin Sarstedt, reached number 3 with his rendition of Hoagy Carmichael's *My Resistance Is Low*.

123

YOU DON'T KNOW

HELEN SHAPIRO

10 August 1961, for three weeks

● ● ●

Columbia DB 4670

Written by John Schroeder and Mike Hawker. Produced by Norrie Paramor.

By reaching number one with her second single while still at school, Helen Shapiro became a national celebrity, the schoolgirl with the grown up voice. Helen was 14 years and 316 days when she hit the top, thus becoming the youngest British artiste to get to number one. But she was still a year older than Frankie Lymon had been when *Why Do Fools Fall In Love* hit number one in 1956 (see no. 48).

Born in Bethnal Green on 28 September 1946, Helen Shapiro was a protégée of the well-known singing coach, Maurice Burman, who introduced her to John Schroeder, then an assistant to Norrie Paramor at Columbia. Her first single was a Schroeder song, *Please Don't Treat Me Like A Child* which cruised happily into the Top 10. For the follow-up, Schroeder and Mike Hawker wrote a ballad, and it took over the number one spot on 10 August 1961. Three days later, in a move apparently unconnected with Miss Shapiro's success, the East Germans began building the Berlin Wall.

124

JOHNNY REMEMBER ME

JOHN LEYTON

31 August 1961, for three weeks
28 September 1961, for one week

● ● ● ●

Top Rank JAR 577

Written by Geoff Goddard. Produced by Joe Meek.

John Leyton, born on 17 February 1939, was a TV actor previously known for his portrayal of Ginger in the BBC TV children's serial *Biggles* when he landed the part of a pop singer called Johnny St. Cyr (pronounced Sincere) in a weekly series, *Harpers West One*. Leyton's manager at the time was a young Australian, on his way to his first million, called Robert Stigwood. Stigwood realised the importance of television exposure and managed to arrange for Leyton to feature his latest single on the show. The song, written by Geoff Goddard and produced by the first great British independent producer, Joe Meek, was a minor-key agony-laden song about a dead love: 'Singing in the sighing of the wind, blowing in the treetops, Johnny Remember Me'. It couldn't miss and it didn't.

John Leyton went on to clock up one more Top 10 hit and seven other lesser chart entries over the next two and a half years. He also landed his biggest film part, appearing with Charles Bronson, Steve McQueen and James Garner in the prisoner of war classic *The Great Escape*. His song went on to feature in the medley of *I Feel Love* (see no. 409), *Love To Love You Baby* and *Johnny Remember Me* which Bronski Beat and Marc Almond took to number 3 in 1985. Their version bore very little resemblance to the original.

125

REACH FOR THE STARS/CLIMB EV'RY MOUNTAIN

SHIRLEY BASSEY

21 September 1961, for one week

●

Columbia DB 4685

Written by *(Reach For The Star)* Udo Jurgens, English lyrics by David West, *(Climb Ev'ry Mountain)* Richard Rodgers and Oscar Hammerstein II. Produced by Norman Newell, with musical direction by Geoff Love.

Shirley Bassey, the most successful solo female artiste in British chart history, is one of many ladies who have hit the top twice,

Three number one stars (left to right) **Mike Sarne**, **Helen Shapiro** *and* **John Leyton** *sit together in what, judging from their clothing, must have been a very cold room.*

but she could be said to be a little ahead of the pack because she took three titles to number one with two hits. Her second number one featured on one side a song written by the man who won the 1966 Eurovision Song Contest for Austria, with English lyrics by Miss Bassey's producer Norman Newell under the pseudonym David West. The other side was a song from *The Sound Of Music*. Despite its fabulous success in album form and on stage and celluloid, *The Sound Of Music* has not supplied as many hits to the single charts as some other less successful shows. The only other hit of a song from the show was Vince Hill's *Edelweiss*, which climbed to number 2 in 1967.

From 14 September to 19 October 1961 the British charts had a new number one each week. There were actually only five records involved in those six weeks of musical chairs, as *Johnny Remember Me* hit the top twice, but there has never in the history of the British charts been a longer run than this one: six weeks of new number ones. The record was equalled in 1968, when again one record (*Mony Mony* – no. 254) featured twice.

126

KON-TIKI

THE SHADOWS

5 October 1961, for one week

Columbia DB 4698

Written by Michael Carr. Produced by Norrie Paramor.

The Shadows' fifth hit was their second to top the chart. It was written by Michael Carr, who had also penned their follow-up to *Apache* (see no 106), the number 5 hit *Man Of Mystery*, which also served as the theme for a series of black and white B-movies based on the stories of Edgar Wallace. Michael Carr was born in Leeds in 1904, but moved to Dublin at a tender age and took to the sea at the age of 18. He became a wind-jammer seaman, film stuntman, cowboy and globe-trotter, experiences which no doubt inspired him to write such hits as *South Of The Border, The Wheel Of The Wagon Is Broken* and *Hang Out The Washing On The Siegfried Line*.

The line-up for this record was still the original Shadows line-up, but by the time the tune was at number one, drummer Tony Meehan had left the Shadows and had been replaced by the drummer from Marty Wilde's Wildcats, Brian Bennett. For Bennett this was a wise move. Marty Wilde had scored his final Top 10 hit at the beginning of 1961, but the Shadows were still making Top 10 hits in 1979.

127

MICHAEL

THE HIGHWAYMEN

12 October 1961, for one week

●

HMV POP 910

A traditional song arranged by Dave Fisher. Produced by Dave Fisher.

Lonnie Donegan covered four American hits in his chart heyday, but the only time he lost out to the original version was when he took on the Highwaymen and their version of the traditional Negro spiritual, *Michael*. The Highwaymen were five students from the Wesleyan University at Middletown, Connecticut, who got together to put on a show for their fellow students in 1959, and were so well received that they decided to carry on performing together. The leader was Dave Fisher who, apart from singing lead tenor, also arranged their songs and played banjo. Bob Burnett, who when not singing or studying was the university pole vault champion, sang and provided the exotic percussion. Steve Butts, crippled as a result of childhood polio, played guitar and sang bass. Steve Trott played guitar and baritone Chan Daniels specialized in an instrument called a charango, made from an armadillo shell.

A visit to New York in November 1960 resulted in a contract with United Artists and a first album from which the title track, *Michael*, was released as a single in America at the beginning of 1961. It was six months before it started to sell heavily, but by September it was number one in the States. It duly repeated its success in Britain, leaving Lonnie Donegan floundering at number 6.

Despite another big American hit, *Cotton-fields* in 1962, the Highwaymen broke up when they graduated that year and never really consolidated their success. Dave Fisher was the only Highwayman who stayed in the music business; Steve Trott became prominent in American legal affairs. In the late '70s the group got back together to re-record *Michael* but it was not a hit.

128

WALKIN' BACK TO HAPPINESS

HELEN SHAPIRO

19 October 1961, for three weeks

● ● ●

Columbia DB 4715

Written by John Schroeder and Mike Hawker. Produced by Norrie Paramor.

Helen Shapiro was still at school when her third single became her second consecutive number one. Another hit from what were rapidly becoming the prolific pens of John Schroeder and Mike Hawker, *Walkin' Back To Happiness* was a lively song in the style of *Don't Treat Me Like A Child* and would have been perfect Eurovision material. It has always seemed odd that while singers like Lulu, Sandie Shaw, Mary Hopkin and Clodagh Rodgers have all sung Britain's Song For Europe, Helen Shapiro was never given the opportunity.

She did have the opportunity to make a film, though, and left school early at the end of 1961 to begin filming *It's Trad, Dad*. The film was successful, making good profits for the producers, but it did not further the careers of its two main stars, Helen Shapiro and Craig Douglas. At the beginning of 1963, six months after her fifth and final Top 10 hit, Helen headlined a nationwide tour on which the Beatles were the main supporting act. Nobody could have coped with that, least of all a 16-year-old girl. Her pop career never recovered from the impact of that tour, so successful for the Beatles and so disastrous for Miss Shapiro. However, she has moved her career solidly into other directions and she remains very much in demand as an actress and singer.

Frankie Vaughan *demonstrates that the Osmonds and David Cassidy were not the first to attract very young fans.*

129

LITTLE SISTER/HIS
LATEST FLAME

ELVIS PRESLEY

9 November 1961, for four weeks

●●●●

RCA 1258

Written by (both sides) Doc Pomus and Mort Shuman. Produced by Steve Sholes and Chet Atkins.

Elvis recorded both sides of his ninth UK number one at sessions in Nashville on 25 and 26 June 1961, while his eighth UK number one was still at the top of the charts. Both sides of the new single were written by Doc Pomus and Mort Shuman, who had also written the English lyrics for that eighth number one, *Surrender* (see no. 119). Between that single and this one, RCA had released the title song of his newest film *Wild In The Country* backed by the first Elvis single ever to feature saxophone, *I Feel So Bad*. Surprisingly it peaked at number 4, becoming the only Elvis single in ten issued between November 1960 and November 1962 not to hit the very top. However RCA were quick

to cover its comparative failure. Only nine weeks after *Wild In The Country* hit the charts its follow-up, *Little Sister/His Latest Flame*, was at number one. It proved to be the first of his longest stretch of successive chart-toppers (five). *His Latest Flame* is sometimes known as *(Marie's The Name) His Latest Flame*, and is a fairly gentle country-flavoured rock number. *Little Sister* was Elvis' first genuine rock number one since *I Need Your Love Tonight* in 1959 (see no. 85), and subsequent cover versions ran the range from Ry Cooder to Robert Plant.

130

TOWER OF STRENGTH

FRANKIE VAUGHAN

7 December 1961, for three weeks

●●●

Philips PB 1195

Written by Burt Bacharach and Bob Hilliard. Produced by Johnny Franz.

A number 5 hit in America for Gene McDaniels was turned into a number one hit in

Britain by Frankie Vaughan. It was yet another number one for Burt Bacharach, the only one not written with Hal David. Co-author of this one was Bob Hilliard who wrote various hits with other partners, like *Seven Little Girls Sitting In The Back Seat*, *Dear Hearts And Gentle People* and *In My Little Corner Of The World*. He died on 1 February 1971.

Frankie Vaughan's career had been in some considerable lull when he recorded *Tower of Strength*. His previous hit had dropped off the charts almost a year earlier, and his previous Top 10 hit, *The Heart Of Man*, was a summer 1959 release. However, *Tower of Strength* was perfect for Vaughan's vigorous style and he quickly cornered the airplay to find himself with the Christmas number one of 1961. After this hit, he was never to be a major chart force again, although he had further Top 10 hits in 1963 and 1967 to bring his total to nine.

As a cabaret performer Frankie Vaughan retained his drawing power for very many years and has never had to wonder where the money to pay the gas bill was coming from.

Another cover version of this song that Frankie swamped was one by Paul Raven, who had to change his name to Gary Glitter a decade later to find Vaughan-type chart fame himself.

Danny Williams *demonstrates the art of dancing while holding a lit cigarette.*

131

MOON RIVER

DANNY WILLIAMS

28 December 1961, for two weeks

● ●

HMV POP 932

Written by Henry Mancini and Johnny Mercer. Produced by Norman Newell.

The fourth Oscar-winning song to top the British charts out of a total of seven to 1987 was the theme from the Audrey Hepburn film *Breakfast At Tiffany's*. It gave Danny Williams his third chart hit and his only number one. In America the hit versions, both of which climbed to number 11 in the Billboard charts, were by composer Henry Mancini and by Jerry Butler, who must be the most successful and influential rock era singer never to have had a hit in Britain. Apart from *Moon River*, Butler also recorded the original version of the Walker Brothers' first number one, *Make It Easy On Yourself* (see no. 203), and many of his other songs, like *For Your Precious Love, He Will Break Your Heart* and *Only The Strong Survive*, are now soul standards. In Britain Danny Williams' only competition was from Henry Mancini, whose version peaked at number 44.

Danny Williams was for a couple of years Britain's answer to Johnny Mathis, with a smooth-as-silk delivery and a choice of material by his experienced producer Norman Newell which accentuated his talents. All the same, for 14 years after his seventh hit, *My Own True Love*, dropped off the charts, Danny Williams disappeared from the chartwatcher's view. He re-emerged in 1977 with *Dancing Easy*, a song that began life as an advertising jingle for Martini.

132

THE YOUNG ONES

CLIFF RICHARD AND THE SHADOWS

11 January 1962, for six weeks

● ● ● ● ● ●

Columbia DB 4761

Written by Sid Tepper and Roy C. Bennett. Produced by Norrie Paramor.

The Young Ones was not only Cliff's second million-selling single but the fourth single in history to enter the charts at number one, the first by a British artist. By the day of its release *The Young Ones* had amassed an all-time record advance for a single to date of 524,000 copies, a record that paled into insignificance two years later when *Can't Buy Me Love* (see no 166) clocked up advance orders of over one million. *The Young Ones* was written by Sid Tepper and Roy Bennett, the Americans who had also written *Travellin' Light* (see no. 92) for Cliff. It was not just Cliff's fifth number one, it was more importantly the title song of his first starring film, which also cast Robert Morley, Carole Gray, Grazina Frame, the Shadows and budding actors Melvyn Hayes and Richard O'Sullivan. In America the film was released as *It's Great To Be Young* so the title tune became an ex-title tune and flopped accordingly.

The Young Ones remained on the charts for 21 weeks equalling *Living Doll* as Cliff's longest continuous chart runner. Twenty-four years later, when Cliff topped the charts with the comedy quartet The Young Ones, they became the only act named after a number one hit to hit the number one spot themselves.

133

ROCK-A-HULA BABY/ CAN'T HELP FALLING IN LOVE

ELVIS PRESLEY

22 February 1962, for four weeks

● ● ● ●

RCA 1270

Written by (*Rock-A-Hula Baby*) Fred Wise, Ben Wiseman and Dolores Fuller, (*Can't Help Falling In Love*) George Weiss, Hugo Peretti and Luigi Creatore. Produced by Steve Sholes.

The third consecutive number one hit to come from the movies was Elvis Presley's tenth number one and his fourth double-sided number one hit.

The film in question was his eighth and most money-spinning film, *Blue Hawaii*. It was not one of the King's best films but it had a very strong soundtrack and crops up on television with monotonous regularity. *Can't Help Falling In Love*, written by George Weiss and *Plume de Ma Tante* hitmakers Hugo and Luigi, was an integral part of the film from the outset and subsequently became one of Elvis' most popular recordings and the closing number in his Las Vegas stage act. *Rock-A-Hula Baby* on the other hand was inserted in the film after regular filming had been completed, to help the film cash in on the twist boom. The *Blue Hawaii* album recorded at Paramount in Hollywood in September 1961 became Presley's biggest ever soundtrack LP.

Can't Help Falling In Love, based on the old French tune, *Plaisir d'Amour*, has subsequently been a British hit for Andy Williams (number 3 in 1970) and the Stylistics (number 4 in 1976) – a rare instance of the same song providing three different Top 10 records at different times. The Stylistics' single was produced by Hugo Peretti and Luigi Creatore, who masterminded the career of the Stylistics during the height of their popularity.

134

WONDERFUL LAND

THE SHADOWS

22 March 1962, for eight weeks

●●●●●●●●

Columbia DB 4790

Written by Jerry Lordan. Produced by Norrie Paramor.

The Shadows' third number one was the second from the pen of Jerry Lordan, who has proved the most successful writer of instrumentals in the history of the British charts. Jerry Lordan had three hits as a singer in 1960, *I'll Stay Single* (which had the next line, 'not one thing'll/make me change my mind'), *Who Could Be Bluer* and *Sing Like An Angel*. But his voice was very lightweight, and his talents clearly lay in writing rather than performing.

Wonderful Land had a horn section added to the basic lead/rhythm bass/drums line-up, an example of the adventurous production style of Norrie Paramor which brought him his 16th number one, to put him at that stage only one behind Mitch Miller's total. *Wonderful Land* stayed at the top for eight weeks, a record for an instrumental second only to Eddie Calvert's *Oh Mein Papa* (see no. 16) which held the top for nine weeks in 1954 and which was another Norrie Paramor production.

While the Shadows' third chart-topper was still riding high, bass guitarist Jet Harris left the group to concentrate on a solo career. He was replaced by another musician from the rapidly thinning ranks of Marty Wilde's Wildcats, Brian 'Licorice' Locking.

135

NUT ROCKER

B BUMBLE AND THE STINGERS

17 May 1962, for one week

●

Top Rank JAR 611

Written by Peter Ilich Tchaikovsky, arranged by Kim Fowley. Produced by Kim Fowley.

For the first time in British chart history, an instrumental took over from another instrumental at number one. B Bumble and the Stingers – the first instrumental one-hit wonder – revamped Tchaikovsky's *Nutcracker Suite* and created a classic from a classic. Mastermind of this hit was Kim Fowley, born in Los Angeles on 27 July 1942, who had already produced another one-hit wonder in America, the Hollywood Argyles (*Alley-Oop*). In Britain, *Nut Rocker* was the zenith of his achievement, but his influence on and involvement with chart acts like P J Proby, the Rockin' Berries, Emerson Lake and Palmer and REO Speedwagon has kept his name in the rock press and cash in his pocket.

His reputation is that of a rather weirder American version of Jonathan King, brilliant at producing hit singles but incapable of creating a long-lasting successful chart act. But at least, unlike Jonathan King, he has one number one hit to his credit. *Nut Rocker* stayed on the charts for 15 weeks in 1962 and when re-issued on the Stateside label in 1972, spent another 11 weeks on the chart and reached number 19.

136

GOOD LUCK CHARM

ELVIS PRESLEY

24 May 1962, for five weeks

●●●●●

RCA 1280

Written by Aaron Schroeder and Wally Gold. Produced by Steve Sholes and Chet Atkins.

Number eleven in the staggering list of Presley number ones was a gentle rock ballad recorded in Nashville on 15 and 16 October 1961. The exact line-up of musicians on this track is unknown, but the Jordanaires were there and are in fact featured even more than usual on this particular cut. The song was written by Aaron Schroeder and Wally Gold, who had already provided Elvis with UK number ones with *I Got Stung* in 1959 (see no. 80) and with their adaptation of *O Sole Mio, It's Now Or Never*, in 1960.

Everything Presley released on singles in 1962 went to the top of the charts, and he was thus at number one for 15 weeks of the year, a record surpassed only by Frankie Laine (27 weeks in 1953), the Beatles (16 weeks in 1963), John Travolta and Olivia Newton-John (16 weeks in 1978) and by Elvis himself (18 weeks in the previous year, 1961, when not all of his singles made number one). Elvis' tally of 15 weeks was equalled by Frankie Goes To Hollywood in 1984, but what has still never been equalled is his total of 33 weeks at number one in a two year period (1961 and 1962). His nearest rival to that record is not Frankie Laine, who did not hit the top either in 1952 or 1954, but the Beatles, with 28 weeks at number one in 1963 and 1964.

Good Luck Charm also completed Elvis' second hat-trick of number ones, a unique achievement at the time and since matched only by the Beatles and Abba.

137

COME OUTSIDE

MIKE SARNE with WENDY RICHARD

28 June 1962, for two weeks

●●

Parlophone R 4902

Written by Charles Blackwell. Produced by Charles Blackwell.

Mike Sarne was born Michael Scheur in 1939 of German extraction. Wendy Richard was just beginning as an actress specializing in the not-so-dumb blonde roles that were still coming her way 20 years later, especially after her success as Miss Brahms in the long-running BBC television series, *Are You Being Served? Come Outside* was the saga of an optimistic boy at a Saturday night dance trying to persuade his date to step into the moonlight with him. It was only the second comedy record (Lonnie Donegan's *My Old Man's A Dustman* was the first) to reach number one and since 1962 only ten comedy records have gone to number one.

Mike Sarne followed up *Come Outside* with *Will I What?* (with Billie Davis) and other less original variations on the theme. When he turned his hand to film directing he succeeded with *Myra Breckinridge* (starring Raquel Welch) in creating what many eminent critics consider the worst film of all time. Wendy Richard now plays Pauline Fowler in the BBC's twice weekly soap *Eastenders* and until her nephew Wicksy (actor Nick Berry) hit the top in 1986, was the only member of the cast with a number one hit. She even re-recorded *Come Outside* at that time with a replacement for Mike Sarne, but it failed to attract the record-buying public the second time around.

138

I CAN'T STOP LOVING YOU

RAY CHARLES

12 July 1962, for two weeks

● ●

HMV POP 1034

Written by Don Gibson. Produced by Sid Feller, orchestra and chorus conducted by Marty Paich.

One of the most influential albums of all time was Ray Charles' 1962 LP *Modern Sounds In Country and Western Music*. For the first time there was acknowledged crossover from rhythm and blues to country and western, meeting pop in the middle. The highlight of the album was Don Gibson's 1957 country ballad, completely reworked by Ray Charles to give him his biggest worldwide hit.

Ray Charles Robinson was born in Albany, Georgia on 23 September 1930. He was blinded by glaucoma at the age of six and orphaned by the age of 14. In the early '50s, after working with a hillbilly band called the Florida Playboys, Charles formed his own trio based on the successful Nat 'King' Cole formula. He dropped his surname to avoid confusion with boxer Sugar Ray Robinson and by 1952 had a recording contract with Atlantic. His career at Atlantic produced two classics *I Got A Woman* and *What'd I Say?*, neither of which hit the British charts, but it was not until he moved to ABC Paramount at the end of 1959 that he really began turning out the hits.

I Can't Stop Loving You has been his only number one in Britain, partly because of a long and ultimately successful fight against drug addiction, which severely restricted his career in the late '60s and '70s. In 1985 he was back at the very top as part of USA For Africa (see no. 548).

Shaving in the shadow of St Paul's is certainly eccentric, but **Frank Ifield** *is merely preparing for a scene in the film* Up Jumped A Swagman, *in which he portrays a singer from Australia recently arrived in London.*

139

I REMEMBER YOU

FRANK IFIELD

26 July 1962, for seven weeks

● ● ● ● ● ● ●

Columbia DB 4856

Written by Johnny Mercer and Victor Schertzinger. Produced by Norrie Paramor.

Frank Ifield was born in Coventry on 30 November 1936, but emigrated from that much-bombed city to Australia with his parents shortly after the war. He began his singing career in Australia, and returned to Britain in 1959 to try to break through in his homeland. Almost immediately he had a small hit with a song called *Lucky Devil*,

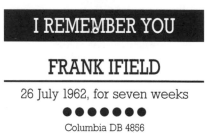

Ray Charles *takes direction from Paul Henreid as he prepares to ride the dodgems for a film. Actor Tom Bell and child star Piers Bishop complete the scene, which is not as unusual as it looks. Though blind, Charles enjoyed driving on a course in his backyard.*

covering the American hit by Carl Dobkins Jr. After that, the success which had seemed so near drifted away, and Ifield looked destined to join the ranks of not-quite-stars like Dickie Pride, Mike Preston and Nelson Keene.

Then, in the middle of 1962, Norrie Paramor and Frank Ifield decided on one more try. Like Connie Francis, four years earlier, they went through the box of old sheet music and came up with *I Remember You*, a song from the 1942 Dorothy Lamour movie *The Fleet's In*. What was different was the yodelling that Ifield put into 'I Remember Yoo-hoo'. Suddenly he was a big star, with a record that stayed at number one for seven weeks and which eventually sold a million copies in Britain alone.

140

SHE'S NOT YOU

ELVIS PRESLEY

13 September 1962, for three weeks

●●●

RCA 1303

Written by Doc Pomus, Jerry Lieber and Mike Stoller. Produced by Steve Sholes and Chet Atkins.

Elvis completed a round dozen of UK number ones with his fourth chart-topper in as many releases (another first for Tupelo's favourite son). The song was not linked to any movie and was one of a dozen or so titles recorded in Nashville (RCA studios) on 19 March 1962. The majority of the titles recorded that day found their way onto the *Pot Luck* album (including *Suspicion* which, like *Wooden Heart*, was 'lost' by RCA as a possible single and became instead a huge hit for unknown Terry Stafford in 1964, at a time when Elvis was running short of strong material). *Pot Luck* was a healthy album seller for Presley in the last half of 1962. Jerry Lieber and Mike Stoller had been asked by Elvis' publisher, Freddy Bienstock, to come up with some new country-flavoured material for this session, and they produced *She's Not You*, together with Doc Pomus, and the song that became its flip, *Just Tell Her Jim Said Hello*, on their own. *She's Not You* thus became the second Elvis number

one for Lieber and Stoller and the fourth for Doc Pomus who had co-written both sides of Elvis' ninth number one *Little Sister/His Latest Flame* (see no. 129), and was partly responsible for his eighth, *Surrender* (see no. 119).

141

TELSTAR

THE TORNADOS

4 October 1962, for five weeks

●●●●●

Decca F 11494

Written by Joe Meek. Produced by Joe Meek.

The third instrumental number one of 1962 was one of the better and more significant records of the early '60s. It was written, produced and arranged by Joe Meek, the man who had earlier hit the top with John Leyton and who had used the five men who now made up the Tornados as session musicians since before Leyton's success. The Tornados (Alan Caddy, Heinz Burt, Roger Jackson, George Bellamy and Clem Cattini) were officially Billy Fury's backing group, but their relationship with Fury was short-lived. *Telstar*, named after the American communications satellite launched earlier in the year, was an organ-dominated instrumental that not only reached number one in England, but went right to the top of the American charts as well.

Telstar was the first major British hit in America for years, and apart from novelties like Lonnie Donegan's *Does Your Chewing Gum Lose Its Flavour*, and Laurie London's *He's Got The Whole World In His Hands* was about the only straight pop hit from Britain since the days of Vera Lynn and David Whitfield. It prepared the way for the Liverpool invasion a year later.

Adding accidentally to the significance of the record, it was during *Telstar's* weeks on top that the first Beatles hit, *Love Me Do*, entered the British charts, and the world of popular music was on the verge of being changed forever.

142

LOVESICK BLUES

FRANK IFIELD

8 November 1962, for five weeks

●●●●●

Columbia DB 4913

Written by Irving Mills and Cliff Friend. Produced by Norrie Paramor.

Following up a monster hit like *I Remember You* is not easy. Frank Ifield, the man with the yodel gimmick, looked a racing certainty for obscurity as rapid as his fame. In the event, not so. Ifield and Paramor came up with the country and western standard *Lovesick Blues*, which had given Hank Williams one of his biggest successes over 10 years earlier. The song had originally been recorded by Emmett Miller in 1928, but despite the many hit versions that have been recorded since, nobody has sold as many copies of *Lovesick Blues* as Ifield.

Ifield was now following in the well-worn footsteps of Cliff Richard, Adam Faith, the Shadows and others in achieving two consecutive number one hits. Only Elvis Presley had completed a hat-trick of number ones (see no. 115), and in retrospect it is amazing to think that the Aussie from Coventry could even have had a chance of completing the hat-trick, for the Liverpool bombshell was on the point of exploding.

143

RETURN TO SENDER

ELVIS PRESLEY

13 December 1962, for three weeks

●●●

RCA 1320

Written by Otis Blackwell and Winfield Scott. Produced by Steve Sholes and Chet Atkins.

Return To Sender was Elvis Presley's fifth

consecutive number one, a record for consecutive chart-toppers that lasted only one year and 363 days, until 10 December 1964, when the Beatles' sixth consecutive number one, *I Feel Fine*, hit the top. *Return To Sender* was from Elvis' 11th film, the uninspiring *Girls! Girls! Girls!*. The main interest in the film is the ineptness of the title as there were actually only two girls featured in the film, played by Stella Stevens and Laurel Goodwin, although in addition to this number one smash, the score included the attractive ballad *Because Of Love* covered on a single by Billy Fury, himself perhaps the greatest British pop singer never to have a number one.

Otis Blackwell, author of such classics as *All Shook Up* and *Great Balls Of Fire*, did not extend himself in concocting with Winfield Scott, this lightweight gentle rocker for the abdicating King to churn off the production line. Amazing to relate, *Return To Sender* was the first Elvis UK number one to feature saxophone. The track was recorded late in 1962 at Paramount Studios in Hollywood, but the line-up of musicians at the session, apart from the Jordanaires on backing vocals as usual, is not clear.

144

THE NEXT TIME/ BACHELOR BOY

CLIFF RICHARD AND THE SHADOWS

3 January 1963, for three weeks

● ● ●

Columbia DB 4950

Written by *(The Next Time)* Buddy Kaye and Philip Springer, *(Bachelor Boy)* Bruce Welch and Cliff Richard. Produced by Norrie Paramor.

Between 8 November 1962 and 10 April 1963, Norrie Paramor produced six of the eight number ones, taking top spot for 16 of those 22 weeks. The only two chart-topping records in that period that he did not produce were one by Elvis (no. 143) and another by Jet Harris and Tony Meehan (no. 146) (who owed their start in the music business to their time as Shadows).

The second of those six Paramor hits was the only Cliff double A-side single which topped the charts. The two songs both came from Cliff's second very successful musical film, *Summer Holiday*. *The Next Time* was a slow romantic ballad performed in Greece against the exotic setting of the Acropolis, with Cliff sporting a rather unflattering English string vest. *Bachelor Boy*, on the other hand, was very much an afterthought. It was written by Cliff – his only number one as a writer – and Bruce Welch after it was discovered that the film was a few minutes too short, and was shot at Pinewood studios as a semi-dance routine with the Shadows rather than incur the extra cost of taking the film crew back to Greece for just one sequence. The ultimate success of the record would perhaps have justified the cost, but few of the hundreds of thousands of fans who saw the film spotted the difference.

145

DANCE ON!

THE SHADOWS

24 January 1963, for one week

●

Columbia DB 4948

Written by Valerie and Elaine Murtagh and Ray Adams. Produced by Norrie Paramor.

Dance On! was a tune found by the manager of Cliff Richard and the Shadows, Peter Gormley, who was listening to the piles of tapes that were always being sent in to his office, and looking for a potential single. It had been written by the three members of the vocal group the Avons, who had hit the Top 3 over Christmas 1959 with their cover version of Paul Evans and the Curls' American Top 10 hit, *Seven Little Girls Sitting In The Back Seat*. Their fourth and final hit had come early in 1961 with their version of Bobby Vee's American smash, *Rubber Ball*. The Avons only reached number 30 with that song, being thoroughly beaten by Bobby Vee, who reached number 4, and by Marty Wilde, who reached number 9. Playing on the Marty Wilde single had been then Wildcats Brian Bennett and Licorice Locking, so perhaps it was apt that the Avons' only connection with a number one hit should come with the help of two of the

people whose *Rubber Ball* had bounced higher than theirs.

As well as being a chart-topping instrumental for the Shadows, Kathy Kirby reached number 11 with her vocal version in 1963. *Dance On!* thus just failed to join the ranks of songs that have been Top 10 hits in both vocal and instrumental versions – songs like *Oh Mein Papa, Annie's Song, Amazing Grace* and *Don't Cry For Me Argentina*.

146

DIAMONDS

JET HARRIS AND TONY MEEHAN

31 January 1963, for three weeks

● ● ●

Decca F 11563

Written by Jerry Lordan. Produced by Dick Rowe.

Terence 'Jet' Harris was born on 6 July 1939 in Kingsbury, Middlesex, and David Joseph Anthony Meehan was born in Hampstead on 2 March 1943. After both had played with assorted groups during 1958, Cliff Richard enlisted them on bass and drums respectively for his backing group The Drifters. They subsequently became The Shadows and had notched up five Top 10 hits by the time that Tony vacated the drumstool in October 1961. Jet Harris remained with the group until March 1962, when he left to pursue a solo career.

After a couple of hits, *Besame Mucho* and *Main Title Theme From The Man With The Golden Arm*, Jet teamed up with Tony, who had since become involved in production work for Decca, and they released the six string bass dominated *Diamonds* at the tail end of 1962.

The tune had been written by singer/songwriter Jerry Lordan who had already supplied the Shadows with *Apache* and *Wonderful Land*. As *Diamonds* hit number one, ironically deposing the Shadows' *Dance On* from the top spot, Jet and Tony spoke out about each other. Jet said 'As a musician, Tony is one of the best: I have learned musical terms and ways that I never knew existed. He's a wizard and impresses me a great deal'. And Tony's thoughts on Jet – 'I have learned a great deal from Jet about stage-work, self-confidence and how to present myself!' After just two more big hits, *Scarlett O'Hara* and *Applejack*, both in 1963, the duo split up.

147

WAYWARD WIND

FRANK IFIELD

21 February 1963, for three weeks

● ● ●

Columbia DB 4960

Written by Stan Labowsky and Herb Newman. Produced by Norrie Paramor.

On 21 February 1963, Frank Ifield succeeded in completing the first hat-trick of number one hits by a British born artist when his version of the Gogi Grant hit of 1956, *Wayward Wind*, reached the very top. It was Ifield's third successive revival of a country song, and in reaching number one with three consecutive singles Ifield joined Elvis Presley on what was then (and still is) a very select list. The song had been written by Newman and Labowsky while they were students at UCLA, but it was not until many years later, when Newman owned a small record label called Era, that it was recorded. Era's first big success was a record called *Suddenly There's A Valley*, released in 1955 by Audrey Brown, renamed Gogi Grant for showbusiness purposes. In searching for a follow-up *The Wayward Wind* was pulled out of Herb Newman's drawer. The song sold millions and topped the American charts for six weeks in 1956, between Elvis Presley's *Heartbreak Hotel* and *I Want You I Need You I Love You*.

Wayward Wind – written originally for a male voice – had climbed to number 9 in Britain in 1956, but Norrie Paramor and Frank Ifield felt the song was right for revival. They went into the Abbey Road studios and recorded the song. It became not only Ifield's third consecutive number one but also the first of seven consecutive number ones over a period of 23 weeks recorded at Abbey Road, by far the most successful run by any studio in the years since the charts began.

Cliff Richard *woos co-star Lauri Peters in* Summer Holiday.

148

SUMMER HOLIDAY

CLIFF RICHARD AND THE SHADOWS

14 March 1963, for two weeks
4 April 1963, for one week

● ● ●

Columbia DB 4977

Written by Bruce Welch and Brian Bennett. Produced by Norrie Paramor.

The title song from the film *Summer Holiday* was written by Bruce Welch and the

Shadows' drummer Brian Bennett while they were on a tour of Britain. The idea came to them while they were rehearsing in the orchestra pit of an empty theatre: Bruce just started singing 'We're all going on a summer holiday, no more working for a week or two', and Brian immediately came up with the 'middle-eight', 'We're going where the sun shines brightly, we're going where the sea is blue . . .'. Over the past quarter of a century it has almost become a traditional song to sing in coaches and cars on the way to the annual holiday. It was the song that the Young Ones (see no. 567) were singing in the double decker bus in the last episode of their notorious TV series as the bus toppled over the edge of the cliff, thus ensuring that no further episodes of the series could be possible.

Cliff Richard is the only act in British chart history to have had more than one chart-topper that has fallen from the top and then climbed back. *Please Don't Tease* (see no. 104) was the first; *Summer Holiday* was the second.

149

FOOT TAPPER

THE SHADOWS

20 March 1963, for one week

●

Columbia DB 4984

Written by Hank B. Marvin and Bruce Welch. Produced by Norrie Paramor.

Norrie Paramor's third consecutive production at the top of the charts is now probably best known for being the signature tune of Radio 2's Saturday morning show, *Sounds Of The Sixties*. It was Bruce Welch's second consecutive number one as a writer (he co-wrote *Summer Holiday*, see no. 148, with Brian Bennett) and as a performer, as the Shadows were taking over from Cliff Richard and the Shadows, who in turn replaced the Shadows a week later. Although Bruce had already written or co-written four of Cliff's number ones, this was the only one of his compositions that the Shadows took to the top.

Foot Tapper featured in the film *Summer Holiday* and so another chart record was established by consecutive number ones coming from the same film. Other films like *Grease* and *Saturday Night Fever* have been more successful in total chart terms, but no other film has provided two number ones in a row, nor three number ones in total (see also no. 144). Two other tunes were featured by the Shadows in *Summer Holiday*. These were called *Round and Round* and *Les Girls*, but neither was released as the A-side of a single.

Foot Tapper was the last of five number ones for the Shadows, although they hit the Top 10 with both of their next two hits, giving them a round dozen of consecutive Top 10 hits. They currently have a tally of 16 Top 10 hits, and in mid-1988 more total weeks on the charts than anybody except Elvis, the Beatles, Frank Sinatra and their one-time boss, Cliff Richard.

150

HOW DO YOU DO IT?

GERRY AND THE PACEMAKERS

11 April 1963, for three weeks

●●●

Columbia DB 4987

Written by Mitch Murray. Produced by George Martin.

Gerry and the Pacemakers may have been the second Merseybeat act to be signed by manager Brian Epstein but they were the first of his Liverpool protégés to score a number one. Vocalist/guitarist Gerry Marsden, an ex-British Railways employee (born 24 September 1942), had been singing with his drummer brother Fred (born 23 November 1940) as the Mars Bars for some years. The Pacemakers were created by adding bassist Les McGuire (born 27 December 1941) and pianist John 'Les' Chadwick (born 11 May 1943) to the line-up. Like countless other Liverpool acts they too had made the trek to Germany to play in Hamburg's Top Ten Club.

Once the Pacemakers had been signed up, producer George Martin began the search for suitable material for a first single. The Beatles had written their own debut disc, *Love Me Do*, which had cracked the Top 20 in October 1962, but Martin was not convinced that McCartney and Lennon had the ability to compose big hits, so as a follow-up to *Love Me Do* he suggested they record a song written by Mitch Murray called *How Do You Do It?*. This they did but their version was never released. Instead the Beatles insisted that their self-penned song *Please Please Me* be issued, proving their point by climbing to number 2. Thus *How Do You Do It?* was handed down to the Pacemakers, who showed the Beatles exactly how to do it!

151

FROM ME TO YOU

THE BEATLES

The Beatles. *The second Liverpool group to get to number one.*

2 May 1963, for seven weeks

●●●●●●●

Parlophone R 5015

Written by John Lennon and Paul McCartney. Produced by George Martin.

When the Beatles' first single *Love Me Do* crept into the Top 50 on 11 October 1962, few people could possibly have guessed that by the end of the next year these four unknown people from somewhere north of Watford would have sold more records in Britain more quickly than anybody in the world before or since, including two singles which, at the time, were the two biggest-selling singles in British history.

From Me To You, the Beatles' third single, was the first of 11 consecutive number one hits for the Fab Four, a record as unlikely ever to be broken. This first number one was on top for seven weeks, which was to be their longest run at the top, equalled only by *Hello Goodbye* (see no. 241) four and a half years later. The Beatles were John Lennon (born 9 October 1940, died 8 December 1980), Paul McCartney (born 18 June 1942), George Harrison (born 25 February 1943) and Ringo Starr (born Richard Starkey on 7 July 1940), who joined the group just weeks before the Beatles bonanza got under way.

Everything was ready for the Beatles. The mediocre quality of pop music in 1962 had created a vacuum that had to be filled from somewhere, and the somewhere turned out to be Liverpool. Even before 1963, Liverpool had provided more than its fair share of musical talent (Frankie Vaughan, Michael Holliday and Billy Fury for example), but during the 'beat group' explosion of 1963/4, Liverpool became the centre of world popular music.

152

I LIKE IT

GERRY AND THE PACEMAKERS

20 June 1963, for four weeks

●●●●

Columbia DB 7041

Written by Mitch Murray. Produced by George Martin.

When Gerry and the Pacemakers took over at the top with their second single they became the first act to score number ones with their first two releases. The Stargazers, Eddie Calvert, Tennessee Ernie Ford and Adam Faith all had reached the summit with their first two hits, but by getting to number one with the only records they had ever released the Pacemakers achieved a feat that was unique at that time.

Like their previous hit, *I Like It* had been recorded at EMI's Abbey Road studios, where the group were to produce their debut album *How Do You Like It?* When released in October the album climbed to number 2, impeded by the Beatles' *Please Please Me* LP. *I Like It* also became writer Mitch Murray's second number one in two months.

The phenomenon of Merseybeat and the hysteria which had begun to occur, particularly at Beatles' concerts, was by now beginning to catch the attention of the British press.

153

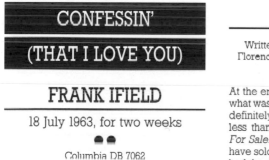

CONFESSIN'
(THAT I LOVE YOU)

FRANK IFIELD

18 July 1963, for two weeks

●●

Columbia DB 7062

Written by Al J. Neiburg, Doc Daugherty and Ellis Reynolds. Produced by Norrie Paramor.

After *Wayward Wind*, Frank Ifield's attempt to score a fourth consecutive number one failed when April 1963's *Nobody's Darlin' But Mine* peaked at number 4. By then Britain's charts were in the grip of the Liverpool sound and pundits wrote off Frank Ifield as somebody who had better start working out his routine for singing his old hits in the clubs, for that was all the future held in store.

However Frank Ifield refused to be written off immediately. Picking up a song written in 1930 and originally titled *Lookin' For Another Sweetie*, he yodelled his way back to the very top of the charts. But when Elvis

eased him out on 1 August, it was indeed the end of the chart-toppers for Frank Ifield. More hits followed, but only one more record, a revival of *Don't Blame Me*, reached the Top 10. Ifield's career is unusual in that he had four number one hits and two Top 10 hits in the space of seven releases in 18 months, but he never reached the Top 20 before or since despite another eight singles that reached the charts. His last hit *Call Her Your Sweetheart* dropped off the charts in February 1967, but his total of 158 weeks on the chart still placed him higher on the all-time list in January, 1988 than, for example, Dean Martin, Boney M or Duran Duran.

154

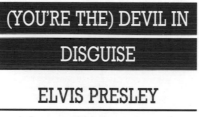

(YOU'RE THE) DEVIL IN
DISGUISE

ELVIS PRESLEY

1 August 1963, for one week

●

RCA 1355

Written by Bill Giant, Bernie Baum and Florence Kaye. Produced by Steve Sholes and Chet Atkins.

At the end of February 1963 Elvis released what was at that time probably his worst and definitely his shortest single at considerably less than two minutes, *One Broken Heart For Sale*. Despite the fact that it would not have sold more than ten copies if it had not had the magic Presley name on the label, it was considered a sensation when this single peaked at number 12 – Elvis had failed to reach the British Top 10 for the first time since the switch to RCA in 1957.

The follow-up to this disaster was eagerly anticipated and the song that was chosen from those recorded at a Nashville session at the end of May 1963 had one important difference from *One Broken Heart For Sale*. The Jordanaires reappeared, having been usurped by the Mello-Men on the previous single. *(You're The) Devil In Disguise* did make number one for one week, but it was already the end of an era. Never again would Elvis be able to claim the top spot as his by right. In fact, of the eight releases between *(You're The) Devil In Disguise* and his next number one *Crying In The Chapel* 2

years later, only one reached the Top 10.

Elvis was not the only American in decline. Such was the domination of the Liverpool groups and British pop at this time that from 26 July 1962 to 25 June 1964, Elvis was the only non-British act to top our charts. Between 3 January 1963 and 25 June 1964, a period of 77 weeks, this one week from August 1963 was the only week when a British record was not on top of our charts.

155

SWEETS FOR MY
SWEET

THE SEARCHERS

8 August 1963, for two weeks

●●

Pye 7N 15533

Written by Doc Pomus and Mort Shuman. Produced by Tony Hatch.

The Searchers was the title of the 1956 John Wayne movie from which Buddy Holly had extracted the line *That'll Be The day* (see no. 64). The group of the same name were the biggest Merseybeat band not to be managed by Brian Epstein. Their manager was the entrepreneur Tito Burns, who like other show biz bosses had been quick to scour Merseyside for the talent that Epstein had missed.

The group line-up on this cover version of the Drifters' original was vocalist/lead guitarist Mike Pender (born Mike Prendergast, Bootle, Liverpool, 3 March 1942), vocalist/rhythm guitarist John McNally (born Walton, Liverpool, 30 August 1941), vocalist/bassist Tony Jackson (born Dingwall, Liverpool, 16 July 1940) and drummer Chris Curtis (born Christopher Crummey, Oldham, 16 August 1941). Having formed in 1962, the group signed to Pye in 1963. They were put in the hands of staff producer Tony Hatch. This hit proved to be the first of the six number ones he has produced to date.

August 8 was also the day of the Great Train Robbery. One member of the gang who committed that crime, Ronald Biggs, became a chart star himself when he appeared on the Sex Pistols single *No One Is Innocent*, a Top 10 hit in 1978.

156

BAD TO ME

BILLY J KRAMER AND THE DAKOTAS

*A battered **Billy J Kramer** wonders if excessive fan enthusiasm is bad for him.*

22 August 1963, for three weeks

● ● ●

Parlophone R 5049

Written by John Lennon and Paul McCartney. Produced by George Martin.

Billy J Kramer and the Dakotas were the first act other than the Beatles to score a number one hit with a Lennon and McCartney composition. Furthermore, the song was one which the Beatles had not released on a single, album or EP. George Martin, by now aware of the phenomenal songwriting abilities of Lennon and McCartney, proceeded to build Billy J's career around their music. His first single, a cover version of *Do You Want To Know A Secret*, a track from the Beatles' *Please Please Me* album, had climbed to number 2. Kramer could also thank Lennon for providing him with something else – a middle initial which stood for nothing whatsoever.

Kramer (born William Howard Ashton in Liverpool, 19 August 1943) had been a guitarist with a number of bands while still working for British Railways. Having become the singer with Liverpool group the Coasters he signed a contract with manager Brian Epstein. Epstein immediately replaced the Coasters with Manchester backing band the Dakotas, having first sacked the Dakotas' vocalist Peter Maclain. The Dakotas were lead guitarist Mike Maxfield, rhythm guitarist Robin MacDonald, bassist Ray Jones and drummer Tony Mansfield, who was the brother of future chart star Elkie Brooks.

157

SHE LOVES YOU

THE BEATLES

12 September 1963, for four weeks
28 November 1963, for two weeks

● ● ● ● ● ●

Parlophone R 5055

Written by John Lennon and Paul McCartney. Produced by George Martin.

In chart terms, this was the Beatles' biggest hit, staying in the Top 50 for 33 weeks (36 if you add its brief re-entry in 1983). It sold over a million copies in Britain alone, and until the follow-up *I Want To Hold Your Hand* (see no. 160) sold even more, it was the biggest selling record in Britain ever. It is also one of only two records to come back to the top of the charts after two other songs had reached number one, the other one being Doris Day's *Secret Love* (see no. 18). Only 19 records have ever regained the top spot, mostly after only one week in a lower position. However, the seven week period while Brian Poole's *Do You Love Me* and *You'll Never Walk Alone* by Gerry and the

Pacemakers were on top of the charts is the longest period ever between spells at number one by the same record.

She Loves You was the record that changed a generation. When *From Me To You* was number one for seven weeks, Beatlemania was rising, but it was no greater than the fan worship that surrounded Cliff Richard earlier or the Bay City Rollers later. But *She Loves You* was something else – the trigger for the swinging '60s. 'She loves you, yeah, yeah, yeah' was the message and the lovable mop-tops were the medium. After almost 20 years the record still sounds outstanding, with the driving rhythm section of John and Ringo, the simple lead of George and the hard-edged vocals of John and Paul. The message was happy, positive, upbeat. The doubts of *Help* and *We Can Work It Out* were yet to come. The despair of *Yesterday* and *Eleanor Rigby* were years ahead. *She Loves You* and *I Want To Hold Your Hand* were the peak of the Beatles' achievements, the songs which most created their image. The only way from there should have been down, but it never happened.

158

10 October 1963, for three weeks

● ● ●

Decca F 11739

Written by Berry Gordy Jr. Produced by Mike Smith.

In 1959 Brian Poole, son of a Dagenham butcher, formed a group with schoolfriends in Barking, Essex. Two years later the line-up was basically the same, but instrumental responsibilities had changed. Alan Howard had swapped sax for bass, Alan Blakely had moved to rhythm guitar, being replaced on drums by Dave Munden, and Ricky West, a trained classical musician, joined to become lead guitarist, allowing Poole to concentrate solely on singing. The BBC Light Programme's *Saturday Club* producer Jimmy Grant saw them at Southend and booked them for several appearances. They turned professional at the end of 1961

following a successful holiday camp season at Butlins in Ayr.

On 1 January 1962, both Brian Poole and the Tremeloes and the Beatles underwent a Decca audition with Mike Smith from the company's A & R team. Head of the department Dick Rowe would only sign one band and having listened to both tapes he chose the one based eight miles from his London office, rejecting the Beatles and securing for himself an everlasting place in rock history.

The band's recording career started with session work; for example, providing the backing for the Vernon Girls' version of *The Locomotion*. Their first four singles all flopped, though their appearance in the film *Just For Fun* with Bobby Vee and the Crickets did give them exposure which helped bring their cover of the Isley Brothers' *Twist And Shout* into the charts. No doubt it would have climbed higher than number 4 were it not for the competition of the Beatles' EP version. They followed this with a group favourite, *Do You Love Me*, a song penned by Tamla Motown's Berry Gordy and an American smash for the Contours. The song gave Brian and the Tremeloes a number one in 16 countries.

159

GERRY AND THE PACEMAKERS

31 October 1963, for four weeks

● ● ● ●

Columbia DB 7126

Written by Richard Rodgers and Oscar Hammerstein II. Produced by George Martin.

You'll Never Walk Alone came from Rodgers and Hammerstein's show *Carousel* (first performed in New York in 1945, although it arrived in London in 1950). In the show it was an inspirational number designed to give courage to the heroine Jan Clayton after the death of her husband, and it was reprised at the end of the show at a high school graduation. All this seems a very long way from the top of the British pop charts, but that is

where the record went to give Gerry and The Pacemakers the then unique record of three consecutive number ones with their first three releases. Another Liverpool band, Frankie Goes To Hollywood equalled the feat in 1984.

Perhaps the strangest part of the story is the way the song was adopted by the faithful home supporters at the Kop End of Anfield, the home of Liverpool Football Club. (The Kop was named after Spion Kop in South Africa where a lot of local men had lost their lives in the Boer War.) The song didn't coincide with any specific success for Liverpool – it was two years since promotion from the Second Division and it was not until the April of 1964 that the club next won the championship; it seemed to be taken up for no particular reason. Ultimately it would be sung by many different sets of fans, although it 'belongs' to the Reds.

The song's connection with football was strengthened further in 1985 when 'The Crowd (lead vocalist Gerry Marsden) took it back to number one with a record whose proceeds all went to the Bradford City Disaster Fund (see no. 551).

The record was at number one on 22 November 1963 when Lee Harvey Oswald fired the shots from the Texas Book Depository Building in Dallas that killed President John F Kennedy.

160

THE BEATLES

12 December 1963, for five weeks

● ● ● ● ●

Parlophone R 5084

Written by John Lennon and Paul McCartney. Produced by George Martin.

When *I Want To Hold Your Hand* took over from *She Loves You* at number one, the Beatles completed a hat-trick of number one hits, to equal the achievements of Elvis Presley, Frank Ifield and Gerry and the Pacemakers. *I Want To Hold Your Hand* also took over from *She Loves You* as the biggest selling single in British history, a record it

The **Dave Clark Five** (Dave Clark on the right) at Heathrow Airport in 1964, the year of their number one.

kept until Paul McCartney's Wings sold over two million copies of *Mull Of Kintyre* (see no. 416). It was also the first time an act had succeeded itself at number one, a record the Beatles kept until John Lennon equalled the feat with *Imagine* and *Woman* in 1981 (see nos 473 and 474).

The main significance of *I Want To Hold Your Hand* is that it is the record that conquered America. On 18 January 1964, two days after the record had dropped off the top of the British charts, it entered the Billboard Hot Hundred and soared quickly to the top. By the end of 1964 the Beatles had achieved six number one hits in America, five more Top 10 hits and no less than 19 other charted sides, on a total of six different labels. Even *Love Me Do* on the now defunct Tollie label reached number one, while its B-side, *P.S. I Love You*, climbed as high as number 10. In later years the Bee Gees and Whitney Houston have equalled the Beatles' record of six consecutive number ones in America, and Christopher Cross has swept the Grammy Awards, but nobody has ever dominated world popular music like the Beatles did in 1964.

161

GLAD ALL OVER

THE DAVE CLARK FIVE

16 January 1964, for two weeks

●●

Columbia DB 7154

Written by Dave Clark and Mike Smith.
Produced by Dave Clark.

The Dave Clark Five, purveyors of the brash, big-beat 'Tottenham Sound', knocked the Fab Four off the top. This was all that journalists needed to begin writing stories proclaiming that the end of the Beatles was nigh. For a while some people believed what they read.

Formed in 1958, the group line-up in '64 was drummer, manager and former film stuntman Dave Clark (born 15 December 1942), vocalist/keyboard player Mike Smith (born 6 December 1943), guitarist Lenny Davidson (born 30 May 1944), bassist Rick Huxley (born 5 August 1942) and saxophonist Denis Payton (born 11 August 1943). They had released 5 singles on 3 labels before *Glad All Over*. Their version of *Do You Love Me* (see no. 158) reached 30 in the charts, paving the way for the big breakthough. In 1964 the USA caught Dave Clark Five fever and on Christmas Day 1965 the group grabbed one week at the top of the American charts with their minor UK hit *Over and Over*. Their sur-

prisingly good film vehicle *Catch Us If You Can* (directed by John Boorman) led to further successes but by 1970 the hits had stopped on both sides of the Atlantic.

Clark invested his earnings wisely. He bought the rights to the '60s pop show *Ready, Steady, Go* which was released on video cassette and reshown on TV in the mid-'80s. In 1986 the musical *Time,* which Clark had been working on as writer and producer since 1980, began a long run at London's Dominion Theatre. The leading role of the Rock Star was taken first by Cliff Richard and then by David Cassidy, both number one hitmakers themselves.

162

NEEDLES AND PINS

THE SEARCHERS

30 January 1964, for three weeks

●●●

Pye 7N 15594

Written by Sonny Bono and Jack Nitzsche.
Produced by Tony Hatch.

The Searchers' second number one was their third single on Pye. It was another old song which, like *Sweets For My Sweet,* had not made any dent on the British charts when originally recorded. In fact, Jackie de Shannon had only reached number 84 in America, so putting it out as a single was a bit of a risk for the Searchers. Their faith in the song was justified as it became their biggest hit and the song that even today people scream for at Searchers gigs.

Written by Jack Nitzsche and Sonny Bono, destined to achieve stardom 18 months later with his wife Cher (see no. 201), *Needles and Pins* was a perfect example of a supreme production that transformed a minor song into a brilliant record. The producer in question, Tony Hatch, actually wrote the Searchers' second single, *Sugar and Spice,* which reached number 2. Had it not been for the domination of the charts at the end of 1963 by the Beatles, the Searchers would have started their chart career with four consecutive number ones. Hatch, thanks largely to his entertaining but blunt comments as a judge on TV talent shows, has come in for occasional ill-informed criticism during his career as a writer, producer and performer, but his production of records like this one, or *Downtown* by Petula Clark, shows that he has been one of the most imaginative and influential record makers in Britain.

163

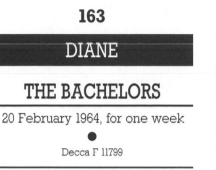

DIANE

THE BACHELORS

20 February 1964, for one week

●

Decca F 11799

Written by Erno Rapée and Lew Pollack. Produced by Michael Barclay.

Totally against the overwhelming Liverpool tidal wave, the Bachelors, three married men from Dublin, built up a highly lucrative career based on sweet harmony versions of old favourites. Starting with *Charmaine* in 1963, they had Top 10 hits with *Diane, I Believe, Ramona* and *Marie* among others. *Diane* was their only number one hit. The song was written in 1927 and originally featured by an off-screen, unidentified female vocalist in the film *Seventh Heaven*.

Originally formed as a novelty instrumental trio called the Harmonichords, the Bachelors were Con Clusky (born 18 November 1941), his brother Declan (born 12 December 1942) and John Stokes (born Sean Stokes on 13 August 1940). Their clean, smiling, image and highly professional stage presence made them particular favourites with TV producers. They were only the second Irish act to top the British charts, after Ruby Murray. Since them, the only Irish group to do so has been the Boomtown Rats (see nos 428 & 440) with whom the Bachelors have only their Irishness in common.

164

ANYONE WHO HAD A

HEART

CILLA BLACK

27 February 1964, for three weeks

● ● ●

Parlophone R 5101

Written by Burt Bacharach and Hal David. Produced by George Martin.

Cilla Black (born Priscilla White on 27 May 1943) was a cloakroom attendant at the famous Cavern Club in Liverpool. She was signed by the Beatles' manager Brian Epstein, and was therefore provided with a Lennon-McCartney song for her first single entitled *Love Of The Loved*, produced by George Martin. This reached number 35. The follow-up was a cover of Dionne Warwick's first US Top 10 single and in Great Britain Cilla clobbered Dionne.

Cilla was thus launched on one of the most impressive recording careers enjoyed by any British female. Her next single was another number one (see no. 170) and the following 15 were all hits, two of them Top 10. In the mid-'70s, the hits stopped coming but Cilla's popularity never waned. Her mastery of 'TV' kept her in the eye of an adoring public and by 1988 she was one of the country's biggest stars in any branch of entertainment. Many of her newer fans probably do not realize what a powerful and dramatic singing voice the hostess of *Surprise, Surprise* and *Blind Date* possesses.

Anyone Who Had A Heart was the first number one by a female soloist since Helen Shapiro at the end of 1961.

165

LITTLE CHILDREN

BILLY J KRAMER AND THE DAKOTAS

19 March 1964, for two weeks

● ●

Parlophone R 5105

Written by Mort Shuman and John Leslie McFarland. Produced by George Martin.

Billy J Kramer and the Dakotas' first three hits had been written by Lennon and McCartney. For their fourth they turned to an American songwriting team containing Mort Shuman, who along with Doc Pomus, had already penned two number ones for

Elvis Presley. Shuman's talent also triumphed for Billy J. In the Merseybeat days there was often no time to rehearse material before it was put onto tape. Kramer claims that *Do You Want To Know A Secret* and *Little Children* were the only numbers he ever rehearsed before stepping into the studio.

Little Children was followed by another Top 10 hit, the Lennon and McCartney composition *From A Window*. Feeling he needed a spell away from the breakneck pace, Kramer and the band spent four months at the North Pier, Blackpool, sharing the bill with comedian Tommy Trinder. Instead of rejuvenating the group, it kept them out of the public eye. The next single, *It's Gotta Last Forever*, failed completely. Kramer returned to the charts with the Bacharach and David song *Trains and Boats and Planes* in 1965 but he and the Dakotas, who in 1963 had had an instrumental hit of their own, *The Cruel Sea*, went their separate ways as soon as the hits began to dry up.

Billy J continues to record occasionally and can still be found performing in clubs and theatres throughout Britain and Europe.

166

CAN'T BUY ME LOVE

THE BEATLES

2 April 1964, for three weeks

● ● ●

Parlophone R 5114

Written by John Lennon and Paul McCartney. Produced by George Martin.

The Beatles' fourth number one was from their first film, *A Hard Day's Night*, and it gave George Martin the unique honour of having produced three consecutive number ones for the second time in 12 months.

Shooting on the film began in March 1964, after the Beatles got back from their first American visit, but much of the music had been recorded earlier. *Can't Buy Me Love* set a still unbeaten record in Britain by having advance sales of over one million copies, and yet it still failed to reach the top in its week of release. It took two weeks to get there, as did every Beatles' number one from *I Want To Hold Your Hand* to *Hey Jude*. It was, in retrospect, a slight let down from the two previous releases, which had been the supreme achievements of the Beatle-mania days. All the same, *Can't Buy Me Love* gave the Beatles yet more Gold Records and their third American number one.

The flip side was a John Lennon song *You Can't Do That*. He described it as his attempt to be Wilson Pickett. Wilson Pickett's last British hit was *Hey Jude*, his attempt to be John Lennon.

Peter and Gordon *(Asher and Waller) together in 1964, the year the world loved* World Without Love.

167

A WORLD WITHOUT LOVE

PETER AND GORDON

23 April 1964, for two weeks

●●

Columbia DB 7225

Written by John Lennon and Paul McCartney. Produced by Norman Newell.

Peter and Gordon's first and most successful hit was a song that Billy J Kramer had turned down, thus allowing two ex-Westminster School boys to be the second act, after Billy J, to top the charts with a Lennon and McCartney composition which the Beatles had not recorded themselves.

Peter Asher (born London 22 June 1944) and Gordon Waller (born Braemar, Scotland, 4 June 1945) were spotted by Norman Newell

at London's Pickwick Club. At that time Peter's actress sister, Jane, had become friends with Paul McCartney and Paul had begun using the Asher family home as a London base. Once Newell had signed the duo to EMI the source of possible songs to record was literally on Asher's doorstep.

In 1967, after seven Top 30 hits including *Woman*, a song that McCartney wrote under the pseudonym Bernard Webb, Peter and Gordon went their separate ways. Asher became producer and Head of A&R with the Beatles' Apple label, where he produced James Taylor's debut album, *Sweet Baby James*. He subsequently became Taylor's manager and also producer and manager of another major American star, Linda Ronstadt. Gordon, on the other hand, has left the entertainment industry. Soon after the duo split, he recorded several solo singles and one solo album, and appeared as Pharaoh in the West End production of *Joseph And The Amazing Technicolor Dreamcoat*, but by the end of the '70s he had settled down to a world without show business.

168

DON'T THROW YOUR LOVE AWAY

THE SEARCHERS

7 May 1964, for two weeks

●●

Pye 7N 15630

Written by Jimmy Wisner and Billy Jackson. Produced by Tony Hatch.

By the time the Searchers had recorded the Orlons' *Don't Throw Your Love Away* a rift had opened within the group. Tony Jackson left to form his own band, the Vibrations, whose subsequent career consisted of little more than one minor hit, *Bye Bye Baby*, at number 38 in October 1964.

While Jackson was fading out, Frank Allen from Cliff Bennett and the Rebel Rousers was being brought in. The Searchers' success continued unabated for another 12 months through classic songs like *When You Walk in The Room* and *Goodbye My Love*. During 1966, their last year of chart success, Chris Curtis vacated the drum seat which was kept warm by Johnny Blunt until

the arrival of Billy Adamson in 1969. In the meantime Curtis had formed the ill-fated Roundabout, a group which failed despite the inclusion of future Deep Purple members Jon Lord and Ritchie Blackmore.

The Searchers' line-up of Pender, McNally, Allen and Adamson remained unchanged for nearly 20 years but in 1986 the act split into two rival camps. Mike Pender formed a new group called Mike Pender's Searchers while the remaining three veterans plus Spencer James continue as the Searchers that ever was.

In April, 1964, just before their second UK number one, **The Searchers** *leave their Chelsea flat to appear on* The Ed Sullivan Show *in New York.*

169

JULIET

THE FOUR PENNIES

21 May 1964, for one week

●

Philips BF 1322

Written by Mike Wilsh, Fritz Fryer and Lionel Morton. Produced by Johnny Franz.

In October 1963 Marie Reidy of 'Reidy's Home Of Music' in Blackburn, Lancashire (the place where they had to count all the four thousand rather small holes, according to the Beatles' *Day In The Life*) telephoned Johnny Franz to ask whether he might be interested in a local group, the Lionel Morton Four. 'Send a tape', replied Mr Franz, and according to his later recollections, 'the tape was so good they were immediately signed to a contract'. The first session produced *Do You Want Me To?* which crept in to the charts at the beginning of 1964, and *Juliet*, the second single, which climbed all the way to number one. It had originally been selected as B-side to *Tell Me Girl*.

Lead singer Lionel Morton had been a choirboy at his local church in Blackburn for seven years which may have helped him when he played the title role in *Jesus Christ Superstar* for a year of the show's lengthy West End run. He was at one time married to the actress Julia Foster. Co-writers of *Juliet* with Lionel were Fritz Fryer (guitar) and Mike Wilsh (keyboards). The fourth Penny was Alan Buck, who had drummed for both Joe Brown's Bruvvers and Johnny Kidd's Pirates before joining the Four Pennies. *Juliet* proved to be the group's only Top 10 hit, although the next three singles all reached the Top 20. One of those singles was *Until It's Time For You To Go*, a song that Elvis Presley took to number 5 in 1972.

170

YOU'RE MY WORLD

CILLA BLACK

28 May 1964, for four weeks

● ● ● ●

Parlophone R 5133

Written by Umberto Bindi, Gino Paoli, English lyrics by Carl Sigman. Produced by George Martin.

You're My World followed hot on the heels of *Anyone Who Had A Heart* and gave Cilla Black her second consecutive number one, and one that would prove to be her last chart topper. The song was an adaptation of an Italian tune by the versatile translator Carl Sigman, whose previous adaptations included *Answer Me*, *The Day The Rains Came* and *It's All In The Game*. *You're My World* was Cilla's only US Top 40 hit and was revived there successfully in 1977 by Helen Reddy.

Among the many smashes Cilla enjoyed in the later '60s were her interpretation of the Bacharach-David classic *Alfie* and a Paul McCartney theme tune for one of her TV series *Step Inside Love*. Her only major error was to compete with the Righteous Brothers' *You've Lost That Lovin' Feelin'*. Her version reached number 2 but it still looked like a failure when it was overtaken by the unknown Americans (see no. 186).

The late Brian Epstein would have been delighted by the sustained success of his only solo female signing although possibly slightly baffled by her apparent reluctance to sing more than occasionally during her numerous TV appearances. Cilla has long been happily married to her second manager, Bobby Willis.

171

IT'S OVER

ROY ORBISON

25 June 1964, for two weeks

● ●

London HLU 9882

Written by Roy Orbison and Bill Dees. Produced by Wesley Rose.

It's Over became The Big O's second number one single four years after *Only The Lonely* glided to the top in November 1960. Like most of his songs *It's Over* had a highly orchestrated arrangement that helped display Orbison's marvellous soaring voice to best effect. His tunes were often referred to as 'pop arias'.

Orbison attained even greater popularity in Great Britain than in his homeland and during his second British tour in 1963 topped the bill over no less than Gerry and The Pacemakers and the Beatles. Orbison's motionless stage persona, with the dark glasses, black outfit and, occasionally, motorcycle leathers, hid a man who was in fact terribly shy. Off-stage Orbison underwent a traumatic three years between 1966 and 1968. First a motorbike accident claimed his wife Claudette (she was the inspiration for the Orbison song *Claudette* that the Everly Brothers had taken to number one) Two years later, two of his three children died in a fire at his home in Nashville.

It's Over was the first American number one hit in the UK for 47 weeks. Strange to relate, it is probably now not as well remembered as most of the lesser hits he scored in the previous four years – items such as *Running Scared*, *Crying* and *In Dreams* – now all standards.

172

THE HOUSE OF THE RISING SUN

THE ANIMALS

9 July 1964, for one week

●

Columbia DB 7301

A traditional song, arranged by Alan Price. Produced by Mickie Most.

The Animals were keyboard player Alan Price (born 19 April 1942), bass player Chas Chandler (born 18 December 1938), guitarist Hilton Valentine (born 2 May 1943), drummer John Steel (born 4 February 1941) and

Hilton Valentine (far left) and Eric Burdon of **The Animals** *present their pooch, Bo Diddley, to actress Susan Hampshire at a gardening competition in Eastbourne. It is less than a month since* The House Of The Rising Sun *topped the chart.*

vocalist Eric Burdon (born 19 May 1941). They started in 1962 doing all-nighters at the Downbeat Club near the Newcastle docks, but when their popularity increased they moved towards the centre of town, graduating to the more up-market Club-A-Go-Go. They became Newcastle's finest live band, performing a varied set ranging from blues standards like *Pretty Thing* to rock 'n' roll favourites such as *Shake Rattle and Roll*.

At the end of 1963 the group had 500 EPs pressed highlighting a selection from their club set. Mickie Most, a freelance record producer in London, obtained a copy and liked it so much he went north to see them live. His belief in the band was reaffirmed. He quickly signed them to Columbia and persuaded them to move to London.

In March the following year the group released their first single, *Baby Let Me Take You Home*, a song Bob Dylan had re-worked for his debut LP and which had started life as a blues number titled *Baby Don't You Tear My Clothes*. The follow-up, *The House Of The Rising Sun*, had been taped at Most's first session with the group and was a traditional piece previously recorded by Josh White and, again, by Dylan for his debut LP. At over four minutes long the record company didn't think *The House Of The Rising Sun* was a wise choice, but the success of the first single gave Most the casting vote and the track, which had been recorded at a Kingsway studio in just two takes, was released.

In the UK it entered at number 31, shot to number 6, then to number one. In America it fared just as well, becoming the first UK record not penned by Lennon/McCartney to make number one in the States since the Beatles instigated the British invasion. Success in America was no longer a Merseyside prerogative.

173

IT'S ALL OVER NOW

THE ROLLING STONES

16 July 1964, for one week

●

Decca F 11934

Written by Bobby Womack and Shirley Womack. Produced by Andrew Loog Oldham.

The first number one by the only group that could ever stand comparison in popularity with the Beatles was a Bobby and Shirley Womack song that was at the same time a small American hit for the Valentinos. It only held the top spot for one week, but with their fourth single the Stones had finally made the big time.

Their first single was Chuck Berry's *Come On* which gave them their first hit, and like the first single of many acts who were to become major chart powers it hung around the lower reaches of the charts for some time without ever getting as high as the Top 10. That single was followed by a Lennon/ McCartney tune which Ringo had sung on the *With The Beatles* album, *I Wanna Be Your Man*. This was the first time that the Stones had to put up with the 'Beatles copiers' tag, which dogged them throughout their career and which John Lennon commented acidly on in his interviews with the magazine that took its name from Mick Jagger and Co, *Rolling Stone*. The group's third single was a magnificent version of the Crickets B-side *Not Fade Away* and to prove the title prophetic they scored the first of five consecutive number ones with their fourth single, *It's All Over Now*. It wasn't, it was only just beginning.

174

A HARD DAY'S NIGHT

THE BEATLES

23 July 1964, for three weeks

●●●

Parlophone R 5160

Written by John Lennon and Paul McCartney. Produced by George Martin.

The title song from the Beatles' first film was their fifth consecutive number one, equalling the record for toppers on the trot held by Elvis Presley. It was their second number one hit from the film, after *Can't Buy Me Love*, which had not been written specifically for the movie.

Dick Lester directed *A Hard Day's Night*, which starred Wilfred Brambell as Paul's Irish grandfather and featured Patti Boyd as a schoolgirl on the train. It is considered one of the best pop films to come out of Britain, and justified its inevitable massive success.

The soundtrack was one of the strongest collections of Beatles songs ever put together. Only seven songs were actually in the film, but these included *And I Love Her* and *If I Fell* as well as the two number one hits. *A Hard Day's Night* was chosen as the title for the film after Ringo, at the end of one long session on the set, quoted from John Lennon's book *In His Own Write* with the comment, 'That was a hard day's night, that was'. Appropriately, Lennon sang lead.

The late Peter Sellers took his version of the song, recorded as an imitation of Laurence Olivier playing Richard III, into the Top 20 a year later. It was the first cover version of a Beatle single to hit the British charts.

175

DO WAH DIDDY DIDDY

MANFRED MANN

13 August 1964, for two weeks

●●

HMV POP 1320

Written by Jeff Barry and Ellie Greenwich. Produced by John Burgess.

Do Wah Diddy Diddy was the first number one to bear a nonsense title. If you met a girl walking down the street singing 'do wah diddy diddy dum diddy do' you'd be far more likely to refer her to a psychiatrist than marry her as vocalist Paul Jones did in the song.

Paul (born Paul Pond, 24 February 1942) was the central attraction of the group, but the backbone of the band was Johannesburg-born keyboard player, Manfred Mann (born Manfred Liebowitz, 21 October 1940). Mann had moved to London in 1961 having studied music at the Vienna State Academy and the Julliard School of Music, New York. In 1962 Mann joined with drummer Mike Hugg (born 11 March 1940) to form the Mann-Hugg Blues Brothers, a jazz/blues instrumental outfit. With the addition of guitarist Mike Vickers (born 18 April 1941), bassist Dave Richmond and Paul Jones, Manfred Mann came into being. Richmond quit after their first two singles flopped, to be replaced by Tom McGuinness (born 3 December 1941). Their third record, *5-4-3-2-1*, the signature tune to ITV's new pop show, *Ready Steady,*

Go, hit big in January 1964. Two releases later Manfred Mann were sitting at the top of the chart with this cover version of a US flop by the Exciters.

Right: **The Honeycombs** *with Ann 'Honey' Lantree on drums, select their equipment in June 1964. Two months later they were number one.*

176

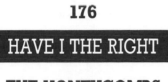

HAVE I THE RIGHT

THE HONEYCOMBS

27 August 1964, for two weeks

●●

Pye 7N 15664

Written by Ken Howard and Alan Blaikley. Produced by Joe Meek.

The Honeycombs had a girl on drums, so in 1964 they were news. There was nothing else very exciting about the group except that they were the first act to be taken over and marketed by Ken Howard and Alan Blaikley, who later achieved massive success with Dave Dee, Dozy, Beaky, Mick, and Tich (see no. 246) and who wrote *I've Lost You*, a number nine hit for Elvis Presley in 1970.

The Honeycombs were Dennis D'Ell (born Dennis Dalziel on 10 October 1943) on lead vocals, Martin Murray (born 7 October 1941) on lead guitar, Alan Ward (born 12 December 1945) on rhythm, John Lantree (born 20 August 1940) on bass and his sister, Ann 'Honey' Lantree (born 28 August 1943) bashing out a rhythm every bit as subtle as Dave Clark's on drums. Martin Murray owned a hairdressing salon where Honey Lantree worked, which was the way the group got together and the origin of the group's name. The fact that Miss Lantree boasted a bee-hive hairdo was probably coincidental.

The Honeycombs' smash repeated its success in many other countries including America (where it reached number 5), Australia and New Zealand. Follow-ups, alas, were less spectacular and a number 12 placing with *That's The Way* a year after their promising start proved to be their swan song.

177

YOU REALLY GOT ME

THE KINKS

10 September 1964, for two weeks

●●

Pye 7N 15673

Written by Ray Davies. Produced by Shel Talmy.

The Kinks in 1964 consisted of Ray Davies (born 21 June 1944, on lead guitar and vocals), his brother Dave (born 3 February 1947, rhythm), Pete Quaife (born 27 December 1943, bass), and Mick Avory (born 15 February 1945, a drummer from Devon who was the band's only non-Londoner). Their first single was the only one with an A-side not written by Ray Davies. It was a version of Little Richard's *Long Tall Sally* and it flopped. Single number two, *You Still Want Me*, also disappeared down the plughole, but single number three was to be a classic of British rock, *You Really Got Me*, as was the fourth, *All Day And All Of The Night*, a re-working of *You Really Got Me* that made number 2 three months later.

Jimmy Page, of the Yardbirds and later Led Zeppelin, is persistently rumoured to have played lead guitar on both this single and Herman's Hermits' *I'm Into Something Good*. Even if these rumours are untrue, Page certainly played lead on Joe Cocker's *With A Little Help From My Friends* (see no. 260), so he got to number one eventually.

178

I'M INTO SOMETHING

GOOD

HERMAN'S HERMITS

24 September 1964, for two weeks

●●

Columbia DB 7338

Written by Carole King and Gerry Goffin. Produced by Mickie Most.

Mickie Most, hot from his success with the Animals, saw the actor Peter Noone on Coronation Street in 1964 and decided he looked like John F Kennedy. Noone was leader of a group called the Heartbeats in Manchester when Most contacted him. Soon Herman's Hermits and 'Hermania' were born. Peter Noone was born on 5 November 1947. His Hermits were Derek 'Lek' Leckenby, (born 14 May 1946), Keith Hopwood (born 26 October 1946), Karl Green (born 31 July 1946) and Barry Whitwam on drums (born 21 July 1946).

Most provided them with *I'm Into Something Good* which is, amazingly enough, the only Goffin/King song ever to top the British charts. It had been a minor hit in the States for a lady named Earl-Jean. The Hermits recorded it (with a little help from session men) and the disc moved rapidly to the top of the charts. It also established them in America where their bouncy unsophisticated style gave them many more hits than in their homeland. *Mrs. Brown You've Got A Lovely Daughter* (originally written for a TV play starring Tom Courtenay) and *I'm Henry VIII I Am* were the biggest of twelve consecutive American Top 20 hits, a better track record than they enjoyed in Britain.

When the Hermits broke up in 1971, Herman had one hit under the name Peter Noone before disappearing from the charts. He emerged at the 1979 World Popular Song Festival in Tokyo singing an Elton John discard called *I'll Stop Living If You Stop Loving Me*, and in 1982 released a solo album after a brief spell fronting a new wave group called the Tremblers. He has also appeared in many musical theatrical productions

around the world, such as the *Pirates of Penzance*. Meanwhile a group named Herman's Hermits with the odd original member soldiers on at oldies gatherings.

179

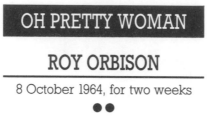

OH PRETTY WOMAN

ROY ORBISON

8 October 1964, for two weeks

London HLU 9919

Written by Roy Orbison. Produced by Wesley Rose.

In the middle of the British domination of the number one position during 1963 and 1964, Roy Orbison managed two chart-toppers and was virtually the only American act whose records were guaranteed to sell in vast quantities at this time.

This was Roy Orbison's final chart-topper, although the hits continued throughout the '60s. His first hit was in 1960, his last at the end of 1969, and yet such was his success in that decade that he remains one of the Top 20 chart acts of all time. In the 1970s and 1980s the popularity of his songs continued, but his own records stopped selling. When

Don McLean's version of *Crying* reached number one (see no. 460), Orbison's compositions had become chart-toppers in three decades, the 1950s *(Claudette)*, the 1960s and the 1980s. In 1981, Orbison had a comeback country hit in America in partnership with Emmylou Harris called *That Loving You Feeling*.

Speaking at Orbison's induction into the rock and roll Hall of Fame in 1987, Bruce Springsteen commented, 'In '75 I went into the studio to make *Born To Run* . . . and most of all I wanted to sing like Roy Orbison. Now everybody knows nobody sings like Roy Orbison.'

180

(THERE'S) ALWAYS SOMETHING THERE TO REMIND ME

SANDIE SHAW

22 October 1964, for three weeks

Pye 7N 15704

Written by Burt Bacharach and Hal David. Produced by Tony Hatch.

*It is 1965 and **Herman's Hermits** really do have something to smile about. After their UK number one in 1964 they had two number ones in America.*

Sandra Goodrich was born in Dagenham, Essex on 26 February 1947. Rather than become a Girl Piper or a Ford factory worker young Miss Goodrich made her way to Adam's Faith's dressing room and sang for the great man. He was impressed and the 17-year-old landed a recording contract. She changed her name to Sandie Shaw, and her second single was a cover version of a small Lou Johnson hit in the USA, written by Burt Bacharach and Hal David. It gave her her first hit and her first number one in only its third week on the chart.

Sandie then proceeded to cut a string of hit singles with the writer/producer Chris Andrews which included her second number one *Long Live Love* (see no. 196). She became the first, and to date only, British female soloist to have three chart-toppers when her Eurovision winner *Puppet On A String* went all the way in 1967 (see no. 232). Madonna, two decades later, was the first girl to equal (and then surpass) Sandie's achievement.

The short-sighted Miss Shaw drew further attention to herself in the early days of her career by never wearing shoes on stage.

181

BABY LOVE

THE SUPREMES

19 November 1964, for two weeks

● ●

Stateside SS 350

Written by Brian Holland, Lamont Dozier and Eddie Holland. Produced by Brian Holland, Lamont Dozier and Eddie Holland.

The Supremes were the first black act to top the UK singles list in nearly four years. *Baby Love* served notice that a new form of rhythm and blues had arrived, a pop-orientated music that was heavy on beat and strong on melody. It became known as 'The Motown Sound' after the label formed by Berry Gordy Jr, and it provided one of the lasting styles of the sixties.

Florence Ballard, Diana Ross and Mary Wilson were the Supremes who made the group's first successful recordings, though

when they had started as the Primettes there had been five and Ross used her real name, Diane Earl. Ballard was the original leader of the group and chose the name the Supremes, but she was gradually phased out for the more glamorous and charismatic Ross, a personal favourite of Gordy. Both he and Smokey Robinson had tried fruitlessly to write and produce for the group. The trio of Holland-Dozier-Holland had better results, providing the Supremes with four years of hits.

The breakthrough came with *Where Did Our Love Go*, an American number one and a British number three. Lyricist Eddie Holland battled with himself for weeks before putting *Baby Love* on paper, considering the song trite. He need not have felt embarrassed. This single was the second of five consecutive American number ones.

182

LITTLE RED ROOSTER

THE ROLLING STONES

3 December 1964, for one week

●

Decca F 12014

Written by Willie Dixon. Produced by Andrew Loog Oldham.

Originally a US soul hit in 1951 for the Griffin Brothers featuring Margie Day, the Willie Dixon song *Little Red Rooster* was covered by Sam Cooke 13 years later. It was this recording, which reportedly featured Billy Preston on keyboards, that brought the song to the attention of the Stones.

The Rolling Stones hold many all time chart records, and among the countless groups of the early and mid-'60s, their consistency and longevity is second to none. They were formed in 1962 and played regularly at London clubs like Wardour Street's Marquee and Giorgio Gomelsky's Crawdaddy Club in Richmond. There they quickly acquired a following and a manager – Andrew Loog Oldham. He juggled the line-up so that by the time they signed with Decca and cut their first single they were five Londoners – Mick Jagger (born on 16 July 1943) on vocals, lead guitarist Keith Richards (born on 18 December 1943), who

dropped the 's' off his surname in imitation of Cliff Richard, drummer Charlie Watts (born 2 June 1941), Bill Wyman (born 24 October 1941) on bass and Brian Jones (born 26 February 1944, died 3 July 1969) on rhythm guitar. This was the line-up on all their number one hits except *Honky Tonk Women* (see no. 274). In the '80s Keith reinstated the final letter of his surname.

183

I FEEL FINE

THE BEATLES

10 December 1964, for five weeks

● ● ● ● ●

Parlophone R 5200

Written by John Lennon and Paul McCartney. Produced by George Martin.

Brian Epstein understood the importance of release dates. In the first five years of Beatlemania, from 1963 to 1967 inclusive, the only year the Beatles did not have the Christmas number one was 1966 when they were too involved in the making of *Sgt Pepper* to release a single. The second of these Christmas hits was *I Feel Fine*. This was the single that put the Beatles one ahead of Elvis in the successive number one stakes. *I Feel Fine* was six out of six for the mop tops – Elvis' greatest run had been five.

The fourth Beatles album *Beatles For Sale* was also released that Christmas and for the first time it was admitted that not all Lennon-McCartney tunes were co-operative efforts. In his liner notes, Beatles publicist Tony Barrow says that various tracks on the LP were considered as potential singles 'until John Lennon came up with *I Feel Fine*'. John Lennon also sang lead on the single, but perhaps the most arresting feature of it was his feed-back guitar work. By the end of their second year as the biggest thing ever to hit British show-business, the Beatles were beginning to be recognized as musicians and not as just pretty faces. George Harrison was the first to attract approving remarks from the critics having always been considered the group's best musician. Before long he was being called one of the best rock guitarists in the world.

184

YEH YEH

GEORGIE FAME AND THE BLUE FLAMES

14 January 1965, for two weeks

●●

Columbia DB 7428

Written by Rodgers Grant, Pat Patrick and Jon Hendricks. Produced by Tony Palmer.

Georgie Fame began life as Clive Powell on 26 June 1943 at Leigh in Lancashire. He sang in his local church choir and taught himself the harmonica and piano, joining his first group, the Dominoes, when aged 14. In the summer of 1959 he played at Butlins holiday camp in Pwllheli and was seen by drummer Rory Blackwell, who invited him to London to join his band as pianist and vocalist.

Lionel Bart heard Powell play and recommended him to impresario Larry Parnes. Parnes changed the youngster's name to Georgie Fame and used his talents on package tours backing stars like Billy Fury and Marty Wilde. He also tried, unsuccessfully, to launch Fame on a solo career as a rock and roll pianist.

In mid-1962 Fame left rock and roll behind and formed the five-man Blue Flames, a rhythm and blues/jazz band. The Blue Flames were Colin Green on guitar, Tony Makins on bass, Peter Coe on sax, Bill Eyden at the drum stool and Ghanaian Speedy Acquaye on congas. Within a short time Fame earned a residency at London's Flamingo Club, whose owner Rik Gunnell became Fame's new manager and secured him a recording deal with Columbia. The band's Flamingo appearances became so popular that he was persuaded early in 1964 to release a live album *Rhythm And Blues At The Flamingo* before he had a hit single. His fourth single with the Blue Flames was *Yeh Yeh*. It climbed quickly to number one and reached number 21 in the States. At the end of 1985, the song climbed back to number 13 when recorded by Matt Bianco.

On 20 January 1965, while *Yeh Yeh* was number one, American DJ Alan Freed, the man who popularized the phrase rock and roll, died of uremia in Palm Springs, aged 42.

185

GO NOW

MOODY BLUES

28 January 1965, for one week

●

Decca F 12022

Written by Larry Banks and Milton Bennett. Produced by Denny Cordell.

The Avengers and Diplomats were two Birmingham based groups that spawned several chart topping stars. The former included Roy Wood and Graham Edge (born 30 March 1942), the latter Bev Bevan and Denny Laine (born 29 October 1944). Wood and Bevan went on to form the Move and ELO. Edge and Laine joined Mike Pinder (born 19 December 1942), Ray Thomas (born 29 December 1942) and Clint Warwick (born 25 June 1949) to form the Moody Blues.

This line-up played extensively on the Midland circuit and gave their first performance at Birmingham's Carlton Ballroom in May 1964. They soon signed with a London manager, Tony Secunda, and secured a deal with Decca. Their first single was the totally unsuccessful *Lose Your Money* but the second release, a cover version of Bessie Banks' soul classic, *Go Now*, gave them a UK smash and an American Top 10 hit.

The next few releases did not fare as well and in August 1966 Warwick gave up music and Laine left to set up his own Electric String Band. He later joined forces with Paul McCartney in Wings (see no. 416). Replacements John Lodge (born 20 July 1943) and Justin Hayward (born 14 October 1946) helped change the Moody Blues' musical style from white R & B to orchestrated rock.

Twenty-one years later, with 40 million-plus album sales for the Moody Blues Mark II worldwide, this appears to have been a wise move.

186

YOU'VE LOST THAT LOVIN' FEELIN'

THE RIGHTEOUS BROTHERS

4 February 1965, for two weeks

●●

London HLU 9943

Written by Phil Spector, Barry Mann and Cynthia Weil. Produced by Phil Spector.

The story of one of the best known records of all time, and the most spectacular production of Phil Spector's long and influential career, begins with the tiny California label, Moonglow Records. It put out the first Righteous Brothers single *Little Latin Lupe Lu* in the spring of 1963. It reached number 49 in the Hot Hundred. It then took luck as much as the soulful voices of the two unrelated brothers to bring them to Phil Spector.

Bill Medley was born on 19 September 1940 in Santa Ana, near Los Angeles. Bobby Hatfield was born on 10 August 1940 in Beaver Dam, Wisconsin, but grew up in Anaheim, in the same Orange County of southern California as Bill Medley. They played with a group called the Paramours, but left as a duo. Soon they were popular in California. Their big break came in 1963 when they performed on the same bill as Phil Spector's top act of the time, the Ronettes. In 1964, they toured the States opening the show for the Beatles, and towards the end of that year TV producer Jack Good signed them as regulars on his rock show *Shindig*. Spector saw them, remembered them from the previous year and took them into his studio. By February 1965 the single was number one in both Britain and America having seen off a cover version by Cilla Black.

They followed their immortal smash with more than a dozen US hits, including another number one, *Soul And Inspiration*, which became one of only two subsequent British Top 20 hits for the duo. In 1968 they split up but reunited in 1974 enjoying one last major American success, *Rock And Roll Heaven*. Medley returned to the charts as

The Seekers *teeter on the edge in February 1965, not knowing if they will be number one in the next week's chart. (They were, and they came down from the roof.)*

half of a duet in 1987 when he and Jennifer Warnes had an international hit with *(I've Had) The Time Of My Life.*

187

TIRED OF WAITING FOR YOU

THE KINKS

18 February 1965, for one week

●

Pye 7 N 15759

Written by Ray Davies. Produced by Shel Talmy.

Tired Of Waiting For You was the second Kinks number one and their third consecutive hit single. Its predecessor, *All Day And All Of The Night,* had only missed the very top by a whisker, but in early 1988 became the first song of the three to return to the Top 10, via the Stranglers.

Tired Of Waiting For You was a gentler item than the first two offerings had been and it can now be seen as the beginning of a long spell of more subtle Ray Davies songs that were to bring the Kinks a most impressive run of '60s and early '70s recording success. Apart from one or two singles, such as the comparatively unsuccessful *Everybody's Gonna Be Happy* and *Till The End Of The Day,* their singles became quieter and the lyrical content, often outstanding, a vital factor in the songs' appeal. In between their second number one and their third, *Sunny Afternoon* (see no. 218) were Davies gems such as the raga rocker *See My Friend* and the witty assaults on the narcissism of Carnaby Street (*Dedicated Follower Of Fashion*), and hypocritical pillars of society (*Well Respected Man*).

Around the time of their second chart-topper the group ditched the pink hunting jackets that manager Robert Wace had originally suggested for them. Wace had been in the band in their early days as the Bo-Weevils and the Ravens at the time they were studying at the Croydon School of Art.

188

I'LL NEVER FIND ANOTHER YOU

THE SEEKERS

25 February 1965, for two weeks

● ●

Columbia DB 7431

Written by Tom Springfield. Produced by Tom Springfield.

I'll Never Find Another You (no relation to *I'd Never Find Another You,* which gave Billy Fury a number 5 hit in 1961/2), was written and produced by Tom Springfield and launched the career of the group that filled the gap in the market when Tom's own group, the Springfields, broke up in 1963. The Springfields were of course the group that featured Tom's sister Dusty as lead vocalist (see no. 213), and without becoming a huge international attraction the trio had achieved considerable success with a series of pop-folk recordings including two British Top 10 entries and one, *Silver Threads And Golden Needles,* that did well in America.

The Seekers, like the Springfields, recorded in a style that owed a little to folk and a little to pop; they sang clear and straightforward melodies with the crystal voice of Judith Durham their instantly recognizable trademark – quite a contrast to the majority of chart groups of the times. The quartet were Australians, although Keith

Potger was actually born in Sri Lanka (2 March 1941). The other three were born in or near Melbourne; Judith on 3 July 1943, Bruce Woodley on 25 July 1942 and Athol Guy on 5 February 1940. Keith Potger's family moved to Melbourne in 1947 and it was in that city that the group was formed. They worked their passage to Britain in 1964, singing on an ocean liner. A booking on *Sunday Night At The London Palladium* was theirs soon after they stepped ashore and next came the recording deal with Springfield.

189

IT'S NOT UNUSUAL

TOM JONES

11 March 1965, for one week

●

Decca F 12062

Written by Les Reed and Gordon Mills. Produced by Peter Sullivan.

It's Not Unusual was originally intended for Sandie Shaw but she turned it down as unsuitable, so Gordon Mills offered it to an unknown Welshman, Tom Jones (born Thomas Jones Woodward on 7 June 1940). Jones' voice and the powerful orchestral arrangement made the song sound so unlike anything Sandie Shaw might have sung that it is hard to understand how it could have been written with her in mind. Still, her loss was Tom Jones' gain and a major career was launched.

The song was played on *Juke Box Jury* with Tom Jones behind the screen listening to the comments of the jury. His appearance on that show probably made the difference – the all-male Welsh miner's son (if he wasn't a miner's son he ought to have been) with the tight trousers and the rabbit's foot swinging from the belt was what the female population of Britain from 8 to 80 had been waiting for. He became the most sophisticated, most sexy and most imitated British singer in pop history and his career was made. With the help of minor surgical alterations to the state of his nose and his tonsils, Tom Jones eventually conquered the whole world to become the All-Round Entertainer that he remains to this day.

Members of the class of '65 take to the Thames. Among the sailing stars are Marianne Faithfull, Lulu, Cathy McGowan, Sandie Shaw and **Unit Four Plus Two.**

190

THE LAST TIME

THE ROLLING STONES

18 March 1965, for three weeks

● ● ●

Decca F 12104

Written by Mick Jagger and Keith Richard.
Produced by Andrew Loog Oldham.

The Last Time gave the Rolling Stones a hat-trick of number ones making them the fifth act on that rapidly expanding list. More important for them, it marked not the last time but the first time a Rolling Stones A-side had been written by the duo that was to become one of the most creative in rock music: Mick Jagger and Keith Richard. At this stage the pair were uncertain about their writing abilities.

While every newspaper was comparing the Stones with the Beatles it is perhaps not surprising that Jagger and Richard were not confident of standing comparison with Lennon and McCartney. The B-side, *Play With Fire*, was credited to Nanker and Phelge, a

pseudonym Mick and Keith used on many early sides.

The Last Time gave the Stones their second Top 10 hit in America, as the follow-up to *Time Is On My Side*. They had to wait for their first number one in the States until the next single (see no. 202), which was recorded in America.

191

CONCRETE AND CLAY

UNIT FOUR PLUS TWO

8 April 1965, for one week

Decca F 12071

Written by Brian Parker and Tommy Moeller. Produced by John L. Barker.

Unit Four Plus Two's brilliantly original number one hit *Concrete And Clay* was one of the few big British hits of 1965 not to be a major smash in America, where it climbed only to number 28. This was primarily because a cover version, by American Eddie Rambeau, climbed to number 39 at the same time, so perhaps combined sales of the two versions were not far short of the successes enjoyed by other British hits of that year.

Unit Four Plus Two was a six man band, as the name suggests. They took their name from the very popular Alan Freeman radio show *Pick Of The Pops* which was divided into four units, Unit Four being the section in which Freeman played the Top 10. The group started out as Unit Four, but then added two more personnel, so adapted the name. The six members were Rod Garwood, Hugh Halliday, Howard Lubin, Buster Miekle, Tommy Moeller and Pete Moules. Russ Ballard, later to compose *So You Win Again* for Hot Chocolate (see no. 408), played on the record but did not join the group full-time until 1967 when its best days were past. In fact, their last chart hit, their fourth, was *Baby Never Say Goodbye*, which lurched onto the chart for one week at number 49 from 17 March 1966, less than a year after *Concrete And Clay* had been at the top of the charts.

American Randy Edelman revived *Concrete And Clay* in 1976 and took it back into the British Top 20, to number 11. In his native America it missed the Top 40 altogether.

192

THE MINUTE YOU'RE GONE

CLIFF RICHARD

15 April 1965, for one week

Columbia DB 7496

Written by Jimmy Gately. Produced by Norrie Paramor.

The first Cliff Richard number one hit that did not feature the Shadows was Cliff's eighth number one and his sixth single release without his long-time backing group. *The Minute You're Gone* was also the second British number one after *Young Love* (see no. 56) to have been recorded earlier by American country superstar Sonny James. His version had reached number 9 on the American country charts in the summer of 1963. Cliff's version was recorded in Nashville, Tennessee, in the summer of 1964, but its release as his 39th single was delayed almost a year.

At the time of its issue, Cliff and the Shadows were coming to the end of their three-month stint at the London Palladium in the pantomime *Aladdin*. Cliff took the title role, the Shads were cast as Wishee, Washee, Noshee and Toshee, Una Stubbs was the romantic interest Princess Dalroubadour and the veteran comedian Arthur Askey played Widow Twankey.

The Minute You're Gone was Cliff's 26th consecutive Top 10 hit. Nevertheless, he was quoted in 1965 as saying that he drew just £10 a week pocket money, despite press insistence that he was a millionaire.

193

TICKET TO RIDE

THE BEATLES

22 April 1965, for three weeks

Parlophone R5265

Written by John Lennon and Paul McCartney. Produced by George Martin.

The Beatles extended their record string of number one hits with consecutive releases to seven with the first offering on single from their second feature film *Help*. The song, *Ticket To Ride*, featured John Lennon on lead vocal which was not unusual, but unexpectedly, Paul McCartney played lead guitar rather than George Harrison. Brian Epstein, the Beatles' manager, won an LP in the music weekly *Melody Maker* for one of the best letters of the week when he wrote pointing out this temporary change of Beatle musical duties.

The *Help* album not only introduced *Ticket To Ride*, the eighth Beatles chart-topper (see no. 200), but the song that within ten years became not only the most covered Beatles composition but one of the most often performed and recorded songs in the history of popular music – Paul McCartney's beautiful ballad *Yesterday*. This was released in 1965 as a single in the States (number one of course) but not in the UK until 1976, six years after the Beatles had broken up. It still made the Top 10.

Yesterday was not actually featured in the movie which was another wacky Dick Lester comedy, co-starring Leo McKern, Eleanor Bron and Victor Spinetti. This film was, inevitably, a major box-office attraction but it lacked some of the fresh and unforced magic of *A Hard Day's Night*.

194

KING OF THE ROAD

ROGER MILLER

13 May 1965, for one week

Philips BF 1397

Written by Roger Miller. Produced by Jerry Kennedy.

Texan Roger Miller, born on 2 January 1936, is a country singer and composer whose songs have embraced comedy (e.g. *You Can't Roller Skate In A Buffalo Herd*) and

Huckleberry Finn, opened on Broadway. It won the Tony Award for Best Musical of the Year.

195

WHERE ARE YOU NOW
(MY LOVE)

JACKIE TRENT

20 May 1965, for one week

●

Pye 7N 15776

Written by Tony Hatch and Jackie Trent.
Produced by Tony Hatch.

The fifth number one to be produced by Tony Hatch was the first hit for the woman who was later to take Mr Hatch to be her lawful wedded husband. Trent's singing talent had become well known through regular appearances on radio and television and Hatch, as well as being staff producer at Pye, was building a reputation as a songwriter, having penned *Sugar and Spice* for the Searchers and *Downtown* for Petula Clark. He had also managed to score an instrumental hit of his own, *Out Of This World*, which had enjoyed one week at number 50 in 1962.

One of Hatch's best known compositions was the theme to the long-running ITV soap opera *Crossroads* which was first broadcast on 2 November 1964. His original theme was rearranged in the '80s but it's unlikely that this was the sole cause for the series' demise in 1988. The tune even popped up as the last track on Paul McCartney and Wing's 1975 number one album, *Venus and Mars*, and the producers of *Crossroads* occasionally substituted this version at the end of particularly emotional episodes.

Two more Top 40 hits followed for Jackie Trent. In 1988 the answer to Trent's musical question of 1965 was Australia, for in the mid-'80s she and her husband moved Down Under. Tony Hatch continues to compose; the theme to the Australian soap opera *Neighbours* is one of his.

extreme sentimentality (e.g. *Little Green Apples*) but not often simultaneously. After a period in the US Army he moved to Nashville in order to hawk his songs around various record companies, and it was as a songwriter that he first found fame. Country singers Ernest Tubb, George Jones and Ray Price and pop stars like Andy Williams all recorded Miller material before he began having American country hits of his own in 1960. His biggest UK success before *King of The Road* had been as the writer of Del Shannon's 1962 number 2 hit, *Swiss Maid*.

Miller scored two US pop hits, *Dang Me* and *Chug-A-Lug*, in 1964. Then came *King of The Road*, a gently swaying saga of a train drifter, the 'road' referred to being the railroad. It was to be a worldwide hit, proving that Peter and Gordon's enthusiasm for the singer they'd seen while touring America was well founded. Four further UK hits followed up to 1969, including a song that took London as its theme, *England Swings*. His career in the US continued, albeit unevenly, through the '70s. In 1985 *Big River*, a Miller musical that he had based on Mark Twain's

196

LONG LIVE LOVE

SANDIE SHAW

27 May 1965, for three weeks

●●●

Pye 7N 15841

Written by Chris Andrews. Produced by Chris Andrews.

Most of Sandie Shaw's singles were written and produced by Chris Andrews, the man who wrote *The First Time*, Adam Faith's final Top 10 hit. He gave Sandie Shaw hits like *I'll Stop At Nothing, Message Understood, Nothing Comes Easy* and *How Can You Tell*. He also wrote *Yesterday Man*, which he sang himself and took to number 3 at the end of 1965. The only one of Miss Shaw's three number ones that he wrote was *Long Live Love*, the only Chris Andrews song ever to top the charts.

Sandie's underrated achievement in being the first solo girl singer to manage three number one British hits is only partly explained by her voice, original and strong though it was (and is). Lulu, for example, recorded songs by Bowie, Neil Diamond and Marty Wilde, and yet her biggest chart success in Britain was her less than memorable Eurovision song *Boom Bang-A-Bang*, which reached number two. Sandie Shaw's choice of writers was always more conservative than Lulu's and over the years Lulu has had the benefit of far more TV exposure than Sandie. So how did Miss Shaw manage three chart toppers? It must have been the bare feet.

197

CRYING IN THE CHAPEL

ELVIS PRESLEY

17 June 1965, for one week
1 July 1965, for one week

●●

RCA 1455

Written by Artie Glenn. Produced by Steve Sholes.

The world of popular music had been turned upside down for the first time since the advent of Elvis himself between the King's 14th and 15th number one successes in the UK. The Beatles, of course, were responsible. Elvis' record sales, while still good by most artists' standards, had taken a major dive and no longer could he rely on his records hitting even the Top 10 every time out. The advent of the British groups was not solely responsible for Elvis' decline – his own career had been artistically off the rails anyway, consisting mainly of feeble movies and weak songs from undistinguished soundtracks which would have sunk completely any performer other than Elvis. But he still retained a devoted following despite his output and the fans rallied round in extremely healthy numbers to make *Crying In The Chapel* his first number one for two years. It was in fact recorded five years before, at the sessions that produced *Surrender* (see no. 119) and his sacred LP *His Hand In Mine*. The song was written in 1952 by Artie Glenn, whose son Darrell and Rex Allen had separate country hits with it in 1953. The same year *Crying In The Chapel* was a R&B and pop hit in the US for the Orioles.

The Hollies line-up on I'm Alive was (left to right) Allan Clarke, Bobby Elliott, Graham Nash, Tony Hicks and Eric Haydock.

198

I'M ALIVE

THE HOLLIES

24 June 1965, for one week
8 July 1965, for two weeks

●●●

Parlophone R 5287

Written by Clint Ballard Jr. Produced by Ron Richards.

Singer/guitarist Graham Nash (born 2 February 1942) and singer Allan Clarke (born 5 April 1942) first sang together at their Salford primary school. Later, as The Two Teens, they performed hits by Lonnie Donegan, Cliff Richard and the Everly Brothers for the Manchester cabaret circuit. Later still, they became the Guytones, the Fourtones (with two other chaps), Ricki and Dane, and by 1961, with bassist Eric Haydock and drummer Donald Rathbone, the Deltas, a title that lasted until Christmas 1962, when they became the Hollies in tribute to Buddy Holly, and were joined by guitarist Tony Hicks (born 16 December 1943).

The Hollies' reputation in the north-west lured EMI staff producer Ron Richards into their territory to hear them and the five-

Disembarking after a successful flight on Trans World Airlines are **The Byrds**, *number one at the time with* Mr Tambourine Man.

Clarke. However, on the *Mr Tambourine Man* single only Roger McGuinn actually performed. The rest of the musicians were session men Leon Russell, Larry Knechtel and Hal Blaine. Blaine has drummed on so many major hits that he could be the most successful chart performer of all time. Hits like *Strangers In The Night, Bridge Over Troubled Water* and *You've Lost That Lovin' Feelin'* all feature Blaine's drumming, as do many of Elvis Presley's later hits.

All the Byrds composed and played on their albums, but after a short while individual feelings replaced group harmonies and the Byrds began to disintegrate. David Crosby left to be part of Crosby, Stills and Nash. The late Gram Parsons, who became the major influence on Emmylou Harris and her pure country-rock style, joined the Byrds but left shortly afterwards with Chris Hillman to form the Flying Burrito Brothers. Soon McGuinn was the only Byrd left, just as he had been on *Mr Tambourine Man.*

200

HELP!

THE BEATLES

5 August 1965, for three weeks

● ● ●

Parlophone R 5305

Written by John Lennon and Paul McCartney. Produced by George Martin.

The title song from their second film gave the Beatles their eighth number one, putting them at the time equal second with Cliff Richard on the list of most chart-toppers in Britain. The Beatles' eight were uniquely consecutive and achieved within a period of just 2 years and 95 days. The other acts to have had eight or more number ones before or since (Elvis, Cliff, Abba and the Rolling Stones) never crammed any eight into so brief a span.

The film *Help!* was originally to be called *Eight Arms To Hold You*, which would have made an interesting title for a love song, possibly breaking lyrical ground that was not actually achieved until *Je T'Aime* in 1969. The Beatles, however, did have another go at writing a song featuring a similar number of limbs when Ringo came up with *Octopus's Garden* on the *Abbey Road* LP.

piece were quickly signed. Their first single, a remake of the Drifters' *Just Like Me,* did reasonably well, rising to number 25, but not well enough to stop drummer Rathbone leaving. He was replaced by former Fentone Bobby Elliott (born 8 December 1942).

The Hollies recorded a string of reworked American rhythm and blues hits like Maurice Williams' *Stay,* Doris Troy's *Just One Look* and the Coasters' *Searchin',* but by 1965 Ron Richards was beginning to find good original songs for them. Several were by Graham Gouldman, who went on to write three number ones with 10 C.C., while *I'm Alive* was by Clint Ballard, the American who also wrote *Good Timin'* for Jimmy Jones and *The Game Of Love* for Wayne Fontana and the Mindbenders.

The group eventually released several of their own compositions as A-sides with no detrimental effect on their remarkable run of hit single consistency. They survived the departure of Eric Haydock (in 1966), replaced by Terry Sylvester, and Graham Nash (in 1968) who moved to America and Crosby, Stills (and Young). Even Allan Clarke took the odd sabbatical but the hits kept coming until 1974.

199

MR TAMBOURINE

MAN

THE BYRDS

22 July 1965, for two weeks

● ●

CBS 201765

Written by Bob Dylan. Produced by Terry Melcher.

In the summer of 1965 folk rock stormed the world. Producer Terry Melcher, the son of 1950s chart-topper Doris Day, took the Bob Dylan song *Mr Tambourine Man* from the album *Bringing It All Back Home* and electrified the jingle-jangle.

The Byrds were Roger McGuinn, a Chicagoan born on 14 July 1942, Gene Clark, David Crosby, Chris Hillman and Michael

Help! was not as successful a film as *A Hard Day's Night*. It was shot in colour, had a much larger budget and made plenty of money, but the Beatles were not happy with it. They gave up films (apart from the self-produced *Magical Mystery Tour* TV film and the *Let It Be* documentary) and got back to what they knew best, composing and recording.

201

I GOT YOU BABE

SONNY AND CHER

26 August 1965, for two weeks

●●

Atlantic AT 4035

Written by Sonny Bono. Produced by Sonny Bono.

Sonny and Cher burst on to the British summer of 1965 with the ultimate hippie anthem, a full two years before hippiedom took over the youth of Europe and America. 'Don't let them say your hair's too long, I don't care, with you I can't go wrong', became the compulsive theme of all young lovers of the mid-60's.

Not that Sonny, at least, was all that young. He was born on 16 February 1935 and had been writing and performing for some years. With Jack Nitzsche he wrote *Needles and Pins,* which became the 162nd British number one when recorded by the Searchers. He thus joined the select group who have written number ones for themselves and for another act. Bono also did some important session work on Phil Spector productions. Lessons he learned from the Tycoon of Teen can be heard throughout *I Got You Babe.*

Sonny and Cher (born Cherilyn LaPierre on 20 May 1946) divorced in 1974 after a decade of substantial record and TV success. Cher began a hectic period as the gossip columnists' delight, her name being linked with many men both eligible and ineligible. By the 1980s, she had become a highly respected actress as well as vocalist (she had had over 20 solo hit singles by early 1988) with an Oscar nomination for her role in the 1983 film *Silkwood*, raves for *Mask,* and awards for *Moonstruck*.

I Got You Babe returned to the number one

spot exactly 20 years later as performed by UB40 with guest vocals by Pretender Chrissie Hynde (see no. 555).

202

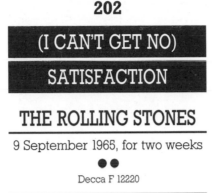

(I CAN'T GET NO)

SATISFACTION

THE ROLLING STONES

9 September 1965, for two weeks

●●

Decca F 12220

Written by Mick Jagger and Keith Richard. Produced by Andrew Loog Oldham.

1965 was the single most important year in the breakthrough of the Rolling Stones. They began writing their own hits with *The Last Time* (see no. 190), they passed the million mark in sales for the first time, achieving this with several discs, and they scaled the summit of the American chart for the first time with *(I Can't Get No) Satisfaction*. This latter title, recorded in Hollywood, remains their calling card. It stated eloquently and forcefully youth's aimless dissatisfaction with love and life in a materialistic society, and in its power suggested the restrained violence that was part of the group's image at the time. Many American radio stations edited out the last verse, which they believed referred to menstruation.

Keith Richard composed the introductory riff and though it became one of the most famous in rock history, Richard at one point thought it might have suited a horn section rather than a guitar. He must have been delighted when Otis Redding used brass to begin his version on his album *Otis Blue.*

Not only is *(I Can't Get No) Satisfaction* the definitive Rolling Stones track, it is one of only two songs to have been a hit in as many as five different years, with charted cover versions by Redding (1966), Aretha Franklin (1967), Bubblerock (Jonathan King under a pseudonym, 1974) and Devo (1978). Only

Right: **Sonny and Cher** *are shown in July, 1965, after having been turned away from The Hilton. The hotel claimed they didn't have a booking; Sonny Bono claimed he and his wife were being discriminated against because of their appearance.*

White Christmas, a chart hit over six different Christmasses since 1952 is superior to the Jagger/Richard *chef d'oeuvre* in this respect.

203

MAKE IT EASY ON

YOURSELF

WALKER BROTHERS

23 September 1965, for one week

●

Philips BF 1428

Written by Burt Bacharach and Hal David Produced by Johnny Franz.

The Walker Brothers were not brothers and none of them were called Walker. They were bassist Scott Walker (born Noel Scott Engel, 9 January 1944), guitarist John Walker (born John Maus, 12 November 1943) and drummer Gary Walker (born Gary Leeds, 3 September 1944). It was Gary who, having come across his future partners singing in Gazzari's, a Los Angeles club, persuaded them that their fortunes were to be made in Britain. Scott had already appeared solo on several of Eddie Fisher's US TV shows (see nos 4 and 10) and had worked with Sonny Bono (see no. 201). John was a TV soap star playing Betty Hutton's son in *Hallo Mom*.

At the time Gary was not the world's greatest drummer, although he had drummed on one tour of England with P. J. Proby. His musicianship was not to be heard on the Walker Brothers' early records and even on stage a second drummer would be hidden in the wings to cover for him. This mattered not, for on arriving in London in 1965 the Walkers cracked the chart with their second single, *Love Her*, a top 20 hit in April. Then came their first number one, a US Top 20 tune for Jerry Butler in 1962. It was the fifth UK chart-topper to be written by Bacharach and David. The Walker Brothers' treatment featured lush orchestration and the rich baritone of Scott.

Ken Dodd *is so excited by his unexpected number one that his hair anticipates punk by more than a decade.*

204

TEARS

KEN DODD

30 September 1965, for five weeks

● ● ● ● ●

Columbia DB 7659

Written by Billy Uhr and Frank Capano. Produced by Norman Newell.

In 35 years of chart history, fewer than 20 acts have hit number one and had a chart career lasting for more than 20 years. Most people would immediately be able to name some of those illustrious names – Elvis, Cliff, the Rolling Stones, Bee Gees, Shadows and Frank Sinatra – but they would probably get stuck before they came up with the name of Ken Dodd.

The chief of the Diddymen, born on 8 November 1932, had his first hit in the summer of 1960, when *Love is Like a Violin* reached the Top 10. His final chart record so far hit the chart 21½ years later, when *Hold My Hand* enjoyed a five week listing over the Christmas period of 1981. A few days later, he joined the even more select band of number one hitmakers to have been honoured by the Queen. His OBE was announced in the 1982 New Year's Honours List.

Ken Dodd's singing career has given him a completely different image from the wild haired purveyor of the tickling stick that we all know and that Mrs Thatcher loves. He has scored 19 hits, four of which reached the Top 10, including the million-selling *Tears*, first recorded by Rudy Vallee three years before Ken was born. None of his hits has been a comedy record. Only *Happiness* (number 31 in 1964) and *Hold My Hand* were even cheerful. The Ken Dodd of the pop charts is a tragic soul, singing songs with titles like *Tears*, *Let Me Cry on Your Shoulder*, *Tears Won't Wash Away My Heartache* and *Broken Hearted*.

205

GET OFF OF MY CLOUD

THE ROLLING STONES

4 November 1965, for three weeks

● ● ●

Decca F 12263

Written by Mick Jagger and Keith Richard. Produced by Andrew Loog Oldham.

The fifth consecutive number one hit for the Stones was their second successive grammatically flawed number one to be recorded in Hollywood. It lasted at the top for one week more than *(I Can't Get No) Satisfaction* even though global sales of *Get Off Of My Cloud* were lower. Again, the singer of the song is portrayed as a discontented soul, this time from the perspective of a disgruntled occupant of the 99th floor of a high-rise block, apparently somewhere in Britain as his financial transactions are made in sterling.

By the end of 1965, the Rolling Stones were probably at the peak of their popularity. They had achieved five number ones in a row, a total only previously reached by Elvis and the Beatles; they had toured America, Australia and Scandinavia with massive success and they had yet to run into serious problems with the laws of drug abuse. Certainly their image was non-conformist and anti-establishment, but at the end of 1965 the Rolling Stones were in danger of achieving conventional acceptance. Before long, Jagger, Richard and the late Brian Jones proved equal to the task of keeping respectability at bay.

206

THE CARNIVAL IS OVER

THE SEEKERS

25 November 1965, for three weeks

● ● ●

Columbia DB 7711

Written by Tom Springfield. Produced by Tom Springfield.

A Russian folk song is not the most obvious source for a British number one, but for Tom Springfield it proved a gold mine. Like Gene Raskin with *Those Were The Days* (see no. 239), Springfield found a Russian folk tune, adapted the melody, added English lyrics and the result was *The Carnival Is Over* – which gave the Seekers their second number one in three singles. The single between *I'll Never Find Another You* (see no. 188) and *The Carnival Is Over* was another Tom Springfield song, *A World Of Our Own*, which climbed to number three.

The Seekers never had another number one, although their popularity and hits continued for some time. *Morningtown Ride* climbed to number two at Christmas 1966. *Georgy Girl,* written by Tom Springfield and Jim Dale for the Lynn Redgrave film of the same name reached number 3. It was the Seekers' biggest American hit, peaking at number 2.

By the time the Seekers broke up they had notched up three more Top 10 hits and a couple of number 11s in the year and a half between March 1966 and September 1967. Their final charting single, *Emerald City,* which only made number 50 for a week in December 1967, was the only one of their nine 45s not to crack the Top 20.

207

DAY TRIPPER/WE CAN WORK IT OUT

THE BEATLES

16 December 1965, for five weeks

● ● ● ● ●

Parlophone R 5389

Written (both sides) by John Lennon and Paul McCartney. Produced (both sides) by George Martin.

The first of four Beatles singles to be officially released as a double A-side duly became their ninth consecutive number one the week after it entered the charts, and it gave them the Christmas number one for the third year in a row.

Both sides became immediate Beatles favourites, and attracted many cover versions. *Day Tripper* hit the charts again in 1967, recorded by Otis Redding, and *We Can Work It Out* came back to chart life twice in the 1970s, once when Stevie Wonder took his version to number 27 in 1971, and again five years later when the Four Seasons followed up four consecutive Top 10 hits with their rendition, which peaked at number 34. A different song of the same title was a minor hit for Brass Construction in 1983. A group called the Vontastics took for themselves a share in the title of Least Successful Chart Act in America when their recording of *Day Tripper* (a Top 10 soul hit) made number 100 for one week only, from 3 September 1966. Thus it was that the most successful and the least successful chart

acts in US chart history both hit with the same song.

208

KEEP ON RUNNING

SPENCER DAVIS GROUP

20 January 1966, for one week

●

Fontana TF 632

Written by Jackie Edwards. Produced by Chris Blackwell.

Chris Blackwell was on the lookout for black talent for his fledgling Island label when he came across the exceptional voice of Steve Winwood at Birmingham's Golden Eagle pub. He immediately signed Winwood and the group he was performing with to Fontana. A year later they were at number one.

Vocalist, guitarist and keyboard player Steve (born 12 May 1948) and his bassist brother Muff (born 15 June 1945) had joined drummer Peter York (born 15 August 1942) and guitarist Spencer Davis (born 17 July 1942) in 1963 to form the Rhythm and Blues Quartet, playing material by the likes of Muddy Waters and Sonny Boy Williamson. On signing a recording contract they changed name and turned professional, releasing a John Lee Hooker song, *Dimples,* as their first single. It flopped but the follow-ups, *Every Little Bit Hurts* and *I Can't Stand It,* fared better. Then with a piece of

Rolling Stones.

inspired musical cross-fertilization producer Blackwell introduced the group to Wilfred 'Jackie' Edwards, a Jamaican ska artist whom he'd discovered during his Island research. Winwood and Davis were off and running.

209

MICHELLE

THE OVERLANDERS

27 January 1966, for three weeks

● ● ●

Pye 7N 17034

Written by John Lennon and Paul McCartney. Produced by Tony Hatch.

The Overlanders were discovered and managed by top rock photographer Harry Hammond. Initially they were a three part harmony group consisting of lead vocalist Laurie Mason, Paul Arnold and Pete Bartholomew. This line-up was extended in 1965 when Terry Widlake and David Walsh joined. The group signed to Tony Hatch at Pye.

Their first eight releases in the UK all failed to chart, but they registered in the States with *Yesterday's Gone,* a bigger hit there for Chad and Jeremy. Despite their lack of chart success at home, their folk beat sound became a popular club attraction, most notably in the northern cabaret clubs and ballrooms where they were always in demand. They even toured as support to the Rolling Stones.

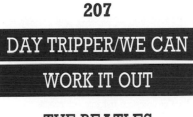

Their one and only triumph on disc came when Hatch and Hammond decided to raid the outstanding recently-released Beatles album, *Rubber Soul*. None of the tracks had been released as singles by the Beatles themselves and a host of lesser acts descended upon the 14 titles with an eye to instant chartdom. *Michelle*, a Paul McCartney ballad sung partly in French, was nabbed by both the Overlanders and by vocal duo David & Jonathan, in reality songwriters Roger Cook and Roger Greenaway (see no. 308). Both versions charted but the Overlanders peaked ten places higher. Their follow-ups however all sank without trace and by the end of the year the group had disbanded, remembered now only as the first act to take a cover of a Beatles LP track to number one.

210

THESE BOOTS ARE MADE FOR WALKING

NANCY SINATRA

17 February 1966, for 4 weeks

● ● ● ●

Reprise R 20432

Written by Lee Hazelwood. Produced by Lee Hazelwood.

Frank Sinatra's eldest daughter, Nancy, to whom one of her father's greatest hits, *Nancy (With The Laughing Face)* was dedicated in 1944, was born in her distinguished father's home state of New Jersey on 8 June 1940. She made her national TV debut in 1960 with her dad and Elvis Presley, the year she married pop singer/actor Tommy Sands, whose own record career was by then on the wane after a storming start with *Teenage Crush* in 1957.

Nancy was one of the first signings to Frank's own Reprise label in 1961, but for five years a series of forgettable recordings of ballads and show tunes advanced her no further than being Frank Sinatra's daughter or Mrs Tommy Sands. She eliminated the latter problem by divorcing Sands in 1965. Then in 1966, Lee Hazelwood, who had supervised twangy guitar man Duane Eddy's recording career in the late '50s and

Nancy Sinatra *with the serious face.*

early '60s, gave her the aggressive and witty *Boots* (his own composition) to record. The result was a number one hit for Nancy on both sides of the Atlantic.

The smash set Nancy off on a healthy string of hits, mainly masterminded by Hazelwood. The next single was really 'Boots 2' entitled *How Does That Grab You Darlin'?* but it made Top 10 US and Top 20 UK. More distinguished was her third British hit, the whimsical *Sugar Town*, which peaked at 5, just before she hit the jackpot in conjunction with her famous parent (see no. 231).

211

THE SUN AIN'T GONNA SHINE ANYMORE

WALKER BROTHERS

17 March 1966, for four weeks

● ● ● ●

Philips BF 1473

Written by Bob Crewe and Bob Gaudio. Produced by Johnny Franz.

After *Make It Easy On Yourself* (see no. 203),

the Walker Brothers put out another heavily emotional ballad as the follow-up. They make the mistake, however, of choosing the basically optimistic song *My Ship Is Coming In* which did not match the fragile and tortured image that Scott Walker had been moulded into, so it only reached number 3.

No such mistakes on the next single. A title as bleak as any that has reached number one, *The Sun Ain't Gonna Shine Anymore*, written by the Four Seasons' masterminds Bob Crewe and Bob Gaudio, gave the Walker Brothers a second number one. By the spring of 1966, Scott Walker was certainly the most popular male vocalist among the female teenage population of Britain and his looks and voice seemed destined to keep him at the top for as long as he wished. But signs of disintegration within the group were already beginning to appear by this time, and when the inevitable parting of the ways took place, not even Scott Walker found sustained success easy to achieve. Maybe he never wanted it, but after several powerful and big-selling albums, some TV shows and a couple of hit singles, he faded. Nothing of great import was heard from any Walker Bro. during the '70s until 1976 when they suddenly reunited out of nowhere, made an album and one excellent Top 10 single *No Regrets* before another lengthy spell of mysterious inactivity, broken this time by Scott on his own and an album entitled *Climate Of Hunter* – a minor LP chart item in 1984.

212

SOMEBODY HELP ME

SPENCER DAVIS GROUP

14 April 1966, for two weeks

● ●

Fontana TF 679

Written by Jackie Edwards. Produced by Chris Blackwell.

The Spencer Davis Group's second number one was, like their first (see no. 208) written by Jackie Edwards. So was their next hit, *When I Come Home*, but this was nothing like as successful as the first two and the band began to write more of their own material. The high chart positions of the next two singles, *Gimme Some Lovin'* and *I'm A Man* (the latter also a hit for Chicago in 1970) proved the wisdom of this change of policy.

By spring 1967, it had become clear that the prodigious talents of Steve Winwood could not be contained within the confines of the Spencer Davis Group, and he left to form Traffic. This move spelt the beginning of the end for the Davis band. Steve's brother Muff also departed, to a behind the scenes role with Chris Blackwell's Island Records. Spencer soldiered on for a while with a variety of replacements but never came up with a combination that recaptured the magic of the Winwood Brothers days.

Traffic became a speedy international success. Their biggest single hit was *Hole In My Shoe*, less than seriously revived by comic hippy neil in 1984. They survived various coming and goings (including Steve's short-lived stint with supergroup Blind Faith in 1969) until the mid-'70s. Winwood lay low for the rest of the decade but came back with a vengeance in the '80s with four hit solo albums and a number one US single, *Higher Love*, in 1986. His elder brother is now head of A&R at CBS Records in London.

Dusty Springfield *and brother Tom share a family moment in 1964, Dusty's first full year as a solo star.*

and September 1965 before achieving her only number one hit in April 1966. *You Don't Have To Say You Love Me* was an adaptation of the Italian song *Io Che No Vivo Senza Ta*.

Often making use of top class writing teams like Bacharach and David or Goffin and King, Dusty's finest hour arrived with her *Dusty In Memphis* album. Produced by Jerry Wexler, it contained the classic single *Son Of A Preacher Man* which made number 9 in December 1968. She faded almost completely from the record scene during the '70s but her reputation as one of the finest singers of her era did not. She eventually returned to prominence in a big way with none other than the Pet Shop Boys (see nos 563 and 593) singing on their 1987 number 2 hit *What Have I Done To Deserve This*. That year she also recorded with Richard Carpenter who obviously considered Dusty one of the few vocalists with whom he could work after the sad death of his sister Karen.

came five singles and nearly two years after their first, but in the meantime the group had been consolidating its position as one of the most popular in the country. Personnel changes were always a feature of Manfred Mann, and by the time *Pretty Flamingo* was recorded, Mike Vickers had left to be replaced by Jack Bruce (born 14 May 1943) who played bass, with Tom McGuinness switching to lead. It was the only occasion in the amazingly varied career of Jack Bruce (Cream, John Mayall, Graham Bond, even the Hollies) when he played on a number one hit single.

This was also the last big Manfred Mann hit featuring Paul Jones as lead singer. A single featuring Jones, *You Gave Me Somebody To Love,* was released after he had left the group that summer, but it climbed no higher than number 36. It is remembered now only as the answer to the trick question, 'What was the last Manfred Mann hit to feature Paul Jones?'. The first single featuring the new lead singer hit the charts the weeks after *You Gave Me Somebody To Love* disappeared. The new singer was Mike d'Abo (born 1 March 1944) and the single was the second Bob Dylan composition that Manfred Mann released as a single, *Just Like A Woman*. The third Dylan-composed single was to give them their biggest hit of all.

213

YOU DON'T HAVE TO SAY YOU LOVE ME

DUSTY SPRINGFIELD

28 April 1966, for one week

●

Philips BF 1482

Written by Pino Donaggio and Vito Pallavicini.
English lyrics by Vicki Wickham and Simon Napier-Bell. Produced by Johnny Franz.

Dusty Springfield (born Mary O'Brien on 16 April 1939 in Hampstead, London) began her career with her brother Tom and Tim Field in the pop-folk group the Springfields. They split in September 1963 after two years of considerable popularity and record sales to match. Four months later Dusty began a solo career that got off to a tremendous start with a number 4 hit *I Only Want To Be With You,* which saw her moving towards a more soulful Tamla Motown sound. She notched up four more Top 10 hits between July 1964

214

PRETTY FLAMINGO

MANFRED MANN

5 May 1966, for three weeks

● ● ●

HMV POP 1523

Written by Mark Barkan. Produced by John Burgess.

The second Manfred Mann chart-topper

215

PAINT IT BLACK

THE ROLLING STONES

26 May 1966, for one week

●

Decca F 12395

Written by Mick Jagger and Keith Richard. Produced by Andrew Loog Oldham.

After *Get Off Of My Cloud* the Rolling Stones slipped. Their next single *Nineteenth Nervous Breakdown* was the first Stones single in two years not to hit number one although it still reached number 2 in the US and the UK. The UK flip side *As Tears Go By* (which had been a hit for Mick Jagger's girlfriend Marianne Faithfull two years before) had been a US Top 10 entry in its own right, but still the follow-up single was crucial. The song chosen was *Paint It Black,* written during the Stones' tour of Australia, recorded in Hollywood and featuring Brian Jones on sitar. Once again there was criticism of the Stones as mere copiers of the Beatles, whose 1965 album *Rubber Soul* had first included George Harrison playing sitar, but the Beatles had never put out a death disc as a single. *Paint It Black* was a death disc.

After *Paint It Black* the Stones went off the boil a bit. Perhaps it was the prosecution of Jagger, Richard and Jones for the use of drugs that caused their standards to drop, but late 1966 and 1967 were not good years for the Stones, artistically or commercially. Mick Jagger sang on the Beatles number one, *All You Need Is Love* (see no. 235) but the next three Stones singles, *Have You Seen Your Mother Baby Standing In The Shadow*, *We Love You* and *Let's Spend The Night Together* gave them Top 10 placings but nothing more.

216

STRANGERS IN THE NIGHT

FRANK SINATRA

2 June 1966, for three weeks

● ● ●

Reprise RS 23052

Written by Bert Kaempfert, Charlie Singleton and Eddie Snyder. Produced by Jimmy Bowen, with orchestral arrangement by Ernie Freeman.

Frank Sinatra's second number one hit came 11 years and 244 days after his first, at that time the longest gap in British chart history between number one hits by the same artist. It came from a most unlikely source, an extremely forgettable James Garner spy film called *A Man Could Get Killed*. Bert Kaempfert, who had also been involved in Elvis Presley's *Wooden Heart* (see no. 115), wrote the complete score for the film, the first Hollywood score he had been asked to compose. Thanks to Ol' Blue Eyes' impeccable performance, the song became far more successful than the film and won four Grammy Awards in 1966. This was a very good year for the Sinatra family. Daughter Nancy had already enjoyed her first number one (see no. 210). By the end of

the 1960s even more success was to be achieved by both she and Frank.

Together they hit the top with *Something Stupid* (see no. 231) while Frank broke all British chart records with his amazingly longlasting hit *My Way*. It set a record 122 weeks of chart life, selling over a million copies in Britain alone. By 1987 the French song, with English lyrics by Paul Anka, was acknowledged as the most recorded composition of all time, ahead of *Yesterday* and *Tie A Yellow Ribbon Round The Old Oak Tree* (see no. 329).

217

PAPERBACK WRITER

THE BEATLES

23 June 1966, for two weeks

● ●

Parlophone R 5452

Written by John Lennon and Paul McCartney. Produced by George Martin.

The tenth consecutive number one for the Beatles was a Paul McCartney song featuring Paul double-tracked singing lead. The song was the first Beatles A-side that could not be interpreted as a love song. This may explain why its initial acceptance was not quite as ecstatic as was usual for a new Fab Four platter.

Nonetheless, *Paperback Writer,* like its seven immediate predecessors in the triumphant line of Beatles releases, reached number one in its second week on the chart. True, it only held the top for two weeks which is the shortest run by any Beatles single at number one (equal with *Hey Jude,* see no. 258), but some of their very best work was still to come. Two months later, the *Revolver* album silenced the doubters. In 1967 the *Penny Lane/Strawberry Fields Forever* single (which, for all its brilliance, became the first Beatles record not to make number one since *Please Please Me* in early 1963) and the masterpiece *Sergeant Pepper's Lonely Hearts Club Band* turned the doubters into believers.

The B-side of *Paperback Writer* was the John Lennon song *Rain.* Possibly no other Beatle single shows the difference between the styles of Lennon and McCartney as much as this, their twelfth single and tenth number one.

218

SUNNY AFTERNOON

THE KINKS

7 July 1966, for two weeks

● ●

Pye 7N 17125

Written by Ray Davies. Produced by Shel Talmy.

The Kinks' third and (to date) last number one was a delightfully laid-back Ray Davies saga of a wealthy layabout fallen on hard times, having been stripped of his assets by the taxman and deserted by his wife who has returned to her parents, alleging drunkenness and cruelty. Nonetheless, the song is strangely positive, with the victim of the situation still able to enjoy the beauty of an English sunny afternoon.

Ray Davies was at his brilliant best in 1966 and 1967. His next two singles, the gloomy *Dead End Street* and the song that made one of London's railway stations seem like a lover's paradise, *Waterloo Sunset*, were, like *Sunny Afternoon*, superb three-minute portraits of aspects of English life. *Autumn Almanac* in late 1967 was the band's eighth consecutive Top 10 single, but the Kinks' admirers had to wait for another three years before Davies came up with further Top 10 gems in *Lola* and *Apeman*.

Since 1972, when *Supersonic Rocket Ship* reached number 12, the Kinks have only made one major impact on the singles chart, even though they have now been going strong as a live band for a quarter of a century. That was in 1983, when another witty slice of English suburban nostalgia, *Come Dancing*, also peaked at number 12. In America, where they have been regular visitors to the album charts in the '80s, this single was their first Top 10 item for 13 years. The line-up of the band has undergone many changes over the years but the cornerstone of the group has always remained the brothers Davies. Ray's songs are constantly appealing to new generations – as the Pretenders, Jam and Stranglers (to name but three) have successfully shown.

219

GET AWAY

GEORGIE FAME WITH THE BLUE FLAMES

21 July 1966, for one week

●

Columbia DB 7946

Written by Clive Powell. Produced by Tony Palmer.

Originally written and performed by Georgie Fame as a commercial jingle for petrol, *Get Away* turned out to be so popular with all those who didn't leave the room to fix a sandwich during the advertisements that Fame decided to uncommercialize the song for general release. It became his second number one smash in five outings, three less substantial chart singles having come between *Get Away* and *Yeh Yeh* (see no. 184).

Fame's final album with the original Blue Flames was the 1966 package *Sweet Things* which consisted mainly of covers of American soul songs. In September Fame disbanded the Blue Flames and devoted more time to working with the Harry South Big Band. The first of three albums on which Fame and South collaborated was released in September 1966, entitled *Sound Venture*. The unusual combination of blues/pop singer with big band was a brave and successful project that followed *Sweet Things* into the album chart Top 10.

Fame's single follow-up to *Get Away* (featuring neither the Blue Flames nor Harry South) was a cover of the Bobby Hebb hit *Sunny* which became a three-way fight when Cher also entered the fray with a single. The final score read Hebb number 12, Fame number 13 and Cher with the bronze at number 32. Georgie's next single, the last before he left Columbia, was pulled from the *Sweet Things* album – Billy Stewart's *Sitting In The Park*. This reached number 12.

220

OUT OF TIME

Chris Farlowe *at home in Islington in 1966, the year* Out Of Time *made him immortal.*

CHRIS FARLOWE AND THE THUNDERBIRDS

28 July 1966, for one week

●

Immediate IM 035

Written by Mick Jagger and Keith Richard. Produced by Mick Jagger.

Chris Farlowe (born John Henry Deighton, 13 October 1940) enjoyed his first musical triumph when his own John Henry Skiffle Group won the English Skiffle Group Contest at Tottenham's Mecca Club in 1957. By 1962 he was lead vocalist with a semi-professional beat group called the Thunderbirds. That same year, following a month long tour of Germany, Farlowe met up with Rik Gunnell, the manager of London's Flamingo and Ram Jam Clubs. Gunnell became the group's manager and they turned pro when their first single, *Air Travel*, was released by Decca in June 1963.

Despite being favourites on the London club circuit, the hit single proved elusive. A cover of *Just A Dream*, Jimmy Clanton's US Top 5 smash from 1958, failed, as did *Buzz With The Fuzz*, a song which looked set to break the run of failures until it was withdrawn by EMI as soon as they worked out the meaning of the mod lyrics.

At the end of 1965 Farlowe moved to the Immediate label, run by the Rolling Stones' manager Andrew Loog Oldham. Here Farlowe found a freedom to record what he wanted and people who believed in his

talents. His second single for Immediate, *Think,* was a song from the Stones LP *Aftermath* and it crept into the charts. Farlowe had a hit at last, at his tenth attempt. The follow-up was another song from *Aftermath,* called *Out of Time.* It made number one in the week that England won the World Cup, giving Jagger and Richard their only chart-topper as writers for another act.

Farlowe's rendition differed greatly from the Stones version on *Aftermath,* but as the 1970 Stones' compilation album *Metamorphosis* shows, Jagger had previously recorded a demo of the song with the same backing track as Farlowe and the Thunderbirds. On the number one hit, Farlowe's voice merely replaced Jagger's.

221

WITH A GIRL LIKE YOU

THE TROGGS

4 August 1966, for two weeks

●●

Fontana TF 717

Written by Reg Presley. Produced by Larry Page.

The Andover-based Troggs were Reg Ball, who modestly changed his named to Reg Presley (lead singer and principal songwriter), Chris Britton (lead guitar), Pete Staples (bass) and Ronnie Bond né Bultis (drums). Originally the Troglodytes, they were spotted by performer-turned-producer Larry Page (who years before had once billed himself as 'Larry Page the teenage rage'). They signed to CBS for whom they released one flop single, a Reg Presley composition.

Fontana were luckier. Page now took the band to the Philips subsidiary and first time out they struck gold. The song was by American Chip Taylor entitled *Wild Thing* and although not a number one, this earthy, extremely basic stomper remains the most famous Troggs recording. The number one arrived next time out via a new Reg effort *With A Girl Like You*, sophisticated only if compared with *Wild Thing*, but similarly irresistible.

The band were chart regulars until the beginning of 1968, the mainstays of Page's own Page One label.

The Troggs *meet a real wild thing (see no. 221).*

222

YELLOW SUBMARINE/
ELEANOR RIGBY

THE BEATLES

18 August 1966, for four weeks

●●●●

Parlophone R 5493

Written (both sides) by John Lennon and Paul McCartney. Produced by George Martin.

The first single that the Beatles released to coincide with the release of the LP from which the tracks came was *Eleanor Rigby* and *Yellow Submarine.* The LP was *Revolver.* It was said at the time that the Beatles issued the single to prevent others from covering songs from their LPs, as had happened, for example, with *Michelle* (see no. 209) and *Girl* from *Rubber Soul,* and was later to happen with *Ob-La-Di Ob-La-Da* (see no. 263) from the white album.

Yellow Submarine was the first Beatles single to feature Ringo singing lead. The enchanting children's singalong number was in stark contrast to *Eleanor Rigby*, an extraordinarily sophisticated song of loneliness that quickly became one of their most covered songs. Although sung by Paul accompanied only by a string quartet, John Lennon later revealed that he made a major writing contribution to the song.

While this single was at number one, the Beatles played their last live date on 29 August 1966 at Candlestick Park in San Francisco.

223

ALL OR NOTHING

THE SMALL FACES

15 September 1966, for one week

●

Decca F 12470

Written by Steve Marriott and Ronnie Lane. Produced by Steve Marriott and Ronnie Lane.

The nattily dressed Small Faces were led by former child actor Steve Marriott (born 30 January 1947). Marriott was later to admit that he could barely play guitar in the early days of the group, but despite that he and his fellow Small Faces, Ronnie Lane (born 1 April 1946), Ian MacLagan (born 12 May 1946) and Kenny Jones (born 16 September 1948) provided the only real competition to the Who in the mid-'60s. Both groups came out of the mod scene in London. The Small Faces had five Top 10 hits between February 1966 and April 1968 with numbers like *Sha La La La Lee, Itchycoo Park* and *Lazy Sunday,* but the only number one was *All Or Nothing,* which dislodged the Beatles at the end of the summer.

In 1969 Marriott left the Small Faces to form Humble Pie with Peter Frampton from the Herd, while Lane and the others joined forces with Rod Stewart and Ronnie Wood to form the Faces. Later Wood went on to become a Rolling Stone. While mainly a singles band, the Small Faces did make an impact in the albums arena when their 1968 album *Ogden's Nut Gone Flake* appeared with a revolutionary circular cover.

Ronnie Lane had two solo hits in 1974, but his career was tragically cut short by multiple sclerosis. He has won enormous admiration for his brave battle against the disease, both on behalf of himself and other sufferers.

224

DISTANT DRUMS

JIM REEVES

22 September 1966, for five weeks

●●●●●

RCA 1537

Written by Cindy Walker. Produced by Chet Atkins.

On 31 July 1964 Jim Reeves was flying to Nashville when his single engine plane encountered a storm. Two days later his body was found in the wrecked aircraft. The country music world had lost one of its greatest performers but a legend was born as a result of the singer's untimely death.

James Travis Reeves (born 20 August 1923, Galloway, Texas) made his first radio broadcast aged 9. An accident prevented him from pursuing a career as a baseball professional so he turned to broadcasting. It was as a DJ on Texas radio station KGRI that he first made his mark. Reeves then landed an announcing job on Texas radio station KWKH, which ran the famous country showcase 'Louisiana Hayride' every Saturday night. Hank Williams failed to arrive one evening and Reeves' bosses asked him to fill in with some songs. A contract with Abbott Records and number one hits on the US country charts followed.

In 1955 he moved to RCA where he managed nine UK hits before his death, including the 1964 winners *I Love You Because* and *I Won't Forget You*. A further 17 hits, including *Distant Drums*, were amassed posthumously between 1964 and 1972. In the USA his success continued into the '80s by the adding of new arrangements to original vocal tracks and by the electronic creation of duets with the living singer Deborah Allen. Record bosses may have gone too far in 1981 when an album of duets was produced by mixing Reeves' voice with that of Patsy Cline, who had herself died in a plane crash in 1963.

225

REACH OUT I'LL BE THERE

THE FOUR TOPS

27 October 1966, for three weeks

● ● ●

Tamla Motown TMG 579

Written by Brian Holland, Lamont Dozier and Eddie Holland. Produced by Brian Holland and Lamont Dozier.

The day after the Beatles reached out for their MBEs at Buckingham Palace, the Four Tops made it to number one. It was the second song penned by Holland, Dozier and Holland to climb to the top (see no. 181) and became Motown's biggest seller at that time.

The Tops, who had originally formed in Detroit as the Four Aims in 1953/54, had their first UK hit with a song that had provided them with their first US number one, *I Can't Help Myself*, in the summer of 1965. Unlike most Tamla Motown groups, and indeed unlike most groups, the Four Tops' line-up has remained unchanged throughout the decades with Levi Stubbs on lead vocals supported by Renaldo Benson, Abdul 'Duke' Fakir and Lawrence Payton. Far

more of a pop outfit than their more socially aware label-mates the Temptations, the Four Tops eventually left Motown in 1972 and, after a mediocre spell with Dunhill, signed to Casablanca records which resulted in a 1981 return to the Top 10 with *When She Was My Girl*. In 1983, after more than 10 years absence, Motown chief Barry Gordy Jr managed to woo the ageing quartet back to his label. Although back where they belong, major record success has not been forthcoming so far. Stubbs was the voice of the man-eating plant Audrey II in the film *Little Shop Of Horrors* in 1986.

226

GOOD VIBRATIONS

THE BEACH BOYS

17 November 1966, for two weeks

● ●

Capitol CL 15475

Written by Brian Wilson and Mike Love. Produced by Brian Wilson.

For a few months in 1966 the Beach Boys (in the UK anyway) were bracketed with the Beatles as progressive music innovators and Brian Wilson ranked with Lennon and McCartney as a songwriter of genius; their album *Pet Sounds* and the single *Good Vibrations* were two of the principal reasons why. The Beach Boys at the time of *Good Vibrations* were brothers Brian Wilson (born 20 June 1942), Dennis Wilson (born 4 December 1944), Carl Wilson (born 21 December 1946), their cousin Mike Love (born 15 March 1941), Al Jardine (born 3 September 1942) and Bruce Johnston (born 27 June 1944).

The Beach Boys were formed in Hawthorne, California in 1961. At high school they were successively Kenny of the Cadets, Carl and the Passions and the Rendletones. They first recorded in 1961 and broke through in the States a year later with the first of many Brian Wilson surfing songs that paid tribute to a life in and around California's rolling waves. It took longer to break in Britain's colder climes but they managed it in 1964 with *I Get Around*.

The four principal themes of early Beach Boy songs of surfing, girls, cars and more girls were less in evidence by 1966. *Good Vibrations* was recorded over six months

during seventeen sessions in four studios. Although the production was difficult and intricate, the extreme length between first session and a final mix has to be put down to the talented yet erratic Brian Wilson.

227

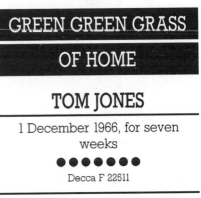

GREEN GREEN GRASS OF HOME

TOM JONES

1 December 1966, for seven weeks

● ● ● ● ● ● ●

Decca F 22511

Written by Claude 'Curly' Putnam Jr. Produced by Peter Sullivan.

Tom Jones' second and so far final number one was a country song about a condemned prisoner, which writer Curly Putnam (see also no. 381) was inspired to write after seeing the 1960 crime classic movie *The Asphalt Jungle*. In that film, which incidentally marked the film debut of Marilyn Monroe, Sterling Hayden played a gangster from Kentucky who dreams one day of going back home to the farm. He finally dies of gunshot wounds having made it back to the green green grass of home.

Green Green Grass of Home was only Tom Jones' second Top 10 hit in Britain, but over the next three and a half years, the lad from Pontypridd chalked up nine more including three consecutive number two hits in 1967 and 1968. Not only that, he signed a contract with ATV to do 17 one-man shows a year for five years for a total of £9 million, at that time by far the largest TV contract ever signed in Britain.

In 1971 and 1972, Tom Jones had two more Top 10 hits, but after that he had to wait for almost 15 years (mainly in Las Vegas) until he crashed back into the UK Top 10 in the spring of 1987 with *A Boy From Nowhere*. This gave him his fifth number 2 hit and pulled him past Roy Orbison and Shirley Bassey in the all time list of Most Weeks On The Chart.

Tom Jones as a grandfather in the late 1980s is just as popular and successful as he was as a sex symbol in the mid-1960s.

It is 1967, the big year for **The Monkees**, but already Mike Nesmith (in the rear wearing glasses) appears unhappy at a London press conference.

228

I'M A BELIEVER

THE MONKEES

19 January 1967, for four weeks

● ● ● ●

RCA 1560

Written by Neil Diamond. Produced by Jeff Barry.

On 5 September 1966 America's NBC television previewed two new series which it hoped would do well, *Star Trek* and *The Monkees*. The Monkees were Mike Nesmith (born 30 December 1942, Houston, Texas), Peter Tork (born Peter Thorkelson 13 February 1944, Washington, D.C.), Mickey Dolenz (born 8 March 1945, Tarzana,

California) and Davy Jones (born 30 December 1946, Manchester, England) and had been brought together by the Screen Gems television company. Nesmith and Tork were musicians, Dolenz and Jones primarily actors. Songs were commissioned from the top songwriters in the business, including Neil Diamond, Goffin and King, Mann and Weil and Boyce and Hart. As soon as the series began airing in Britain the Monkees repeated the success they had begun to achieve in the USA two months earlier. Initially Screen Gems only allowed the Monkees to sing, not play, on their records, which upset Tork and Nesmith especially. It was the company's heavy control of its stars' careers which finally led to the departure of first Tork, then Nesmith, in 1969, but not before the group had produced a run of excellent hit singles which proved their abilities were not merely manufactured.

Both *Star Trek* and *The Monkees* continue to be shown around the world. In 1986, as the fourth Star Trek movie, *The Journey Home*, was being produced, the Monkees, minus Nesmith, set out on a revival tour and released the single *That Was Then, This Is Now*, a minor hit in October of that year.

229

THIS IS MY SONG

PETULA CLARK

16 February 1967, for two weeks

● ●

Pye 7N 17258

Written by Charles Chaplin. Produced by Ernie Freeman.

Petula Clark, whose only other British number one had been *Sailor* (see no. 113) in 1961, returned to the top almost six years later with this theme tune of the film *A Countess From Hong Kong*, starring Marlon Brando and Sophia Loren and directed by the man who played a cameo role as a sea-sick waiter, Charlie Chaplin. Chaplin also wrote the theme song which has sold more copies world-wide than even his famous *Limelight* theme. Being well into his seventies when he wrote the tune, he is probably the oldest person ever to write a number one hit.

Petula Clark first recorded *This Is My Song* in French, Italian and German for the European market. Then she made an English version and thus managed to top the charts virtually all the way across Europe in four different languages. Her British success was despite strong competition from Harry Secombe, whose version climbed to number 2 to give him his biggest pop hit ever.

Petula Clark's last British hit was her version of *I Don't Know How to Love Him*, but her career continues in full swing. She celebrated her 48th birthday by starring as Maria in the London revival of *The Sound Of Music*, and seems likely to extend indefinitely her showbusiness successes which began with her first film at the age of 11, made before the end of World War II.

230

RELEASE ME

ENGELBERT HUMPERDINCK

2 March 1967, for six weeks

● ● ● ● ● ●

Decca F 12541

Written by Eddie Miller and Dub Williams. Produced by Charles Blackwell.

The transformation of Gerry Dorsey into Engelbert Humperdinck is one of the most famous 'if at first you don't succeed' stories in show business. Arnold George Dorsey was born in Madras, India (venue of a Boomtown Rats concert in February 1982) on 2 May 1936, and moved with his family to England shortly after the end of the war. After completing his National Service in 1956, he began a show business career as Gerry Dorsey, which lasted for nine years and covered occasional recording contracts, sporadic TV and radio spots and endless shows in provincial theatres on pop package tours. There was also a lot of resting between engagements.

In 1965, he met one of his former roommates, Gordon Mills, who was by then managing Tom Jones. Mills took Gerry Dorsey on to his management roster and changed his name to Engelbert Humperdinck, which was the name of the German composer (1854-1921) who wrote the opera *Hansel and Gretel*. He recorded a couple of almost successful singles, one of which, *Dommage Dommage*, was a big hit in Europe. Then he stood in for Dickie Valentine, who was ill, on *Sunday Night At The*

1967 Variety Club winners **Engelbert Humperdinck** *[Show Business Personality of the Year] and Carol White [Most Promising Star] display their awards.*

London Palladium and sang his latest single, *Release Me*. Over a year later it finally dropped off the chart after the longest single stay in the Top 50 ever by any record in Britain.

231

SOMETHING STUPID

NANCY SINATRA AND FRANK SINATRA

13 April 1967, for two weeks

● ●

Reprise RS 23166

Written by C. Carson Parks. Produced by Jimmy Bowen and Lee Hazelwood.

For the first time two acts who had already achieved a number one hit in their own right combined to record yet another number one. The act was a father and daughter pairing, a combination which had never topped the charts before or has since. By taking their only single to the summit they became the first act to be one hit wonders on both sides of the Atlantic.

Nancy Sinatra's producer Lee Hazelwood found the tune, and it was Nancy who showed it to her father. Frank Sinatra was the one who suggested they record it as a duet. The session turned out to be not only an artistic duet, but also a producer's duet, which went remarkably smoothly considering that both producers are known for their strong individual style, and it was the first time either of them had come up against eight track studio equipment. Despite reservations by some executives that the lyrics were unsuitable for close relatives to sing to each other, nobody mentioned their doubts to Frank Sinatra, who after all owned the Reprise company. So the record was released and sold millions at a rate that would even have been very impressive for Sinatra père in his bobbysoxer heyday. In the mid-'60s it was remarkable.

232

PUPPET ON A STRING

SANDIE SHAW

27 April 1967, for three weeks

● ● ●

Pye 7N 17272

Written by Bill Martin and Phil Coulter. Produced by Ken Woodman.

Britain's first Eurovision Song Contest winner made Sandie Shaw the first female solo artist to have three number ones. The contest was first staged in 1956 and by 1967 had expanded to become one of the year's biggest annual TV extravaganzas. As a parade of the year's most brilliant new compositions it has always been hopelessly inadequate but as compulsive viewing it delivers every year.

Sandie's victory was achieved with a song strong enough to have succeeded even without the Eurovision hype behind it. It became a vast European smash and for the following year or two the competition threatened to achieve musical credibility as performers of the stature of Cliff Richard and Olivia Newton John represented the UK. Before long a return to songs of total anonymity disposed of the threat.

In March 1968 Shaw married the fashion designer Jeff Banks. Her last Top 10 hit to date was *Monsieur Dupont* in 1969. The '70s were a quiet period for the singer. She divorced and concentrated on bringing up her daughter, Grace. In the early '80s musicians who had merely been children when she was at the height of her fame sought her out. First to do so was Martyn Ware of Heaven 17 who produced Sandie singing Cilla Black's *Anyone Who Had A Heart* (see no. 164). Then, in 1984, after 14 years' absence, Sandie returned to live performance and the charts with the Morrissey composition *Hand In Glove*, backed by the Smiths.

233

SILENCE IS GOLDEN

THE TREMELOES

18 May 1967, for three weeks

● ● ●

CBS 2723

Written by Bob Gaudio and Bob Crewe.
Produced by Mike Smith.

Having split from lead vocalist Brian Poole, the Tremeloes were expected to fade into obscurity. Instead, an astute image change launched them into a chart career that outdid anything they achieved backing Brian Poole. They even managed to claim three American hits in the process. The membership had changed: Alan Howard had left the band before Brian Poole departed to pursue a solo career that never took off, and his replacement, Mick Clark, only lasted a short while before moving aside for new lead singer Len 'Chip' Hawkes (born 11 November 1946).

Their first release, still on Decca, was Paul Simon's composition, *Blessed*. It sank without a trace. The Trems grew longer hair and wore trendier clothes and put out their version of their favourite track from the Beatles' *Revolver* album, *Good Day Sunshine*. Another miss. They switched labels to CBS and found the Cat Stevens song, *Here Comes My Baby*. Their up-tempo cover entered the Top 10 as its author's own *Matthew And Son* slipped down to number five.

Their follow-up song had been the flip of the Four Seasons' smash *Rag Doll*, a plaintive ballad called *Silence Is Golden*. The group amazed their fans and indeed most observers of the music industry by their superb vocal harmonies, the feature of the single that captivated the punters who propelled the platter to number one in just three weeks. A third Top 10 hit, *Even The Bad Times Are Good*, followed before the summer was finished.

234

A WHITER SHADE OF PALE

PROCOL HARUM

8 June 1967, for six weeks

● ● ● ● ● ●

Deram DM 126

Written by Keith Reid and Gary Brooker.
Produced by Denny Cordell.

From June to September the number one

spot was occupied by three songs which together sum up the summer of 1967, the Summer of Love. Flower power, peace and love, together with many exotic substances, were in the air. *A Whiter Shade Of Pale*, with its tantalizingly meaningless lyrics and haunting melody lifted from Bach, matched the mood of the era perfectly.

Procol Harum was created to record the songs of lyricist Keith Reid and vocalist/keyboard player Gary Brooker (born 29 May 1945). Brooker was a former member of the respected Southend R & B quartet the Paramounts who had received bad publicity when it was alleged their 1964 Top 40 version of Jerry Lieber and Mike Stoller's composition *Poison Ivy* had been hyped into the charts. The other musicians who appeared on the number one were organist Matthew Fisher (born 7 March 1946), guitarist Ray Royer (born 8 October 1945), drummer Bobby Harrison (born 28 June 1943) and bassist Dave Knights (born 28 June 1945). By the time the band's debut album had been recorded, Royer and Harrison had been replaced by two former Paramounts, BJ Wilson and Robin Trower. In March 1969 Knights and Fisher quit, and in came the fourth Paramount, Chris Copping. Until 1971, when Trower left, Procol Harum were the Paramounts in all but name.

Discounting the 1972 chart revival of *A Whiter Shade Of Pale*, Procol Harum scored only five hits in their ten year existence. Their last hit, *Pandora's Box* in 1974, neatly rounded off their chart career, for it was produced by the writers of *Poison Ivy*, Lieber and Stoller.

235

ALL YOU NEED IS LOVE

THE BEATLES

19 July 1967, for three weeks

● ● ●

Parlophone R 5620

Written by John Lennon and Paul McCartney.
Produced by George Martin.

1 June 1967 was the day of the release in Britain of the *Sergeant Pepper's Lonely Hearts Club Band* LP, the album that completed the process of transformation of the Beatles. The transformation was from a group who prided themselves in the early days on their ability to reproduce on stage any sound they put down on record, into a group who had given up live performances in favour of the sophistication of recording techniques to produce brilliant popular music. *Sergeant Pepper* not only led the way for groups to spend more time in the studios exploring new ideas in sound, it also was one of the very first 'concept' albums.

Just 24 days after the release of *Sgt Pepper*, the Beatles appeared on a BBC-TV show *Our World* that was beamed live by satellite to all five continents. They sang *All You Need Is Love* in the Abbey Road studio, and within two weeks it became their next single and their 12th number one.

236

SAN FRANCISCO (BE SURE TO WEAR SOME FLOWERS IN YOUR HAIR)

SCOTT McKENZIE

9 August 1967, for four weeks

● ● ● ●

CBS 2816

Written by John Phillips. Produced by Lou Adler and John Phillips.

San Francisco is the best remembered dippy hippy anthem of that dopey era. It is however a popular oldie to this day not just as a wacky slice of social history but because the melody is one of the best ever crafted by the leader of The Mamas and Papas, John Phillips. Scott McKenzie's gentle vocal refrain and the production skills of Lou Adler (The Mamas and Papas' producer, still three years away from his remarkably successful association with Carole King) and Phillips also stand up well over the years.

McKenzie (born in Virginia on 10 January 1944) and Phillips sang together in the early '60s as part of a folk group called the Journeymen. When that outfit broke up Phillips formed The Mamas and Papas with his wife-to-be Michelle Gilliam, Denny Doherty and Cass Elliott. This quartet took off in early 1966 with the first of a line of hit singles, a Phillips composition entitled *California Dreamin'*. *Monday Monday* was the song that broke them big in England. McKenzie in the meantime had got no closer to international acclaim than an audition to be a Monkee (see no. 228) but this changed when his old mate handed him the tribute to San Francisco.

The hit bears the longest title of any song to reach number one in Britain. It was followed by another Phillips number, *Like An Old Time Movie*, which did just enough (one week at number 50) to keep Scott off the one-hit wonder list. After that, chart silence from the Voice Of Scott McKenzie (as he was billed on his second hit), but he is now back on the road with Phillips as a fully fledged part of the reformed The Mamas and Papas. He gets to sing his hit every night.

237

THE LAST WALTZ

ENGELBERT HUMPERDINCK

6 September 1967, for five weeks

●●●●●

Decca F 12655

Written by Les Reed and Barry Mason. Produced by Peter Sullivan.

After *Release Me* Engelbert Humperdinck found another country standard called *There Goes My Everything*, which had been a country smash for Jack Greene in 1966. That climbed to number 3. Next Engelbert chose a new song by the very successful British songwriters Les Reed and Barry Mason called *The Last Waltz*. Within weeks it became the standard closing tune for every dance up and down the nation, and Engelbert had a hit that eventually sold even more copies worldwide than *Release*

Me. It was a monster hit in Europe, too, where Mireille Mathieu recorded a French version, *La Dernière Valse*, which even reached the British Top 50. Of all the late '60s ballads which seemed to dominate world markets as the Liverpool tide subsided, *The Last Waltz* is probably the best known, probably the biggest seller and certainly the biggest hit ever written by the prolific Les Reed and Barry Mason.

It was the last waltz for a revolutionary too. Che Guevara was killed by anti-guerrilla forces in Bolivia on 9 October 1967. On the other hand, it was the first waltz for the Cunard liner, the *Queen Elizabeth II*, which was launched at the Clydebank shipyard on 20 September.

238

MASSACHUSETTS

THE BEE GEES

11 October 1967, for four weeks

●●●●

Polydor 56 192

Written by Barry, Robin and Maurice Gibb. Produced by Robert Stigwood and the Bee Gees.

The quite remarkable career of the Bee Gees first kicked into top gear with their third British and fourth American hit single, *Massachusetts*. The Bee Gees are the three brothers Gibb whose parents must have forseen future royalties as they had the presence of mind to be in residence in the tax haven of the Isle of Man when the boys were born. Barry on 1 September 1947 and twins Robin and Maurice on 22 September 1949.

There was little money around in Gibb circles in those days, however, and the family emigrated to Australia in 1958 just after the birth of their fourth son, Andy. Down Under the boys' musical abilities soon surfaced and as the Gibbs, then as the BGs, and finally as the Bee Gees they became well known. They first recorded in 1963 and had several Aussie chart entries before deciding to return to Britain in early 1967.

Back home they approached the London based Australian impresario/manager Robert Stigwood who was at the time linked to Brian Epstein's NEMS organization which, of course, included the Beatles among its

clients. Stigwood was impressed and the Bee Gees' second British release, *New York Mining Disaster 1941 (Have You Seen My Wife Mr. Jones)*, became a Top 20 hit in both Britain and America.

Massachusetts, like every Bee Gee hit of the past twenty-plus years was written by all or some of the Gibb brothers, in this case by all three. They had never actually been to the state in question when they wrote the song but liked the sound of the name. At this early stage of their career the Bee Gees were actually five strong, the Gibbs being supported in performance by guitarist Vince Melouney and drummer Colin Petersen.

239

BABY NOW THAT I'VE FOUND YOU

THE FOUNDATIONS

8 November 1967, for two weeks

●●

Pye 7N 17366

Written by Tony Macaulay and John McLeod. Produced by Tony Macaulay.

The Foundations produced six chart hits in two years from September 1967 to September 1969, but none was as big as the first of them all, *Baby Now That I've Found You*, which also gave Tony Macaulay the first of four number one hit productions. The Foundations were Clem Curtis (born 28 November 1940) on vocals, Eric Allandale (born 4 March 1936) on trombone, Pat Burke (born 9 October 1937) on flute, Mike Elliott (born 6 August 1929) on tenor sax, Sri Lankan Tony Gomez (born 13 December 1948), who played organ, Tim 'Sticks' Harris (born 14 January 1948) on drums, Peter Macbeth (born 2 February 1943) on bass and Alan Warner (born 21 April 1941) who played lead guitar.

Their second biggest hit came a year later, in 1968, with *Build Me Up Buttercup*, a song by Macaulay and Mike d'Abo, the lead singer of Manfred Mann. It reached number 2 in Britain and number 3 in America, but some of the gilt came off the gingerbread (for the writers anyway) when the song, like many other hits before it, became the subject of a plagiarism suit.

While the Foundations were on top of the British charts, a major force in rock journalism was born. The first edition of *Rolling Stone* was launched by editor/publisher Jann Wenner in San Francisco on 18 November 1967.

240

LET THE HEARTACHES BEGIN

LONG JOHN BALDRY

22 November 1967, for two weeks

● ●

Pye 7N 17385

Written by Tony Macaulay and John McLeod. Produced by John McLeod.

It was perhaps apt that this song was at number one when the first heart transplant was performed by Dr Christian Barnard at the Groote Schuur Hospital, South Africa, on 3 December 1967. However, this record has more claims to fame than just that. First, it was one of the few occasions when writers have ousted another of their songs at the top. Macaulay and McLeod joined Bacharach and David, Lennon and McCartney and Bruce Welch as writers who replaced themselves at number one. Macaulay and McLeod set an unequalled record, however, by taking over from each other as writer/producers at number one. The same producer has often produced consecutive number one hits, but this is the only occasion when one half of a writing team has written and produced a song that took over from his partner's production at the top.

Long John Baldry himself, born on 12 January 1941, is the tallest act ever to make number one. His height is variously reported between 6'6" and 6'9" but even the former height is about double that of Little Jimmy Osmond when *Long Haired Lover From Liverpool* ruled (see no. 324). Baldry sang with various distinguished blues groups in the '60s including the Hoochie Coochie Men, Steampacket (a touring R&B revue that at various times included Julie Driscoll, Brian Auger and Rod Stewart) and Bluesology, whose pianist Elton John took his second name from Baldry's first. None of Baldry's blues recordings made the charts

and it was a switch to tear-jerking ballads such as *Let The Heartaches Begin* that brought him to national attention. He was never really happy with his new role as MOR emoter and he eventually returned to his musical roots. No more chart records but no more having to wear the bow ties either.

241

HELLO GOODBYE

THE BEATLES

6 December 1967, for seven weeks

● ● ● ● ● ● ●

Parlophone R 5655

Written by John Lennon and Paul McCartney. Produced by George Martin.

Between *All You Need Is Love* and *Hello Goodbye* the Beatles' world changed. Brian Epstein, the rich man of *Baby, You're A Rich Man* (the flip side of *All You Need Is Love*), died in August 1967, and the complete domination of the world's record shops achieved by *Sgt. Pepper* meant that the world was looking forward to the Beatles' next record with all the anticipation that was there in 1963 and 1964. But with Epstein dead, the Beatles had nobody to tell them what to do, and therein lay the seeds of their disintegration.

Hello Goodbye was probably their most straightforward single since *Help!* (see no. 200). It was nowhere near as inventive as *Strawberry Fields Forever* or *Eleanor Rigby* but it stayed at number one for seven weeks, the longest run by any Beatles single since *From Me To You*. Originality was expressed on the other side, *I Am The Walrus*, a track from their TV film *Magical Mystery Tour*, which hit the screens on Boxing Day 1967. *Magical Mystery Tour* was panned by the critics and the leadership that Paul McCartney had assumed after the death of Brian Epstein took its first knock.

242

THE BALLAD OF BONNIE AND CLYDE

GEORGIE FAME

24 January 1968, for one week

●

CBS 3124

Written by Mitch Murray and Peter Callender. Produced by Mike Smith.

Georgie Fame's record career with CBS was not quite as memorable as his days from 1964-66 had been with Columbia, but while there he did add his name onto the still short (and then even shorter) list of acts who have managed to go all the way to number one three times. Fame was the seventeenth to do it.

The Ballad Of Bonnie And Clyde was inspired by the film *Bonnie And Clyde* which was a movie sensation of 1967. The Arthur Penn film starred Warren Beatty and Faye Dunaway as a glamorous pair of 1930s bank-robbers and was a huge box-office success around the world. British writers Mitch Murray (see nos 152 and 152) and Peter Callender wrote a witty jazz flavoured pop song that gave away most of the film's plot in three minutes and it proved ideal for the Fame vocal style. It was also his biggest hit to date in the United States, reaching number 7. In both Britain and America it did considerably better on record than the music that was actually in the film, *Foggy*

Georgie Fame *is congratulated by his girlfriend Carmen as his latest single reaches number one.*

Mountain Breakdown, a guitar/banjo instrumental by bluegrass masters Lester Flatt and Earl Scruggs.

Since his third chart-topper, Fame's biggest single has been a 1971 duet with Alan Price, *Rosetta*. He has become a highly-regarded jazz and sophisticated pop vocalist, whose interpretation of the works of composers such as George Gershwin forms a major part of his contemporary stage act. He made a brief return to the pop charts in 1986 as a guest vocalist on *New York Afternoon* by Mondo Kane.

having consecutive catalogue numbers (CBS 3124 and 3125) at number one. CBS obviously liked the song. They reissued the Robert Knight original on their Monument label in 1974 and made the Top 20 with it. In 1981 a third CBS version of the song, this time by Rex Smith and Rachel Sweet, also hit the charts. This is the only time that there have been as many as three chart versions of a song all from the same record company.

Esther and Abi Ofarim *pose in London while they were number one with* Cinderella Rockefella.

243

EVERLASTING LOVE

THE LOVE AFFAIR

31 January 1968, for two weeks

●●

CBS 3125

Written by Buzz Cason and Mac Gayden. Produced by Mike Smith.

To cover this Robert Knight American hit, producer Mike Smith saw no reason to use the members of the teeny-bopper group Love Affair on the record. So apart from lead singer Steve Ellis, Mike Smith used session musicians rather than the members of the group whose instrumental talents at the time were charitably described as limited. The roster of major hits whose credited performers are nowhere near the studio at the time is long and legendary, but to admit the practice in 1968 was daring. It made no difference, however, as the record made it all the way to the top. What was more amazing was that Love Affair – by now using a higher percentage of their membership on record – managed four more Top 20 hits before breaking up and fading into the further recesses of the pop memory.

Not that *Everlasting Love* was a bad record. Far from it. Ellis had a powerful and expressive voice. Producer Mike Smith was enjoying his second consecutive number one while CBS joined Philips, RCA and MGM in

244

MIGHTY QUINN

MANFRED MANN

14 February 1968, for two weeks

●●

Fontana TF 897

Written by Bob Dylan. Produced by Mike Hurst.

With the arrival of new vocalist, Old Harrovian and ex-Band of Angels member Mike D'Abo, Manfred Mann changed record labels and began working with producer Mike Hurst, late of the Springfields. After three vocal Top 10ers and an instrumental hit, *Sweet Pea*, the group returned to the top for their third number one.

Mann had already had hits with two other Dylan songs, *If You Gotta Go Go Now*, and *Just Like A Woman*, but *Mighty Quinn* had lain incomplete on tape for months before Manfred could convince both producer and band that the song would make a hit single.

By now bassist Jack Bruce had left to form Cream, his replacement being Klaus Voorman, the longtime Beatles' friend and designer of their *Revolver* LP sleeve. But by 1969, after 17 hit singles, Manfred decided to dissolve the group and return to his first love, jazz. With Mike Hugg he created Emanon, which evolved into Manfred Mann Chapter Three. Then came a move into heavy rock via Manfred Mann's Earth Band and, between 1973 and 1979, five more Top 50 singles with Chris Thompson on vocals. One of these, a cover version of Bruce Springsteen's *Blinded By The Light*, gave the group something which the Boss has never had, a US number one.

245

CINDERELLA

ROCKEFELLA

ESTHER AND ABI OFARIM

28 February 1968, for three weeks

●●●

Philips BF 1640

Written by Mason Williams. Produced by Abi Ofarim and Chaim Somel.

Only two husband and wife teams have ever topped the charts, and such is the transitoriness of life that both couples are now divorced. Sonny and Cher split up amidst vast publicity, but Esther and Abi Ofarim managed to go their own ways comparatively quietly, some years after their big success.

Esther Ofarim was born Esther Zaled in Safed, Israel on 13 June 1943, and her husband Abraham Reichstadt was born in Tel

Aviv on 5 October 1939. Their marriage entitled Esther to leave the Israeli Army after serving only four months of her National Service, and enabled the pair to concentrate on a musical career. By 1963 they were a top attraction in Israel and rather confusingly, that year Esther Ofarim represented Switzerland in the Eurovision Song Contest. Their reputation throughout Europe grew as they recorded in French, German and English as well as Hebrew, and by mid-1967 they were appearing frequently on television programmes throughout Europe. It was one such appearance on the *Eamonn Andrews Show* that brought *Cinderella Rockefella* to the notice of the British public. The song had been written by Mason Williams, American composer and guitarist who hit in Britain with his *Classical Gas* later in 1968, and had been recorded by Esther and Abi in 1967. It was not issued as a single until early 1968, when public demand created the hit.

246

LEGEND OF XANADU

DAVE DEE, DOZY, BEAKY, MICK AND TICH

20 March 1968, for one week

●

Fontana TF 903

Written by Ken Howard and Alan Blaikley.
Produced by Steve Rowland.

Ken Howard and Alan Blaikley, whose knack for writing instantly memorable and entertainingly original pop songs brought them their first chart-topper in 1964 with the Honeycombs (see no. 176), had their greatest and longest-lasting run of pop success with a manically-monikered group from Wiltshire previously named Dave Dee and the Bostons.

Using the band's existing nicknames, Howard and Blaikley rechristened the group, who were ex-policeman Dave Dee (born David Harman, 17 December 1943), Dozy (born Trevor Davies, 27 November 1944), Beaky (born John Dymond, 10 July 1944), Mick (born Michael Wilson, 4 March 1944) and Tich (born Ian Amey, 15 May 1944).

Their first hit, *You Make It Move,* was followed by a similar sounding Top 10er *Hold*

Tight. The early DD, D, B, M and T style consisted of shouted vocals and a heavy beat which gradually evolved into a series of more intricate mini-epics of which *Legend* was the masterpiece. They'd come close to the top before and surprised no one when *Legend* went all the way. Within a year fortunes waned and by 1970 Dave Dee had split to have one solo hit, *My Woman's Man,* while D, B, M and T soldiered on, also scoring one hit, *Mr President.* Dave Dee has been a recording executive with several companies and the rest of the group, with a new Mick, are now based in their own club in Marbella, Spain.

247

LADY MADONNA

THE BEATLES

27 March 1968, for two weeks

●●

Parlophone R 5675

Written by John Lennon and Paul McCartney.
Produced by George Martin.

The Beatles' final number one on the Parlophone label, their fourteenth was by no means their most successful single. Certainly it reached the top, one place higher than their classics like *Penny Lane/Strawberry Fields Forever* and *Let It Be,* but *Lady Madonna* only stayed on the chart for a total of eight weeks, the shortest-lived Beatles single ever. At the time, only three other number one hits had stayed on the charts for eight weeks or less. Two of those were Christmas hits – Dickie Valentine's *Christmas Alphabet* (see no. 40) (seven weeks) and Winifred Atwell's *Let's Have Another Party* (see no. 26), which was listed for eight weeks. The other short-running chart topper was Frankie Laine's *Hey Joe* (see no. 13), which hit the top when the chart was only a Top 12.

Between *Hello Goodbye* and *Lady Madonna,* the double EP *Magical Mystery Tour* had been released and climbed to number 2. The set included one of the Beatles' most covered songs, *Fool On The Hill,* as well as their only instrumental release, *Flying.* The hostile critical reception of the *Magical Mystery Tour* film followed by the mediocre chart performance of *Lady*

Madonna, made late 1967 and early 1968 the low point of the Beatles' amazing career but for the Beatles even a nadir was a number one hit.

248

CONGRATULATIONS

CLIFF RICHARD

10 April 1968, for two weeks

●●

Columbia DB 8376

Written by Bill Martin and Phil Coulter.
Produced by Norrie Paramor.

Cliff Richard's first attempt to win the Eurovision Song Contest resulted in his first number one hit for three years but not in a second consecutive Eurovision victory for Britain. The winner of the 1968 contest, held in London's Albert Hall on 6 April, was the Spanish songstress Massiel, whose *La La La* pipped Cliff at the post amidst cries of foul from the British press about the tactical voting of some of the foreign delegations.

Not that it really mattered. *Congratulations* was easily the biggest hit in Europe of all the Eurovision songs of 1968. Cliff eventually recorded several different versions of the song for release around the world. *Congratulations* very quickly rolled to one million plus sales.

Congratulations was Cliff's 41st British single, and it proved to be his biggest worldwide seller to date, even reaching number 99 in the American Hot Hundred. In later years, both *Devil Woman* and *We Don't Talk Anymore* (see no. 441) have overhauled the sales figures of *Congratulations,* but all the same it remains one of the biggest hits in the history of the Eurovision Song Contest.

249

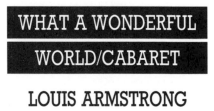

WHAT A WONDERFUL WORLD/CABARET

LOUIS ARMSTRONG

24 April 1968, for four weeks

● ● ● ●

HMV POP 1615

Written by (What A Wonderful World)
George David Weiss and George Douglas,
(Cabaret) – John Kander and Fred Ebb.
Produced by Bob Thiele.

Despite a remarkably strong rumour to the
contrary, Armstrong's biographer James
Lincoln Collier maintains that it is 'almost
certainly untrue' that Daniel Louis Armstrong was born neatly on 4 July 1900. Collier
maintains 'Satchmo' was born in 1898 on an
unknown date (many Americans without an
official birthday chose 4 July as a date of con-
venience). If, as seems likely, Collier is correct then Armstrong was in fact just over 69
years old when he had his first number one,
making him the oldest ever artist to reach
the top . It took Armstrong 15 years 127 days
after his initial singles chart entry with *Takes
Two To Tango* to make the top. His
American 1964 number one, *Hello Dolly*,
peaked in Britain at number four.

Armstrong the musician and the man
achieved far more than mere chart success,
as an American at a time when the USA was
moving to the front of world events, as a
black man who, during a period of
increased black consciousness and liberation, rose from the background of poverty
and a family history of slavery to become an
unofficial ambassador for his country, but
more than anything as a magnificent jazz
trumpeter and vocalist whose genius gave
pleasure to millions for decades Armstrong
stands as a shining light in the cultural
history of the 20th century.

What A Wonderful World received fresh
exposure in America in 1988 through the
movie *Good Morning Vietnam*.

250

YOUNG GIRL

UNION GAP featuring
GARY PUCKETT

22 May 1968, for four weeks

● ● ● ●

CBS 3365

Written by Jerry Fuller. Produced by Jerry
Fuller.

The group that sold more singles in
America in 1968 than the Beatles were led
by a man who spent his childhood in Hib-
bing, Minnesota, the same town that was
home to the young Bob Zimmerman (aka
Bob Dylan). The group were billed as Union
Gap on their first chart hit, *Woman Woman,*
but like the Supremes and the First Edition
they subsequently changed the billing on
the record label to feature their lead singer
more prominently as their success grew.
Young Girl was their second hit, and by the
time they hit the charts for a third time the
outfit was known as Gary Puckett and the
Union Gap.

Whatever the billing the line-up was the
same for all the singles. Gary Puckett was
the vocalist, Dwight Bement played bass,
Canadian Kerry Chater handled rhythm
guitar duties, Paul Whitbread was the drummer and Gary Withem played keyboards.
They wore American Civil War uniforms
and gave themselves military ranks (from
General Puckett down to Privates Whitbread and Withem) to remind their more
erudite fans that they had taken their name
from the site of a famous Civil War battle.

The group got together in San Diego, California in 1967, and through producer and
songwriter Jerry Fuller, who auditioned
them one night in a bowling alley, they
landed a recording contract almost immediately. Within a few months of formation
they had received their first Gold Disc for
Woman Woman.

251

JUMPING JACK FLASH

THE ROLLING STONES

19 June 1968, for two weeks

● ●

Decca F 12782

Written by Mick Jagger and Keith Richard.
Produced by Jimmy Miller.

This was the Stones' first number one for two
years, but what a record! To get the summer

Louis Armstrong *addresses his 1968 birthday
luncheon.*

parties of 1968 going (in those pre-disco
days) all you needed were copies of *Simon
Says* by the 1910 Fruitgum Co., *Son Of Hickory Holler's Tramp* by O C Smith, and this
one. Thirteen years later, *Jumping Jack
Flash* was still the number used by the
Stones to close the show on their American
tour, still the number the fans were waiting
for.

The first batch of the Rolling Stones drug
problems were over by now, certainly for
Mick Jagger and Keith Richard, whose jail
sentences of one year and three months respectively imposed in June 1967 had been
overturned on appeal. Brian Jones also had
a nine month jail sentence reduced on
appeal to merely a fine, but the strain of the
court appearances told on him, an asthmatic, more than on the others. He spent
much of the early part of 1968 in hospitals trying to recover his fitness, both mental and
physical, but in May 1968, just a few days before the release of *Jumping Jack Flash*, he
was arrested once again on drugs charges.
Exactly a year after it dropped from the top
he drowned in his swimming pool. By that
time he had already left the Stones but had
shown few signs of sorting out his problems.

252

BABY COME BACK

THE EQUALS

3 July 1968, for three weeks

●●●

President PT 135

Written by Eddie Grant. Produced by Ed Kassner.

If anyone could be dubbed the 'leader' of a group called the Equals then it was vocalist Derv Gordon who, with his guitarist twin brother Lincoln was born in Kingston, Jamaica on 29 June 1948. The other Equals were guitarist Eddie Grant (born Guyana, 5 March 1948), drummer John Hall (born London, England, 25 October 1947) and guitarist Pat Lloyd (born London, England, 17 March 1948).

The Equals had spent two years recording ska/pop tunes for President Records with some European success when an old song, *I Get So Excited,* became a minor UK hit. Then *Baby Come Back* was re-released, providing the label with its only number one to date. Other hits followed, including *Viva Bobby Joe* and *Black Skinned Blue Eyed Boys.* The group then became embroiled in a long legal dispute with President, making it impossible for them to release any records. After an out of court settlement the group resumed work but the damage had been done. The Equals had been forgotten, but one member, Eddie Grant, eventually more than matched the band's achievements with his own pop/reggae material (see no. 510).

253

I PRETEND

DES O'CONNOR

24 July 1968, for one week

●

Columbia DB 8397

Written by Les Reed and Barry Mason. Produced by Norman Newell.

The talents of songwriters Reed and Mason had already assisted the careers of Tom Jones and Engelbert Humperdinck before lifting comedian and compere Des O'Connor (born Stepney, London, January 1932) to the top.

O'Connor was an all-round entertainer who made his showbusiness debut in October 1953 at the Palace Theatre, Newcastle, after a spell working as a Butlin's Red Coat. He played a minor part in the history of rock'n'-roll by virtue of the fact that in 1958 he was the linkman on the only British tour under-taken by Buddy Holly. In the early '60s he was the compère of TV's *Sunday Night At The London Palladium,* one of the most popular variety shows of the era. By 1963 he'd been given his own TV series, an excellent vehicle for promoting his vocal prowess, but it wasn't until the final weeks of 1967 that his records began to sell. In a hit-making career of just over three years he managed seven Top 30 hits including the unforgettable *Dick-A-Dum-Dum* and the nostalgic *1-2-3 O'Leary* in which the word 'O'Leary' is made to rhyme with 'Mary'. The ballad *I Pretend* stayed on the charts for 36 weeks, a total bettered by only five other number one singles. It was the seventh and final number one production by Norman Newell.

254

MONY MONY

TOMMY JAMES AND THE SHONDELLS

31 July 1968, for two weeks
21 August 1968, for one week

●●●

Major Minor MM567

Written by Bobby Bloom, Richie Cordell, Bo Gentry and Tommy James. Produced by Bo Gentry and Richie Cordell.

Tommy James (born Tommy Jackson, 29 April 1946, Dayton, Ohio) and the Shondells first graced the UK charts in 1966 with their US number one, *Hanky Panky,* which climbed to a more modest 38 while the English football team were winning the World Cup. *Mony Mony* was their only other British chart entry, but it was a big hit. In America they were vastly more popular with 19 hit singles between *Hanky Panky* in 1966 and *Come To Me* in 1970.

The Shondells were from Pittsburgh, originally named the Raconteurs. They were Mike Vale (bass), Pete Lucia (drums), Eddie Gray (guitar) (not the Leeds United footballer) and Ronnie Rosman (organ). James and the group parted company in 1969 and that was the last the charts any-where heard of the Shondells. James has had thirteen solo US hits since 1970, but only one, *Draggin' The Line,* made the Top 10.

Mony Mony lives as a standard rock'n'roll dance number. Billy Idol brought it back to the Top 10 in 1987. Other James/Shondells hits have been given new leases of life over the years, such as *I Think We're Alone Now* by Tiffany in 1987/88 and *Crimson & Clover* by Joan Jett and the Blackhearts in 1982.

255

FIRE

THE CRAZY WORLD OF ARTHUR BROWN

14 August 1968, for one week

●

Track 604022

Written by Vincent Crane, Arthur Brown, Peter Ker and Michael Finesilver. Produced by Kit Lambert.

When Arthur Brown (born 24 June 1944) and his manager Vincent Crane wrote *Fire* and built a stage act featuring facial make-up, a burning hat and many stage effects which later lived on through Alice Cooper and others, they hoped they were creating a hit and launching Brown on a successful chart career. On both points they were wrong. Yes, the song was a hit, but two other writers, Peter Ker and Michael Finesilver, sued successfully to show that *Fire* was not an original creation but a variation of their song *Fire*. Furthermore, the song was Brown's only hit, and he never really set the world alight as successfully as he had his hat. The *New Statesman,* no less, thought that 'Arthur Brown could easily be the first genuine artist to come out of our local underground. He's disconcerting, even faintly perverse, but distinctly original and very very English'. But once again the *New Statesman* merely showed that its finger was not really on the pulse of British popular music, not even at their local underground.

The record was produced by the late Kit Lambert, manager of the Who. On Arthur Brown's LP, associate producer credits went to Pete Townsend of the Who, but the official producer of the single was Kit Lambert who owned the Track label.

256

DO IT AGAIN

THE BEACH BOYS

28 August 1968, for one week

Capitol CL 15554

Written by Brian Wilson and Mike Love. Produced by Brian Wilson.

The LP *Sergeant Pepper's Lonely Hearts Club Band* may have been the peak of the Beatles' recording career but it played a part in the downfall of the Beach Boys. Brian Wilson, who had seen the Beatles as rivals, suffered a mental breakdown following the relative commercial failure of his group's *Pet Sounds* album in America. Under his direction the Beach Boys had drifted away from their surfing image into more esoteric and less commercial waters. This proved too much for some fans to swallow, and the band's popularity waned in the USA after their number one hit *Good Vibrations.*

Support held up well in the UK however. A track pulled off their 1966 *Summer Days* album, *Then She Kissed Me*, went Top 10 in 1967, as did the rather muddled Brian Wilson creation *Heroes And Villains*. Three more medium-sized hits followed before *Do It Again*, a nostalgic look back at days of sun and surf, surprised even Beach Boy fans by snatching seven days of chart heaven.

In the late summer of 1987 the Beach Boys

climbed back up to number 2 as guest artists on the Fat Boys' rap version of the Surfaris' 1963 instrumental hit *Wipe Out.* Always a major concert attraction, the Beach Boys have continued as living legends to this day both home and away, although this is sadly not true in the case of Dennis, drowned off Marina Del Rey, California, in 1983.

257

I'VE GOTTA GET A
MESSAGE TO YOU

THE BEE GEES

4 September 1968, for one week

Polydor 56 273

Written by Barry, Robin and Maurice Gibb. Produced by Robert Stigwood and the Bee Gees.

A critic once observed that the Bee Gees of the late '60s were a gloomy bunch. When asked by Barry Gibb what songs could be cited to justify this remark, he replied, 'New York Mining Disaster 1941. . .I've Gotta Get A Message To You . . .' 'And that's it!' Barry concluded.

The critic could be forgiven for having been overly affected by the two singles. They both concerned personal dilemmas of a desperate nature, the first that of a miner trapped below the surface and the second that of a killer who is about to be executed. At least the Gibbs were romantic to the end: both men facing death wanted to communicate with their women.

I've Gotta Get A Message To You came at a crucial time for the Bee Gees. After hitting the American Top 20 with their first five singles there and the British equivalent with four out of the first five UK releases, they had suffered their first international miss, *Jumbo. Message* proved them more than one-year wonders, marking their breakthrough to the US Top 10 and their return to the number one spot in Britain.

258

HEY JUDE

THE BEATLES

11 September 1968, for two weeks

Apple R 5722

Written by John Lennon and Paul McCartney. Produced by George Martin.

This song was inspired by Paul McCartney's fondness for Julian Lennon, son of John and Cynthia. While driving to Cynthia's house for a visit after she and John had broken up, he started singing 'Hey Jules.' He changed the title to *Hey Jude,* thinking Jude a name with a more singable flavour than Jules. Paul was uncertain about some of the lyric's obscure lines, such as 'the movement you need is on your shoulder,' but John and Yoko Ono considered them marvellously avant-garde. The Beatles' 15th number one, *Hey Jude* was the longest chart-topper ever, at approximately seven minutes ten seconds. It ruled the roost for nine weeks in the US, the Beatles' longest run at number one, but was cut short after two weeks in the UK by McCartney's own production, *Those Were The Days* by Mary Hopkin.

Hey Jude was the initial offering on the Beatles' Apple label, part of a debut issue of four. Despite being the first single for the company, it retained Parlophone's numbering system. Wilson Pickett scored a Top 20 hit with his soulful cover version mere months later. *Hey Jude* became the title track of an American anthology of Beatles singles.

259

THOSE WERE THE
DAYS

MARY HOPKIN

25 September 1968, for six weeks

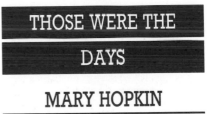

Apple 2

Written by Gene Raskin and Alexander Vertinski. Produced by Paul McCartney.

Though fourteen years separated their number ones, **Mary Hopkin** *and* **Vera Lynn** *appeared together at the 1969 Women of the Year Luncheon.*

Mary Hopkin (born 3 May 1950, Pontardawe, Wales) was one of a number of acts who found fame following an appearance on a TV talent show. Sixties model and future chart star Twiggy telephoned Paul McCartney after seeing Hopkin win a round of *Opportunity Knocks.* She was immediately signed to the Beatles' Apple label.

It was McCartney who chose to record *Those Were The Days,* a Russian folk song entitled *Darogoi Dlimmoyo (Dear For Me)* written by Alexander Vertinski with English lyrics by American Gene Raskin. After its release on 16 August, it climbed the charts and toppled her mentor's single *Hey Jude,* from the summit. Technically this cannot be included on the list of those instances where consecutive label catalogue numbers have appeared at number one because in June EMI and Apple had agreed that all future Beatle discs would appear on the Apple label with Parlophone numbers. Nonetheless *Hey Jude* was definitely Apple 1 in all but number.

Those Were The Days sold four million worldwide and was Hopkin's biggest success. Her follow up was a McCartney composition, *Goodbye,* but this time the Beatles'

own *Get Back* won out, keeping Hopkin in second place. Her debut album, *Postcard,* contained neither of these tracks but did include a version of Ray Noble's *Love Is The Sweetest Thing,* which Peter Skellern took to number 60 in 1978. After a number of years out of the limelight Hopkin was telephoned by Skellern in 1983 and asked to join his group Oasis which also comprised Julian Lloyd Webber, Mitch Dalton, and Bill Lovelady. Despite the impressive line-up they produced no single hits.

260

WITH A LITTLE HELP FROM MY FRIENDS

JOE COCKER

6 November 1968, for one week

●

Regal Zonophone RZ 3013

Written by John Lennon and Paul McCartney. Produced by Denny Cordell.

Ex-gas fitter Joe Cocker (born John Cocker, Sheffield, 20 May 1944) is respected as one of the world's greatest rock vocalists. Few could have so successfully turned this sing-along track of the Beatles' *Sergeant Pepper* LP into a soulful ballad.

Cocker had formed his first band, an R & B combo called Vance Arnold and the Avengers, in 1963. The following year he cut his first single, a version of the Beatles' *I'll Cry Instead,* using the name Joe Cocker. Working with numerous musicians he became well known on the London club circuit, gaining the attention of Eric Clapton and Jimi Hendrix. Having recorded *Marjorine,* a mildly successful single, with Procol Harum's producer Denny Cordell, Cocker decided to record the stage favourite *With A Little Help From My Friends.* The musicians who can be heard on this track are guitarist Jimmy Page, drummer BJ Wilson, plus bassist Chris Stainton and keyboard player Tom Eyre of Cocker's Grease Band. The backing singers were Madeline Bell, Rosetta Hightower and Sunny Wheetman.

Top 40 hits *Delta Lady* and *The Letter* followed, and a memorable appearance at the 1969 Woodstock Festival confirmed Cocker

as a major talent. For a while he seemed destined for superstardom but the singer hid himself away for most of 1970, unhappy with the pressures of fame. He returned to record with the likes of Albert Lee and Leon Russell but was not to have another UK hit single until he teamed up with Jennifer Warnes to sing *Up Where We Belong,* the theme to the 1982 film *An Officer And A Gentleman.* This duet reached the Top 10 in 1983. In 1987 his revival of Ray Charles' *Sticks And Stones* brought him back to the Top 75 as a solo act as well as his Top 50 release *Unchain My Heart.*

261

THE GOOD THE BAD AND THE UGLY

HUGO MONTENEGRO AND HIS ORCHESTRA AND CHORUS

13 November 1968, for four weeks

●●●●

RCA 1727

Written by Ennio Morricone. Produced by Hugo Montenegro.

The Good The Bad And The Ugly was the first instrumental number one since 3 April 1963, when the Shadows' *Foot Tapper* gave way four weeks before the Beatles had their first chart-topper. It had as its unlikely birthplace a spaghetti western starring Clint Eastwood. Montenegro himself was born in New York in 1925, but moved to California after serving in the US Navy and became known for the scores to films like *Hurry Sundown* and TV series like *The Man From U.N.C.L.E.* He also acted as arranger and conductor for label-mate Harry Belafonte.

The Good The Bad And The Ugly featured Elliott Fisher on electric violin, Manny Klein on piccolo trumpet, Tommy Morgan on electronic harmonica and Arthur Smith on ocarina, the instrument that produced the haunting introduction to the record. The grunting noises were by Ron Hicklin, who led the chorus. Whistler Muzzy Marcellino also features on the record.

Hugo Montenegro managed to avoid the

stigma of being a one hit wonder on 8 January 1969, when his theme to Clint Eastwood's next spaghetti western *Hang 'Em High* reached number 50, only to disappear from the charts the next week.

262

LILY THE PINK

SCAFFOLD

11 December 1968, for three weeks
8 January 1969, for one week

● ● ● ●

Parlophone R 5734

Written by John Gorman, Mike McGear and Roger McGough. Produced by Norrie Paramor.

The Scaffold were Liverpudlians John Gorman, poet Roger McGough and Paul McCartney's younger brother Michael, who called himself Mike McGear. They first hit the charts with *Thank U Very Much,* a Top 5 hit at Christmas 1967 with the enigmatic first line, 'Thank U very much for the Aintree Iron'. Other unusual singles, like *2 Day's Monday,* failed completely, but at Christmas in 1968 they achieved their only number one, the saga of Lily The Pink and her Medicinal Compound.

It was the late Norrie Paramor's final number one production, his 27th, a total which is still the record today. At the time it meant that he had produced slightly more than one in ten number one hits, a phenomenal achievement. It was Paramor's only number one as an independent producer after years as a staff producer at EMI. Uncredited vocals in the background in the verse about Jennifer Eccles and her terrible freckles were by Graham Nash of the Hollies, whose single *Jennifer Eccles* had been a Top 10 hit earlier that year. Also on background vocals was Norrie Paramor's production assistant, Tim Rice. The production had been completed and was ready to be pressed when Mike McGear decided that what it really needed was a bass drum. The drum was added, the tape remixed and the single sold a million. Without that bass drum, would it have hit the charts quite so hard? Nobody will ever know.

Marmalade *show off the latest in late-Sixties designer jackets.*

263

OB-LA-DI OB-LA-DA

MARMALADE

1 January 1969, for one week
15 January 1969, for two weeks

● ● ●

CBS 3892

Written by John Lennon and Paul McCartney. Produced by Mike Smith.

The Beatles had released five singles and an EP since February 1967, none of which appeared on a UK album. Three tracks on side one of *The Beatles* double-album, released in 1968, would have made good singles: *While My Guitar Gently Weeps, Back In The USSR* (which eventually made the Top 20 when released in 1976) and the reggae tinged *Ob-La-Di Ob-La-Da.* It was left to this Scottish group to take the latter tune to the top of the pile.

Marmalade grew out of the band Dean Ford and the Gaylords, formed in 1961. The line-up in 1968 was vocalist Dean Ford (born Tom McAleese, 5 September 1946), guitarists Junior Campbell (born 31 May 1947) and Pat Fairley (born 14 April 1946), bassist Graham Knight (born 8 December 1946) and drummer Alan Whitehead (born 24 July 1946). This quintet had eight Top 30 hits, including *Reflections Of My Life* and *Rainbow,* both of which made number 3. The group became the toast of Thailand following the Bangkok Music Festival in 1971 be-

fore songwriter Campbell moved off for a mildly successful solo career. Fellow Scot Hughie Nicholson was brought in and three more hits ensued, but by 1974 only Dean Ford remained from the original Marmalade line-up.

Graham Knight returned in 1976 to help the group to one more success with the Macaulay/Greenaway song *Falling Apart At The Seams,* by which time even Dean Ford had left. With various personnel the group has continued into the '80s, at one point attempting a comeback with a medley of their old hits called *Golden Shreds.*

264

ALBATROSS

FLEETWOOD MAC

29 January 1969, for one week

●

Blue Horizon 57 3145

Written by Peter Green. Produced by Mike Vernon.

When guitar virtuoso Peter Green left John Mayall's Bluesbreakers in 1967 (he had originally been recruited to replace Eric Clapton) he invited drummer Mick Fleetwood (who had played a very brief stint with Mayall), bassist John McVie, and guitarists Jeremy Spencer and Danny

Kirwan to join him in a group which was originally known as Peter Green's Fleetwood Mac. The hits followed including this beautiful instrumental which has twice been a massive UK seller. It returned to the charts in 1975, failing by just one place to become the only re-issued chart-topper to make number one again. Then in 1970 Green left the group in a whirl of religious, moral and personal dilemmas. In 1971 Spencer, an avid New Testament reader who had once got the group banned from the Marquee Club by going on stage with a wooden dildo hanging from his fly, disappeared a couple of hours before a gig in LA and was found later in the week with The Children of God religious sect.

Fleetwood and McVie brought in vocalist Christine Perfect, who became John McVie's wife. After more personnel changes they enlisted the American duo Lindsay Buckingham and Stevie Nicks. Massive success followed with the zenith being the huge-selling album *Rumours* in 1977. In 1987 Lindsay Buckingham left the group to go solo.

1967 and **The Move** *are not in a good mood. They are on their way to the High Court to face an injunction to cease circulating their promotional postcard that rudely portrayed Harold Wilson.*

265

BLACKBERRY WAY

THE MOVE

5 February 1969, for one week

Peter Sarstedt *shares an orange juice with Chief Wolf Robe of Tulsa, Oklahoma.*

●

Regal Zonophone RZ 3015

Written by Roy Wood. Produced by Jimmy Miller.

In the mid-'60s the Cedar Club was the favourite haunt of all the local groups from the Birmingham area. It was here that the Move were formed. Roy Wood (born 8 November 1948), Carl Wayne (born 18 August 1944), Curtis 'Ace' Kefford (born 10 December 1946), Bev Bevan (born 24 November 1944) and Trevor Burton (born 9 March 1949) had all appeared in various Birmingham outfits, but none had gained national fame.

The group moved to London, became a regular act at the Marquee and signed with manager Tony Secunda. Their new wave sound and sensational TV appearances, in which they smashed TVs, cars and effigies of Hitler, brought attention to their early singles, and the first four all made the Top 10. One of them, *Flowers In The Rain*, gained immortality as the first record ever played on Radio One. In Spring 1968, Kefford left suffering from nervous exhaustion but the group decided against bringing in a new member. Instead Burton switched from guitar to bass. *Wild Tiger Woman* became their first flop in the summer and the band threatened to call it a day if their next single didn't fare any better.

The next release was *Blackberry Way*. Written like all their previous hits by Roy Wood and with Richard Tandy joining the band for this one record playing keyboards,

the song gave the Move their only number one.

Early in 1970 Wayne left following a disagreement over whether or not the group should continue a season of cabaret. He was replaced by Jeff Lynne. By 1972, the Move's final year, the group consisted of Wood, Bevan and Lynne. Their final LP *Message From The Country,* featuring oboes, violins and flutes underlined their new and experimental direction. This trio formed the nucleus of the Electric Light Orchestra and in July 1972 the Move's last single was slipping down the charts as ELO's first single climbed them.

266

(IF PARADISE IS) HALF

AS NICE

AMEN CORNER

12 February 1969, for two weeks

● ●

Immediate IM 073

Written by Lucio Battisti, English lyric by Jack Fishman. Produced by Shel Talmy.

Amen Corner were under the control of Welshman Andy Fairweather-Low and comprised Dennis Byron (drums), Alan Jones and Mike Smith (saxophones), Neil Jones (guitar), Clive Taylor (bass) and Blue Weaver (keyboards). Their producer Shel Talmy worked with the Who, Kinks, Easybeats and Manfred Mann before leaving the record industry in the early '70s to write a novel *The Ichabod Deception*.

Based in Cardiff, the band first sprang to prominence with the blues-based hit *Gin House* which climbed to number 12 in 1967. Their style changed to bubblegum pop and they made numbers 3 and 6 in 1968 with *Bend Me Shape Me* and *High In The Sky* respectively. The following year, after changing labels from the Decca subsidiary Deram to Immediate, they scored their only number one. The follow-up single *Hello Suzie* made number 4 in the June of the same year but there were no more hits, although a reissue of their chart-topper staggered to number 34 in 1976. Fairweather-Low had solo success in the '70s with Top 10 singles *Wide Eyed And Legless* and *Natural Sinner*.

267

WHERE DO YOU GO TO, MY LOVELY?

PETER SARSTEDT

26 February 1969, for four weeks

●●●●

United Artists UP 2262

Written by Peter Sarstedt. Produced by Ray Singer.

Peter Sarstedt's elder brother Richard had already had a number one hit, *Well I Ask You* (see no. 122) in 1961, under the name Eden Kane. Seven and a half years later his brother Peter stuck with the family name to release a single and establish a record that has only once been matched. They were the first brothers to have separate solo number ones in Britain, a feat that was equalled by Donny and Little Jimmy Osmond at the end of 1972. Paul McCartney and his brother Mike McGear have also had separate number one hits, but McGear's was only as part of a group. The same holds true for Michael Jackson and his many brothers.

In 1976 the third Sarstedt brother, Clive (for some reason calling himself Robin for recording purposes), reached number

Desmond Dekker.

three with his version of *My Resistance Is Low,* enabling the Sarstedt clan to become the only trio of brothers in British chart history to rack up separate solo hits. The Osmonds and the Jacksons (two brothers and a sister each with solo hits) come close to the Sarstedt record, as do the Gibbs, of whom Andy and Robin have hit as soloists while Barry has charted in partnership with Barbra Streisand. But no family has yet quite matched this Sarstedt achievement.

Peter's hit was a continental café-flavoured ballad about a poor little rich girl. He was never able to repeat its huge success, but has remained active on the record and performance scene, both solo and in conjunction with his brothers.

268

I HEARD IT THROUGH THE GRAPEVINE

MARVIN GAYE

26 March 1969, for three weeks

●●●

Tamla Motown TMG 686

Written by Norman Whitfield and Barrett Strong. Produced by Norman Whitfield.

Marvin Gaye (born Marvin Pentz Gay, 2 April 1939) was not the only Motown act to record *Grapevine*. The Miracles and the Isley Brothers both attempted it before him, the Temptations and the Undisputed Truth after him. It was Gladys Knight and The Pips, however, who produced the first hit version in 1967 when their gospel-flavoured interpretation gave them a minor UK chart entry and a US number 2 smash. Though not a *Billboard* number one, it was Motown's biggest American seller at that time.

The strength of the song was proved by Gaye's deeply soulful rendition on his *In The Groove* LP, producing a classic single whose US sales surpassed even Knight's record. Gaye had been an underrated artist in the UK, where his greatest success had been a 1967 Top 20 duet with Kim Weston, *It Takes Two*. In America he'd been charting regularly since 1962 with songs such as *Stubborn Kind Of Fellow* and *How Sweet It Is*.

Then came *Grapevine* and other successes, including his only UK Top 10 hit after splitting from Motown, 1982's *Sexual Healing*. His 1973 winner *Let's Get It On* replaced his *Grapevine* as Motown's best seller in America.

During an argument on 1 April 1984 Marvin Gaye Snr shot his son dead, one day before the singer's 45th birthday. *Grapevine* returned to the British Top 10 in 1986 revitalized by its use in a jeans commercial.

269

THE ISRAELITES

DESMOND DEKKER AND THE ACES

16 April 1969, for one week

●

Pyramid PYR 6058

Written by Desmond Dekker and Leslie Kong. Produced by Leslie Kong.

Discounting Marmalade's version of Lennon and McCartney's *Ob-La-Di Ob-La-Da, The Israelites* was reggae's first number one and Desmond Dekker the genre's first star.

Dekker (born Kingston, Jamaica, 1943), a former welder, joined Jamaican studio group The Aces in the mid-'60s. Their 1967 debut UK hit, *007 (Shanty Town),* was produced by Dekker's musical mentor, the Chinese/Jamaican Leslie Kong. The Aces scored a string of successes in their homeland from 1967 to 1969 while in Britain it looked as if *007* had been a one-off hit. Then came *The Israelites,* which also achieved Top 10 status in the USA, a rare achievement for a reggae song.

Dekker came close to topping the chart again in 1970 when his song *You Can Get It If You Really Want,* from the film *The Harder They Come,* went to number 2, denied the ultimate glory by Freda Payne. In 1971 Leslie Kong died of a heart attack, an event which sent Dekker's career into decline. Despite two Top 20 hits in 1975, *Sing A Little Song* and a reissue of his number one, Desmond Dekker had by then been replaced as the king of reggae by fellow Jamaican Bob Marley.

270

GET BACK

THE BEATLES WITH BILLY PRESTON

23 April 1969, for six weeks

●●●●●●

Apple R 5777

Written by John Lennon and Paul McCartney. Produced by George Martin.

After 13 consecutive number ones that reached the top in their second week on the charts, the Beatles finally came straight into the chart at number one with a song performed live on the roof of the Apple offices in London in February 1969. The version which was released was not recorded on the roof: that was produced as usual by George Martin at Abbey Road.

Billy Preston, who joined Tony Sheridan as the only individuals to have a performing credit on a Beatles' single, was born in Houston, Texas on 9 September 1946. He had by 1969 established a reputation as a brilliant session keyboards man, and it was George Harrison who brought him into the Beatle empire. John Lennon said of Billy Preston, 'we might have had him in the group', but the group was already breaking up. Preston put out a brilliant single on Apple in mid-1969, *That's The Way God Planned It,* which made number 11. Despite vocal and instrumental number ones in America in the early '70s, he faded chartwise in Britain until the beginning of 1980 when the born-again Christian reached number two in duet with Stevie Wonder's ex-wife Syreeta with the aptly titled *With You I'm Born Again.*

271

DIZZY

TOMMY ROE

4 June 1969, for one week

●

Stateside SS 2143

Written by Tommy Roe and Freddy Weller. Produced by Steve Barri.

Thomas David Roe, born in Atlanta, Georgia on 9 May 1942, was one of the ranks of pop stars who admit that their biggest influence was Buddy Holly. *Dizzy* was a brilliant piece of pure bubblegum, but early Tommy Roe hits, especially his first, *Sheila,* were virtual duplications of Buddy Holly's phrasing, arrangements and sound. His first break came when, like Bobby Vee, he was asked to stand in on a date which Buddy Holly had been booked for, and a year later Roe recorded and released *Sheila* on the tiny Judd label in Georgia. The record failed to attract any interest, but within two years Roe had signed with ABC-Paramount who re-recorded and re-released *Sheila.* This time it was a hit and Roe was on his way.

His career was not very consistent after that; some big hits like *The Folk Singer* in 1963 in Britain, and *Sweet Pea* and *Hooray For Hazel* in 1966 in the States but a lot of failures until Roe and Freddie Weller wrote *Dizzy.* Roe thus had his first number one seven years after his first hit. Co-writer Freddy Weller is now a country singer after a spell as one of Paul Revere's Raiders.

272

THE BALLAD OF JOHN AND YOKO

THE BEATLES

11 June 1969, for three weeks

●●●

Apple R 5786

Written by John Lennon and Paul McCartney. Produced by George Martin and the Beatles.

The last number one hit by the Fab Four in fact featured a Fab Two as only John and Paul actually played on *The Ballad Of John And Yoko,* a hastily concocted but irresistibly catchy paean to some of the then recent events of John Lennon's life, the principal one being his marriage to the avant-garde Japanese artist, Yoko Ono.

The chorus had lines like 'Christ, you know it ain't easy' and 'The way things are going/ They're going to crucify me', which imme-diately caused the media to criticize the increasingly erratic John Lennon, and to raise again the furore caused by his 'We're bigger than Jesus' remark in America a few years earlier. Not that this bothered the Beatles. By the time this record was released they had all but split up. The later singles, *Something* and *Let It Be,* were both recorded before *The Ballad Of John And Yoko,* which incidentally was the 14th of the Beatles' 17 number ones to reach the top in its second week on the chart.

And so the Beatles' reign of unprecedented success was over. John and Yoko climbed into their bag, Paul married Linda, George dug deeper into Indian music and Ringo went into films. Despite the brilliance and phenomenal success of many of their individual records since 1969, nothing has recreated the magic that 'the new Beatles single' always did.

273

SOMETHING IN THE AIR

THUNDERCLAP NEWMAN

2 July 1969, for three weeks

●●●

Track 604-031

Written by Speedy Keen. Produced by Pete Townshend.

This hit made Pete Townshend the only member of the original Who to have any connection with a number one single. The nearest his group ever came was number 2 with their 1965 song *My Generation.*

'Before I met Peter I knew nothing,' admitted the former pub pianist and Bix Beiderbecke fan Andy 'Thunderclap' Newman. Vocalist and drummer Speedy Keen had first met the Who in Ealing, London when they were known as the High Numbers. They had remained firm friends and a Keen composition, *Armenia, City In The Sky,* even appeared on the 1968 *The Who Sell Out* album. The third member of Thunderclap Newman was guitarist Jimmy McCulloch who later joined Wings. He died in 1979.

Townshend also produced *Accidents,* the follow-up to *Something In The Air,* which lasted just one week in the Top 50. The group split up soon after. Keen released an interesting though unsuccessful album, *Previous Convictions,* and Newman took up the saxophone and went back to the pub circuit.

274

HONKY TONK WOMEN

THE ROLLING STONES

23 July 1969, for five weeks

●●●●●

Decca F 12952

Written by Mick Jagger and Keith Richard. Produced by Jimmy Miller.

Just three weeks after the last Beatles chart-topper slid from the number one position, the last Rolling Stones number one (so far) took over. They went out with a bang, at least, as five weeks was their longest ever run at number one. The Stones' chart career is amazing in its consistency. Eight number ones put them fifth on the all time list, but their unbeaten record is that over a period of 14 years 8 months, every single official release by the Rolling Stones made the Top 10. When *Respectable* peaked at number 23 in late 1978, it marked the first time that the Stones had missed the Top 10 since *I Wanna Be Your Man* peaked at number 12 at the end of 1963. It was also the lowest chart placing they had ever had – apart from a Decca cash-in single of *Out Of Time* – in a 15 year career. But they were still making Top 10 hits in the 1980s.

Honky Tonk Women was the only Stones number one after Brian Jones left the group, 20 days before *Honky Tonk Women* reached the top. The replacement Stone on this record is Mick Taylor (born 17 January 1941), who came from John Mayall's Bluesbreakers. Taylor left the Stones at the end of 1974, and his replacement was, and still is, Ronnie Wood from the Faces.

Creedence Clearwater Revival *(left to right: Tom Fogerty, Doug Clifford, John Fogerty and Stu Cook) together during their brief but beautiful heyday.*

275

IN THE YEAR 2525
(EXORDIUM AND
TERMINUS)

ZAGER AND EVANS

30 August 1969, for three weeks

●●●

RCA 1860

Written by Rick Evans. Produced by Denny Zager and Rick Evans.

The record that gave way to the Rolling Stones at the top of the American charts took over from them in Britain. One of the weirdest and therefore best known one-hit-wonder records in British pop history, *In The Year 2525* was a bleak vision of man's future written by Evans in half an hour one day in Lincoln, Nebraska. Denny Zager (born 1944) and Rick Evans (born 1943) had originally been part of a group called the Eccentrics, a country outfit from Nebraska, but had been performing as a duo for some years before the success of *In The Year 2525.* In November 1968, they borrowed $500 to record the song in Texas. They formed their own company, and hawked the initial pressing of

1000 copies around record shops and local radio stations. They sent copies of the record to all the major record companies as well, but it was RCA in New York that took the bait, and signed Zager and Evans to a national deal.

The result was a national release in June 1969 and a number one hit in America by July. In the UK, it also hit the top very quickly, but they disappeared just as fast, to join the growing list of one hit wonders. Exordium and Terminus.

276

BAD MOON RISING

CREEDENCE
CLEARWATER REVIVAL

20 September 1969, for three weeks

●●●

Liberty LBF 15230

Written by John Fogerty. Produced by John Fogerty.

At the time of *Bad Moon Rising* Creedence Clearwater Revival consisted of John Fogerty (born 28 May 1945), brother Tom (born 9 November 1941), Doug Clifford (born 24 April 1945) and Stu Cook (born 25 April 1945). Their debut UK hit had been

Serge Gainsbourg *and* **Jane Birkin** *are shown in 1972 with the consequences of their heavy breathing.*

Proud Mary, the saga of a Mississippi paddlesteamer. It had climbed to number 8 and would eventually become their best-known composition partly through inclusion in Elvis Presley's stage repertoire and a successful reworking by Ike and Tina Turner which cracked the US Top 5 in 1971.

Creedence were at their best live and had appeared at the Denver Pop Festival, the Atlanta Pop Festival and the Atlantic City Pop Festival within the space of five weeks during the summer of 1969. Then came *Bad Moon Rising,* the second of three consecutive number 2 hits in their native USA where they never enjoyed a number one single. All the same, for a few months in 1970 they were probably the most popular active rock band in the world. Eight more chart hits by mid-1971 completed Creedence's rise in Britain. In October 1972 the group issued a press statement announcing that they would be working on solo projects for a while but the band was never revived.

Twelve years after its initial success *Bad Moon Rising* was used imaginatively during an horrific yet hilarious scene of metamorphosis in the film *An American Werewolf in London.*

John Fogerty, the driving force and major talent of CCR has enjoyed considerable solo success since his group's demise, most notably via his 1985 album, *Centerfield.*

277

JE T'AIME ... MOI MON PLUS

JANE BIRKIN AND SERGE GAINSBOURG

11 October 1969, for one week

●

Major Minor MM 645

Written by Serge Gainsbourg. Produced by Jack Baverstock.

In the week ending Saturday 11 October 1969, two events occurred that persuaded the older generation in Britain that the country was going to the dogs. Firstly, the 50p piece was introduced as a forerunner to full decimalization of the coinage. Secondly *Je T'aime* reached the top of the charts.

Mind you, it had everything going for it. A very strong tune (which charted under the title *Love At First Sight* by a group called Sounds Nice when the BBC banned the original), a beautiful English girl, recently seen roaming naked with David Hemmings in the Antonioni film *Blow Up,* and for the first but not the last time on a hit record, grunts and groans sounding remarkably like a lady and gentlemen getting to know each other very well indeed. Of course, it sold like hot cakes, and the only surprising thing is that Fontana, who originally issued the record, were overcome with a fit of morality and deleted it when it was at number 2 in the charts. Major Minor, who had no such scruples, took over the master and were rewarded by a number one hit in the record's second week on their label.

Birkin and Gainsbourg, who were not married but who were enjoying a long-lasting relationship at the time, never repeated their chart success, and go down in the books as one-hit wonders. The record was however reissued in 1974 on the Antic label and enjoyed a further chart run. This makes *Je T'Aime. . .Moi Non Plus* not only the only French language chart-topper but also the only number one to hit the chart on three different labels. In racking up a total of 34 weeks on the chart, Birkin and Gainsbourg achieved the longest total chart run of any one hit wonder.

Jane Birkin, who married James Bond composer John Barry before meeting Serge Gainsbourg, is still based in France. These days she is a successful actress, having for example played the part of the murderess Christine Redfern in the Agatha Christie film, *Evil Under The Sun.*

278

I'LL NEVER FALL IN LOVE AGAIN

BOBBIE GENTRY

18 October 1969, for one week

●

Capitol CL 15606

Written by Burt Bacharach and Hal David. Produced by Kelso Hurston.

With this song from their musical *Promises Promises* Bacharach and David notched up their sixth number one composition maintaining their third position in the league of most successful number one songwriting partnerships.

Bobbie Gentry *poses in London in 1968 before working on a television programme.*

Bobbie Gentry (born Roberta Lee Streeter, 27 July 1944) began playing piano at the age of seven, going on to study music at the Los Angeles Conservatory of Music. After seeing the film *Ruby Gentry* she decided to jettison her own surname in favour of Ruby's and by 1966 she was singing and writing songs for her own song and dance group.

Bobbie had approached Capitol Records with an eye to selling songs to other artists. Instead they asked her to sing them herself. Bobbie's first hit was the mysterious *Ode To Billy Joe,* a UK Top 20 smash and US number one in 1967. There were no more British hits until this one, a song of disillusionment whose listeners felt sure that the singer would one day change the view expressed in the title. A cover of the Everlys' *All I Have To Do Is Dream* (see no. 73) with Glen Campbell put her back in the Top 10 in December, but apart from a minor hit in 1970, that was it. Bobbie did fall in love again. After divorcing millionaire Bill Harrah she married singer Jim Stafford in 1978.

279

SUGAR SUGAR

THE ARCHIES

25 October 1969, for eight weeks

●●●●●●●●

RCA 1872

Written by Jeff Barry and Andy Kim. Produced by Jeff Barry.

The Archies, a cartoon TV series featuring the adventures of comic book teenager Archie and his friends, was an ideal project for musical supervisor Don Kirshner. He'd been responsible for the early Monkees shows (see no. 228) and had found real-life musicians difficult to manipulate. Two dimensional characters proved far less troublesome. Session singers Ron Dante and Toni Wine were hired to be the singing voices of the Archies and when the fictional group sang *Sugar Sugar* in their series it rocketed to number one in both the US and UK. The Archies had other hits in America but not in Britain.

Ron Dante achieved the rare chart honour of appearing in the same Top 10 with two different groups, the Archies and the Cuff-Links, whose single *Tracy* peaked at number 4. Dante's talents also stretched to production, and in partnership with Barry Manilow he produced *Mandy,* Manilow's first US chart-topper and a UK number 5 hit in 1975. Canadian Andy Kim, who co-wrote *Sugar Sugar,* also returned to the top of the US charts when his self-penned *Rock Me Gently* went all the way in 1974. Kim just missed out in Britain. The single stalled at number 2.

Only 10 discs have enjoyed a longer run of consecutive weeks at number one than *Sugar Sugar.* The Archies' eight week stay at the top is the longest of any one-hit wonder to date.

280

TWO LITTLE BOYS

ROLF HARRIS

20 December 1969, for six weeks

●●●●●●

Columbia DB 8630

Written by Theodore F Morse and Edward Madden. Produced by Martin Clarke.

Rolf Harris' recording of the 1903 song about the two boys Joe and Jack, who share horses at all possible moments in their lives, from nursery to battlefield, was a perfect Christmas number one. Although music has never been his only interest, nor even the principal reason for his continuing success today, Rolf Harris has always been good at putting unusual songs across.

His first hit, which also reached number 3 in the American charts, was *Tie Me Kangaroo Down, Sport,* a piece of Aussie nonsense to rank with Slim Dusty's *A Pub With No Beer. Sun Arise,* a number 3 hit in Britain in 1962, was an aboriginal chant made very commercial. *Two Little Boys* was his only major hit that did not have an Australian background.

After his chart-topper, Rolf Harris seems to have forsaken the charts (apart from joining Gerry Marsden and company as part of the Crowd, see no.551), making him one of only ten acts who have failed to follow up a number one by the end of 1987. His many other activities, his work in TV and cabaret, his painting and writing, leave him little time to do so.

281

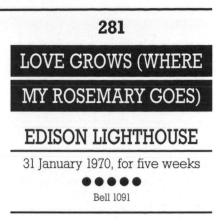

LOVE GROWS (WHERE MY ROSEMARY GOES)

EDISON LIGHTHOUSE

31 January 1970, for five weeks

●●●●●

Bell 1091

Written by Barry Mason and Tony Macaulay. Produced by Tony Macaulay.

In 1970 if you wanted a hit record you got Tony Burrows to sing lead. The king of the session singers, Burrows sang lead with the hastily assembled group Edison Lighthouse as well as on the Pipkins' Top 10 hit of the spring *Gimme Dat Ding* and various other singles. *Love Grows* raced to the number one position in its second week on the chart, which was at the time the quickest rise by an act new to the charts. Seeing that Edison Lighthouse only existed in the studio, it was a tribute to the song itself and to the usual faultless Tony Macaulay production that it climbed so quickly. It was in brief, a perfect light pop song, and it sold accordingly.

A group of four anonymous-looking people, none of them Tony Burrows, was put together and given the name Edison Lighthouse to cash in on the success of *Love Grows.* It didn't work because the voice was wrong. One brief week at number 10 with a song called *It's Up To You Petula* at the beginning of 1971 is all that stands between Edison Lighthouse and the paradoxical immortality of being a one-hit wonder.

282

WAND'RIN' STAR

LEE MARVIN

7 March 1970, for three weeks

●●●

Paramount PARA 3004

Written by Alan Jay Lerner and Frederick Loewe. Produced by Tom Mack.

Lerner and Loewe set out to write hit musicals, not hit singles, yet they managed two number ones. The first came in 1958 via Vic Damone (see no. 72). The second was from the soundtrack of *Paint Your Wagon* as performed by Lee Marvin. It was common film practice for an actor who could act but couldn't sing to mime to the vocal track of a more talented singer. However Marvin's gruff drawl was perfect for the singing voice of the character that he played and the adage that 'it ain't what you do it's the way that you do it' was proved correct once more.

Marvin had often been cast as a tough guy, his most famous role at that time having been Frank Ballinger in the TV cop series *M Squad*. The B-side of *Wand'rin' Star* featured Marvin's co-star, Clint Eastwood, making a rare appearance on disc with *I Talk To The Trees*. This title was listed on the chart along with the A-side for two weeks but had been removed by the time the single reached the top so the star of *The Good The Bad And The Ugly* (see no. 261) was prevented from becoming a number one hit-maker. Undaunted, Eastwood continued his acting career and in 1986 became Mayor of Carmel, California.

Marvin died on 29 August 1987.

283

BRIDGE OVER TROUBLED WATER

SIMON AND GARFUNKEL

28 March 1970, for three weeks

●●●

CBS 4790

Written by Paul Simon. Produced by Paul Simon, Art Garfunkel and Roy Halee.

One song regularly voted into the Top 10 of Favourite Records Of All Time by readers of magazines and listeners to radio stations is Paul Simon's *Bridge Over Troubled Water.* Paul Simon (born 13 October 1942) and Arthur Garfunkel (born 5 November 1942) worked together since they were kids growing up together in New York, and they even had a pop hit in America, *Hey School-girl,* under the names of Tom & Jerry. It reached number 54 on the Billboard charts in 1957.

Their first US hit as Simon and Garfunkel was *Sounds Of Silence,* which topped the charts there. It was covered in Britain by the Bachelors after the original version failed to make any impression. Simon and Garfunkel's parade of British hits began with the follow up, *Homeward Bound.* Their soundtrack for the film *The Graduate* was a landmark in the use of rock in the movies, and their final studio album, *Bridge Over Troubled Water* was the biggest selling album in Britain in the '70s.

The title track, featuring Art Garfunkel's voice at its very best, gave them the biggest single hit of their careers. The inspiration for the song was a New York doo-wop gospel recording, *Oh Mary Don't You Weep,* performed by the Swan Silvertones. That song contained the lines, 'I'll be your bridge over deep water if you trust in me'.

After the LP, the pair went their separate ways, Art Garfunkel into films *(Catch 22, Carnal Knowledge)* and on to solo recording successes (see nos. 379 and 436). Paul Simon recorded a series of high quality solo albums, culminating in 1986 in the number one album *Graceland,* which featured one of his biggest selling solo singles *You Can Call Me Al.*

In 1981 the duo reunited briefly for a highly successful concert in New York's Central Park in front of an estimated 500,000 people and later made key European appearances, but they did not get back together on a permanent basis.

284

ALL KINDS OF EVERYTHING

DANA

18 April 1970, for two weeks

●●

Rex R 11054

Written by Denny Lindsay and Jackie Smith. Produced by Ray Horricks.

All Kinds of Everything was the second Eurovision Song Contest winner to top the UK charts (see no. 232) and was the first by a foreign entrant do to so. Before Dana's success on behalf of Ireland the highest position that any foreign Eurovision song had achieved was number 17 when Italy's Gigliola Cinquetti struck lucky with *Non Ho L'Eta Per Amarti* in 1964.

Dana (born Rosemary Brown, Belfast, Northern Ireland, 30 August 1951) was still at school when she was chosen to represent the Irish Republic in the 1970 contest held in Amsterdam. She charmed the judges with *All Kinds Of Everything,* a pretty 'list' song about the objects and emotions which reminded her of a loved one. The UK entry that year, *Knock Knock Who's There* by Mary Hopkin (see no. 259), was beaten into second place whereas the year before Lulu's *Boom Bang A Bang* had tied for victory with the Spanish, Dutch and French entries.

Dana followed up with another Top 20 hit, *Who Put The Lights Out?,* after which four years of silence ensued. She then signed with Dick Leahy's GTO label, leading to further hits such as *Fairy Tale* in 1976. In the decade that has passed since then she has continued to record, scoring the odd minor hit, but her career now consists mainly of pantomime appearances and guest spots on television shows which have helped to keep her in the public eye.

285

SPIRIT IN THE SKY

NORMAN GREENBAUM

2 May 1970, for two weeks

●●

Reprise RS 20885

Written by Norman Greenbaum. Produced by Eric Jacobson.

A song by an unknown New England Jew praising Jesus and telling the world he was 'gonna recommend you to the Spirit In The Sky' was one of the most unlikely number ones of all time.

Norman Greenbaum (born in Malden, Massachusetts on 20 November 1942) moved to LA in 1966 and put together a good time jug band, one step beyond Lovin' Spoonful, called Dr. West's Medicine Show and Junk

Band, which astonished America with the most unlikely hit of 1966, *The Eggplant That Ate Chicago*, which peaked at number 52. The group split up in 1967, but three years later Greenbaum came up with a solo album, *Spirit In The Sky,* whose title track, with its reverberating fuzz guitar riff, stormed to number 3 in America, and all the way to the top in Britain. The record was, accidentally, the start of the 'God Rock' boom, which included shows like *Godspell* and *Jesus Christ Superstar* as well as singles like *Put Your Hand In The Hand* and *Amazing Grace* (see no. 312). *Jesus Christ Superstar* even featured the guitar effect on some tracks, consciously borrowed from *Spirit In The Sky.*

Norman Greenbaum's second album was coincidentally given the same title as the song that knocked him off the top in Britain – *Back Home.* His first follow-up single *Canned Ham* also seemed an unusual subject for someone of his religious background. Greenbaum proved to be a one-hit wonder, but the song did not. Dr & the Medics (see no. 571) revived the song and took it back to number one in the summer of 1986.

286

BACK HOME

THE ENGLAND WORLD CUP SQUAD

16 May 1970, for three weeks

● ● ●

Pye 7N 17920

Written by Bill Martin and Phil Coulter. Produced by Bill Martin and Phil Coulter.

Back Home was the song with which England's finest proved that having a number one single was easier than defending a two goal lead against West Germany. In their delicate illustration of the art of voice control on those awkward high notes, Bobby Moore and the lads showed themselves marginally defter with a 4/4 arrangement than a 4-4-2, even if the former was engineered by two Scotsmen in Martin and Coulter. In Mexico the 1970 squad was plagued by an unhappy list of misfortunes including the Ramsey substitutions against West Germany, Moore and a missing

bracelet, stomach troubles, and Peter Bonetti, and were ultimately unable to repeat the success of the 1966 team who lifted the Jules Rimet trophy with the aid of a Russian linesman and Geoff Hurst.

After many flops the group reformed for the 1982 finals in Spain, this time sporting entirely new personnel, led by the permed (and ultimately unfit) generalissimo himself, Kevin Keegan (he later made an extremely ill-advised bid for solo glory but was mercifully brought down outside the Top 40). Keegan, supported by the likes of Paul Mariner (who borrowed Rod Stewart's hairstyle for the occasion), Mick Mills and Peter Shilton took *This Time (We'll Get It Right)* up to the number 2 spot where they stalled, as they did on the pitch, from a lack of fire power when it counted. Their 1986 comeback single *We've Got The Whole World At Our Feet* raised serious doubts about the act's long-term musical future, as it peaked at a position that painfully reminded fans of the truly great days – 66.

287

YELLOW RIVER

CHRISTIE

6 June 1970, for one week

●

CBS 4911

Written by Jeff Christie. Produced by Mike Smith.

Yellow River was written for the Tremeloes who turned it down, so Jeff Christie decided that the only way he could get the song recorded was to do it himself. He put together a three-piece group consisting of himself, Mike Blakely, a brother of a Trem, and Chris Elms and managed to persuade Mike Smith, the Tremeloes' producer (see no. 233), to record them. This was a good move as Smith had already produced five number ones, including the only four UK-produced CBS number ones to date (nos 233, 242, 243 and 263). The success of *Yellow River* meant that from the middle of 1967 until the beginning of 1972, almost five years, Mike Smith was the only British producer to come up with a number one for CBS, and he did it five times.

Perhaps it is not surprising that a group put together so hurriedly to record rather than

Like many hits of the late '60s and early '70s, In The Summertime *by* **Mungo Jerry** *has recently been adapted for a commercial.*

to perform did not last long. The follow-up to *Yellow River* was *San Bernadino,* a song very similar to its chart-topping predecessor. It reached number 7. But that was the end of the story, apart from one week at number 47 over a year later with a song called *Iron Horse.* All the same, it might have given Christie some satisfaction that this last week on the charts was some eight months after the last Tremeloes hit had dropped off the chart. They should never have turned down *Yellow River.*

288

IN THE SUMMERTIME

MUNGO JERRY

13 June 1970, for seven weeks

● ● ● ● ● ● ●

Dawn DNX 2502

Written by Ray Dorset. Produced by Barry Murray.

Mungo Jerry were Colin Earl on piano, Paul King on banjo and jugg, Mike Cole on bass and leader Ray Dorset supplying vocals and guitar. As there was no drummer he was also the group 'stomper'.

Dorset had been doing live shows since the age of 14 and his band The Good Earth were a popular live attraction, able to do shows anywhere in the UK at short notice with a set that ranged from rock-a-billy to blues and skiffle. Dorset learnt his songwriting skills when the band backed Jackie Edwards, the man who supplied Spencer Davis with their two number ones. In 1969 he wrote *In The Summertime,* coming up with the riff one night on his guitar and producing the words the following day at work.

Early in 1970 the group went into the Pye recording studios and cut several songs with Barry Murray, one of their early managers. Both he and the record company thought that *Summertime* was a hit and it was released just as the group, still called The Good Earth, stole the show at June's Hollywood Festival in Newcastle, playing on a bill that included Traffic, Black Sabbath, Free and the Grateful Dead. Their Saturday performance went down so well that they were quickly added to the Sunday line-up.

After the festival, with the acetate of the single already pressed, the band held a ballot and changed their name to Mungo Jerry, one of the cats in the T.S. Eliot verses. Widespread radio exposure plus news of their Hollywood performance helped the song debut at 13. It quickly rose to the top spot and Dorset, who had a job as a laboratory researcher, had to ask for time off work to record *Top Of The Pops.* The song became the best-selling single in the UK that year and it topped the charts in 26 countries, enabling Dorset to give up his job and concentrate on his passion for music.

Elvis' penultimate UK number one (his 16th) took place five years after his previous chart-topper, *Crying In The Chapel* (see no. 197). A lot had happened in those five years. Elvis' career had slipped to its lowest point (1967) with the quality of his output on both wax and celluloid mediocre at best. Then in 1968 he began a major comeback that was to continue until his death in 1977. He recorded songs that were not featured in abysmal films, and more important, gave up making the abysmal films. He starred in his own excellent TV spectacular and returned to live concerts in Las Vegas in 1969.

In June 1969 *In The Ghetto* made number 2 in Britain – his first to get higher than number 13 for three years. In November he was very unlucky to miss number one with *Suspicious Minds,* one of the best singles of his entire career, although this track did bring him back to the US top spot for the first time since *Good Luck Charm* in 1962.

The Wonder Of You was the single that did the trick for him in Britain and it did so in style, staying at the top for no less than six weeks. It was recorded live at the International Hotel, Las Vegas, as part of four days of recording of Presley concerts there from 16-19 February 1970. The Joe Guercio Orchestra, the Sweet Inspirations (a black girl vocal group), The Imperials Quartet (a white vocal group) and Millie Kirkham (vocals) were all with Elvis during these shows and key rhythm section players were James Burton (guitar), Glen D. Hardin (piano), Jerry Scheff (bass) and Ronnie Tutt (drums). *The Wonder Of You* was written by Baker Knight and was originally a hit in 1959 and again in 1964 for Ray Peterson in the US, and for Ronnie Hilton and Peterson in the UK in 1959. On Elvis' version Glen D. Hardin (a former Cricket) is credited with the arrangement of the track.

The Miracles were the first group to be signed to Berry Gordy Jr's Tammie Records in 1958, yet they had to wait over a decade to score their first number one in both the UK and USA.

William 'Smokey' Robinson (born Detroit, Michigan, 19 February 1940) had been singing with high-school group the Matadors for three years before meeting Gordy, then an independent producer. The group, which at one time contained Robinson's wife, Claudette, changed name in 1958 and at the time of *Tears Of A Clown* consisted of tenor Bobby Rogers, baritone Ronnie White and bass Warren 'Pete' Moore with Smokey taking lead vocals.

By 1970 Robinson, an exceptional songwriter and producer, had become Vice President of Tamla Motown. In fact he was set to quit singing to concentrate on his other work when UK Motown executive John Marshall, having already revitalized a 1965 Miracles recording, *Tracks Of My Tears,* pulled this song from their 1967 *Make It Happen* album with even greater success, pushing it to number one within six weeks and doing the same in the USA two months later.

Robinson eventually left the group in 1972, his replacement being Billy Griffin. *Tears Of A Clown* provided co-writer Stevie Wonder with his first number one credit of any kind, his *Yester-Me, Yester-You, Yesterday* having peaked at number 2 nine months before. Both Wonder and Robinson would see their names credited as the writers of number one songs again, but not until the 1980s (see nos. 480 and 538). Wonder had imagined a fairground calliope in composing *The Tears Of A Clown's* famous introduction; Robinson thought of the heartbroken clown Pagliacci when penning the lyrics.

289

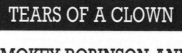

THE WONDER OF YOU

ELVIS PRESLEY

1 August 1970, for six weeks

●●●●●●

RCA 1974

Written by Baker Knight. Produced by Elvis Presley and Felton Jarvis, arranged by Glen D. Hardin.

290

TEARS OF A CLOWN

SMOKEY ROBINSON AND THE MIRACLES

12 September 1970, for one week

●

Tamla Motown TMG 745

Written by Henry Cosby, William Robinson and Stevie Wonder. Produced by Henry Cosby and William Robinson.

291

BAND OF GOLD

FREDA PAYNE

19 September 1970, for six weeks

●●●●●●

Invictus INV 502

Written by Ron Dunbar and Edith Wayne. Produced by Brian Holland, Lamont Dozier, and Eddie Holland.

Freda Payne's only number one, indeed only Top 30 single, was put out on the label formed by the record's famous ex-Motown producers Holland-Dozier-Holland. The label had several successes, notably *Band Of Gold* and The Chairman Of The Board's *Give Me Just A Little More Time,* but was unable to keep on producing the necessary goods through the 1970s and folded. While still with Invictus, Payne achieved a number 33 with *Deeper And Deeper.* The next year *Cherish What Is Dear To You* crept up to number 46, and was to prove to be the last of Payne's appearances on the British singles chart. In America she had one of the major protest hits of the Vietnamese war, *Bring The Boys Home.* By the mid-'70s she had returned to the stage, where she had originally started her career.

Band Of Gold had a comparatively unusual lyric concerning the failure of a couple to consummate their marriage on their wedding night, and the ultimate failure of the marriage itself. The song was covered by Bonnie Tyler in 1986 with a thumping Hi-NRG interpretation by Jim Steinman; it failed to dent the charts. Belinda Carlisle's version also flopped.

292

WOODSTOCK

MATTHEWS' SOUTHERN COMFORT

31 October 1970, for three weeks

Uni UNS 526

Written by Joni Mitchell. Produced by Ian Matthews.

Woodstock is the story in song of the Woodstock Music Festival, which ran for three days from 15 August 1969 on a farm belonging to Max Yasgur near Woodstock in upper New York State. The festival attracted about 400,000 fans, who came to see acts such as Jimi Hendrix, the Who, Joe Cocker, Jefferson Airplane, Santana, Country Joe and The Fish and the newly formed Crosby, Stills and Nash. At the time Joni Mitchell was close to this 'supergroup' trio and was originally scheduled to be at Woodstock with them. However, other commitments kept her away from the show, and she had to

be content with watching news reports of it on television in her hotel room in New York City. Then she wrote the song.

Ian Matthews left the folk rock band Fairport Convention in 1969. His first solo album, released at the beginning of 1970, was called *Matthews' Southern Comfort.* His band took the name of the album, and on this single the line-up was Ian Matthews on vocals, Gordon Huntley, Ramon Duffy, Andy Leigh, Carl Barnwell and Mark Griffiths. It was to be their only hit, making them at the time the 15th member of that exclusive one-hit fraternity and the fourth act to qualify during 1970, a year which in retrospect can be seen to have lacked any musical direction at all.

In 1971 Matthews dissolved his band to go solo and without setting the world on fire with his music has remained a respected performer on both sides of the Atlantic. He had one Top 20 hit in the States as a solo artist – *Shake It* in 1978/79. Few people will remember that *Woodstock* was at number one when Charles de Gaulle died on 9 November 1970 at a place which has been

Voodoo Chile *by* **Jimi Hendrix***, which had nothing to do with black magic in South America, originally appeared on* Electric Ladyland.

less often celebrated in song than Woodstock, Colombey-les-deux-Eglises.

293

VOODOO CHILE

JIMI HENDRIX

21 November 1970, for one week

●

Track 2095 001

Written by Jimi Hendrix. Produced by Jimi Hendrix.

Like Otis Redding, Jim Reeves and Laurel and Hardy, Jimi Hendrix had his biggest

British singles chart hit posthumously. James Marshall Hendrix was born in Seattle, Washington on 27 November 1942 (the sleeve notes of his debut album erroneously give his year of birth as 1947), and apart from a brief two year residence in the US paratroopers, which ended for medical reasons in 1963, he went immediately into music. He played tours of the South, backing acts like B.B. King, Little Richard, Jackie Wilson, the Isley Brothers and Wilson Pickett. In the mid-'60s Hendrix, then operating under the name Jimmy James, met Chas Chandler at the Cafe Wha in Greenwich Village. Chandler was impressed and took the young guitar virtuoso to England where they quickly formed The Experience, who backed Hendrix during his breakthrough in Britain.

Although not primarily a singles artist, Hendrix had four Top 10 singles in 1967 and 1968. He met an untimely death on 18 September 1970 in the London apartment of Monika Danneman, where he choked on his own barbiturate-induced vomit. He was 27.

Time has not erased his reputation as one of the most skilled and original performers of the electric guitar, whose scintillating live act earned him the soubriquet 'The Black Elvis'.

294

I HEAR YOU KNOCKIN'

DAVE EDMUNDS

28 November 1970, for six weeks

●●●●●●

MAM 1

Written by Dave Bartholomew and Pearl King. Produced by Dave Edmunds.

Dave Edmunds (born 15 April 1944) first tasted chart success as one-third of the Cardiff-based trio, Love Sculpture. Their version of Khachaturyan's *Sabre Dance*, featuring some breakneck guitar work by Edmunds, made the Top 10 in 1968. The band's short career established Edmunds as one of the country's top musicians.

Between 1968-70 Edmunds spent a great deal of time in his own Rockfield studios in South Wales, learning and perfecting his production skills. He taught himself how to recreate the sounds of his heroes, idols such as the Everly Brothers, Phil Spector and the

Clive Dunn*'s fictitious granddaughters all tell him he's 'lovely'.*

Beach Boys. One of the first productions at the studio was his own version of the Smiley Lewis 1955 soul hit *I Hear You Knockin'*, written by Fats Domino's co-writer Dave Bartholomew and Pearl King. When released the song wasted no time at all moving to the top. It smashed in at 16, then pole-vaulted to number one. Two years later Edmunds returned to the Top 10 with the Spector-sounding *Baby I Love You* and *Born To Be With You*.

Dave's occasional collaborations with Nick Lowe were formalized in 1980 when they formed Rockpile with Billy Bremner and Terry Williams. This line-up had played on most of Lowe's and Edmunds' solo work for some time and were widely acclaimed as a fine live band. Unfortunately the band split after one LP, a sad loss to all rock fans.

Since then Edmunds has become one of the world's leading producers, helping break the Stray Cats and working with the Fabulous Thunderbirds, the Everlys, Chet Atkins, Carl Perkins and others. In 1986 he returned to number one as producer for Shakin' Stevens' *Merry Christmas Everyone*.

295

GRANDAD

CLIVE DUNN

9 January 1971, for three weeks

●●●

Columbia DB 8726

Written by Herbie Flowers and Kenny Pickett. Produced by John Cameron and Clive Dunn.

Clive Dunn, born in 1919, was a good deal younger than Louis Armstrong (see no. 249) when he achieved his number one but his popular image of a bumbling senior citizen may have fooled many into thinking he really was a grandad.

Dunn became known to TV viewers in the early '60s through appearances in the situation comedy *Bootsie and Snudge.* In 1965 he landed the role of Lance-Corporal Jones in *Dad's Army,* the long-running BBC sitcom set in wartime. For ten years he played the butcher and eager member of the Home Guard whose catch phrase, 'They don't like it up 'em', became known to millions. Dunn certainly knew about the reality of warfare as he had served in the 4th Hussars during the Second World War and was unfortunate enough to be captured in Greece. *Grandad* was written for him by Kenny Pickett and guitarist Herbie Flowers, at that time a member of Blue Mink and a future member of Sky. Coming at the height of *Dad's Army's* popularity, the song used Dunn's image to perfection and climbed to the top after six weeks.

When *Dad's Army* ended the BBC gave Dunn his own children's series, also called *Grandad,* and in 1978 he was awarded an OBE for his services to TV and the theatre. Clive Dunn the pop star remains a one-hit wonder.

296

MY SWEET LORD

GEORGE HARRISON

30 January 1971, for five weeks

●●●●●

Apple R 5884

Written by George Harrison. Produced by George Harrison and Phil Spector.

George Harrison's first solo effort after the break-up of the Beatles was a triple album, *All Things Must Pass.* The first single from the album was *My Sweet Lord,* which took Harrison to number one in only his second week on the chart as a solo performer. The album was undoubtedly Harrison's masterpiece, although he was certainly helped by the musicians on the album who included Ringo Starr, Klaus Voorman (who also played on John Lennon's *Imagine* and Nilsson's *Without You*), Billy Preston, Eric Clapton, Dave Mason, Gary Brooker, Bobby Keyes and Carl Radle among others.

However, the vast success of *My Sweet Lord* was soured by the fact that the estate representing the deceased writer of the Chiffons' hit *He's So Fine* successfully sued George Harrison for breach of copyright, and what is more, Bill Martin and Phil Coulter rightfully demanded and got royalties for the track *It's Johnny's Birthday* on the *Apple Jam* third LP of the three record set, which was to the tune of Cliff Richard's 1968 chart-topper *Congratulations.* A track on a later Harrison album *This Song,* wryly commented on the dangers of breach of another writer's copyright.

In 1987 George made a strong chart comeback. Teamed with ELO's Jeff Lynne his single *Got My Mind Set On You* was kept at number 2 for four weeks by T'Pau (see no. 600). During the '80s he became a major independent film producer with his company, Handmade Films, responsible for many major features including Monty Python and Madonna vehicles.

It was recorded at Pye, originally in a 16 track studio, but the band weren't happy with the sound and they re-recorded it at the 8 track studio where they had cut *Summertime.* When it rose to number one they became one of the few acts whose first two releases both topped the charts. At the time only Gerry and the Pacemakers had achieved this feat. Since then John Travolta and Olivia Newton-John, Frankie Goes to Hollywood and George Michael have equalled it. The band's third single, *Lady Rose,* climbed to number 5 only.

After an Australian tour, arguments over whether or not they should hire a drummer led to King and Earl leaving. Dorset retained the name Mungo Jerry and in 1973 scored with *Alright Alright Alright,* the group's fourth and final Top 10 entry. Since the hits stopped in April 1974, Dorset has remained involved in the industry. He has continued to sell in Europe and had a big smash with *It's A Secret,* a number one in South Africa.

In 1980 Dorset provided Kelly Marie with her breakthrough UK hit (see no. 400). Recently he wrote the theme tune to the TV series *Prospects,* and also *Wizbit,* the Paul Daniels show. His diverse songwriting talents have also spread into the field of sport: he has written theme songs used by the Wigan football and rugby teams when they run on to the pitch.

and using the name Toby Tyler he sang in the London folk clubs. In late 1965 he was signed to Decca under the name Marc Bolan, and after two flop singles in seven months he was dropped. In 1967 he joined John's Children, only staying for three months. Bolan left in the summer, initially to form a five-piece rock 'n' roll outfit, but the funds wouldn't stretch that far so he ended up with Tyrannosaurus Rex, an acoustic duo with percussionist Steve Peregrine-Took. This line-up became a fashionable act, often appearing at London's hippie hang-out, the Middle Earth. For the first time Bolan made inroads into the chart, *Deborah* and *One Inch Rock* making the Top 40 and the LP *Unicorn* just falling short of the Top 10. Part of this success was due to Radio One's John Peel, a staunch supporter of the band. After *Unicorn* Took left and was replaced by Mickey Finn.

By 1970 Tony Visconti had become their producer. After the *Beard Of Stars* LP Bolan realised that his acoustic approach was probably limiting his audience. As he always intended to make trends and not follow them, he decided to return to an electric guitar. Under the shorter name of T Rex, and on the Regal Zonophone spin-off label Fly, the first single release was *Ride A White Swan.* It climbed the charts to 6, slipped out of the Top 10, then rose once more peaking at 2. With one fell swoop T Rex had achieved their long-expected breakthrough. The record company wisely released the follow-up while *Ride A White Swan* was still on its 20 week chart run. *Hot Love,* with its catchy sing-a-long chorus, not only made number one but stayed there for six weeks, becoming the fifth best-selling single of the year, creating mass interest in T Rex.

297

BABY JUMP

MUNGO JERRY

6 March 1971, for two weeks

●●

Dawn DNX 2505

Written by Ray Dorset. Produced by Barry Murray.

Mungo Jerry decided to wait until the massive international sales of *In The Summertime* had died down before releasing the follow-up, which explains the long gap between these two singles. *Baby Jump* had been written in 1968/9 and was a concert favourite under a different title. When the band agreed that this would be the follow-up Dorset re-wrote the lyrics and came up with the new title, *Baby Jump.*

298

HOT LOVE

T REX

20 March 1971, for six weeks

●●●●●●

Fly BUG 6

Written by Marc Bolan. Produced by Tony Visconti.

Marc Bolan was born in Hackney, London on 30 September 1947, and he grew up around Soho where his mother ran a market stall. He left school in his early teens and did various casual jobs including work as a model. His first taste of fame was when his photo appeared in *Town* magazine as an example of the 'mod look'.

One of his early influences was Donovan,

299

DOUBLE BARREL

DAVE AND ANSIL COLLINS

1 May 1971, for two weeks

●●

Technique TE 901

Written by Winston Riley. Produced by Winston Riley.

The Jamaican duo of Dave and Ansil Collins

came from nowhere in the spring of 1971 to hit with only the second West Indian reggae record to top the British charts, two years after the first – Desmond Dekker's *Israelites* (see no. 269). There was considerable confusion about who they were and how to spell Ansil (Ansel? Ansell? Ansill?), but their anonymity made no difference to the record's success. Apart from its British sales, *Double Barrel* also climbed to number 22 in the American charts, to become one of the first reggae hits over there.

The early success of reggae in Britain in the first years of the 1970s was helped by the popularity of the music among a growing section of white youth – the skinheads. But of course the music in its basic form is primarily appreciated by its creators, the Jamaican people. The Jamaican population in Britain is not large enough to ensure national chart success for most reggae hits, and the few that do break into other sections of the market tend to be light on some of the rougher and less comprehensible aspects of the music. This did not appear to be the case with the Collins hit.

Here Hank Medress of the Tokens *(The Lion Sleeps Tonight)* and Dave Appell were working as producers for Bell Records. They had a demo of a song written by Irwin Levine and Toni Wine called *Candida,* performed by a group called Dawn. The record company liked the song but not the lead vocals. The producers persuaded Orlando to sing lead, which he did but merely as a favour, not expecting any long commitment. The tape was then sent to California where Vincent and Hopkins added their background vocals.

When released Bell had a massive international hit even they could not have expected. The follow-up single, another Irwin Levine tune, this time in collaboration with L. Russell Brown, was recorded in the same informal manner but once it had topped the charts in both America and the UK Bell realized the trio would have to become a 'real' group, if only to stop the endless succession of fake Dawns springing up on either side of the Atlantic. The trio, who still had not met when *Knock Three Times* was recorded, agreed, and so Dawn was properly born.

where the rougher-edged versions of the same song by composer Lally Scott and by Mac and Katie Kissoon failed to attract much attention.

It was released in the UK at the end of May 1971, and within three weeks was at number one, where it stayed for five weeks. After this hit Britain took them a little more seriously, and further hits followed. The follow-up *Tweedle Dee Tweedle Dum* reached number 2. Had it made number one it would have joined *Chirpy Chirpy Cheep Cheep* as one of the very few songs with nonsense titles to reach number one. As it is *Chirpy Chirpy Cheep Cheep* was the fourth and last nonsense title to get to the top, after *Do Wah Diddy Diddy, Mony Mony* and *Ob-la-di Ob-la-da.* Their third Top 10 hit had yet another nonsense title, *Soley Soley,* and it was not until their fourth chart hit *Sacramento* that they ventured into a recognized language. But by then the hits were coming to an end.

300

KNOCK THREE TIMES

DAWN

15 May 1971, for five weeks

●●●●●

Bell 1146

Written by Irwin Levine and L. Russell Brown. Produced by Dave Appell and the Tokens.

Dawn were Tony Orlando (born Michael Anthony Orlando Cassavitis, 3 April 1944) and backing singers Joyce Vincent (born 14 December 1946) and Thelma Hopkins (born 28 October 1948).

Orlando was only 17 when his song *Bless You* made the Top 10 in late 1961. The song was his second hit single in America, the first, the Goffin/King composition *Halfway To Paradise,* having been covered for the UK market by Billy Fury. One more minor hit followed but by 1963 Orlando quit his recording career to work for music publishers Robins, Feist and Miller. Early 1970 found him working for a subsidiary of Columbia Records, April Blackwood.

301

CHIRPY CHIRPY CHEEP CHEEP

MIDDLE OF THE ROAD

19 June 1971, for five weeks

●●●●●

RCA 2047

Written by Lally Scott. Produced by Giacomo Tosti and Ignacio Greco.

Middle of the Road were very unlikely hit makers. They were a group of four Scots, Ken Andrew, Eric and Ian Lewis and Sally Carr, who performed with reasonable success in Europe but who were completely unknown in Britain. They had originally concentrated on Latin-American music and were for a time known as Los Caracas, but it was as Middle of the Road that they recorded a song they had heard in Italy. The record was released in Europe and became a big hit in Spain and Belgium,

302

GET IT ON

T REX

24 July 1971, for four weeks

●●●●

Fly BUG 10

Written by Marc Bolan. Produced by Tony Visconti.

The line-up for this song had been together as T Rex since December 1970. Members were Bolan and Mickey Finn (who was described as adding 'vocal percussion' to this track) with Steve Collins and Bill Legend, who both joined the group following a *Melody Maker* ad and auditions.

Get It On was an early taster for the LP *Electric Warrior.* Its rapid ascent to the top of the charts confirmed Bolan's status as the UK's most popular star. In December T Rex claimed two of the year's Top 10 best-selling singles; *Get It On* was at 10, *Hot Love* five places higher. In December the band claimed its first LP chart-topper when *Electric Warrior* forced *Led Zeppelin IV* to move aside and settled in for a lengthy six week run.

Get It On was Bolan's only Stateside hit, but the song reached the Top 10 twice. The T Rex original halted at 10; in 1985 the Power Station, featuring Robert Palmer as lead vocalist, took it to a new peak of 9.

During the song's four week supremacy George Harrison held the precursor to Live Aid – the concert for Bangladesh took place in Madison Square Garden on 1 August. The show's profits and the live triple album provided money for the relief of this desperate country.

303

I'M STILL WAITING

DIANA ROSS

21 August 1971, for four weeks

● ● ● ●

Tamla Motown TMG 781

Written by Deke Richards. Produced by Deke Richards and Hal Davis.

When Diana Ross and the Supremes parted company at the turn of the decade, Motown hoped it would have two star attractions

Middle of the Road *achieved three European million sellers in 1971.*

In Britain **Diana Ross** *has had two number ones solo and one with the Supremes. In America the respective totals are five and twelve, with an additional chart-topping duet with Lionel Richie.*

instead of one, but faced the prospect both might fade. Ross' debut disc, *Reach Out and Touch* was not a good start. Intended to entreat parents of drug addicts to be understanding to their children, it was too vague to inspire the mass audience and was only a minor hit. Diana's extended reading of Marvin Gaye and Tammi Terrell's 1967 classic *Ain't No Mountain High Enough* provided her with the smash she needed. But after the next hit, *Remember Me*, there was no obvious follow-up and nothing new awaiting release.

BBC Radio 1 breakfast show DJ and self-confessed Diana Ross freak Tony Blackburn told Tamla Motown he would make the album track *I'm Still Waiting* his Record of the Week, playing it every morning for five days, if the company would release it as a single. The label did, Blackburn did, and the result was Tamla Motown's biggest UK seller to date.

The record was not a major hit in the United States, and when Ross performed it in her British act by request, she was baffled though pleased by the standing ovations greeting it. She had unknowingly found a personal anthem.

304

HEY GIRL DON'T BOTHER ME

THE TAMS

18 September 1971, for three
weeks

●●●

Probe PRO 532

Written by Ray Whitley. Produced by Rick
Hall.

The Tams, five men from Atlanta, Georgia,
were already around 30 years old when
they recorded *Hey Girl Don't Bother Me.*
This gave them their fifth American hit, but
in the UK they had failed to make any
impact. In 1968, the Tams' seventh American
hit, *Be Young Be Foolish Be Happy* proved
to be their last Stateside chart outing, but
still nothing had hit the British charts. Then
in 1970, Stateside re-issued *Be Young Be
Foolish Be Happy* in the UK, and for no
obvious reason it reached number 32. Floyd
Ashton (born 15 August 1933), Horace Key
(born 13 April 1934), Charles Pope (born 7
August 1936), his brother Joseph Pope (born
6 November 1933) and Robert Smith (born 18
March 1936) were now stars in Britain too.

In 1971 *Hey Girl Don't Bother Me* was re-
issued on their Probe label, and it soared to
the very top. No one could have foreseen
that their harmless dance record *There
Ain't Nothing Like Shaggin'* would become a
1987 hit due to the idiomatic British use of the
word 'shag', and its resultant BBC ban.

305

MAGGIE MAY

ROD STEWART

9 October 1971, for five weeks

●●●●●

Mercury 6058 097

Written by Rod Stewart and Martin
Quittenton. Produced by Rod Stewart.

Professional Scotsman Rod Stewart was in
fact born in London on 10 January 1945 to
parents who owned a newsagents shop on
the Archway Road in Holloway, North
London. Stewart attended the same second-
ary school as Ray Davies of the Kinks. On
leaving he tried his hand at a few profess-
ions like fence-erecting and grave-dig-
ging. Stewart also had a successful trial at
Brentford FC but left after becoming dis-
illusioned with the wages and eventually
took the only option left – 'what can a poor
boy do but play for a rock and roll band'?
This Stewart did with a vengeance, going
through the ranks of several bands, most
notably the Jeff Beck Group and the Faces,
before pursuing solo glory.

Maggie May was originally put out as a
B-side to *Reason To Believe,* but airplay and
consumer reaction forced the BMRB to flip
the listings. It was taken from his third solo
album *Every Picture Tells A Story,* which
gave him the British acclaim his previous
two efforts had accorded him in the USA. At
one point Stewart occupied the number one
spot on both the singles and albums charts
on both sides of the Atlantic.

306

COZ I LUV YOU

SLADE

13 November 1971, for four weeks

●●●●

Polydor 2058 155

Written by Noddy Holder and Jim Lea.
Produced by Chas Chandler.

Slade members are Noddy Holder (born
Walsall, Staffordshire on 15 June 1950) on
lead vocals and guitar, Jimmy Lea (born
Wolverhampton, Staffs. on 14 June 1952) on
bass and piano, Dave Hill (born Castle
Fleet, Devon on 4 April 1952) on guitar and
Don Powell (born Bilston, Staffs. on 10 September 1950). The four came together in the
late 1960s and formed The 'N Betweens
(their penchant for the grammatical tom-
foolery already being apparent), a cover
group working with obvious club material
like Beatles and Motown numbers. After
changing their name to Ambrose Slade they
were spotted at Rasputin's Club in Bond
Street in February 1969 by Chas Chandler.

The former member of the Animals was
searching for something to follow Jimi Hendrix. Chandler became their manager and
producer and it was his ear for a brilliant
commercial production that was a vital
ingredient to their success.

Get Down And Get With It, an old Little
Richard song written by Bobby Marchan,
gave them their first chart action, rising to
number 16. It established the boot-stomping
routine that was to become one of their
trade-marks. Then Holder and Lea's *Coz I
Luv You* brazenly thundered to the top and
the '70s were blown wide open for Noddy
and the Boyz (sic).

307

ERNIE (THE FASTEST MILKMAN IN THE WEST)

BENNY HILL

11 December 1971, for four weeks

●●●●

Columbia DB 8833

Written by Benny Hill. Produced by Walter
Ridley.

Benny Hill was born Alfred Hawthorne Hill
in Southampton on 25 January 1925. After
leaving school he found work as a milkman,
so was well qualified to sing about the profession in later years.

After the war Hill built his reputation as a
troop comedian by touring Britain's variety
halls. He soon realized that his style of
comedy, a mixture of slapstick, eccentric
characters and suggestive songs, was well
suited to the medium of television. After
many guest appearances he was given his
own BBC TV series, *The Benny Hill Show.*
This switched to Thames Television in 1969,
the year in which he was named ITV Entertainer of the Year by the Variety Club of
Great Britain. It was likely that many had forgotten that he had had a sprinkling of hit
singles in the early '60s with titles like
Gather In the Mushrooms and *Transistor
Radio.* Now at the peak of his popularity a
new single was likely to do well but even so
Ernie, a comedy song full of bawdy innuen-

dos, surprised most people by getting to number one.

As the years progressed Hill began to ration his eagerly awaited TV appearances to just one or two special programmes every year and by the '80s he'd become a cult figure in America through reruns of his old shows. Benny Hill makes almost no live appearances these days but in March 1987 he was persuaded to perform in a live promotional showcase for Thames Television at the Lincoln Centre, New York.

308

I'D LIKE TO TEACH THE WORLD TO SING

THE NEW SEEKERS

8 January 1972, for four weeks

●●●●

Polydor 2058 184

Written by Roger Cook, Roger Greenaway, William Backer, and Billy Davis. Produced by David Mackay for Leon Henry Productions

The most successful advertising jingle in history began as *I'd Like To Buy The World A Coke*, was transmogrified into *I'd Like To Teach The World To Sing* and gave the original jingle artists, the Hillside Singers, a big hit in America. It also gave the New Seekers their biggest hit on both sides of the Atlantic.

Advertising jingles had succeeded before. Georgie Fame's *Get Away* (see no. 219) was based on an advertisement for petrol. Cliff Adams' *Lonely Man Theme* in 1960 was probably the first chart hit advertising theme tune. It was the background music for the Strand cigarette advertisement whose punch line 'You're Never Alone With A Strand' became a national catchphrase, so much so that the advertisement featured in Cliff Richard's first starring movie *The Young Ones*. The advertisement also turned off the customers in such vast numbers that the Strand cigarette disappeared before cigarette advertising on TV went the same way.

The New Seekers were formed on the break-up of the Seekers (see nos 188 and 206) by Seeker Keith Potger. They were Eve

Graham (born 13 April 1943), Lyn Paul (born 16 February 1949), Peter Doyle (born 28 July 1949), Marty Kristian (born 27 May 1947) and Paul Layton (born 4 August 1947). The girls had been in an unsuccessful group called The Nocturnes before Potger created the New Seekers. The men, an Australian, a German and a Briton, took very much a back seat to the girls, on whose charms the group sold records by the bucketful. *I'd Like To Teach The World To Sing* was their third hit, and to follow up the corny commerciality of a Coke jingle, only one option was possible – they sang 1972's Song For Europe, *Beg, Steal Or Borrow*.

309

TELEGRAM SAM

T REX

5 February 1972, for two weeks

●●

T Rex 101

Written by Marc Bolan. Produced by Tony Visconti

T Rex's third consecutive number one came after a label change from Fly to EMI, where for this single only they were on the T Rex label. During the switchover period Fly put out another track from the *Electric Warrior* album, *Jeepster*, as an unauthorized single. Despite no promotion at all by the band it went to number 2. After *Telegram Sam* moved to the top spot, Fly delved into the band's back catalogue for further material to release. This proved an excellent idea as *Debora/One Inch Rock*, by now four years old, made the Top 10 single charts. On the album lists they claimed two number ones. After Deep Purple lasted seven days, the hits LP *Bolan Boogie* put the group back on top, this time for three weeks.

Telegram Sam was the first single from *Slider*, EMI's album of new material that emerged in August. It contained the same line-up as *Electric Warrior*, but it wasn't as successful either artistically or commercially, perhaps because it was the third T Rex LP in five months.

Right: **Chicory Tip**, the first number one hitmakers named after a vegetable.

310

SON OF MY FATHER

CHICORY TIP

19 February 1972, for three weeks

●●●

CBS 7737

Written by Giorgio Moroder, Peter Bellotte and Michael Holm. Produced by Roger Easterby and Des Champ.

The first UK produced CBS number one not originated by Mike Smith was a record co-written by a man destined to become one of the world's most successful producers, Giorgio Moroder (see nos 409, 456 and 579). *Son Of My Father,* a Top 80 hit in the USA when recorded by Giorgio himself, was covered for the British market by a group of unknowns from Maidstone, Kent.

Chicory Tip vocalist Peter Hewson, guitarist Rick Foster and bassist Barry Mayger had been playing together for seven years. They were joined by drummer Brian Shearer 18 months before the success of *Son Of My Father.* The single is notable as the first chart topper to feature a synthesizer, an instrument which first came to public attention when a primitive model was featured on the Beatles' *Abbey Road* album. It was exploited by Moroder on hits he produced for Sparks, the Three Degrees, Donna

Summer, Blondie and others. The Moog synthesizer featured on this disc was played not by a member of Chicory Tip but by engineer and soon-to-be producer Chris Thomas (see no 449).

Son Of My Father sold a million but after two more Top 20 hits over the next 18 months Chicory Tip disappeared from the charts.

Nilsson *took a Badfinger song and made it better.*

311

WITHOUT YOU

NILSSON

11 March 1972, for five weeks

●●●●●

RCA 2165

Written by Pete Ham and Tom Evans. Produced by Richard Perry.

Harry Nilsson, known officially merely as Nilsson, was born in Brooklyn, New York City on 15 June 1941. He was in the late '60s and early '70s a respected and much covered singer-songwriter, but ironically neither of the two songs for which he is best known were written by him.

His first hit, both in America and the UK, was the theme song of the Dustin Hoffman-Jon Voigt movie *Midnight Cowboy*. The song was called *Everybody's Talking*, written by Fred Neil, and it stayed 15 weeks on the British charts without ever climbing higher than number 23.

Without You is track one on side two of Nilsson's best album *Nilsson Schmilsson*, recorded in London in June 1971. It was written by two members of the Apple group Badfinger who had played on George Harrison's *All Things Must Pass* album and had scored the first of their three Top 10 hits with the theme tune from the Peter Sellers-Ringo Starr film *The Magic Christian*. Also playing bass on *Without You* is Klaus Voorman, who designed the *Revolver* album cover and was spoken of as a possible replacement for Paul McCartney. It was not the Beatles connection that made the hit. Nilsson's *Without You* is quite simply one of the great pop records of the 1970s.

312

AMAZING GRACE

THE PIPES AND DRUMS AND MILITARY BAND OF THE ROYAL SCOTS DRAGOON GUARDS

15 April 1972, for five weeks

●●●●●

RCA 2191

Traditional. Produced by Peter Kerr.

The act with the longest name ever to reach number one did so with the first chart topper to feature the traditional instrument of Scotland, the Scottish bagpipe. The hymn, *Amazing Grace,* had become known to record buyers through Judy Collins' vocal version, which clocked up 67 weeks on the chart between December 1970 and January 1973 but only climbed as high as number 5.

The Royal Scots' instrumental version first appeared on the album *Farewell To The Greys.* The LP was a tribute to the Royal Scots Greys (2nd Dragoon) which on 2 July 1971 had amalgamated with the 35th Caribiniers (Prince of Wales Dragoon Guards) to form a new regiment. At the time of their success the band was stationed in West Germany and so was unaware that a track from its album was gaining tremendous radio listener reaction, beginning on BBC Radio Two. Public demand forced RCA to release the cut as a single and within three weeks it marched to the top of the chart.

Amazing Grace, in both its vocal and instrumental versions, was on the charts for 94 weeks, making it the second most popular chart melody next to *My Way.*

313

METAL GURU

T REX

20 May 1972, for four weeks

●●●●

EMI MARC 1

Written by Marc Bolan. Produced by Tony Visconti.

This was T Rex's fourth consecutive number one, discounting the two unofficial releases put out by the band's former record company Fly. As it was released on EMI instead of the T Rex label it gave the band the obscure record of having three successive number ones on three different labels, all within the space of ten months. Rod Stewart equalled this unlikely record in 1977, but it took him almost five years and his number ones were not with consecutive issues.

Bolan seemed secure as the UK's major star, but when he and producer Tony Visconti split in 1974 his success began to falter. In December that year Mickey Finn quit and despite new line-ups Bolan only entered the Top 20 two more times, once in 1975 and once the following year with *I Love To Boogie.*

1977 looked as though it was going to be his comeback year. He did a UK tour with the Damned as support and moved into television, hosting a six week television series with stars like David Bowie and newcomers like the Jam and the Stranglers. Bolan died on 16 September when the car in which he was travelling hit a tree. He was still only 29. Since then his records have continued to sell. Most of his output is under the safe and caring hands of John Bramley at Marc On Wax, who put out the Top 5 compilation LP *20th Century Boy* in 1985.

314

VINCENT

DON MCLEAN

17 June 1972, for two weeks

●●

United Artists UP 35359

Written by Don McLean. Produced by Ed
Freeman.

Don McLean (born 2 October 1945, New
Rochelle, New York) had taken to making
music when ill health precluded him from
outdoor activities. His boyhood idol had
been Buddy Holly (see nos 64 and 84) and
McLean's memories of hearing of his hero's
death in 1959 moved him to write *American
Pie,* a UK number 2 and a US chart-topper in
1972, and the song by which he will

probably be best remembered.

However it was the next track to be lifted
from his *American Pie* album that gave him
his first UK number one, although McLean
himself thought that *Vincent,* written about
the 19th century artist Van Gogh, drew too
detailed a picture and left little to the listener's imagination. Amsterdam's Van Gogh
museum disagreed and played the disc
daily.

In 1973 came the *Don Maclean* album, consisting of songs about the singer's reaction to
fame. The press and music business disliked the cynicism and the singer/song-
writer's popularity took a dip until 1980 (see
no. 460). In the meantime Perry Como had
recorded McLean's *And I Love Her So* and
made it a Top 10 hit in 1973. Don was also the
inspiration for Roberta Flack's US number
one, *Killing Me Softly With His Song.* Lori
Lieberman had seen McLean perform
American Pie at the Troubadour, Los
Angeles and asked Charles Fox and Norman Gimbel to write a song to fit her
feelings.

The longest chart-runner by **T Rex,** *Ride A
White Swan, was not one of their four number
ones.*

315

TAKE ME BACK 'OME

SLADE

1 July 1972, for one week

●

Polydor 2058 231

Written by Noddy Holder and Jim Lea.
Produced by Chas Chandler.

By the time *Take Me Back 'Ome* became the
second Slade single to reach the top within

Slade needed help to celebrate their three number ones in 1973.

City, Utah, 9 December 1957). Donny's first number one was an Anka song which the Canadian had taken to number 2 in the USA and 33 in the UK in 1960.

Donny was the youngest of the brothers who had been singing as the Osmonds since 1960, although Donny had to wait until he was six before he was allowed to join Alan, Wayne, Merrill and Jay on stage. Encouraged by parents Olive and George the boys performed at various Mormon functions, which led to a residency at Disneyland. Regular appearances on the Andy Williams and Jerry Lewis TV shows made the Osmonds household names by the end of the '60s. Yet it was not until 1971, having signed a recording contract with MGM, that they scored their first hit, *One Bad Apple,* featuring a lead vocal from Donny which sounded remarkably like Michael Jackson. A US number one, the single failed to register in the UK charts. Donny also scored three solo Top 10 hits in America during 1971, including the number one *Go Away Little Girl.* The Goffin-King song was the first composition in the rock era to be number one for two different artists, having earlier been a success for Steve Lawrence. The wave of Osmondmania took 12 months to cross the Atlantic but when it did it swept *Puppy Love* a 1960 Paul Anka hit, all the way to the top.

317

SCHOOL'S OUT

ALICE COOPER

12 August 1972, for three weeks

Warner Brothers K 16188

Written by Alice Cooper and Michael Bruce. Produced by Bob Ezrin.

Vincent Furnier, the minister's son from Detroit, became Alice Cooper, the group took his name and the world was outraged. Members of Parliament teamed up with ordinary mothers to prevent Alice Cooper from touring Britain and the record shot to the top, the free publicity tailor-made for a number one hit.

Furnier, born on Christmas Day 1945, formed a group in 1965 called the Earwigs, who proved to be a rather less commercial

eight months (the two number ones had been separated by a number 4 called *Look Wot You Dun*) the Wolverhampton boys' style was firmly established. In an attempt to grab a slice of the adolescent market manager Chas Chandler had first abbreviated the group's name to Slade and then emphasized their skinhead bovver boy image with closely cropped hair, Doc Martens and Ben Shermans.

The crunching rock Slade played was in good company at the top of the singles chart in 1973 with other ear-bashers like Suzi Quatro, Sweet, Gary Glitter and Wizzard all making it to the number one spot. Of all these groups it was Slade who held complete dominance until the end of 1974. With Noddy Holder's distinctive rasping vocals and the calculating lack of subtlety in their arrangements and song titles, they bulldozed their way to fourth place in the league table of acts with consecutive Top 5 releases, behind such luminaries as the Beatles (22), Presley (20), Cliff Richard (19) but ahead of people like the Rolling Stones (10).

316

PUPPY LOVE

DONNY OSMOND

8 July 1972, for five weeks

● ● ● ● ●

MGM 2006 104

Written by Paul Anka. Produced by Mike Curb and Ray Ruff.

Paul Anka had dropped to number 15 after his nine week run at number one with *Diana* (see no. 63) when Olive Osmond gave birth to her seventh son, Donald (born Salt Lake bunch of insects than the Crickets or the Beatles. It is alleged that they became Alice Cooper after a session with a Ouija board when a spirit named Alice Cooper told them that she was Vincent Furnier. They were discovered by Frank Zappa in Los Angeles at a Lenny Bruce Memorial gig when the entire audience, except Zappa and Shep Gordon, who became the group's manager, walked out. With a pedigree like that how could they fail? By killing chickens on stage they established a reputation that began to draw the crowds, and the quality of the music improved to a point where only a small percentage of the audience walked out. By this time they had a recording contract, and life began to look good for Alice Cooper – Vincent Furnier, Glen Buxton, Dennis Dunaway, Michael Bruce and Neal Smith. But it didn't last. The hype was too total and even Alice himself began to hate his image; he took up golf and made half-hearted attempts to become adorable. By 1982 he was back to touring in the old unpleasant style in pursuit of past glories but he had been rumbled by then – he really is a nice guy who should leave animal destruction to Ozzy Osbourne.

318

YOU WEAR IT WELL

ROD STEWART

2 September 1972, for one week
●
Mercury 6052 171

Written by Rod Stewart and Martin Quittenton. Produced by Rod Stewart.

You Wear It Well was the second consecutive solo number one for the gravelly-voiced rocker who was once so poor that while hitching round Europe some years earlier he had had to be repatriated from Spain because he was destitute. Legend has it that he still owes British Airways the cost of the flight home. *You Wear It Well* was the first single issued off his album *Never A Dull Moment* which dominated the album listings at the end of 1972. It was similar to its predecessor *Maggie May* both in its Stewart/Quittenton composition and its style. The backing cast of the single cited Ste-

Rod Stewart *is shown singing at the Wembley Empire Pool to benefit the Stars Organisation for Spastics.*

wart's history in previous bands, featuring Ronnie Wood of the Faces on acoustic guitar and Mickey Waller, from Stewart's days with Steam Packet, on the drums.

After *You Wear It Well* Stewart was absent from the top slot for three years before *Sailing* glided to the top. In the meanwhile he notched up an impressive seven appearances in the Top 10 in various guises. There were three solo hits (*Angel/What Made Milwaukee Famous* – no.4, *Oh No Not My Baby* – no.6, and *Farewell/Bring It On Home To Me/You Send Me* – no. 7), a number 3 hit with *In A Broken Dream* as lead singer for Python Lee Jackson and a similar role for the Faces. Their three Top 10 hits were all during this period of Stewart's absence from number one, the most successful of which was *Cindy Incidentally* which made number 2.

319

MAMA WEER ALL CRAZEE NOW

SLADE

9 September 1972, for three weeks

●●●

Polydor 2058 274

Written by Noddy Holder and Jim Lea. Produced by Chas Chandler.

Mama Weer All Crazee Now was Slade's second consecutive number one single, following directly on from the equally badly spelled *Take Me Back 'Ome.* They were never to achieve the elusive hat-trick of consecutive number ones, a feat managed by eleven other acts. Only T. Rex (4), Presley (5), The Rolling Stones (5) and The Beatles (11) have managed more than three on the trot. The single that followed *Mama Weer All Crazee Now* into the charts was *Gudbuy T'Jane* which 'only' reached the number 2 spot. Had it made top spot it would have given Slade an uninterrupted run of five chart toppers.

Most of Slade's song titles have either a deliberate misspelling, a grammatical error or a forced colloquialism. (The title of their 1987 album *You Boyz Make Big Noize* was

coined by the studio tea-lady on hearing Noddy and Co at work.) They seem to share this tendency with Prince, who seems to be the only other chart act continually and deliberately to perform surgery on the English language.

320

HOW CAN I BE SURE

DAVID CASSIDY

30 September 1972, for two weeks

●●

Bell 1258

Written by Felix Cavaliere and Eddie Brigati. Produced by Wes Farrell.

After their experience with the Monkees, the television company Screen Gems knew what might happen when they launched the Partridge Family in 1970.

David Cassidy (born 12 April 1950), the son of the actor Jack Cassidy, played the whiter-than-white Keith Partridge, the guitarist/vocalist with a fictional family group that included his mother, played by David's real stepmother Shirley Jones. The original series ran from 1970 to 1974 in the USA but in Britain it was first aired by the BBC in 1971, who decided to drop it after one series. Clamour from fans, who had already bought the Partridges' US number one single *I Think I Love You* and made it a number 19 hit in the UK, caused ITV to buy the series. By the time *How Can I Be Sure* had become a hit in Britain David Cassidy's career in the USA was taking a nosedive. His biggest solo hit had been a cover of the Association's *Cherish,* which made the US Top 10 in 1971. None of his subsequent efforts even reached the Top 20. *How Can I Be Sure,* a US hit for the Young Rascals in 1967, had been covered by Dusty Springfield in the UK in 1970. In the US Cassidy's version got no higher than 25.

Rolling Stone magazine printed an article in March 1972 which not only reported Cassidy's dissatisfaction with his squeaky-clean image but published semi-nude photographs. By co-operating the singer effectively destroyed his US career at the age of twenty-one.

321

MOULDY OLD DOUGH

LIEUTENANT PIGEON

14 October 1972, for four weeks

●●●●

Decca F 13278

Written by Nigel Fletcher and Robert Woodward. Produced by Stavely Makepiece.

Lieutenant Pigeon was formed in Coventry out of the group Stavely Makepiece. Under this guise three schoolboy friends, drummer Nigel Fletcher, pianist Robert Woodward and bass guitarist Stephen Johnson released one unsuccessful single, *Edna.* The change of name to Lieutenant Pigeon improved their luck and gave them a number one in their fifth week on the chart.

Mouldy Old Dough was indeed old by the time it had climbed to the top, having been released eight months earlier. It contained almost no other vocal content than its title, a corruption of 'vo-de-o-do', the phrase well loved by megaphone toting band vocalists of the '20s and '30s. Rob Woodward's piano teacher mum, Hilda, appeared on this hit which was recorded in the front room of the Woodward's semi. Thus Lieutenant Pigeon became the only number one hit combo to feature a mother and son.

The group continued their success with *Desperate Dan,* a similar sounding tune which made it to the Top 20, but the following months saw the popularity of Lieutenant Pigeon dropping.

322

CLAIR

GILBERT O'SULLIVAN

11 Nobember 1972, for two weeks

●●

MAM 84

Written by Gilbert O'Sullivan. Produced by Gordon Mills.

Gilbert O'Sullivan's first number one single came almost exactly two years after his first chart appearance with *Nothing Rhymed*, which climbed to number 8. In between, O'Sullivan had another three Top 10 hits as well as a Top 20 success. Simultaneous with the success of *Clair* was the Irishman's only chart-topping album, *Back To Front*, which remained on chart for a fine 64 weeks. *Clair* was not the obvious love story but was inspired by the young daughter of O'Sullivan's manager Gordon Mills for whom Gilbert babysat. This angle gave the song a wider audience than it would have received had it been a traditional romance. Chuck Berry with *Memphis Tennessee* and the Brotherhood of Man with *Save Your Kisses For Me* (see no. 387) have also put a twist involving infants at the end of a musical tale.

Gordon Mills, who managed Tom Jones and Engelbert Humperdinck as well as Gilbert O'Sullivan, created a large public company on the back of their successes. He died, his fortunes having fallen, in 1986.

323

MY DING-A-LING

CHUCK BERRY

25 November 1972, for four weeks

●●●●

Chess 6145 019

Written by Chuck Berry. Produced by Esmond Edwards.

It is a strange twist of fate that Chuck Berry had his only British number one with *My Ding-A-Ling*, a comparatively inconsequential piece of ribaldry that had been in and out of Berry's live set since he turned professional in the 1950s. The song was recorded live at the Lanchester Arts Festival in 1972 and went to the top of the singles listings on both sides of the Atlantic. Berry's previous singles had included many historic recordings but none ever made the very top, although a double A-side combination of *Memphis Tennessee/Let It Rock* had climbed to number 6 in October 1963 and *No Particular Place To Go* made number 3 in May of the following year.

Berry was born Charles Edward Berry in St. Louis, Missouri on 18 October 1931 and learned guitar through his teens, copying the patterns of the Delta blues players of the '30s. After a spell in reform school, a marriage and brief employment at General Motors, he signed to Chess records in 1955 with the backing of Muddy Waters. From there he helped define rock and roll, influencing artists like the Beatles and the Rolling Stones with his reshaped 12 bar boogie.

324

LONG HAIRED LOVER FROM LIVERPOOL

LITTLE JIMMY OSMOND

23 December 1972, for five weeks

●●●●●

MGM 2006 109

Written by Christopher Dowden. Produced by Mike Curb and Perry Botkin.

Born on 16 April 1963, Jimmy Osmond was the youngest of Olive and George Osmond's eight sons. By reaching the top at the tender age of nine years, two-hundred and fifty one days, he took over the title of Youngest Number One Hitmaker from Frankie Lymon, who'd made his appearance at the top at the advanced age of 13 (see no. 48).

Little Jimmy's triumph came at the end of the first year of Osmondmania. His big brothers had amassed five Top 40 hits in eight months. Two of them, *Down By The Lazy River* and *Crazy Horses* featured Alan, Wayne, Merrill, Jay, and Donny Osmond. The other three, *Puppy Love* (see no. 316), *Too Young* and *Why* were credited to Donny alone. The day that Little Jimmy became the second Osmond to make it to the top Donny's *Why* stood at number 5 and the Osmonds' *Crazy Horses* at nine. Never before had a family so dominated the chart. A rush of Christmas spirit also returned *Puppy Love* and *Too Young* to the listings so that for three festive weeks five Osmond discs could be found in the Top 50.

Little Jimmy Osmond enjoyed two more Top 20 hits before getting on with the task of becoming big Jimmy Osmond. After a spell as an actor he is now a successful TV director in the USA.

325

BLOCKBUSTER

SWEET

27 January 1973, for five weeks

●●●●●

RCA 2305

Written by Nicky Chinn and Mike Chapman. Produced by Phil Wainman.

There are only four acts that have spent more than 150 weeks on the singles charts and less than ten on the albums charts. Three of that list, Bill Haley, David Whitfield and Guy Mitchell, were all stars before the LP lists began, so they can be honourably excused. The fourth name in this select group is Sweet, whose album success was limited to two weeks in 1974 and a hits retrospective a decade later. On the singles charts, however, they were one of the top acts of the early '70s.

They were formed in 1968 with Brian Connolly on vocals, Steve Priest on bass, Andy Scott on guitar and Mick Tucker on drums. In 1970 they joined forces with the then unknown writers Nicky Chinn and Mike Chapman, who penned all their early hits and provided them with *Blockbuster*, the longest running number one of the year and a song that used an air raid siren a decade before Frankie's *Relax*. After this number one they had three consecutive singles stall at 2. *Ballroom Blitz* even entered that high and failed to improve, an anomaly that has only ever happened to the Beatles with *Let It Be* (Lee Marvin stayed at number one), and Wham! with *Last Christmas* (prevented by Band Aid).

In 1975 the band decided to split from the Chinn/Chapman stable and at first this seemed to be a wise move as their own composition *Fox On The Run* shot to their customary number two slot. However they lost sales in an effort to find a more musically appreciative audience. Their last Top 10 hit came in 1978 with *Love Is Like Oxygen*, taken from Joan Collins' 'come-back' movie *The Bitch*. In their time Sweet were at the forefront of the glam rock movement, and unlike Slade, Gary Glitter and Marc Bolan they were a big American success, claiming four Top 10 hits, more than all the others put together.

326

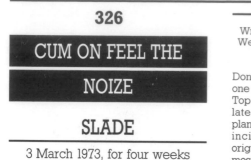

CUM ON FEEL THE NOIZE

SLADE

3 March 1973, for four weeks

● ● ● ●

Polydor 2058 339

Written by Noddy Holder and Jim Lea. Produced by Chas Chandler.

As Slade headed the singles listings on 29 March 1973 the last US soldier left Vietnam. *Cum On Feel The Noize* signalled a new low in Slade's always eccentric spelling but marked the zenith of their action-packed chart career, for they were now in the middle of the most successful post-Beatles run of any group. Their work was remarkable not in its cleverly crafted constitution mixing heavy metal and a pseudo-rebellious teenage stance, but in that it enjoyed both critical and public acclaim. The latter was obviously reflected in the seal of commercial approval their offerings found from the masses who bought them to number one; but Slade also found themselves blessed with the former, probably because there was no other act around at the time who were able to come near their raw energy and eternal enthusiasm. On stage they were as thunderous as on record, and they remained a popular live act long after the chart heroics were memories. In the 1980s they were still being booked to appear at prestigious rock festivals like Donnington.

327

THE TWELFTH OF NEVER

DONNY OSMOND

31 March 1973, for one week

●

MGM 2006 199

Written by Jay Livingston and Paul Francis Webster. Produced by Mike Curb and Don Costa.

Donald Clark Osmond's second number one was his fourth solo UK hit. All had been Top 10ers and all had been cover versions of late '50s/early '60s ballads. Mike Curb planned the release of the remakes to co-incide with the seasons in which the originals were popular. To be fair to Donny, most of them will be best remembered in their original versions, the definitive *The Twelfth of Never* having been recorded in 1957 by Johnny Mathis. Oddly his version was never a hit in the UK and only managed a lowly placing of 51 in the USA. It had a longer life as a key part of *Johnny's Greatest Hits,* for many years the longest runner in US chart history. Cliff Richard had had the first UK success with the song, making the Top 10 in the autumn of 1964.

Before long Donny recorded with his sister Marie, who had a solo hit in November of 1973 with *Paper Roses.* Their four hits together were also cover versions. Donny and Marie achieved the fairly interesting feat of successfully covering consecutive US number ones, namely Dale and Grace's *I'm Leaving It (All) Up To You* and Nino Tempo and April Stevens' *Deep Purple,* both American chart toppers at the end of 1963.

328

GET DOWN

GILBERT O'SULLIVAN

7 April 1973, for two weeks

● ●

MAM 96

Written by Gilbert O'Sullivan. Produced by Gordon Mills.

Gilbert O'Sullivan's second consecutive and final number one was *Get Down.* Unlike all the other songs with *Get Down* in the title, like KC and the Sunshine Band's *Get Down Tonight* or Kool & The Gang's *Get Down On It,* O'Sullivan's song had nothing to do with dancing at the discotheque. It was a plea to his dog to get down off the furniture.

Get Down represented the peak of Gilbert O'Sullivan's popularity. Only one more Top 10 hit was to follow, and two years later the hits stopped. There then followed a bitter dispute with manager and producer Gordon Mills which resulted in a widely-reported court case early in 1982 with claims and counterclaims about how much money O'Sullivan had earned and how much of his earnings he had been able to get his hands on. In May 1982, the law found in favour of Gilbert (real name Ray O'Sullivan) describing him as 'a patently honest and sincere man' who had not received a just proportion of the vast income his songs had generated. Well before the case came to court, O'Sullivan had left MAM and even scored his 15th hit, *What's In A Kiss* on CBS, at the end of 1980, his first hit for over five years.

329

TIE A YELLOW RIBBON ROUND THE OLD OAK TREE

DAWN FEATURING TONY ORLANDO

21 April 1973, for four weeks

● ● ● ●

Bell 1287

Written by Irwin Levine and L Russell Brown. Produced by Hank Medress and David Appell.

Whilst the pioneers of glam rock were dominating the charts, the song that kept Sweet's *Hell Raiser* and Gary Glitter's *Hello Hello I'm Back Again* off the number one spot was the heart-rending story of a convicted criminal returning home to his loved one after serving a three year jail sentence. Songwriters Irwin Levine and L. Russell Brown turned this tale into *Tie A Yellow Ribbon Round the Old Oak Tree,* 1973's best selling single on either side of the Atlantic. World sales for the single topped six million, but more importantly for Dawn it resurrected their US career. By the end of 1975 they had sold over 25 million records worldwide. It became Dawn's biggest selling single and according to the *Guinness Book of Records* is one of the most recorded songs of all-time, with over 1,000 versions.

The task of following up this monster smash proved difficult in the UK, but not in America. One Top 20 entry and a minor Top 40 effort was all they could muster over here, but in their native homeland they enjoyed several big chart hits including their final number one *He Don't Love You (Like I Love You)*, written by Clarence Carter, Curtis Mayfield and Jerry Butler.

By the end of their career the group's billing had changed to Tony Orlando and Dawn. It is therefore ironic to reflect that the forgotten singers in the group, Joyce Vincent and Thelma Hopkins, appeared on more number ones than the highlighted Orlando, their vocals having graced the Four Tops' *Reach Out I'll Be There* and *I Heard It Through The Grapevine* by Marvin Gaye.

330

SEE MY BABY JIVE

WIZZARD

19 May 1973, for four weeks

● ● ● ●

Harvest HAR 5070

Written by Roy Wood. Produced by Roy Wood.

Roy Wood was born in Birmingham on 8 November 1946, attending Mosley College Of Art before being expelled. He then drifted through local bands before joining Birmingham super-group the Move in 1966. Five years later, with musical differences arising between members of the group, Wood left to found the Electric Light Orchestra with the idea of forming a group to create on stage the sort of lush orchestral sounds the Beatles were achieving with numbers like *Strawberry Fields Forever*. After just one album with ELO in their year of inception, *Message From The Country*, and two Top 10 singles, Wood left the group in the hands of Jeff Lynne and formed Wizzard. The latter initially were a large band sporting a French Horn player, an electric cellist and two drummers. After a disappointing first album, Wood refined Wizzard to a more basic combination and immediately scored the group's first number one with *See My Baby Jive*. This success introduced Wood to a newer, younger audience than the Move and with Wood's ear for a commercial melody gave Wizzard another number one and a Top 5 hit the same year.

Wizzard *blew it and got to number one anyway.*

331

CAN THE CAN

SUZI QUATRO

16 June 1973, for one week

●

RAK 150

Written by Nicky Chinn and Mike Chapman. Produced by Nicky Chinn and Mike Chapman.

Suzi Quatro (born Detroit, Michigan, 3 June 1950) was the daughter of Art Quatro, leader of a mildly famous jazz band of the 1950s. Suzi made her musical debut aged eight playing bongos in dad's band. Assuming the name Suzi Soul she became a TV go-go dancer at 14. A year later she teamed up with sisters Patti and Nancy to form her first group, the Pleasure Seekers. This band stuck together for five years, playing across the USA and overseas, including one trip to entertain the troops in Vietnam.

The group had changed their name to Cradle and were performing in a Detroit club in 1970 when Suzi was signed by producer Mickie Most to his RAK Records. Leather-clad Suzi hit the road in 1972 as support act to Slade, accompanied by drummer Dave Neal, keyboard player Alistair Mackenzie and guitarist (and future husband) Len Tuckey. Her debut single *Rolling Stone* flopped in 1972, and for a year Suzi's self penned singles sank without trace. Then Most teamed her with writers and producers Chinn and Chapman who had just written their first number one for Sweet (see no. 325). The result was *Can The Can*.

332

RUBBER BULLETS

10 C.C.

23 June 1973, for one week

●

UK 36

Written by Kevin Godley, Lol Creme and Graham Gouldman. Produced by 10 C.C. at Strawberry Studios.

Rubber Bullets represented a first taste of number one hit-making for the four members of 10 C.C. which must have been particularly gratifying for Eric Stewart, the only member of the group who does not have writing credit on this song. Stewart had been a member of Wayne Fontana and the Mindbenders, who reached number two with *The Game Of Love* in 1965. When the Mindbenders split from their leader their first solo hit, *A Groovy Kind Of Love*, reached number 2 in 1966. The Mindbenders later broke up and Eric Stewart formed Hotlegs with Kevin Godley and Lol Creme. Their only hit, *Neanderthal Man*, in 1970, also reached number 2. When 10 C.C.'s first hit, *Donna*, also reached number 2, Eric Stewart must have felt doomed never to reach the very top. 23 June 1973 not only gave him and 10 C.C. their first number one, but it also gave Jonathan King's label, UK, its only number one. None of Jonathan King's many efforts under other names and on other labels ever reached number one, and this record is his only claim to a number one hit.

333

SKWEEZE ME PLEEZE ME

SLADE

30 June 1973, for 3 weeks

●●●

Polydor 2058 377

Written by Noddy Holder and Jim Lea. Produced by Chas Chandler.

Slade's penultimate number one put them in the select club of three artists who have had two singles to enter straight at number one. The others are Elvis Presley with three, and The Jam also with three. As with *Mama Weer All Crazee Now*, *Skweeze Me Pleeze Me* also preceded a follow-up single that stalled at number 2, thus again preventing Slade from achieving the elusive hat-trick of chart toppers with consecutive releases. This time it was *My Frend Stan* that couldn't quite make it.

While Slade were enjoying unchallenged supremacy in the singles listings, they were also proving themselves no slouches in the long-playing stakes. During the halcyon years of 1972-1974 the five albums released by the Wolverhampton group included three consecutive number ones (*Slayed?* in 1972, *Sladest* the following year and then *Old New Borrowed And Blue* in 1974), a number 2 (*Slade Alive* from 1971) and a number 6 (*Slade In Flame*, Christmas of 1974).

334

WELCOME HOME

PETERS AND LEE

21 July 1973, for one week

●

Philips 60006 307

Written by Jean-Alphonse Dupre, Stanislas Beldone, English lyrics by Bryan Blackburn. Produced by Johnny Franz.

Until they joined forces in 1970, the blind Lenny Peters had been a pub pianist in London's East End and Di Lee had been half a dancing duo called the Hailey Twins. In April 1970 they made their first public appearance together as guests on a Rolf Harris stage show in Bournemouth. After three years of touring clubs and theatres they were spotted by TV host Hughie Green, who put them on his ITV *Opportunity Knocks* talent show. Following their first appearance on 12 February 1973 TV viewers voted for them to return time and time again.

Welcome Home, Peters and Lee's first single, took two months to climb to the top and was the tenth and final number one production by Philips' resident A&R man Johnny Franz. The production on this ballad bore all his hallmarks, including lush orchestration and a choir of backing singers. Over the next three years Peters and Lee became stalwarts of television variety shows and scored four more hits including the 1974 number three smash, *Don't Stay Away Too Long*.

335

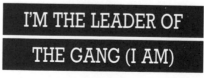

I'M THE LEADER OF THE GANG (I AM)

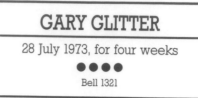

GARY GLITTER

28 July 1973, for four weeks

●●●●

Bell 1321

Written by Gary Glitter and Mike Leander. Produced by Mike Leander.

Gary Glitter was born Paul Raven 8 May 1944. As a youngster he hung out at the Two I's coffee bar in Soho along with all the other fashionable rockers including Cliff Richard, the Shadows and Marty Wilde. His first single, released in 1959 by Decca, has been critically acclaimed as one of the worst singles of all time, with Glitter himself admitting the disc's lack of artistic credibility. During the '60s he released a succession of flop R&B singles under his real name, despite working with top producers Ron Richards (the Hollies) and George Martin. The closest he came was with *Walk On Boy*, which would have been a hit if the chart had been just a few places bigger.

He was nonetheless never short of work, helping out on *Ready Steady Go!* and spending a five year stint in Germany working in clubs, learning his skills as a live entertainer. He returned to the UK in 1969 and renewed his partnership with producer Mike Leander, whom he first met in 1964. As Paul Monday he released his falsetto reworking of *Amazing Grace* and a squatter's anthem entitled *We're All Living In One Place*. Unfortunately the public would have nothing of it. As MCA weren't too keen either, he left to join Bell records.

Glitter and Leander decided the best move would be to return to their rock 'n' roll roots. They decided to write audience participation rock similar to that of their heroes Elvis, Little Richard and Gary US Bonds. They played all the instruments on the early hits, the first of which was *Rock 'n' Roll Parts 1 + 2*. This broke after becoming an anthem in the clubs where it put rock 'n' roll back on the dance floors. Having at last made the charts Gary Glitter now found himself competing with Marc Bolan as flavour of the month. His next three singles all made the Top 10, two stalling at the runner-up spot, and he was duly rewarded for all his efforts when *I'm The Leader of the Gang (I Am)* smashed in at 2 and took that final step to the top where it remained for four weeks. It may not have been the best of all his records, but it is Glitter's favourite 'because it was my first (number one)'. The song remains the anthem of his followers. When Glitter hits the stage, the whole auditorium erupts into chants of 'leader', 'leader', 'leader'.

336

YOUNG LOVE

DONNY OSMOND

25 August 1973, for four weeks

●●●●

MGM 2006 300

Written by Carole Joyner and Ric Cartey. Produced by Mike Curb and Don Costa.

Donny Osmond had already revived one former UK number one, *Why*, and successfully hoisted it back into the Top 5. Britain's favourite Mormon was at the peak of his popularity in 1973 so when he covered Tab Hunter's 1957 smash (see no. 56) it raced back to the top. For a tune to have appeared at the top via two different acts was not unique. *Answer Me, Cherry Pink And Apple Blossom White* and *Singing The Blues* had all been manoeuvred to number one in two versions, but the gap between their appearances at the top had been two weeks at the most. Sixteen years and one hundred and thirty-six days separated Tab and Donny.

Donny's final solo hit of the '70s, the fittingly-titled *Where Did All The Good Times Go*, fell off the chart in the second week of 1975 although he continued to have success with his brothers and in partnership with his sister Marie until 1976. Marie and Donny hosted their own variety show on American television until the end of the '70s. Donny married, had three children and dropped out of the music business to concentrate on TV production. In 1987 a new deal with Virgin generated further recordings.

Top right: **Donny Osmond**'s co-producer Don Costa helmed many memorable hits, including Frank Sinatra's My Way.

Right: **Gary Glitter** smiles at the thought of his third number one in a year.

Simon Park *minus his orchestra.*

337

ANGEL FINGERS

WIZZARD

22 September 1973, for one week

●

Harvest HAR 5076

Written by Roy Wood. Produced by Roy Wood.

Roy Wood is one of the very few people who have been bona fide members of two different groups that have had number one hits (not including charity groups). The list includes Paul McCartney (Beatles and Wings), Denny Laine (Moody Blues and Wings), Bev Bevan (Move and ELO) and Roy Wood (Move and Wizzard).

Angel Fingers was Wizzard's second consecutive number one hit, and it marked the peak of Roy Wood's chart success. 1973 was dominated by the RAK/Bell/Donny Osmond school of teenypop, but Roy Wood managed to introduce subtleties of production into his basically simple pop tunes that make them stand the test of time. He also knew he was not producing great art and was happy to joke about his music. *I Wish It Could Be Christmas Every Day* (number 4 at Christmas 1973 and a hit again over the Yuletides of 1981 and 1984) features Wizzard with 'vocal backing by the Suedettes plus the Stockland Green Bilateral School First Year Choir, with additional noises by Miss Snob and Class 3C'.

Roy Wood is still active in the recording studios and on television. At the end of 1986 he joined forces with Dr. & The Medics on a remake of Abba's first hit, *Waterloo*, which briefly climbed into the Top 50.

338

EYE LEVEL

SIMON PARK ORCHESTRA

29 September 1973, for four weeks

● ● ● ●

Columbia DB 8946

Written by Simon Park and Jack Trombey. Produced by Simon Park.

The 50th and final number one for EMI's legendary Columbia label was performed by an orchestra led by a graduate of Music at Winchester College, Oxford, Simon Park (born Market Harborough, March 1946) who had begun playing the piano at the age of five.

Eye Level was the first TV theme to have topped the chart. The music was used for the ITV series *Van Der Valk,* which was based on the detective thriller novels of Nicholas Freeling. Just as the actor who played Van Der Valk, Barry Foster, pretended to be a Dutchman, the Dutch co-writer of this tune, Jan Stoeckhart, pretended to be an Englishman when he assumed the *nom de plume* Jack Trombey.

The single was initially released during Van Der Valk's first series and reached number 41 in November 1972. Viewing figures for the second series increased and the theme tune was re-released by public demand. This time it climbed all the way to the top. At that time the 308 days that had elapsed from first chart entry to chart peak placed the single second to *Rock Around The Clock* on the list of tardiest number ones. Bill Haley's classic had taken 322 days.

339

DAYDREAMER/PUPPY SONG

DAVID CASSIDY

27 October 1973, for three weeks

● ● ●

Bell 1334

Written by (Daydreamer) Terry Dempsey, (Puppy Song) Harry Nilsson. Produced by Rick Jarrard.

The BBC broadcast the 500th edition of its long-running pop show *Top of the Pops* on 4 October 1973. Among those appearing on that special one hour programme were Gary Glitter, Slade and the Osmonds. It was this last act, and Donny Osmond in particular, who were Cassidy's main rivals in the teen heart-throb stakes so David's managers, Screen Gems, used the event for a cunning publicity stunt.

Cassidy appeared to be jetting in especially for the show. An aeroplane was seen taxiing to a halt and when the doors opened, out jumped David for an apparent live performance of both sides of his new single. But the singer had in fact already been in the UK for several days and had taped the songs the day before they were transmitted. Screen Gems' ploy worked. The double A-side entered the chart at number 8. The following week it was at the top.

His appeal soon began to diminish. It was thought that after his version of the Beach Boys' *Darlin'* had fallen off the chart at the end of 1975 that was the last of David Cassidy.

This was a hasty assumption. In 1985 the singer returned to the Top 10 with his own composition, *The Last Kiss,* which featured backing vocals by the teen hero for a later generation, George Michael. In 1987 Cassidy took over the lead role in the West End musical *Time* from Cliff Richard.

340

I LOVE YOU LOVE ME LOVE

GARY GLITTER

17 November 1973, for four weeks

● ● ● ●

Bell 1337

Written by Gary Glitter and Mike Leander. Produced by Mike Leander.

Four songs entered the charts at number one during 1973. Three were by Slade; the fourth was *I Love You Love Me Love,* Gary Glitter's second consecutive number one.

Many of Glitter's hits were linked to his live shows. Several started out as lines he would speak between songs. Glitter did say that he was the 'leader of the gang', he did tell the audience 'you're beautiful', and when he asked them 'do ya wanna touch?', they all shouted 'yeah'. Glitter would then team up with Leander to build a song around the phrase. They both thought that *I Love You Love Me Love* would make a great song title. When asked what the next single was going to be called they gave this nonsensical title and 250,000 labels were duly printed before the song was written.

Glitter and Leander still believed this was a number one single, feeling more secure about it than any other hit before or after. What they couldn't have guessed was its rapid sales. It quickly pushed past one million and became a massive international success. It remains in the UK's Top 40 bestselling singles of all-time. It was covered in America by Joan Jett, who also took a cover of *Do You Wanna Touch?* into the Top 20.

341

MERRY XMAS EVERYBODY

SLADE

15 December 1973, for five weeks

● ● ● ● ●

Polydor 2058 422

Written by Noddy Holder and Jim Lea. Produced by Chas Chandler.

Slade's last number one single was produced and written by the same personnel that gave them all of their six chart-topping singles. It was also the only single to come straight in at the top spot directly after the previous number one had also done this. *Merry Xmas Everybody* was the biggest of Slade's successes, selling a million in its original version. It was re-recorded by the Wolverhampton lads and the Reading Choir for Christmas 1980. The 1973 original

was followed by three consecutive Top 5 singles for Slade before the hits gradually tailed off. Since 1975 there have been four Top 10s and four Top 20s by Slade, a significant achievement for a group whose red letter days have long since passed and a testament to the shrewd talents of Holder and Lea. *Merry Xmas Everybody* has now reappeared at six Christmases since 1973 and has become the first Christmas record to clock up 30 weeks on the charts.

342

YOU WON'T FIND ANOTHER FOOL LIKE ME

NEW SEEKERS

19 January 1974, for one week

●

Polydor 2058 421

Written by Tony Macaulay and Geoff Stephens. Produced by Tommy Oliver.

The New Seekers matched the original Seekers by hitting the top twice when the Tony Macaulay/Geoff Stephens song *You Won't Find Another Fool Like Me* reached number one in its ninth week on the chart.

By this stage, the break-up of the New Seekers seemed to be inevitable. Earlier releases had billed them first as 'The New Seekers featuring Marty Kristian' and then as 'Eve Graham and the New Seekers'. Lyn Paul was also looking for the opportunity to break out from the confines of the group, so it was not surprising when the follow-up to their second chart-topper, another long-titled hit called *I Get A Little Sentimental Over You*, became the final single before the split.

The solo careers of the individual New Seekers never really took off, so in 1976 they reformed on a new label, CBS. They enjoyed three more Top 50 hits and 18 more weeks on the charts over the next two years. Since then their only brush with the charts has been as a part of Ferry Aid. We await with interest the formation of the New New Seekers.

343

TIGER FEET

MUD

26 January 1974, for four weeks

● ● ● ●

RAK 166

Written by Nicky Chinn and Mike Chapman. Produced by Nicky Chinn and Mike Chapman.

Mud were the third act that the writing team of Chinn and Chapman ('Chinnichap') took to the top, Suzi Quatro and Sweet having already reached number one with the duo's compositions by the time *Tiger Feet* stomped to the top spot for a month. Similarly Mickie Most's record label RAK had already had a number one with Quatro, but Mud were to become their biggest success. *Tiger Feet* was the first number one hit amongst ten Top 20 hits that the alliance between Mud, Chapman and Chinn, and RAK produced between March 1973 and July 1975.

Mud had first broken into the singles chart in 1973 when *Crazy* and *Hypnosis* reached numbers 12 and 16 respectively. *Dyna-mite* hinted at the greater success that would lay ahead for the group when it reached number 4 towards the end of the year. It was the first of eight consecutive Top 10 singles, including three number ones, between October 1973 and June 1975.

344

DEVIL GATE DRIVE

SUZI QUATRO

23 February 1974, for two weeks

● ●

RAK 167

Written by Nicky Chinn and Mike Chapman. Produced by Nicky Chinn and Mike Chapman.

Suzi Quatro's second chart-topper was

Chinn and Chapman's fourth number one composition. It was also the fifth time in chart history that consecutive label numbers had become number one hits. *48 Crash* and *Daytona Demon* had come between Quatro's *Can The Can* and *Devil Gate Drive*. All four songs portrayed Suzi as an aggressive rocker.

In the mid-'70s Suzi Quatro took her stage act back home to America but wasn't able to sell her image in the same successful manner as she had done in Britain. At the same time she began to lose touch with her UK audience and for a couple of years looked like sliding off the charts for good, along with the rest of the glam rockers.

But in 1978 she returned with a softer persona and the singles *If You Can't Give Me Love* and a duet with Smokie's vocalist Chris Norman, *Stumblin' In,* the latter providing her with that elusive US hit. An acting career followed. She appeared in several episodes of the TV series *Happy Days* in the role of Leather Tuscadero. Stage roles included the part of Annie Oakley in a West End revival of the musical *Annie Get Your Gun.*

345

JEALOUS MIND

ALVIN STARDUST

9 March 1974, for one week

●

Magnet MAG 5

Written by Peter Shelley. Produced by Peter Shelley.

Alvin Stardust (born Bernard Jewry in 1942) had first seen chart action in 1961 as Shane Fenton. Although Jewry was the vocalist with Shane Fenton and the Fentones he was in fact the second singer to bear that name, the first having died suddenly before the group's success. In the summer of 1962 *Cindy's Birthday,* the band's biggest hit, dropped out of the charts. From then until the winter of 1973 the world heard nothing of Bernard Jewry.

Producer Peter Shelley had persuaded Michael Levy to start an independent label called Magnet in mid-1973. He had already heard Stardust's demo of *My Coo-Ca-Choo.* Released as a single and given the cata-

logue number MAG 1, the song bounded up to the number 2 position. Stardust's black leather clothes and his imaginative way of holding the microphone soon became well-known. *My Coo-Ca-Choo,* which resembled *Spirit In The Sky* (see no. 285) in melody if not in sentiment, was considered a better song than the follow-up, *Jealous Mind,* but it was the second disc that won Stardust seven days at the top.

Shelley wrote six consecutive Top 20 hits for Stardust before the singer decided to look elsewhere for material, a decision which led to six years of chart obscurity. He renewed his career in 1981 by making a bizarre move to independent Stiff Records and recording a Top 10 version of Nat King Cole's *Pretend.* Three more hitless years followed until he signed with Chrysalis with whom he was able to produce further Top 10ers like *I Feel Like Buddy Holly,* a song which name-checks not only Lubbock's finest son but also Paul McCartney.

346

BILLY DON'T BE A

HERO

PAPER LACE

16 March 1974, for three weeks

● ● ●

Bus Stop BUS 1014

Written by Mitch Murray and Peter Callander. Produced by Mitch Murray and Peter Callander.

Paper Lace joined Mary Hopkin and Peters and Lee as number one hitmakers who owed their initial success to the TV talent show *Opportunity Knocks.* Like them they got to the top with their very first hit. The group, based in the lacemaking city of Nottingham, were singer/drummer Phil Wright (born 9 April 1950), bassist Cliff Fish (born 13 August 1949), and guitarists Chris Morris (born 1 November 1954), Michael Vaughan (born 27 July 1950) and Carlo Santanna (born 29 June 1947).

Billy was Murray and Callander's second number one composition (see also no. 242). Murray had also co-written Gerry and the Pacemakers' first two number ones in 1963

(see nos 150 and 152). *Billy* emulated its UK success in the USA when Bo Donaldson and the Heywoods rushed out a cover version. A vengeful Paper Lace quickly released their UK number 3 hit *The Night Chicago Died* in America. The ploy worked and the band enjoyed seven days atop the Billboard Hot One Hundred. But fortunes were waning in Britain, where they managed to score only one more Top 20 hit before becoming entangled in legal problems with their record label. Save for a 1978 version of *We've Got The Whole World In Our Hands* accompanied by Nottingham Forest FC, Paper Lace have not visited the charts again.

347

SEASONS IN THE SUN

TERRY JACKS

6 April 1974, for four weeks

● ● ● ●

Bell 1344

Written by Jacques Brel, English lyrics by Rod McKuen. Produced by Terry Jacks.

Winnipeg born Terry Jacks was the first Canadian act since Paul Anka to score a UK number one. Terry and his wife Susan had seen UK chart action as the Poppy Family in 1970 with the Top 10 tune *Which Way You Going Billy,* a single that Mrs Jacks had originally intended to release under her own name, Susan Pesklevits.

While in session with the Beach Boys in 1973 (see nos 226 and 256) Terry Jacks recorded the French song *Le Moribond* (The Dying Man), adapted into English by poet Rod McKuen. Jacks had wanted the Beach Boys to record the tune but they were not keen. A year later Jacks was persuaded to release the track himself. It gave him a number one hit in Canada on his own Goldfish label and bowled over the rest of the world on Bell, reaching the very top in both the US and UK. Another Brel song, the equally mournful *If You Go Away,* provided him with a further Top 10er in 1974, but after two seasons in the charts it was Jacks who went away.

348

WATERLOO

ABBA

4 May 1974, for two weeks

● ●

Epic EPC 2240

Written by Bjorn Ulvaeus, Benny Andersson and Stig Anderson. Produced by Bjorn Ulvaeus and Benny Andersson.

Benny Andersson (born in Stockholm on 16 December 1946) began his musical career with a group called the Hep Stars, who were for some years very popular in Sweden. Bjorn Ulvaeus (born in Gothenberg on 25 April 1948) was with an outfit called the Hootenanny Singers but in the late '60s the two combined to form the duo Bjorn and Benny. It was hardly the obvious foundation for the most popular group in the world since the break-up of the Beatles. By the early '70s Bjorn and Benny had achieved considerable popularity in Scandinavia at which time they brought their girlfriends into the group. They were Agnetha Faltskog (born in Jonskoping on 5 April 1950) and Annifrid Lyngstad (born in Norway on 15 November 1945) and by the original ploy of taking the initial letters of the quartet's first names, the name Abba was born. Up to this moment the only thing that could be said about the new group was the startling lack of originality dis-

*Eurovision Song Contest winners **ABBA** are shown in Brighton, Agnetha still wearing her identity pass.*

played by all concerned throughout their musical careers. The music that Abba actually produced was therefore all the more unexpected.

Waterloo was Sweden's Eurovision entry for 1974. It won easily and became probably the biggest international hit in the history of the contest. It created a new stereotype of Eurovision song, which continued into 1981 with Bucks Fizz, another two men-two girls group.

*Here's looking at **Paper Lace**.*

349

SUGAR BABY LOVE

THE RUBETTES

18 May 1974, for four weeks

● ● ● ●

Polydor 2058 442

Written by Wayne Bickerton and Tony Waddington. Produced by Wayne Bickerton.

When songwriters try to sell their compositions they don't send along pieces of sheet music. They record demonstration tapes on which either they or other musicians performed their songs. Bickerton and Waddington had hired six session musicians, singer Paul da Vinci, keyboard players Bill Hurd and Peter Arnisson, guitarist Tony Thorpe, bassist Mick Clarke and drummer John Richardson to perform their songs. The session men really liked one tune, *Sugar Baby Love,* and approached Polydor to release it as a single. They did and it was a hit.

The musicians hurriedly formed themselves into a group and adopted the name the Rubettes. Da Vinci had aspirations to become a solo star and declined the offer to join the new band, so guitarist Alan Williams was brought in as the sixth Rubette. After

two more hits with Polydor the group moved to State records, owned by Bickerton and Waddington, their first single for the label being *I Can Do It,* a Top 10 hit in 1975. Meanwhile Paul da Vinci managed a Top 20 entry on his own with *Your Baby Ain't Your Baby Anymore.* The Rubettes carried their success through to 1977 by which time they had discarded their white stage berets and rock and roll pastiches for casual clothes and a softer, more thoughtful sound. Their final chart appearance came in April 1977 when *Baby I Know* made the Top 20.

350

THE STREAK

RAY STEVENS

15 June 1974, for one week

●

Janus 6146 201

Written by Ray Stevens. Produced by Ray Stevens.

The eclectic Ray Stevens (born Ray Ragsdale, Clarksdale, Georgia, 1939) has recorded for at least eight labels and in as many different styles. He took music seriously, having studied the subject at Georgia State University, but many of his biggest hits were novelty records. Stevens' first US success came in 1961 with *Jeremiah Peabody's Poly-Unsaturated Quick Dissolving Fast Acting Pleasant Tasting Green and Purple Pills,* the longest unbracketed title in chart history. Many American successes followed. In 1970 he managed his first UK hit with the optimistic pop song *Everything Is Beautiful.* A year later he rushed the stage with the number 2 hit *Bridget The Midget,* a song about a cabaret dwarf. *The Streak* concerned the short-lived fad of running naked in public places, the more observers the better. This was his greatest international hit, but his finest musical moment came in 1975 when his bluegrass version of the Johnny Mathis hit *Misty* was awarded a Grammy for the Best Arrangement Accompanying a Vocalist.

Stevens' streak of success ended in 1977, although he continued to score US country hits, mainly with novelty songs. A man who made the Top 40 imitating a group of chickens clucking Glenn Miller's *In The Mood* is assured of a place in chart history.

351

ALWAYS YOURS

GARY GLITTER

22 June 1974, for one week

●

Bell 1359

Written by Mike Leander and Gary Glitter. Produced by Mike Leander.

After two highly successful slow songs, *I Love You Love Me Love* and *Remember Me This Way,* Gary Glitter and writing partner Mike Leander decided an uptempo song was needed. They released *Always Yours* and claimed their third number one. Once more the tune was an ode to the fans. Glitter usually pre-announced it with a grin on his face by saying 'I'm Yours, Always Yours'. The follow-up *Oh Yes! You're Beautiful* peaked at 2, the closest he has ever come to getting a fourth number one. Within a year his run of Top 10 hits ended. His first 11 hits all made the Top 10 and this remains a record.

Years later Glitter faced bankruptcy. It wasn't that he had failed to receive his royalties, it was merely that he somehow managed to spend them. However, he is one of those performers who are never forgotten and in 1984 he had his most successful comeback. That June he cracked the Top 40 with *Dance Me Up.* In December he had his first Top 10 hit for nine years, taking the festive *Another Rock 'n' Roll Xmas* to number 7. Glitter remained an eager concert performer, and appeared at Wembley as part of the bill for Wham!'s final concert.

352

SHE

CHARLES AZNAVOUR

29 June 1974, for four weeks

●●●●

Barclay BAR 26

Written by Charles Aznavour and Herbert Kretzmer. Produced by Eddie Barclay, arranged by Del Newman.

The theme from the TV series *The Seven Faces Of Woman* gave French superstar Charles Aznavour his biggest international hit. In Britain, it was his only hit apart from *The Old Fashioned Way,* which despite climbing no higher than number 38 in the charts, gave Aznavour 15 weeks of chart glory, one week longer than *She.*

Charles Aznavour (born 22 May 1924) is the only French solo singer to top the British charts, although Serge Gainsbourg partnered his English friend, Jane Birkin, to number one in 1969. It gave Eddie Barclay and his Barclay Records, which had for years been hugely successful in France, their biggest international hit, and put the not obviously attractive Aznavour into the upper reaches of worldwide superstardom. Aznavour is now beyond needing chart success, like Sinatra, Tom Jones and a few others. This is lucky for him as he has had none since 1974.

She joined Anthony Newley's *Why* as the shortest title to reach number one, although less than 9 months later, a two letter title took over the honour of being the shortest at number one. British lyricist Herbert Kretzmer, in 1982 the Daily Mail TV critic, had come near to a number one in 1960 with his witty words for Peter Sellers and Sophia Loren's hit *Goodness Gracious Me,* but this time he reached the very top.

353

ROCK YOUR BABY

GEORGE MCCRAE

27 July 1974, for three weeks

●●●

Jayboy BOY 85

Written by Harry W Casey and Richard Finch. Produced by Harry W Casey and Richard Finch.

Eras in popular music are quite often signalled by individual records. *Rock Your Baby* clearly began the disco craze of the seventies. The first number one by a black artist since *My Ding-a-Ling* in 1972, it was followed by five soul and reggae chart-toppers by the end of the year.

Rock Your Baby was originally intended for McCrae's wife Gwen, but when she couldn't make the session, engineer H W Casey cut the record with George, allegedly on scrap tape. The unusual production, distinguished by a lengthy introduction and the vocalist's falsetto delivery, found fast favour in Puerto Rican and gay clubs in New York. Purchases by their clientele forced the record onto WABC, then the nation's most important Top 40 outlet. Other radio stations had to follow suit, and *Rock Your Baby* became a worldwide smash with total sales estimated in excess of ten million.

McCrae had come a long way from his first group, The Fabulous Stepbrothers. Ironically, his producer and record company went on to more lasting success than he did. Casey won fame as KC of KC and the Sunshine Band while TK, an American label distributed in Britain by Jayboy, was a leading label of the mid-seventies.

354

WHEN WILL I SEE YOU
AGAIN

THE THREE DEGREES

17 August 1974, for two weeks

● ●

Philadelphia International PIR 2155

Written by Kenny Gamble and Leon Huff. Produced by Kenny Gamble and Leon Huff.

There have been four groups who begin with 'Three' in the singles chart: Three Kayes, who later became The Kaye Sisters, Three Good Reasons, Three Dog Night and The Three Degrees. Of these only the latter two have broken into the Top 10, Three Dog Night with Randy Newman's *Mama Told Me Not To Come* (number 3 in August 1970) and The Three Degrees, whose first Top 10 was also their first and only number one. The Three Degrees remain by far the most successful of the four groups with a triple connotation. They were the poppiest part of the popular Philadelphia International roster.

Consisting of Fayette Pickney, Sheila Fer-

The Three Degrees *shown during their most precious moments – August 1974.*

guson and Valerie Thompson, The Three Degrees went on to three more Top 10 successes after *When Will I See You Again.* During this period they earned the reputation as Prince Charles' favourite pop group and Sheila Ferguson was invited to dance with the heir to the throne. They have not been seen on the chart since 1979, although they continued to tour the cabaret circuit regularly.

355

LOVE ME FOR A
REASON

THE OSMONDS

31 August 1974, for three weeks

● ● ●

MGM 2006 458

Written by Johnny Bristol. Produced by Mike Curb.

The five singing Osmonds were Alan (born 22 July 1949), Wayne (born 28 August 1951), Merrill (born 30 April 1953), Jay (born 2 March 1955) and Donny (born 9 December 1957). Older brothers Virl and Tommy were involved with running the Osmonds' management company.

The writer of *Love Me For A Reason,* Johnny Bristol was one of the great Motown writer/producers of the late '60s. He was fated to have only one hit featuring his own vocal chords, *Hang On In There Baby,* which like *Love Me For A Reason* entered the chart on 25 August 1974. It peaked at 3. The producer of *Love Me For A Reason,* Mike Curb, was the President of MGM Records. He won greater responsibility when he became Lieutenant Governor of California.

This was the last number one by any of the Osmond configurations. In all the family mustered a handsome 26 hits in just over four-and-a-half years. The last of these was the Osmonds' 1976 number 37 *I Can't Live A Dream.* The Osmonds broke up in 1980, only to reform without Donny two years later. Since 1982 they've been a country act and in 1984 and '85 returned to Britain to appear at the annual Country Music Festival in Wembley.

356

KUNG FU FIGHTING

CARL DOUGLAS

21 September 1974, for three weeks

● ● ●

Pye 7N 45377

Written by Carl Douglas. Produced by Biddu.

Kung Fu Fighting was recorded in ten minutes flat, sold nearly ten million copies worldwide and was a number one hit both in the UK and USA. Not bad for a song that was intended to be a B-side.

Carl Douglas was born in Jamaica but was living in London when he and Indian-born producer Biddu began working together. The pair had previously collaborated on the film *Embassy*; Biddu had written the title song and Douglas had supplied the vocals. During a recording session for the singer's single *I Want To Give You My Everything*, Douglas asked his producer if he could write the B-side. Kung Fu, a martial art not unlike karate, was being taught throughout Britain in 1974, having risen to popularity through the violent Bruce Lee films. Carl Douglas had written a song about the fad and presented it, along with a handful of others, to Biddu. The tune was recorded and little else thought about it.

Pye flipped the single to feature *Kung Fu Fighting* as the A-side and, after a slow start, it began selling. By climbing to the top it gave Biddu the distinction of being the first Asian to produce a number one hit.

357

ANNIE'S SONG

JOHN DENVER

12 October 1974, for one week

●

RCA APBO 0295

Ken Boothe *nabbed the only number one on the famous reggae label Trojan.*

Written by John Denver. Produced by Milt Okun.

John Denver was born John Deutschendorf in New Mexico in 1933, but took his stage name from the biggest city in Colorado, the state whose natural beauty inspired many of his songs. It is an astonishing fact that this song of praise to his wife Ann is his only solo hit in Britain. Over seven years later a duet with Placido Domingo, *Perhaps Love*, brought him back into the charts, but his American hits like *Rocky Mountain High*, *Take Me Home Country Roads* (covered by Olivia Newton-John) and *Sunshine On My Shoulder* all failed in Britain.

Probably John Denver has reconciled himself to this failure. In the States his popularity in the early '70s was such that he eventually rated a cover of *Time* magazine. He wrote songs for other artistes, for example *Leavin' On A Jet Plane* for Peter, Paul and Mary. He starred in the box-office smash movie *Oh God* with George Burns and continues to play sell-out concerts all over America and many other parts of the world.

358

SAD SWEET DREAMER

SWEET SENSATION

19 October 1974, for one week

●

Pye 7N 45385

Written by D.E.S. Parton. Produced by D.E.S. Parton and Tony Hatch

Like Showaddywaddy before them, Manchester-based soft-soul band Sweet Sensation were winners of the ITV talent show *New Faces*. One of the panel of judges was Tony Hatch, who took the group under his wing to produce his seventh and final number one to date.

At the time of their success Sweet Sensation was an eight-man outfit comprising four vocalists and four musicians. The singers were Vincent James, Junior Daye, St. Clair Palmer and Marcel King, who at 16 was the youngest member. The music came from Barry Johnson on bass, Leroy Smith on piano, Roy Flowers on drums and guitarist

Gary Shaugnessy, the only white member of the band. Producer and writer D.E.S. Parton was in fact David Parton who would score a Top 10 hit of his own two years later by covering *Isn't She Lovely*, a track from Stevie Wonder's double album *Songs In The Key of Life*.

The group had only one further success, *Purely By Coincidence*, which reached number 11. Indeed it was pure coincidence that Ken Boothe, who replaced Sweet Sensation at number one, enjoyed just one more hit, that at number 11. Although they tried for a third hit Sweet Sensation's next single release, *Boom Boom Boom*, bombed.

359

EVERYTHING I OWN

KEN BOOTHE

26 October 1974, for three weeks

● ● ●

Trojan TR 7920

Written by David Gates. Produced by Lloyd Chalmers.

Ken Boothe was born in Jamaica in 1949. In 1967 he recorded a version of Sandie Shaw's *Puppet On A String*, but the first the British charts knew of him was when his reggae version of Bread's *Everything I Own* climbed to the summit seven years later. The song was written by Bread's lead singer David Gates and it had already been a number 32 hit for the group in 1972. Throughout his version Ken Boothe sings 'Anything I Own' rather than 'Everything I Own', thus making this record one of the few in which the title is never actually sung. There are other examples of this at number one, like *Space Oddity*, *The Ballad Of John And Yoko*, *Bohemian Rhapsody* and *The Chicken Song*, but Ken Boothe's record is the only one on which the title should have been sung but by mistake wasn't.

Ken Boothe seemed to have the makings of a regular chartbuster, with a smooth style and a choice of material that showed the breadth of his musical taste. But after only one more hit, *Crying Over You*, he dropped off the charts at the end of February 1975 for ever. The song, however, came back to life in 1987 when Boy George (see no. 586) took his version of *Everything I Own* to number one, following the Boothe arrangement rather than Bread's original, the 11th song to hit number one in two different versions. David Gates returned to the top spot as a writer with Telly Savalas' reading of *If* (see no. 367).

360

GONNA MAKE YOU A STAR

DAVID ESSEX

16 November 1974, for three weeks

●●●

CBS 2492

Written by David Essex. Produced by Jeff Wayne.

David Cook's first musical occupation was as a jazz drummer in the '60s band the Everons. Derek Bowman, then theatre critic for the *Daily Express*, was told about the group. When he saw them at a pub in Leytonstone he was immediately impressed with the charismatic drummer. When Cook (born 23 July 1947) left the band Bowman became his manager, persuading the youngster to change his name to Essex, one he felt was more suited to both music and theatre.

Initial releases on Fontana, then Decca, all failed. Somewhat disappointed with his singer's lack of chart success Bowman turned to the world of theatre in which he himself had more interest. Essex's first role was in a provisional production of the American musical *The Fantastics*. A part in *Oh Kay* by P.G. Wodehouse/George and Ira Gershwin soon followed. His first lead was in an American show *Your Own Thing*. The big break came in October 1971 when he landed the role of Jesus in *Godspell* at Chalk Farm's Roundhouse Theatre. The reviews were ecstatic. When film producer David Puttnam saw the show he offered Essex the part of Jim McClain in his forthcoming production *That'll Be The Day*. Essex took a seven week break from *Godspell* to shoot the film and wrote *Rock On* for the soundtrack. The song was released worldwide by CBS in August 1973 and became a massive international hit, putting Essex in the envia-

ble position of being a star of cinema, theatre and music.

Lamplight and *America* followed *Rock On* into the UK charts, and as soon as he had finished filming *Stardust*, the follow-up to *That'll Be The Day*, Essex concentrated on his career as a pop singer. *Gonna Make You A Star* was recorded at Advision Studios and featured Herbie Flowers' infectious bass riff.

361

YOU'RE THE FIRST THE LAST MY EVERYTHING

BARRY WHITE

7 December 1974, for two weeks

●●

20th Century BTC 2133

Written by Barry White, Tony Sepe and Peter Radcliffe. Produced by Barry White.

Big Barry is by far the most successful of any of the Whites to appear in the British singles chart. Of the other four (Chris, Snowy, Tam and Tony Joe) only Snowy has had more than one chart entry, and even his second and final hit only peaked at number 66.

Barry first appeared in 1973 with *I'm Gonna Love You Just A Little Bit More Baby* which made number 23 and set the standard for the title length of White's singles. The longer the title the better White's chances of a hit. His shorter titles (there are three of four words each) tended not to get quite as high as songs like *You See The Trouble With Me* (number 2 in 1976) and *Can't Get Enough Of Your Love Babe* (number 8 in 1974), although quite against form *It's Ecstasy When You Lay Down Next To Me*, which ought by rights to have been a sure-fire number one, stalled at a disappointing number 40.

Barry White was born in Galveston, Texas in 1944 and between the years of 1973 and 1978 notched up a creditable five Top 20s, four Top 10s and a number one. His smash instrumental *Love Theme* by the Love Unlimited Orchestra was another Top 10er. Barry White is also the answer to the bizarre trivia question 'who had a bigger UK hit with *Just*

The Way You Are than its composer Billy Joel?'

362

LONELY THIS CHRISTMAS

MUD

21 December 1974, for four weeks

●●●●

RAK 187

Written by Nicky Chinn and Mike Chapman. Produced by Nicky Chinn and Mike Chapman.

Mud's first two chart-topping singles were separated by two more Top 10 hits, *The Cat Crept In* (number 2) and *Rocket* (number 6). The group were now in the middle of their glorious but short-lived run of success. This spot of delicate Yuletide emotional blackmail, like their first two number ones, came from the combination of the pens of Chapman and Chinn and the presses of Mickie Most's RAK.

Mud consisted of Les Gray on lead vocals, Rob Davis on guitar, Roy Stiles on bass and Dave Mount on drums. In 1987 long after the

Barry White *had his first, his last, his every number one in 1974.*

glitter of the charts had faded a reformed group billed as 'Les Gray's Mud' could be found playing in supper clubs, as well as college dances and Student Union Christmas parties for students with long memories. Like Gary Glitter, the group are able to capitalize on being a nostalgic remnant so that for the next few holiday seasons people will murmur the chorus of *Lonely This Christmas.*

363

DOWN DOWN

STATUS QUO

18 January 1975, for one week

●

Vertigo 6059 114

Written by Francis Rossi and Robert Young. Produced by Status Quo.

In 1975 Status Quo were guitarist/vocalist Francis Rossi (born Michael Rossi 29 May 1949), guitarist/vocalist Rick Parfitt (born 12 October 1948), bassist/vocalist Alan Lancaster (born 7 February 1949) and drummer John Coghlan (born 19 September 1946). Rossi met Lancaster at school and formed the Scorpions when the pair were but 13-years-old. Coghlan was recruited in 1965 and the name changed to the Spectres. Three flop singles were released through Pye and the name was changed again to Traffic Jam. Under this guise they recorded the prophetically titled *Almost There But Not Quite.* 1967 saw the arrival of Parfitt and a final name change to Status Quo.

The early Quo were purveyors of psychedelic bubble gum music and scored two Top 10 hits with *Pictures of Matchstick Men* and *Ice In The Sun.* But they soon became disenchanted with their pop image and replaced their Carnaby Street clothes with T-shirts and jeans. The band kept a low profile for two years while they perfected their harder, 12 bar boogie sound. A Top 20 entry, *Down The Dustpipe,* heralded the change which was complete by the time Quo had moved to Vertigo Records in 1972. Their first single for the label, *Paper Plane,* hit the Top 10 and was third in an unbroken run of 32 Top 40 hits, a feat no other group can boast. *Down Down* was fifth in this sequence.

Lancaster and Coghlan grew tired after

years of touring and quit the group in the '80s. After a brief retirement, Rossi and Parfitt revived the Quo with fresh members and returned to the charts in 1986 with *In The Army Now,* a number two hit and their biggest for six years.

364

MS GRACE

THE TYMES

25 January 1975, for one week

●

RCA 2493

Written by John Hall and Johanna Hall. Produced by Billy Jackson.

With *Ms Grace* the Tymes joined the Dave Clark Five, Bobbie Gentry, Paper Lace, the Osmonds and Barry White on the list of acts who have scored only one number one in the UK and one in the USA, but with different singles. The Tymes took longer about it than the others, having topped the American chart back in 1963 with *So Much In Love,* a UK number 21. By remaining at the top for just seven days on both sides of the Atlantic they made the list with the minimum credentials.

Tymes members George Hilliard and Norman Bennett had been singing together since they met at summer camp in 1956. They formed the Latineers with Donald Banks and Albert Berry. In 1960, when George Williams joined as lead vocalist, the group assumed their more familiar moniker. Hits were always sporadic for the Tymes, one of their best known being their 1969 Top 20 uptempo version of *People,* the Barbra Streisand classic from the musical *Funny Girl. You Little Trust Maker* reintroduced the group to the charts in September 1974, to be followed three months later by *Ms Grace.* The original title had been *Miss Grace* but was altered in the wake of women's liberation.

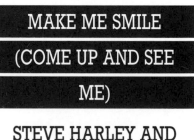

365

JANUARY

PILOT

1 February 1975, for three weeks

● ● ●

EMI 2255

Written by David Paton. Produced by Alan Parsons.

With perfect timing *January* reached number one on 1 February, to give Alan Parsons his first number one production ever. His second followed immediately but his third is yet to come. Pilot were David Paton, Ian Bairnson, Billy Lyle and Stuart Tosh. They first hit the charts with *Magic* at the end of 1974, which spent 11 weeks on the chart without reaching the Top 10 but promised great things for the future. The great things came with *January* which hit number one in its third week on the charts. It was a major surprise when neither of the next two singles hit the Top 30 and the band died a natural death. The song's arranger Andrew Powell went on to record Kate Bush, and both David Paton and Ian Bairnson played on her first LP which included *Wuthering Heights* (see no. 420), but as a group Pilot was grounded.

January was the first month to appear in a number one title apart from Rod Stewart's *Maggie May.* A year later, the Four Seasons took *December '63* (see no. 385) to number one, but otherwise months have been unsuccessful chart sorties.

366

MAKE ME SMILE (COME UP AND SEE ME)

STEVE HARLEY AND COCKNEY REBEL

22 February 1975, for two weeks

EMI 2263

Written by Steve Harley. Produced by Steve Harley and Alan Parsons.

Alan Parsons' second consecutive chart-topper as a producer was the only number one by a group who at one time looked set to be very big indeed. The line-up for *Make Me Smile (Come Up And See Me)* was Steve Harley, Stuart Elliott on drums, Jim Cregan on guitar, Duncan Mackay on keyboards and George Ford on bass. Tina Charles (see no. 386) sang back-up vocals. Jim Cregan later joined Rod Stewart and played on *Da Ya Think I'm Sexy?* (see no. 429) while Duncan Mackay moved up to Strawberry Studios when Kevin Godley and Lol Creme left 10 C.C., and is to be heard on *Dreadlock Holiday* (see no. 426). If this band had stayed together they might have lived up to the promise of the first few hits. However, after only one more single taken from their album *The Best Years Of Our Lives*, a Top 20 hit called *Mr. Raffles (Man It Was Mean)*, Cockney Rebel disbanded.

Steve Harley had one more Top 10 hit on his own in 1976 with the George Harrison composition *Here Comes The Sun*. It was to be a further decade, in 1986, before Harley reappeared in the Top 10, this time in partnership with Sarah Brightman singing the title number from the fabulously successful musical *Phantom Of The Opera*.

367

TELLY SAVALAS

8 March 1975, for two weeks

●●

MCA 174

Written by David Gates. Produced by Snuff Garrett.

A catch phrase of 'who loves ya baby' and a shaven head brought TV policeman Kojak to the public's attention, and it was primarily on the back of Kojak's popularity that actor Telly Savalas had his first and only British

number one single. Savalas had first taken his hair off for Burt Lancaster's *Birdman Of Alcatraz* (1962) and it became his trademark in a long and varied career which included *Horror Express, A Town Called Bastard* and *Genghis Khan*. He also made an appearance in *On Her Majesty's Secret Service* (1969) and the *The Great Muppet Movie* (1979). Although in most of the films Savalas's bald head and stocky build made him an ideal villain, in real life it was a different story.

Telly Savalas (real name Aristotle Savalas) was born on 21 January 1925 in Garden City, New York, from Greek stock. He graduated from Columbia University and went straight into action as a GI in World War II. He was injured in action and thus decorated with the Purple Heart. After the war he joined the Information Services of the State Department and went on to work as a senior director for ABC News. While at ABC he won the Peabody Award for one of his series, *Your Voice Of America*. He was in his late 30s when he turned to acting, first on TV and later in feature films.

368

THE BAY CITY ROLLERS

22 March 1975, for six weeks

●●●●●●

Bell 1409

Written by Bob Crewe and Bob Gaudio. Produced by Phil Wainman.

The Bay City Rollers (original name the Saxons) hailed from Edinburgh and were Leslie McKeown (born 12 November 1955) on lead vocals, Eric Faulkner (born 21 October 1955) and Stuart Wood (born 25 February 1957) on guitars, Alan Longmuir (born 20 June 1953) on bass, and his brother Derek (born 19 March 1955) on drums. By the time *Bye Bye Baby* hit the top the Rollers' first five singles had already been Top 10 hits, four of them in 1974. In that year the revamped Rollers, backed with slick material mostly from the pens of Bill Martin and Phil Coulter, who had previously written Sandie Shaw's Eurovision winner *Puppet On A String*, and management from Tam Paton.

Despite accusations that they didn't actually play on their own records, the Bay City Rollers became a group with an hysterical following, their young audience imitating their trademark tartan clothing. At their heady peak the Bay City Rollers were not just a British, but a worldwide teen sensation.

369

MUD

3 May 1975, for two weeks

●●

RAK 201

Written by Sonny West, Norman Petty and Bill Tilghman. Produced by Nicky Chinn and Mike Chapman.

Oh Boy was the last of Mud's three number ones and was actually issued after the group had moved away from Chinn and Chapman and RAK to a new home at the Private Stock label. The song also had the distinction of being the only chart-topper that Chinn and Chapman produced but did not write. It was issued by RAK as a follow-up to the number 3 hit *The Secrets That You Keep*. This was a comparatively long title for Mud, who would here appear to be the antithesis of Barry White. Ten of their 15 chart singles had either one or two word titles. This was the second time *Oh Boy* had been a major hit. The first time around, in 1958, it climbed to number 3 for the Crickets.

After *Oh Boy* Mud did not re-ascend the heights they had previously reached. They still managed another four Top 10 singles, three on the new label, one an earlier RAK recording, between June 1975 and November 1976. They are able to look back proudly at a career that boasts three number ones, six Top 10s and three Top 20s in three years. Only one of their singles in this period failed to make the Top 30.

370

STAND BY YOUR MAN

TAMMY WYNETTE

17 May 1975, for three weeks

●●●

Epic EPC 7137

Written by Billy Sherrill and Tammy Wynette. Produced by Billy Sherrill.

Tammy Wynette (born Virginia Wynette Pugh, 5 May 1942) had been divorced from her husband, country singer George Jones, for exactly two months when this song of female devotion became her only number one. It had been recorded seven years earlier. Tammy's chart career is unusual in that each of her three hit singles, *Stand By Your Man, D.I.V.O.R.C.E.,* and *I Don't Want*

The supremely talented and occasionally successful **Johnny Nash** *learns that* Tears On My Pillow *will be the last of his six Top 10 hits.*

To Play House were re-releases of American country hits from 1967/68.

Tammy was well qualified to sing about the subject of marriage, having gone through the process five times, beginning at the age of 17. By 20 she had three children. Working as a beautician in Birmingham, Alabama, she supplemented her income by plugging records and singing in local clubs and bars. She then came to the attention of Epic producer Billy Sherrill, who signed her to the label in 1966. Her relationship with George Jones was at first musical, but matrimony followed in 1969.

On 6 July 1978 Tammy decided to stand by yet another man, friend and record producer George Richey. The pair married in the singer's luxury Florida home. Her biography, also called *Stand By Your Man,* was adapted for film in 1982.

371

WHISPERING GRASS

WINDSOR DAVIES AND DON ESTELLE

7 June 1975, for three weeks

●●●

EMI 2290

Written by Fred and Doris Fisher. Produced by Walter Ridley.

TV comedy writers Jimmy Perry and David Croft had a long association with the BBC, responsible as a team or with other writers for such series as *Are You Being Served?, Hi De Hi, 'Allo 'Allo* and *Dad's Army.* Each of these series spawned one hit: *Are You Being Served Sir?* by John Inman, *Hi De Hi (Holiday Rock)* by Paul Shane and the Yellowcoats, *Je T'Aime (Allo Allo)* by Rene and Yvette and, indirectly, *Grandad* by Clive Dunn (see no. 295). *It Ain't Half Hot Mum,* set in wartime India, starred Windsor Davies and Don Estelle, who respectively played the bullying Battery Sgt Major Williams and the diminutive and cowardly Private 'Lofty' Sugden. They became the most successful of Perry and Croft's creations by scoring two hits.

Whispering Grass had been made popular four decades earlier by one of the most suc-

cessful singing groups of the pre-chart era, the Inkspots. When the cast of *It Ain't Half Hot Mum* were asked to record an album of army concert party favourites, *Whispering Grass* was a natural choice but in this version Estelle's beautiful tenor was juxtaposed with Davies' gruff spoken voice. When released as a single it climbed to the top of the charts within a month. The follow-up, *Paper Doll,* reached number 41 in autumn 1975 but subsequent solo efforts by Don Estelle failed to chart. However the Davies/Estelle partnership had been formed and the pair continued to appear together in pantomime and cabaret for several years.

372

I'M NOT IN LOVE

10 C.C.

28 June 1975, for two weeks

●●

Mercury 6008 014

Written by Graham Gouldman and Eric Stewart. Produced by 10 C.C.

I'm Not In Love was 10 C.C.'s second number one single, coming two years after 1973's *Rubber Bullets.* It was also the second release for their new label Mercury who had signed them from Jonathan King's UK label. The track was taken from their *Original Soundtrack* album, a set that had yielded up a number 7 for the group in the shape of *Life Is A Minestrone* and would give them a number 5 later in the year with *Art For Art's Sake.*

With hindsight *I'm Not In Love* can be seen as one of the outstanding songs of the 1970s and certainly one of the best of 10 C.C.'s influential output. The string of successful singles the group put together between 1972 and 1978 made them the most consistent hitmakers of any British group in the 1970s. They can list three number ones and eight Top 10s.

I'm Not In Love also enjoyed a further brief spell of chart success in 1987 when two-time Eurovision winner Johnny Logan took his version into the Top 50. Godley and Creme split from Gouldman and Stewart in 1976, creating two hit acts. They were together on 1987's smash compilation album *Changing Faces.*

373

TEARS ON MY PILLOW

JOHNNY NASH

12 July 1975, for one week

●

CBS 3220

Written by Ernie Smith. Produced by Johnny Nash.

John Lester Nash Jr, born in Houston, Texas on 19 August 1940, first hit the British charts in 1968 when his reggae-flavoured *Hold Me Tight* reached number 5 in the autumn of that year. He had been a successful recording star in America since the end of 1957 when his first hit, *A Very Special Love*, reached number 46 in the Billboard charts. At the end of 1958 he released a single with ABC Paramount stable mates Paul Anka and George Hamilton IV called *The Teen Commandments,* which gave him his biggest hit until *Hold Me Tight* and which is now a collectors' item.

A succession of hits followed *Hold Me Tight*, oddly enough in batches of three every three years. After three hits in 1968/69, and three more in 1972 (including his US number one hit *I Can See Clearly Now), Tears On My Pillow* was the first of three hits in 1975-6. 1979 passed without Nash's distinctive voice returning to the charts. He remains one of the most successful reggae acts in British chart history, and his early recordings of the late Bob Marley's songs certainly contributed to the subsequent success that came to Marley and the Wailers a little later.

374

GIVE A LITTLE LOVE

THE BAY CITY ROLLERS

19 July 1975, for three weeks

● ● ●

Bell 1425

Written by Johnny Goodison and Phil Wainman. Producer by Phil Wainman.

Give A Little Love was the Bay City Rollers' second consecutive number one single. In a year's time they had the last of their ten consecutive Top 10 singles, *I Only Wanna Be With You.* By then Alan Longmuir had left because he felt that at 26 he was too old for the group. He was replaced by 18-year-old Ian Mitchell, who himself left and was replaced by Pat McGlynn. When McGlynn quit in 1977 the group continued as a four piece. They met with little success when their record company tried to give them a more adult image. During the last year of their huge British success, they also managed a number one single in the USA, but it was all downhill after this, and after two chart appearances at number 16 and 34 in 1977 they did not appear in the chart again.

375

BARBADOS

TYPICALLY TROPICAL

9 August 1975, for one week

●

Gull GULS 14

Written by Jeffrey Calvert and Max West. Produced by Jeffrey Calvert and Max West.

Jeffrey Calvert and Max West, two recording engineers, used spare studio time to record their own compositions. One of those was a Christmas novelty tune, *The Ghost Song,* which was recorded for Mickie Most's RAK label but was finished too late to be released for the 1974 festive season. Having failed to cash in on the Christmas market they then made a bid for summer success with a piece of ersatz reggae entitled *Barbados,* featuring spoken vocals by Captain Tobias Wilcock of Coconut Airways.

Although it was far from the genuine article, *Barbados* had originally been scheduled for release with legendary reggae label Trojan Records. At the last moment Gull stepped in with a better offer. As perfect for summer as *In The Summertime* had been in 1970, the single took off as soon as it was released but had to hold at number 2 for a couple of weeks before the Rollers lost their grip on the top spot.

Apart from Calvert and West, who aspired to emulate the success of writers/producers

Mike Chapman and Nicky Chinn, Typically Tropical was an aggregation of session musicians. Even at the time it seemed unlikely that they could follow up their hit and plans to revitalize *The Ghost Song* came to nothing. Typically Tropical remain one hit wonders to this day.

Typically Tropical *flew higher than any other act for seven days in August, 1975.*

376

CAN'T GIVE YOU ANYTHING (BUT MY LOVE)

THE STYLISTICS

16 August 1975, for three weeks

● ● ●

Avco 6105 039

Written by Hugo Peretti, Luigi Creatore and George David Weiss. Produced by Hugo Peretti and Luigi Creatore.

The leftovers of two defunct Philadelphia groups, the Percussions and the Monarchs, combined at the beginning of the 1970s to create the Stylistics, a five man vocal group which built its hits around the falsetto singing of their lead vocalist, Russell Thompkins Jr. The other members of the group, James Dunn, Aaron Love, Herbie Murrell and James Smith, provided a slick backing but the only real distinction of the group sound was Thompkins' lead vocal.

When first they signed for Hugo and Luigi's Avco label, their singles were produced by Thom Bell, and in the main written by Bell and Linda Creed. Records like *I'm Stone In Love With You* and *You Make Me Feel Brand New* made the Stylistics one of the hottest groups in the world by the mid-'70s, and when Hugo and Luigi themselves (with more than a little help from the late Van McCoy) took over production of Stylistics singles, the hits carried on uninterrupted. *Can't Give You Anything (But My Love)* was the group's tenth chart single and was co-written by George David Weiss, who had also co-written *Can't Help Falling In Love* for Elvis Presley (see no. 133). It was no surprise, therefore, that the Stylistics recorded *Can't Help Falling In Love* in 1976 and made it one of those very rare songs to have been a Top 10 hit three times.

377

SAILING

ROD STEWART

6 September 1975, for four weeks

●●●●

Warner Brothers K 16600

Written by Gavin Sutherland. Produced by Tom Dowd.

Sailing had more weeks on the chart than any record from the second half of the '70s except Boney M's *Rivers of Babylon/Brown Girl In The Ring*. It had 11 weeks in its first go, which included four weeks at number one and 20 weeks in the second run the following year when it crawled back to number 3. The comeback was spurred by the use of the record as the theme for a BBC television series about HMS Ark Royal.

This song originally appeared on an album by the Sutherland Brothers. Sutherland knew he had penned a catchy tune and used it with joke lyrics for a flimsy single

distributed as a Christmas greeting, now a collectable for trivia buffs and Stewart aficionados.

Rod, who realized his recording career needed a shot in the arm, went to record in the United States with legendary producer Tom Dowd. Arriving at the Muscle Shoals Studio he inquired where the famous rhythm section was. Told he was looking at them, he blurted out in surprise that they were white men. He had assumed such soulful players had to be black.

Stewart intended his version of *Sailing* to be 'one for the terraces', a record whose popularity would be enhanced by its use by football crowds. He was proved correct by supporters around the country.

378

HOLD ME CLOSE

DAVID ESSEX

4 October 1975, for three weeks

●●●

CBS 3572

Written by David Essex. Produced by Jeff Wayne.

Since *Gonna Make You A Star* reached the top in 1974, David Essex had finished filming *Stardust* and had twice made the Top 10. *Hold Me Close* proved to be his final number one.

He was involved in Jeff Wayne's massively popular *War Of The Worlds* LP, but he then changed careers once more, returning to the theatre in 1978 to win the Variety Club Personality of the Year award for his portrayal of Che Guevara in *Evita*. His single *Oh What A Circus* from *Evita* reached number 3 in the autumn of 1978. In 1980 the theme from his motorcycle movie *Silver Dream Machine* gave him his eighth Top 10 hit. 1982 found him hosting his own TV series *The David Essex Showcase*, a programme which concentrated on new acts such as Mari Wilson and Philip Jap. Later that same year he appeared as the poet Byron in the Young Vic's production of *Childe Byron,* and he rounded off a hectic 12 months by having one of his biggest hits to date, *A Winter's Tale,* which was kept from the top only by Renée and Renato's immortal love duet.

Probably his most ambitious project started in 1983 when he began work on a musical based on 1789's mutiny on H.M.S. Bounty. The show opened in London's Piccadilly Theatre in 1984 with Essex as Fletcher Christian and Frank Finlay as Captain Blythe. *Tahiti,* taken from the musical, brought his Top 10 tally into double figures.

379

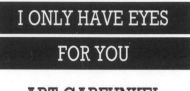

ART GARFUNKEL

25 October 1975, for two weeks

●●

CBS 3575

Written by Harry Warren and Al Dubin. Produced by Richard Perry.

After splitting with Paul Simon, Art Garfunkel followed a film career, starring in such successes as *Catch 22* and the Jack Nicholson – Ann-Margret – Candice Bergen film *Carnal Knowledge.* He recorded only sporadically and his first solo hit in Britain came after Paul Simon had already had four solo outings on our charts, including two Top 10 hits. Garfunkel did better than his former partner, however, by reaching the very top with this song from the 1930s which had been an American hit for the Flamingos in 1959.

The writers of this song, Harry Warren and Al Dubin, also wrote such standards as *September In The Rain* and *You're Getting To Be A Habit With Me,* but *I Only Have Eyes For You* was their only major success on the British charts. Art Garfunkel's chart career then went into total collapse until his next hit and his next number one in 1979 (see no. 436). Once again, eyes were the secret of his success.

380

SPACE ODDITY

DAVID BOWIE

8 November 1975, for two weeks

●●

RCA 2593

Written by David Bowie. Produced by Gus Dudgeon.

Space Oddity was for years the only record to go to number one as a re-issue. As it first charted in 1969, it had the further distinction of being the only single to have taken more than one year to reach number one after its initial appearance in the best-sellers, until equalled by John Lennon's *Imagine*. It was a slower moving hit than even these statistics suggest. Bowie wrote the number in 1968 for a proposed German television special, *Love You Till Tuesday*.

Space Oddity was eventually released to tie in with the 1969 Apollo moon landing, but Americans shied away from the terrible tale of Major Tom; they wished Neil Armstrong and company success, not doom. The single finally charted in Britain the first week of September, but then dropped out. It re-entered later in the month, eventually earning a placing at number 5. The song finally made the American Top 10 in 1972. Upon re-issue as part of a series of RCA oldies it made its glorious British flight in 1976. Bowie re-recorded it in sparser style for a 1980 B-side. That year his *Ashes to Ashes* (see no. 464), which continued the story of Major Tom, became the only sequel to a number one hit to make number one itself.

Space Oddity was the only Bowie A-side produced by Gus Dudgeon, who later worked on Elton John's hits, including, ironically, *Rocket Man*. Rick Wakeman plays synthesizer on this disc.

381

D.I.V.O.R.C.E.

BILLY CONNOLLY

22 November 1975, for one week

Polydor 2058 652

Written by Billy Connolly, Claude Putnam Jr and Bobby Braddock. Produced by Phil Coulter.

Six months after Tammy Wynette hit the top of the charts with her classic moral clarion call (see no. 370), Billy Connolly adapted one of her biggest American hits to his own purposes and took it all the way to the top, bleeped language and all. The Big Yin transformed the original song into the saga of a scruffy Scottish dog breaking up an otherwise happy and civilized Glasgow couple.

Billy Connolly has been so successful as a comedian that his record sales, though considerable, are merely a sideline. He has had only four chart singles but has enjoyed greater success as an album artist, achieving three Top 10 LPs. After *D.I.V.O.R.C.E.*, he attacked another Tammy Wynette song, *No Charge*, which reached number one when covered by J.J. Barrie (see no. 389). Billy Connolly's version was called *No Chance (No Charge)*. After *In The Brownies* in 1979, a song based in part on the Village People's *Y.M.C.A.* (the only initial song beside *D.I.V.O.R.C.E.* to hit number one), he absented the singles charts until 1985 when his TV theme *Super Gran* reached number 32.

382

BOHEMIAN RHAPSODY

QUEEN

29 November 1975, for nine weeks

●●●●●●●●●

EMI 2375

Written by Freddie Mercury. Produced by Roy Thomas Baker and Queen.

Only eighteen months after their first hit, *Seven Seas Of Rhye*, Queen topped the list with a single that was a technical masterpiece of popular music. Not since *Rose Marie* by Slim Whitman had dominated the chart for 11 weeks in 1955 had a record remained at the top for so long. Any other group may have been cowed by such early success but for vocalist Freddie Mercury

*The first solo number one by **Art Garfunkel** was originally a hit in America by Ben Selvin and his Orchestra in 1934.*

(born Frederick Bulsara, 5 September 1946), guitarist Bryan May (born 19 July 1947), bassist John Deacon (born 19 August 1951) and drummer Roger Taylor (born 26 July 1949) it was simply the start of a career which saw them become one of the most popular groups in the world.

Queen grew out of the art school band Smile which Mercury formed in the early 1970s. They evolved their sound characterized by Freddie Mercury's dramatic vocals and Bryan May's distinctive guitar sound, partly achieved by employing a coin as a plectrum. Whether it was the mock gospel of *Somebody To Love*, the rock and roll pastiche of *Crazy Little Thing Called Love* or the disco influenced *Another One Bites The Dust* (the last two being US number ones), the act was always identifiable as Queen.

A promotional video for television was made for Bo Rhap, as the group affectionately referred to the song, and it is generally agreed to have been the first pop video to assist the success of a single. The trend for video production grew until by the mid-'80s any hit which didn't have an accompanying video was an exception to the rule.

383

MAMMA MIA

ABBA

31 January 1976, for two weeks

● ●

Epic EPC 3790

Written by Stig Anderson, Benny Andersson and Bjorn Ulvaeus. Produced by Benny Andersson and Bjorn Ulvaeus.

The record that changed Abba from just another European group into the Superswedes whose sales exceeded those of Volvo was *Mamma Mia*. Not that *Mamma Mia* was itself a massive worldwide smash, but by giving Abba their second number one in Britain almost two years after the first, it established a base of international popularity on which they built their incredible sales of the late '70s and early '80s.

Between *Waterloo* and *Mamma Mia* had been some flops and three hits. Two of those hits did not even make the Top 30, but *SOS*, the release before *Mamma Mia*, climbed to number 6 to return Abba to the Top 10 after 18 months' absence. When *Mamma Mia* hit the top Abba became the first act to have a

number one hit after their Eurovision number one, a feat that has since been equalled by Brotherhood Of Man, Cliff Richard and Bucks Fizz but never by a foreign act. Abba have changed the popular music of recent years by making record executives realize that European groups can sell, whether or not they are Abba imitators. Acts like Europe, a-ha and Kraftwerk owe a lot of their international success to the success of Abba, which really began with *Mamma Mia,* the 383rd record and 400th different song to reach number one.

384

FOREVER AND EVER

SLIK

14 February 1976, for one week

●

Bell 1464

Written by Bill Martin and Phil Coulter. Produced by Bill Martin and Phil Coulter.

Slik, the last of the '70s teen groups were, like the Bay City Rollers, from Scotland. Bill Martin and Phil Coulter wrote and produced them, as they had the Rollers, so not surprisingly they also sounded like the Bay City Rollers.

Martin and Coulter had parted company with the Rollers bandwagon some 12 months before their association with Slik and had been looking for another musical vehicle. They'd long been associated with Eurovision, having written the UK entries in 1966 and 1968 (see nos 232 and 248) and had also masterminded hits for Irish artist Kenny. When Kenny left RAK records, Martin and Coulter simply retained the name, to which they owned the rights, and dumped it on another bunch of young hopefuls who hit with *The Bump* and *Fancy Pants*.

Then came Slik, who were guitarist James 'Midge' Ure, keyboard player Billy McIsaac, drummer Kenny Hyslop and bassist Jim McGinlay. Dressed in smart baseball outfits they were leapt upon by the pop press who applauded them as The Next Big Thing. However Slik were not to be stars forever and ever. Their follow-up, *Requiem,* clambered to number 24 and that was it.

Ure, who nearly joined the Sex Pistols, was able to demonstrate his talent later with New Wavers the Rich Kids, then with New Romantics Visage and electropoppers Ultravox, who had a massive number 2 hit with *Vienna* in 1981. Hyslop also managed to

*Midge Ure (centre front) led **Slik** on their ascent to the top in 1976.*

revive his career by joining Simple Minds that same year. Midge Ure was not to be associated with another number one until almost nine years later. It was to be the biggest selling single in the UK to date (see no. 543).

385

DECEMBER '63 (OH WHAT A NIGHT)

THE FOUR SEASONS

21 February 1976, for two weeks

● ●

Warner Bros K 16688

Written by Bob Gaudio and Judy Parker. Produced by Bob Gaudio.

The Four Seasons emanated from New Jersey and named themselves after the cocktail lounge in a bowling alley. The original line-up was Frankie Valli (born Francis Castelluccio in Newark, 3 May 1937), Tommy DeVito, Nick DeVito and Hank Megenski. The group achieved huge success in the early '60s with hits like *Sherry, Let's Hang On,* and *Rag Doll* but the line up that operated by then had changed to Valli, Tommy DeVito, Bob Gaudio (born in The Bronx, New York on 17 November 1942) and Nick Massi. They achieved considerable credibility, that helped them survive a turbulent period in pop music's history, when the Rolling Stones announced that the Four Seasons was the only American group worth paying any attention to.

In the year before their only British number one single they had two Top 10 hits with *Night* and *Who Loves You,* but by now the group was really five Seasons featuring Valli, Gaudio, Don Ciccone, John Paiva and Gerry Polci, the last-named handling the lead vocal on *December '63.* The follow-up was *Silver Star* which made number 3 in the same year. Valli was not through, however, landing a Top 10 theme tune, *Grease,* in 1978.

Brotherhood of Man *hitching a ride back from the Eurovision Song Contest.*

386

I LOVE TO LOVE (BUT MY BABY LOVES TO DANCE)

TINA CHARLES

6 March 1976, for three weeks

● ● ●

CBS 3937

Written by Jack Robinson and James Bolden. Produced by Biddu.

With *I Love To Love* Tina Charles emerged from the legion of studio session singers to become, albeit briefly, Britain's foremost female disco star. Her loud and full-throated voice had anonymously graced many hits, most notably *I'm On Fire,* a Top 5 hit released under the group name *5000 Volts* in 1975. At the beginning of 1976 she began working with Indian producer Biddu, who had provided Carl Douglas with a number one hit in both the UK and USA 18 months earlier (see no. 356). The partnership worked and a star was born.

Tina only made the Top 10 on two further occasions with *Dr Love* and *Dance Little Lady Dance,* although a remixed version of *I Love To Love* sold over 600,000 copies across Europe when released in 1986. Unfortunately Tina's career was held back by a lack of good material and the birth of her first baby in 1977. A friend at the time of her number one was Trevor Horn. Horn had long been a pal of musician and jingle writer Geoff Downes, whom he recruited to Tina's tour band. Downes and Horn began writing songs with Bruce Wooley, including *Baby Blue,* a minor hit for Dusty Springfield in 1979 (see no. 213). But the Downes-Horn partnership was to produce greater success once they had assumed the group identity of the Buggles (see no. 444).

387

SAVE YOUR KISSES FOR ME

BROTHERHOOD OF MAN

27 March 1976, for six weeks

● ● ● ● ● ●

Pye 7N 45989

Written by Tony Hiller, Martin Lee and Lee Sheriden. Produced by Tony Hiller.

More than *Waterloo,* more than *Puppet On A String,* more than *Non Ho L'Eta Per Amarti, Save Your Kisses For Me* was a

runaway Eurovision Song Contest winner even before the voting had started. The coy little song of Daddy going to work and leaving his 3-year-old daughter at home for the day not only smashed through the charts and into the hearts of Europe, but marked an astonishing and surprisingly long-lived comeback for Brotherhood of Man.

In 1970 Brotherhood of Man were a two man, two girl vocal group rather hurriedly put together around a session hit, *United We Stand,* that reached number 10 in Britain. It was used as an anthem of gay liberation in America in the early seventies. There is nothing in the lyrics to assume that the subject might be homosexuality, but it's an easy song to sing along with and the group's name could be made to fit the cause.

388

FERNANDO

ABBA

8 May 1976, for four weeks

● ● ● ●

Epic EPC 4036

Written by Stig Anderson, Benny Andersson and Bjorn Ulvaeus. Produced by Benny Andersson and Bjorn Ulvaeus

Abba's third number one, their second in succession, was *Fernando*. It knocked Brotherhood of Man off the top, but they retaliated by modelling their style ever closer on Abba, and even coming up with two more chart-toppers, *Angelo* and *Figaro* (see nos 410 and 418) whose titles bore a more than coincidental similarity to *Fernando*.

Fernando was a gentle anti-war song, featuring the only mistake in English in Bjorn Ulvaeus' lyrics, when he wrote 'Since many years I haven't seen a rifle in your hand'. It may seem churlish to point out the mistakes in English, but it is worth mentioning only because it is unique. How many English writers could write nine number one hits in a foreign language virtually without error? Albert Hammond (writer of *When I Need You* – no. 401) speaks fluent Spanish, but even he prefers to write about the rain in Southern California rather than the rain in Spain. Abba have also had hits with song titles in Italian, *Mamma Mia*, and French,

Voulez-vous, but the nearest they have got to their native Swedish was their ode to Stockholm, *Summer Night City*.

389

NO CHARGE

J J BARRIE

5 June 1976, for one week

●

Power Exchange PX 209

Written by Harlan Howard. Produced by Bill Amesbury.

Canadian J J Barrie (born Barrie Authors, 7 July 1933, Ottawa, Ontario) made it to the top with a cover version of a Melba Montgomery country hit which was also a US success for Tammy Wynette and her daughter, Tina. It was only the second song he had ever recorded.

Barrie, a former comedian and manager of Blue Mink, had not intended to become a singer when he released his first single *Where's The Reason?* in 1976. He and Terry Britten had written the song for Glen Campbell and had sent him a demonstration tape, but Campbell's producer saw no reason why Barrie shouldn't put the song out himself.

Then came the somewhat sentimental *No Charge*, a version of which Barrie had once included in his comedy routines. The uncredited female vocalist who contributed greatly to the single's success is Vicky Brown, the wife of early '60s rocker Joe Brown. Comedian Billy Connolly wasted no time in lampooning the song in the way he had Tammy Wynette's *D.I.V.O.R.C.E.* (see no 381). The Scotsman's version, titled *No Chance (No Charge)*, also made the Top 30. Barrie re-released *Where's The Reason?* as a follow-up but it failed again. Then in 1977, as a tribute to the late Bing Crosby, Barrie recorded his song *So Long Bing*. Ten albums and many singles later, J J remains a one-hit wonder. Harlan Howard is the writer of many country classics, including *Busted* and *The Chokin' Kind.*

390

COMBINE HARVESTER

(BRAND NEW KEY)

THE WURZELS

12 June 1976, for three weeks

● ● ●

EMI 2450

Written by Melanie Safka. Produced by Bob Barratt.

While the scorching summer of 1976 created havoc for real farmers, the trio who made their career singing about that industry found it a time of celebration. The Wurzels, who started out in 1966 as Adge Cutler's backing band, were Tommy Banner, Tony Baylis and Pete Budd. They had been managed since the late '60s by John Miles, and they secured a record deal with EMI after Bob Barratt heard a tape of theirs and saw potential in their distinctive brand of entertainment. The group decided to continue after Cutler's death in a car crash in 1974, and it was Barratt who suggested they put new lyrics to Melanie's US number one and UK Top 5 hit *Brand New Key*. The Wurzels totally re-wrote the lyrics, though Melanie still received all the songwriting royalties, and the result was *Combine Harvester,* the saga of a West Country farmer courting his lady love.

The song charted after extensive radio play. It was one of those few comedy records that can withstand a certain number of repeated plays.

Although the Wurzels had been a popular club act in the south for over ten years, and had even appeared on the Simon Dee and David Frost television shows, the number one hit broke them beyond their native West Country. Their immortal *Top of the Pops* appearances featured a full-size combine harvester as a prop, and they were quickly signed up to promote farming equipment. They appeared on many television variety shows.

The trio were determined not to become a novelty act and very nearly returned to the top spot with their follow-up, *I Am A Cider Drinker,* based on George Baker's *Una Paloma Blanca.* Their last hit was in June

1977 but they have by no means disappeared. They still record and perform with unending enthusiasm.

391

YOU TO ME ARE
EVERYTHING
REAL THING

26 June 1976, for three weeks

● ● ●

Pye International 7N 25709

Written by Ken Gold and Micky Denne.
Produced by Ken Gold.

The Real Thing were four Liverpool lads who first came to public notice on the Hughie Green talent show *Opportunity Knocks.* Success was not immediate for the group even after they had been spotted by the ex-Radio Luxembourg DJ Tony Hall. Chris Amoo, his brother Eddie, Dave Smith and Ray Lake were signed unsuccessfully to a couple of major labels before a move to Pye changed their luck. Linking up with producer Ken Gold, they took one of his songs to the very top as their first chart entry. Eight other hits followed over a three year period, including *Can't Get By Without You,* which reached number 2, and *Can You Feel The Force?* which reached number 5. Another label change in 1980 to Calibre resulted in one more small hit, *She's A Groovy Freak.*

It was six years before the public heard much more of the Real Thing, although they had toured with David Essex in the interim. In 1986 PRT re-mixed the group's three biggest hits of ten years earlier, two of which became Top 10 hits all over again. *You To Me Are Everything (The Decade Remix)* climbed to number 5 and stayed on the charts for 13 weeks, two weeks more than the chart-topping original. On the Jive label a new release, *Straight To The Heart,* gave the foursome a hit on their fourth different label. Probably the major event of the '80s for the band came when an Afghan hound bred by Chris Amoo emerged as the Crufts Supreme Champion for 1987.

Somehow **Demis Roussos** *fits into Johnny Fingers' pyjamas and Bob Geldof gets into Roussos' kaftan, but certainly Fingers' suit didn't come from Bob?!?*

392

THE ROUSSOS
PHENOMENON EP
DEMIS ROUSSOS

17 July 1976, for one week

●

Philips DEMIS 001

Written by *(Forever and Ever)* Stylianos Vlavianos and Robert Constandinos, *(Sing An Ode To Love)* Stylianos Vlavianos, Robert Constandinos and Charalampe Chalkitis, *(So Dreamy)* Stylianos Vlavianos and Robert Constandinos, *(My Friend The Wind)* Stylianos Vlavianos and Robert Constandinos. Produced by Demis Roussos.

Demis Roussos (born 15 June 1947 in Alexandria) and Vangelis Papathanassiou were members of Aphrodite's Child, whose million-selling single *Rain and Tears* hit the British Top 30 late in 1968. Demis had to wait another eight years to get to number one with an EP of songs he had recorded between 1973 and 1976. Vangelis was patient until 1981 when his solo chart debut was made with the theme to the film *Chariots of Fire,* a US chart-topper the following year.

At seventeen and a half stones Roussos was possibly the heaviest number one hitmaker. His EP was certainly heavy on playing time, clocking in at 14 minutes and 44 seconds. Britons taking holidays in Greece had been enchanted by his flowing robes and ethereal voice for many years and had been returning home with suitcases full of Roussos albums. Philips decided to market his appeal in the UK and his chart account was opened with the 1975 Top 10 hit *Happy To Be On An Island In The Sun.* His number one EP was followed by a number 2 smash, *When*

Forever Has Gone. It is Roussos who has been gone from the charts since 1977. His name returned to the headlines in the most dramatic of circumstances in 1985 when he was hijacked along with the passengers and crew of the airliner in which he was travelling. For several days he was held hostage at Beirut airport until he and his fellow prisoners were released unharmed.

393

DON'T GO BREAKING MY HEART

ELTON JOHN AND KIKI DEE

24 July 1976, for six weeks

●●●●●●

Rocket ROKN 512

Written by Elton John and Bernie Taupin. Produced by Gus Dudgeon.

Elton John was the world's most prominent and best-selling recording artist in the early and mid-'70s. But for all his global success he had never reached number one in his home country, coming closest with the 1972 number 2 *Rocket Man.* In March of 1976 he recorded his part of the duet at Eastern Sound in Toronto, Canada. The tape was then brought to London where Kiki Dee added her vocal. As usual, Gus Dudgeon produced and Bernie Taupin supplied the lyric. The difference was the use of the songwriting pseudonyms Anne Orson and Carte Blanche, which Elton and Bernie sometimes used when penning material for Kiki.

Elton's first release on his Rocket label, the record exploded in the summer, going to number one in Britain for six weeks and America for four. It penetrated international markets previously closed to Elton as a soloist. *Don't Go Breaking My Heart* was the world number one for 1976.

There was never a proper follow-up. The pair considered recording the Four Tops' *Loving You Is Sweeter Than Ever* but didn't get around to it until 1981. The release of *Don't Go Breaking My Heart* came as Elton entered a period of voluntary retirement,

with no original studio material emerging for two years. John has had five solo number ones in America and appeared there on the chart-topping AIDS relief disc, *That's What Friends Are For* by Dionne and Friends.

394

DANCING QUEEN

ABBA

4 September 1976, for six weeks

●●●●●●

Epic EPC 4499

Written by Stig Anderson, Benny Andersson and Bjorn Ulvaeus. Produced by Benny Andersson and Bjorn Ulvaeus.

Abba completed their first hat-trick of number ones in Britain with *Dancing Queen,* which also became their only American number one. Abba had been quoted as saying that they would never tour America until they had a number one hit there, so the success of *Dancing Queen* gave them the excuse to sample the delights of motels and fast food in the United States.

The follow-up to *Dancing Queen* was their only single in three years not to make the top. It was called *Money Money Money* and reached number 3. It confirmed the jinx on 'money' records. The Bay City Rollers followed up two number ones with *Money Honey* which also reached number 3. Elvis Presley's first flop after five consecutive number ones in 1961 and 1962 was *One Broken Heart For Sale,* and only the Beatles with *Can't Buy Me Love* have managed to sing about money without a drop in popularity.

395

MISSISSIPPI

PUSSYCAT

11 October 1976, for four weeks

●●●●

Sonet SON 2077

Written by Werner Theunissen. Produced by Eddy Hilberts.

Pussycat became the third European act to hit number one in Britain in 1976 and the first Dutch stars to hit the very top of the British charts. The song they took to the top was the third number one about an American state, after *Carolina Moon* (see no. 75) and *Massachusetts* (see no. 238)

The group began life in Limburg in south Holland. The line-up on *Mississippi* was Lou Willé, his wife and lead singer Tony, her two sisters Marianne Hensen and Betty Dragstra and three men who had begun their rock career as a band called Scum, Theo Wetzels, Theo Coumans and John Theunissen. The three sisters were the most in any number one group, but still below the brothers record, which stands at five for both the Jacksons and Osmonds. The siblings had been telephone operators in Limburg, where Lou Willé played with his brothers in a group called Ricky Rendell and his Centurions until he married Tony and helped create a band called Sweet Reaction.

When this band signed to EMI-Bovema in the Netherlands producer Eddy Hilberts took them into the studio. He changed their name to Pussycat and gave them a song written six years earlier by Werner Theunissen, guitar tutor to the three sisters and no relation to John Theunissen. The song, *Mississippi,* was their first single. It sold a reputed four and a half million copies worldwide, making Pussycat the biggest thing to come out of Limburg since the cheese.

396

IF YOU LEAVE ME NOW

CHICAGO

13 November 1976, for three weeks

●●●

CBS 4603

Written by Peter Cetera. Produced by James Guercio.

Chicago began life in the late '60s as Chicago Transit Authority, which persuaded one co-author to release a couple of singles under the name Huddersfield Transit Authority. For a while it looked as though the two organizations would enjoy equal success in the UK, but then CTA became just plain Chicago and charted with the Spencer Davis hit, *I'm A Man*. The follow-up *25 or 6 to 4* was another Top 10 hit. Six hitless years followed for both Huddersfield and Chicago. At the end of 1976 *If You Leave Me Now* climbed to the very top.

The prime movers of Chicago were Pete Cetera, the vocalist (born 13 September 1944), Robert Lamm on keyboards (born 13 October 1944) and Terry Kath on guitar (born 31 January 1946, died 23 January 1978 in a shooting accident). The rest of the line-up was Lee Loughnane, Jim Pankow, Walter Parazaider, Dan Seraphine and Laudir Oliviera, a Brazilian who joined in 1974. Most of their album titles consisted of their name and a Roman numeral. *If You Leave Me Now* came from *Chicago X*.

397

UNDER THE MOON OF LOVE

SHOWADDYWADDY

4 December 1976, for three weeks

●●●

Bell 1495

Written by Tommy Boyce and Curtis Lee. Produced by Mike Hurst.

In 1973 two rival Leicester bands, the Hammers and the Choice, decided to marry their fortunes to create an eight-piece rock and roll group called Showaddywaddy. This explains why the band had two of everything; vocalists Dave Bartram and Buddy Gask, drummers Romeo Challenger and Malcolm Allured, guitarists Trevor Oakes and Russ Field and bassists Rod Deas and Al James.

Showaddywaddy achieved their big break on ITV's talent show *New Faces*. A recording contract with Bell followed immediately and the band's debut single, the self-penned *Hey Rock and Roll*, leaped to number 2 in 1974. The group persisted with their own compositions but with diminishing success. Then in 1975 they released a version of

Eddie Cochran's *Three Steps To Heaven* (see no. 102). It stopped one step below the original, kept off the top by Windsor Davies and Don Estelle, but Showaddywaddy had hit upon the formula which was to provide them with a run of nine Top 10 singles. Each one was a pop version of a rock and roll classic. *Under The Moon Of Love* had been a hit for writer Curtis Lee, who had also hit the US Top 10 in 1961 with *Pretty Little Angel Eyes,* Showaddywaddy's final Top 10er in 1978. By 1980 Shakin' Stevens replaced the group as Britain's most successful rock and roll revivalist.

398

WHEN A CHILD IS BORN (SOLEADO)

JOHNNY MATHIS

25 December 1976, for three weeks

●●●

CBS 4599

Written by Fred Jay and Di Damicco Ciro. Produced by Jack Gold.

Eighteen years and 216 days after the first chart appearance of Johnny Mathis (born in San Francisco on 30 September 1935) he finally hit the number one spot with a million-selling Christmas hit. Eighteen years earlier he had enjoyed another seasonal success, *Winter Wonderland*.

Mathis racked up nine hits between May 1958 and the end of 1960, including three Top 10 hits. Then the bottom fell out of the Mathis market and apart from one week at number 49 on 4 April 1963, he was hitless until early 1975 when his remake of the Stylistics' 1972 hit *I'm Stone In Love With You* climbed to number 10. However, Johnny always remained a star. His albums never stopped selling. Most noteworthy was *Johnny's Greatest Hits,* which stayed on the American charts for 490 weeks from April 1958.

The German, Michael Holm, had an earlier international hit with *When A Child Is Born*. In 1981 Mathis popped back at number 74 with a duet version of this song with Gladys Knight.

399

DON'T GIVE UP ON US

DAVID SOUL

15 January 1977, for 4 weeks

●●●●

Private Stock PVT 84

Written by Tony Macaulay. Produced by Tony Macaulay.

David Soul (born David Solberg, Chicago, Illinois, 28 August 1943) was known to British TV viewers as Detective Ken Hutchinson, the blond half of *Starsky and Hutch*. Listeners to *Don't Give Up On Us* may have been startled to learn that David Soul had in fact begun as a singer not an actor. He'd been cutting folk and pop singles throughout the '70s but without any luck. In desperation he sent a photograph of himself to the famous New York entertainment agency William Morris. His ploy of disguising his face with a ski mask caught their imagination and he was immediately contracted to become The Covered Man, the resident singer on the Merv Griffin TV Show.

Soul completed a series of *Starsky and Hutch* before deciding to try his hand at recording once more. His first album for Private Stock had already been released before he was teamed with prolific hit writer Tony Macaulay (see nos 239, 240 and 281). *Don't Give Up On Us* also reached number one in the singer's homeland four months later.

400

DON'T CRY FOR ME ARGENTINA

JULIE COVINGTON

12 February 1977, for one week

●

MCA 260

Written by Tim Rice and Andrew Lloyd Webber. Produced by Tim Rice and Andrew Lloyd Webber.

Julie Covington *added to her mystique by declining to appear on Top of the Pops.*

This hit tune from the phenomenally successful musical *Evita* was not given its title, which has now passed into the realms of popular cliché, until almost the final take of the final recording session of the original *Evita* album.

An extensive search for a woman to take the title role on the record ended when the performance of Julie Covington in the TV series *Rock Follies* persuaded Lloyd Webber and Rice that this was the singer they needed. The recording went very well, but for the strongest tune they wanted a title that would make the song a hit out of the context of *Evita*. Covington even recorded the title line as 'It's Only Your Lover Returning'. This didn't sound right. With the deadline for completion of the album approaching it was decided that *Don't Cry For Me Argentina* would have to do, a good title for the storyline but a rotten one (so everybody thought) for a single.

Nobody need have worried. The single sold 980,000 copies in the UK alone and was the biggest-selling single by a female vocalist until it was overtaken in 1985 by Jennifer Rush's *Power Of Love* (see no. 558). Julie Covington did not want the title role when *Evita* was produced in London. The search for the star ended with Elaine Paige, who went on to record, with Barbara Dickson, the biggest-selling single ever by a female vocal duo (see no. 545).

401

WHEN I NEED YOU

LEO SAYER

19 February 1977, for three weeks

● ● ●

Chrysalis CHS 2127

Written by Albert Hammond and Carole Bayer Sager. Produced by Richard Perry.

Leo Sayer, born in Shoreham, Sussex on 24 May 1948, first came to the notice of the record-buying public early in 1973. That was when the début solo LP by Roger Daltrey of the Who was released featuring songs by Leo Sayer and Dave Courtney. A single culled from the LP, *Giving It All Away*, took Roger Daltrey to number 5 in the late spring of that year. Leo Sayer, like Sandie Shaw, had been discovered by Adam Faith, but unlike Miss Shaw, Sayer was also managed by Faith, who by the early '70s had given up singing.

At the end of 1973 Leo Sayer's first single *The Show Must Go On* was released. He performed the song in whitened face and a clown's outfit and it shot to number 2. In America it was covered by Three Dog Night who took it to the Top 5. It might have been difficult to throw off the clown image, which like Gilbert O'Sullivan's short trousers and pudding basin haircut was fine for attracting public attention but not much good for sustaining a musical career. However, Sayer followed up with hit after hit – *One Man Band* (another song originally recorded by Roger Daltrey), *Long Tall Glasses, Moonlighting* and his first American chart-topper *You Make Me Feel Like Dancing*. After three number 2 hits in his first five singles, Sayer must have despaired of ever topping the charts. But on 19 February 1977 his sixth hit (the first he had not co-written) gave the Chrysalis label their first number one.

402

CHANSON D'AMOUR

MANHATTAN TRANSFER

2 April 1977, for five weeks

● ● ● ● ●

Atlantic K 10886

Written by Wayne Shanklin. Produced by Richard Perry.

Americans Tim Hauser, Janis Siegel, Laurel Masse and Alan Paul had to work hard before charming their way to the top of the charts. Hauser was the most experienced of the group, having begun his career with R&B group the Criterions in the late '50s. As session singers, Siegel and Masse had been heard on hundreds of advertising jingles. Paul had specialized in musicals and film work.

Manhattan Transfer first formed in 1969, although only Tim Hauser remained from those days. They honed their kitsch image in New York's gay bars reviving swing and doo-wop classics of the '40s and early '50s. The quartet broke through in Britain and France before achieving success in the US singles chart. *Chanson d'Amour* was originally an American hit for Art and Dotty Todd. The Man Tran version, producer Richard Perry's second consecutive number one, will be best remembered for its 'rat tat tat tat tat', hook line. Further hits included ballads such as *Walk In Love*, up-tempo numbers like *Spice of Life* and revivals of songs like *On A Little Street in Singapore*. A 1981 reworking of the Ad Libs' classic *The Boy From New York City* made the American Top 10, their best US showing. Manhattan Transfer continue today, Cheryl Bentyne having replaced Laurel Masse in 1979.

403

KNOWING ME

KNOWING YOU

ABBA

2nd April 1977, for five weeks

● ● ● ● ●

Epic EPC 4955

Written by Benny Andersson, Stig Anderson and Bjorn Ulvaeus. Produced by Benny Andersson and Bjorn Ulvaeus.

Despite the small hiccup in Abba's stream of chart successes when *Money Money Money* reached only number 3, the boys and girls from snowy Sweden showed their ability to bounce back when their next single, *Knowing Me Knowing You*, hit the top on 2 April 1977, in its sixth week on the chart. It then stayed there for five weeks, and became the first number one in Abba's second hat-trick of chart-toppers. That second threesome took 46 weeks to complete, the third slowest trio after the Beatle's *Lady Madonna/Hey Jude/Get Back* run which covered 56 weeks, and Police, who took 52 weeks in 1979 and 1980 over the hat-trick. The Beatles took 46 weeks over their *Help/Day Tripper/Paperback Writer* hat-trick as well. John Lennon completed his posthumous threesome in seven weeks.

404

FREE

DENIECE WILLIAMS

7 May 1977, for two weeks

●●

CBS 4978

Written by Deniece Williams, Hank Redd, Nathan Watts and Susaye Green. Produced by Maurice White and Charles Stepney.

Indiana-born Deniece Williams never intended to make her living through music, having trained to be a nurse in Chicago. To earn extra cash she took a job in a record shop, where her boss heard her singing. He invited two friends over from a local record label, Toddlin' Town, which led to Deniece cutting her first tracks. Stevie Wonder heard them (see nos 499 and 538) and for four years she sang with him as a member of his vocal backing group Wonderlove. It was Wonder who convinced Deniece she had the potential to become a star. A meeting with Maurice White, leader of soul/funk outfit Earth, Wind and Fire, led to her signing with CBS. White masterminded Deniece's debut album *This Is Niecy*, on which *Free* was the standout ballad.

That's What Friends Are For provided a further Top 10 hit in 1977 and a duet with Johnny Mathis (see no 398), *Too Much Too Little Too Late*, climbed to number 3 a year later. Despite some US success there were no hits between 1979 and 1983. Then came a

song from the 1984 film *Footloose*, *Let's Here It For The Boy*, which returned Deniece to the top.

405

I DON'T WANT TO TALK ABOUT IT/FIRST CUT IS THE DEEPEST

ROD STEWART

21 May 1977, for four weeks

●●●●

RIVA 7

Written by *(I Don't Want To Talk About It)* Danny Whitten, *(First Cut Is The Deepest)* Cat Stevens. Produced by Tom Dowd.

Here was a case where the artist really had to thank his fans for his number one. Without their participation, *I Don't Want To Talk About It* would never even have been released. It originally appeared on the album *Atlantic Crossing* leading off the slow side of the set that included *This Old Heart Of Mine* and concluded with *Sailing*. The massive success of the latter track tended to obscure the remaining material, and Stewart's new

Kenny Rogers *discusses the shortcomings of his departed* Lucille.

label Riva began issuing singles from the following album, *Night On The Town* in the summer of 1976.

But at the Christmas concerts Rod gave in London that year he and his associates were startled when fans sang along with the chorus of *I Don't Want To Talk About It*, even continuing when Rod dropped out to watch them. Clearly the artist had a potential hit of which he had been unaware. The track was made his next single, and it went to number one for four weeks. Since so many fans already had *Atlantic Crossing*, a track from *Night On The Town*, *First Cut Is The Deepest*, was made part of a double-A disc, but *Talk* was far and away the lead side.

Sadly, Danny Whitten, a member of Neil Young's Crazy Horse and author of the song, did not live to see it become a hit. He was dead of a drug overdose.

406

LUCILLE

KENNY ROGERS

18 June 1977, for one week

●

United Artists UP 36242

Written by Roger Bowling and Hal Bynum. Produced by Larry Butler.

Kenneth Donald Rogers (born Houston, Texas, 21 August 1938) came close to having a number one with the First Edition in 1969 when *Ruby Don't Take Your Love To Town*, a song about a crippled Vietnam veteran, was kept at bay by the Archies and Rolf Harris. The First Edition, a country/pop outfit, had formed themselves in 1967 out of the New Christy Minstrels and were the first group to sign to Frank Sinatra's Reprise label (see nos 210, 216 and 231). Rogers' distinctive gravelly voice was always to the fore, propelling them to several hits in the USA. When the group broke up in the mid-'70s Rogers found no problem in securing a solo recording contract with United Artists. Minor US country successes followed until *Lucille* became his first solo smash hit winning him the 1977 Grammy Award for Best Country Vocal Performance.

The *Lucille* referred to in this tear-jerking chart-topper had walked out on her man and their four hungry children at an inconvenient moment. In Britain BBC Radio Two DJ Terry Wogan found the sentiment irresistible and played the single at every opportunity, assisting the record's progress and returning the bearded six foot country star to the UK chart after an absence of seven years.

407

SHOW YOU THE WAY TO GO

THE JACKSONS

25 June 1977, for one week

●

Epic EPC 5266

Written by Kenny Gamble and Leon Huff. Produced by Kenny Gamble and Leon Huff.

Jermaine Jackson married Berry Gordy's daughter and stayed with Motown when his brothers moved to Epic. The remaining quartet of Jackie (born 4 May 1951), Tito (born 15 October 1953), Marlon (born 12 March 1957) and Michael (born 29 August 1958) added their youngest brother Randy (born 29 October 1962) on bongos. A newcomer, Gerald Brown, replaced Jermaine on base. The new line-up was called the Jacksons since Motown contested ownership of the original name.

Neither the Jackson 5 nor the Jacksons had had a number one single before *Show You The Way To Go* went to the top in 1977, immediately after the group had finished their first UK concerts for five years. Despite the many hits that followed the Jacksons have not had another British number one single, their highest effort being *Shake Your Body (Down To The Ground)*, a number 4 in 1979. Legendary Philadelphia writers/producers/executives Kenny Gamble and Leon Huff achieved with this single the number one that eluded them with the O'Jays and Billy Paul. They had previously succeeded with the Three Degrees (see no. 354).

408

SO YOU WIN AGAIN

HOT CHOCOLATE

2 July 1977, for three weeks

● ● ●

RAK 259

Written by Russ Ballard. Produced by Mickie Most.

There have been five other 'Hot' groups in the singles chart besides the Chocolate one: Hot Blood, Hot Butter, Hotlegs, Hotshots and Hot Streak. None of them has a record of chart success that can come anywhere near Hot Chocolate's. Although *So You Win Again* was their only number one, they had twelve Top 10 singles, plus another seven Top 20s and six Top 40s. Hot Chocolate were one of only three acts to put in a chart appearance in every year of the 1970s – the illustrious company they keep in this exclusive club being Diana Ross and Elvis Presley.

Formed by lead singer Errol Brown in 1970, Hot Chocolate were Patrice Olive (bass), Larry Ferguson (keyboards), Tony Connor (drums) and Harvey Hinsley (guitar). One-time member Tony Wilson, who played bass and composed most of the early material together with Brown, left in 1975 to go solo. He became the first British signing to Albert Grossman's Bearsville label, for which he released an album in 1976 called *I Like Your Style*. In 1987 Errol Brown had a solo career and a Top 40 hit *Personal Touch*.

409

I FEEL LOVE

DONNA SUMMER

23 July 1977, for four weeks

● ● ● ●

GTO GT 100

Written by Giorgio Moroder, Pete Bellotte and Donna Summer. Produced by Giorgio Moroder and Pete Bellotte.

Giorgio Moroder was first heard of as the composer and original performer of the Chicory Tip hit *Son Of My Father* (see no. 310). Five and a half years later he re-emerged as the composer and producer of many hits for disco goddess Donna Summer, whose *I Feel Love* was only marginally more subtle than her semi-pornographic *Love To Love You Baby*, her first British hit at the beginning of 1976. Moroder and Donna Summer have both gone on to even greater heights of success, but this summertime Summer hit remains their only number one collaboration in Britain. It had the mournful honour of being at number one on 16 August 1977, when Elvis Presley died.

By 1987 Donna Summer had racked up a total of 28 hits in Britain, as well as one more in duet with Barbra Streisand, the powerful *No More Tears (Enough Is Enough)*, which climbed to number 3 in Britain and gave her her third number one of 1979 in America. Summer was born LaDonna Gaines on the last day of 1948 in Boston, Massachusetts and thus was already in her late twenties before her chart breakthrough. Her massive success with a string of disco hits have subsequently made her the fifth most successful female vocalist in British chart history, and although her tally of only seven Top 10 hits (including that duet with Ms Streisand) is not particularly impressive, her list of chart entries is longer than that of any other woman except Diana Ross.

410

ANGELO

BROTHERHOOD OF MAN

20 August 1977, for one week

●

Pye 7N 45699

Written by Tony Hiller, Martin Lee and Lee Sheridan. Produced by Tony Hiller.

The sad story of the Mexican shepherd boy Angelo gave Brotherhood of Man their second number one and confirmed their style of music as Abba-inspired. Their Eurovision chart-topper of 1976, *Save Your Kisses For Me* (see no. 387) was obviously in the style of Abba, but then so were practically all the successful Europop songs of the mid-'70s. Brotherhood Of Man's third post-Eurovision single had been an imaginative cover of Diana Trask's big US country hit, *Oh Boy (The Mood I'm In)*, which led fans to assume that the Abba influence had waned as far as the Brotherhood were concerned. This proved not to be the case when their next single, *Angelo*, came out. But they answered their critics in the best possible way – the record shot to number one.

Angelo lived high on a mountain in Mexico, and when he and his rich girlfriend ran away together, they ran and ran until they reached the coast where they chose to die in the sand. The cause of death is not stated, but one must suspect exhaustion.

411

FLOAT ON

THE FLOATERS

27 August 1977, for one week

●

ADC 4187

Written by Arnold Ingram, James Mitchell Jr and Marvin Willis. Produced by Woody Wilson.

Led by Cancerian Larry Cunningham, the Floaters formed in Detroit 10 years before their one and only British hit single. *Float On* was lifted from their 1977 album *Floaters*, and had originally been composed as an instrumental track. All that could be heard of the group was the occasional chant of 'float, float on' in the background. They had intended to use the music throughout the album as a linking device but James Mitchell of the Detroit Emeralds heard the melody and persuaded them to record ad lib vocals. The Floaters now had a song with which they could introduce themselves. Thus the world learned that Ronnie was an Aquarian who liked 'a woman who can hold her own' and that Charles was a Libran who liked 'a woman who carries herself like Miss Universe'. Paul wasn't so choosy. He was a Leo and liked 'all women of the world'. And finally there was Larry, a Cancerian, who needed 'a woman that loves everything and everybody'. Whether they found their heart's desires we will never know for after 11 weeks on the chart *Float On* floated off leaving the Floaters high and dry as one-hit wonders.

412

WAY DOWN

ELVIS PRESLEY

3 September 1977, for five weeks

●●●●●

RCA PB 0998

Written by Layng Martine, Jr. Produced by Elvis Presley and Felton Jarvis.

Elvis' 17th and final UK number one was the single that had been issued shortly before his tragic death on 16 August 1977. It had not shown signs of being more than a minor chart entry when the King died and immediately it shot to number one. It was ironic that his death should have resulted in his equalling the Beatles' all-time record of 17 number one records. The song was written by Layng Martine, Jr and is the only Elvis number one to carry a production credit, as follows: 'Executive producer: Elvis Presley; Associate Producer: Felton Jarvis.' Vocal accompaniment is by J D Sumner and the Stamps quartet, Kathy Westmoreland, Sherrill Neilson and Myrna Smith. The track was recorded at Elvis' home, Graceland, in Memphis during sessions at the end of October 1976. James Burton is one of the guitarists on the sessions. These were the last studio recordings of Presley's life – all that was to come in 1977 were some indifferent concert tapings of previously recorded material. Since his death Elvis has had several more hits, two of which made the Top 10. An 18th number one is obviously not impossible but as the years go by, it becomes less and less likely. It is probably right that Elvis and the Beatles should remain the all-time joint UK number one champions.

413

SILVER LADY

DAVID SOUL

8 October 1977, for three weeks

●●●

Private Stock PVT 115

Written by Tony Macaulay and Geoff Stephens. Produced by Tony Macaulay.

The co-star of Paul-Michael Glaser in *Starsky and Hutch*, David Soul is not the only singing policeman to find success in the singles chart – Don Johnson (*Miami Vice*) and Dennis Waterman (*The Sweeney*) have both had hits. Soul is not even the first law-enforcer to get himself a number one, since Telly Savalas and Lee Marvin (one-time star of the *Streets Of San Francisco*) had already beaten him to it.

Silver Lady was David Soul's second chart-topping single. Sandwiched between the two number ones was a number 2, *Going In With My Eyes Open*. Soul thus belongs to a group of chart acts like Slade who were only prevented from getting the elusive hat-trick of number ones with consecutive releases by the 'failure' at number 2 of one of the records in the sequence. After *Silver Lady* Soul had another Top 10 and a Top 20 before he disappeared from the charts. His enviable record of all his singles becoming at least Top 20s not only reflects the fact that he could actually sing properly (unlike Savalas) but also makes him the most successful of the singing detectives.

414

YES SIR I CAN BOOGIE

BACCARA

29 October 1977, for one week

●

RCA PB 5526

Written by Frank Dostal and Rolf Soja. Produced by Rolf Soja.

Astonishingly, it took 414 number ones over nearly 25 years for the first female vocal duo, Maria Mendiola and Mayte Mateus, to hit the very top. There have been plenty of male vocal duos at the top, from the Everly Brothers to Typically Tropical, plenty of male/female vocal duos at the top, beginning with Sonny and Cher, and even female vocal trios such as the Supremes and the Three Degrees. But it took two leggy Spanish girls singing a Dutch production in English to make the breakthrough in the British charts, and by an extraordinary co-incidence one record that their success kept out of the top spot was *Black Is Black*, a song originally recorded by a German/Spanish vocal group in English but this time revived by La Belle Epoque, a French female vocal duo.

Baccara were also the first Spanish act to hit the top in Britain. They remained the only Spaniards to have a number one until Julio Iglesias actually sang in his native tongue four years later (see no. 490).

415

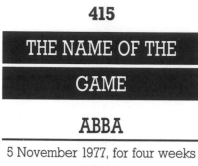

THE NAME OF THE GAME

ABBA

5 November 1977, for four weeks

●●●●

Epic EPC 5750

Written by Stig Anderson, Benny Andersson and Bjorn Ulvaeus. Produced by Benny Andersson and Bjorn Ulvaeus.

It was perhaps fitting that one of the biggest chart names of all time should be at number one on 14 November 1977, the 25th birthday of the singles charts in Britain. Abba's sixth number one hit brought them level with Slade in the all-time rankings, behind only Elvis and the Beatles (17 each), Cliff Richard (then 9 number ones) and the Rolling Stones (8). Abba have now overtaken the Stones but look very unlikely indeed to pass Cliff for the bronze medal position. While he has gone on to score a tenth chart-topper (see no. 441) as well as another in cahoots with the Young Ones (see no. 567), Abba have split, and another Abba single, let alone another chart-topper, seems unlikely.

Abba's achievements in opening the doors of the British charts to the sounds of Europe should not be underestimated. Before the Swedish quartet burst onto the scene, hits by European acts in Britain were very rare indeed. None had topped the charts.

Another Abba chart achievement is less well known. Apart from their 19 Top 10 hits (peaking at every position between 1 and 7), Abba never even reached the Top 20 with their other six entries. The best of the rest was *Head Over Heels*, which stopped at number 25. No other act has such a sharply divided success rating.

416

MULL OF KINTYRE/ GIRLS' SCHOOL

WINGS

3 December 1977, for nine weeks

●●●●●●●●●

Capitol R 6018

Written by Paul McCartney and Denny Laine. Produced by Paul McCartney.

Paul McCartney had registered ten post-Beatle Top 10 singles by the end of 1976, but none of them had gone all the way. Three, *Another Day*, *Silly Love Songs* and *Let 'Em In*, had peaked at number 2. To add to this frustration, he had scored five US chart-toppers in the same period, *Silly Love Songs* being America's number one of the year 1976. The pattern changed drastically with *Mull Of Kintyre*. McCartney wrote the song because he felt Scotland needed a contemporary anthem and, quite simply, because he loved his home there. Denny Laine helped complete the composition. At the time, the line-up of Wings was undergoing change and the trio on this record of Paul, Linda and Denny Laine was as small as the group ever got.

Paul was not certain that *Mull Of Kintyre* would be a hit, so he made it part of a double A-side with the up-tempo *Girls' School*. In the States his doubts were proved justified. *Mull Of Kintyre* did not capture the American imagination and it was left to the other side to peak at a rather lowly number 33. In Britain, it was obvious that *Mull Of Kintyre* was the popular side. It was the first single to sell more than two million copies in the United Kingdom, surpassing the Beatles' *She Loves You* to become the nation's all-time number one until Band Aid came along.

Wings (left to right: Paul McCartney, Linda McCartney, and Denny Laine) receive international awards for Band on the Run and Red Rose Speedway, not knowing that their biggest domestic success, Mull of Kintyre, is coming up.

417

UPTOWN TOP RANKING

ALTHIA AND DONNA

4 February 1978, for one week

Lightning LIG 506

Written by Althia Forest, Donna Reid and Errol Thompson. Produced by Joe Gibson.

After the first wave of reggae in 1969/70, chart reggae music had begun to move away from its authentic roots and began making compromises for the pop market. Bob and Marcia's 1970 *Young Gifted and Black* even included a string section. By 1974 there were two distinct categories of successful reggae: 'lovers' rock' (*Everything I Own, Tears On My Pillow*) and quirky novelties. Althia Forest and Donna Reid's hit, a Jamaican number one, was one of the quirkiest of them all.

Althia was 17 and Donna 18, both just out of school in Kingston, Jamaica, when the record began taking off. Producer Joe Gibson supplied the tune, to which the women added slang words that they'd heard on out-of-town trips. The title *Uptown Top Ranking* actually describes what a non-urban Jamaican does when he goes into the city to show off.

Finding initial radio support from BBC Radio One's John Peel the song was 'playlisted', that is placed on the list of singles that must be featured on daytime Radio One shows, a rare achievement for a reggae single. The song became a national talking point because no one understood the lyrics. Curiosity value hoisted it to the top after seven weeks on the chart. Althia and Donna became one-hit wonders, the novelty having worn off.

418

FIGARO

BROTHERHOOD OF MAN

11 February 1978, for one week

Pye 7N 46037

Written by Tony Hiller, Martin Lee and Lee Sheriden. Produced by Tony Hiller.

The third number one for Brotherhood Of Man was the third produced by Tony Hiller and the third written by Messrs Hiller, Sheriden and Lee. It was their second consecutive number one about a foreign man with a six-letter name ending in O. It must be admitted that *Figaro* was not as strong a song as *Angelo* and despite being a happy, uncontroversial record for the discos, immaculately performed and produced, it stayed at the top for one week only before being pushed out by *Take A Chance On Me* by the group the Brotherhood so successfully imitated, Abba.

The follow-up to *Figaro, Beautiful Lover* also sang the praises of foreign men (is this what the British public wants to hear?) but only just made the Top 20. The next single peaked at 41. Their last listed title *Lightning Flash* saw its light go out at number 67 in July 1982.

419

TAKE A CHANCE ON ME

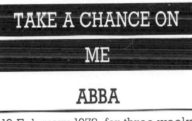

ABBA

18 February 1978, for three weeks

●●●

Epic EPC 5950

Written by Benny Andersson and Bjorn Ulvaeus. Produced by Benny Andersson and Bjorn Ulvaeus.

Abba completed a hat-trick of increasing uncertainty on 18 February 1978. The first record of the hat-trick had the positive title *Knowing Me Knowing You* and stayed at the top for five weeks. The second record had the less certain but still unworried title *The Name Of The Game*, and stayed on top for four weeks. The third record was much less optimistic, pleading *Take A Chance On Me*, which the British public did for three weeks. Logically, Abba should have recorded

Maybe Baby and *God Only Knows* as their next two singles, which would have held the top spot for two weeks and one week respectively, but they didn't. They recorded *Summer Night City* which became the first of six consecutive Abba singles to hit the Top 5 without any reaching the very top. It was therefore quite a surprise to chart-watchers if not to Epic Records executives when at the end of 1980 two singles from the *Super Trouper* album hit number one, to put Abba back on top after two and a half years.

420

WUTHERING HEIGHTS

KATE BUSH

11 March 1978, for four weeks

●●●●

EMI 2719

Written by Kate Bush. Produced by Andrew Powell.

Wuthering Heights, a musical version of the classic Brontë novel, launched the career of one of the most original talents to hit popular music in the 1970s. With its weird but haunting chorus of 'Heathcliff, it's me, I'm Cathy come home again' it became an airplay favourite almost at once and a number one hit in its fifth week on the charts. It appeared as the final track on the first side of *The Kick Inside*, Kate Bush's debut LP, which also included her second single and second Top 10 hit, *The Man With The Child In His Eyes*. Dave Gilmour of Pink Floyd had discovered and nurtured the teenage Ms Bush and played guitar on *Wuthering Heights*.

Whilst a tally of sixteen hits is impressive enough, Kate's real strength lies in the LP market where her *Never For Ever* album was the first by a female singer to hit the top. *Hounds Of Love* and the compilation *The Whole Story* brought her level with Barbra Streisand who also has three long playing chart-toppers. Even more spectacular is the fact that Kate writes all her own material.

Eight years on from *Wuthering Heights* Kate received the prestigous BPI award for Best female vocalist while the award for Best Male vocalist went to Peter Gabriel. Coincidentally, Kate has duetted on many Gabriel tracks including two top ten hits, *Don't Give Up* and, although uncredited, *Games Without Frontiers*.

When the **Bee Gees** *got to the top with* Night Fever *9 years and 231 days after* Massachusetts *headed the class theirs was the second longest gap between number ones, surpassed only by Frank Sinatra's wait.*

421

MATCHSTALK MEN

AND MATCHSTALK

CATS AND DOGS

BRIAN AND MICHAEL

8 April 1978, for three weeks

●●●

Pye 7N 46035

Written by Michael Coleman. Produced by Kevin Parrott.

The song with the second longest title to reach number one was the saga of the Ancoats painter L S Lowry, whose death on 23 February 1976 inspired Mick Coleman to write the song. He took it to producer Kevin Parrott and the pair recorded the song. Parrott decided that Brian and Michael sounded more commercial than Kevin and Michael, so the chance of a Kevin reaching number one was lost. A year later, Australian Kevin Johnson had a number 23 hit in 1975 and England soccer captain Kevin Keegan would climb to number 31 with *Head Over Heels In Love* in 1979, but otherwise Mr Parrott seems to have been correct in his opinion of the lack of commerciality of the name Kevin.

Matchstalk Men (not to be confused with Status Quo's 1968 debut hit *Pictures of Matchstick Men*) features the St Winifred's School Choir (see no. 472) singing with Brian and Michael. The subsequent careers of both Kevin Parrott and Mick Coleman have continued to involve children. All follow-ups to their number one were failures, but Kevin produced a hit by the Ramblers from the Abbey Hey Junior School, *The Sparrow*, which reached number 11 at the end of 1979. Mick Coleman also wrote *Hold My Hand*, recorded at Christmas 1981 by both Ken Dodd (who made it a hit) and the St Winifred's School Choir (who flopped).

422

NIGHT FEVER

THE BEE GEES

29 April 1978, for two weeks

●●

RSO 002

Written by Barry, Robin and Maurice Gibb. Produced by Barry, Robin and Maurice Gibb, Karl Richardson and Albhy Galuten.

The Bee Gees were at the Chateau d'Herouville in France working on the follow-up to their *Children of the Universe* album when they received a phone call from manager Robert Stigwood. He was making a film of a Nik Cohn article in *New York* magazine and needed a few songs. He couldn't send them a script but needed the numbers within a fortnight.

The Gibbs worked in the black music based groove that had recently brought them great success with *Jive Talkin'* and *You Should Be Dancing*. Without really knowing how the songs would be used, they presented Stigwood with *How Deep Is Your Love, Staying Alive, Night Fever, More Than A Woman,* and *If I Can't Have You,* the last of which was ultimately given to Yvonne Elliman. Stigwood was unhappy he did not have a title track for the film, which he thought he would call *Saturday Night.* The Bee Gees noted they did have a song called *Night Fever,* so the movie became *Saturday Night Fever.*

The double album soundtrack went on to become the world's biggest-ever seller, nearing the 30 million mark (later eclipsed by *Thriller*). The Gibbs became so associated with the film many people assumed they had appeared in it, but this was not so.

423

RIVERS OF BABYLON

BONEY M

13 May 1978, for five weeks

●●●●●

Atlantic/Hansa K11120

A traditional song, arranged by Frank Farian and Hans-Georg Mayer. Produced by Frank Farian.

German-born Franz Reuther adopted the name Frank Farian in order to improve his chances as a pop singer, but his career did not live up to his expectations. Farian faired better with Boney M, a disco hit machine he created. Montserrat-born Maizie Williams, Bobby Farrell from the Antilles and two Jamaicans, Liz Mitchell and Marcia Barrett, began their string of successes with *Daddy Cool* in 1976.

Rivers Of Babylon, Boney M's only Top 30 success in America, was fifth in a sequence of nine consecutive UK Top 10 hits the quartet managed between 1976 and 1979. It had been on the chart for some months before DJs and dancers started to flip the disc to feature the B-side, *Brown Girl In The Ring*. Suddenly the single, which had fallen to number 20, began to turn around. Chartwatchers agonized as fresh airplay lifted the disc from 6 to 5, then 4, then 3 and finally to number 2, blocked from returning to the number one position by the Commodores' *Three Times A Lady*. It gradually slid down the charts to depart only after the Christmas parties of 1978 had been forgotten, 40 weeks after entering. This was the second longest consecutive chart run by a number one (after *Release Me*, see no. 203). More importantly *Rivers Of Babylon* became the second biggest-selling disc in the UK at that time. Only *Mull Of Kintyre* had sold more.

most successful chart act in recording history, if statistics are cunningly manipulated. Together they released only two singles, both of which topped the charts for a combined total of 16 weeks. No other act has done so well with 100% of their singles releases. Individually, John Travolta starred in two of the biggest box office successes of all time, *Saturday Night Fever* and *Grease*, as well as the film which did for country music what his earlier two had done for disco and '50s rock 'n' roll, *Urban Cowboy*. Miss Newton-John's acting career has been less spectacular, but this has been more than compensated for by her singing career. She has had hits with Cliff Richard and with ELO (see no. 461) but on her own has become the most successful female singer the US record charts have ever seen, winning three Grammies in 1974 and topping the charts with monotonous regularity. As the '80s got into their stride Olivia's hits got even bigger. At the end of 1981 *Physical* stayed at number one in America for no less than ten straight weeks. In the UK her solo offerings have never done quite as well, though this is the country of her origin (she is technically British, having emigrated with her family from the UK to Australia when she was four). She has also received an OBE.

Olivia Newton-John *and* **John Travolta** *are shown at the Hollywood party celebrating the premiere of Grease.*

THREE TIMES A LADY

THE COMMODORES

19 August 1978, for five weeks

● ● ● ● ●

Motown TMG 1113

Written by Lionel Richie, Jr. Produced by James Carmichael and the Commodores.

The world owes this classic love song to Leo Sayer, who had nothing to do with the writing or making of it. In 1977 the Grammy Award for Best Rhythm and Blues Song went to Sayer and Vini Poncia for Leo's worldwide hit *You Make Me Feel Like Dancing*. Among the defeated writers were the Commodores. Shaken that white men could defeat him in this category, Commodore Lionel Richie vowed to write pop. It had always been the intention of the Commodores to earn as much as the top rock bands. Now Richie set out to develop his craft as a songwriter for all formats.

Three Times A Lady followed *Sweet Love* and *Just To Be Close To You*, all hit Commodore ballads that originally appeared as the

YOU'RE THE ONE THAT

I WANT

JOHN TRAVOLTA AND OLIVIA NEWTON-JOHN

17 June 1978, for nine weeks

● ● ● ● ● ● ● ● ●

RSO 006

Written by John Farrar. Produced by John Farrar.

John Travolta (born 18 February 1954) and Olivia Newton-John (born in Cambridge on 26 September 1948) lay claim to being the

Bob Geldof of the **Boomtown Rats** *(Pete Briquette is shown kneeling) preparing to set their* Rat Trap.

last track on side one of an album. The group figured that after a few up-tempo dance numbers, this was wise placement. The tracks were always far too long for single release, and it was left to co-producer James Carmichael to edit them. Richie was only too willing to let him handle the chore, but with the passage of time and the development of his reputation and skills he finally began to write ballads with the proper length in mind.

Three Times A Lady replaced *I'm Still Waiting* as Motown's best UK seller. It was also number one in America.

426

DREADLOCK HOLIDAY

10 C.C.

23 September 1978, for one week

●

Mercury 6008 035

Written by Eric Stewart and Graham Gouldman. Produced by Eric Stewart and Graham Gouldman.

By the time *Dreadlock Holiday* visited the top of the charts for a brief week in 1978,

10 C.C. had lost Kevin Godley and Lol Creme who had gone off to develop their new instrument the Gizmo. The two remaining members, Stewart and Gouldman, cut the album *Deceptive Bends* in 1977 and then took four new members on board for 1978's *Bloody Tourists*, including *Dreadlock Holiday*. After this they could only manage a number 50 in 1982. 10 C.C. had tallied three number ones and eight Top 10s between 1972 and 1978.

Godley and Creme had two Top 10 singles, *Under Your Thumb* (number 3) and *Wedding Bells* (number 7) in 1981. In the '80s they became award-winning leaders in video direction. The clip from their own *Cry* helped it become both a UK and US success. Eric Stewart has recently worked with Paul McCartney, and Graham Gouldman has teamed up with Andrew Gold to hit the Top 20 under the name Wax.

427

SUMMER NIGHTS

JOHN TRAVOLTA AND OLIVIA NEWTON-JOHN

30 September 1978, for seven weeks

● ● ● ● ● ● ●

RSO 18

Written by Warren Casey and Jim Jacobs. Produced by Louis St. Louis.

The only male/female duo to have two number one hits is John Travolta and Olivia Newton-John. In achieving their second number one they broke all sorts of chart records. They hit number one with every single record they have ever released, which has never been done by any other act that has released more than one single. They reached number one with their first and last chart hits, equalling the record set by Kay Starr in the '50s. They also find themselves on the short list of artists who hit number one with their first two releases (5 acts), artists who failed to follow up a number one (9 acts) and artists with 15 or more weeks on top in one year (5 acts). Olivia Newton-John, who has never climbed higher than number two in Britain as a solo singer, has also achieved one-hit wonder status in combination with Electric Light Orchestra (see no. 461). John

Travolta, a novice singing star in the tradition of Tab Hunter and Lee Marvin has also achieved a number two hit as a solo artist.

Grease, from which both the duo's chart-toppers came, has proved to be the most successful film in terms of original hits in the annals of the British charts. Two number ones, two number 2s (*Hopelessly Devoted To You* and *Sandy*), a number 3 (Frankie Valli's *Grease*) and a number 11 (*Greased Lightnin'*) give it a list of hits that far outstrips its nearest rivals, *Summer Holiday* and *The Young Ones*.

428

RAT TRAP

THE BOOMTOWN RATS

18 November 1978, for two weeks

● ●

Ensign ENY 16

Written by Bob Geldof. Produced by Mutt Lange.

The Boomtown Rats had Top 20 hits with their first four releases but even this streak did not prepare them for the success of *Rat Trap*. The third A-side from the Top 10 album *Tonic For The Troops*, it was put out to show that the Irish sextet wasn't just a pop band.

Viewing a videotaped Rats performance at the Hammersmith Odeon months later, lead singer and writer Bob Geldof noticed that even shortly after the release of *Tonic* concert-goers were calling for *Rat Trap*. At the time, this indication of a possible hit was missed.

When *Rat Trap* replaced *Summer Nights* at the top it was hailed as the triumph of local talent over a highly hyped Hollywood hit. Conveniently overlooked was the fact that the Boomtown Rats were, in fact, Irish, though they had come to London specifically for the purpose of making it in the international capital of rock music. *Rat Trap* was the first New Wave number one.

With the success of *Rat Trap* Geldof, already a proven charismatic figure on *Top of the Pops*, found himself in heavy demand from television chat hosts who were relieved to find an articulate representative of, if not spokesman for, New Wave.

429

DA YA THINK I'M SEXY

ROD STEWART

2 December 1978, for one week

●

Riva 17

Written by Rod Stewart and Carmen Appice.
Produced by Tom Dowd.

The question of unintentional plagiarism raised in the *My Sweet Lord* case surfaced again with Rod Stewart's 1978 disco hit. The artist originally claimed full credit for himself and band member Appice until a complaint was made that the music was clearly borrowed from Jorge Ben's *Taj Mahal*, a tribute to the American blues singer who himself used the name of the Indian monument. The issue never blew up in the media because Stewart donated the song to UNICEF in the historic January 1979 United Nations concert. There was, however, a temporary wrangle over how much of the song's rights he had actually assigned to the children's charity.

Da Ya Think I'm Sexy was a startling departure for Stewart, placing him directly in the mainstream of the 1978 disco boom. He enjoyed soul and disco chart success with this multi-million seller. Ironically, it temporarily took his career off the rails. He became broadly typed as a leering stud. In seven years he had only missed the Top 10 once, and then only by one place. For the following three years he fell short, often well short, every time.

430

MARY'S BOY CHILD – OH MY LORD (medley)

BONEY M

9 December 1978, for 4 weeks

● ● ● ●

Atlantic/Hansa K11221

Written by Jester Hairston, Frank Farian and
Fred Jay. Produced by Frank Farian.

The fifth tune to top the charts in two versions (see no. 65) was Boney M's second number one. Like their first it had a religious theme. Between these two divine chart-toppers had come *Rasputin*, a song about the diabolical priest from 19th century Russia. That Rasputin only made it to number 2 in the charts didn't necessarily prove that good always triumphs over evil. It helped Boney M spend 54 weeks on the charts of 1978, a feat matched by no other act.

The following year Frank Farian's foursome actually made a concert tour of the USSR, where they briefly rivalled Abba for jukebox popularity. In the UK only two more Top 10 hits followed *Mary's Boy Child*. Farian led his protégés back to the previously fruitful formula of singalong religion with singles such as *I'm Born Again* and *Children of Paradise* but these failed to impress record buyers in the way *Mary's Boy Child* or *Rivers of Babylon* had. The idea of combining an old hit song with one of the producer's own was used again by Michael Zager in his supervision of the Detroit Spinners (see no. 455).

431

YMCA

VILLAGE PEOPLE

6 January 1979, for three weeks

● ● ●

Mercury 6007 192

Written by Jacques Morali, Henri Delolo and
Victor Willis. Produced by Jacques Morali.

When Frenchman Jacques Morali saw Felipe Rose wearing Indian dress in a New York gay discotheque, then saw him in a second club a week later with other costumed characters, he got an idea. He told *Rolling Stone*, 'I say to myself, "You know, this is fantastic – to see the cowboy, the Indian, the construction worker with other men around." And also, I think to myself that the gay people have no group, nobody to personalize the gay people, you know?'

What a New Yorker might take for granted the foreigner saw as an exciting fantasy: a group of young men dressed as stereotypical American males. He recruited an ensemble, mostly models, to front songs

Village People.

about US gay capitals. The name Village People represented the men of Greenwich Village in New York City. When the first album sold 100,000 copies and a single, *San Francisco (You've Got Me)* made the British charts, Morali quickly found himself Village persons who could sing as well as pose, retaining Felipe Rose and lead vocalist Victor Willis. The unpredictable happened. *Macho Man* became a pop hit in America and *YMCA* an international smash, selling several million copies, including approximately 150,000 in one day in Britain alone over the 1978 Christmas period. All types of audiences could relate to this ode to the Mecca of Manhood, and the group quickly became a mass appeal fad. In so doing they lost touch with their original supporters and went the way of all fads, falling out of fashion and, even worse, the charts.

432

HIT ME WITH YOUR

RHYTHM STICK

IAN AND THE BLOCKHEADS

27 January 1979, for one week

●

Stiff BUY 38

Written by Ian Dury and Chas Jankel.
Produced by Chas Jankel.

Before this major hit, Ian Dury (born 12 May 1942) had been best known as the leader of one of the earliest new wave bands, Kilburn and the High Roads, named after the college where Drury had taught art.

year during a 'jam session' at the Warehouse in Old Kent Road Jankel produced the strong disco melody which Dury took, added lyrics to, and titled *Hit Me With Your Rhythm Stick*.

With no album imminent, the track was released as a single and in early 1979 the group spent a week at number one. On their last day at the top Sid Vicious died from a heroin overdose at the age of 21.

433

HEART OF GLASS

BLONDIE

3 February 1979, for four weeks

●●●●

Chrysalis CHE 2275

Written by Chris Stein and Deborah Harry.
Produced by Mike Chapman.

Blondie were lead singer Debbie Harry (born Miami, Florida, 1 July 1945), guitarist Chris Stein (born 5 January 1950), guitarist Frank Infante, keyboard player Jim Destri, bassist Nigel Harrison, and drummer Clem Burke. Debbie had begun taking the vocal spotlight as early as 1967 when she fronted New York folk/rock band Wind In The Willows. At the end of 1973 Harry and Stein formed the Stillettos, from which Blondie emerged in 1974.

New Wave music was proving more marketable in the UK than in the USA. Having gained a recording deal with the London-based label Chrysalis in 1977, the group quickly produced two albums, *Blondie* and *Plastic Letters*. The latter included their first UK hit, a version of Randy and the Rainbows' *Denise*. Retitled *Denis*, it climbed to number 2 in 1978. Ex-Mud and Suzi Quatro producer Mike Chapman was brought in for the third album, *Parallel Lines*. Two cuts from the LP had already been released as singles before *Heart of Glass*, which successfully attracted a new audience of disco fans to make it Blondie's first number one. Its appeal also crossed over to the other side of the Atlantic where it became not only the group's first US success but a number one.

In 1975 Chas Jankel (born 16 April 1952) joined the outfit. During the next 18 months Ian Dury and the Kilburns built up a huge cult following with their early brand of punk. In 1977 Dury signed a publishing deal with Blackhill Music and manager Andrew King. Having been rejected by all the majors the group, now called Ian and the Blockheads, signed to the newly-formed Stiff Records run by Managing Director Dave Robinson, Dury's former manager. The young record company had little money and the group signed for the paltry fee of £5000 inclusive of studio costs.

University and pub gigs and the infamous Stiff Tour payed off when the debut album *New Boots And Panties* charted in October 1977. No singles were taken from the set. In April 1978, the Top 10 45 *What A Waste* created widespread interest in the group, giving the LP long term sales. Later that

434

TRAGEDY

THE BEE GEES

3 March 1979, for two weeks

●●

RSO 27

Written by Barry, Robin and Maurice Gibb.
Produced by The Bee Gees, Karl Richardson
and Albhy Galuten.

The Bee Gees dominated the international
record business in 1978 as no act had done
since the heyday of the Beatles. Not only
was *Saturday Night Fever* the best-selling
album of all-time, several records the
brothers wrote and produced in varying
combinations with different artists were
worldwide hits and the title song of the film
Grease allegedly earned writer and co-producer Barry Gibb more money than anyone
had ever received from a single song.

The age-old show business question asking
what one does for an encore was never
more apt. The Bee Gees replied with *Spirits
Having Flown*, an album recorded in Florida with Galuten and Richardson. They
chose to change pace with the first single
from the set, preceding the LP's release
with *Too Much Heaven*. This ballad, its
publishing rights donated to UNICEF,
reached number 3 in Britain and one in
America.

The second single from the package,
Tragedy, scaled the summit in both
countries. At the time the group was concerned that every single they released be a
potential US number one. In this case they
got the top spot at home, too. *Tragedy* was
the last UK smash in the late '70s string of
Bee Gees hits. Their first number one of the
'80s would come, not with their own voices,
but with that of Barbra Streisand.

435

I WILL SURVIVE

GLORIA GAYNOR

17 March 1979, for four weeks

●●●●

Polydor 2095 017

Written by Dino Fekaris and Freddie Perren.
Produced by Dino Fekaris in association with
Freddie Perren.

Like *Kung Fu Fighting* and *Juliet, I Will Survive* was originally intended as the B-side of
a single but won through. Gaynor had
achieved dance-floor fame via side one of
her debut LP which contained three segued
tracks, *Honey Bee, Never Can Say Goodbye*
and *Reach Out I'll Be There*. All were edited
for single release, the second climbing to
number 2. She assumed the title of Disco
Queen in 1975 only to have the crown
snatched from her head by the sensuously
moaning Donna Summer (see no. 409). Subsequent offerings failed to enrapture disco
devotees causing most fans to believe that
she had in fact said goodbye.

Substitute, a single from her album *Love
Tracks*, was released in 1979, but it was the
B-side that gained attention. The Who, Clout
and Liquid Gold have all made the Top 10
with songs titled *Substitute* but none has
reached number one, so it was perhaps a
wise move to promote *I Will Survive*
instead. The track topped the stack in both
the UK and the USA, rekindling the flame of
Gaynor's career. Her follow-up, *Let Me
Know (I Have The Right)* was too similar to
make much impact. *I Am What I Am*, a song
from the musical *La Cage Aux Folles*, put
the singer back into the Top 20 in 1983 but
she again made the mistake of trying to
repeat the formula by releasing *Strive*. It
sank without trace and Gloria Gaynor's chart
career went under for the third time.

436

BRIGHT EYES

ART GARFUNKEL

14 April 1979, for six weeks

●●●●●●

CBS 6947

Written by Michael Batt.
Produced by Michael Batt.

This number one removed Art Garfunkel
from the list of one-hit wonders where he
had been languishing since 1975. It represented great personal triumphs for both
Garfunkel and Mike Batt, yet it was nearly
never a single. The vocalist, always inten-
sely concerned with his image and craft,
did not feel the theme from the cartoon film
Watership Down would make a worthy
single. He also had no intention of putting it
on his new album, *Fate For Breakfast*. It was
only when CBS executives in the UK showed
him photographs of fans queuing to see the
film that he relented.

Bright Eyes became the biggest-selling
single of 1979 and the last hit (until Culture
Club's *Karma Chameleon*, see no. 527) to
last as long as six weeks at the top. It also
went to number one in several other
European countries, but it never made the
American Hot 100.

This second solo UK number one gave Garfunkel a 2-0 edge over ex-partner Paul
Simon. Even during their glorious partnership their only British number one was a solo
vocal by Art, making the tally 3-0, most odd
in view of Simon's esteemed reputation as a
writer and great success as an album artist.
For Mike Batt it was an even sweeter
triumph. His eight hits as the Wombles had
typed him as a lightweight, despite a few
other successes. *Bright Eyes* established
him as a serious talent.

437

SUNDAY GIRL

BLONDIE

26 May 1979, for three weeks

●●●

Chrysalis CHS 2320

Written by Chris Stein. Produced by Mike
Chapman.

The fourth track to be taken from the album
Parallel Lines gave Blondie their second
number one. A simple melodic song, it
served to broaden the appeal of the group
still further. *Parallel Lines* wound up being
the best-selling album of 1979.

A great deal of media attention began to be
focused upon photogenic vocalist Debbie
Harry, whose previous employment had
included stints as a barmaid, a Bunny girl
and a BBC New York office worker. Just as
Alice Cooper (see no. 317) had originally
been the name for a whole group, not simply

its lead singer, Blondie strove hard for their title to be used in reference to a band. But when the general public referred to Blondie they meant the peroxide blonde Debbie Harry who was now appearing on bedroom wall posters throughout the world.

Blondie spent a total of 43 weeks in the Top 75 in 1979. For the first time in history three acts ended the year with exactly the same tally of weeks on chart. It isn't easy to spend ten months of the year in the charts but in 1979 Abba, Blondie and Chic made it seem as simple as ABC.

438

RING MY BELL

ANITA WARD

16 June 1979, for two weeks

●●

TK TKR 7543

Written by Frederick Knight.
Produced by Frederick Knight.

Anita Ward was a young teenager singing *a cappella* gospel in a Memphis, Tennessee church choir when Chuck Holmes discovered her and got her a recording contract. Very little happened for a long time, as acknowledged by Miss Ward on the liner notes to her *Songs Of Love* album which included *Ring My Bell*. 'Special thanks to my manager Chuck Holmes', she wrote, 'for his persistent determination' which eventually led to producer Frederick Knight and recording sessions in Jackson, Mississippi.

The result of those sessions was a mediocre collection of songs, written for the most part by Frederick Knight, Chuck Holmes and Anita herself, with one outstanding track, *Ring My Bell*. It was perfect midsummer disco music and it raced to the top of the charts. The hook was the synthesizer of Carl Marsh which produced a sound – impossible to translate into words but instantly recognizable to the ear – which became almost as copied as Donna Summer's referee's whistle. After the success of *Ring My Bell*, absolutely nothing. Anita Ward is now a member of the one-hit wonder club, with little prospect of releasing herself from it. A sad fate for a girl who used three studios, four engineers, two remixers and a 'midnight mix by Richie Rivera' as well as a producer to come up with a number one.

Gary Numan of **Tubeway Army** *gets to grips with his own success.*

439

ARE 'FRIENDS' ELECTRIC?

TUBEWAY ARMY

30 June 1979, for four weeks

●●●●

Beggars Banquet BEG 18

Written by Gary Numan.
Produced by Gary Numan.

As a child Gary Numan (born 8 March 1958) was very interested in gadgets. One of his earliest musical memories was of the Shadows performing on TV, though it was the guitars that intrigued him more than their music. By the age of 15 he started writing lyrics. In February 1978 he recorded his first song *That's Too Bad* at Spacewood Studios in Cambridge. His dad paid for the session and on the day of release Gary quit his job at W.H.Smith to concentrate fully on a career in music with his group Tubeway Army.

The band consisted of Gary's uncle, Jeff

Lidyard (born 1 September 1950) on drums and Paul Gardiner (born 1 May 1958), a friend, on bass. Numan handled vocals, guitar and keyboards. Gardiner heard that local record shop Beggars Banquet were forming their own label and Numan sent them the punk demo of *That's Too Bad*, not because he favoured that style of music, simply because he realized it was more likely to secure a deal. His plan worked and the single was released, selling a respectable 7000 copies.

With his dad once again paying studio fees the debut LP *Tubeway Army* was recorded in just three days, and in early 1979 the follow-up *Replicas* was recorded in a 16-track demo studio in London over a period of five days. The first single, from the album *Down In The Park*, flopped. The second, chosen by Numan, was *Are 'Friends' Electric?*, a merger of two songs, one a ballad with spoken lyrics and one with the basic melody riff.

Sales of 20,000 picture discs put the song in the charts, it shot up the Top 40 and following a charismatic *Top of the Pops* performance it reached number one, staying there long enough to be matched by *Replicas* on the LP lists.

440

I DON'T LIKE MONDAYS

THE BOOMTOWN RATS

28 July 1979, for four weeks

●●●●

Ensign ENY 30

Written by Bob Geldof. Produced by Phil Wainman.

Bob Geldof had been in Atlanta, Georgia, doing an university interview, when a story came in over the news service. A young girl in San Diego, California named Brenda Spencer was shooting from her bedroom window at children in the school playground across the street. In mid-massacre, so to speak, she had been telephoned by a journalist and paused to answer the phone. The journalist asked her why she was killing people, and her answer was, 'I don't like

Mondays'. Geldof turned the tragedy into a dramatic million-seller that was chosen as Best Single of 1979 in the British Rock And Pop Awards, sponsored by Radio One, *Nationwide* and the *Daily Mirror*.

I Don't Like Mondays was a hit in many countries, the US being a glaring exception. Fear of lawsuits and charges of bad taste as much as any aversion to New Wave kept the radio stations from playing the record. The unofficial boycott was front page news in *Variety*, the only time the Rats earned such prominent coverage in the show business bible.

The Boomtown Rats were Bob Geldof on vocals, Pete Briquette (born Pat Cusack) on bass, Johnny 'Fingers' Maylett on piano, Gary Roberts and Gerry Cott on guitars and Simon Crowe on drums. They gave *Mondays* its pre-release première at the 1979 Loch Lomond festival.

441

WE DON'T TALK ANYMORE

CLIFF RICHARD

25 August 1979, for four weeks

● ● ● ●

EMI 2975

Written by Alan Tarney. Produced by Bruce Welch.

Twenty years and 25 days after his first number one hit (see no. 88) Cliff Richard reached the top for the tenth time with his biggest-selling worldwide hit. It marked a second period of strong resurgence for the ageless Cliff, who came up with seven more Top 10 hits over the next four years. Among those hits was his ninth number 2 hit, his version of his own favourite song of all time, Shep and the Limelight's *Daddy's Home*. This just failed to push Human League off the top at Christmas 1981. The seventh of those comeback Top 10 hits, *Please Don't Fall In Love*, which reached number 7 at the end of 1983, was the 50th single featuring Cliff to hit the Top 10, one of which was a duet with Phil Everly. Cliff's 50th solo Top 10 hit came on 4 July 1987 when a song written and produced by Alan Tarney, *My Pretty*

One, leapt to number 10. On his 47th birthday in October 1987, Cliff was enjoying his 51st solo Top 10 hit with another Tarney effort, *Some People*, which climbed as high as number 3, his biggest hit since *Daddy's Home*.

In 1986 Cliff's record contract with EMI lapsed but he still managed to hit the Top 10 twice, in collaboration with first the Young Ones (see no. 567) and secondly with Sarah Brightman. With the latter he went to number 3 with *All I Ask Of You* from *Phantom Of The Opera*, establishing the bizarre record of hitting the Top 10 with a song from one West End show while actually starring in another (*Time*).

During the weeks that *We Don't Talk Anymore* was at number one Norrie Paramor, the man who was most responsible for the recording success of Cliff Richard and the Shadows, died. He was then, and remains now, the man who has produced the most British number one hits.

442

CARS

GARY NUMAN

22 September 1979, for one week

●

Beggars Banquet BEG 23

Written and produced by Gary Numan.

Gary Numan was not idle while *Are 'Friends' Electric?* was in the chart. He found 14 spare days in which to record the LP *The Pleasure Principle*. Tubeway Army had in reality been disbanded for several months so it was no surprise when Numan took solo credit for *Cars*, a song he originally recorded on a bass guitar and which he claimed took as long to write as it did to play. Four weeks after it charted both the single and LP were number one.

As a performer Numan had not played live for over a year, and even then only the occasional pub gig, yet in September he started a challenging UK tour filling theatres like the Hammersmith Odeon. In the following spring he toured America, where *Cars* had made the Top 10.

His singles and LPs continued to make the Top 10 into the early 1980s. In 1987 a remixed

version of *Cars*, described as the 'E Reg. version' climbed back into the Top 20. The flip side was *Are 'Friends' Electric?*. In 1984 he invested all his profits into his own record label Numa. The only real luxury he has ever afforded himself has been his aeroplane. He remains the only pop star to have flown around the world solo and these days, besides recording, does low level aerobatics displays in a World War II Spitfire.

443

MESSAGE IN A BOTTLE

POLICE

29 September 1979, for three weeks

● ● ●

A&M AMS 7474

Written by Sting. Produced by Police and Nigel Gray.

With *Message In A Bottle* Herb Alpert and Jerry Moss' A&M label scored their first UK number one after 13 years of trying. Just a few months earlier Deptford group Squeeze had come close with two consecutive number 2 singles, but it was Police who finally made the grade.

The line-up of vocalist/bassist Sting (born Gordon Sumner, Newcastle, 2 October 1951), guitarist Andy Summers (born Blackpool, 31 December 1942) and drummer Stewart Copeland (born Alexandria, Virginia, 16 July 1952) had been performing together since the summer of 1977 although the group had been formed by Sting, Copeland and Corsican guitarist Henry Padovani sixth months before. Before Padovani left in August 1977 the trio recorded one single, *Fall Out*, for Illegal Records, a label set up by Copeland and his brother Miles. It was not a hit at the time but did enter the Top 50 when re-released after the success of *Message In A Bottle*.

Before reaching the top of the chart each of the Police men had served their musical apprenticeship. Summers had changed his name to Somers in 1964 and joined Zoot Money's Big Roll Band. He played in a variety of groups throughout the '60s and

'70s, including Eric Burdon's New Animals. He joined Police in July 1977. Copeland had been with Curved Air since 1974 and Sting had joined semi-professional Newcastle outfit Last Exit in 1974. In 1976 he left his job as a teacher to move to London and concentrate on music. The public soon got the message!

444

VIDEO KILLED THE RADIO STAR

BUGGLES

20 October 1979, for one week

●

Island WIP 6524

Written by Bruce Woolley, Trevor Horn and Geoff Downes. Produced by Trevor Horn and Geoff Downes.

Having worked together briefly in Tina Charles' band (see no. 386) Trevor Horn and Geoff Downes had gone their separate ways, Downes to become an advertising jingles producer and Horn to become resident bass player at the Hammersmith Palais. In 1978 they began writing songs with Bruce Woolley and formed the idea of a studio band called the Buggles. No sooner had Woolley left to form his own outfit, the

Dr Hook *lead singers Dennis Locorriere and Ray Sawyer.*

Camera Club, than Downes and Horn won a recording contract with Island after label boss Chris Blackwell heard a demo of *Video Killed The Radio Star*. Three months later the duo were number one.

After one album and three more hit singles the Buggles took part in a seemingly bizarre move, replacing Rick Wakeman and Jon Anderson in Yes, one of the '70s biggest album-sellers. It seemed crazy but it worked for a while. Following the demise of Yes in 1981, Downes and guitarist Steve Howe joined ex-Family/King Crimson/Uriah Heep bassist John Wetton and ex-ELP drummer Carl Palmer to form the successful supergroup Asia.

445

ONE DAY AT A TIME

LENA MARTELL

27 October 1979, for three weeks

● ● ●

Pye 7N 46021

Written by Kris Kristofferson. Produced by George Elrick.

One track from Lena Martell's 13th LP for Pye was the Kris Kristofferson gospel song, *One Day At A Time*. Miss Martell had been for some years (as 13 LPs would indicate) a consistent seller in the easy listening category. Her LPs contain her versions of the popular middle-of-the-road hits of the day, all exquisitely performed and painstakingly produced, but never expected to contain a track which could have given Miss Martell a hit in the singles charts. *One Day At A Time* changed all that. Considerable TV and radio exposure for her version of the song, which had never been a British hit before, created a public demand which suddenly gave Lena Martell her one and only British hit single.

The Andrew Lloyd Webber-Tim Rice combination has launched the careers of many a female vocalist – Yvonne Elliman, Helen Reddy and Julie Covington to name but three. But for Lena Martell they were not so lucky. Her version of *Don't Cry For Me Argentina* was the follow-up to *One Day At A Time* and it missed completely. But her albums still sell as well as ever.

446

WHEN YOU'RE IN LOVE WITH A BEAUTIFUL WOMAN

DR HOOK

17 November 1979, for three weeks

● ● ●

Capitol CL 16039

Written by Even Stevens. Produced by Ron Haffkine.

The core of Dr Hook was formed in 1969 when folk guitarist/vocalist Dennis Locorriere (born 13 June 1949) and R&B singer/guitarist Ray Sawyer (born 1 February 1937) began performing together in New Jersey. The act was originally known as Dr Hook and The Medicine Show. Several musicians passed through the group but the other performers on this single are guitarist Rik Elswit, drummer John Wolters, bassist Jance Garfat and keyboard player Billy Francis.

Dr Hook's first and probably best loved hit was *Sylvia's Mother*. The song, written by the man who had helped gain them their recording contract, *Playboy* cartoonist Shel Silverstein, ascended to number 2 in 1972. This was followed by a four year gap until their next success, another number 2 hit, the sentimental *A Little Bit More*. However their American Top 10 career had continued with a wry comment on rock music, *Cover Of The Rolling Stone* and a version of the Sam Cooke song *Only Sixteen* (see no. 89).

When You're In Love With A Beautiful Woman entered the charts in September and two months later reached the summit. But just a year after their number one Dr Hook were struggling to make even the Top 50. Not even a change of label could revive their fortunes.

447

WALKING ON THE MOON

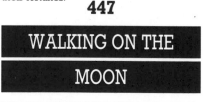

POLICE

8 December 1979, for one week

●

A&M AMS 7494

Written by Sting. Produced by Police and Nigel Gray.

Police's second number one followed hard upon their first (see no 443). Like its predecessor it had originally been a track on their number one album *Reggatta De Blanc*.

Police singles followed a strange pattern. Three tracks from their debut album *Outlandos d'Amour* had been released in 1978. *Roxanne* and *So Lonely* had had no initial success. In between had come *Can't Stand Losing You*, a minor hit. Both the group and their manager Miles Copeland were dismayed by the poor public reaction to their blend of rock and reggae. For a while Sting laid down his bass guitar and took up acting, appearing in two films, the 'road' movie *Radio On* and the mod nostalgia film *Quadrophenia*. It was during this time that the trio first bleached their hair for a TV chewing-gum advert and decided to remain blond.

A successful tour of the USA in 1978 gave Police new confidence and the single *Roxanne* began to sell in America. Re-promoted in Britain it climbed to number 12. *Can't Stand Losing You* was revitalized and did even better by reaching number 2. The music press, after a year of giving them the cold shoulder, were now in hot pursuit of Police and turned Sting into the rival of Debbie Harry in the pin-up stakes. Two number ones followed and, in for a penny, in for a pound, A&M then reactivated *So Lonely* which duly made the Top 10 at the beginning of 1980.

448

ANOTHER BRICK IN THE WALL (PART II)

PINK FLOYD

15 December 1979, for five weeks

● ● ● ● ●

Harvest HAR 5194

Police *(left to right: Stewart, Sting and Andy) check each other out.*

Written by Roger Waters. Produced by Roger Waters, Bob Ezrin and Dave Gilmour.

Led by the enigmatic Syd Barrett, Pink Floyd had first checked into the charts in 1967 with the psychedelic Top 20 hits *Arnold Layne* and *See Emily Play*. Twelve years of singles silence followed until a track from the album *The Wall* gave the Floyd the biggest surprise of their long career and provided producer Bob Ezrin with his second number one (see no. 317).

In addition to guitarist Barrett (born 4 January 1946) the Floyd of 1967 had been bassist Roger Waters (born 6 September 1944), keyboard player Richard Wright (born 28 July 1945) and drummer Nick Mason (born 27 January 1945). Failing health in late 1967 forced Barrett to be replaced by

Dave Gilmour (born 6 March 1944). Like Yes and Led Zeppelin, the Floyd built a reputation through the early '70s as an albums-only outfit with LPs like *Atom Heart Mother* and *Wish You Were Here*, both number ones. In 1973 their classic *Dark Side of The Moon* album, engineered by Alan Parsons, only made it to number 2 but stayed in the LP charts for an unearthly 294 weeks, selling an estimated thirteen million copies worldwide. It holds the record for most weeks in the Billboard Top 200, passing 700 weeks in late 1987.

In 1982 a film of *The Wall* was released, produced by Alan Parker and starring Boomtown Rats leader Bob Geldof (see nos. 428 and 440) in the role of Pink. The name was a reference to the ill-informed question 'which one's Pink?'.

The debut album, Pretenders, *entered the LP chart at the top, the first new number one of the new decade.*

449

BRASS IN POCKET

THE PRETENDERS

19 January 1980, for two weeks

● ●

Real ARE 11

Written by Chrissie Hynde and James Honeyman-Scott. Produced by Chris Thomas.

The Pretenders that appeared on *Brass In Pocket* were vocalist/guitarist and ex-*New Musical Express* journalist Chrissie Hynde (born Akron, Ohio), guitarist and keyboard player James Honeyman-Scott, bassist Pete Farndon and drummer Martin Chambers.

The band had previously issued a cover of the Kinks' *Stop Your Sobbing* and an original song *Kid*. Both had nudged into the Top 40 and gained the group critical acclaim. *Brass In Pocket* was nearly frozen out during the Christmas period but eventually climbed to the top of the tree after ten weeks on the chart.

On 15 June 1982 Farndon announced he was leaving the band. The following day Honeyman-Scott died of a drug overdose. The tribute single *Back On The Chain Gang*, with Billy Bremner on guitar and Tony Butler on

bass, gave the Pretenders their biggest US hit when it climbed to number 5. Tragedy struck again when on 15 April 1983 Farndon was also found dead following an overdose. Martin Chambers stepped down in mid-decade leaving founder Chrissie the great and last remaining original Pretender. She dissolved the group in 1985, only to return in 1986 with three new Pretenders.

Chrissie Hynde was married to Jim Kerr of Simple Minds on 9 May 1984.

450

THE SPECIAL A.K.A.

LIVE (EP)

THE SPECIALS

2 February 1980, for two weeks

● ●

2 Tone CHS TT7

Written by *(Too Much Too Young)* Jerry Dammers and Lloyd Chalmers, *(Guns Of Navarone)* Dmitri Tiompkin and Paul Francis Webster, *(Long Shot Kick De Bucket)* Sydney Roy Crooks and Jackie Robinson, *(The Liquidator)* Harry Johnson, *(Skinhead Moonstomp)* Monty Naismith and Roy Ellis. Produced by Jerry Dammers and Dave Jordan.

The Special A.K.A. Live was the only number one for the Coventry-based Chrysalis subsidiary Two Tone Records which in 1979/80 led to a shortlived ska revival. Both Madness (see no. 501) and the Beat achieved their initial success on Two Tone before moving to Stiff and Go Feet respectively. The Specials had scored their first Top 10 hit in 1979 when *Gangsters* climbed to number 6. This single was unusual because the B-side featured a different act to the A-side, namely the Selecter.

Special A.K.A. had been performing for three years when in 1980 they adopted the name their loyal fans used for their favourite group, the Specials. The musicians who appear on this EP were vocalist Terry Hall, keyboard player Jerry Dammers, vocalist/guitarist Lynval Golding, percussionist/guitarist Neville Staples, drummer John

Bradbury, guitarist Roddy Radiation, bassist 'Sir' Horace 'Gentleman' Parker, flugel horn player Dick Cuthell and trombonist Rico Rodriguez, a Jamaican who had played on many of the original ska hits of the late '60s. *Too Much Too Young* and *Guns Of Navarone* had been recorded at the Lyceum, London and the other songs at Tiffany's, Coventry. The group would score three more Top 10ers before appearing at the top yet again just 18 months later.

451

COWARD OF THE

COUNTY

KENNY ROGERS

16 February 1980, for two weeks

● ●

United Artists UP 614

Written by Roger Bowling and B. E. Wheeler. Produced by Larry Butler.

Lucille (see no. 406) had launched Kenny Rogers' solo career in both the UK and his native USA in 1977. In America he had developed into a major artist with a string of country hits to his name. In Britain, where the market for country music is smaller, he was less successful until *Coward of the County* brought him back to the public's attention. Like *Lucille*, Coward was a sentimental 'story song', the variety of country tune most likely to succeed in the UK, and in 1981 Rogers starred in a TV movie based upon the lyrics of the song.

At the end of 1980 Kenny Rogers scored his first international pop success, *Lady*, penned by Lionel Richie. A US number one and a UK Top 20 hit, it put the singer in the superstar league. Duets with Scotland's Sheena Easton (*We've Got Tonight*) and fellow country/MOR superstar Dolly Parton (*Islands In The Stream*) continued to broaden his appeal. By 1983 his stature was such that RCA had to pay a reported sum of twenty million dollars to lure him away from UA. Despite recording an album with ex-Beatles producer George Martin in 1986, Rogers has had no UK chart success since 1983. He has still made a fortune in the US, donating a portion of it to fighting hunger.

452

ATOMIC

BLONDIE

1 March 1980, for two weeks

● ●

Chrysalis CHS 2410

Written by Chris Stein and Debbie Harry. Produced by Mike Chapman.

Three must have been Blondie's lucky number. *Atomic*, the third track to be lifted from the *Eat To The Beat* album, entered the chart at number three and was their third number one. The single's high chart debut meant that Debbie Harry had entered the list in a higher position than any other female. This was in the days before Madonna altered nearly all the records for achievements by female artists.

Like their first chart-topper, *Heart Of Glass* (see no. 433), *Atomic* was a disco hit. It seemed that Blondie would always do best with songs you could dance to rather than rock numbers like their two preceding singles *Dreaming* and *Union City Blue*.

In 1980 Debbie Harry appeared in two feature films, Mark Reichert's thriller *Union City*, for which Blondie supplied the theme tune, and Alan Rudolph's *Roadie*, which starred US rocker Meat Loaf and included guest appearances by Alice Cooper (see no. 317) and Roy Orbison (see nos 108, 171 and 179).

453

TOGETHER WE ARE

BEAUTIFUL

FERN KINNEY

15 March 1980, for one week

●

WEA K 79111

Written by Ken Leray. Produced by Carson Whitsett, Wolf Stephenson and Tommy Couch.

Together We Are Beautiful had been recorded by British vocalist Steve Allan 18 months before Fern Kinney hit the charts, and at the beginning of 1979 he enjoyed two weeks of chart action with his version. Some 364 days after Mr Allan dropped out of the charts for ever, Fern Kinney's rendition came on to the charts via the discos, and within a month was number one. Six weeks later, she became the 28th current member of the one-hit wonder club, the third consecutive female vocalist to join this exclusive band, and the first of five one-hit wonders of 1980.

In her native land Miss Kinney is not quite as obscure as she has been for all but 11 weeks of her life in Britain. She was first noticed when she had a big disco hit with her version of King Floyd's 1970 American R&B number one, *Groove Me*.

454

GOING

UNDERGROUND/

DREAMS OF

CHILDREN

THE JAM

22 March 1980, for three weeks

● ● ●

Polydor POSP 113

Written by Paul Weller (both sides). Produced by Vic Coppersmith-Heaven.

The Jam were the most successful English New Wave band. Much of that success was due to the songwriting talents of leader Paul Weller, whose songs combined the articulacy of Ray Davies with the 'Fire And Skill' of Pete Townshend (the motto 'Fire And Skill' was written on the group's bass amp). The trio from Sheerwater, Surrey, were Weller on guitar and vocals, bassist Bruce Foxton, and drummer Rick Buckler. Their very first single, *In The City*, reached number 40 in May 1977. *Going Underground/Dreams Of Children* was their first number one, going straight in at the top on 22 March

1980. Their tenth single, it capitalized upon the success of their previous hit, *The Eton Rifles*, and was typically Wellerian in composition, dwelling upon urban alienation and resignation. Their earlier chart success had been based upon a trio of similarly-titled songs which all charted again when they were re-issued in April 1980 – *All Around The World*, *The Modern World*, and *News Of The World*. They share this titular similarity with the 'world' songs of Ronnie Hilton (*Two Different Worlds*, *Around The World*, and *The World Outside*), although nobody can match the Jam's succession of 'London' songs – *In The City*, *A-Bomb In Wardour Street*, *Strange Town*, and *Down In the Tube Station At Midnight*.

455

WORKING MY WAY

BACK TO YOU

DETROIT SPINNERS

12 April 1980, for two weeks

● ●

Atlantic K 11432

Written by Sandy Linzer and Denny Randell. Produced by Michael Zager.

The Spinners were called the Motown Spinners and then the Detroit Spinners in Britain

Budding star **Fern Kinney** *is shown as she appeared on* Top of the Pops.

to avoid confusion with the folk singers of the same name. They survived several personnel changes and finally achieved their British number one 25 years after the original group began singing together in high school in Ferndale, Michigan. At that point they went by yet another name, the Dominicos.

Initially protégés of Harvey Fuqua, they scored their first American Top 40 hit in 1961 on his Tri-Phi label with *That's What Girls Are Made For*. When Fuqua went to Motown so did the Spinners, who hit the 40 again in 1965 with *I'll Always Love You* and then in 1970 with the Stevie Wonder-produced *It's A Shame*. This disc, also co-written by Wonder, gave the group their first British entry. In 1972, now on Atlantic Records, they began a memorable string of hits with producer Thom Bell, including *Could It Be I'm Falling In Love*, *Ghetto Child*, and their US number one with Dionne Warwicke, *Then Came You*.

Great glory in Britain was reserved for their work with yet another mentor, Michael Zager. He coupled the old Four Seasons hit *Working My Way Back To You* with his own *Forgive Me Girl* to reach the top spot, though oddly his own composition was not credited on the original label. A medley of old and new was not only appealing to listeners, it gave Zager a share of the composer's royalties, and he repeated the trick later in 1980 by joining *Cupid* with *I've Loved You For A Long Time*.

456

CALL ME

BLONDIE

26 April 1980, for one week

Chrysalis CHS 2414

Written by Giorgio Moroder and Debbie Harry. Produced by Giorgio Moroder.

Call Me, from the soundtrack of Peter Schrader's *American Gigolo*, saw a temporary divorce between Blondie and producer Mike Chapman, who had masterminded their first three number ones. For their fourth they teamed up with the king of disco production, Giorgio Moroder. He shared the writing credits with Debbie Harry, who

became the first woman in British chart history to pen three number ones. She nearly didn't make it; Moroder had wanted Stevie Nicks to provide vocals on the track but Fleetwood Mac's songthrush had declined the offer.

Call Me proved to be the most successful of all Blondie singles in their native USA where it topped the Billboard Hot 100 for six weeks and ended the year as the Best Selling Single of 1980. It bears no connection with the Europop hit of the same title, which the Italian singer Spagna took to number 2 in 1987.

457

GENO

DEXY'S MIDNIGHT RUNNERS

3 May 1980, for two weeks

● ●

Late Night Feelings R 6033

Written by Kevin Rowland and Al Archer. Produced by Pete Wingfield.

Singer and guitarist Kevin Rowland (born 17 August 1953) was the uncompromising leader of the Birmingham-based Midnight Runners, whose street gang image was taken from the Martin Scorsese film *Mean Streets*. In addition to Rowland the group line up in 1980 was trombonist Big Jimmy Patterson, saxophonists Steve Spooner and JB, organist Peter Saunders, bassist Peter Williams and drummer Andy Growcott.

It was Bernie Rhodes, manager of the successful new wave/punk band the Clash, who steered the Runners' early career by arranging a recording deal with EMI. Their first single, *Dance Stance*, name-checked several Irish authors and grazed the Top 40. Then came their first number one. It was written about one of Rowland's heroes, Geno Washington, who in the mid-'60s led the Ram Jam Band, a UK soul outfit whose club reputation was second to none.

Having completed recording their debut album, *Searching For The Young Soul Rebels*, Rowland took charge of the master tapes from producer Pete Wingfield and refused to return them until EMI agreed to provide him with a more favourable con-

tract. Having just scored a number one he was in a strong position and got his own way. After two more Top 20 hits Rowland decided to sack every member of the group save one. Surprisingly, this didn't affect his ability to come up with number one hits (see no. 506).

458

WHAT'S ANOTHER

YEAR

JOHNNY LOGAN

17 May 1980, for two weeks

● ●

Epic EPC 8572

Written by Shay Healy. Produced by Bill Whelan and Dave Pennefather.

The Irish entry in the 25th Eurovision Song Contest was sung by an Australian, Johnny Logan. There have been many precedents for a country to be represented by an artist of different national origin, though the notion seems odd in Britain, which traditionally has given the nod to native performers. Logan is now, it should be added, a naturalized Irishman.

The photogenic and personable Logan, real name Sean Sherrard, proved an overnight sensation with his well-made recording of the title. The single shot in and out of the charts so quickly that it registered only eight weeks on the chart in all. For the next seven years Johnny had the dubious distinction of the shortest chart career of any artist with a number one hit to his credit.

He might have shed that title earlier had it not been for legal complications. He had previously contracted to another record company. With two different labels throwing out releases to capitalize on the Eurovision victory, radio programmers and record buyers alike, rarely excited about follow-ups to Eurovision winners anyway, threw up their hands in despair and ignored them all.

In 1987 Johnny Logan was once again the Irish entrant for Eurovision, this time with a self-penned song called *Hold Me Now*. It proved an easy winner, making Logan the first act ever to win the contest twice. The recording climbed to number 2 in Britain, kept off the top by Whitney Houston (see no. 591), but removing Logan's name from the list of one-hit wonders.

459

THEME FROM M*A*S*H* (SUICIDE IS PAINLESS)

MASH

31 May 1980, for three weeks

●●●

CBS 8536

Written by Mike Altman and Johnny Mandel. Produced by Thomas Z. Shepherd.

The film *M*A*S*H** (which stands for Mobile Army Surgical Hospital) starred Donald Sutherland. Sutherland also starred in *The Eagle Has Landed* with Michael Caine, the star of *Alfie*, which inspired Burt Bacharach and Hal David to write the song which proved to be a hit for Cilla Black. Another co-star of *The Eagle Has Landed* was Jenny Agutter, who also starred in *The Railway Children*, directed by Lionel Jeffries who featured in *Chitty Chitty Bang Bang* written by Ian Fleming whose James Bond books have, in their film versions, provided theme song hits for Nancy Sinatra, Shirley Bassey, John Barry, Sheena Easton, Carly Simon, Wings, Matt Monro and others. Elliot Gould, another star of *M*A*S*H**, was married to Barbra Streisand who starred in *Hello Dolly* which provided a hit for Louis Armstrong who starred in *High Society*, a film which contained the hit song *Samantha*, a hit for Bing Crosby and Grace Kelly, and for Kenny Ball who also had a hit with *March Of The Siamese Children* from *The King And I* which originally starred (in the Broadway production) Gertrude Lawrence, who was portrayed in the biopic *Star* by Julie Andrews, who has never had a hit single.

The M*A*S*H* theme single came from nowhere, via Noel Edmonds' persistent plugging, to reach number one a decade after it was recorded. It was co-written by the son of the film's director, Robert Altman, but all it proves is that films feature a lot of music, some good, some bad.

460

CRYING

DON McLEAN

21 June 1980, for three weeks

●●●

EMI 5051

Written by Roy Orbison and Joe Melson. Produced by Larry Butler.

The odyssey of this track to number one rivals that of Kraftwerk's *The Model* (see no. 494) as one of the strangest ever. Originally recorded in 1978 as part of the *Chain Lightning* album, it was rejected by McLean's American record company, whose chief executive suggested it be sped up to make it more commercial. McLean resisted, having intentionally dropped the Latin beat of Roy Orbison's 1961 original to create a reflective ballad. He was further resistant to change because he thought *Crying* was one of his best performances as a singer.

Over a year later, McLean made a personal trip to Israel, stopping over in Northern Europe for a television appearance that would pay for the journey. One of the numbers he performed was *Crying*, which received such viewer reaction the cut was released as a single. When it went Top 5 in a couple of countries, EMI put it out in Britain where it went to number one. With this success McLean made a deal with a new US record company and enjoyed an American Top 5 hit in 1981. American buyers were unaware it had taken three years and an international trek to get there. Always a top concert attraction around the world, McLean was now restored as a media favourite.

The seven years and 357 days that had elapsed between McLean's number one hits was the fourth longest in chart history. He had gone to number one in Ireland during the interim with *Mountains O'Mourne*.

Johnny Logan *seems to know seven years will pass before his next big hit.*

461

XANADU

OLIVIA NEWTON-JOHN AND ELECTRIC LIGHT ORCHESTRA

12 July 1980, for two weeks

●●

Jet 185

Written by Jeff Lynne. Produced by Jeff Lynne.

'The most dreadful, tasteless movie of the decade. Indeed, probably of all time,' Felix Barker wrote in the London *Evening News*, dismissing the Olivia Newton-John film *Xanadu*. Barker's criticism was only slightly more severe than the general public's reaction to the musical extravaganza, in which Olivia, a daughter of Zeus, inspired Gene Kelly to open a roller disco in California.

The film may have been a folly but the music from it was spectacularly successful. Four tracks became hits in both Britain and the

United States, with *Xanadu* a UK number one and *Magic* an American chart-topper. But whereas *Magic* was Olivia's solo, *Xanadu* was a duet with the Electric Light Orchestra. Indeed, the record was written and produced by ELO leader Jeff Lynne. It was Newton-John's third UK number one, all in tandem with somebody else. For the ELO, who had two hits from the film on their own, it was their first appearance in the number one position in any form. They had previously scored 13 Top 10ers without ever going all the way.

462

USE IT UP AND WEAR IT OUT

ODYSSEY

26 July 1980, for two weeks

●●

RCA PB 1962

Written by Sandy Linzer and L Russell Brown. Produced by Sandy Linzer.

Though it had occasionally happened through the years, in the post-punk era it became commonplace: an American record could get to number one in Britain without even penetrating the Top 100 at home. It was so with three 1980 number ones, *Together We Are Beautiful* by Fern Kinney, *Theme From M*A*S*H* by Mash and *Use It Up And Wear It Out* by Odyssey.

In the last case the clear reason was that the British chart reflected sales with no airplay factor. If a disco record caught on and sold, it made the chart. In the States, the radio spin element was also important. *Use It Up And Wear It Out* had in fact done fairly well in the US disco chart but was blocked from spreading to pop because the other side *Don't Tell Me, Tell Her* was the stronger deck on black radio. There was no such divided chart action in Britain. *Use It Up And Wear It Out* which had received heavy disco attention on import, won quick radio acceptance from programmers fond of the group's 1975 Top 5 hit *Native New Yorker*. Odyssey were happy to have a number one but slightly dismayed that the side of their work they preferred, the ballad, was not recognized. They need not have worried:

the follow-up, the down tempo *If You're Looking For A Way Out*, was also one of the year's Top 40 sellers.

This triumph was also sweet for co-writer Sandy Linzer. The veteran author had helped pen the Detroit Spinners' number one only three months earlier. His patience had paid off.

463

THE WINNER TAKES IT ALL

ABBA

9 August 1980, for two weeks

●●

Epic EPC 8835

Written by Benny Andersson and Bjorn Ulvaeus. Produced by Benny Andersson and Bjorn Ulvaeus.

Abba's return to the top after a 2½ year absence was a surprise to chart form-watchers who felt that they would fade slowly into the sunset after a long, hugely successful but no longer chart-topping career. The first of two singles taken from Abba's *Super Trouper* album changed all that by leap-frogging to the top in only its second week on the chart. The group had come a long way since those far off days of Hep Stars, Hootenanny Singers and the Anni-Frid Four.

By the time the group recorded *Super Trouper* both romantic partnerships within Abba had come to an end: Benny and Frida, Bjorn and Agnetha were no longer lovers and/or husband and wife. Yet the quartet seemed to be able to handle the complications of such breakdowns with the skill with which they made records – families had broken up but the hits kept coming. *The Winner Takes It All* was Abba's eighth number one.

464

ASHES TO ASHES

DAVID BOWIE

23 August 1980, for two weeks

●●

RCA BOW 6

Written by David Bowie. Produced by David Bowie and Tony Visconti.

Eleven years after he left Major Tom stranded in *Space Oddity*, David Bowie continued his saga on an even more pessimistic note. Left 'floating in my tin can' in 1969, out of radio contact with Ground Control, Major Tom now stood revealed as 'a junkie . . . hitting an all-time low'.

The hapless astronaut moaned 'I've never done good things/I've never done bad things/I've never done anything out of the blue.' Bowie told the *New Musical Express* the words could be applied to himself, representing a 'continuing, returning feeling of inadequacy over what I've done'. Reflecting the discontent many thoughtful artists feel, he added 'I'm not awfully happy with what I've done in the past.' At least he gave himself credit for 'the idea that one doesn't have to exist purely on one defined set of ethics and values, that you can investigate other areas and other avenues of perception and try and apply them to everyday life.'

The New Romantic movement, which owed its existence to Bowie's past, was just beginning to exert its influence, and Bowie turned to it for his *Ashes To Ashes* video. He wore a Pierrot costume and featured the mentor of the movement, Steve Strange. Unlike *Space Oddity*, *Ashes to Ashes* was not a great success in the United States, but there Bowie scored an even more important triumph when he successfully took over the title role in the Broadway production of *The Elephant Man*.

465

START

THE JAM

6 September 1980, for one week

●

Polydor 2059 266

Written by Paul Weller. Produced by Vic Coppersmith-Heaven.

Born on 23 May 1958, Paul Weller's main

influence in music has, he says, been Ray Davies of the Kinks, and his favourite record of all time is the Kinks' *Waterloo Sunset*, a song about London, the city that has been the subject of many of the Jam's biggest hits. Ray Davies and the Kinks emerged from a bleak period in the early '70s to become a very popular live act in America and a big influence on '80s rock. The influence of Ray Davies is sometimes direct, as for example with the Pretenders and their versions of his compositions *Stop Your Sobbing* and *I Go To Sleep*, and sometimes indirect, as for example through the songs of Paul Weller.

The Jam have a remarkable chart pedigree. It took them nine singles to reach the Top 10, but since the success of *The Eton Rifles* at the end of 1979 they hit the Top 10 with every single, usually in the first week on the chart. They hit the very top three times. Like Gary Numan, Jam tended to sell in vast quantities in the week the new single was released, and sales then tailed off. This also meant they entered the chart at their highest position and just went down from there. Both *Start* (which took two weeks to reach number one) and their third number one, *A Town Called Malice/Precious* (see no. 495) lasted only eight weeks on the chart, the fewest number of weeks of chart action for any number one since the introduction of the Top 75, and second only to *Christmas Alphabet* (see no. 40) since the chart began. Ferry Aid's *Let It Be* (see no. 588) subsequently broke this Jam in and out speed record.

466

FEELS LIKE I'M IN LOVE

KELLY MARIE

13 September 1980, for two weeks

● ●

Calibre PLUS 1

Written by Ray Dorset. Produced by Pete Yellowstone.

Ray Dorset, former lead singer of Mungo Jerry and composer of their two number ones decided to write a song for Elvis Presley to record. In the summer of 1977 he came up with *Feels Like I'm In Love*. Elvis had been one of his idols and he had recorded his favourite Elvis tune *Baby Lets Play House* on Mungo Jerry's only hit album. Dorset intended to send the demo of *Feels Like I'm In Love* to Presley's management. Sadly The King's untimely death ruled this out and the song ended up as a B-side of a Mungo Jerry single released in France.

Several people wanted to buy the rights for the song from Dorset but he refused. It was Elliott Cowen from publishers Red Bus Music who suggested that the tune would be ideal for Scottish songstress Kelly Marie and would undoubtedly break her in the UK.

Kelly was born Jacqueline McKinnon on 23 October 1957 in Paisley, Scotland. She enjoyed European success when *Who's That Lady With My Man* won her a French gold disc and made many of the European charts. *Feels Like I'm In Love* took months to break, selling well in the North before finally charting. When it reached the top it gave the Calibre label a number one with its first single and placed Dorset among the select group of singer/songwriters whose compositions have been number ones for themselves and other performers. Kelly Marie had two more Top 30 entries and another minor hit.

467

DON'T STAND SO
CLOSE TO ME

POLICE

27 September 1980, for four weeks

● ● ● ●

A&M AMS 7564

Written by Sting. Produced by Police and Nigel Gray.

1980's best-selling single, a mildly controversial song about the secret love between a teacher and his pupil, entered the chart at number one. It was the third time that Police had gone to the top of the class, making them the eighth act to achieve this hat-trick. *Don't Stand So Close To Me* was the first track to be released from *Zenyatta Mondatta*, a set which eventually attained triple platinum status in the UK. This song also took

Police into the US Top 10 for the first time.

Between *So Lonely*, their last single, and *Don't Stand So Close To Me* had come an unusual release known as the *Six Pack*. It contained each of the group's five hit singles to date plus a new single reworking a track from *Reggatta De Blanc*, *The Bed's Too Big Without You*. Issued as a limited edition it was immediately acquired by fans and record collectors alike who saw that this would eventually become a valuable item. The collection entered the charts at number 17 and sold well for four weeks.

This year drummer Stewart Copeland released a ten-inch album on the Kryptone label under the name Klark Kent. He had been issuing singles using this pseudonym for two years and one of them, *Don't Care*, had scraped into the Top 50 in 1978.

468

WOMAN IN LOVE

BARBRA STREISAND

25 October 1980, for three weeks

● ● ●

CBS 8966

Written by Barry and Robin Gibb. Produced by Barry Gibb, Karl Richardson and Albhy Galuten.

At the peak of their success in 1978 the Bee Gees were approached to produce Bob Dylan and Barbra Streisand. Shortly thereafter Dylan began his series of religious albums, but Streisand remained interested. She was in the duet phase of her career, having recently scored with team-ups co-starring Neil Diamond and Donna Summer. Though two tracks from the *Guilty* album featured Barry Gibb and became American hits, the international number one was *Woman In Love*. Streisand (born 24 April 1942), who had enjoyed a US Top 5 smash in 1964 with *People*, had made her British chart debut in 1966 with *Second Hand Rose*. The 14 year 279 day interval between her first chart appearance and her first number one was the fourth longest wait in UK history.

Considered by many to have the finest female voice of her time, Streisand co-operated with other artists so often because she preferred filming to making records, and sometimes had to be lured into the studio. She has also recently avoided the Broadway stage, where she first won acclaim in 1962 for a supporting role in the musical *I Can Get It For You Wholesale*.

The success of the Streisand-Gibb collaboration was such that the *Guilty* album remained in the British album chart well into 1982.

469

THE TIDE IS HIGH

BLONDIE

15 November 1980, for two weeks

Chrysalis CHS 2465

Written by John Holt. Produced by Mike Chapman.

Blondie were reunited with Mike Chapman, the producer of their first three number ones, for this fifth and final chart-topper. It completed a hat-trick of number ones (see nos 452 and 456) which together perched on the summit for just five weeks, the shortest-lived threesome to date. A reggae song, it had been written by John Holt, ex-lead singer with the Paragons. He had become a hit-maker in his own right in 1975 when his reggae version of Kris Kristofferson's *Help Me Make It Through The Night* had made it to number 2. Mike Chapman could now boast nine number ones as a producer putting him behind only George Martin, Norrie Paramor and Johnny Franz on the list of British producers of number ones.

The follow-up to *The Tide Is High, Rapture*, also came from the album *Autoamerican*. It only made number 5 in the UK but topped the US chart, completing a hat-trick for Blondie in America.

470

SUPER TROUPER

ABBA

29 November 1980, for three weeks

●●●

Epic EPC 9089

Written by Benny Andersson and Bjorn Ulvaeus. Produced by Benny Andersson and Bjorn Ulvaeus.

The second single from the *Super Trouper* album was the title track. It gave Abba their ninth number one. It took a week longer than *The Winner Takes It All* to climb to the top, but was only knocked off the top by the tragedy of John Lennon's death. It was perhaps a fitting reminder to the biggest group in the world since the break-up of the Beatles that the Fab Four still stood taller than any other group in popular music history.

The final Abba album *The Visitors*, released in 1981, failed to yield a number one single. By the end of 1982 the group had disbanded in all aspects except a final press announcement. That year Frida Lyngstad was the first Abba member to have a solo hit. Agnetha Faltskog followed with three small hits in 1983. Bjorn and Benny went on to co-write the musical *Chess* with Tim Rice, which yielded not only their tenth chart-topper as writers (see no. 545), but also a single that sold more copies than any Abba single, Murray Head's *One Night In Bangkok*.

Abba have still not officially disbanded, but it seems very unlikely that the four super-Swedes (one of whom is Norwegian) will get back together in the recording studios. Their songs will no doubt return to the charts, though. Already, there have been chart cover versions of their *Waterloo* (by Dr and the Medics) and *The Day Before You Came* (by Blancmange). The Abba song-book is likely to prove a rich source of hits for many years to come.

471

(JUST LIKE) STARTING OVER

JOHN LENNON

20 December 1980, for one week

●

WEA/Geffen K 79186

Written by John Lennon. Produced by John Lennon, Yoko Ono and Jack Douglas.

(Just Like) Starting Over had peaked at number 8 in the British chart and had fallen back to number 21 when the tragic news of Lennon's murder broke. The next week the song was at number one, to give John Lennon his first British chart-topper since the Beatles split, one week too late.

The long-awaited *Double Fantasy* album had many fine tracks and all-in-all proved that John Lennon was in pretty good musical form after his long lay-off. But *(Just Like) Starting Over* was by no means the best track on the album, and its original peak position of number 8 was a truer reflection of its real merit as a hit single. Both *Woman* (see no. 474) and *Watching The Wheels*, the second and third singles from the album, would have been most people's choices for release before *(Just Like) Starting Over*.

But what does that matter? The death of John Lennon deprived the world of a man who had made a matchless contribution to 20th-century music and who clearly still had a great deal more to give.

472

THERE'S NO-ONE QUITE LIKE GRANDMA

ST WINIFRED'S SCHOOL CHOIR

27 December 1980, for two weeks

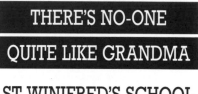

Music for Pleasure FP 900

Written by Gordon Lorenz. Produced by Peter Tattersall.

One hit wonders come in all shapes and sizes, but probably the smallest in individual shape but the largest in total size was a girls' school choir whose first single was at the time the only single ever released, or ever planned for release, by the budget LP label Music for Pleasure. MFP's 100 per cent success with single releases was not unique, however. The T Rex label only ever issued one single, *Telegram Sam* (see no. 309) and that was a number one hit too.

At Christmas 1981 the girls issued an LP which sold well and another single, also on MFP, featuring the song that Ken Dodd turned into a minor hit, *Hold My Hand*, but it flopped completely. MFP's reign as the joint most successful singles label of all time was over. The St Winifred's girls are only just one-hit wonders, though. The children singing on the Brian and Michael hit, *Matchstalk Men And Matchstalk Cat And Dogs* (see no. 421) are the St Winifred's School Choir, who thus become the only act whose only chart appearances have been on two one-hit wonder singles.

There's No-One Quite Like Grandma was, incidentally, the 500th track to be listed at number one, thanks to double-sided hits and two EPs which swelled the total above 472.

473

IMAGINE

JOHN LENNON

10 January 1981, for four weeks

● ● ● ●

Parlophone R 6009

Written by John Lennon. Produced by John Lennon, Yoko Ono and Phil Spector.

The death of John Lennon created a demand for his records that compares only with the sales of Elvis records in 1977, and one result was that Lennon's masterpiece, *Imagine*, reached number one in Britain.

It was originally recorded in 1971 for the album of which it was the title track, but it was not released as a single in Britain until 1975, when it reached number 6. It was released then only because Lennon had gone into retirement which was to last until 1980, so *Imagine* was actually his final single release for five years. Produced by Phil Spector, who had also worked on the Beatles' *Let It Be* album and George Harrison's *All Things Must Pass*, the *Imagine* album featured many of the musicians who were on George's album including Klaus Voorman and Alan White on the title track.

Imagine was the second of three consecutive number ones for John Lennon, and on 7 February 1981 he equalled a record set by the Beatles at the end of 1963 when he took over from himself at the top of the charts.

474

WOMAN

JOHN LENNON

7 February 1981, for two weeks

● ●

Geffen K 79195

Written by John Lennon. Produced by John Lennon, Yoko Ono and Jack Douglas.

By far the strongest song on the *Double Fantasy* LP, it is hard to understand why *Woman* was not released as the first single off the album. When it was released it quickly completed a hat-trick of number ones for John Lennon within a period of seven weeks, which is by far the quickest hat-trick of number ones ever completed.

The sales of John Lennon records in the weeks after his death were staggering. On 10 January, in the chart which first reflected immediate post-Christmas sales, three of the Top 5 singles were by Lennon – *Imagine, Happy Christmas (War Is Over)* and *(Just Like) Starting Over*. That same week, the *Double Fantasy* album was at number 2 in the LP charts behind Abba. *Imagine* was at number 39 and *The Beatles 1962-1966* was at number 58. By the beginning of February there were five Lennon singles in the Top 40, the extra two being *Woman* and *Give Peace A Chance*. There were also three Lennon albums in the Top 15, as well as two Beatles albums in the Top 75. A little later came the Roxy Music single (see no. 476) and even the John Lennon/Elton John live duet single of *I Saw Her Standing There*. In chart terms it was the most spectacular monopoly of the charts since the Beatles in their heyday – small compensation for the loss of such a musical giant.

475

SHADDUP YOU FACE

JOE DOLCE MUSIC THEATRE

21 February 1981, for three weeks

● ● ●

Epic EPC 9518

Joe Dolce *plays in the recorded audience reaction on* Shaddup You Face.

Written by Joe Dolce. Produced by Joe Dolce and Ian McKenzie.

The unlikely one-hit wonder who kept John Lennon songs off the top for three weeks early in 1981 was an Italian-American born in Painesville, Ohio in 1947. From 1966 he was in a group called Sugarcreek, who recorded an unsuccessful album on the Metromedia label in America in 1969. By 1974, Joe Dolce had formed a 'poetry-music fusion group' and was touring the East Coast of America, 'creating popular songs out of poetry classics' by Dylan Thomas, Yeats and Sylvia Plath.

1978 found Joe Dolce in Australia where he formed the Joe Dolce Music Theatre Show, and created the character Giuseppi. As Giuseppi he recorded *Shaddup You Face*, which became a big hit in Australia and was picked up by Epic for the UK market. It became the first comedy record to hit the top since *D.I.V.O.R.C.E.* (see no. 381) and Joe Dolce became the first one-hit wonder of 1981 when all his follow-up singles, including the weird *Reggae Matilda*, missed and the face of Joe Dolce was shut up.

Shakin' Stevens *had three number ones in less than a year.*

476

JEALOUS GUY

ROXY MUSIC

14 March 1981, for two weeks

● ●

Polydor ROXY 2

Written by John Lennon. Produced by Bryan Ferry and Rhett Davies.

The murder of John Lennon moved many artists to write songs about the man and their emotions following his death. Paul McCartney and Ringo Starr joined George Harrison on his tribute single *All Those Years Ago*, Lennon's close friend Elton John penned *Empty Garden* and Mike Oldfield released *Moonlight Shadow*.

The only words printed on the sleeve of this single were the title, the artist and the phrase 'a tribute'. When Lennon was murdered Roxy Music were in Germany rehearsing for a television show. Like many artists that week they decided to include a Lennon number in their set and chose *Jealous Guy* from the *Imagine* album. It was so well received that upon returning to Britain they cut the tune at a studio near Phil Manzanera's home in Chertsey. Three weeks after release it had climbed to the top, giving Roxy Music their only number one. Within 18 months the group would be no more.

After their first six Top 30 singles Roxy Music were rested while lead singer Bryan Ferry developed his solo career. In 1979 Ferry reunited with guitarist Phil Manzanera, saxophonist Andy Mackay and drummer Paul Thompson to take up where they had left off. Their new, more sophisticated sound propelled them to ten more Top 40 hits before Ferry slunk off once more, resurfacing in 1985 with a number one album, *Boys And Girls*, and three Top 30 singles.

477

THIS OLE HOUSE

SHAKIN' STEVENS

28 March 1981, for four weeks

● ● ● ●

Epic EPC 9555

Written by Stuart Hamblen. Produced by Stuart Colman.

Shakin' Stevens was born Michael Barrett in Cardiff on 4 March 1951, so he was not yet four years old when Rosemary Clooney took the song *This Ole House* to number one (see no. 25). He apparently never heard the song until the end of 1980, by which time he had had two small hits, *Hot Dog* and *Marie Marie*. He took the song to his producer Stuart Colman and the rest is history.

Stevens' first break in the business came in 1969 when he appeared on the same bill (rather lower down) as the Rolling Stones at the Saville Theatre. But he failed to capitalize on that opportunity and found himself trailing up and down the country, playing in thousands of half-empty halls for almost eight years. The second big break came in 1977 when he was one of three artists asked to play the title role in the West End musical *Elvis*. He was very successful and it led to a residency on Jack Good's revamped *Oh Boy* TV show and another series called *Let's Rock*. That led to the Epic recording contract and a lot of hard work by Stevens, his manager Freya Miller and his record company to turn Shaky into a recording star. It finally paid off with *This Ole House* which thus became the sixth song in British chart history to hit number one in two different versions.

478

MAKING YOUR MIND

UP

BUCKS FIZZ

18 April 1981, for three weeks

● ● ●

RCA 56

Written by Andy Hill and John Danter. Produced by Andy Hill.

Bucks Fizz (Bobby Gee, Mike Nolan, Cheryl Baker and Jay Aston) won the Eurovision

Song Contest in 1981 with *Making Your Mind Up*. They became the fourth British winners, after Sandie Shaw, Lulu and Brotherhood Of Man, and the fourth British act to take their Eurovision song to number one (Lulu failed to top the charts with her Eurovision title, but Cliff topped the charts with the runner-up *Congratulations*). *Making Your Mind Up* was in fact the first UK entry to reach the British Top 10 since *Save Your Kisses For Me* (see no. 387) in 1976. For the first time since 1968 Eurovision provided a number one hit in consecutive years, but unlike 1980's Johnny Logan, Bucks Fizz were conspicuously successful with their follow-up singles.

Perhaps it was the song, far stronger than most Eurovision Europop entries and a runaway winner in Dublin, or perhaps it was the way Cheryl and Jay discarded their skirts as they sang the song. The most likely reason for their continued success was that they filled a widening gap in the young teen market. By the end of 1981 only Shakin' Stevens and Dollar could begin to match Bucks Fizz in the pre-pubescent popularity stakes.

479

STAND AND DELIVER

ADAM AND THE ANTS

9 May 1981, for 5 weeks

● ● ● ● ●

CBS CBSA 1065

Written by Adam Ant and Marco Pirroni. Produced by Chris Hughes.

The event that Adam Ant says made him want to become a rock star was a Roxy Music concert at the Rainbow in 1972. It took a while for the then 18-year-old Stuart Goddard to metamorphose into Adam and to find his Ants, but by the start of 1981, 'Marco, Merrick, Terry Lee, Gary Tibbs and yours truly' had become Britain's most successful chart act, following in the tradition of Herman's Hermits, T Rex and the Bay City Rollers as teeny bop heroes.

Stand And Deliver was the first of Adam and the Ants' number one hits. It came in the middle of a year in which their records racked up a total of 91 weeks on the chart (a figure that has only ever been beaten three

times). This averaged out at almost two records on the charts each week throughout the year. Several of their late 1980 and 1981 hits were recorded a few years earlier, before Marco Pirroni joined the group, when the height of their ambition was, according to some liner notes, to perform in 'a very clandestine atmosphere, where Antpeople gather to be entertained'. There was nothing very clandestine about Antmania in 1981. Ants records sold in massive quantities and *Stand And Deliver* went to number one in its first week of chart action, only the third time that an act had gone straight to number one with their first chart-topper.

Adam Ant's Stand And Deliver *was the longest running number one in the calendar year of 1981.*

480

BEING WITH YOU

SMOKEY ROBINSON

13 June 1981, for two weeks

● ●

Motown TMG 1223

Written by William 'Smokey' Robinson. Produced by George Tobin in association with Mike Piccirillo.

Smokey Robinson's first number one solo single came about as a consequence of a song he had written over a dozen years be-

fore. *More Love* had been a US Top 40 hit for Robinson and the Miracles in 1967. Kim Carnes took it to the Top 10 in 1980 in a version produced by George Tobin, who had overseen Robert John's US number one *Sad Eyes*. Robinson always made a point of sending additional songs to artists who had hits with his material. In this case he sent a batch to Tobin, who was well known for the firm control he asserted over his charges. The embarrassed producer had to reply that he was no longer working with Carnes, but that he would love to cut the number *Being With You* with Smokey himself. Robinson, who had liked the Carnes version of *More Love*, consented, and enjoyed his biggest success since the 1970 winner *Tears Of A Clown*.

Ironically, *Being With You* was held at number 2 in America by the number one hit of 1981, *Bette Davis Eyes* by . . . Kim Carnes. The success of *Being With You* prompted Motown to celebrate Smokey's 25th anniversary in show business, though literally speaking they were jumping the gun by nearly a year.

481

ONE DAY IN YOUR LIFE

MICHAEL JACKSON

27 June 1981, for two weeks

● ●

Motown TMG 976

Written by Sam Brown III and Renée Armand. Produced by Sam Brown III.

Michael Jackson was born on 29 August 1958, two weeks before Cliff Richard first hit the charts in Britain. At the age of 11 he sang lead on the first hit (and first American number one) for the Jackson Five, *I Want You Back*. For several years, even after Michael's voice broke, Motown had the hottest black act in the world with the Jackson family, who hit the charts both as a group and with Michael's solo hits, none of which ever reached number one in Britain.

Michael and his brothers, excluding Jermaine, had moved to Epic in 1976, but Motown still had a lot of old material on file.

For no apparent reason a five-year-old single – *One Day In Your Life* – was reactivated and this time hit the very top. For the only time in the label's history, Tamla Motown achieved consecutive number ones in Britain. Both were solo records by lead singers of successful Motown groups, but the Michael Jackson track was so old that one fifth of all Motown singles were released between the day *One Day In Your Life* hit the British market and the day it became a hit.

482

GHOST TOWN

THE SPECIALS

11 July 1981, for three weeks

● ● ●

2 Tone CHS TT 17

Written by Jerry Dammers. Produced by John Collins.

A police drugs raid in St Paul's, Bristol sparked off a series of riots in Britain's decaying inner cities the like of which had never been seen before in mainland Britain. The Specials second number one, although written before these events, provided a haunting commentary to that troubled summer.

Even before *Ghost Town* had made it to the top, Neville Staples, Terry Hall and Lynval Golding had announced their departure from the band to form the Fun Boy Three. This trio scored seven hits in 18 months, their biggest being *It Ain't What You Do It's The Way That You Do It* (in partnership with Bananarama) and a version of *Our Lips Are Sealed*, originally a hit for the American quintet the Go-Gos. The Specials lived on, having reverted to their previous name, the Special AKA. Their first release after the split was *The Boiler*, featuring spoken vocals from Rhoda Dakar. The single dealt graphically with the subject of rape and was consequently banned by almost all radio stations. Even so it climbed to number 35. Although in the early days the band's ska style had attracted many skinheads it had always allied itself with the anti-fascist and anti-apartheid movements and in 1984 came up with one of its finest singles, *Nelson Mandela*.

483

GREEN DOOR

SHAKIN' STEVENS

1 August 1981, for four weeks

● ● ● ●

Epic EPCA 1354

Written by Bob Davie and Marvin Moore. Produced by Stuart Colman.

Shakin' Stevens' architecture fixation, which began with *This Ole House* (see no. 477), continued with *Green Door*, the second '50s song the Welsh rocker resurrected and took to the top. *Green Door* had not been a number one the first time round in 1956. Three versions had made the chart, the most successful being by Frankie Vaughan. It gave the high-kicking singer his first Top 10 hit stopping at number 2. The original version by American Jim Lowe climbed to number 8. Another British cover, by Glen Mason, hit number 24.

Green Door was the follow-up to his own favourite of Stevens' recordings, *You Drive Me Crazy*. Shaky took it to number 2 but couldn't quite push it up that final notch. *Green Door* arrived on the charts at number 22 and leapt to the summit the following week. At the time that jump of 21 places was second only to the 26 place climb made by Elvis Presley's *Surrender* (see no. 119) twenty years earlier. By late 1987 this leap was the fourth biggest of all time.

The original *Green Door* artist, Jim Lowe, became a famous DJ on WNEW-New York. Ironically the producer of Stevens' version, Stuart Colman, was also a radio celebrity.

484

JAPANESE BOY

ANEKA

29 August 1981, for one week

●

Hansa HANSA 5

Written by Bobby Heatlie. Produced by Neil Ross.

There was no sense writing to *Jim'll Fix It* asking for a number one record, so Scottish folk singer Mary Sandeman went out and got it herself. A respected traditional vocalist who sang with the Scottish Fiddle Orchestra, Sandeman felt she'd like the thrill of having a pop hit record but didn't want to do so under her own name. Mary had taught herself to sing in Gaelic; pretending she was Japanese for a few minutes was by comparison easy.

Having recorded *Japanese Boy* she needed an oriental-sounding name to use as a pseudonym. She looked through the Edinburgh phone book and found Anika. Rather than risk upsetting the real Anika, she changed the middle vowel and became Aneka. She wore a kimono and Japanese wig on *Top of the Pops* to further the illusion. Ironically, the Japanese music business wasn't too impressed, thinking the record sounded more like a Chinese effort. But the single was a hit on the European continent as well as in the UK. It was the first number one in Britain by a British artist for Hansa, a large German-based company.

When her game was over Sandeman remarked she found singing to Edinburgh Festival Fringe audiences more frightening than *Top of the Pops*. She returned to performing her Gaelic music.

485

TAINTED LOVE

SOFT CELL

5 September 1981, for two weeks

● ●

Some Bizzare BZS 2

Written by Ed Cobb. Produced by Mike Thorne.

Synthesizer player Dave Ball (born Blackpool, 3 May 1959) and vocalist Marc Almond (born Southport, 9 July 1959) began making music together while students at Leeds Polytechnic. Having released an unsuccessful EP on their own Big Frock label they signed to Lincoln-based Some Bizzare and recorded two songs, *The Girl With The*

Patent Leather Face and *Memorabilia*, the latter becoming a Top 30 dance hit in the USA.

Gravitating to London as part of the so-called futurist movement Soft Cell gained much music press coverage. It was therefore not surprising that their next single should do well. What was unexpected was its source: northern soul. The pair knew Gloria Jones' version of Ed Cobb's song from their trips to Leeds discotheques and their dramatic reworking stormed the charts after a histrionic performance on BBC TV's *Top Of The Pops*.

Tainted Love was 1981's best seller. In the USA it remained on the Billboard Hot One Hundred for a remarkable 43 weeks, the all-time longevity record. There were eight more UK Top 30 hits for Soft Cell. *Tainted Love* itself returned to the charts on two further occasions. After the duo split in 1984 Ball concentrated on production. Although Almond guested on Bronski Beat's medley single of 1985, which contained a reworking of Donna Summer's 1977 number one *I Feel Love* (see no. 409), he was unable to reproduce the success of Soft Cell either on his own or as Marc and the Mambas.

486

PRINCE CHARMING

ADAM AND THE ANTS

10 September 1981, for four weeks

● ● ● ●

CBS CBSA 1408

Written by Marco Pirroni and the Ants. Produced by Chris Hughes, Marco Pirroni and the Ants.

The songwriting talent of Marco Pirroni, former guitarist with Siouxsie and the Banshees, was once again in evidence on Adam and the Ants' second number one. Although the melody was remarkably similar to that of Rolf Harris' *War Canoe*, Harris took no legal action.

The Ants will be best remembered for their elaborate theatrical image which was under the control of Adam, a former art student. The promotional videos for both *Prince Charming* and *Stand And Deliver* were directed by Mike Mansfield but were

based on detailed storyboards drawn by Adam. The fairy tale *Prince Charming* video featured the singer as a Prince with Stuart Goddard's boyhood heroine, Diana Dors, playing the part of the Fairy Godmother. Lulu starred in the video for the follow-up single *Ant Rap*, released at the end of 1981. This time the motifs were castles, dungeons and damsels in distress but unlike his last two efforts the song had absolutely nothing to do with the pictures that accompanied it. The record stopped short of number one, peaking at 3. Within weeks Ants Merrick, Miall and Tibbs had been ousted. Future singles would be credited simply to Adam Ant but Marco Pirroni would remain as Ant's colleague.

487

IT'S MY PARTY

DAVE STEWART with BARBARA GASKIN

17 October 1981, for four weeks

● ● ● ●

Stiff BROKEN 2

Written by Herb Wiener, Wally Gold and John Gluck Jnr. Produced by Dave Stewart.

The town of Hatfield is famous for Hatfield House, seat of the Marquess of Salisbury, and for the British Aerospace factory by the A1 where the first flights of such famous aircraft as the Vampire and the Comet took place. In British chart history it is known as the home town of the Zombies and Scots-born Donovan. It is also featured heavily on the motorway signs known to millions of drivers coming out of London – 'Hatfield and the North'.

The motorway sign became the name of a travelling band in the early 1970s. Hatfield and The North were Richard Sinclair, Phil Miller, Pip Pyle and Dave Stewart, who played piano, organ and tone generator. A female vocal backing group, The Northettes, worked with the band. They were Amanda Parsons, Ann Rosenthal and Barbara Gaskin.

The band broke up, hitless but with a cult following, in the mid-'70s. In 1981 Dave Stewart emerged on a new chart version of Jimmy Ruffin's Top 10 hit of 1966 and 1974, *What Becomes Of The Broken Hearted?*,

which featured Hatfield-born Colin Blunstone, an ex-Zombie, on vocals. A few months later an extraordinary version of Lesley Gore's 1963 smash, *It's My Party* climbed right to the top with vocals by Northette Barbara Gaskin.

488

EVERY LITTLE THING SHE DOES IS MAGIC

POLICE

14 November 1981, for one week

●

A&M AMS 8174

Written by Sting. Produced by Hugh Padgham and Police.

The lead-off tracks from the two previous Police albums, *Reggatta De Blanc* and *Zenyatta Mondatta*, had both topped the charts (see nos 443 and 407). Their 1981 *Ghost In The Machine* album saw the group

*The number one by **Soft Cell** was penned by a former member of the Four Preps, who fell just short at two in 1958 with Big Man.*

collaborating with a new producer but it was not this fact that prevented *Invisible Sun*, the initial release from the set, from getting to number one. Police always made quality videos to accompany their songs but the footage of riots in Northern Ireland used in the video for *Invisible Sun* caused the BBC and IBA to prevent it being shown on British television. The single peaked at number 2, kept off the very top by Adam and the Ants' *Prince Charming*.

A second single, *Every Little Thing She Does Is Magic,* was released with almost embarrassing haste, entering the charts just four weeks after *Invisible Sun*. With a cheery video shot both in and outside George Martin's recording studio in Montserrat this happy-go-lucky image proved to be what the fans wanted. The single leapt to number one in the UK and number 3 in the USA, where *Invisible Sun* hadn't even been released. The follow-up *Spirits In The Material World* made the top 20 on both sides of the Atlantic.

For a while the band pursued individual projects. Sting acted in the BBC TV drama *Artemis '81* and the feature film *Brimstone and Treacle*, which spawned his Top 20 solo hit, *Spread A Little Happiness*. Andy Summers teamed up with Robert Fripp for the instrumental album *I Advanced Masked*. It was another 10 months before Police enjoyed their final spell at the top.

489

UNDER PRESSURE

QUEEN AND DAVID BOWIE

21 November 1981, for two weeks

● ●

EMI 5250

Written by Queen and David Bowie. Produced by Queen and David Bowie.

Under Pressure marked only the second occasion in which two makers of number one hits came together for the first time to record another number one. The previous case was when Frank Sinatra and daughter Nancy teamed up on *Something Stupid* (see no. 231). Bowie, like Frank, had scored two

prior number ones: Queen, like Nancy, had achieved one.

Under Pressure was written and recorded when Bowie and Queen met in a German studio. Since it was an act of on-the-spot inspiration, no album was ever recorded. Indeed, no B-side was made. Since it was Queen's session, one of their tracks went on the flip and they got lead billing on the disc.

Because *Another One Bites The Dust* had been a long-lived hit in the United States in late 1980, selling over three million copies in that country alone, the *Queen's Greatest Hits* album planned for Christmas had to be postponed until 1981, even in Britain; imports would otherwise have flooded America. EMI had a long time to plan their UK marketing strategy and pressed hundreds of thousands of *Hits* in anticipation of a television campaign. This meant they could not put *Under Pressure* on the album: the LP was already sitting in the warehouse. In the States, where no such problem existed, the cut did appear on the set.

490

BEGIN THE BEGUINE (VOLVER A EMPEZAR)

JULIO IGLESIAS

5 December 1981, for one week

●

CBS CBSA 1612

Written by Cole Porter, Spanish lyrics by Julio Iglesias. Produced by Ramon Arousa.

On 12 October 1935 the new musical *Jubilee,* with music and lyrics by Cole Porter and book by Moss Hart, opened at the Imperial Theatre, New York. The show was a comparative failure but it has two claims to theatrical immortality. Firstly, it featured Montgomery Clift, one of Adam Ant's heroes, in his first professional role as Prince Peter, and secondly the hit song of the show was *Begin The Beguine*.

Despite countless versions of the song recorded since 1935, no version appeared on the British charts until a man who had been Real Madrid's reserve team goalkeeper translated the words rather loosely into Spanish and romped up to number one.

Julio Iglesias, born on 23 September 1943, had been the idol of Spanish middle-of-the-road fans for some time, filling the niche in Spanish hearts that Charles Aznavour (see no. 352) had cornered in France. CBS also claim that by 1980 Iglesias was the top-selling male singer in the world and 'the top-selling artist in the history of CBS records – ever'. Names on CBS include Barbra Streisand, Simon and Garfunkel, Frankie Laine, Guy Mitchell and Adam and the Ants, so the sales of Julio Iglesias records must indeed have been quite sensational.

491

DON'T YOU WANT ME?

HUMAN LEAGUE

12 December 1981, for five weeks

● ● ● ● ●

Virgin VS 466

Written by Jo Callis, Phil Oakey and Philip Adrian Wright. Produced by Martin Rushent and Human League.

It had been a poor year for sales of singles. The synthesizer-based band the Human League scored the only million-seller to be released during 1981 with this unusual love/hate duet between League leader Philip Oakey (born 2 October 1955) and Susanne Sulley (born 22 March 1963). Susanne and her friend Joanne Catherall (born 18 September 1962) had been recruited to the group as dancers after Oakey saw the pair gyrating at a nightclub in his native Sheffield. The line-up on *Don't You Want Me?* included Ian Burden (born 24 December 1957), Jo Callis (born 2 May 1951) and Adrian Wright (born 30 June 1956).

The Human League never quite attained the popularity of Abba, whom Oakey at the time named as his chief musical influence, even though *Don't You Want Me?* made it to number one in the USA and their next two UK singles *Mirror Man* and *(Keep Feeling) Fascination* both climbed to number 2. Nor was their success as financially rewarding as it might have been because the group had handed over a percentage of income from record sales to Martyn Ware and Ian Craig Marsh, former group members who were later to find fortune as Heaven 17.

After an extended chart absence the

Human League returned to the Top 10 in 1986 when they collaborated with prolific US producers Jimmy 'Jam' Harris and Terry Lewis to record the single *Human*. This semi-eponymous record returned them to the top of the American charts.

492

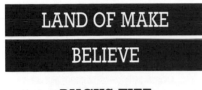

LAND OF MAKE BELIEVE

BUCKS FIZZ

16 January 1982, for two weeks

● ●

RCA 163

Written by Andy Hill and Peter Sinfield. Produced by Andy Hill.

The group responsible for bringing the 1982 Eurovision Song Contest to Harrogate managed a second number one early in 1982 with a song which rapidly became a favourite on children's television and radio shows. It was a children's song along the lines of the Seekers' *Morningtown Ride* (a number 2 hit 15 years earlier) and even ended with a poem read by 11-year-old Abby Kimber, a member of the Mini-Pops children's group who had some success with their album over Christmas 1981. To complete the child connections, the wife of Bobby Gee of Bucks Fizz had her first baby a few days before the record hit the top.

The Eurovision Song Contest has proved a mixed blessing for the British contestants. The established acts, like Sandie Shaw, Lulu, Cliff Richard, Olivia Newton-John and the Shadows all found that Eurovision gave them one hit single but little more. The unknowns like Co-Co, the Allisons or Prima Donna have mostly disappeared back into obscurity once the last television set was switched off. Only Brotherhood of Man and Bucks Fizz have successfully used Eurovision to launch a career. Dana from Ireland also turned one Eurovision success into the basis of a good career, as did the quartet from Sweden who won in 1974, Abba.

493

OH JULIE

SHAKIN' STEVENS

30 January 1982, for one week

●

Epic EPCA 1742

Written by Shakin' Stevens. Produced by Stuart Colman.

Elvis Presley's 17th number one *Way Down* (see no. 412) was on top when Sir Freddie Laker inaugurated his London to New York Skytrain on 25 September 1977. Shakin' Stevens' third number one, *Oh Julie*, was on top when Laker Airways went bankrupt four years later. Airlines may come and airlines may go, but rock and roll goes on forever.

After the comparative failure of Shaky's follow-up to *Green Door* (see no. 483), a revival of *It's Raining* that only just made the Top 10, Epic decided to put out a self-penned song to revive the Shaky fortunes, and it did just that. It was very much in the rock idiom that Shaky had so completely appropriated from the fading Showaddywaddy, and it sneaked a week at the top at a time when outstanding singles were in very short supply.

One unlikely fact about Shakin' Stevens is that his real name at the time *Oh Julie* reached the top was Clark Kent, a name he adopted by deed poll a few years ago.

494

THE MODEL/ COMPUTER LOVE

KRAFTWERK

6 February 1982, for one week

●

EMI 5207

Written by Ralf Hutter, Karl Bartos and Emil Schultz. Produced by Ralf Hutter and Florian Schneider.

The Model is one of the strangest success stories of recent years. A 1978 track that had received considerable club play, it was placed on the B-side of the new number *Computer Love* when that title was issued in 1981. Buyers are more likely to purchase a single if they are partial to the B-side as well as the top deck.

The tactic was only partially successful, as *Computer Love* was only a minor hit. But it refused to die and featured in sales reports for several months. Clubs still preferred *The Model*. Finally the picture sleeve was altered with the colours changed, the title *Computer Love* taken off the front and the words *The Model* put in the computer screen. Sufficient sales pushed the record into the Top 75 and subsequent radio plays exploded the disc. Though a double-sided hit, this was never a double-A: *The Model* was always the official B-side. The group's time had simply come; the synthesizer music long championed by the German ensemble had come to dominate the UK market.

During the first two months of 1982 the BMRB altered its method of chart computation. The traditional Monday-Saturday tally was dropped in favour of Friday-Thursday on the grounds that the sales diary collectors charged too much for Saturday working. With the impact of weekend sales and *Top of the Pops* appearances now delayed until a fortnight after they occurred, bizarre yo-yo performances were observed. *The Model* went 10-2-3-1, the first single to drop on the chart and then to go number one since the 1981 re-appearance of *Imagine*.

495

A TOWN CALLED MALICE/PRECIOUS

THE JAM

13 February 1982, for three weeks

● ● ●

Polydor POSP 400

Written by Paul Weller (both sides). Produced by Pete Wilson and The Jam.

This was the second Jam single and the 13th chart single to come straight in at number

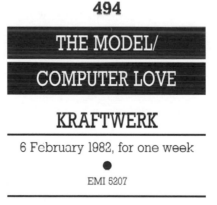

one. It proved one of the most notable singles ever because of the number of statistical minutiae it helped create. Only Slade had bettered the Jam's achievement of two immediate number ones, entering on top with three. Elvis Presley was the only other artist to manage two. As previously stated the Jam's two instant successes were also among the fastest moving number ones ever. *A Town Called Malice/Precious* lasted a mere eight weeks on the chart, four of which were in the Top 10, and of that four three were spent at number one. This single is also significant for ensuring that nos 494 and 495 were the only two consecutive number ones to be double-sided hits. Furthermore this Jam outing was also the reason for the reclassification of permissable methods of sales calculation after EMI objected to *A Town Called Malice/Precious* being available in a studio-recorded 7-inch version and a live 12-inch version. The feeling was that the Jam's fans were buying both versions of the single and so stopping EMI's big seller of the moment, the Stranglers' *Golden Brown*, from reaching number one. In future different performances of the same song were charted separately. By the end of 1982 the Jam had come up with a third single that entered the chart at number one (see no. 511).

496

THE LION SLEEPS TONIGHT

TIGHT FIT

6 March 1982, for three weeks

● ● ●

Jive 9

Written by Hugo Peretti, Luigi Creatore, George David Weiss, Solomon Linda, Paul Campbell and Albert Stanton. Produced by Tim Friese-Greene.

Jive's first number one was a version of a chart stalwart. Based on the Zulu folk tune *Wimoweh*, it had been popularized in pre-rock days by Pete Seeger's quartet the Weavers. Karl Denver first hit the Top 5 with the tune in 1962, pursued up the UK charts by a US number one version with new lyrics by the Tokens, *The Lion Sleeps Tonight*.

Robert John took the song back into the US Top 3 in 1972 and ten years later Tight Fit wailed their own way to success.

Tight Fit was not a new chart name. A group of session musicians had produced two successful medleys of '60s hits using this moniker. Jaap Eggermont's Star Sound beat Tight Fit in the medley stakes by grabbing two number 2 hits so Jive changed their tactics. *The Lion Sleeps Tonight* was recorded with vocals by City Boy's Roy Ward and a photogenic group was put together to promote it. The resulting trio comprised model Steve Grant and dancers Julie Harris and Denise Gyngell. The latter had been rejected from the Bucks Fizz auditions. 'I'm sure we're going to have at least five hits', dreamed Julie Harris at the time. Yet after just one more Top 5 smash, *Fantasy Island*, Harris and Gyngell were out, replaced by Vicki Pemberton and Carol Stevens. This Tight Fit line-up was completely unsuccessful so Steve Grant moved on to form a high-energy disco troupe called Splash.

497

SEVEN TEARS

THE GOOMBAY DANCE BAND

27 March 1982, for three weeks

● ● ●

Epic EPCA 1242

Written by Wolff-Ekkehardt Stein and Wolfgang Jass. Produced by Jochen Petersen.

The Goombay Dance Band, a German-based outfit fronted by the fire-eating 35-year-old Oliver Bendt, took up the mantle of Boney M to top the British charts with a piece of Caribbean Europop. Only a few weeks after Kraftwerk had become the first German act to hit number one in the UK, the Goombay Dance Band became the second. They proved to be another group like Tight Fit, who had a different line-up in the studios from the one on TV and live dates.

The Goombay Dance Band officially comprises Bendt, his wife Alicia, Dorothy Hellings, Wendy Doorsen and Mario Slijngaard. The Bendt's two children, Danny and Yasmin, often appear on stage as background

vocalists. Bendt learned his fire-eating and his calypso rhythms on St Lucia in the West Indies, and by 1980 had established his band as one of the most successful acts in Germany. *Seven Tears* was originally recorded in Germany in mid-1980, and its success soon after its release in January 1982 was the culmination of a long and determined effort by their management and their record company to move into the slot that Boney M had begun to vacate. After many flops in Britain their patience was rewarded.

498

MY CAMERA NEVER LIES

BUCKS FIZZ

17 April 1982, for one week

●

RCA 202

Written by Andy Hill and Nicola Martin. Produced by Andy Hill.

My Camera Never Lies was the third number one in a 12-month period for Bucks Fizz. They became the first act to achieve three number ones within a year since Shakin' Stevens. Of all the Eurovision winners, only Abba have scored more number ones. Brotherhood Of Man also managed three, but theirs came over a two-year period.

The melody of *My Camera Never Lies* was written by Andy Hill and the lyrics by Nicola Martin. Hill took Bucks Fizz into the studio and recorded the boys' lines first, since they were the most straightforward. He then cut the girls' part. Finally came the complicated middle sections where the members are chanting 'my cam-e-ra' at each other. Hill gave the quartet full credit for mastering this complex sequence without much rehearsal. With the success of this single Bucks Fizz suddenly found themselves critical as well as commercial favourites, positively reviewed in music papers usually damning of middle-of-the-road pop.

The glory days did not last long. A highly-publicized and messy split in the group when Jay Aston left did not help. More serious and upsetting was the coach crash the group were involved in while on tour in the north east. Mike Nolan suffered severe injuries, and it was not known for several months whether he would be able to perform again. However, a Top 10 hit in 1986 with the adventurous *New Beginning (Mamba Seyra)* proved that Bucks Fizz were not ready to be written off just yet.

499

EBONY AND IVORY

PAUL McCARTNEY with STEVIE WONDER

24 April 1982, for three weeks

● ● ●

Parlophone R 6054

Written by Paul McCartney. Produced by George Martin.

The final track on the second side of *Tug Of War*, the album that reunited George Martin and Paul McCartney in the recording studio, featured Stevie Wonder (born Steveland Morris Judkins on 13 May 1950 in Saginaw, Michigan). When *Ebony And Ivory* was released as a single, Motown refused to allow Wonder full billing on the label, so Paul McCartney with (rather than and) Stevie Wonder was the name of the act that shot to the top to give McCartney his 24th songwriting credit at number one and his first on his own.

McCartney and Wonder have between them enjoyed over 1150 weeks on the British charts, and yet together they remain one-hit wonders. A second duet on *Tug Of War*, *What's That You're Doing?* was not issued as a single. When it came to making the *Ebony And Ivory* video it was impossible to get the two superstars in the same place at the same time. The final video, which features the two of them at the piano keyboard, was put together by technical wizardry and a lot of crossed fingers. Few viewers realized that the two stars were never together for the filming.

At this stage neither Paul McCartney nor Stevie Wonder had ever had a solo number one hit. Wonder had co-written *Tears Of A Clown* (see no. 290) for Smokey Robinson and the Miracles, and now had co-performed a hit he had not written. He had to wait another two and a half years for his solo

hit (see no. 538), but when it came, it proved to be one of the biggest-selling singles of all time. Paul McCartney's solo number one (see no. 530) would arrive a few months before Wonder's, but curiously in sales terms it was not one of his biggest smashes.

500

A LITTLE PEACE

NICOLE

15 May 1982, for two weeks

● ●

CBS A 2365

Written by Ralph Siegel and Bernd Meinunger, English lyrics by Paul Greedus. Produced by Robert Jung.

For the third consecutive year the winner of the Eurovision Song Contest also won a place at the top of the charts. Seventeen-year old Nicole Hohloch from Saarbrücken was a popular winner for Germany in the contest held in Harrogate on 24 April 1982. She became the sixth winner to top the British charts in the 27 years of the competition and the first of those six performers who didn't sing in English to win. Sweden's Abba won in 1974 with *Waterloo* (see no. 348) but the Contest rules at that time allowed entrants to sing in languages other than their native tongue, something which is currently verboten.

For co-writer Siegel it was a triumph through persistence. He'd composed Germany's Eurovision entry for four years in a row and had come second in 1980 and 1981 before finally providing the winning song in 1982. Siegel thought highly of the work of British songwriter Paul Greedus, which included the 1976 Top 10 hit *Fairytale* for former Euro victor Dana (see no. 284), and asked him to put English lyrics to his song. Greedus continued his connection with Eurovision by producing Britain's 1983 entry, *I'm Never Giving Up* by Sweet Dreams.

Nicole's chart career is extraordinary. She has only had two hits. Her first, *A Little Peace*, hit the very top and her second, *Give Me More Time*, spent just one week in August 1982, at number 75.

501

HOUSE OF FUN

MADNESS

29 May 1982, for two weeks

● ●

Stiff BUY 146

Written by Mike Barson and Lee Thompson. Produced by Clive Langer and Alan Winstanley.

This only number one for the north London ska band was written by their keyboard player Mike Barson and their saxophonist Lee Thompson. It occurred right in the middle of their 23-hit singles chart career, being both preceded and followed by 11 hits. No less than 15 of the 23 were Top 10 items, and for the period from their first chart entry (1 September 1979 – *The Prince*) until their November 1986 swansong ([*Waiting For] The Ghost Train)* no other act had more weeks on the UK singles chart than Madness.

Six members of Madness emerged from the Camden Town band the Invaders – Barson and Thompson, bassist Mark Bedford, vocalist Graham 'Suggs' McPherson, guitarist Chris Foreman and drummer Daniel Woodgate. By the time of *House Of Fun* (a celebration of a young man's introduction into the wicked adult world) they had become a seven piece with the addition of singer/trumpeter/dancer Chas Smash aka Carl Smyth.

Madness were by far the most popular all-white ska group of their day, retaining influences of that West Indian music right through to their more serious and sophisticated later recordings on their own Zarjazz label. Their 'nutty' image, zany videos and good time act were an integral part of their appeal. Their musical versatility was beyond doubt as they pushed single after single (some purely instrumental) into the best-sellers before their final split in 1986, though Barson had left at the end of 1983.

Charlene *came out of virtual retirement to sing live on* Top of the Pops.

502

GOODY TWO SHOES

ADAM ANT

12 June 1982, for two weeks

●●

CBS A 2367

Written by Adam Ant and Marco Pirroni. Produced by Adam Ant, Marco Pirroni and Chris Hughes.

The third number one to feature the lead vocals of Stuart Goddard (born 3 November 1954) aka Adam Ant was the only one of the three to be credited to him alone. However Adam's chief sidekick in the Ants, Marco Pirroni, was still greatly in evidence on *Goody Two Shoes* and the sound of the third chart-topper was much in the tradition of the first two. As he had with *Prince Charming* (see no. 486) and as he was to do in 1983 with a number 5 hit *Puss 'N' Boots,* Adam drew inspiration for his 1982 number one from the world of pantomime and children's fantasy. The song discussed the clean-living life of

its subject – 'don't drink, don't smoke, what do you do?' – a life whose virtues Ant himself often extolled.

It was all downhill after *Goody Two Shoes* as far as Adam's chart fortunes were concerned. His follow-up *Friend Or Foe* reached number 9, and the one after that *Desperate But Not Serious* only 33. *Puss 'N' Boots* restored some honour but it was his last Top 10 success. But Ant/Goddard is still a significant talent both visually and vocally. No leader of a group who made an impact achieved by only a score of record acts in UK music history should be written off. His recent work as an actor supports this positive view.

503

I'VE NEVER BEEN TO ME

CHARLENE

26 June 1982, for one week

●

Motown TMG 1260

Written by Ron Miller and Ken Hirsch. Produced by Ron Miller, Berry Gordy and Don Costa.

Charlene Duncan is a true UK one-hit wonder with no other claim to record fame beyond her week of glory with *I've Never Been To Me*. The disc was originally recorded in 1976 and issued in America on the Prodigal label, a little known label within the Motown Corporation. It limped to 97 in the US in 1977. Veteran Motown producer Ron Miller must have long consigned Charlene's recording career to the out-tray when, in 1982, a Florida radio station suddenly began playing *I've Never Been To Me* to phenomenal audience reaction. Motown re-released the single on the parent label and this time it went to number 3 in the States and those vital two places higher in the UK.

It took some time for Motown to rediscover their new hit act, for she had married and settled in England. Charlene was actually working in an Ilford sweetshop when news of her belated triumph reached her. She promoted her hit and went back into the studio in the hope of sustaining her success.

Motown even teamed Charlene with Stevie Wonder and a duet entitled *Used To Be* made number 46 in America in late 1982.

Charlene's hit is a saga of a woman failing to discover herself and true happiness despite an action-packed lifestyle that included making love to a priest in the sun, visits to the 'Isle of Greece' and being undressed by kings. Halfway through a tear-jerking monologue Charlene points out that the life of a mundane housewife is actually more rewarding. This is probably just as well as Charlene's long-term fortunes in the music world were not improved even by this monster smash.

Two of the men at the controls of this recording had already experienced number one success in Great Britain, Don Costa as producer of Paul Anka (see no. 63) and Donny Osmond (see nos. 327 & 366) and Berry Gordy as writer of no. 158 for Brian Poole. Charlene's hit took almost six years to reach the top but another Gordy song, *Reet Petite,* was to take even longer after the original recording date to do so (see no. 582). Of course, as the founder of the fabulously successful Tamla Motown group of companies, Gordy has had several other links with the UK top slot.

504

HAPPY TALK

CAPTAIN SENSIBLE

3 July 1982, for two weeks

●●

A&M CAP 1

Written by Richard Rodgers and Oscar Hammerstein II. Produced by Tony Mansfield.

Guitarist/bassist/vocalist Captain Sensible began life as Ray Burns, who became part of the important punk band the Damned in 1976 (original line-up Burns/Sensible, Rat Scabies, Dave Vanian, Brian James). The group made their debut supporting the Sex Pistols at the 100 Club in July of that year. Their early recordings on Stiff were commercial failures and despite their highly praised and explosive stage act, the Damned disbanded in 1978, personality clashes within the group adding to their frustration. However they soon re-emerged with Algy Ward and then Paul Gray replacing Brian James, and this time around they hit the charts with both singles and albums on Chiswick. The individual members of the band had on several occasions made their own extra-Damned recordings, but none proved to be as overwhelmingly popular as Captain Sensible's version of a Rodgers and Hammerstein standard from *South Pacific*. It outsold every Damned single released before or since and is about as removed from the Damned style as could be.

The Captain signed with A & M for solo projects in 1982, by which time the Damned were with Bronze. He declared his loyalty to the group stating that they were 'the first real punk band and they'll be the last whatever happens'. Almost immediately his irresistible version of *Happy Talk* zoomed to number one, making a record leap in its second chart week from 33 to the top. He thus provided both Rodgers and Hammerstein with their fifth number one, the legendary pair's first for 19 years (see no. 159).

Sensible remained with the Damned until the end of 1984, but there was a conflict of both interest and style between his two careers. Solo-wise his only other major hit, *Glad It's All Over*, owed a lot to the *Damned On 45* flip side which consisted of a medley of 15 Damned songs plus *Happy Talk*. He has advertised Weetabix and apeared on countless pop and children's TV shows as all-round good egg and japer. Burns has made cricket records under the name Percy Pavilion.

Sans Sensible, the Damned scored their biggest hit yet when a revival of Barry Ryan's 1968 winner *Eloise* reached number 3 in 1986.

505

IRENE CARA

17 July 1982, for three weeks

● ● ●

RSO RSO 90

Written by Michael Gore and Dean Pitchford. Produced by Michael Gore.

Irene Cara broke into the limelight as Coco Hernandez in *Fame,* the hit Alan Parker

Eileen was a girl Kevin Rowland of **Dexys Midnight Runners** grew up with and immortalized in their second number one.

movie about a New York drama school. She also sang the title song which became her first hit record, reaching number 4 in the US in the year of the film's release, 1980. It failed to make any impression in Britain at that time but more than made up for this two years later, when the spin-off TV series of *Fame* became an enormous hit, making a chart recording act out of the cast as 'Kids From Fame' and making Irene's original movie song the hit it should have been in the first place. The fast moving disco winner was written by Lesley Gore's brother Michael and lyricist Dean Pitchford. It was nominated for an Oscar. (Lesley Gore's first hit record *It's My Party*, a 1963 US number one, was a chart-topper in the UK 18 years later – see no. 487.)

Irene started performing when she was just seven, appearing on Spanish-language radio and TV shows in New York. She made her Broadway debut a year later (an orphan in *Maggie Flynn* starring Jack Cassidy and Shirley Jones – father and stepmother of David Cassidy, see nos. 320 and 330). Already a seasoned concert performer, by the age of 12, she began writing songs. By the time the big break of *Fame* came along, she had already appeared in several films, including the lead role in the musical *Sparkle,* and TV series such as *Roots: The Next Generation.* The soundtrack of *Fame* provided her with a second, lesser, hit single on

both sides of the Atlantic, the ballad *Out Here On My Own*, but her second significant hit came from another movie, 1983's *Flashdance.* Irene did not act in this film but her interpretation of *Flashdance. . .What A Feeling* gave her an American chart-topper and a number 2 in Britain. This time around the song sung by Irene Cara won the Oscar.

506

DEXYS MIDNIGHT RUNNERS AND THE EMERALD EXPRESS

7 August 1982, for four weeks

● ● ● ●

Mercury DEXYS 9

Written by Kevin Rowland, Jimmy Patterson and Kevin Adams. Produced by Clive Langer and Alan Winstanley.

After *Geno* (see no. 457), his first number one hit with Dexys (then sporting an apostrophe), Kevin Rowland's follow-up singles enjoyed only moderate acclaim until the release of this Celtic soul masterpiece. Teamed with a group of fiddlers named the Emerald Express (who received equal billing on the label) a totally new-look (gypsy) and nearly all-new-personnel, Runners climbed all the way back to *Geno* heights with the saga of young love and lust inspired by a girl Rowland grew up with.

The album that contained *Come On Eileen, Too-Rye-Ay,* was also a huge success, reaching number 2 and remaining on the charts for nearly a year. It reflected Rowland's passion at the time for Celtic influenced folk music allied on occasion to a powerful rock beat. Both single and album did very well in America, the former repeating its British chart achievement between Michael Jackson's two *Thriller* number ones in April 1983. Producers Langer and Winstanley's second number one came just three months after their first (no. 501).

One more Top 10 hit followed *Come On Eileen,* the group's revival of Ulsterman Van Morrison's *Jackie Wilson Said,* but since late 1982 there has not been a great rush to the stores for Dexys product. The group did earn a Top 20 placing at the end of 1986 with *Because Of You,* the theme from *Brush Strokes,* a TV comedy series about a painter/decorator. The decline in their fortunes was not arrested by an extraordinary change of image for the 1985 album *Don't Stand Me Down.* A 4-piece line-up were portrayed on the cover in neat unexciting suits and ties (but no tie for violinist Helen O'Hara).

507

EVE OF THE TIGER

SURVIVOR

4 September 1982, for four weeks

● ● ● ●

Scotti Brothers SCT A 2411

Written by Frankie Sullivan and Jim Peterik. Produced by Jim Peterik and Frankie Sullivan.

The incredible box-office success of Sylvester 'Sly' Stallone's films about the fictitious heavyweight boxer Rocky spilled over into the record charts on more than one occasion. *Gonna Fly Now,* the theme of the first movie, was a US number one in 1977. The song meant little in England, despite further

exposure in *Rocky II.* For *Rocky III,* the saga of Rocky's punch-up with Mr T. in the guise of Clubber Lang, Stallone commissioned a theme from Chicago band Survivor.

Since 1981 Survivor consisted of keyboardist Jim Peterik, lead guitarist Frankie Sullivan, vocalist David Bicker, bassist Stephan Ellis and drummer Marc Droubay. They had only enjoyed moderate record sales, with one US Top 40 hit to their name, though leader Peterik had been with the Ides Of March in his University of Illinois days when that group had a number 2 US success with *Vehicle. Rocky III* ensured Survivor's survival. Peterik and Sullivan came up with a song inspired by a line that cropped up several times in the film's screenplay. It captured the drive, pace and violence of the boxer's life to a (Mr) T. It became champ of the American charts in July and scored a second knock-out against all-comers in England by September. Survivor (with Jimi Jamieson now lead singer) were retained by Sly for *Rocky IV* in 1985 and their *Burning Heart* did almost as well (number 5 UK, number 2 US).

508

PASS THE DUTCHIE

MUSICAL YOUTH

2 October 1982, for three weeks

● ● ●

MCA YOU 1

Written by Jackie Mittoo, Fitzroy Simpson and Lloyd Ferguson. Produced by Peter Collins.

The BBC TV News doesn't often feature stories from the record charts but an exception was made in the first week of October 1982 for five unknown black youths dancing outside the Houses Of Parliament singing a song that would have been totally incomprehensible to the occupants of those buildings. The boys were the Birmingham based Musical Youth and the unusual interest in their success was a fair reflection of the unexpectedness of it.

Musical Youth were all pupils at Duddeston Manor School in Birmingham. The line-up included two sets of brothers, Kelvin and Michael Grant and Junior and Patrick Waite plus Dennis Seaton. Their ages ranged from 16 down to only 11 and great media interest centred around the fact that the youngest

members would be breaking the law were they to work more than a certain number of days, even though they were top of the pops.

The original lead vocalist was Junior and Patrick's father, Fred, who had sung with the Techniques in his native Jamaica. The group appeared in several pubs in and around Birmingham even though Kelvin was only 8 when they started out. They recorded a single *Political/Generals* for Birmingham's 021 Records and secured a session on John Peel's Radio 1 show. In early 1982 Fred backed away from the limelight and Dennis Seaton took over as lead singer. A recording contract was signed with MCA who thus enjoyed their first number one single since *Don't Cry For Me Argentina* over five years earlier. The record's leap from 26 to 1 in its second chart week was one of the most spectacular and surprising vaults to the top.

The contagious reggae anthem *Pass The Dutchie* was a re-write of an old Mighty Diamonds tune by Jackie Mittoo. It had originally been called *Pass The Kutchie* but the key word was tactfully altered to Dutchie – a Jamaican cooking pot. Kutchie refers to a different kind of pot altogether and was hardly the sort of thing youngsters should have been singing about.

The group enjoyed seven more hits in the following 18 months, but none had the astonishing impact of their debut. *Pass The Dutchie* went Top 10 in the States and they sang with Donna Summer on her minor hit *Unconditional Love.* Since then the group has floundered and disbanded.

509

DO YOU REALLY

WANT TO HURT ME

CULTURE CLUB

23 October 1982, for three weeks

● ● ●

Virgin VS 518

Written by Culture Club (Boy George, Jon Moss, Roy Hay and Michael Craig). Produced by Steve Levine.

George O'Dowd, born 14 June 1961 in South London, was a figure on the glitzy fringe of

London's club scene from the end of the '70s before he became professionally involved with music. Thanks solely to his extraordinary appearance he had become a well-known personality in nightspots such as Billy's and Blitz, where his penchant for make-up, dresses and outlandish headgear made him a centre of attention and a magnet for photographers and gossip. He was eventually spotted by Bow Wow Wow (and ex-Sex Pistols) manager Malcolm McLaren who asked him to tour with Bow Wow Wow purely because of his startling visual impact.

It transpired that O'Dowd (who had long called himself Boy George) could actually sing. He formed his own group with bassist Mikey Craig, In Praise Of Lemmings, who became Sex Gang Children with the addition of John Suede (guitar) and Jon Moss (drums). Suede was eventually replaced by Roy Hay (guitar and keyboards) and George renamed the band Culture Club in 1981.

In early 1982 Culture Club made some demos which impressed Virgin. Two of the tracks became the band's first two A-sides, although neither *White Boy* nor *I'm Afraid Of Me* charted. The principal interest in the band was still the look of George himself until they came up with the music to match third time around. *Do You Really Want To Hurt Me* made the breakthrough even to those who had not to date clapped eyes on George and Culture Club. When those who bought the gentle, sensitive and unthreatening single, masterfully produced by Steve Levine and dominated by George's excellent white soul vocals, actually saw the outfit that had created it, there was little doubt that an act out of the ordinary was off and running. Sure enough, *Do You Really Want To Hurt Me* became a worldwide bestseller and Boy George was on the way to international superstardom.

510

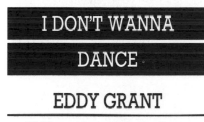

I DON'T WANNA DANCE

EDDY GRANT

13 November 1982, for three weeks

Ice ICE 56

Written by Eddy Grant. Produced by Eddy Grant.

With his fifth British hit ex-Equal Eddy Grant became the twelfth former member of a number one group to take the top as a solo act. The Equals (see no. 252) had long since gone the way of all flesh by the time Eddy's solo career took shape and from his initial breakthrough in 1979 with *Living On The Front Line* Grant built up a substantial list of recording successes whose peak to date came in late 1982 and early 1983 with the singles *I Don't Wanna Dance* and *Electric Avenue.* The second of these reached number 2 both sides of the Atlantic.

The Guyana-born Edmond Montague Grant based himself in Barbados where he recorded his heavy reggae-rock hits, writing, arranging and producing the material himself for his own label. Among his other noteworthy recordings were *Living On The Front Line* which popularized that expression describing ghetto life, and *Walking On Sunshine*, taken to the Top 10 in a cover by Rocker's Revenge. His theme for Michael Douglas' movie *Romancing The Stone* made the US Top 30 despite appearing in the film for only seconds. *Gimme Hope Jo'anna* returned Eddy to the Top 10 in 1988

511

BEAT SURRENDER

THE JAM

4 December 1982, for two weeks

●●

Polydor POSP 540

Written by Paul Weller. Produced by Peter Wilson.

The fourth and final number one for the Jam was also the last new single release of their five-year recording career. They achieved a mass invasion of the singles charts in early 1983 as *Beat Surrender* was slipping out of the Top 75, but this was with 13 re-issues of previous hits. On 22 January 1983, they made chart history by entering the lists with nine titles simultaneously, adding one more the following week and three more the week after that, giving them, on 5 February, a record 13 hits at once. None got higher than 21 this time around, but it was an astounding accomplishment bearing in mind that all 13 had been substantial hits at least once before and not that long before either.

Beat Surrender gave the Jam co-ownership of another record by hitting number one first week out. This was the Jam's third number one to do this, equalling the '70s achievement of Slade (nos. 326, 333 and 341). Jam fans however knew that this was the group's swansong because two months before *Beat Surrender* came out they had amazed the music world by announcing their imminent break-up. A UK chart career of 18 hit singles and 8 hit albums was over, spectacular indeed despite the Jam's failure to make any impact in the United States.

Since the Jam's demise Bruce Foxton (three minor hit singles) and Rick Buckler have not suffered from over-exposure but Paul Weller has continued to make his presence felt, if not quite at Jam level. From March 1983 his new recording unit, The Style Council, formed around Weller and ex-Merton Parka Mick Talbot, have consistently hit the singles and album charts with a series of recordings that owe little to the abrasive and frantic sound of the Jam. Weller has not yet returned to the very top of the singles lists but the Council's *Our Favourite Shop* was a number one album in 1985.

512

SAVE YOUR LOVE

RENÉE & RENATO

18 December 1982, for four weeks

●●●●

Hollywood HWD 003

Written by John Edward and Sue Edward. Produced by John Edward.

Contrary to popular belief, Renée and Renato, the act who gave British music lovers one of the most mind-boggling Christmas number one hits since the inception of the charts, are strictly speaking not one-hit wonders as a follow-up single by the disparate duo entitled *Just One More Kiss* lurched up to no. 48 in February 1983. It was however downhill fast from there.

Roman-born Renato Pagliari was a waiter with a powerful set of lungs living in Birmingham who was originally only appreciated by his fellow pasta pushers. Legend

1977, Genesis simply continued as a trio of Collins, Mike Rutherford and Tony Banks. It was then that the band matched and eventually surpassed the achievements of the Peter Gabriel era. They enjoyed hit singles and albums and sold-out concert tours around the world.

The three members of Genesis have all undertaken individual projects while the group continues to prosper. In early 1981, Phil's first solo album, *Face Value,* entered the British album charts at number one in its first week, propelled there in part by the number 2 single *In The Air Tonight.* His second album *Hello, I Must Be Going* (November 1982) was nearly as big as the first and included *You Can't Hurry Love.*

514

DOWN UNDER

MEN AT WORK

29 January 1983, for three weeks

● ● ●

Epic EPC A 1980

Written by Colin Hay and Ron Strykert.
Produced by Peter McIan.

Men At Work were an Australian quintet formed by lead singer Colin Hay and lead guitarist Ron Strykert at La Trobe University, Melbourne. Joined by keyboard and woodwind player Greg Ham, drummer Jerry Speiser and bassist John Rees, they first performed as Men At Work at the Cricketers Arms pub in Melbourne. CBS Australia teamed them up with an American producer, Peter McIan, and the result was the album *Business As Usual* which contained two enormous hit singles, *Who Can It Be Now* and *Down Under.* A US tour as support to Fleetwood Mac, plus heavy exposure of the video on MTV, enabled the first of these to go all the way to number one in America, although in Britain it could only reach a modest 45 placing at the end of 1982.

The second single more than made up for this quiet UK debut by zipping to the very top in the fifth week after its release. It also became Men At Work's second straight US number one. It was Australia's first visit to the UK summit since Rolf Harris in 1969 (see no. 280), although Joe Dolce's 1981 hit (no. 475) was recorded Down Under and semi-

(or at least the sleevenote of his album) has it that his break came when he was asked to fill in for a guest singer who had failed to arrive. His reception that night was ecstatic and follow-up appearances in local cabaret venues soon meant that saltimbocca alla Romana's loss was (among other places) the Winter Gardens, Margate's gain. There he met Hilary Lefter who became Renée on Renato's recording of *Save Your Love.* Unfortunately Lefter left before the record made its surprise impact upon the Christmas market; 28-year-old Val Penny and wig were drafted in to mime for the video. *Just One More Kiss,* recorded before the R & R split, featured the original Renée, but after that Renato preferred to continue Renée-less.

513

YOU CAN'T HURRY LOVE

PHIL COLLINS

15 January 1983, for two weeks

● ●

Virgin VS 531

Written by Brian Holland, Lamont Dozier and Eddie Holland. Produced by Phil Collins, assisted by Hugh Padgham.

Phil Collins, drummer and vocalist of Gene-

Renee and Renato. *The first of the first pair of successive number one 'love' titles since the Sixties.*

sis, became one of the biggest international stars of the '80s. He enjoyed his first UK number one with his fifth solo release, the first that was not one of his own compositions. *You Can't Hurry Love* was one of the many classic Motown hits written by Holland-Dozier-Holland, who unbelievably only enjoyed two British number ones (see nos. 181 & 225) before Collins' success. The original 1966 version of the song had been a UK Top 3 hit for Diana Ross and The Supremes as well as their seventh US chart-topper.

Phil Collins was born in Chiswick on 30 January 1951. He began drumming at the age of five and at 14 he entered stage school. His brief stage career included the part of the Artful Dodger in the West End production of *Oliver.* By the late '60s he was devoting his creative energies entirely to music, his early bands including the Real Thing (not *the* Real Thing, see no. 391), Hickory and Flaming Youth, a studio aggregation that made one highly acclaimed concept album in 1969 entitled *Ark II.* A year later came the vital career move – Phil auditioned for Genesis and became their drummer in September 1970. He made his vocal debut for the band on the *Nursery Cryme* album, released in 1974. Genesis were on the way to becoming a significant international act when front man Peter Gabriel quit in 1975. Many felt that was the end of the group but after a period of re-thinking, the band re-emerged with Collins as the 'new' lead singer. When guitarist Steve Hackett left in

Aussies the Bee Gees and Olivia Newton-John had been at the top more recently. *Down Under*, a reggae influenced rock number about Australians who travel overseas and then come home, was certainly the first smash to mention Vegemite.

Men At Work never enjoyed such international acclaim again although their second album *Cargo* delivered three medium-sized hit singles. Speiser and Rees left the band in 1984 and Colin Hay issued solo work in 1986.

515

TOO SHY

KAJAGOOGOO

19 February 1983, for two weeks

● ●

EMI 5359

Written by Kajagoogoo (lyrics by Limahl and Nick Beggs). Produced by Nick Rhodes and Colin Thurston.

Kajagoogoo were a quintet from Leighton Buzzard in Herttfordshire. Originally named Art Nouveau, they consisted of Limahl (lead vocalist), Nick Beggs (bass, vocals), Steve Askew (E Bow and Guitar), Stuart Crawford Neale (synthesizers, vocals) and Jez Strode (drums and electronic programming). Limahl (real name Chris Hamill – Limahl is an anagram of Hamill) was the last to join via an advertisement in the music press.

The group had already had demo tapes rejected by EMI when Wigan-born Limahl, working part-time as a waiter in London's Embassy Club, spotted Duran Duran's Nick Rhodes. He persuaded Rhodes that he and his band were, at worst, the next sensation but one. EMI showed new interest in the band with the promise of Rhodes and Duran producer Colin Thurston at the recording helm. Their first single *Too Shy* hit the jackpot, achieving something that the well-established Duran Duran had not at that point done – the number one singles spot. The song had originally been called *Shy Shy* after a phrase in the chorus, but was altered to avoid confusion with Duran Duran and Talk Talk.

The group had a further six single hits in the UK, and *Too Shy* was a substantial hit in the States, but they were not destined for lasting fame. Limahl left the group in 1984. He subsequently enjoyed world-wide success with the Giorgio Moroder production and composition *Never Ending Story*, while the remaining members of the band soldiered on for a while as Kaja.

516

BILLIE JEAN

MICHAEL JACKSON

5 March 1983, for one week

●

Epic EPC A 3084

Written by Michael Jackson. Produced by Quincy Jones.

1983 was the year in which Michael Jackson stopped being a mere superstar and became a phenomenon. This was achieved primarily through his album *Thriller*, which five years on remains the best-selling album in history. Its stupendous success in virtually every country of the world set new commercial standards for all contemporary artists as well as for Jackson's own subsequent releases. *Thriller* is reputed to have sold about 40 million copies – thus making it possible that Epic will become the first record company to apologize for a mere 20 million sale should any of Jackson's follow-ups, such as his 1987 album *Bad*, perform only half as well.

Michael's previous solo album *Off The Wall*, also produced immaculately by Quincy Jones, had contained four UK Top 10 hits and a fifth that made no. 41. The most successful single, *Don't Stop Till You Get Enough*, had peaked at no. 3. The first single cut from *Thriller*, a duet between Jackson and Paul McCartney entitled *The Girl Is Mine*, topped out at no. 8. *Billie Jean* was the song that kicked *Thriller* into the stratosphere. It told the (fictitious) tale of a woman who attempts to blame Jackson for her illegitimate offspring. The basic rhythm line of the song was laid down by Jackson on a drum machine and enhanced later by drummer Leon Ndugu Chancler, bassist Louis Johnson of the Brothers Johnson, guitarist Dean Parks, veteran jazzman Tom Scott on lyricon

Michael Jackson *popularized the promotional video more than anyone else with his three clips from* Thriller, *beginning with* Billie Jean.

Bonnie Tyler *(no. 517) achieved the total eclipse of Michael Jackson.*

and Greg Smith and Bill Wolfer on synthesizer. Jerry Hey arranged the string charts

The hits kept on coming from *Thriller*. A record-breaking seven titles became US Top 10 items, with five (a sixth reached no. 11) doing so in Britain. Jackson waited nearly five years before releasing another solo package. In the intervening years he hogged headlines for his personal eccentricities rather than for his music, although he did participate rather half-heartedly in a Jacksons tour and album in 1984. Tales of oxygen cylinders, plastic surgery, chimpanzees and remains of the Elephant Man cannot diminish the extraordinary impact of *Thriller*, his masterpiece.

517

TOTAL ECLIPSE OF THE HEART

BONNIE TYLER

12 March 1983, for two weeks

●●

CBS TYLER 1

Written by Jim Steinman. Produced by Jim Steinman.

Bonnie Tyler was born on 8 June 1953, in Skewen, South Wales, near Swansea. At 17 she won a local talent contest and began singing in Welsh nightclubs, including the Townsman Club in Swansea where she was seen by Ronnie Scott and Steve Wolfe. They had written a song called *Lost In France* and asked Bonnie to record it. It became her first hit single, reaching number 9 in late 1976. Scott and Wolfe were Bonnie's managers, songwriters and producers from 1976 to 1981, but after the debut hit her only major achievement was the 1978 monster *It's A Heartache,* which gave Bonnie her first taste of Stateside success. When Tyler severed connections with her management in 1981, she had been all but forgotten for three years.

Searching for a major producer, Bonnie's new manager, David Aspden, approached Meat Loaf mastermind Jim Steinman. Steinman, based in New York, is a producer who thinks big and who attempts to bring a sense of grand theatre to his work in the recording studio. This he did for Bonnie with *Total Eclipse Of The Heart.* The six-track extravaganza raced past all opposition to the top, denying none other than Michael Jackson more than a solitary week at the top with *Billie Jean.* The Steinman-produced album *Faster Than The Speed Of Night* was only the second by a British female to top the album charts since the listings began in 1958 (Kate Bush's *Never For Ever* was the first). The single also went all the way to number one in America.

In early 1984 Bonnie enjoyed a British Top 10 hit with Shakin' Stevens, a revival of the 1960 Brook Benton/Dinah Washington classic *A Rockin' Good Way.* Over a year after that she was up at number 2 with a Steinman song from the movie *Footloose* that she had recorded back in 1983, *Holding Out For A Hero.* Since then her husky tones have only graced the less glamorous end of the Top 75 via another Steinman epic *Loving You's A Dirty Job But Somebody's Gotta Do It,* a duet with Todd Rundgren.

518

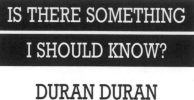

IS THERE SOMETHING I SHOULD KNOW?

DURAN DURAN

26 March 1983, for two weeks

●●

EMI 5371

Written by Duran Duran. Produced by Duran Duran and Ian Little.

At the height of their popularity, from the end of 1982 until about halfway through 1985, Duran Duran could claim to be as popular with younger rock fans as any other group in the world. *Is There Something I Should Know?* was their eighth British release and the first to go all the way, topping their previous high of number 2 with *Save A Prayer.*

Duran Duran was founded in Birmingham in 1978. Their image was from the word go 'New Romantic', in sharp contrast to the less delicate attitudes portrayed by many of the successful punk groups of the era. Their name was that of the villain in Jane Fonda's 1968 movie *Barbarella,* for Barbarella's in Birmingham was the name of the club in which they performed most in their early days. The line-up that made the first Duran record had evolved by the summer of 1980: Simon Le Bon (vocals), Nick Rhodes (synthesizers and keyboards) and the unrelated Taylors, John (bass), Andy (guitar) and Roger (drums). They began their chart career in early 1981 with *Planet Earth,* which climbed to number 12. Their third single, *Girls On Film,* was the first to take them into the Top 10, helped by a controversial video directed by Godley and Creme (see nos 332 and 372).

It was videos, particularly those directed by Russell Mulcahy, that broke the band in the States. Duran Duran paid as much attention to their visual appeal as they did to their sound and the booming MTV channel in America gave hefty exposure to their 1982 Sri Lanka-lensed video *Hungry Like The Wolf.* This set them off on a run of big US hits. Alex Sadkin, who before his accidental death in 1987 became a fully-fledged producer of Duran Duran and other major artists, is credited on this track as co-mixer with Ian Little.

519

LET'S DANCE

DAVID BOWIE

9 April 1983, for three weeks

●●●

EMI America EA 152

Written by David Bowie. Produced by David Bowie and Nile Rodgers.

Bowie's third solo British number one was the first not to mention his famous creation Major Tom, who nevertheless still made the charts again in 1983 courtesy of German singer/songwriter Peter Schilling's hit *Major Tom (Coming Home). Let's Dance* was lyrically a less complex theme than those of *Space Oddity* and *Ashes To Ashes.* It was the title track of his first album for EMI America, and the pairing of Bowie with Chic's Nile Rodgers at the desk resulted in one of the most instantly appealing Bowie LPs yet. He promoted it with a mammoth international trek, the *Serious Moonlight Tour,* that kind of lunar illumination being a line of the *Let's Dance* lyric. *Let's Dance* became Bowie's second US number one.

When the International Association for the Study Of Popular Music met in Reggio, Italy, in 1983, Mr Wim van der Plas delivered a paper entitled 'Can Rock Be Art?', in which he debated whether the role of rock music as a revolutionary medium within a capitalist society could be considered art. Van der Plas stated that Bowie's *Let's Dance* video made a 'statement about the true state of affairs in the world' by depicting a black woman on her knees scrubbing a car-filled motorway; he closed his paper quoting the hit thus: 'The question of rock and art can be summarized quite succinctly: Put on your red shoes and dance the blues'. Quite.

520

TRUE

SPANDAU BALLET

30 April 1983, for four weeks

●●●●

Reformation SPAN 1

Written by Gary Kemp. Produced by Tony Swain, Steve Jolley and Spandau Ballet.

Five-man North London group Spandau Ballet made their first live appearance in private in November 1979 before an audience of invited friends, primarily pacesetters of the contemporary fashion scene. They were soon well-established as part of the circuit of outrageous West End club life, their position when signing their first recording deal powerful enough for their own Reformation label to be given top billing over that of the company that signed them, Chrysalis.

Tony Hadley (vocals), Kemp brothers Martin (bass) and Gary (guitar and keyboards), Steve Norman (sax, percussion) and John Keeble (drums) had a major hit first time out with *To Cut A Long Story Short.* They had established a run of nine consecutive chart records when their greatest success, the thoughtful Gary Kemp ballad *True,* appeared as both the title track of their third album and a single in Spring 1983. Both LP and 45 topped their respective charts.

Spandau were now challenging Duran Duran for New Romantic/teeny fan supremacy but although their next two singles reached 2 and 3 respectively in the UK, they never quite touched their mid-1983 heights again. A further blow to their career came when a drawn out dispute with Chrysalis prevented the release of any new Spandau product for over a year. It therefore said a lot for the loyalty of the group's fans, and for the quality of their music, when a late 1986 comeback album on CBS, *Through The Barricades,* together with the title track single, returned them to Top 10 status.

521

CANDY GIRL

NEW EDITION

28 May 1983, for one week

●

London LON 21

Written by Maurice Starr and Michael Jonzun. Produced by Maurice Starr and Michael Jonzun.

Candy Girl was the New Edition's first record, and although it was only a moderate success in their native America, it became one of the more unexpected number one hits of 1983 in the UK.

The five boys, Ralph Tresvant (lead vocalist), Michael Bivins, Ronald DeVoe, Ricky Bell and Bobby Brown, were all aged between 13 and 15 in 1983. They won a talent contest at their school in Roxbury, Massachusetts, and were spotted by writer/producer Maurice Starr. Michael Bivins' uncle was taken aboard as manager and Starr, working with his brother Michael Jonzun, an established figure on the New York disco scene via his act the Jonzun Crew, gave the boys material to record and worked with them to create a Jackson Five type stage act.

Streetwise Records of New York snapped up the New Edition's first recording and were quickly rewarded when the single broke into the dance charts, and then the black charts, where it scooted all the way to number one. It failed to cross over in a big way to the pop charts (a mere no. 46) but its success in Britain was some compensation. Since then the quintet (incidentally the fifth five-piece to hit number one in the first four months of 1983) have had consistent US chart action in black, dance and pop lists, but only one more sizeable UK hit with *Mr. Telephone Man* in 1985. Brown left to go solo in 1986.

522

EVERY BREATH YOU

TAKE

POLICE

4 June 1983, for four weeks

●●●●

A&M AM 117

Written by Sting. Produced by Hugh Padgham and Police.

Police fans had been forced to wait over 18 months for their idols' fifth album, *Synchronicity.* The first track to be stripped from the set, *Every Breath You Take,* charged up the charts to give the band their fifth and final number one to date. Sting would later affectionately refer to the song's lyrics in his 1985 solo hit *Love Is The Seventh Wave.*

From the time that *King Of Pain* slipped off the Top 75 in February 1984 speculation grew as to whether Police would record together again. Fears were compounded when Sting produced a solo album and appeared at the Live Aid concert without Summers or Copeland. A project to produce a collection of old songs gave a glimmer of hope but was aborted after just one track had been recorded. This new version of their third number one, *Don't Stand So Close To Me,* was released in 1986 and became their least successful single for A & M, managing a position of just 24. A Greatest Hits package, an LP that looks like being their last, was put out at the end of that year.

523

BABY JANE

ROD STEWART

2 July 1983, for three weeks

●●●

Warner Bros W 9608

Written by Rod Stewart and Jay Davis. Produced by Rod Stewart and Tom Dowd; co-produced by Jim Cregan and George Tutko.

Rod Stewart records, by his own very high standards, had not been selling at quite the rate of yore after his fifth number one hit *Da Ya Think I'm Sexy?* (see no. 429) in 1978. In the following four-and-a-half years he only once graced the UK Top 10 with *Tonight I'm Yours (Don't Hurt Me)* in 1981. Thus it was that his sixth number one *Baby Jane* was rather unjustly hailed as a comeback for the oft-imitated gravel larynx.

In truth, Rod had never really been away. His status as one of the most photographed personalities of the entertainment business had never faltered, and his tours were never less than massively successful. Two of his early '80s singles, *Passion* and *Young Turks*, had gone Top 5 Stateside. But a number one in either Britain or America is a great boost to any act of whatever standing at any time and Rod's excitement at hitting the top with *Baby Jane* was obvious during his tour to promote the *Body Wishes* album from which the single came.

Baby Jane took Stewart's total weeks at number one to 18, level with the Rolling Stones, who had needed eight number one hits to amass their 18 weeks. Besides the Stones, only Elvis, the Beatles, Abba and Cliff had now had more number ones, and only Slade the same number. Rod himself has not added to this tally since 1983, although he missed out by only one place in summer 1986 with *Every Beat Of My Heart*.

524

WHEREVER I LAY MY HAT (THAT'S MY HOME)

PAUL YOUNG

23 July 1983, for three weeks

●●●

CBS A 3371

Written by Marvin Gaye, Norman Whitfield and Barrett Strong. Produced by Laurie Latham.

Paul Young burst into prominence, apparently from nowhere, with his heartfelt rendition of an old Marvin Gaye B-side. The Luton-raised vocalist had, however, been recording for over five years with first Street Band and then the Q-Tips, without ever enjoying the acclaim that *Wherever I Lay My Hat* brought him with his third solo single.

Street Band were a heavy metal meets R&B

influenced pop band for whom Paul sang and played harmonica and occasional bass and keyboards. They signed for the small Logo label in 1978 and hit the Top 20 with their first single – but not with the intended A-side. It was the flip, the throwaway novelty item *Toast*, that appealed to radio, landing the band with an identity crisis when none of the music they really wanted to play met with any chart success whatsoever.

A disheartened Street Band split by the end of 1979 and Young and Mick Pearl (bass) of the group set about forming a new outfit. The result was the Q-Tips, an 8-piece that made its recording debut in March 1980. Their work was principally inspired by and/or featured '60s soul classics but none of their revivals or original material clicked. Again, a discouraged Paul Young-fronted band broke up.

Paul's fortunes changed completely when he took up a solo deal with CBS. After near misses with *Iron Out The Rough Spots* and *Love Of The Common People* (later to become a number 2 hit for Paul Young the star) he broke through all the way with the Motown ballad. His solo recording career maintained a good striking rate for the next four years, including a US chart-topper with *Every Time You Go Away*.

525

GIVE IT UP

K C & THE SUNSHINE BAND

13 August 1983, for three weeks

●●●

Epic EPC A 3017

Written by H.W. Casey and Debra Carter. Produced by H.W. Casey and Richard Finch.

Writer/producer Harry Wayne 'KC' Casey began scoring fairly regularly on international charts with his combo KC and the Sunshine Band in the mid-'70s. In the United States his efforts led to no less than five number one singles between 1975 and 1980. His only British number one to date was provided by a track from his 1982 album *All In A Night's Work*.

Casey (vocals and keyboards) and bassist

Richard Finch were the founders and constant driving forces behind the band's success. Their made-for-discos recordings swept Europe before they took off in the States, *Queen Of Clubs* being the song that launched them in Britain and on the Continent some months ahead of their American breakthrough with *Get Down Tonight*. The band varied in size from 7 members to 11, but Casey and Finch were writers and producers of all their major titles, nearly all irresistible dance fodder for the clubs.

On 15 January 1982, Casey was badly injured in a car accident seven blocks from his Hialeah, Florida home. It took him nearly a year to recuperate and it was during this time that the Irish and then British offices of Epic records decided to push *Give It Up* as a single. Epic in the US were nonetheless unimpressed and KC released the track on his own label, Meca, making the US Top 20 in early 1984 with the track credited just to KC. With or without the Sunshine Band, KC has not charted on either side of the Atlantic since then.

526

RED RED WINE

UB 40

3 September 1983, for three weeks

●●●

DEP International DEP 7

Written by Neil Diamond. Produced by UB 40 and Ray 'Pablo' Falconer.

Neil Diamond's first British number one as a writer was the January 1967 Monkees monster *I'm A Believer* (see no. 228). He had to wait over 16 years for his second, again with a song he had written in the '60s. The title was *Red Red Wine*, which had already been a minor hit twice in the UK, by Jimmy James and the Vagabonds in 1968 and Tony Tribe a year later. Diamond's own version had created just a ripple on the US Hot 100 in 1968.

The team that brought Neil's songwriting back to the heights were the Birmingham octet UB 40. The name is taken from the British Government dole registration card, a sad set of digits known only too well to many youngsters when unemployment was at its very worst in Britain in the early '80s. They began their recording career with the small Graduate label but later graduated to their own record company, DEP International. The band's first hit was a double-sider *King/Food For Thought* and from that excellent start in March 1980 they soon established themselves as one of the most consistent hitmakers of their time. Many of their songs contained a political or social message, their first chart-topper being an exception, unless it can be construed as a plea for temperance.

Their canny combination of pop melodies (mainly original) and dub reggae rhythms was the creation of the sons of Scottish folk singer Iain Campbell, Ali (vocals and rhythm guitar) and Robin (lead guitar), Astro (MC & trumpet), Michael Virtue (keyboards), Brian Travers (sax), Norman Hassan (percussion), Earl Falconer (bass) and Jim Brown (drums). Ray 'Pablo' Falconer was Earl's brother and UB 40's sound engineer.

527

KARMA CHAMELEON

CULTURE CLUB

24 September 1983, for six weeks

●●●●●●

Virgin VS 612

Written by Culture Club (Boy George, Jon Moss, Roy Hay, Michael Craig) and Phil Pickett. Produced by Steve Levine.

Between their first hit (see no. 509) and their second number one *Karma Chameleon* Boy George and Culture Club had rocketed to superstardom, their flamboyant lead singer having one of the most instantly recognizable faces in the western world by late 1983. A succession of outstanding records, of which *Karma Chameleon* was by some distance the most popular single, coupled with George's devastating visual appeal, placed the 22-year-old and his group briefly on a pinnacle that few personalities in any field achieve in a lifetime. Problems were looming, yet during the six weeks that Culture Club were back leading the pack, it seemed that the charming Boy George, all innocence wrapped up in drag, was a man totally in control of what had to be a long and colourful career, loved by old and young alike. The band's records sold in every

In 1985 **Billy Joel** *married his* Uptown Girl *video co-star, Christine Brinkley.*

major world market and George's impact on fashion and appearance was sensational.

Culture Club were supported by the powerful larynx of Helen Terry, for this hit and on others, as well as for stage appearances. Co-composer of *Karma Chameleon* Phil Pickett, who had been a member and writer for the three-hit mid-'70s pop band Sailor, played keyboards on this smash. Jud Lander supplied harmonica. There were noises made later by the composers of the 1960 Jimmy Jones hit *Handy Man* that *Karma Chameleon* was a little too close to *Handy Man* for comfort.

528

UPTOWN GIRL

BILLY JOEL

5 November 1983, for five weeks

●●●●●

CBS A 3775

Written by Billy Joel. Produced by Phil Ramone.

William Martin Joel (born in Hicksville, Long Island, New York, 9 May 1949) took his first piano lessons at the age of four and formed his first rock and roll band, the Echoes, when he was 14. He underwent serious training for life both by playing piano in all-night bars and by becoming an amateur boxer (22 wins in 28 fights, one broken nose). His first recordings were made as a member of the Hassles and then of heavy rock trio Attila, but these and his first solo album *Cold Spring Harbor* (1972) did not last the distance. He was saved by the bell, however, when CBS Records spotted him at a Puerto Rican song festival. In 1974 he recorded his *Piano Man* album and the title song, recalling many of his experiences in those all-night bars, gave him his first single hit in the States.

His 1977 album *The Stranger* was his first teaming with ace producer Phil Ramone. This proved to be his passport to international acceptance. One of the album's songs, *Just The Way You Are,* was his first UK hit and has since been recorded by scores of other artists, becoming a genuine standard.

His first American number one, 1980's *It's Still Rock And Roll To Me,* was his last hit in Britain for nearly three years until the fantastic success of his *An Innocent Man* album lifted his status in Europe to something approaching American level. The album featured Billy playing and singing in the style of many of his heroes from the '50s and '60s, such as the Drifters, Otis Redding and Little Anthony and the Imperials. His tribute to the Four Seasons, *Uptown Girl,* dedicated to his girlfriend Christine Brinkley, was the most popular track of all and became the second best-selling single of 1983 in Britain.

Joel, who married model Brinkley aboard a yacht in the middle of New York Harbour in 1985, has compiled a substantial list of album and singles hits since *Uptown Girl.*

529

ONLY YOU

FLYING PICKETS

10 December 1983, for five weeks

●●●●●

10 Records TEN 14

Written by Vince Clarke. Produced by Flying Pickets and John Sherry.

The last four months of 1983 contained just three number one singles. Following the long runs at the top of Culture Club and Billy Joel, *a cappella* vocal sextet the Flying

Pickets finished the year in triumphant style with a revival of the not very old Yazoo number 2 hit, composed by the male half of that duo, Vince Clarke. The female half was Alison 'Alf' Moyet.

The number one Christmas hit of 1983 was sung by Rick Lloyd, Ken Gregson, Gareth Williams, David Brett, Brian Hibbard and Red Stripe. They met when acting in a touring play about the 1984-5 miners' strike entitled *One Big Blow* with the 7:84 theatre company. In the play they were required to sing *a cappella*. This led to performances in pubs and clubs as an unaccompanied vocal sextet and an album *Live At The Albany Empire,* in which they gave new life to several pop classics such as *Not Fade Away, To Know Him Is To Love Him* and *Da Doo Ron Ron.* They were then signed to Virgin's 10 label where they struck gold.

Not surprisingly, their appeal on record has proved to be limited, and apart from the immediate follow-up to *Only You,* which reached the Top 10, they have made no significant chart dent since. Nonetheless they

Pipes of Peace *gave* **Paul McCartney** *the unique sweep – number one as a soloist and as part of a duo, trio, quartet and quintet.*

continue to have strong international live appeal and are doubtless relieved that the temptations of excessive commercial success in a capitalist society have passed them by. Hibbard and Stripe have recently been replaced by Hereward Kaye and Gary Howard.

530

PIPES OF PEACE

PAUL McCARTNEY

14 January 1984, for two weeks

● ●

Written by Paul McCartney. Produced by George Martin.

Paul McCartney's first UK number one under just his own name completed a unique full house of chart achievements. When *Pipes Of Peace* made it to the top he became the first performer to have got there as a soloist, as part of a duo (with Stevie Wonder – see no. 499), as part of a trio (with Wings – see no. 416), as part of a quartet (see 16 of the 17 Beatles number ones) and as part of a quintet (the Beatles with Billy Preston – see no. 270). He later did it with even larger aggregations on charity records such as *Do They Know It's Christmas?* (see no. 543).

He also became the third solo Beatle to reach number one, leaving only Ringo out in the cold (though Starr's *Photograph* and *You're Sixteen* both went all the way Stateside). This gave the Beatles yet another record in that no other group had seen three ex-members in solitary splendour at the summit.

Pipes Of Peace was Paul's 25th number one as a writer, bringing him to within one of John Lennon's record total. It was George Martin's 27th number one as a producer, tying him with the late Norrie Paramor as production champ. The single was given a huge boost by its imaginative video showing Paul in the guise of two soldiers on opposing sides in the trenches of World War I. The album from which the single came, also entitled *Pipes Of Peace,* was the sequel to his highly acclaimed previous effort, *Tug Of War.* It included a US number one duet with Michael Jackson, *Say, Say, Say.*

531

RELAX

FRANKIE GOES TO HOLLYWOOD

28 January 1984 for five weeks

● ● ● ● ●

ZTT ZTAS 1

Written by Peter Gill, Holly Johnson and Mark O'Toole. Produced by Trevor Horn.

The rise and fall of the Liverpool quintet Frankie Goes To Hollywood, their name taken from a headline about the young Sinatra's entry into the movie business, is one of the more remarkable stories of recent recording history.

Vocalist Holly (christened William) Johnson spent a year with Scouse band Big In Japan in 1976/77. When Big In Japan became Pink Military, Holly went solo for a while. As just plain Holly he released two singles, both duds. The other four Frankies had even less experience before linking up with Holly to become the sensation of 1984. Paul Rutherford (billed with Frankie as 'vocals and "I came to dance"'), Mark O'Toole (bass), Brian Nash (guitar) and Peter Gill (drums) had all played in local bands of striking anonymity.

The five became one in late 1982 and played their first gig as support to Hambi And The Dance, as obscure a start to a career as it is possible to get. The break came when they appeared on Channel 4's rock show *The Tube* where their unsubtle sexual antics made as big an impression as their funk. Ex-Buggle (see no. 444) Trevor Horn, chief of the new Zang Tumb Tumm organization was watching and wanted them for his label. Horn was by now one of the country's most sought-after producers thanks to work with Dollar, Spandau Ballet, Yes and ABC, and a healthy recording debut seemed assured.

Not even Horn could have anticipated just how healthy. It took some time for their first single, *Relax,* to emerge, and when it did, in November 1983, its early progress was sluggish. It pottered around the lower regions of the Top 75 until one morning Radio One's breakfast DJ Mike Read realized just what the lyrics were saying. He unilaterally declared his disgust and his refusal to play the disc led to an all-out BBC ban. This was just what the record needed. A struggling platter became a huge number one and the Frankie saga was off and running.

532

99 RED BALLOONS

NENA

3 March 1984, for three weeks

● ● ●

Epic A 4074

Written by Joern-Uwe Fahrenkrog-Peterson, Carlo Karges (English lyrics by Kevin McAlea). Produced by Rheinhold Heil and Manne Praeker.

The Nena that gave the world *99 Red Balloons* was a group, not a girl singer. Few realized this fact even when the quintet became the fourth German act to top the British singles charts, following in the footsteps of Kraftwerk (see no. 494), the Goombay Dance Band (see no. 497) and Nicole (see no. 500), all of whom got there in a golden period for Deutschrock between February and May 1982.

Confusingly, Nena was also the professional name of the band's vocalist, Gabriele Kerner. Her male colleagues were Rolf Brendel (drums), Jurgen Dehmel (bass), Joern-Uwe Fahrenkrog-Peterson (keyboards) and Carlo Karges (guitar). The last two were the composers of the number one. The band was formed in Berlin in 1982.

In its original German form, *99 Luftballons*, the record became a massive hit in the United States, rising to number two. English fans were deemed too insular and/or ignorant to cope with a German lyric, so Kevin McAlea was drafted in to translate. It is still doubtful whether many Brits who bought it appreciated the anti-nuclear message of what was to most just a very catchy pop record. Nena, the group, remain popular in Germany, but have enjoyed no repetition of their success in English language markets.

Right: **Lionel Richie's** *six week run at number one, Motown's longest, was matched four months later by Stevie Wonder. Far right: Gabriele Kerner loaned her nickname* **Nena** *to her group.*

533

HELLO

LIONEL RICHIE

24 March 1984 for six weeks

● ● ● ● ● ●

Motown TMG 1330

Written by Lionel Richie. Produced by Lionel Richie and James Anthony Carmichael.

Lionel Brockman Richie Jr. (born Tuskegee, Alabama, 20 June 1949) found considerable fame and fortune as a member of the Commodores (see no. 425) before establishing himself as America's leading black balladeer and one of the most successful songwriters that vast country has ever produced.

His break with the group came in 1982, but he had broken through as an individual writer and performer before the split. He had written and produced a US number one single for Kenny Rogers in 1980 (*Lady*), and the title song he composed for the Brooke Shields film *Endless Love* in 1981, which he sang sans Commodores but with Diana Ross, had been the longest-running American number one in Motown's history. The solo route beckoned and no one could blame Lionel for taking it when he did.

His solo recording career got off to a hot start with the single *Truly* and the album *Lionel Richie.* Hotter yet was the monumentally popular second album *Can't Slow Down.* The collection included several uptempo offerings, but it was the soulful and sentimental *Hello* that became the favourite track in Britain.

Richie has delighted mantlepiece-manufacturers by the number of awards he has won for his writing and performing (including an Oscar for *Say You, Say Me*). The highlight of his personal career to date, however, was his appearance before a television audience literally measured in billions at the closing ceremony of the 1984 Los Angeles Olympic Games when he performed an extended version of *All Night Long* with 200 break-dancers, athletes from all over the world and a spaceship. He was also a driving force behind the American answer to Band Aid, U.S.A. for Africa's *We Are The World* (see no. 648).

534

THE REFLEX

DURAN DURAN

5 May 1984, for four weeks

●●●●

EMI DURAN 2

Written by Duran Duran. Produced by Alex Sadkin, Ian Little and Duran Duran.

After their first number one (see no. 518) Duran Duran had to wait over a year for their second. In between the two peaks their faces became known beyond the confines of the pop world. Simon le Bon and Nick Rhodes in particular were rarely out of the popular press, the former for his ocean yachting exploits, and all five for various liaisons and/or marriages with members of the opposite sex. Duran Duran by mid-1984 meant glamour and jet-setting as well as huge record sales. Their many young admirers were known as Durannies.

The Reflex was first heard on their third album *Seven And The Ragged Tiger*. The first two singles from this album had done well, but the decision to call in Chic genius Nile Rodgers (see no. 519) to remix *The Reflex* made the third single the biggest of all. It also became their first American number one.

In 1986 the group began to disintegrate with members recording in two separate units. Andy and John Taylor teamed with Robert Palmer and Chic's Tony Thompson and Bernard Edwards as Power Station, while the other three recorded as Arcadia. Both new acts had hits, but not in the Duran league.

Duran Duran re-grouped and continued where they had left off with *View To A Kill* from the James Bond movie, but the end of Duran Duran Mark I was not long delayed. During the recording of their *Notorious* album, which did not quite measure up to the highest expectations, Andy Taylor left for America and a solo career, and Roger Taylor gave up music in favour of the country life. Le Bon, Rhodes and the sole surviving Taylor, John, continue Duran Duran as a trio.

The Reflex contains the credit 'Mixed by Nile Rodgers and Jason Corsaro'. Producer Alex Sadkin, who went on to further success with acts such as Simply Red and Foreigner

(see no. 544), was killed in a car crash in 1987, a sad loss to the music business.

535

WAKE ME UP BEFORE YOU GO-GO

WHAM!

2 June 1984, for two weeks

●●

Epic A 4440

Written by George Michael. Produced by George Michael.

The George Michael success story shifted into top gear when the sixth Wham! single surpassed all of the duo's previous efforts to rush to number one in its second week of release. From now until Wham!'s demise the only record to keep a Wham! single from number one was the freak Band Aid mega-seller (see no. 543) which itself included vocals by George Michael.

George Michael Panos (born 26 June 1963) and Andrew Ridgely (born 26 January 1963) met at Bushey Heath Comprehensive school in Hertfordshire when both were young teenagers. They played together in groups and remained friends after leaving school. In 1982 they made a demo of *Wham! Rap* with George on vocals and bass, Andrew handling guitar and drum machine. A new label, Innervision, showed interest and released the track, but without much response from media or public. Next time out, they did better. *Young Guns (Go For It)* entered the Top 10 at the end of 1982. Once the boys' energetic routines and smouldering looks were seen on television, a young following grew quickly. Their first single was re-worked to become their second Top Tenner and by summer 1983 they had made it four out of four. Their debut LP *Fantastic* entered the album charts at number one, an outstanding feat for an act's first LP.

However, problems developed between the duo and their label. Wham! signed with former Marc Bolan manager Simon Napier-Bell, who fought to get them released from Innervision. While the dispute blazed Wham! hit the road for their first tour, the highly theatrical *Club Fantastic Tour*, featur-

ing among other side attractions backing singer/dancers Pepsi and Shirlie, later to score hits as a duo themselves.

When finally free to sign a new deal, Wham! did so with Epic. The first single was the slick and tuneful party item *Wake Me Up Before You Go-Go*. All at once it was noticed that George Michael was a man of many talents. Speculation about the future of Andrew Ridgely in such a subordinate role began to surface.

536

TWO TRIBES

FRANKIE GOES TO HOLLYWOOD

16 June 1984, for nine weeks

●●●●●●●●●

ZTT ZTAS 3

Written by Holly Johnson, Peter Gill and Mark O'Toole. Produced by Trevor Horn.

Frankie Goes To Hollywood's second single and second chart-topper crashed straight in at number one and held down the top spot for a further two months. Its nine-week stretch there was the longest since Travolta and Newton-John's glorious summer of '78 (see no. 424).

Where *Relax* had dealt with (mainly gay) sex, *Two Tribes* tackled politics with about the same depth of intellect and with even greater public approval. The record was a masterpiece of production and marketing. No-one saw fit to ban it, although the Godley and Creme video showing Reagan and Chernenko lookalikes fighting hand to hand raised a few hackles. The band's contribution to *Two Tribes* was merely the first phase of the recording. Horn then spent weeks juggling with sound, adding, subtracting, mixing and remixing. Actor Patrick Allen's reading of extracts from government civil defence leaflets became an integral part of the 'song'.

When *Two Tribes* was released in a blaze of publicity, Frankie-mania gave *Relax* yet another sales boost. There was, after all, nothing else for Frankie fans to buy at that point, on disc, anyway. (Frankie merchandising, in particular 'Frankie Say' T-shirts, was shipping nearly as fast as the records.) For the weeks of 7 and 14 July FGTH held down both numbers one and two in the singles chart, hitherto a mountain climbed only by the Beatles (for three weeks in 1963 and for three in 1967) and an ex-Beatle (John Lennon, two weeks in 1981). Another factor contributing to the massive and long-running sales of Frankie product was Horn's wheeze of putting out as many as seven different mixes of the singles. Some Frankie nutters bought the lot.

537

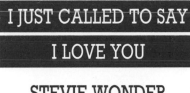

CARELESS WHISPER

GEORGE MICHAEL

18 August 1984, for three weeks

●●●

Epic A 4603

Written by George Michael and Andrew Ridgeley. Produced by George Michael.

George Michael's first number one as a writer and producer had been knocked off the top after just two weeks by the explosion of Frankie Goes To Hollywood's *Two Tribes*. It must therefore have been particularly satisfying for Michael to be the man to bring *Two Tribes*' nine-week run to a close.

Careless Whisper is the only George Michael song for which his Wham! partner gets equal writing credit. Ironically, it was the first released under George's name alone. It was written long before the boys became famous, when they were still Bushey schoolboys. As a bushy adult, George had recorded the sensitive ballad as a solo item in America in 1983, but he did not consider that version good enough to release. His 1984 re-recording in England was obviously of sufficient quality to continue his winning streak.

Naturally, the non-contribution of Ridgely to this smash fuelled yet more rumours that the days of Wham! were numbered, but although George himself was now a personality known better to the non-rock public than his group, there was still no official talk of a split. Indeed, in America, where the band broke through in November 1984 with *Wake Me Up Before You Go-Go* (see no. 535), *Careless Whisper* was

released under the name 'Wham! featuring George Michael' where it duplicated its British success with ease in early 1985.

538

I JUST CALLED TO SAY

I LOVE YOU

STEVIE WONDER

8 September 1984, for six weeks

●●●●●●

Motown TMG 1349

Written by Stevie Wonder. Produced by Stevie Wonder.

Musical giant Stevie Wonder at last achieved one of the few honours to have eluded him – a British number one single – with the ballad *I Just Called To Say I Love You* from the soundtrack of the film *The Woman In Red*. It did the trick for him 18 years and 318 days after his UK chart debut with *Uptight*. At the time this was a record gap between an act's British chart debut and first number one (see no. 582 for the latest record holder).

He had actually written it in outline some seven or eight years before, but it had never made it on to any of his albums. It more than made up for its long gestation period when it surfaced as part of Stevie's soundtrack for the Gene Wilder picture. Up against the toughest opposition in years (Phil Collins, Ray Parker Jr, Kenny Loggins and Lee de Carlo, Snow and Pitchford) Stevie won his first Oscar.

Save this extraordinary lack of solo number ones, Stevie's UK chart career has been long and loud. *I Just Called To Say I Love You* was his 15th Top 10 hit and since 1966 he had charted at least once every year except 1983. He had, of course, shared top spot honours with Paul McCartney in 1982 (see no. 499) and *The Woman In Red* album was his 11th UK best-seller. *I Just Called To Say I Love You* sold over a million copies in Britain alone and was his 8th US number one. Impressive though these and other Stevie statistics are, his music sings for itself, and will never need the support of figures to demonstrate its timeless qualities.

539

FREEDOM

WHAM!

20 October 1984, for two weeks

●●

Epic A 4743

Written by George Michael. Produced by George Michael.

When Wham!'s second consecutive number one single peaked it seemed to some chart observers that George Michael was attempting to establish a personal stranglehold on every alternate chart-topper. *Freedom*, released worldwide under the Wham! moniker, stormed to number one in two weeks flat.

Gimmicky marketing techniques were by now hardly necessary to sell a Wham! or George Michael product but Epic broke new ground by releasing two different picture discs of *Freedom*, one George-shaped, one Andrew-shaped. The song itself was in the *Go Go* mould. The message of the lyric appeared to be that George wanted to tie himself down to one particular lover, but in fact the hook line of the song stated exactly the opposite, viz. 'I don't want your freedom'. This semantic point never developed into a major issue, or even into a minor one.

Because of Wham!'s long chart runs their American release dates fell spectacularly behind their British ones. *Freedom* did not escape there until the following summer. Like the minor confusion in the lyric, this had no detrimental effect on the sales.

540

I FEEL FOR YOU

CHAKA KHAN

10 November 1984, for three weeks

●●●

Warner Bros W 9209

Written by Prince. Produced by Arif Mardin.

American superstar Prince's only connection with a UK number one single remains his writing of Chaka Khan's *I Feel For You*. Khan's triumph ended a barren 20-month spell for female artists at the top. She also brought recent number one debutant Stevie Wonder (see no. 538) back to the summit, for it is he who plays harmonica on the track. Another famous name involved is Grandmaster Melle Mel whose opening rap around Chaka's name was as striking an intro as you (or Miss Khan) could wish for.

Chaka was born Yvette Marie Stevens on 23 March 1953 in Great Lakes, Illinois. She first came to prominence as the lead singer of soul/funk band Rufus, whose first hit *Tell Me Something Good* was a Stevie Wonder song. Chaka's powerful voice and voluptuous appearance were crucial to Rufus' popularity, which took a dive when she left them, not totally amicably, in 1978.

Her debut solo album yielded an international smash single *I'm Every Woman*, bringing her to the attention of a substantial British audience in early 1979 for the first time. Rufus had never charted at all in the UK at that point and Chaka had only one modest chart recognition as vocalist on a Quincy Jones single. Her albums and singles over the next three years were not major sellers and it took a temporary reunion with Rufus to bring her back into the limelight via *Ain't Nobody*, a number 8 hit in spring 1984. This proved to be the prelude to greater things.

The *I Feel For You* album matched the quality of her best days with Rufus. Chaka's power-packed vocals allied to electronic breakdance rhythms found immediate favour both sides of the Atlantic. She has had erratic record sales since, and has not always been the most consistent of live performers, but her original and dominating vocal stylings, an influence on many lesser artists, ensure continued interest in her work.

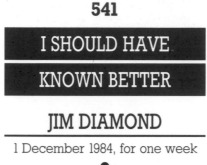

541

I SHOULD HAVE KNOWN BETTER

JIM DIAMOND

1 December 1984, for one week

●

A & M AM 220

Written by Jim Diamond and Graham Lyle.
Produced by Pip Williams.

Scotsman Jim Diamond guaranteed himself a permanent place in rock history when he declared, just one week after reaching number one for the first time, that he hoped *I Should Have Known Better* would not still be there the following week. This rarer than rare statement from a newcomer to the hall of fame was not made because Jim disliked his own record, but because the Band Aid single was about to be released. With an admirable display of unselfishness he hoped that *Do They Know It's Christmas?* would take the minimum time possible to outstrip his sales and thus earn the maximum publicity possible for Bob Geldof's Band Aid campaign.

As things turned out, the Band Aid milestone was not issued in time to make the 8 December chart and Jim had the less satisfying experience of having to make room at the top for Frankie Goes To Hollywood's third, final and shortest run at number one.

Diamond first made waves as half of PhD, a synthesizer-orientated duo who reached the Top 3 in spring 1982 with *I Won't Let You*

Frankie Goes to Hollywood *employing some unconvincing bouncers.*

Down. The other 50 per cent was classically-trained pianist Tony Hymas. Diamond's high plaintive vocals were the most arresting feature of the hit. For a while they enjoyed great acclaim all over Europe. Diamond's voice was heard to equal effect on his first and biggest solo hit, for which he chose a title that the Beatles had used for one of the well-known songs from *A Hard Day's Night.*

Without joining the big league of really hefty sellers, Jim has come up with three chart entries since *I Should Have Known Better,* including the theme song from the TV series *Boon, Hi Ho Silver,* a Top 10 entry.

542

THE POWER OF LOVE

FRANKIE GOES TO HOLLYWOOD

8 December 1984, for 1 week

●

ZTT ZTAS 3

Written by Peter Gill, Holly Johnson, Mark O'Toole, Brian Nash. Produced by Trevor Horn.

Frankie concluded their staggering year by equalling the 21-year-old record set by fellow Liverpudlians Gerry and the Pacemakers of making number one with each of their first three single releases. It was, however, a bit of a narrow squeak and even as *The Power Of Love* reached number one it was clear that the near 2,000,000 sales of *Two Tribes* were a thing of their past and that the Frankie bubble was already a little deflated.

Having done their best to offend with sex and politics (see nos. 531 and 536) the quintet attempted to cause waves with religion third time out. This was done primarily through their video for the song which featured an original interpretation of the Nativity. Complaints were virtually nil. There were more about the artwork of their first album *Welcome To The Pleasuredome,* released with *The Power Of Love* and an instant number one.

By extraordinary coincidence, one of the titles on the 12-inch version of *Relax* was a

Band Aid. *The only single to go top three two Christmasses in a row.*

cover of Gerry's 1964 composition *Ferry Cross The Mersey.* Great interest centred around Frankie's fourth single. Could they make it four in a row? Gerry's fourth hit had peaked at number 2 back in 1964 and when FGTH's next, the title track from their double album, did the same, the two bands from the same city but different generations were still locked in a tie for the best ever start to a singles career. Frankie finally topped the Pacemakers when *Rage Hard,* (released no less than 18 months after *Pleasure Dome!*) staggered to number 4, compared with Gerry's number 6 fifth time out.

That was about the last major achievement of FGTH's meteoric career. Without Trevor Horn at the controls their recordings became parodies of their early successes, and Frankie say that's all folks.

543

DO THEY KNOW IT'S CHRISTMAS?

BAND AID

15 December 1984, for five weeks

●●●●●

Phonogram FEED 1

Written by Bob Geldof and Midge Ure. Produced by Midge Ure.

Bob Geldof's inspired conception and organization of the first and greatest of the all-star charity singles led to the setting of numerous recording achievements that in many cases are unlikely ever to be surpassed. The greatest achievement of all, however, remains the skill with which the lead singer of the Boomtown Rats (see nos. 428 and 440) captured the imagination and the hearts of millions for an indisputably worthy cause. Inevitably lesser men followed in his footsteps with the result that two or three years later it almost seemed that a record whose royalties were *not* going to charity was an endangered species, but nothing can dim the glory of Bob Geldof, KBE, in creating Band Aid and the Live Aid follow-up concert of 13 July the following year.

Moved by the desperate pictures on TV of the terrifying famine in Ethiopia, Geldof resolved to make some personal effort, however small, to fight the disaster. He had the idea of raising funds through a one-off record featuring many of music's big contemporary names and contacted Midge Ure (see nos 384, 557), with whom he wrote a suitable song for the project. In days he assembled a staggering line-up of talent, cut the record (produced by Ure) and began to realize the enormity of what he had set in motion when the sales exceeded his most optimistic forecasts.

Do They Know It's Christmas? entered the chart at number one, the first time this had

Foreigner knocked the all-time best-seller out of number one.

A Girl Like You, a 1981 ballad, broke the all-comers' record by staying at number 2 for 10 consecutive weeks in the US and gave them their first major British hit. *I Want To Know What Love Is* did even better, going all the way in both countries.

Foreigner were joined on the single by Tom Bailey of the Thompson Twins, Jennifer Holliday and the New Jersey Mass Choir. This hit gave producer Alex Sadkin (see no. 534) his second UK number one in eight months.

been done by a new recording act. It quickly became the biggest selling single of all time in the UK, with the total by Christmas 1987 standing at over 3,500,000. It affected the lives of millions, not least that of Bob Geldof, who dedicated the best part of two years of his life to his new cause. He had always maintained that he was primarily an entertainer who intended to get back to his proper job as soon as he could leave his foundation in safe hands, but the greatness thrust upon him has made it difficult for the public to re-accept him as a rock singer.

The performers credited on the Band Aid single are as follows:

Adam Clayton, Bono (U2); Phil Collins; Bob Geldof, Johnny Fingers, Simon Crowe, Peter Briquette (Boomtown Rats); David Bowie; Paul McCartney; Holly Johnson (Frankie Goes To Hollywood); Midge Ure, Chris Cross (Ultravox); Simon Le Bon, Nick Rhodes, Andy Taylor, John Taylor, Roger Taylor (Duran Duran); Paul Young; Tony Hadley, Martin Kemp, John Keeble, Gary Kemp, Steve Norman (Spandau Ballet); Glenn Gregory, Martyn Ware (Heaven 17); Francis Rossi, Rick Parfitt (Status Quo); Sting; Jon Moss, Boy George (Culture Club); Marilyn; Keren, Sarah and Siobhan (Bananarama); Jody Watley (then Shalamar); Paul Weller (Style Council); Robert 'Kool' Bell, James Taylor, Dennis Thomas (Kool and The Gang); George Michael.

544

I WANT TO KNOW
WHAT LOVE IS

FOREIGNER

19 January 1985, for three weeks

●●●

Atlantic A 9596

Written by Mick Jones. Produced by Alex Sadkin and Mick Jones.

Mick Jones of Foreigner became the first Jones to write a number one hit single when his dramatic gospel-flavoured ballad *I Want To Know What Love Is* ended the noble Band Aid five-week supremacy. Born 27 December 1944 in London, Mick's first taste of the music business was behind the counter in a Woking record shop. He topped this achievement as a guitarist with Nero and The Gladiators, a group lumbered with a Roman stage costume gimmick, that enjoyed two minor UK chart entries in 1961. From there he went to France where he worked with Johnny Hallyday, then back to England as part of Spooky Tooth, and then over to the States where he teamed up with Leslie West for a while.

Foreigner Mark I was formed in New York in 1976. It consisted of Jones, Lou Gramm (vocals), Ian MacDonald (guitar, keyboards), Al Greenwood (keyboards), Ed Gagliardi (bass) and Dennis Elliott (drums). MacDonald and Elliott were Londoners, the other three native New Yorkers. They won a deal with Atlantic and placed four of their first five singles in the American Top 10, enjoying only modest success in the UK.

In 1980 the group shrank and reformed. As a quartet consisting of Jones, Gramm, Elliott and Rick Wills (bass), they broadened their musical horizons, not now concentrating primarily on heavy rock numbers. *Waiting For*

545

I KNOW HIM SO WELL

ELAINE PAIGE AND BARBARA DICKSON

9 February 1985, for four weeks

●●●●

RCA CHESS 3

Written by Benny Andersson, Tim Rice and Bjorn Ulvaeus. Produced by Benny Andersson, Tim Rice and Bjorn Ulvaeus.

The tenth number one single for Abba masterminds Benny and Bjorn was the first not performed by the Swedish supergroup, although like their other nine it featured lead vocals by two women. Lennon and McCartney remain the only writers to have hit the top more often than Andersson and Ulvaeus.

This time around, however, they had to share the writing limelight with lyricist Tim Rice (see no. 400) with whom they had written the musical *Chess*. The *Chess* album produced two simultaneous hit singles, the other being Murray Head's *One Night In Bangkok*. Head's track only reached number 12 in the UK, but generally did better than *I Know Him So Well* around the world and topped the charts in 11 countries, reaching number 3 in the States. *I Know Him So Well* became the all-time best-selling single by a female duo in Britain. It was sung by two of the most popular female vocalists in the country whose principal successes had hitherto been in the theatre (both have won awards for leading West End roles, Barbara in *Blood Brothers* and Elaine in *Evita*), in concert and on album. Both had enjoyed major solo chart singles such as *January February* and *Answer Me* (Barbara, born in Dunfermline on 27 September 1947) and *Memory* (Elaine, born in Barnet on 5 March 1948).

I Know Him So Well was recorded in Abba's Polar studio in Stockholm. Because of their hectic schedules neither girl was present for the other's vocal contribution but they have twice performed the song together in concert and many times on television around the world. Elaine went on to play the role of Florence for over a year in the West End production of *Chess*.

546

YOU SPIN ME ROUND (LIKE A RECORD)

DEAD OR ALIVE

9 March 1985, for two weeks

● ●

Epic A 4861

Written by Dead Or Alive (Pete Burns, Stephen Coy, Tim Lever, Michael Percy). Produced by Mike Stock, Matt Aitken and Pete Waterman.

You Spin Me Round (Like A Record) was not only the first number one to mention the most vital item of music business software ever invented, it made slower uninterrupted progress to the top than any previous hit. It did not get there until its 14th week in the Top 75, having entered the chart before any of the three hits that preceded it at number one. Peter Burns was once quoted in *Sounds* as saying he would perform an intimate physical act with one of the authors of this book if it would help him to get a hit record, but this unusual promotional offer was neither accepted nor necessary.

Dead Or Alive provided studio genii Stock-Aitken-Waterman with the first of their number one successes. The credit 'produced by Stock-Aitken-Waterman' was to become a dominating feature in the industry over the next three years, but here the single label stated 'directed by Mike Stock and Matt Aitken; A Pete Waterman production'. *Youthquake,* the album that contained *You Spin Me Round* was, on the other hand, 'produced by Stock-Aitken-Waterman'.

Dead Or Alive consisted of Peter Burns (vocals), Stephen Coy (drums), Tim Lever (keyboards) and Michael Percy (bass). They were formed in Liverpool in 1982. They have enjoyed respectable international sales since they spun at the top, and have made a particularly good impression on the US dance charts.

547

EASY LOVER

PHILIP BAILEY (DUET WITH PHIL COLLINS)

23 March 1985, for four weeks

● ● ● ●

CBS A 4915

Written by Philip Bailey, Phil Collins and Nathan East. Produced by Phil Collins.

Earth, Wind and Fire co-lead vocalist and percussionist Philip Bailey (born in Denver, Colorado on 8 May 1951) launched his solo recording career in late 1984, turning to Phil Collins (see no. 513) for the production duties. Not surprisingly, Phil's contribution to Bailey's album *Chinese Wall* consisted of more than supervision of the sound. He played drums throughout, co-wrote the track that became the album's biggest hit and even sang on it himself. Hitherto Bailey's greatest UK success had come via the Earth Wind and Fire hits *September* and *Let's Groove,* both number 3 hits for the soul/funk band, which usually consisted of nine members.

Philip Bailey joined the Los Angeles-based Earth Wind and Fire in 1972. The band had been founded by Maurice White three years before and was just beginning to take off when Bailey came aboard. His vocal acrobatics were perhaps seen at their best on the sixth EWF album *That's The Way Of The World* from which came the single *Shining Star,* their only US chart-topper to date, which Bailey co-wrote with White and keyboardist Larry Dunn. The single did not even chart in the UK.

Easy Lover was actually credited to Bailey with the credit 'duet with Phil Collins' in miniscule print on the label. It is remembered as a fully-fledged duet.

Elaine Paige *and* **Barbara Dickson** *made the best-selling single by a female duo.*

USA For Africa. *Michael Jackson (front row, second from right) and co-writer Lionel Richie had both previously penned number ones on their own.*

548

WE ARE THE WORLD

U.S.A FOR AFRICA

20 April 1985, for two weeks

● ●

CBS US AID 1

Written by Michael Jackson and Lionel Richie. Produced by Quincy Jones.

The second all-star charity single to reach number one was for the same cause as the first (see no. 543). Bob Geldof's enormous success with *Do They Know It's Christmas?*, which had sold over a million copies in the United States as well as the unparalleled three-million plus in Britain, had started a train of conscience in the music industry which was shortly to lead to the triumph of Live Aid. USA For Africa (United Support of Artists for Africa) was another step on the road to that magnificent event and a direct result of the Geldof/Ure initiative. For once, the music business would not criticize the use by one act of another's idea.

Those who set the music world's battle against Ethiopian famine in motion on the other side of the Atlantic were Harry Belafonte, Ken Kragen (manager of Lionel Richie), Richie himself and Michael Jack-son. The latter two wrote the anthemic song and most of the hottest music names in America came to the A&M studios in Hollywood under the supervision of Quincy Jones on the night of 28 January 1985. An inevitable worldwide number one, *We Are The World* topped the US parade for four weeks and the British for two. (The American charts had not been so kind to the Band Aid record, which despite its huge sale got no higher than number 13.)

The soloists on the single (in order) are: Lionel Richie, Stevie Wonder, Paul Simon, Kenny Rogers, James Ingram, Tina Turner, Billy Joel, Michael Jackson, Diana Ross, Dionne Warwick, Willie Nelson, Al Jarreau, Bruce Springsteen, Kenny Loggins, Steve Perry, Daryl Hall, Huey Lewis, Cyndi Lauper, Kim Carnes, Bob Dylan, Ray Charles.

Others credited on the single:
Dan Aykroyd, Harry Belafonte, Lindsey Buckingham, Sheila E, Bob Geldof, John Oates (Hall & Oates), Jackie Jackson, La Toya Jackson, Marlon Jackson, Randy Jackson, Tito Jackson, Waylon Jennings, The News (Huey Lewis and), Bette Midler, Jeffrey Osborne, The Pointer Sisters, Smokey Robinson.

549

MOVE CLOSER

PHYLLIS NELSON

4 May 1985, for one week

●

Carrere CAR 337

Written by Phyllis Nelson. Produced by Yves Dessca.

The fifth Nelson to appear in the British single charts was the first to make number one, Phyllis succeeding where Bill, Ricky, Sandy and Willie have all to date failed. *Move Closer* is however Phyllis' only hit in the UK so far and by the beginning of 1988 she had been on the one-hit wonder list for almost three years.

Phyllis was born in Jacksonville, Florida where she sang with her brothers and sisters in the Nelson Five. Realizing that she would have done better to have been born in Nelsonville and to have sung with the Jackson Five, she moved to Philadelphia where she joined a group called Brown Sugar. She also sang back-up for Major Harris and after a stint with another act named Philly Cream she made her first solo records, *Don't Stop The Train* becoming a big dancefloor hit.

She began to make a national name for herself when her recording of *I Like You* came on to the US dance charts in late 1985 and proceeded to climb to number one. It also crossed over with some success to the Hot 100. It was however a ballad, her own composition, that brought her to the attention of British fans. *Move Closer* made leisurely progress up the UK chart, grabbing just one week in pole position after a 10-week climb. In America the track made little impression, possibly because Phyllis was only established as a dance record act and her supporters in that field found little to jump around to in *Move Closer*.

550

19

PAUL HARDCASTLE

11 May 1985, for five weeks

● ● ● ● ●

Chrysalis CHS 2860

Written by Paul Hardcastle, William Coutourie and Jonas McCord. Produced by Paul Hardcastle.

London-born (10 December 1957) producer and keyboard player Paul Hardcastle achieved his first number one production with his own name in the artist slot as well. However he is not a performer in the conventional sense on this smash, the title of which refers to the average age of American soldiers in the Vietnam war.

To an electro-funk rhythm track, Hardcastle made use of the speaking voices of American commentators and soldiers (and the singing voices of a female chorus) to spell out some of the unpleasant facts of being a soldier in the conflict that tore America apart in the '60s. In World War II, states the record, the average age of the combat soldier was 26; in Vietnam he was Nineteen – N- N- N- N- Nineteen. The electronic stutter that preceded the title word many times during the track became a catch phrase within days of the record's release. *19* inspired a hit parody by impressionist Rory Bremner operating as the Commentators entitled *N- N- Nineteen Not Out* referring to the England cricket team's batting average.

Hardcastle has notched up a string of chart

records in Britain, under his own name, under a pseudonym (Silent Underdog), and as producer of other artists, but none has yet repeated the phenomenal success of his digitally titled monster, which made the Top 20 in the country where the soldiers of the hit were born.

19 (the title on the label is displayed as a number, not as a word) can claim to be the shortest title of any British number one, with only *If* (see no. 367) as a possible challenger. But *If* has two more letters in its title than *19*.

551

YOU'LL NEVER WALK ALONE

THE CROWD

15 June 1985, for two weeks

● ●

Spartan BRAD 1

Written by Richard Rodgers and Oscar Hammerstein II. Produced by Graham Gouldman and Ray Levy.

The third number one single recorded by a hastily assembled aggregation of stars in aid of a particular cause came about as a result of the fire that destroyed a stand at Bradford City Football Club, killing over 50 people. A fund was started to provide financial compensation for the relatives of the victims and to help Bradford City to their recovery from the disaster. One of the principal sources of income for the fund was the Crowd's recording of the song that Gerry and the Pacemakers had taken to number one in 1963, *You'll Never Walk Alone* (see no. 159).

The line-up for this single was put together by Graham Gouldman of 10 C.C. (who had been a co-writer and co-producer of three previous chart-toppers, nos. 332, 372 and 426) and Ray Levy. The cast list was not as distinguished as those of the two Ethiopian famine records, but neither this nor the more parochial nature of the cause seemed to affect the British public's desire to contribute via the Crowd. Naturally, appeal outside the UK was limited.

Over 50 artists (many not really connected

with the music business) are credited on the sleeve with the inclusion of Gerry Marsden as lead vocalist the point of greatest interest. Gerry became the first artist in history to hit number one twice with two different versions of the same song, a feat to be equalled a year later (see no. 567). Rodgers and Hammerstein were each at number one for the sixth time, the fifth as a team, a mere three years since their comeback via Captain Sensible (see no. 504). Zak Starkey, son of Ringo Starr, is also on the record, which made him and his dad the first father-son team to feature on number ones, with the older Starr leading 17-1.

List of artists credited on the sleeve with helping the Crowd (not all of whom are actually performing on *You'll Never Walk Alone*):

Gerry Marsden, Tony Christie, Denny Laine, Tim Healy, Gary Holton, Ed Stewart, Tony Hicks, Kenny Lynch, Colin Blunstone, Chris Robinson, A. Curtis, Phil Lynott, Bernie Winters, Girls School, Black Lace, John Otway, Rick Wakeman, Barron Knights, Tim Hinkley, Brendan Shine, John Verity, Rolf Harris, Rob Heaton, Patrick McDonald, Smokie, Bruce Forsyth, Johnny Logan, Colbert Hamilton, Dave Lee Travis, Rose Marie, Frank Allen, Jim Diamond, Graham Gouldman, Pete Spencer, Chris Norman, Gerard Kenny, the Nolans, Graham Dene, Suzy Grant, Peter Cook, The Foxes, Jess Conrad, Kim Kelly, Motorhead, John Entwistle, Jimmy Henney, Joe Fagin, David Shilling, Karen Clark, Gary Hughes, Zak Starkey, Eddie Hardin, Paul McCartney, Kiki Dee, Keith Chegwin.

552

FRANKIE

SISTER SLEDGE

29 June 1985, for four weeks

● ● ● ●

Atlantic A 9547

Written by Joy Denny. Produced by Nile Rodgers.

North Philadelphia family act Sisters Sledge first recorded in 1971 but by the time they came to public attention in 1975 with their first US chart record *Love Don't You Go*

Through No Changes On Me they had shortened their name by one letter to Sister Sledge. They are not related to Percy of *When A Man Loves A Woman* fame nor is their number one related to Connie Francis' 1959 US Top Tenner of the same title.

Their 1975 American charter was hardly a major breakthrough for the girls. It was a Top 40 soul hit but only reached number 92 on the Hot 100. They achieved much greater chart recognition in England when *Mama Never Told Me* broke out of the clubs into the Top 20 in the summer of that year, a track that never registered anywhere in their home country. From 1976-1979 they had the odd success on the US soul charts but never pop.

Then in 1979 Joni (who sings lead on *Frankie*), Debbie, Kim and Kathy Sledge burst out of the medium time with their album *We Are Family*. The major factor responsible was the Chic production team of Nile Rodgers (see nos 519 and 534) and Bernard Edwards. The album went to number 3 in America, with two of its singles *He's The Greatest Dancer* and the title track, making the Top 10. Both were also substantial hits in the UK, as was a third cut, *Lost In Music*.

Apart from 1984 remixed versions of old hits, the girls failed to capitalize on *We Are Family* until the unexpected rise of *Frankie*, taken from their album *When The Boys Meet The Girls*. Nile Rodgers was back at the helm but even his wizardry did not help a great deal in the States where *Frankie*, the one track from the package to chart, limped only to number 75.

Sister Sledge *as they appeared in 1979, their most successful year: (left to right) Kathie, Kim and Jonie.*

553
THERE MUST BE AN ANGEL (PLAYING WITH MY HEART)
EURYTHMICS
27 July 1985, for one week

●

RCA PB 40247

Written by David A. Stewart and Annie Lennox. Produced by David A. Stewart.

Waitress Annie Lennox from Aberdeen met itinerant musician David Stewart in a restaurant in his home town of Sunderland. Stewart had at one time been part of Longdancer, the first group signed to Elton John's Rocket Records. The worker/customer relationship developed into a romantic and professional association, the latter beginning with the Tourists in 1977. The group, which also included Stewart's fellow Wearsider Peet Coombes, enjoyed five hit singles and three albums in 1979/80, their most notable waxing being their revival of the Dusty Springfield debut hit *I Only Want To Be With You*. The Tourists became the third act to take the song to number 4, versions by both Dusty (1963) and the Bay City Rollers (1976) having reached that exact position before them.

A legal bust-up with their label Logo, and the end of their romance led to the demise of the Tourists but from these two wreckages Eurythmics (they insist there is no 'The' in their group name) were born in 1981. They were now simply a professional duo starting again. It was a struggle which took its toll on the physical and mental health of both performers in Eurythmics' early days. In 1981 *Never Gonna Cry Again* scraped into the Top 75 and over a year later *Love Is A Stranger* nearly reached the Top 50. *Sweet Dreams (Are Made Of This)* changed everything. Stark image (Annie) plus economic electro-production (Dave) plus Annie's intense interpretation of their haunting song took them all the way bar one place in the UK and all the way bar nothing in the States.

554
INTO THE GROOVE
MADONNA
3 August 1985, for four weeks

●●●●

Sire W 8934

Written by Madonna and Steve Bray. Produced by Madonna and Steve Bray.

The phenomenon that is Madonna reached the top of the British pops for the first time with her seventh consecutive hit single. It featured in the movie in which she starred with Rosanna Arquette, *Desperately Seeking Susan*. During the four weeks that *Into The Groove* led the pack, Madonna's debut hit from early 1984, *Holiday*, re-entered the charts and rose all the way to number 2, beating its first-time peak by four places. On 17 August 1985 Madonna became the only female and the fourth act ever to hold down both number one and 2 positions in the UK singles chart simultaneously.

The lady who became the biggest female record star the music industry has ever known was born Madonna Louise Veronica Ciccone on 8 August 1958 (probably!) in Detroit, Michigan. She moved to New York in 1977, looking for stardom. She enrolled at a dance theatre and met disco star Patrick Hernandez (who had had a big international hit with *Born To Be Alive* in 1979). He took her to Paris where she sang back-up vocals on various tracks but she did not feel she was in the right place at the right time to satisfy her ambitions and she soon returned to New York. With a drummer friend from way back, Steve Bray, she produced a series of dance-orientated demo tapes of original songs which in turn led to a deal with Sire Records.

As an unknown aiming for the top she presented herself to and was accepted by Michael Jackson's then manager Freddy DeMann. Her first single *Everybody* (late 1977) did next to nothing, and the next *Burning Up* little better. Her first album, *Madonna*, appeared in 1983 with her third single *Lucky Star*. Again, little response. It was one of the two tracks on the album written by outsiders that got her away. *Holiday* by Curtis Hudson and Lisa Stephens took her to number 6 in the UK and to number 16 in the States.

She was now off and running and the hits just kept on coming. Second time around *Lucky Star* scored, as did a second non-Madonna composed track from the LP, *Borderline* (by Reggie Lucas). The first mega-smash was her fourth hit, *Like A Virgin* (number 3 UK, number one US) produced by the ubiquitous Nile Rogers. In Britain the next three, *Material Girl, Crazy For You* and *Into The Groove* all did as well or better than the one before.

Her looks excited as much interest as her music. By the middle of 1985 Madonnamania was an international phenomenon.

555

I GOT YOU BABE

UB 40
Guest vocals by
Chrissie Hynde

31 August 1985, for one week

●

DEP International DEP 20

Written by Sonny Bono.
Produced by UB 40 and Ray 'Pablo' Falconer.

Exactly 20 years after *I Got You Babe* topped the charts for its originators Sonny and Cher (see no. 201), UB 40, with Pretenders leader Chrissie Hynde credited as guest vocalist, took the song back to number one. Sonny Bono's most famous composition thus became the eighth song to head the list via two different versions. Both UB 40 and Hynde had had one previous chart-topper (see nos 526 and 449).

In the two years since *Red Red Wine* UB 40 had added impressively to their list of hit singles, five more in all, including top ten entries *Please Don't Make Me Cry* and *If It Happens Again.* Three of these hits were from *Labour Of Love,* the same album that had featured *Red Red Wine,* an LP that consisted entirely of UB 40's versions of songs recorded by reggae artists between 1969 and 1972. They returned to their own writing talents for their next album, *Geffrey Morgan* (sic), a top three item, including *If It Happens Again,* apparently a statement of their intentions were Margaret Thatcher to be re-elected.

In 1985 they made three visits to the States and the video for *I Got You Babe* was shot during a concert at Jones Beach on Long Island, where Chrissie Hynde joined the band on stage. The record itself was cut at UB 40's own studio, the Abattoir in Birmingham.

UB 40 have always run themselves as a collective, resisting all attempts to have any one member of the group pushed to the fore or act as a representative for all. They regarded their friends behind the scenes as equal contributors to the band's fortunes. Thus the tragic death of their co-producer Ray 'Pablo' Falconer in a car crash in late 1987 was a blow that hit them more than such a disaster might hurt other groups.

556

DANCING IN THE
STREET

DAVID BOWIE AND
MICK JAGGER

7 September 1985, for four weeks

● ● ● ●

EMI America EA 204

Written by Ivy Hunter, William Stevenson and Marvin Gaye. Produced by Clive Langer and Alan Winstanley.

Old-timers Mick Jagger and David Bowie proved that a duo with the combined age of

David Bowie *and* **Mick Jagger** *made a marvellous present for* Dancing In The Street's *twenty-first birthday.*

an octogenarian could bop with the best of them. Their dynamic collaboration on disc and on video brought in yet more thousands of much needed dollars, pounds, yen, marks, francs etc., for the Live Aid appeal via their vibrant revival of the Martha and the Vandellas classic *Dancing In The Street.*

The hit came straight into the chart at number one and held off all opposition for a month. Jagger had not been part of such a smash since the eighth and final Stones number one *Honky Tonk Women* in 1969 (see no. 274) and even by Bowie's more recent standards (three number ones since 1975), this was a major landmark of his output.

The original version of *Dancing In The Street* only made number 28 when it was first issued in 1964, but five years later it did better, climbing to fourth place. The 1985 cover gave Marvin Gaye a posthumous number one as a co-composer and Brits Langer and Winstanley their third as producers (see nos 501 and 506). Yet again Nile Rodgers' name appeared on the credits of a chart-topper; this time he was listed under 'additional production' along with Jagger, Steve Thompson and Michael Barbiero (see nos 519, 534 and 552).

The only Stones single to chart after the Jagger/Bowie smash was, coincidentally, another cover version, this time of the Bob and Earl standard *Harlem Shuffle.* Mick's energies have been devoted almost exclusively to a solo career since 1986. The two superstars having not reunited for further chart attacks, they remain (as a combo) on the list of one-hit wonders.

557

IF I WAS

MIDGE URE

5 October 1985, for one week

●

Chrysalis URE 1

Written by Midge Ure, and Danny Mitchell. Produced by Midge Ure.

After being a major force behind two number one records, Ultravox star Midge Ure finally made it to the heights in his own right with a fairly conventional (by his standards) ballad. His love song spent only one week at the top but it was long overdue major personal recognition for the man who had co-written and produced Britain's all-time best-selling single (see no. 543) and been a part of the briefly famous Slik (see no. 384).

Midge was born in Lanarkshire and cast aside an engineering apprenticeship in Glasgow in favour of the gamble of the music business. He joined a band called Salvation who became Slik and in the hands of producer/writers Bill Martin and Phil Coulter scored their big hit in 1976. The group collapsed after a year or so and Midge joined up with ex-Sex Pistol Glen Matlock to form the Rich Kids with Steve New and Rusty Egan. They never enjoyed the good fortune their energetic 'power pop' recordings deserved and they split in 1978, having only once reached the Top 30. It was Midge's arrival in the ranks of the reformed Ultravox, who had just lost former leader John Foxx, that brought the first taste of real success for both him and the electronic band. This came with their 1980 album *Vienna,* whose title track reached number 2 early the following year.

A string of Ultravox hits followed all composed by the four members Ure, Chris Cross, Billie Currie and Warren Cann. Their 1982 album *Quartet* was produced by George Martin in Montserrat. Midge found time to work with Steve Strange in the studio group Visage, who clocked up seven hits from 1980-84. He enjoyed a solo Top 10 hit in 1982 with the Tom Rush song *No Regrets* (also a 1976 hit for the Walker Brothers) but only resumed his parallel individual recording projects in earnest with his 1985 album *The Gift* whence came *If I Was.* The hit features Level 42's Mark King on bass.

Jennifer Rush *recorded the best-selling single by a woman in UK history.*

558

THE POWER OF LOVE

JENNIFER RUSH

12 October 1985, for five weeks

●●●●●

CBS A 5003

Written by Candy de Rouge, Gunther Mende, Jennifer Rush and Mary Susan Applegate. Produced by Gunther Mende and Candy de Rouge.

The only million seller of 1985 was the largest-selling single ever by a woman in the UK, beating Julie Covington's 980,000 (see no. 400). It also set an all time record in the slowness of its progress to the top, taking no less than 16 weeks to make it. It charted on 29 June at number 65 and in its twelfth chart week had only progressed to number 42, staying for nine consecutive weeks in the forties. The following week it broke into the all-important Top 40 at number 36 which automatically increased its airplay dramatically. It then accelerated with remarkable zest: 15 to 2 to 1, where it remained for a further month. Its progress on the way down was also extremely dilatory and it chalked up 32 weeks in all before departing. At the end of 1986 it returned for another wander around the lower regions.

The song was the second with the title *The Power Of Love* to make number one, following only ten months after Frankie Goes To Hollywood's hit of the same name. A third song with the same title by Huey Lewis and the News was a number one in America in August 1985, but in the UK it failed to go beyond number 11. There is no logical explanation for the sudden rush to use this title which had never provided anyone with a British hit before 1984.

Jennifer was a native of Queens, New York, but she recorded her gigantic Euro-smash in Germany. Her passionate reading of a sensual ballad supported by a powerful synthesized programme struck a chord in the hearts of Eurolovers once trendy radio stations permitted them to hear it, but her heart-rending voice of experience left her fellow Americans less moved. They only let her emote her way to number 57. She at least had the satisfaction of seeing off a rival version by Air Supply, but had reason to feel hard done by when Laura Branigan's version went Top 30 in late 1987.

Not surprisingly her records since have never quite matched her devastating debut, but she did make the Top 40 in the States with a duet with Elton John entitled *Flames Of Paradise,* and remains an important European act.

559

A GOOD HEART

FEARGAL SHARKEY

16 November 1985, for two weeks

●●

Virgin VS 808

Written by Maria McKee. Produced by David A. Stewart.

Ex-Undertone Feargal Sharkey outstripped every chart performance of his former band with his third solo hit. In the producer's chair was Eurythmic David A. Stewart (see no. 553) whose masterly work on Lone Justice singer-songwriter Maria McKee's bright philosophical gem brought the Ulsterman a far wider audience than seven years of highly rated work with the Undertones.

The Undertones were formed in the mid-'70s in Derry. The original line-up was Sharkey (vocals), brothers John (rhythm guitar) and Damian (lead guitar/keyboards) O'Neill, Mickey Bradley (bass) and Billy Doherty (drums). Their first record *Teenage Kicks* was released on a Northern Ireland independent label and subsequently nationwide on Sire. It achieved an encouraging 31 placing in late 1978.

Regular chart singles followed, but only 1980's *My Perfect Cousin* scraped into the Top 10. Success was never quite consistent or substantial enough to hold them together and they split up in 1983. Feargal, who was the only non-composing Undertone, teamed up with Vince Clarke in the Assembly. The only Assembly single ever released, *Never Never* reached number 4 in 1983. They disbanded before most fans had realized who the group was. Feargal moved to Madness' (see no. 501) label Zar jazz which issued the first single to come out under his own name, *Listen To Your Father*. Although this was a medium-sized hit, Sharkey released no Zarjazz follow-up. Instead he moved to Virgin where one more hit in the twenties preceded *A Good Heart*. His follow-up *You Little Thief* went Top 5 in early 1986. He premiered the track on British TV live from a jumbo jet several miles up in the air.

560

I'M YOUR MAN

WHAM!

30 November 1985, for two weeks

●●

Epic A 6716

Written by George Michael. Produced by George Michael.

By George Michael's standards, there was a long gap between his third and fourth number one singles. His first three number ones (2 with Wham! and one solo – see nos 535, 537 and 539) had all occurred within a four and a half month period whereas his next (a Wham! hit) was over a year coming. There had been no dip in his or his group's popularity however. The late 1984 Wham! single *Last Christmas* had been released simultaneously with the Band Aid megasmash (see no. 543) and was held at number two becoming the first single to sell a million in the UK without reaching the top. Its royalties went to Band Aid. *I'm Your Man*, the first Wham! release since *Last Christmas*, took only two weeks to overcome all opposition.

During 1985 George appeared at Live Aid with Elton John singing Elton's *Don't Let The Sun Go Down On Me*. This collaboration was extended further when George appeared on a track from Elton's *Ice On Fire* album, *Wrap Her Up*, which was issued as a single, reaching number 12 a few weeks after *I'm Your Man* peaked.

At the end of 1985 *Last Christmas* made the Top 10 for the second time. The song became the centre of a court battle when Barry Manilow's publishers unsuccessfully claimed that the tune was a lift of Barry's *Can't Smile Without You*. It charted again over Christmas 1986, reaching number 47.

In March 1986, George finally confirmed that months if not years of rumours that Wham! would split were now correct. 'It's the most amicable split in pop history' he said in one television interview.

561

SAVING ALL MY LOVE FOR YOU

WHITNEY HOUSTON

14 December 1985, for two weeks

●●

Arista ARIST 640

Written by Michael Masser and Gerry Goffin. Produced by Michael Masser.

Whitney Houston was born in New Jersey in 1963, the daughter of Cissy Houston, the cousin of Dionne and Dee Dee Warwick. Her mother was the lead singer of the Sweet Inspirations from 1967-70 and their work included backing vocals for Aretha Franklin and Elvis Presley. Cissy went solo in 1970 but despite the widespread respect her soulful voice earned her within the music industry she never made a major breakthrough on her own. It was left to her daughter to earn the family fortune.

Whitney began her showbiz career as a fashion model, became a studio vocalist and made her chart debut duetting with Teddy Pendergrass in 1984 on the medium-sized US hit *Hold Me*. She then progressed to cutting her own album which, thanks to the superb team of writers, musicians and producers assembled around her by Clive Davis of Arista Records, became the most successful debut LP of all time.

The first American hit single was *You Give Good Love,* a number 3. The second, and the first in the UK, was the ballad of a mistress' dilemma *Saving All My Love For You*, which topped the charts in both countries. The latter originally appeared on a Marilyn McCoo and Billy Davis, Jr album. Two more American number ones, *How Will I Know*, and *The Greatest Love Of All*, emerged. *Whitney Houston* went on to sell in excess of 13 million copies around the world, the all-time number one by a woman.

Michael Masser and Gerry Goffin had teamed for a US number one before. In 1976 their song *Theme from 'Mahogany' – Do You Know Where You're Going To* had done the trick for Diana Ross. Goffin was most celebrated for his '60s work with his then wife Carole King and had previously been at the top of the UK charts back in 1964 thanks to Herman's Hermits (see no. 178).

562

MERRY CHRISTMAS EVERYONE

SHAKIN' STEVENS

28 December 1985, for two weeks

●●

Epic A 6769

Written by Bob Heatlie. Produced by Dave Edmunds.

Nearly four years went by between Shakin' Stevens' third and fourth number ones but during that time he established himself as one of the most consistent hit-makers the British charts had ever seen. Between *Oh Julie* (see no. 493) and *Merry Christmas Everyone* Shaky added another 11 consecutive hits to his tally, seven of them Top 10 and two of them Top 2, as well as a Top 5 hit in duet with Bonnie Tyler (see no. 517). One of the biggest in this string had been his 1982 Christmas offering *The Shakin' Stevens EP*, which featured *Blue Christmas* as the lead track.

Technically, Shaky did not have the 1985 Christmas number one with *Merry Christmas Everyone,* because he did not displace Whitney Houston from the top until the chart dated 'the 28th December', but this fact could hardly have caused Stevens, producer Dave Edmunds or writer Bob Heatlie many sleepless nights as they soared into the new year ahead of all rivals. Both Edmunds (see no. 294) and Heatlie (see no. 484) had made number one in their *Merry Christmas Everyone* modes once before.

Since his fourth chart-topper (only Elvis, Cliff and Rod Stewart of male singers have had more) Shaky has shown no sign of letting up in his assault on the best-sellers. His audience has grown to embrace fans of all ages and his live concerts go from strength to strength. He is a supreme entertainer, combining a sense of humour with brilliantly-chosen material from the past three decades and an energetic and immaculately executed performance.

563

WEST END GIRLS

PET SHOP BOYS

11 January 1986, for two weeks

● ●

Parlophone R 6115

Written by Neil Tennant and Chris Lowe. Produced by Stephen Hague.

Neil Tennant and Chris Lowe met in August 1981 in a hi-fi shop in the Kings Road, Chelsea. Neil had once been a member of a Newcastle group, Dust, from which he progressed not to another group but to

publishing, working for Marvel Comics and winding up as an Assistant Editor on the teen fan mag *Smash Hits*. Chris, five years Neil's junior, was a former trombonist turned keyboard player whose early professional days included a stretch with septet One Under The Eight.

Now calling themselves the Pet Shop Boys, a name that they claim has no significance beyond being inspired by a friend who worked in a pet shop, they worked together on songs and productions when architectural study (Chris) and journalism (Neil) permitted. A 1983 trip to New York for *Smash Hits* gave Neil the chance to meet producer Bobby 'O' Orlando and in 1984 Orlando and the Pet Shop Boys recorded the first version of *West End Girls* which did quite well in Europe but nothing in England, where it was released by Epic.

The duo took the decision to devote their energies full-time to the PSB. Neil wrote a farewell article in *Smash Hits* entitled 'Why I Quit Smash Hits To Be A Teen Sensation!'. They signed with EMI. Their first Parlophone single *Opportunities (Let's Make Lots Of Money)* came out in June 1985 but followed the Epic effort into oblivion. The choice for the second EMI single was a re-recording of *West End Girls* and the reaction from the public could hardly have been in greater contrast to that which had greeted the original version. The single, produced by Stephen Hague, was an eerie half-spoken, half-sung portrait of city life into which were poured real street sounds and synthetic electronic sounds. It entered the chart at the end of November 1985 and just under two months later emerged top of the heap during the post-Christmas shakeout.

564

THE SUN ALWAYS

SHINES ON T.V.

A-HA

25 January 1986, for two weeks

● ●

Warner Brothers W 8846

Written by Pal Waaktaar. Produced by Alan Tarney.

Norway's contribution to the history of popular music had consisted mainly of a string of glorious disasters in the Eurovision Song Contest until 1985. That year a female duo named Bobbysocks represented Norway, although one girl was Swedish. They defied precedent and prediction by winning the annual event that everyone loves to hate with *Let It Swing*. Despite this sensational victory the Bobbysocks' single only made number 45 in the UK charts and it was left to Pal Waaktaar, Magne 'Mags' Furuholmen and Morten Harket to do for Norway what only Abba and Blue Swede had previously done for Scandinavian pop groups – top the charts in Britain and/or America. a-ha did this in both countries.

a-ha emerged from a Norwegian band named Bridges, formed in 1979. Included in the line-up were Pal (vocals/guitar) and Mags (keyboards). Morten was at the time with the awkwardly named soul band Souldier Blue, but when he met Pal and Mags the three musicians decided to try their luck as a new combination. Visits to London in 1982 and 1983 won them management and a record contract, the latter with WEA.

Their first recording sessions in London went badly although *Take On Me* sold well in Norway. It flopped twice in the UK and when even their second single failed to click in Norway it seemed as if the torch of their nation's pop music was still in the clutch of one half of the Bobbysocks. a-ha's manager Terry Slater still had faith in *Take On Me* and he persuaded Alan Tarney (see no. 441) to re-cut the song with the trio. This version was issued in Britain and the States in May 1985.

The response of the British public was no greater than it had been to the original version, but in America, thanks in part to a stunning video made by Steve Barron, the Tarney-produced *Take On Me* made number one within three months. The message finally reached the UK, and with persistent re-promotion by WEA *Take On Me* charted in September, rising to number 2 during a 19-week run in the best-sellers.

The photogenic threesome soon became teen idols whose looks as much as their music guaranteed them enormous sales with their follow-up. *The Sun Always Shines On T.V.* nipped to number one in the UK in a mere four weeks and since then they have come up with a healthy sequence of Top 10 items, including a James Bond title song in 1987, *The Living Daylights*. Lead vocalist Morten Harket has even achieved the honour of an entry in *Who's Really Who*.

565

WHEN THE GOING GETS TOUGH, THE TOUGH GET GOING

BILLY OCEAN

8 February 1986, for four weeks

●●●●

Jive JIVE 114

Written by Wayne Braithwaite, Barry J. Eastmond, R. J. 'Mutt' Lange and Billy Ocean. Produced by Robert John 'Mutt' Lange.

Billy Ocean was born Leslie Sebastian Charles on 21 January 1950 in Trinidad. He was raised in England and first came to the attention of British record buyers in 1976. A run of disco-influenced hit singles that began with the number 2 smash *Love Really Hurts Without You* took him away from the world of sessions as a back-up vocalist or as an imitator of the stars on cheap albums of cover versions of current hits. These successes (all on the GTO label) ground to a halt by early 1980 and nothing was heard of Billy for over four years.

In 1984 Billy signed a new deal with Jive records and quickly registered a huge come-back with a composition he co-wrote with producer Keith Diamond, *Caribbean Queen (No More Love On The Run)*. This single (originally recorded as *European Queen...*) made number 6 in Britain but, more important, number one in America.

Phase two of Billy's record career now swung into impressive action. The fifth of his Jive hits (all co written by him), produced by 'Mutt' Lange, whose only previous number one in the UK had been with the Boomtown Rats (see no. 428), proved to be the one that did the ultimate trick for him in the UK, boosted by its inclusion in the Michael Douglas movie *The Jewel Of The Nile*. Douglas sang backing vocals on the record. In the US it only made number 2, but Billy was more than compensated for this minor disappointment by the Stateside achievement of his follow-up *There'll Be Sad Songs (To Make You Cry)* which went one better, though eleven worse in Britain.

The origin of the saying that inspired Ocean's only British chart-topper to date is not certain but it has been attributed to Joseph P. Kennedy, father of the American President, and one time US Ambassador to Britain. Whoever came up with it, he/she was indirectly responsible for the second longest title to a UK number one of all time, its 37 letters tying it with Brian and Michael's hit (see no. 421) and second only to Scott McKenzie's (see no. 236) although pedants argue that as 33 letters of the title of *San Francisco (Be Sure To Wear Some Flowers In Your Hair)* are in brackets, Ocean and Brian and Michael should be considered joint holders of this uncoveted honour.

566

CHAIN REACTION

DIANA ROSS

8 March 1986, for three weeks

●●●

Capitol CL 386

Written by Barry, Robin and Maurice Gibb. Produced by Barry Gibb, Karl Richardson and Albhy Galuten.

Chain Reaction had Bee Gees stamped indelibly all over it. Since those halcyon days of the late '70s when *Saturday Night Fever* reached epidemic proportions, the Bee Gees own recording career had gone into a temporary recession. All three Gibb brothers were involved in solo projects, Robin having the most success with a number one in Germany, *Juliet*. Their great achievements lay in revitalizing the careers of Barbra Streisand (see no. 468) and Dionne Warwick and providing the Kenny Rogers – Dolly Parton duo with their US number one *Islands In The Stream*. In 1986 they turned their attention to the most charted female vocalist of all time, Diana Ross.

In 1980 Nile Rodgers and Bernard Edwards of Chic had provided a similar boost to the Ross career with the album *Diana*, which spawned three Top 20 hits including *Upside Down*, which peaked at number 2. Since the end of 1982 however, Miss Ross had been absent from the British Top 40. The album with Barry Gibb supervising was called *Eaten Alive*. The first single released from it, Michael Jackson's title track, flopped badly, appearing on our charts for only one

week at number 71. *Chain Reaction*, released at the very beginning of the new year, brought the album out of the bargain buckets and into the charts and became the first Ross chart-topper since *I'm Still Waiting* (see no. 303) 14 years and 172 days earlier. This was the longest wait between number one hits ever recorded. To add to the oddness of the feat, neither of Diana Ross' two British chart-toppers made the top half of the US top 100, which she has topped five times as a soloist, twelve times with the Supremes and once with Lionel Richie.

567

LIVING DOLL

CLIFF RICHARD AND THE YOUNG ONES FEATURING HANK MARVIN

29 March 1986, for three weeks

●●●

WEA YZ 65

Written by Lionel Bart. Produced by Stuart Colman.

The most indestructible British pop star of all time, Cliff Richard OBE broke yet more new ground in the 29th year of his career when he zoomed up to the top of the charts for the 11th time, accompanied by his colleague from way back, Hank B Marvin, and the comedy quartet named after one of Cliff's other number ones (see no. 132). Marvin, with five Shadows number ones and seven other Cliff-and-Shads number ones, was actually gracing the summit for the 13th time.

Living Doll was unlike any of Cliff's previous successes in that the song had already been a number one single for him (a mere 27 years earlier). Gerry Marsden, in his role as lead singer of the Crowd (see no. 551) had beaten Cliff to the honour of becoming the first to hit the top twice with the same song, but Gerry's wait between successes had been a less staggering 22 years. It is probable, nay certain, that the vast majority of the purchasers of the mark II *Living Doll* were not even born when Cliff and the Drifters (as

Hank's group then was) first took it to the top (see no. 88).

The record was the fifth number one made for charity and the fourth that fought famine in Ethiopia (see nos 543, 548 and 556). The disc was Stuart Colman's fourth chart-topper as a producer (his other three all being with Shakin' Stevens) and Lionel Bart's third as a writer (once before, obviously, with *Living Doll* and once with Anthony Newley – see no. 100).

Although the vocal performance on the 1986 version by Cliff and Hank's lead guitar work were both beyond criticism, it has to be said that the anarchic contribution of the Young Ones was the major selling factor. Nigel Planer, Adrian Edmondson, Rik Mayall and Christopher Ryan had established themselves both collectively and individually as leaders of Alternative Comedy and they were at their destructive best on *Living Doll* both on record and in the video. They re-appeared as cod heavy metal act Bad News in 1987, causing great damage to Queen's *Bohemian Rhapsody*. Planer (who played Che Guevara during the West End run of *Evita)* had a number 2 in 1984 with *Hole In My Shoe* in his guise as moronic hippy, neil. Meanwhile Cliff moves inexorably on towards his 100th hit.

568

A DIFFERENT CORNER

GEORGE MICHAEL

19 April 1986, for three weeks

● ● ●

Epic A 7033

Written by George Michael. Produced by George Michael.

The fabulously successful George Michael notched up his fifth number one as a writer and producer, and his second in two solo outings. Like *Careless Whisper* (see no. 537) this was a reflective ballad, in sharp contrast to the uptempo Wham! hits. *A Different Corner* took a mere three weeks to reach the summit, banging another nail into the Wham! coffin which had already been assembled via George's March announcement that the duo's days together would end in June.

There was still one more Wham! chart-

topper to come (see no. 572) but the success of *A Different Corner* naturally provided a superb launch-pad for George's official solo career. Much interest centred around the release of the third George Michael single as he seemed to be a dead cert to equal the best-ever starts to a singles career by Gerry and the Pacemakers in 1963 and Frankie Goes To Hollywood in 1984, both acts having hit number one with their first three releases. Alas, George narrowly missed this distinction, partly because his next single, *I Want Your Sex*, received only restricted airplay because of its lyrical content. George maintained that it was a plea for safe sex and monogamy, but opposition was just enough to spoil his track record. His next single *Faith,* released in autumn 1987, also fell just short of the ultimate honour.

A Different Corner was the first single to be issued in the United States as a George Michael record. It climbed to number 7.

569

ROCK ME AMADEUS

FALCO

10 May 1986, for one week

●

A & M AM 278

Written by Rob and Ferdi Bolland and Falco. Produced by Rob and Ferdi Bolland.

Falco, born in Vienna as Johann Holzel, is the most successful pop export Austria has ever produced, in as much as he is the first native of that country to reach number one in both Britain and America. However mention must be made here of Austrian zither genius Anton Karas, whose *The Third Man* music (*The Harry Lime Theme*) made number one in America in 1950, and probably would have done in Britain had record charts been in operation then.

The song that elevated Falco to worldwide attention was his tribute to another Austrian whose musical achievements put even Falco and Karas into the shade, viz Wolfgang Amadeus Mozart. The Peter Shaffer play *Amadeus* about the rivalry between Mozart and fellow composer Salieri had been an international hit in the early '80s and by the time Falco's dance smash had broken around the world there can have been few

unaware of the great composer's middle name. Purchasers of Falco's album *Falco 3* were treated to a potted history of Mozart during the eight-minute-plus mix of *Rock Me Amadeus,* recited in English by a voice bearing a remarkable resemblance to that of Kermit the Frog, but the American edit mix that topped the singles lists concentrated on rhythm rather than history.

Falco's first breakthrough outside German-speaking territories came in 1983 when a song he co-wrote and recorded, *Der Kommissar* went Top 5 in the United States. It was however an English act, After The Fire, who had the hit; Falco's own version was a Top 10 dance chart item, but an English translation by After The Fire leader Andrew Piercy made the difference as far as the pop charts were concerned. Neither version made much impact in the UK. Falco had a second consecutive US dance hit with *Maschine Brennt* but after that zilch until *Rock Me Amadeus.*

His immediate follow-up *Vienna Calling* was a substantial hit in both Britain and America, but subsequent releases, though often enormous hits in Germany and Austria, have made little impression. Mozart remains internationally popular.

570

THE CHICKEN SONG

SPITTING IMAGE

17 May 1986, for three weeks

● ● ●

Virgin SPIT 1

Written by Philip Pope, Robert Grant and Doug Naylor. Produced by Philip Pope.

From the *Economist* magazine to the top of the charts is an unusual progression, but it was the route taken by Peter Fluck and Roger Law, the inventors and designers of the Spitting Image puppets, whose late night Sunday television show *Spitting Image* is compulsory viewing for politicians and other public figures who are the likely targets of the Fluck and Law lampooning. They began by designing models for the front covers of the *Economist* in the early '70s, but developed into television in the '80s with what they see as the logical next step for political cartooning.

The television shows feature a huge cast of writers and impressionists, and the musical contributions are very often the lowlight of the evening. The simply appalling *Chicken Song* was designed to be a lampoon of songs like Black Lace's longlasting Eurohit *Agadoo*, but either too many or too few people saw the joke, and Spitting Image's first single shot to the number one spot in only its second week of chart life. *Agadoo* had peaked at number 2.

Spitting Image continues as a television programme into the late '80s. As long as they continue to feature dreadful songs there is every possibility they will rack up a few more hits. They deprived themselves of one-hit wonder status at Christmas 1986 when their double-sided hit *Santa Claus Is On The Dole/First Atheist Tabernacle Choir* reached number 22.

571

SPIRIT IN THE SKY

DOCTOR AND THE MEDICS

7 June 1986, for three weeks

● ● ●

IRS/MCA IAM 113

Written by Norman Greenbaum. Produced by Craig Leon.

The tenth song to make number one in two different versions was Norman Greenbaum's *Spirit In The Sky* (see no. 285). His 1970 chart-topper was resurrected by the band who described themselves as 'a cross between Valerie Singleton and a slug'. Doctor and the Medics consisted of six multi-coloured people, namely Clive Jackson known professionally as the Doctor, sisters Collette and Wendi (the Anadin Brothers), Steve the guitarist, Vom the drummer and Richard Searle on bass. Their first single was *The Druids Are Coming*, with the even more paranoid title *The Goats Are Trying To Kill Me* on the flip side. If the Druids ever came it was without the great British public knowing anything about it, as the record failed to get anywhere near the charts.

The six-foot-five Doctor (a fully qualified St. John's Ambulance Brigade first aider) is one of the tallest people ever to reach the top of

the charts, but despite the ease with which his group accomplished the feat with their first hit, subsequent singles have made less rapid headway. The follow-up, also from their first album *Laughing At The Pieces*, was called *Burn* but failed to catch fire and was extinguished at number 29. Their next chart hit was another revival of a previous number one, this time Abba's *Waterloo* (see no. 348), for which they enlisted the help of another highly-painted and flare-trousered number-one hitmaker, Roy Wood. It has proved so far to be their Waterloo, their final battle with the charts.

572

THE EDGE OF HEAVEN

WHAM!

28 June 1986, for two weeks

● ●

Epic FIN 1

Written by George Michael. Produced by George Michael.

The final official Wham! single release followed the golden route taken by three of the previous four to the top of the pops. It had

been over six months since Wham!'s penultimate winner *I'm Your Man* (see no. 560) but hardly a cold spell for George Michael who had the solo *A Different Corner* slotted into the number one position almost exactly halfway between the two final Wham! offerings (see no. 568). He was now moving into the very big league indeed, with six number ones under his belt.

The 7-inch version of *The Edge Of Heaven*, which featured Elton John on piano, initially appeared only in double-pack form with the second disc headed by *Where Did Your Heart Go*, a cover of a Was (Not Was) song. Before long the two A-sides were issued on one disc, at which stage *The Edge Of Heaven* became the A-side of the A-sides, for those who were either too slow or too unenthusiastic to purchase *Battlestations* and a reworking of *Wham! Rap* (both Michael songs).

Wham! went out in style at the end of June in front of 72,000 fans at Wembley Stadium for 'The Final' show (Elton John again making a guest appearance). Their farewell album (also called *The Final*) was a compilation of some of their greatest cuts and was available as either a straightforward double LP or as a super-glamorous boxed set with gold

Wham! *also had three consecutive number ones in America from* Make It Big.

Madonna. *The top star of the mid-Eighties.*

vinyl discs and items of Wham! memorabilia. Both sold prodigiously.

That was it for the duo who had gone about as far as they could go in just four years (in less than two in America). George Michael has continued to be a major force in the music industry, Andrew Ridgely somewhat less so; both can be proud to have been half of Wham! whatever their future individual exploits.

573

PAPA DON'T PREACH

MADONNA

12 July 1986, for three weeks

● ● ●

Sire W 8636

Written by Brian Elliott, additional lyrics by Madonna. Produced by Madonna and Stephen Bray.

Madonna's second number one was a heart-wrenching song about a girl's plea to her father not to criticize her for becoming pregnant. It was more tuneful and thoughtful than many of her other hits, but still recorded with at least one eye on the dancefloor.

Virtually a year had passed since *Into The Groove* (see no. 554) but in between her first two number ones Madonna had moved into undisputed worldwide superstardom. She actually had eight Top 5 UK hits in 1985, a record not even Elvis Presley had ever matched in a calendar year. In that year she also beat by four chart weeks Ruby Murray's 30-year-old record of 80 chart weeks in one year by a female artiste (see no. 29). Another major event in her life that took place in 1985 was her marriage to the excitable actor Sean Penn.

True Blue, her third album, featured *Papa Don't Preach* and indeed two other number one hits. It was itself an instant LP chart-topper when issued in June 1986. The first single from the multi-platinum set was *Live To Tell* from Penn's film *At Close Range*, in which Madonna did not appear. This 45 narrowly missed repeating its US number one success in the UK. *Papa Don't Preach*, issued just two months later, did not falter at the final hurdle, extending her sequence of consecutive Top 5 hits to eleven.

Among the background vocalists on *Papa Don't Preach* was Siedah Garrett (see no. 596). She warbled on most of the *True Blue* tracks, including all three number one singles (see also nos 577 and 589).

574

THE LADY IN RED

CHRIS DE BURGH

2 August 1986, for three weeks

● ● ●

A&M AM 331

Written by Chris de Burgh. Produced by Paul Hardiman.

Chris de Burgh, born Christopher John Davidson on 15 October 1950, is an Irishman who spent part of his childhood in Argentina. During the late 1970s and early 1980s he built up an enormous following among album buyers but rarely made it into the singles charts. His first British LP chart placing was with his 1981 set *Best Moves*, and subsequent albums *The Getaway* and *Man On The Line* enjoyed lengthy runs on the charts. With his single releases he was less successful. In Australia, he had a massive smash with *Don't Pay The Ferryman*, which only reached number 48 in Britain. *High On Emotion*, his only other chart single before *The Lady In Red*, rose higher on foreign emotion than it did on the British stiff upper lip.

De Burgh was the first act to crash into the Swiss album charts at number one and one year was the best-selling English speaking male LP artist in Germany. With the consistent success of his albums and his worldwide tours, it was only a matter of time before the big hit single arrived in Britain.

In 1986 he released his album *Into The Light*. The single from it was a song he wrote for his wife, *The Lady In Red*. It was undoubtedly the most romantic male vocal since Stevie Wonder's *I Just Called To Say I Love You*, and it crossed over from the mums of Radio Two to the younger singles buyers of Radio One. *Into The Light* became his most successful album and his 1986 British tour was a sell-out.

Apart from this one big hit, which hit the Top 10 in America too, Chris de Burgh has yet to put a single in the Top 40, although his popularity at Christmas 1986 finally placed his 1975 single *A Spaceman Came Travelling* on the charts. Chris de Burgh is not a singles hitmaker but is likely to remain a firmly established favourite with his enormous album buying followers.

575

I WANT TO WAKE UP WITH YOU

BORIS GARDINER

23 August 1986, for three weeks

● ● ●

Revue REV 733

Written by Mac David. Produced by Willie Lindo.

Jamaican Boris Gardiner has had probably the most confusing chart career of any of the number one hitmakers. His first chart hit was in 1970, when an instrumental entitled *Elizabethan Reggae* crept into the Top 50 (as it then was) for one week and then disappeared. The record was credited to one Byron Lee, whose name was listed as the artist on the labels of the first copies pressed. When the record re-entered the charts another week later, the instrumentalist credited was still Mr Lee. It was not until the sixth week of its chart life that *Elizabethan Reggae* was credited to the real performer, Boris Gardiner, but even then his name was spelt Gardner, and it was as Boris Gardner that he was known to British chart freaks until the summer of 1986.

16 years and 87 days after Gardner/Lee fell off the charts, the gentle reggae love ballad *I Want To Wake Up With You* entered the British charts, and for the first time Boris Gardiner was correctly billed. As if to celebrate the record swept quickly right to the top, and put Boris at that time third in the list of slowest number one hitmakers, behind only Stevie Wonder and Johnny Mathis. Within six months he had been overtaken by both Jackie Wilson and Ben E. King, but neither of them had hit with both an instrumental and a vocal hit. Of all the number one hitmakers only Russ Conway, Fleetwood Mac, Manfred Mann and the Shadows have had both vocal and instrumental hits, apart from Boris Gardiner. (Elton John, who is half a chart-topping act, has also had solo vocal and instrumental hits.) By the end of 1986, Gardiner had hit the charts twice more and his name was clearly established and correctly spelt everywhere.

576

DON'T LEAVE ME THIS WAY

COMMUNARDS WITH SARAH JANE MORRIS

13 September 1986, for four weeks

● ● ● ●

London LON 103

Written by Kenny Gamble, Leon Huff and Carry Gilbert. Produced by Mike Thorne.

Bronski Beat's lead singer James William Horsburgh Somerville left at the height of his band's success to form the Communards with Richard Coles and an all female backing band. After two singles sold disappointingly it looked as though Jimi had made the wrong commercial move. But Sarah Jane Morris' unusually deep voice complemented Somerville's higher pitched vocal range, and their galloping remake of the Harold Melvin and the Bluenotes Top 5 hit of 1977 climbed to number one and went on to outsell all other singles of 1986.

Nine years before, soul singer Thelma Houston (Whitney's aunt and Cissy's sister) had also recorded the song, and although her Motown version had only climbed to number 13 in Britain, it hit the very top in America. Harold Melvin's single did not breach the Top 40 there.

The Communards took their name from the Paris Commune, a revolutionary experiment which was proclaimed on 28 March 1871 after the Franco-Prussian War, and crushed exactly two months later. The 1986 Communards were also politically active through their involvement with the Red Wedge, a group of like-minded pop people who toured the country promoting political awareness among the young. *Don't Leave Me This Way* was itself an apolitical song, but was poignantly dedicated to the Greater London Council which was at the time in the process of being abolished by the government.

577

TRUE BLUE

MADONNA

11 October 1986, for one week

●

Sire W 8550

Written by Madonna and Stephen Bray. Produced by Madonna and Stephen Bray.

True Blue, the title song and third single from Madonna's third album, may only have held down the top spot for one week but it was enough to give Ms. Ciccone a clutch of new chart-history distinctions.

Madonna became the only female recording artist to achieve three number one singles in the UK since Sandie Shaw was the first to do so in 1967. In the 19 years between *Puppet On A String* (see no. 232) and *True Blue* the two girls from Abba and Debbie Harry with Blondie had enjoyed nine and five number ones respectively, but throughout that period Sandie's feat had remained unique. Madonna also became only the second lady writer to have had a hand in three number ones, equalling Debbie Harry in that respect. Stephen Bray, a mere male, promoted from being plain Steve first time out (see no. 554), achieved his second with the catchy song with a late '50s feel. *True Blue* just failed to become her fifth Stateside number one, but the next single from the album, *Open Your Heart,* which did not go all the way in Britain, did.

In 1986 Madonna starred in a non-musical movie with husband Sean Penn entitled *Shanghai Surprise.* It was produced by George Harrison's film company Handmade Films. The main surprise turned out to be that the film flopped. This had no effect whatsoever on Madonna's power as a record star.

578

EVERY LOSER WINS

NICK BERRY

18 October 1986, for three weeks

● ● ●

BBC RESL 204

Written by Simon May, Stewart James and Bradley James. Produced by Simon May, Stewart James and Bradley James.

The twice-weekly soap opera *EastEnders* has proved to be the most successful programme ever shown on BBC television. With average audiences around the 20 million mark, the Tuesday and Thursday episodes regularly took the top two positions in JICTAR ratings throughout 1986 and 1987. The biggest audiences of all came in the autumn of 1986 when 17-year-old Michelle, daughter of Arthur and Pauline Fowler and already the mother of 'Dirty Den' Watts' baby, married Lofty Holloway the asthmatic barman at Den's pub, the Queen Victoria. The saga spun out over several weeks as first Arthur stole the money to pay for the reception, then Michelle left Lofty standing at the altar and then finally she decided to go through with the wedding.

Nick Berry plays Simon Wicks, fellow barman and best man to Lofty. During the episodes between Michelle jilting Lofty and finally marrying him, Lofty consoled himself by playing over and over again *Every Loser Wins.* The viewers loved it. The record climbed from number 65 to number 4 in one week, the biggest ever leap within the charts. It went on to give BBC records its only number one to date.

Despite the best efforts of Anita Dobson and other EastEnders stars Nick Berry is still the only member of the cast to top the charts since Wendy Richard (aka Pauline Fowler) got there with Mike Sarne back in 1962 (see no. 137).

579

TAKE MY BREATH AWAY

BERLIN

8 November 1986, for four weeks

● ● ● ●

CBS A 7320

Written by Giorgio Moroder and Tom Whitlock. Produced by Giorgio Moroder.

Giorgio Moroder's fourth chart-topper as a writer and his third as a producer was the song that won the Academy Award for Best Song at the presentation ceremony in March 1987. *Take My Breath Away* was the love theme from the Paramount film *Top Gun,* which also featured songs by Kenny Loggins, Teena Marie, Cheap Trick and Harold Faltermeyer. The flip side of the 7-inch single was credited to 'Giorgio Moroder (featuring Joe Pizzulo)', and Berlin themselves were only on CBS by courtesy of Phonogram. All in all it was not a deliberate part of Berlin's career progression, and yet it gave them their biggest worldwide hit, topping the charts on both sides of the Atlantic.

Berlin, the only chart-topping act named after an European city, are from Los Angeles. They began as a six-piece band whose first American hit came in 1983 with a song called *Sex,* which withdrew after climbing only to number 62. By the time *Take My Breath Away* was recorded, they were a three-piece outfit, Terri Nunn on vocals, John Crawford on bass and Rob Brill on drums. In their second week at number one the top five singles all featured female vocalists. Kim Wilde, Bangles, Mel and Kim and Swing Out Sister were the acts holding on to the positions from 2 to 5, an unprecedented domination of the charts by the 'weaker' sex.

580

THE FINAL COUNTDOWN

EUROPE

6 December 1986, for two weeks

● ●

Epic A 7127

Written by Joey Tempest. Produced by Kevin Elson.

The second Swedish act to top the British charts were the five man rock band Europe. Their music has been described by Bjorn Ulvaeus, a member of the only other Swedish outfit to take a record to number one in England, as 'melodic hard rock . . . that's the way music should sound today'.

Europe arose out of a four man band formed by Joakim Larsson called Force. Larsson grew up in the north Stockholm suburb of Upplands Väsby, the fastest growing industrial and business centre in Sweden. He changed his name to Joey Tempest and in the early 1980s Force rocked their way through gig after gig, playing mainly Tempest originals based on the sound of '70s bands like Slade and Sweet. In 1982 a Swedish daily newspaper organized a rock band contest, the prize being the chance of a recording contract. Tempest changed the name of his band to Europe, entered the competition and won. From then on, success beckoned ever more strongly.

By 1986 the band had grown to five people – Joey Tempest, Mic Michaeli, Ian Haughland, John Leven and Kee Marcello. Only Tempest survived from the original group Force. *The Final Countdown* was the band's first big hit outside Sweden. It eventually sold well over two million copies and topped the charts in 13 countries.

Europe *also had a number one in the US* Radio and Records *chart*, Carrie.

581

CARAVAN OF LOVE

THE HOUSEMARTINS

20 December 1986, for one week

Go! Discs GOD 16

Written by Ernie Isley, Chris Jasper and Marvin Isley. Produced by John Williams.

The Isley Brothers spin-off trio, the younger generation Isley Jasper Isley, issued their *Caravan Of Love* album in 1985, brushed the British charts at the end of 1985 and climbed to number 52 during five weeks of chart action. Early in 1986 Hull's most successful four-piece band, the Housemartins, debuted in the charts with the oddly titled

Sheep, which ran out of support at number 54. Their follow-up, however, was a Top 3 hit: *Happy Hour*. Norman Cook, Paul Heaton, Stan Cullimore and Hugh Whittaker were suddenly the flavour of the month.

An *a cappella* section had been a popular part of Housemartins' concerts; *Caravan of Love* had been a big number one on the US black music chart. When at Christmas 1986, the avowedly Christian Housemartins put out an *a cappella* version of the same song nobody was really surprised to see it at the very top of the lists. The only surprise was that it could only hold on for one week before being flattened by the Jackie Wilson phenomenon.

The sleeve notes stated, with great historical inaccuracy that 'a cappella is a musical form, using voices alone, which started in the small Northern town of Hull at the beginning of the twentieth century. Suitably shamefaced and apologetic for their dark past involving "pop" instruments such as the electronic guitar and the electronic bass guitar, the Housemartins now proudly present for your listening pleasure and spiritual regeneration a selection of their favourite *a cappella* numbers. May they touch your heart. Power to the people. Respect for the

steeple.' By the next Christmas not only had drummer Hugh Whittaker been replaced by Dave Hemingway, but their current hit, *Build*, featured all those electronic instruments and more that the Housemartins had apologized for when they made *Caravan Of Love*.. The group then disbanded.

582

REET PETITE

JACKIE WILSON

27 December 1986, for four weeks

●●●●

SMP SKM 3

Written by Berry Gordy and Tyran Carlo. Produced by Carl Davis.

29 years and 42 days after it first hit the chart

at the end of 1957, Jackie Wilson's *Reet Petite* outsold all other singles in Britain to become the 582nd chart-topper. The 64th number one, *That'll Be The Day* by the Crickets, was at the top of the charts when *Reet Petite* originally came into the British Top 30 on 15 November 1957. Its reappearance at the end of 1986 beat all re-issue statistics by several years.

Jack Leroy Wilson was born in Detroit, Michigan on 9 January 1934, and at first seemed likely to become a world champion boxer rather than a million-selling recording star. However, 'Sonny' Wilson's professional welterweight career was less than impressive; he won only two of his ten fights. By 1951, Wilson turned to singing and was soon discovered by Johnny Otis. Billy Ward, then leader of the highly successful Dominoes, also heard and liked Wilson's voice. For five years Wilson became a Domino, firstly singing back-up vocals for lead vocalist Clyde McPhatter. From 1953 Jackie sang lead after McPhatter's departure to the Drifters. In 1956 Billy Ward and his Dominoes reached no. 13 on the American pop charts with *St. Therese Of The Roses,* the first Jackie Wilson lead vocal to make a national impact. The success of this single encouraged him to go solo. His very first single was *Reet Petite,* written by Tamla Motown founder Berry Gordy and Wilson's cousin Billy Davis, who penned it under the name Tyran Carlo. Although that single was far more successful in Britain, where it reached number 6 first time out, he was launched on a career that was to bring six American Top 10 hits and 14 other Top 40 hits over the next ten years.

Despite his artistic success, his life was tragic. On 15 February 1961 he was shot by a fan in New York, and although he appeared to have made a good recovery, he was never fully fit again. On 29 September 1975 he suffered a massive heart attack while on stage in New Jersey. He fell and hit his head and lapsed into a coma. He eventually regained consciousness, but his health was irreparably damaged. It was almost a mercy when he died, aged 50, on 21 January 1984. Three years later, this great and underrated talent finally hit number one with one of the very best of all the British chart-toppers.

The two hit-makers whose discs took the longest to get to number one . . . **Jackie Wilson** *with* Reet Petite *and* **Ben E King** *with* Stand By Me.

583

JACK YOUR BODY

STEVE 'SILK' HURLEY

24 January 1987, for two weeks

● ●

DJ International LON 117

Written by Steve 'Silk' Hurley. Produced by Steve 'Silk' Hurley.

As the old song says, 'They do things they don't do on Broadway, in Chicago'. While hip-hop was happening in New York, the windy city became the birthplace of House Music, a hybrid of Hi-NRG and soul music designed with the feet in mind. House hit the dancefloors of Great Britain in 1986 and the charts via Farley 'Jackmaster' Funk's *Love Can't Turn Around,* a song that borrowed copiously from JM Silk's *I Can't Turn Around.*

JM Silk are Keith Nunnally and Steve 'Silk' Hurley. It was a solo Hurley who took House music to the top of the singles chart for the first time, although officially *Jack Your Body* should have been an album hit instead. The record sold heavily on 12-inch, becoming the first number one to register over half its sales in the larger format, but the playing time of the 12-inch disc was over 26 minutes, exceeding Gallup's regulation 25 minutes for a single. The 12-inch record should really have been considered an album, and this being the case, the 7-inch on its own would have peaked at a mere number 7 on the singles chart.

Hurley now joins the growing list of one-hit wonders. He nearly added himself to the list of instrumental number ones, which has remained unchanged since Simon Park's *Eye Level* (see no. 338), but the repetitious chanting of the title words denies *Jack Your Body* the chance of being considered a true instrumental.

584

I KNEW YOU WERE
WAITING (FOR ME)

GEORGE MICHAEL AND ARETHA FRANKLIN

7 February 1987, for two weeks

●●

Epic DUET 2

Written by Simon Climie and Denis Morgan. Produced by Narada Michael Walden.

Aretha Franklin was born on 25 March 1925 in Detroit, one of the five children of the Reverend CL Franklin, America's best-selling maker of recorded sermons. *Aretha* started singing in church before going on to a secular career. Signed to CBS by John Hammond, she broke through on *Aretha* with sides produced by Jerry Wexler. One of these, *Respect*, became a US number one.

However, it took a duet with George Michael to get the Queen Of Soul to the top of the singles chart in Britain, 19 years and 244 days after her solo chart debut. Aretha Franklin's highest placing before *I Knew You Were Waiting For Me* was a number 4 hit in August 1968, *I Say A Little Prayer*. For her partner on *I Knew You Were Waiting (For Me)* the top of the chart was not a new position; Michael had visited the peak six times before, four times as half of Wham! and twice as a solo artist in his own right. This was the first of the seven number ones he was involved with which he had neither written nor produced. For Narada Michael Walden this was the first of three number ones in 5 months.

585

STAND BY ME

BEN E KING

21 February 1987, for three weeks

●●●

Atlantic A9361

Written by Jerry Lieber, Mike Stoller and Ben E King. Produced by Jerry Lieber and Mike Stoller.

For the second time in two months a record over 25 years old stood at the very top of the charts. 25 years and 244 days after the record first entered the British lists, *Stand*

By Me went all the way. The reason was that it was featured in a TV jeans ad, the springboard for the successful Rob Reiner hit revivals of *I Heard It Through The Grapevine* and *When A Man Loves A Woman*. In America it had just been a re-released hit as the theme of the successful Rob Reiner film, *Stand By Me*. In the States its re-release took the record to number 9, five places lower than it had managed in 1961, but it still became only the third record to hit the American Top 10 on two entirely different occasions. Chubby Checker's *The Twist* and Bobby 'Boris' Pickett's *Monster Mash* had previously performed this feat.

Ben E King, born Benjamin Earl Nelson in North Carolina in 1938, first sang professionally with the New York group, the Crowns. In 1959 they were signed to Atlantic as the Drifters, and Ben E King became the sixth singer in three years to sing lead on a Drifters single. The new Drifters' first single was *There Goes My Baby* which failed to chart in Britain despite climbing to number 2 in America. King's supreme moment with the Drifters was his wonderful lead vocal on *Save The Last Dance For Me* late in 1960. The record climbed to number 2 in Britain and one place higher in their homeland. Even before it reached the top of the charts, King had left the Drifters to go solo. He kicked off his career with what became a standard, *Spanish Harlem*, backed with a lesser tune called *First Taste Of Love*, which was the hit side in England. Then came *Stand By Me*, a record that was covered with remarkable lack of success by Cassius Clay, aka Muhammad Ali, and later taken into the British charts by such diverse talents as Kenny Lynch and John Lennon.

586

EVERYTHING I OWN

BOY GEORGE

14 March 1987, for two weeks

●●

Virgin BOY 100

Written by David Gates. Produced by Steve Levine.

Since his peak of success as lead singer of Culture Club, life had treated George O'Dowd very badly indeed. A very highly

Boy George *may not have realized he was singing a tribute to one of David Gates' deceased relatives*

publicized and self-destructive involvement with drugs kept Boy George on the front pages of the tabloids for weeks, during which time it seemed not only his career but his life was damaged beyond repair. Boy George had other ideas.

Covering the David Gates song that Ken Boothe had already taken to number one twelve and a half years earlier (see no. 359), Boy George rose rapidly to the top, to make *Everything I Own* the 11th song to hit number one in two different versions. It was also the first of those 11 songs which did not hit the top at the time it first charted. The original version, by writer Gates' group Bread, peaked at number 32 two years before Ken Boothe's reggae-tinged version climbed to number one. Boy George borrowed the Boothe arrangement rather than a slice of the Bread version.

Culture Club was by now officially dead, but Boy George was launched on a successful solo career. With *Everything I Own* he became the first male soloist known professionally only by his first name to top the charts, and by the end of 1987 he had racked up four single hits, including the aptly-titled Christmas hit *To Be Reborn*.

587

RESPECTABLE

MEL AND KIM

28 March 1987, for one week

●

Supreme SUPE 111

Written by Mike Stock, Matt Aitken and Peter Waterman. Produced by Mike Stock, Matt Aitken and Peter Waterman.

The first official Stock/Aitken/Waterman production to hit the very top was the second chart single for London born sisters Mel and Kim Appleby. Kim, born in 1962, is the elder by five years, but both got their start in show business through modelling assignments. In Mel's case, the most publicized sessions were for *Penthouse* and *Mayfair* magazines which do not feature a lot of clothing in most of their photographs. The mastermind of Mel's brief but sensational career in front of the camera was her mother Gladys, who originally sent snaps of her daughter to a national newspaper. Sister Kim was at the time working in a clothes factory, which was obviously of little use to Mel, who preferred the night clubs of London's West End. 'We were very streetwise', she says of her life before Stock, Aitken and Waterman.

Their first hit was *Showing Out (Get Fresh At The Weekend),* which peaked at number 3 late in 1986. That was followed by *Respectable,* which in turn was followed by their appearance on the Ferry Aid single, with which they knocked themselves off the top. Their third single was the title track from their first album, *F.L.M.,* which gave them their third Top 10 hit. Life for Mel and Kim was indeed Fun, Love and Money.

588

LET IT BE

FERRY AID

4 April 1987, for three weeks

● ● ●

Sun AID 1

Written by John Lennon and Paul McCartney. Produced by Mike Stock, Matt Aitken and Pete Waterman.

The sixth charity number one was in aid of the relatives and dependents of the victims of the Zeebrugge Ferry disaster. The Townsend Thorensen ship, 'Herald of Free Enterprise' capsized on 6 March 1987, killing almost 200 people. Ferry Aid was organized by the *Sun* newspaper, several of whose readers were on board the doomed ship as a result of a cheap travel offer the Sun had run. The single contributed over £700,000 pounds to the Fund.

The hit itself created several chart records. It entered at number one, the third charity disc to do so, but lasted only seven weeks on the chart in all, equalling the shortest chart run ever by a number one. It gave Stock, Aitken and Waterman their second consecutive number one as producers, and it gave Lennon his 27th number one as a writer and McCartney his 26th, to stretch them even further ahead of the pack. It also became the only song originally released as a single by the Beatles to enjoy a higher chart placing in the cover version. The Beatles *Let It Be* had peaked at number two.

Among the number one hitmakers who made up Ferry Aid were Paul McCartney, Mel and Kim (who thus knocked themselves off the top), Kate Bush, Boy George, Suzi Quatro, Alvin Stardust, Bonnie Tyler, Bucks Fizz, Dr and the Medics, Frankie Goes To Hollywood and the New Seekers. Other stars singing along included Kim Wilde, Edwin Starr and Mark Knopfler.

589

LA ISLA BONITA

MADONNA

25 April 1987, for two weeks

● ●

Sire W 8378

Written by Madonna and Patrick Leonard. Produced by Madonna and Patrick Leonard.

Madonna's third number one from *True Blue* finally established her as the all-time distaff champ. Her career total of four put her out on her own ahead of Sandie Shaw as far as solo performers were concerned and

of Debbie Harry writer-wise. The co-writer and co-producer of *La Isla Bonita,* and keyboard player on the track was Patrick Leonard, the third male partner for the lady in these two departments in four chart-toppers. Guitarist Bruce Gaitsch was given a writing credit on the album version of *La Isla Bonita* but not on the single, hence his non-inclusion in the singles credits above.

La Isla Bonita is a lament for a little island, San Pedro, which appears to be within the tropics and, of course, Spanish or Spanish-speaking. There is no San Pedro island listed in the Times Atlas of the World, which includes some extremely obscure places, so one must assume that the island is either a figment of Madonna's imagination or very small indeed.

Madonna undertook a world tour in 1987 which included concerts at London and Leeds in Britain. The UK press gave her more space and attention than they normally allotted to all the members of the Royal Family combined. Her music received only a small proportion of the coverage, often being ignored by journalists who were more interested in watching her jog or in her marital problems. Anyone taking time to listen to the *True Blue* album properly would realize that that approach to Madonna was unjustified. Underneath all the hoopla was a talented professional very much in control.

590

NOTHING'S GONNA STOP US NOW

STARSHIP

9 May 1987, for four weeks

● ● ● ●

Grunt FB 49757

Written by Diane Warren and Albert Hammond. Produced by Narada Michael Walden.

Narada Michael Walden's production of Starship's *Nothing's Gonna Stop Us Now,* from the hit movie *Mannequin,* marked a remarkable triumph for Starship's lead singer, Grace Slick (born 10 October 1939). Like the Grateful Dead, who achieved their first ever

American Top 10 album in 1987, Grace Slick was at the peak of her fame 20 years earlier as lead singer with Jefferson Airplane, the West Coast hippie band of the late '60s. Jefferson Airplane never had a hit single in Britain despite a succession of classic releases, two of which *(White Rabbit* and *Somebody To Love)* reached the Top 10 in America. After two massive albums, *Surrealistic Pillow* and *After Bathing At Baxter's,* the band wound down and gradually evolved into Jefferson Starship, led by Slick and Paul Kantner (born 3 March 1941), with former Airplane colleague Marty Balin (born 30 January 1943) back in evidence by the time their 1974 album *Dragonfly* was released. In 1975, Balin's composition *Miracles* took Jefferson Starship to number 3 in the American singles chart, but there were still no ripples on this side of the Atlantic.

In 1980 Jefferson Starship finally broke into the British charts with their fifth American hit *Jane,* which levelled out at number 21. In 1985 they changed their name yet again, to Starship, and kicked off with consecutive American number ones, *We Built This City* and *Sara.* Both records were hits in Britain, but neither made the Top 10. In 1987 Starship scored their third American chart-topper and their first in Britain. The title of the song was right for Grace Slick and co., *Nothing's Gonna Stop Us Now.* Grace became the oldest woman ever to sing lead on a UK number one.

the producer's chair for most of the tracks. The first single from the new album was the 33-letter title *I Wanna Dance With Somebody (Who Loves Me),* which gave Walden his second consecutive number one production and his third of the year. When Stock, Aitken and Waterman equalled Walden's feat later in the year, 1987 became the first year since 1963 in which two production teams had each produced number ones for three different acts.

I Wanna Dance With Somebody (Who Loves Me) featured several famous names behind the Houston vocals. Apart from Narada Michael Walden himself on drums, Michael's brother Randy Jackson played bass synth, and 1975 *Swing Your Daddy* hit-maker Jim Gilstrap sang back-up vocals. Other tracks on the album featured Kenny G on sax, Jellybean in the production booth and Roy Ayers on vibes. Whitney's version of the 545th number one *I Know Him So Well,* the final track on side two of the album, was a duet with her mother Cissy Houston. The singles culled from *Whitney* to follow up her second chart-topper were also successful. *Didn't We Almost Have It All?* hit the Top 20 and *So Emotional* climbed into the Top 5. *Whitney* was the first album in history to enter both the UK and US LP lists at number one. (Weeks later *Bad* duplicated this feat.)

Firm back into the charts at number 74. Loosely based on an old German folk-song, *I Am The Music Man, Star Trekkin'* put to music the antics of the Starship Enterprise from the television and film series *Star Trek.* All the same, most people would have felt that a song with a tune as subtle as a nursery rhyme and with lyrics about 'klingons on the starboard bow' and 'life, Jim, but not as we know it' was unlikely to boldly go where only 591 records had gone before – namely to the very top.

But the Firm did just that. The next week the record had soared to number 13, a rise of 61 places, the second biggest climb in the history of the charts. One week later it hit the top spot, becoming only the 20th record to rise from outside the Top 10 straight to number one. It also beat the chart record set by Charlene's *I've Never Been To Me* (see no. 503) which had entered the charts at number 73, the lowest original chart entry by a number one until the Firm rewrote the record books. Whether the Firm will put together any more such revolutionary singles in the future remains to be seen. After *Star Trekkin'* dropped out of orbit their chart career slipped into a Black Hole for the rest of 1987.

593

IT'S A SIN

PET SHOP BOYS

4 July 1987, for three weeks

● ● ●

Parlophone R 6158

Written by Neil Tennant and Chris Lowe. Produced by Julian Mendelsohn and Stephen Hague.

It's A Sin was written at the same time as the Pet Shop Boys' previous chart-topper *West End Girls* (see no.863), but was not issued until 18 months later. It was the first track released from their album *Actually* and stormed to the top in only its second week on the chart. By topping the charts for a second time the Pet Shop Boys became only the third male duo ever to hit the top more than once, but they remain a long way behind the Everly Brothers and Wham!, both of whom have four chart-toppers to their credit. Those who wish to count T Rex as a duo would also add them to that list of quadruple chart-toppers.

591

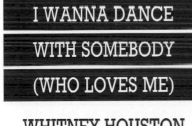

I WANNA DANCE WITH SOMEBODY (WHO LOVES ME)

WHITNEY HOUSTON

6 June 1987, for two weeks

● ●

Arista RIS 1

Written by George Merrill and Shannon Rubicam. Produced by Narada Michael Walden.

To follow her massive album *Whitney Houston* Miss Houston recorded the album *Whitney* with Narada Michael Walden in

592

STAR TREKKIN'

THE FIRM

20 June 1987, for two weeks

● ●

Bark TREK 1

Written by Grahame Lister and John O'Connor. Produced by Grahame Lister and John O'Connor.

The Firm first hit the charts in 1982 with their song in praise of the George Cole character from the TV series *Minder, Arthur Daley (E's Alright).* The song was so obviously a one-off hit that no chart fan was surprised when five years went by without further contributions to *British Hit Singles* by the Firm. But on 6 June 1987 another song based on a long-running television series brought the

Although *It's A Sin* is an out and out disco stomper, it has a serious lyric, inspired by vocalist Neil Tennant's strict Catholic upbringing. His school, St. Cuthbert's Grammar School in Newcastle upon Tyne, may have been a strictly religious one, but it has also become known as something of a breeding ground for pop stars, as Gordon Sumner, aka Sting, was a pupil there a few years before Tennant.

'A real over-the-top Pet Shop Boys record' is how Tennant describes his second chart-topper. 'When we were making it we did not apply any notions of taste.' The accompanying video was directed by Derek Jarman in the same vein, with hooded monks, a church consumed by fire and cameos of the seven deadly sins. Their next single, a number 2 hit featuring Dusty Springfield, was perhaps aptly titled *What Have I Done To Deserve This?*

594

WHO'S THAT GIRL

MADONNA

25 July 1987, for one week

●

Sire W 8341

Written by Madonna and Patrick Leonard. Produced by Madonna and Patrick Leonard.

Madonna's lead over the field as the all-time female number one champ was extended yet further when the title track from her 1987 movie *Who's That Girl* became her fifth British chart-topper, as writer, performer and producer. In all three categories all other solo females trail her.

Who's That Girl was a comedy featuring Griffin Dunne and Sir John Mills. The latter's closest personal links with the hit parade

Los Lobos, *Spanish for 'the wolves'.*

had come in 1962 with his daughter Hayley's transatlantic smash *Let's Get Together*. The new film was Madonna's second successive box-office disappointment. Her quite staggering popularity on disc cut no ice with the critics and their lack of enthusiasm was somehow conveyed to the public. Vincent Canby, film critic of *The New York Times,* wrote a perceptive piece arguing that the essence of Madonna's screen persona had already been captured in her videos, most notably *Open Your Heart.*

For all that the single could hardly have been bigger. It kicked off the soundtrack album which contained three other Madonna titles plus numbers from Duncan Faure, Club Nouveau, Michael Davidson, Scritti Politti and Coati Mundi, and this too was a hefty seller.

595

LA BAMBA

LOS LOBOS

1 August 1987, for two weeks

● ●

Slash/FFRR/London LASH 13

A traditional song, arranged by Ritchie Valens. Produced by Mitchell Froom.

Los Lobos are five Spanish Americans whose revival of the Ritchie Valens classic *La Bamba* was the first song ever sung completely in Spanish to top the charts. Julio Iglesias' *Begin The Beguine* (see no. 490) was mainly in Spanish, but *La Bamba* was the first chart-topper since the infamous *Je T'Aime . . . Moi Non Plus* (see no. 277) to be performed entirely in a foreign language. It was the title song from the biopic about Ritchie Valens, who died aged 17 in the plane crash that also killed Buddy Holly and the Big Bopper. By taking over at the top from Madonna's *Who's That Girl,* also a film title song, the British charts had consecutive number ones from the movies for the first time since *Summer Holiday* (see no. 148) was succeeded by *Foot Tapper* (see no. 149) almost a quarter of a century earlier.

The song had, surprisingly, not been a hit for Valens the first time around, and its only previous appearance on the British charts had been in 1964, when the Crickets took the song to number 21 as their final hit. The

Valens version did enjoy a few weeks of chart glory in the summer of 1987 in the wake of Los Lobos' success, and this chart reappearance by the late rock star, 28 years and 142 days after his previous chart entry, created a gap between hits only exceeded by Eartha Kitt.

596

I JUST CAN'T STOP

LOVING YOU

MICHAEL JACKSON WITH SIEDAH GARRETT

15 August 1987, for two weeks

● ●

Epic 6502027

Written by Michael Jackson. Produced by Quincy Jones and Michael Jackson.

Michael Jackson's third solo number one was not a solo hit at all. Taken from *Bad,* the follow-up album to his all-time best seller *Thriller, I Just Can't Stop Loving You* featured Jacko in duet with Siedah Garrett, a fact that was mentioned on the single record sleeve but not on the label itself. Siedah Garrett had earlier sung without credit on Dennis Edwards' 1984 hit *Don't Look Any Further,* so she was no doubt accustomed to lack of recognition by now. She was also used to the number one spot. Although Michael Jackson had been there four times before (twice solo, once with the Jacksons and once with USA For Africa), so had Siedah Garrett. She had sung backing vocals on all of Madonna's chart-toppers except her very first, *Into The Groove* (see no. 554), and had last been at the top of the charts only two weeks earlier when *Who's That Girl* (see no. 594) was ruling the roost. Miss Garrett featured on all the tracks on Madonna's *True Blue* album except for *White Heat,* which was the only track on the LP to feature Michael's brother, Jackie Jackson, on background vocals. It was only by chance that Michael rather than Jackie was thus the first Jackson she sang with.

Michael Jackson's third number one was rapidly followed by a number 3 hit when the title track from *Bad* was released a few weeks later. Sister Janet also hit the Top 10 again in 1987 when her *Let's Wait A While* climbed to number 3 as one of seven singles from her album, *Control.* The Jackson family have few rivals to the title of Most Charted Family, although by the end of 1987 the leader of their greatest competition in that category, Donny Osmond, was back in the chart after a 13-year gap with *Groove.*

597

NEVER GONNA GIVE YOU UP

RICK ASTLEY

29 August 1987, for five weeks

● ● ● ● ●

RCA PB 41447

Written by Mike Stock, Matt Aitken and Peter Waterman. Produced by Mike Stock, Matt Aitken and Peter Waterman.

Rick Astley, born in the Lancashire town of Newton-le-Willows on 6 February 1966, became the third act shaped by the hot production team of Stock, Aitken and Waterman to hit the top in 1987. Like the first of those acts, Mel and Kim (see no. 587), Rick Astley also appeared as part of the second act, Ferry Aid (see no. 588), but being a complete unknown at the time did not get any part of the label credit. *Never Gonna Give You Up* had already been made and was living in the can. It was recorded in October 1986 and mixed on New Year's Day 1987, then held for release until summer. By the time it had kept all competition at bay for five weeks, the longest stay on top since Jennifer Rush's *The Power Of Love,* the record had outsold all other singles of 1987. His second single, *Whenever You Need Somebody,* crashed into the chart at number 11, many commentators speculated that it would be the 600th number one, but it could only climb to number 3. After his appearance on the Miss World TV show in November it went back to number 3 and *Never Gonna Give You Up* re-entered the Top 40.

Astley had graduated from playing drums to singing lead with a band called FBI, the same progression Phil Collins made through Genesis. Rick was spotted by Peter Waterman in a Warrington club in 1985.

598

PUMP UP THE VOLUME/ANITINA (THE FIRST TIME I SEE SHE DANCE)

M/A/R/R/S

3 October 1987, for two weeks

● ●

4 AD AD 707

Written by (*Pump Up The Volume*) Steven and Martyn Young/A.R.Kane/C.J.Mackintosh/John Fryer/Dave Darrell, (*Anitina*) A.R.Kane/Colourbox. Produced by (*Pump Up The Volume*) Martyn Young, (*Anitina*). Produced by Martin Young.

The legal profession looked set to become the prime beneficiary of the dance smash *Pump Up The Volume* created by members of two groups signed to the avant-garde label 4AD, home of the Cocteau Twins, the Birthday Party, This Mortal Coil, Colourbox and A.R. Kane, among others. M/A/R/R/S was an amalgamation of the two last-named acts plus scratch deejay C.J. Mackintosh, under the supervision of Colourbox producer/leader Martyn Young.

The aspect of the record that excited lawyers was the fact that *Pump Up The Volume* sampled sounds from other recordings. This technique, the electronic process of lifting sounds from one record and inserting them into another, had become a common feature of dance records by 1987. The trouble with *Pump Up The Volume* was that Pete Waterman of the phenomenally successful Stock-Aitken-Waterman production team (see nos 587, 588, 597) felt that Martyn Young's use of a second or two of a Stock-Aitken-Waterman hit (under their own name) *Roadblock* was a breach of their copyright. When Young in retaliation claimed that SAW had nicked some of *Pump Up The Volume* on a re-mix of a dance hit by Sybil, battle was joined. At one point an injunction placed by Waterman on the M/A/R/R/S single prevented *Pump Up The Volume* from being distributed for five days. This almost certainly kept Stock-Aitken-

Rick Astley *had the best-selling number one of 1987.*

Waterman protégé Rick Astley (see no. 597) on top for one more week than might otherwise have been the case, though of course this had not been the motive behind Waterman's injunction.

Anitina... was listed as being at number one together with this controversial slice of sound but clearly *Pump Up The Volume* was the side that sold the single. M/A/R/R/S have apparently expressed a desire to remain one-hit wonders stating they would credit future singles to different planets.

599

YOU WIN AGAIN

THE BEE GEES

17 October 1987, for four weeks

● ● ● ●

Warner Brothers W8351

Written by Barry, Robin and Maurice Gibb. Produced by Arif Mardin with Barry, Robin and Maurice Gibb, co-produced by Brian Tench.

The return of the Bee Gees to the top of the charts eight years and 215 days after their previous, fourth, number one (see no. 434) established more chart records fot the Manx-born Gibb brotherhood. Only five acts have ever suffered through a lean period of more than seven years between number one hits, and when *You Win Again* climbed to the top, the Bee Gees did it for the second time. The gap between their second and a third number ones had been even longer, 9 years and 231 days. *You Win Again,* the first single release from their album *E.S.P.,* finally fell from the top 20 years and 34 days after their first chart-topper, *Massachusetts* (see no. 238) reached number one, making them only the third act, after Elvis and Cliff, to achieve a 20-year span of number one hits. The record was the seventh number one written by Barry and Robin Gibb (and the sixth for Maurice), putting Barry and Robin behind only Lennon, McCartney, Andersson and Ulvaeus on the all time list of successful writers. The three brothers in harness, with six co-written number ones, rank behind only the Lennon/McCartney and Jagger/Richard partnerships.

You Win Again stayed on top for four weeks, equalling the longest run at number one by any Bee Gees hit, and bringing them level with Rod Stewart and T Rex at the top of the list of acts who have hit number one on the most labels – three.

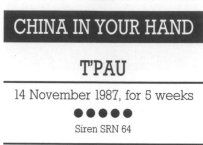

600

CHINA IN YOUR HAND

T'PAU

14 November 1987, for 5 weeks

● ● ● ● ●

Siren SRN 64

Written by Carol Decker and Ron Rogers. Produced by Roy Thomas Baker.

Thirty-five years to the day after the British charts were first published in the *New Musical Express* the Shropshire band T'Pau

T'Pau *held off George* (Got My Mind Set On You) *Harrison to claim Britain's 600th number one.*

claimed the six hundredth number one with the third release from their debut album *Bridge Of Spies.* Named after Mr Spock's Vulcan friend in the *Star Trek* TV series T'Pau took tapes of their album to most of the record companies in Britain. They were turned down many times before being signed by Siren, a Virgin company. At first it seemed that most of the record companies in Britain were right to have turned T'Pau down, because when their first single, *Heart And Soul,* was released in January 1987, it sank more rapidly than the Titanic and a second single also failed. However *Heart And Soul* went Top 5 in America. This success bounced back across the Atlantic and T'Pau had a re-promoted smash in their home country.

T'Pau are songwriters Carol Decker (vocals) and Ron Rogers (rhythm guitar and some bits), Tim Burgess (drums and percussion), Michael Chetwood (keyboards), Paul Jackson (bass) and native Shropshire lad Taj Wyzgowski (who plays 'guitar solos and other bits'). When *China In Your Hand* leapt from number 5 to number one on 14 November, producer Roy Thomas Baker achieved a chart-topper for the first time since *Bohemian Rhapsody* 12 years earlier.

PART

2

The Six Hundred Number Ones Listed Alphabetically By Artist

The information given in this part of the book is as follows: the date that the record first reached number one, the title, label, catalogue number and the number of weeks at number one.

We have also listed acts under the name they used for their number one hits, which is not necessarily their usual styling. For example, Ian Dury is listed under 'Ian And The Blockheads', which is how he was billed for *Hit Me With Your Rhythm Stick*. Cross-reference will also be found under 'Blockheads' and 'Ian Dury'.

─────────────── **A** ───────────────

ABBA *Sweden/Norway male/female vocal/ instrumental group*

4 May 74	WATERLOO	Epic EPC 2240	2 wks
31 Jan 76	MAMMA MIA	Epic EPC 3790	2 wks
8 May 76	FERNANDO	Epic EPC 4036	4 wks
4 Sep 76	DANCING QUEEN	Epic EPC 4499	6 wks
2 Apr 77	KNOWING ME KNOWING YOU	Epic EPC 4955	5 wks
5 Nov 77	THE NAME OF THE GAME	Epic EPC 5750	4 wks
18 Feb 78	TAKE A CHANCE ON ME	Epic EPC 5950	3 wks
9 Aug 80	THE WINNER TAKES IT ALL	Epic EPC 8835	2 wks
20 Nov 80	SUPER TROUPER	Epic EPC 9089	3 wks

ACES *– see Desmond DEKKER & THE ACES*

ADAM and the ANTS *UK, male vocal/ instrumental group*

9 May 81	STAND AND DELIVER	CBS A 1065	5 wks
19 Sep 81	PRINCE CHARMING	CBS A 1408	4 wks
12 Jun 82	GOODY TWO SHOES	CBS A 2367	2 wks

A-HA *Norway, male vocal/instrumental group*

25 Jan 86	THE SUN ALWAYS SHINES ON T.V.	Warner Bros W8846	2 wks

ALTHIA and DONNA *Jamaica, female vocal duo*

4 Feb 78	UP TOWN TOP RANKING	Lightning LIG 506	1 wk

AMEN CORNER *UK, male vocal/instrumental group*

12 Feb 69	(IF PARADISE IS) HALF AS NICE	Immediate IM 073	2 wks

ANEKA *UK, female vocalist*

29 Aug 81	JAPANESE BOY	Hansa/Ariola HANSA 5	1 wk

ANIMALS *UK, male vocal/instrumental group*

9 Jul 64	HOUSE OF THE RISING SUN	Columbia DB 7301	1 wk

Paul ANKA *Canada, male vocalist*

30 Aug 57	DIANA	Columbia DB 3980	9 wks

ANTS *– see ADAM and the ANTS*

ARCHIES *US, male/female vocal group*

25 Oct 69	SUGAR SUGAR	RCA 1872	8 wks

Louis ARMSTRONG *US, male vocalist*

24 Apr 68	WHAT A WONDERFUL WORLD/CABARET	HMV POP 1615	4 wks

Rick ASTLEY *UK, male vocalist*

29 Aug 87	NEVER GONNA GIVE YOU UP	RCA PB 41447	5 wks

Winifred ATWELL *UK, female instrumentalist – piano*

3 Dec 54	LET'S HAVE ANOTHER PARTY	Philips PB 268	5 wks
13 Apr 56	POOR PEOPLE OF PARIS	Decca F 10681	3 wks

Charles AZNAVOUR *France, male vocalist*

29 Jun 74	SHE	Barclay BAR 26	4 wks

─────────────── **B** ───────────────

BACCARA *Spain, female vocal duo*

29 Oct 77	YES SIR, I CAN BOOGIE	RCA PB 5526	1 wk

BACHELORS *Ireland, male vocal group*

20 Feb 64	DIANE	Decca F 11799	1 wk

Philip BAILEY *US, male vocalist*

23 Mar 85	EASY LOVER	CBS A 4915	4 wks

Billed 'with Phil Collins'. See also Phil COLLINS

Long John BALDRY *UK, male vocalist*

22 Nov 67	LET THE HEARTACHES BEGIN	Pye 7N 17385	2 wks

BAND AID *International, male/female vocal/ instrumental charity group*

15 Dec 84	DO THEY KNOW IT'S CHRISTMAS?	Mercury FEED 1	5 wks

J J BARRIE *Canada, male vocalist*

5 Jun 76	NO CHARGE	Power Exchange PX 209	1 wk

Shirley BASSEY *UK, female vocalist*

20 Feb 59	AS I LOVE YOU	Philips PB 845	4 wks
21 Sept 61	REACH FOR THE STARS/CLIMB EV'RY MOUNTAIN	Columbia DB 4685	1 wk

BAY CITY ROLLERS *UK, male vocal/ instrumental group*

22 Mar 75	BYE BYE BABY	Bell 1409	6 wks
19 Jul 75	GIVE A LITTLE LOVE	Bell 1425	3 wks

BEACH BOYS *US, male vocal/instrumental group*

17 Nov 66	GOOD VIBRATIONS	Capitol CL 15475	2 wks
28 Aug 68	DO IT AGAIN	Capitol CL 15554	1 wk

BEAKY *– see Dave DEE, DOZY, BEAKY, MICK and TICH*

BEATLES *UK, male vocal/instrumental group*

2 May 63	FROM ME TO YOU	Parlophone R 5015	7 wks
12 Sep 63	SHE LOVES YOU	Parlophone R 5055	4 wks
28 Nov 63	SHE LOVES YOU	Parlophone R 5055	2 wks
12 Dec 63	I WANT TO HOLD YOUR HAND	Parlophone R 5084	5 wks
2 Apr 64	CAN'T BUY ME LOVE	Parlophone R 5114	3 wks
23 Jul 64	A HARD DAY'S NIGHT	Parlophone R 5160	3 wks
10 Dec 64	I FEEL FINE	Parlophone R 5200	5 wks
22 Apr 65	TICKET TO RIDE	Parlophone R 5265	3 wks
5 Aug 65	HELP!	Parlophone R 5305	3 wks
16 Dec 65	DAY TRIPPER/WE CAN WORK IT OUT	Parlophone R 5389	5 wks
23 Jun 66	PAPERBACK WRITER	Parlophone R 5452	2 wks
18 Aug 66	YELLOW SUBMARINE/ELEANOR RIGBY	Parlophone R 5493	4 wks
19 Jul 67	ALL YOU NEED IS LOVE	Parlophone R 5620	3 wks
6 Dec 67	HELLO GOODBYE	Parlophone R 5655	7 wks
27 Mar 68	LADY MADONNA	Parlophone R 5675	2 wks
11 Sep 68	HEY JUDE	Apple R 5722	2 wks
23 Apr 69	GET BACK	Apple R 5777	6 wks

11 Jun 69   THE BALLAD OF JOHN AND YOKO.................................
                                              Apple R 5786   3 wks
Get Back is 'with Billy Preston'. See also George HARRISON, John LENNON, Paul McCARTNEY, Paul McCARTNEY with Stevie WONDER, WINGS

BEE GEES *UK, male vocal/instrumental group*
11 Oct 67   MASSACHUSETTS...................... Polydor 56 192   4 wks
4 Sep 68   I'VE GOTTA GET A MESSAGE TO YOU.......................
                                              Polydor 56 273   1 wk
29 Apr 78   NIGHT FEVER................................ RSO 002   2 wks
3 Mar 79   TRAGEDY....................................... RSO 27   2 wks
17 Oct 87   YOU WIN AGAIN.................... Warner Bros W 8351   4 wks

Harry BELAFONTE *US, male vocalist*
22 Nov 57   MARY'S BOY CHILD............................. RCA 1022   7 wks

Tony BENNETT *US, male vocalist*
13 May 55   STRANGER IN PARADISE............... Philips PB 420   2 wks

BERLIN *US, male/female vocal/instrumental group*
8 Nov 86   TAKE MY BREATH AWAY................. CBS A 7320   4 wks

Chuck BERRY *US, male vocalist/instrumentalist – guitar*
25 Nov 72   MY DING-A-LING............................ Chess 6145 019   4 wks

Nick BERRY *UK, male vocalist*
18 Oct 86   EVERY LOSER WINS.................. BBC RESL 204   3 wks

Jane BIRKIN & Serge GAINSBOURG *UK/France female/male vocal duo*
11 Oct 69   JE T'AIME ... MOI NON PLUS.........................
                                              Major Minor MM 645   1 wk

Cilla BLACK *UK, female vocalist*
27 Feb 64   ANYONE WHO HAD A HEART..........................
                                              Parlophone R 5101   3 wks
28 May 64   YOU'RE MY WORLD.................. Parlophone R 5133   4 wks

BLOCKHEADS   *– see IAN and the BLOCKHEADS*

BLONDIE *US/UK, female/male vocal/instrumental group*
3 Feb 79   HEART OF GLASS.................... Chrysalis CHE 2275   4 wks
26 May 79   SUNDAY GIRL.................... Chrysalis CHS 2320   3 wks
1 Mar 80   ATOMIC............................. Chrysalis CHS 2410   2 wks
26 Apr 80   CALL ME.......................... Chrysalis CHS 2414   1 wk
15 Nov 80   THE TIDE IS HIGH.............. Chrysalis CHS 2465   2 wks

BLUE FLAMES   *– see Georgie FAME*

BONEY M *West Indies, male/female vocal group*
13 May 78   RIVERS OF BABYLON.......... Atlantic/Hansa K 11120   5 wks
9 Dec 78   MARY'S BOY CHILD – OH MY LORD (medley)............
                                              Atlantic/Hansa K 11221   4 wks

BOOMTOWN RATS *Ireland, male vocal/instrumental group*
18 Nov 78   RAT TRAP.......................... Ensign ENY 16   2 wks
28 Jul 79   I DON'T LIKE MONDAYS............. Ensign ENY 30   4 wks

Pat BOONE *US, male vocalist*
15 Jun 56   I'LL BE HOME................. London HLD 8253   5 wks

Ken BOOTHE *Jamaica, male vocalist*
26 Oct 74   EVERYTHING I OWN................. Trojan TR 7920   3 wks

David BOWIE *UK, male vocalist*
8 Nov 75   SPACE ODDITY........................ RCA 2593   2 wks
23 Aug 80   ASHES TO ASHES.................. RCA BOW 6   2 wks
9 Apr 83   LET'S DANCE............ EMI America EA 152   3 wks
See also David BOWIE and Mick JAGGER, QUEEN and David BOWIE

David BOWIE and Mick JAGGER *UK, male vocal duo*
7 Sep 85   DANCING IN THE STREET... EMI America EA 204   4 wks
See also David BOWIE, QUEEN and David BOWIE, ROLLING STONES

BOY GEORGE *UK, male vocalist*
14 Mar 87   EVERYTHING I OWN................ Virgin BOY 100   2 wks
See also CULTURE CLUB

BRIAN and MICHAEL *UK, male vocal duo*
8 Apr 78   MATCHSTALK MEN AND MATCHSTALK CATS AND DOGS........................ Pye 7N 46035   3 wks

BROTHERHOOD OF MAN *UK, male/female vocal group*
27 Mar 76   SAVE YOUR KISSES FOR ME.......... Pye 7N 45569   6 wks
20 Aug 77   ANGELO............................ Pye 7N 45699   1 wk
11 Feb 78   FIGARO............................ Pye 7N 46037   1 wk

Crazy World Of Arthur BROWN *UK, male vocal/instrumental group*
14 Aug 68   FIRE............................. Track 604022   1 wk

BUCKS FIZZ *UK, male/female vocal group*
18 Apr 81   MAKING YOUR MIND UP.............. RCA 56   3 wks
16 Jan 82   LAND OF MAKE BELIEVE........... RCA 163   2 wks
17 Apr 82   MY CAMERA NEVER LIES........... RCA 202   1 wk

BUGGLES *UK, male vocal duo*
20 Oct 79   VIDEO KILLED THE RADIO STAR.......................
                                              Island WIP 6524   1 wk

B. BUMBLE and the STINGERS *US, male instrumental group*
17 May 62   NUT ROCKER................. Top Rank JAR 611   1 wk

Kate BUSH *UK, female vocalist*
11 Mar 78   WUTHERING HEIGHTS............ EMI 2719   4 wks

BYRDS *US, male vocal/instrumental group*
22 Jul 65   MR TAMBOURINE MAN.............. CBS 201765   2 wks

— C —

Eddie CALVERT *UK, male instrumentalist – trumpet*
8 Jan 54   OH MEIN PAPA.................. Columbia DB 3337   9 wks
27 May 55   CHERRY PINK AND APPLE BLOSSOM WHITE...........
                                              Columbia DB 3581   4 wks

CAPTAIN SENSIBLE *UK, male vocalist*
3 Jul 82   HAPPY TALK...................... A&M CAP 1   2 wks

Irene CARA *US, female vocalist*
17 Jul 82   FAME............................ RSO 90   3 wks

David CASSIDY *US, male vocalist*
30 Sep 72   HOW CAN I BE SURE................ Bell 1258   2 wks
27 Oct 73   DAYDREAMER/THE PUPPY SONG...... Bell 1334   3 wks

CHARLENE *US, female vocalist*
26 June 82   I'VE NEVER BEEN TO ME.......... Motown TMG 1260   1 wk

Ray CHARLES *US, male vocalist/instrumentalist – piano*
12 Jul 62   I CAN'T STOP LOVING YOU......... HMV POP 1034   2 wks

Tina CHARLES *UK, female vocalist*
6 Mar 76   I LOVE TO LOVE (BUT MY BABY LOVES TO DANCE)................CBS 3937   3 wks

CHECKMATES   *– see Emile FORD and the CHECKMATES*

CHER   *– see SONNY and CHER*

CHICAGO *US, male vocal/instrumental group*
16 Oct 76   IF YOU LEAVE ME NOW.............. CBS 4603   3 wks

CHICORY TIP *UK, male vocal/instrumental group*
19 Feb 72   SON OF MY FATHER................. CBS 7737   3 wks

CHRISTIE *UK, male vocal/instrumental group*
6 Jun 70   YELLOW RIVER..................... CBS 4911   1 wk

Petula CLARK *UK, female vocalist*
23 Feb 61   SAILOR........................... Pye 7N 15324   1 wk
16 Feb 67   THIS IS MY SONG.................. Pye 7N 17258   2 wks

Dave CLARK FIVE *UK, male vocal/instrumental group*
16 Jan 64   GLAD ALL OVER.................... Columbia DB 7154   2 wks

Rosemary CLOONEY *US, female vocalist*
26 Nov 54   THIS OLE HOUSE.................. Philips PB 336   1 wk
14 Jan 55   MAMBO ITALIANO.................. Philips PB 382   1 wk
4 Feb 55   MAMBO ITALIANO.................. Philips PB 382   2 wks

Eddie COCHRAN *US, male vocalist*
23 Jun 60   THREE STEPS TO HEAVEN....... London HLG 9115   2 wks

Joe COCKER *UK, male vocalist*
6 Nov 68   WITH A LITTLE HELP FROM MY FRIENDS.................
Regal-Zonophone RZ 3013   1 wk

COCKNEY REBEL   *– see Steve HARLEY and COCKNEY REBEL*

Alma COGAN *UK, female vocalist*
15 Jul 55   DREAMBOAT........................ HMV B 10872   2 wks

Dave and Ansil COLLINS *Jamaica, male vocal duo*
1 May 71   DOUBLE BARREL.................... Technique TE 901   2 wks

Phil COLLINS *UK, male vocalist*
15 Jan 83   YOU CAN'T HURRY LOVE............ Virgin VS 531   2 wks
See also Philip BAILEY

COMETS   *– see also BILL HALEY and his COMETS*

COMMODORES *US, male vocal/instrumental group*
19 Aug 78   THREE TIMES A LADY............. Motown TMG 1113   5 wks
See also Lionel RICHIE

COMMUNARDS *UK, male vocal/instrumental duo*
13 Sep 86   DON'T LEAVE ME THIS WAY.... London LON 103   4 wks
Billed as 'with Sarah Jane Morris', UK, female vocalist.

Perry COMO *US, male vocalist*
6 Feb 53   DON'T LET THE STARS GET IN YOUR EYES.............
HMV B 10400   5 wks
28 Feb 58   MAGIC MOMENTS................... RCA 1036   8 wks

Billy CONNOLLY *UK, male vocalist*
22 Nov 75   D.I.V.O.R.C.E..................Polydor 2058 652   1 wk

Russ CONWAY *UK, male instrumentalist – piano*
27 Mar 59   SIDE SADDLE.................. Columbia DB 4256   4 wks
19 Jun 59   ROULETTE....................Columbia DB 4298   2 wks

Alice COOPER *US, male vocalist*
12 Aug 72   SCHOOL'S OUT.................. Warner Brothers K 16188   3 wks

Don CORNELL *US, male vocalist*
8 Oct 54   HOLD MY HAND.................... Vogue Q 2013   4 wks
19 Nov 54   HOLD MY HAND.................. Vogue Q 2013   1 wk

Julie COVINGTON *UK, female vocalist*
12 Feb 77   DON'T CRY FOR ME ARGENTINA....... MCA 260   1 wk

Floyd CRAMER *US, male instrumentalist – piano*
18 May 61   ON THE REBOUND.................. RCA 1231   1 wk

CREEDENCE CLEARWATER REVIVAL *US, male vocal/instrumental group*
20 Sep 69   BAD MOON RISING.................... Liberty LBF 15230   3 wks

CRICKETS *US, male vocal/instrumental group*
1 Nov 57·   THAT'LL BE THE DAY............ Vogue Coral Q 72279   3 wks
See also Buddy HOLLY

CROWD *Multi-national male/female vocal/instrumental charity group*
15 Jun 85   YOU'LL NEVER WALK ALONE... Spartan BRAD 1   2 wks

CULTURE CLUB *UK, male vocal/instrumental group*
23 Oct 82   DO YOU REALLY WANT TO HURT ME......................
Virgin VS 518   3 wks
24 Sep 84   KARMA CHAMELEON.................... Virgin VS 612   6 wks
See also BOY GEORGE

—————————— **D** ——————————

DAKOTAS   *– see Billy J. KRAMER and the DAKOTAS*

Vic DAMONE *US, male vocalist*
27 Jun 58   ON THE STREET WHERE YOU LIVE............................
Philips PB 819   2 wks

DANA *UK, female vocalist*
18 Apr 70   ALL KINDS OF EVERYTHING............ Rex R 11054   2 wks

Bobby DARIN *US, male vocalist*
3 Jul 59   DREAM LOVER.......................... London HLE 8867   4 wks
16 Oct 59   MACK THE KNIFE...................... London HLE 8939   2 wks

Windsor DAVIES and Don ESTELLE *UK, male vocal duo*
7 Jun 75   WHISPERING GRASS........................... EMI 2290   3 wks

Spencer DAVIS GROUP *UK, male vocal/ instrumental group*
20 Jan 66   KEEP ON RUNNING......................... Fontana TF 632   1 wk
14 Apr 66   SOMEBODY HELP ME.................... Fontana TF 679   2 wks

DAWN *US, male/female vocal group*
15 May 71   KNOCK THREE TIMES....................... Bell 1146   5 wks
21 Apr 73   TIE A YELLOW RIBBON ROUND THE OLD OAK
             TREE................................ Bell 1287   4 wks

Doris DAY *US, female vocalist*
16 Apr 54   SECRET LOVE........................... Philips PB 230   1 wk
7 May 54   SECRET LOVE........................... Philips PB 230   8 wks
10 Aug 56   WHATEVER WILL BE WILL BE.... Philips PB 586   6 wks

Chris DE BURGH *Ireland, male vocalist*
2 Aug 86   THE LADY IN RED........................... A&M AM 331   3 wks

DEAD OR ALIVE *UK, male vocal/instrumental group*
9 Mar 85   YOU SPIN ME ROUND (LIKE A RECORD)....................
             Epic A 4861   2 WKS

Dave DEE, DOZY, BEAKY, MICK and TICH *UK, male vocal/instrumental group*
20 Mar 68   THE LEGEND OF XANADU............ Fontana TF 903   1 wk

Kiki DEE   *– see Elton JOHN and Kiki DEE*

Desmond DEKKER and the ACES *Jamaica, male vocal/instrumental group*
16 Apr 69   THE ISRAELITES........................... Pyramid PYR 6058   1 wk

John DENVER *US, male vocalist*
12 Oct 74   ANNIE'S SONG........................... RCA APBO 0295   1 wk

DETROIT SPINNERS *US, male vocal group*
12 Apr 80   WORKING MY WAY BACK TO YOU – FORGIVE
             ME GIRL........................... Atlantic K 11432   2 wks

DEXYS MIDNIGHT RUNNERS *UK, male vocal/instrumental group*
3 May 80   GENO................................... R 6033   2 wks
7 Aug 82   COME ON EILEEN.................... Mercury DEXYS 9   4 wks
Come On Eileen with EMERALD EXPRESS, UK, male/female vocal/instrumental group

Jim DIAMOND *UK, male vocalist*
1 Dec 84   I SHOULD HAVE KNOWN BETTER A&M AM 220   1 wk

Barbara DICKSON   *– see Elaine PAIGE and Barbara DICKSON*

DOCTOR and the MEDICS *UK, male/female vocal/instrumental group*
7 Jun 86   SPIRIT IN THE SKY............................... IRS IRM 113   3 wks

DR HOOK *US, male vocal/instrumental group*
17 Nov 79   WHEN YOU'RE IN LOVE WITH A BEAUTIFUL
             WOMAN........................... Capitol CL 16039   3 wks

Ken DODD *UK, male vocalist*
30 Sep 65   TEARS........................... Columbia DB 7659   5 wks

Joe DOLCE MUSIC THEATRE *US, male vocalist*
21 Feb 81   SHADDUP YOU FACE.................... Epic EPC 9518   3 wks

Lonnie DONEGAN *UK, male vocalist*
12 Apr 57   CUMBERLAND GAP.................... Pye Nixa B 15087   5 wks
28 Jun 57   GAMBLIN' MAN/PUTTING ON THE STYLE................
             Pye Nixa N 15093   2 wks
31 Mar 60   MY OLD MAN'S A DUSTMAN......... Pye 7N 15256   4 wks

DONNA   *– see ALTHIA and DONNA*

Carl DOUGLAS *UK, male vocalist*
21 Sep 74   KUNG FU FIGHTING.................... Pye 7N 45377   3 wks

Craig DOUGLAS *UK, male vocalist*
11 Sep 59   ONLY SIXTEEN........................... Top Rank JAR 159   4 wks

DOZY   *– see Dave DEE, DOZY, BEAKY, MICK and TICH*

DREAMWEAVERS *US, male/female vocal group*
16 Mar 56   IT'S ALMOST TOMORROW........ Brunswick 05515   2 wks
6 Apr 56   IT'S ALMOST TOMORROW............ Brunswick 05515   1 wk

Clive DUNN *UK, male vocalist*
9 Jan 71   GRANDAD........................... Columbia DB 8726   3 wks

DURAN DURAN *UK, male vocal/instrumental group*
26 Mar 83   IS THERE SOMETHING I SHOULD KNOW...............
             EMI 5371   2 wks
5 May 84   THE REFLEX........................... EMI DURAN 2   4 wks

Ian DURY   *– see IAN and the BLOCKHEADS*

———————— E ————————

EDISON LIGHTHOUSE *UK, male/female vocal/ instrumental group*
31 Jan 70   LOVE GROWS (WHERE MY ROSEMARY GOES)........
             Bell 1091   5 wks

Dave EDMUNDS *UK, male vocalist/multi-instrumentalist*
28 Nov 70   I HEAR YOU KNOCKIN'........................... MAM 1   6 wks

Tommy EDWARDS *US, male vocalist*
7 Nov 58   IT'S ALL IN THE GAME........................... MGM 989   3 wks

ELECTRIC LIGHT ORCHESTRA   *– see Olivia NEWTON-JOHN and ELECTRIC LIGHT ORCHESTRA*

EMERALD EXPRESS *– see DEXYS MIDNIGHT RUNNERS*

ENGLAND WORLD CUP SQUAD *UK, male vocal group*
16 May 70   BACK HOME..Pye 7N 17920   3 wks

EQUALS *UK, male vocal/instrumental group*
3 Jul 68   BABY COME BACK.........................President PT 135   3 wks
See also Eddy GRANT

David ESSEX *UK, male vocalist*
16 Nov 74   GONNA MAKE YOU A STAR................CBS 2492   3 wks
4 Oct 75   HOLD ME CLOSE.................................CBS 3572   3 wks

Don ESTELLE *– see Windsor DAVIES and Don ESTELLE*

EUROPE *Sweden, male vocal/instrumental group*
6 Dec 86   THE FINAL COUNTDOWN..............Epic A 7127   2 wks

EURYTHMICS *UK, female/male vocal/instrumental duo*
27 Jul 85   THERE MUST BE AN ANGEL (PLAYING WITH MY HEART)...................................RCA PB 40247   1 wk

EVANS *– see ZAGER and EVANS*

EVERLY BROTHERS *US male vocal/instrumental duo*
4 Jul 58   ALL I HAVE TO DO IS DREAM.London HLA 8618   7 wks
5 May 60   CATHY'S CLOWN.........................Warner Bros WB 1   7 wks
2 Mar 61   WALK RIGHT BACK.................Warner Bros WB 33   3 wks
20 Jul 61   TEMPTATION.............................Warner Bros WB 42   2 wks

------------------------- **F** -------------------------

Adam FAITH *UK, male vocalist*
4 Dec 59   WHAT DO YOU WANT..............Parlophone R 4591   3 wks
10 Mar 60   POOR ME.................................Parlophone R 4623   1 wk

FALCO *Austria, male vocalist*
10 May 86   ROCK ME AMADEUS...........................A&M AM 278   1 wk

Georgie FAME *UK, male vocal/instrumentalist*
14 Jan 65   YEH YEH.......................................Columbia DB 7428   2 wks
21 Jul 66   GET AWAY.....................................Columbia DB 7946   1 wk
24 Jan 68   THE BALLAD OF BONNIE AND CLYDE.......................
                                                                CBS 3124   1 wk
Yeh Yeh and Get Away credit the BLUE FLAMES, UK, male instrumental backing group

Chris FARLOWE and the THUNDERBIRDS *UK, male vocal/instrumental group*
28 Jul 66   OUT OF TIME........................... Immediate IM 035   1 wk

FERRY AID *International male/female charity group*
4 Apr 87   LET IT BE..Sun AID 1   3 wks

FIRM *UK, male/female vocal/instrumental group*
20 Jun 87   STAR TREKKIN'....................................Bark TREK 1   2 wks

Eddie FISHER *US, male vocalist*
30 Jan 53   OUTSIDE OF HEAVEN.........................HMV B 10362   1 wk
26 Jun 53   I'M WALKING BEHIND YOU.............HMV B 10489   1 wk

FLEETWOOD MAC *UK, male instrumental group*
29 Jan 69   ALBATROSS........................Blue Horizon 57 3145   1 wk

FLOATERS *US, male vocal/instrumental group*
27 Aug 77   FLOAT ON..ABC 4187   1 wk

FLYING PICKETS *UK, male vocal group*
10 Dec 83   ONLY YOU................................10 Records TEN 14   5 wks

Emile FORD and the CHECKMATES *UK, male vocal/instrumental group*
18 Dec 59   WHAT DO YOU WANT TO MAKE THOSE EYES AT ME FOR..Pye 7N 15225   6 wks

Tennessee Ernie FORD *US, male vocalist*
11 Mar 55   GIVE ME YOUR WORD................Capitol CL 14005   7 wks
20 Jan 56   SIXTEEN TONS............................Capitol CL 14500   4 wks

FOREIGNER *UK/US, male vocal/instrumental group*
19 Jan 85   I WANT TO KNOW WHAT LOVE IS......................
                                                            Atlantic A 9596   3 wks

FOUNDATIONS *UK, male vocal/instrumental group*
8 Nov 67   BABY NOW THAT I'VE FOUND YOU......................
                                                            Pye 7N 17366   2 wks

FOUR PENNIES *UK, male vocal/instrumental group*
21 May 64   JULIET..Philips BF 1322   1 wk

FOUR SEASONS *US, male vocal/instrumental group*
21 Feb 76   DECEMBER '63 (OH WHAT A NIGHT)........................
                                                        Warner Bros K 16688   2 wks

FOUR TOPS *US, male vocal group*
27 Oct 66   REACH OUT I'LL BE THERE...............................
                                                    Tamla Motown TMG 579   3 wks

Connie FRANCIS *US, female vocalist*
16 May 58   WHO'S SORRY NOW..............................MGM 975   6 wks
26 Sep 58   CAROLINA MOON/STUPID CUPID.... MGM 985   6 wks

FRANKIE GOES TO HOLLYWOOD *UK, male vocal/instrumental group*
28 Jan 84   RELAX!...ZTT ZTAS 1   5 wks
16 Jun 84   TWO TRIBES.......................................ZTT ZTAS 3   9 wks
8 Dec 84   THE POWER OF LOVE........................ZTT ZTAS 5   1 wk

Aretha FRANKLIN *– see George MICHAEL and Aretha FRANKLIN*

------------------------- **G** -------------------------

Serge GAINSBOURG *– see Jane BIRKIN and Serge GAINSBOURG*

Boris GARDINER *Jamaica, male vocalist*
23 Aug 86   I WANT TO WAKE UP WITH YOU........................
                                                            Revue REV 733   3 wks

Art GARFUNKEL US, male vocalist
25 Oct 75   I ONLY HAVE EYES FOR YOU.............CBS 3575   2 wks
14 Apr 79   BRIGHT EYES.........................CBS 6947   6 wks
See also SIMON and GARFUNKEL

Siedah GARRETT – see Michael JACKSON

Barbara GASKIN – see Dave STEWART with Barbara GASKIN

Marvin GAYE US, male vocalist
26 Mar 69   I HEARD IT THROUGH THE GRAPEVINE.....................
Tamla Motown TMG 686   3 wks

Gloria GAYNOR US, female vocalist
17 Mar 79   I WILL SURVIVE..............Polydor 2095 017   4 wks

Bobby GENTRY US, female vocalist
18 Oct 69   I'LL NEVER FALL IN LOVE AGAIN......................
Capitol CL 15606   1 wk

GERRY and the PACEMAKERS UK, male vocal/instrumental group
11 Apr 63   HOW DO YOU DO IT?.................Columbia DB 4987   3 wks
20 Jun 63   I LIKE IT.........................Columbia DB 7041   4 wks
31 Oct 63   YOU'LL NEVER WALK ALONE Columbia DB 7126   4 wks

Gary GLITTER UK, male vocalist
28 Jul 73   I'M LEADER OF THE GANG (I AM).....Bell 1321   4 wks
17 Nov 73   I LOVE YOU LOVE ME LOVE.............Bell 1337   4 wks
22 Jun 74   ALWAYS YOURS........................Bell 1359   1 wk

GOOMBAY DANCE BAND Germany/Montserrat, male/female vocal/instrumental group
27 Mar 82   SEVEN TEARS................Epic EPC A 1242   3 wks

GORDON – see PETER and GORDON

Eddy GRANT Guyana, male vocalist/instrumentalist
13 Nov 83   I DON'T WANNA DANCE..................Ice ICE 56   3 wks
See also EQUALS

Norman GREENBAUM US, male vocalist
2 May 70   SPIRIT IN THE SKY......................Reprise RS 20885   2 wks

---------------------- **H** ----------------------

Bill HALEY and his COMETS US, male vocal/instrumental group
25 Nov 55   ROCK AROUND THE CLOCK..... Brunswick 05317   3 wks
6 Jan 56   ROCK AROUND THE CLOCK..... Brunswick 05317   2 wks

Paul HARDCASTLE UK, male producer/instrumentalist – keyboards
11 May 85   19.........................Chrysalis CHS 2860   5 wks

Steve HARLEY and COCKNEY REBEL UK, male vocal/instrumental group
22 Feb 75   MAKE ME SMILE (COME UP AND SEE ME)..............
EMI 2263   2 wks

Jet HARRIS and Tony MEEHAN UK, male instrumental duo – bass guitar and drums
31 Jan 63   DIAMONDS.........................Decca F 11563   3 wks
See also SHADOWS

Rolf HARRIS Australia, male vocalist
20 Dec 69   TWO LITTLE BOYS.....................Columbia DB 8630   6 wks

George HARRISON UK, male vocalist
30 Jan 71   MY SWEET LORD.....................Apple R 5884   5 wks
See also BEATLES

Jimi HENDRIX EXPERIENCE US/UK, male vocal/instrumental group
21 Nov 70   VOODOO CHILE.....................Track 2095 001   1 wk

HERMAN'S HERMITS UK, male vocal/instrumental group
24 Sep 64   I'M INTO SOMETHING GOOD. Columbia DB 7338   2 wks

HIGHWAYMEN US, male vocal group
12 Oct 61   MICHAEL.....................HMV POP 910   1 wk

Benny HILL UK, male vocalist
11 Dec 71   ERNIE (THE FASTEST MILKMAN IN THE WEST)......
Columbia DB 8833   4 wks

Ronnie HILTON UK, male vocalist
4 May 56   NO OTHER LOVE.....................HMV POP 198   6 wks

Michael HOLLIDAY UK, male vocalist
14 Feb 58   THE STORY OF MY LIFE.......... Columbia DB 4058   2 wks
29 Jan 60   STARRY EYED.....................Columbia DB 4378   1 wk

HOLLIES UK, male vocal/instrumental group
24 Jun 65   I'M ALIVE.....................Parlophone R 5287   1 wk
8 Jul 65   I'M ALIVE.....................Parlophone R 5287   2 wks

Buddy HOLLY US, male vocalist
24 Apr 59   IT DOESN'T MATTER ANYMORE. Coral Q 72360   3 wks
See also CRICKETS

HONEYCOMBS UK, male/female vocal/instrumental group
27 Aug 64   HAVE I THE RIGHT.....................Pye 7N 15664   2 wks

Mary HOPKIN UK, female vocalist
25 Sep 68   THOSE WERE THE DAYS..................... Apple 2   6 wks

HOT CHOCOLATE UK, male vocal/instrumental group
2 Jul 77   SO YOU WIN AGAIN..................RAK 259   3 wks

HOUSEMARTINS UK, male vocal group
20 Dec 86   CARAVAN OF LOVE..................... Go! Discs GOD 16   1 wk

Whitney HOUSTON US, female vocalist
14 Dec 85   SAVING ALL MY LOVE FOR YOU......................
Arista ARIST 640   2 wks
6 Jun 87   I WANNA DANCE WITH SOMEBODY (WHO LOVES ME).....................Arista RIS 1   2 wks

HUMAN LEAGUE UK, male/female vocal/instrumental group
12 Dec 81   DON'T YOU WANT ME?..................Virgin VS 466   5 wks

Engelbert HUMPERDINCK *UK, male vocalist*
2 Mar 67   RELEASE ME.................................Decca F 12541   6 wks
6 Sep 67   THE LAST WALTZ.........................Decca F 12655   5 wks

Tab HUNTER *US, male vocalist*
22 Feb 57   YOUNG LOVE.............................. London HLD 8380   7 wks

Steve 'Silk' HURLEY *US, male vocalist*
22 Jan 87   JACK YOUR BODY.............. DJ International LON 117   2 wks

Chrissie HYNDE   *– see PRETENDERS, UB40*

---- **I** ----

IAN and the BLOCKHEADS *UK, male vocal/
instrumental group*
27 Jan 79   HIT ME WITH YOUR RHYTHM STICK Stiff BUY 38   1 wk

Frank IFIELD *UK, male vocalist*
26 Jul 62   I REMEMBER YOU.................Columbia DB 4856   7 wks
8 Nov 62   LOVESICK BLUES.................Columbia DB 4913   5 wks
21 Feb 63   WAYWARD WIND.................Columbia DB 4960   3 wks
18 Jul 63   CONFESSIN'.........................Columbia DB 7062   2 wks

Julio IGLESIAS *Spain, male vocalist*
5 Dec 81   BEGIN THE BEGUINE (VOLVER A EMPEZAR)............
                                CBS A 1612   1 wk

---- **J** ----

Terry JACKS *Canada, male vocalist*
6 Apr 74   SEASONS IN THE SUN............................ Bell 1344   4 wks

Michael JACKSON *US, male vocalist*
27 Jun 81   ONE DAY IN YOUR LIFE............ Motown TMG 976   2 wks
5 Mar 83   BILLIE JEAN...........................Epic EPC A 3084   1 wk
15 Aug 87   I JUST CAN'T STOP LOVING YOU Epic 650202 7   2 wks
*I Just Can't Stop Loving You with Siedah Garrett.
See also JACKSONS*

JACKSONS *UK, male vocal group*
25 Jun 77   SHOW YOU THE WAY TO GO........ Epic EPC 5266   1 wk
See also Michael JACKSON

Mick JAGGER   *– see David BOWIE and Mick
JAGGER, ROLLING STONES*

JAM *UK, male vocal/instrumental group*
22 Mar 80   GOING UNDERGROUND/DREAMS OF CHILDREN...
                            Polydor POSP 113   3 wks
6 Sep 80   START.................................. Polydor 2059 266   1 wk
13 Feb 82   A TOWN CALLED MALICE/PRECIOUS........................
                            Polydor POSP 400   3 wks
4 Dec 82   BEAT SURRENDER......................Polydor POSP 540   2 wks

Tommy JAMES and the SHONDELLS *US,
male vocal/instrumental group*
31 Jul 68   MONY MONY.................... Major Minor MM 567   2 wks
21 Aug 68   MONY MONY.................... Major Minor MM 567   1 wk

Billy JOEL *US, male vocalist/instrumentalist – piano*
5 Nov 83   UPTOWN GIRL.............................. CBS A 3775   5 wks

Elton JOHN and Kiki DEE *UK, male/female
vocal duo*
24 Jul 76   DON'T GO BREAKING MY HEART........................
                            Rocket ROKN 512   6 wks

JOHNSTON BROTHERS *UK, male vocal group*
11 Nov 55   HERNANDO'S HIDEAWAY.............Decca F 10608   2 wks

Jimmy JONES *US, male vocalist*
7 Jul 60   GOOD TIMIN'...................................MGM 1078   3 wks

Tom JONES *UK, male vocalist*
11 Mar 65   IT'S NOT UNUSUAL.......................Decca F 12062   1 wk
1 Dec 66   GREEN GREEN GRASS OF HOME................................
                            Decca F 22511   7 wks

---- **K** ----

KAJAGOOGOO *UK, male vocal/instrumental group*
19 Feb 83   TOO SHY.....................................EMI 5359   2 wks

KALIN TWINS *US, male vocal duo*
22 Aug 58   WHEN.................................Brunswick 05751   5 wks

Kitty KALLEN *US, female vocalist*
10 Sep 54   LITTLE THINGS MEAN A LOT..... Brunswick 05287   1 wk

Eden KANE *UK, male vocalist*
3 Aug 61   WELL I ASK YOU...............................Decca F 11353   1 wk

KC and the SUNSHINE BAND *US, male vocal/
instrumental group*
13 Aug 83   GIVE IT UP.............................Epic EPC A 3017   3 wks

Jerry KELLER *US, male vocalist*
9 Oct 59   HERE COMES SUMMER................London HLR 8890   1 wk

Chaka KHAN *US, female vocalist*
10 Nov 84   I FEEL FOR YOU.......................Warner Bros W 9209   3 wks

Johnny KIDD and the PIRATES *UK, male
vocal/instrumental group*
4 Aug 60   SHAKIN' ALL OVER...........................HMV POP 753   1 wk

KIM   *– see MEL and KIM*

Ben E KING *US, male vocalist*
21 Feb 87   STAND BY ME........................ Atlantic A 9361   3 wks

KINKS *UK, male vocal/instrumental group*
10 Sep 64   YOU REALLY GOT ME.....................Pye 7N 15673   2 wks
18 Feb 65   TIRED OF WAITING FOR YOU........ Pye 7N 15759   1 wk
7 Jul 66   SUNNY AFTERNOON........................Pye 7N 17125   2 wks

Fern KINNEY *US, female vocalist*
15 Mar 80   TOGETHER WE ARE BEAUTIFUL.... WEA K 79111   1 wk

KRAFTWERK *Germany, male vocal/instrumental
group*
6 Feb 82   THE MODEL/COMPUTER LOVE............EMI 5207   1 wk

Billy J. KRAMER and the DAKOTAS *UK, male vocal/instrumental group*

22 Aug 63	BAD TO ME	Parlophone R 5049	3 wks
19 Mar 64	LITTLE CHILDREN	Parlophone R 5105	2 wks

———— L ————

Frankie LAINE *US, male vocalist*

24 Apr 53	I BELIEVE	Philips PB 117	9 wks
3 Jul 53	I BELIEVE	Philips PB 117	6 wks
21 Aug 53	I BELIEVE	Philips PB 117	3 wks
23 Oct 53	HEY JOE	Philips PB 172	2 wks
13 Nov 53	ANSWER ME	Philips PB 196	8 wks
19 Oct 56	A WOMAN IN LOVE	Philips PB 617	4 wks

LEE – *see PETERS and LEE*

John LENNON *UK, male vocalist*

20 Dec 80	(JUST LIKE) STARTING OVER	Geffen K 79186	1 wk
10 Jan 81	IMAGINE	Parlophone R 6009	4 wks
7 Feb 81	WOMAN	Geffen K 79195	2 wks

See also the BEATLES

Jerry Lee LEWIS *US, male vocalist/instrumentalist – piano*

10 Jan 68	GREAT BALLS OF FIRE	London HLS 8529	3 wks

Johnny LEYTON *UK, male vocalist*

31 Aug 61	JOHNNY REMEMBER ME	Top Rank JAR 577	3 wks
28 Sep 61	JOHNNY REMEMBER ME	Top Rank JAR 577	1 wk

LIEUTENANT PIGEON *UK, male/female instrumental group*

14 Oct 72	MOULDY OLD DOUGH	Decca F 13278	4 wks

Los LOBOS *US, male vocal/instrumental group*

1 Aug 87	LA BAMBA	London LASH 13	2 wks

Johnny LOGAN *Ireland, male vocalist*

3 May 80	WHAT'S ANOTHER YEAR	Epic EPC 8572	2 weeks

LOVE AFFAIR *UK, male vocal/instrumental group*

31 Jan 68	EVERLASTING LOVE	CBS 3125	2 wks

Frankie LYMON – *see TEENAGERS featuring Frankie LYMON*

Vera LYNN *UK, female vocalist*

5 Nov 54	MY SON MY SON	Decca F 10372	2 wks

———— M ————

Paul McCARTNEY *UK, male vocalist*

14 Jan 84	PIPES OF PEACE	Parlophone R 6064	2 wks

See also Paul McCARTNEY with Stevie WONDER, BEATLES, WINGS

Paul McCARTNEY with Stevie WONDER *UK/US, male vocal duo*

24 Apr 82	EBONY AND IVORY	Parlophone R 6054	3 wks

See also Paul McCARTNEY, Stevie WONDER, BEATLES, WINGS

George McCRAE *US, male vocalist*

27 Jul 74	ROCK YOUR BABY	Jayboy BOY 85	3 wks

Scott McKENZIE *US, male vocalist*

9 Aug 67	SAN FRANCISCO (BE SURE TO WEAR SOME FLOWERS IN YOUR HAIR)	CBS 2816	4 wks

Don McLEAN *US, male vocalist*

17 Jun 72	VINCENT	United Artists UP 35359	2 wks
21 Jun 80	CRYING	EMI 5051	3 wks

MADNESS *UK, male vocal/instrumental group*

29 May 82	HOUSE OF FUN	Stiff BUY 146	2 wks

MADONNA *US, female vocalist*

3 Aug 85	INTO THE GROOVE	Sire W 8934	4 wks
12 Jul 86	PAPA DON'T PREACH	Sire W 8636	3 wks
11 Oct 86	TRUE BLUE	Sire W 8550	1 wk
25 Apr 87	LA ISLA BONITA	Sire W 8378	2 wks
25 Jul 87	WHO'S THAT GIRL	Sire W 8341	1 wk

MANFRED MANN *South Africa/UK, male vocal/instrumental group*

13 Aug 64	DO WAH DIDDY DIDDY	HMV POP 1320	2 wks
5 May 66	PRETTY FLAMINGO	HMV POP 1523	3 wks
14 Feb 68	MIGHTY QUINN	Fontana TF 897	2 wks

MANHATTAN TRANSFER *US, male/female vocal group*

12 Mar 77	CHANSON D'AMOUR	Atlantic K 10886	3 wks

MANTOVANI *UK, orchestra*

14 Aug 53	MOULIN ROUGE	Decca F 10004	1 wk

See also David WHITFIELD

MARCELS *UK, male vocal group*

4 May 61	BLUE MOON	Pye International 7N 25073	2 wks

Kelly MARIE *UK, female vocalist*

13 Sep 80	FEELS LIKE I'M IN LOVE	Calibre PLUS 1	2 wks

MARMALADE *UK, male vocal/instrumental group*

1 Jan 69	OB-LA-DI OB-LA-DA	CBS 3892	1 wk
15 Jan 69	OB-LA-DI OB-LA-DA	CBS 3892	2 wks

M/A/R/R/S *UK, male scratch/instrumental group*

3 Oct 87	PUMP UP THE VOLUME/ANITINA	4AD AD 707	2 wks

Lena MARTELL *UK, female vocalist*

27 Oct 79	ONE DAY AT A TIME	Pye 7N 46021	3 wks

Dean MARTIN *US, male vocalist*

17 Feb 56	MEMORIES ARE MADE OF THIS	Capitol CL 14523	4 wks

Al MARTINO *US, male vocalist*

14 Nov 52	HERE IN MY HEART	Capitol CL 13779	9 wks

Lee MARVIN *US, male vocalist*

7 Mar 70	WAND'RIN' STAR	Paramount PARA 3004	3 wks

MASH *US, male vocal/instrumental group*

31 May 80	THEME FROM 'M*A*S*H' (SUICIDE IS PAINLESS)	CBS 8536	3 wks

Johnny MATHIS *US, male vocalist*
25 Dec 76   WHEN A CHILD IS BORN (SOLEADO)...........................
CBS 4599   3 wks

MATTHEWS SOUTHERN COMFORT *UK,*
male vocal/instrumental group
31 Oct 70   WOODSTOCK.................................... Uni UNS 526   3 wks

MEDICS   *– see DR. and the MEDICS*

Tony MEEHAN   *– see Jet HARRIS and Tony MEEHAN*

MEL and KIM *UK, female vocal duo*
28 Mar 87   RESPECTABLE................................ Supreme SUPE 111   1 wk

MEN AT WORK *Australia, male vocal/instrumental group*
29 Jan 83   DOWN UNDER.............................. Epic EPC A 1980   3 wks

George MICHAEL *UK, male vocalist*
18 Aug 84   CARELESS WHISPER......................... Epic A 4603   3 wks
19 Apr 86   A DIFFERENT CORNER..................... Epic A 7033   3 wks
See also George MICHAEL and Aretha FRANKLIN, WHAM!

George MICHAEL and Aretha FRANKLIN *UK/US, male/female vocal duo*
7 Feb 87   I KNEW YOU WERE WAITING (FOR ME)...................
Epic DUET 2   2 wks

See also George MICHAEL, WHAM!

MICHAEL   *– see BRIAN and MICHAEL*

MICK   *– see Dave DEE, DOZY, BEAKY, MICK and TICH*

MIDDLE OF THE ROAD *UK, male/female vocal/instrumental group*
19 Jun 71   CHIRPY CHIRPY CHEEP CHEEP......... RCA 2047   5 wks

Roger MILLER *US, male vocalist*
13 May 65   KING OF THE ROAD......................... Philips BF 1397   1 wk

MIRACLES   *– see Smokey ROBINSON and the MIRACLES*

Guy MITCHELL *US, male vocalist*
13 Mar 53   SHE WEARS RED FEATHERS.. Columbia DB 3238   4 wks
11 Sep 53   LOOK AT THAT GIRL..................... Philips PB 162   6 wks
4 Jan 57   SINGING THE BLUES......................... Philips PB 650   1 wk
18 Jan 57   SINGING THE BLUES......................... Philips PB 650   1 wk
1 Feb 57   SINGING THE BLUES......................... Philips PB 650   1 wk
17 May 57   ROCK-A-BILLY................................ Philips PB 685   1 wk

MONKEES *US/UK, male vocal/instrumental group*
19 Jan 67   I'M A BELIEVER.................................. RCA 1560   4 wks

Hugo MONTENEGRO *US, orchestra*
13 Nov 68   THE GOOD THE BAD AND THE UGLY.......................
RCA 1727   4 wks

MOODY BLUES *UK, male vocal/instrumental group*
28 Jan 65   GO NOW.....................................Decca F 12022   1 wk

Jane MORGAN *US, female vocalist*
23 Jan 59   THE DAY THE RAINS CAME....... London HLR 8751   1 wk

Sarah Jane MORRIS   *– see COMMUNARDS*

MOVE *UK, male vocal/instrumental group*
5 Feb 69   BLACKBERRY WAY............ Regal Zonophone RZ 3015   1 wk

MUD *UK, male vocal/instrumental group*
26 Jan 74   TIGER FEET....................................RAK 166   4 wks
21 Dec 74   LONELY THIS CHRISTMAS...................RAK 187   4 wks
3 May 75   OH BOY..RAK 201   2 wks

MUNGO JERRY *UK, male vocal/instrumental group*
13 Jun 70   IN THE SUMMERTIME.................Dawn DNX 2502   7 wks
6 Mar 71   BABY JUMP........................Dawn DNX 2505   2 wks

Ruby MURRAY *UK, female vocalist*
18 Feb 55   SOFTLY SOFTLY......................... Columbia DB 3558   3 wks

MUSICAL YOUTH *UK, male vocal/instrumental group*
2 Oct 82   PASS THE DUTCHIE........................ MCA YOU 1   3 wks

---

N

Johnny NASH *UK, male vocalist*
12 Jul 75   TEARS ON MY PILLOW........................... CBS 3220   1 wk

Phyllis NELSON *US, female vocalist*
4 May 85   MOVE CLOSER.................................Carrere CAR 337   1 wk

NENA *Germany, male/female vocal/instrumental group*
3 Mar 84   99 RED BALLOONS..............................Epic A 4074   3 wks

NEW EDITION *US, male vocal group*
28 May 83   CANDY GIRL....................................... London LON 21   1 wk

NEW SEEKERS *UK, male/female vocal/instrumental group*
8 Jan 72   I'D LIKE TO TEACH THE WORLD TO SING...............
Polydor 2058 184   4 wks
19 Jan 74   YOU WON'T FIND ANOTHER FOOL LIKE ME..........
Polydor 2058 421   1 wk

Anthony NEWLEY *UK, male vocalist*
5 Feb 60   WHY..Decca F 11194   4 wks
28 Apr 60   DO YOU MIND..................................Decca F 11220   1 wk

Olivia NEWTON-JOHN and ELECTRIC LIGHT ORCHESTRA *UK, female vocalist and male vocal/instrumental group*
12 Jul 80   XANADU... Jet 185   2 wks
See also John TRAVOLTA and Olivia NEWTON-JOHN

NICOLE *Germany, female vocalist*
15 May 82   A LITTLE PEACE.............................. CBS A 2365   2 wks

NILSSON *US, male vocalist*
11 Mar 72   WITHOUT YOU................................. RCA 2165   5 wks

Gary NUMAN *UK, male vocalist*
30 Jun 79   ARE 'FRIENDS' ELECTRIC?.................................
Beggars Banquet BEG 18   4 wks
22 Sep 79   CARS........................ Beggars Banquet BEG 23   1 wk
Are 'Friends' Electric? by Gary Numan under the name
TUBEWAY ARMY

─────────── **O** ───────────

Billy OCEAN *UK, male vocalist*
8 Feb 86   WHEN THE GOING GETS TOUGH, THE TOUGH
GET GOING............................. Jive JIVE 114   4 wks

Des O'CONNOR *UK, male vocalist*
24 Jul 68   I PRETEND.................... Columbia DB 8397   1 wk

ODYSSEY *US, female/male vocal group*
26 Jul 80   USE IT UP AND WEAR IT OUT........ RCA PB 1962   2 wks

Esther and Abi OFARIM *Israel, female/male*
vocal duo
28 Feb 68   CINDERELLA ROCKEFELLA........ Philips BF 1640   3 wks

Roy ORBISON *US, male vocalist*
20 Oct 60   ONLY THE LONELY........... London HLU 9149   2 wks
25 Jun 64   IT'S OVER................... London HLU 9882   2 wks
8 Oct 64   OH PRETTY WOMAN.................. London HLU 9919   2 wks
12 Nov 64   OH PRETTY WOMAN................... London HLU 9919   1 wk

Tony ORLANDO   *– see DAWN*

Donny OSMOND *US, male vocalist*
8 Jul 72   PUPPY LOVE..................... MGM 2006 104   5 wks
31 Mar 73   THE TWELFTH OF NEVER.............. MGM 2006 199   1 wk
25 Aug 73   YOUNG LOVE.................. MGM 2006 300   4 wks
See also OSMONDS

Little Jimmy OSMOND *US, male vocalist*
23 Dec 72   LONG HAIRED LOVER FROM LIVERPOOL.................
MGM 2006 109   5 wks

OSMONDS *US, male vocal/instrumental group*
31 Aug 74   LOVE ME FOR A REASON............ MGM 2006 458   3 wks
See also Donny OSMOND

Gilbert O'SULLIVAN *Ireland, male vocalist*
11 Nov 72   CLAIR........................ MAM 84   2 wks
7 Apr 73   GET DOWN....................... MAM 96   2 wks

OVERLANDERS *UK, male vocal/instrumental*
group
27 Jan 66   MICHELLE........................ Pye 7N 17034   3 wks

─────────── **P** ───────────

PACEMAKERS   *– see GERRY and the*
PACEMAKERS

Elaine PAIGE and Barbara DICKSON *UK,*
female vocal duo
9 Feb 85   I KNOW HIM SO WELL.................. RCA CHESS 3   4 wks

PAPER LACE *UK, male vocal/instrumental group*
16 Mar 74   BILLY DON'T BE A HERO.......... Bus Stop BUS 1014   3 wks

Simon PARK ORCHESTRA *UK, orchestra*
29 Sep 73   EYE LEVEL................. Columbia DB 8946   4 wks

Freda PAYNE *US, female vocalist*
19 Sep 70   BAND OF GOLD............................ Invictus INV 502   6 wks

PET SHOP BOYS *UK, male vocal/instrumental duo*
11 Jan 86   WEST END GIRLS.................. Parlophone R 6115   2 wks
4 Jul 87   IT'S A SIN....................... Parlophone R 6158   3 wks

PETER and GORDON *UK, male vocal duo*
23 Apr 64   A WORLD WITHOUT LOVE..... Columbia DB 7225   2 wks

PETERS and LEE *UK, male/female vocal duo*
21 Jul 73   WELCOME HOME........................ Philips 6006 307   1 wk

PILOT *UK, male vocal/instrumental group*
1 Feb 75   JANUARY............................... EMI 2255   3 wks

PINK FLOYD *UK, male vocal/instrumental group*
15 Dec 79   ANOTHER BRICK IN THE WALL (PART II).................
Harvest HAR 5194   5 wks

PIRATES   *– see Johnny KIDD and the PIRATES*

PLATTERS *US, male/female vocal group*
20 Mar 59   SMOKE GETS IN YOUR EYES.... Mercury AMT 1016   1 wk

POLICE *UK, male vocal/instrumental group*
29 Sep 79   MESSAGE IN A BOTTLE.............. A&M AMS 7474   3 wks
8 Dec 79   WALKING ON THE MOON....... A&M AMS 7494   1 wk
27 Sep 80   DON'T STAND SO CLOSE TO ME.................
A&M AMS 7564   4 wks
14 Nov 81   EVERY LITTLE THING SHE DOES IS MAGIC.................
A&M AMS 8174   1 wk
4 Jun 83   EVERY BREATH YOU TAKE.............. A&M AM 117   4 wks

Brian POOLE and the TREMELOES *UK,*
male vocal/instrumental group
10 Oct 63   DO YOU LOVE ME........................... Decca F 11739   3 wks
See also TREMELOES

Perez PRADO *Cuba, orchestra*
29 Apr 55   CHERRY PINK AND APPLE BLOSSOM WHITE..........
HMV B 10833   2 wks

Elvis PRESLEY *US, male vocalist*
12 Jul 57   ALL SHOOK UP.....................HMV POP 359   7 wks
24 Jan 58   JAILHOUSE ROCK.....................RCA 1028   3 wks
30 Jan 59   ONE NIGHT/I GOT STUNG..................RCA 1100   3 wks
15 May 59   A FOOL SUCH AS I/I NEED YOUR LOVE TONIGHT..
RCA 1113   5 wks
3 Nov 60   IT'S NOW OR NEVER.......................... RCA 1207   8 wks
26 Jan 61   ARE YOU LONESOME TONIGHT........ RCA 1216   4 wks
23 Mar 61   WOODEN HEART.......................... RCA 1226   6 wks
1 Jun 61   SURRENDER........................... RCA 1227   4 wks
9 Nov 61   HIS LATEST FLAME/LITTLE SISTER. RCA 1258   4 wks
22 Feb 62   ROCK-A-HULA BABY/CAN'T HELP FALLING IN
LOVE...........................RCA 1270   4 wks

24 May 62	GOOD LUCK CHARM	RCA 1280	5 wks
13 Sep 62	SHE'S NOT YOU	RCA 1303	3 wks
13 Dec 62	RETURN TO SENDER	RCA 1320	3 wks
1 Aug 63	(YOU'RE THE) DEVIL IN DISGUISE	RCA 1355	1 wk
17 Jun 65	CRYING IN THE CHAPEL	RCA 1455	1 wk
1 Jul 65	CRYING IN THE CHAPEL	RCA 1455	1 wk
1 Aug 70	THE WONDER OF YOU	RCA 1974	6 wks
3 Sep 77	WAY DOWN	RCA PB 0998	3 wks

Billy PRESTON – see BEATLES

Johnny PRESTON US, male vocalist

17 Mar 60	RUNNING BEAR	Mercury AMT 1079	2 wks

PRETENDERS UK/US, male/female vocal/instrumental group

19 Jan 80	BRASS IN POCKET	Real ARE 11	2 wks

See also UB40

PROCOL HARUM UK, male vocal/instrumental group

8 Jun 67	A WHITER SHADE OF PALE	Deram DM 126	6 wks

Gary PUCKETT – see UNION GAP featuring Gary PUCKETT

PUSSYCAT Holland, male/female vocal/instrumental group

4 Sep 76	MISSISSIPPI	Sonet SON 2077	4 wks

— Q —

Suzi QUATRO US, female vocalist/instrumentalist – bass guitar

16 Jun 73	CAN THE CAN	RAK 150	1 wk
23 Feb 74	DEVIL GATE DRIVE	RAK 167	2 wks

QUEEN UK, male vocal/instrumental group

29 Nov 75	BOHEMIAN RHAPSODY	EMI 2375	9 wks

See also QUEEN and David BOWIE

QUEEN and David BOWIE UK, male vocal/instrumental group and male vocalist

21 Nov 81	UNDER PRESSURE	EMI 5250	2 wks

See also QUEEN, David BOWIE, David BOWIE and Mick JAGGER

— R —

Marvin RAINWATER US, male vocalist

25 Apr 58	WHOLE LOTTA WOMAN	MGM 974	3 wks

Johnnie RAY US, male vocalist

30 Apr 54	SUCH A NIGHT	Philips PB 244	1 wk
16 Nov 56	JUST WALKIN' IN THE RAIN	Philips PB 624	7 wks
7 Jun 57	YES TONIGHT JOSEPHINE	Philips PB 686	3 wks

REAL THING UK, male vocal/instrumental group

26 Jun 76	YOU TO ME ARE EVERYTHING	Pye Int 7N 25709	3 wks

Jim REEVES US, male vocalist

22 Sep 66	DISTANT DRUMS	RCA 1537	5 wks

RENEE and RENATO UK, female/male vocal duo

18 Dec 82	SAVE YOUR LOVE	Hollywood HWD 003	4 wks

Cliff RICHARD UK, male vocalist

31 Jul 59	LIVING DOLL	Columbia DB 4306	6 wks
30 Oct 59	TRAVELLIN' LIGHT	Columbia DB 4351	5 wks
28 Jul 60	PLEASE DON'T TEASE	Columbia DB 4479	1 wk
11 Aug 60	PLEASE DON'T TEASE	Columbia DB 4479	2 wks
29 Dec 60	I LOVE YOU	Columbia DB 4547	2 wks
11 Jan 62	THE YOUNG ONES	Columbia DB 4761	6 wks
3 Jan 63	THE NEXT TIME/BACHELOR BOY		
		Columbia DB 4950	3 wks
14 Mar 63	SUMMER HOLIDAY	Columbia DB 4977	2 wks
4 Apr 63	SUMMER HOLIDAY	Columbia DB 4977	1 wk
15 Apr 65	THE MINUTE YOU'RE GONE	Columbia DB 7496	1 wk
10 Apr 68	CONGRATULATIONS	Columbia DB 8376	2 wks
25 Aug 79	WE DON'T TALK ANYMORE	EMI 2975	4 wks

See also Cliff RICHARD and the YOUNG ONES. The SHADOWS appear on all Cliff's number ones up to and including Summer Holiday. See also SHADOWS

Cliff RICHARD and the YOUNG ONES UK, male vocal group

29 Mar 86	LIVING DOLL	WEA YZ 65	3 wks

See also Cliff RICHARD

Wendy RICHARD – see Mike SARNE with Wendy RICHARD

Lionel RICHIE US, male vocalist

24 Mar 84	HELLO	Motown TMG 1330	6 wks

See also COMMODORES

RIGHTEOUS BROTHERS US, male vocal duo

4 Feb 65	YOU'VE LOST THAT LOVIN' FEELIN'		
		London HLU 9943	2 wks

Smokey ROBINSON US, male vocalist

13 Jun 81	BEING WITH YOU	Motown TMG 1223	2 wks

See also Smokey ROBINSON and the MIRACLES

Smokey ROBINSON and the MIRACLES US, male vocal group

12 Sep 70	TEARS OF A CLOWN	Tamla Motown TMG 745	1 wk

See also Smokey ROBINSON

Lord ROCKINGHAM'S XI UK, orchestra

28 Nov 58	HOOTS MON	Decca F 11059	3 wks

Tommy ROE US, male vocalist

4 Jun 69	DIZZY	Stateside SS 2143	1 wk

Kenny ROGERS US, male vocalist

18 Jun 77	LUCILLE	United Artists UP 36242	1 wk
16 Feb 80	COWARD OF THE COUNTY	United Artists UP 614	2 wks

ROLLING STONES UK, male vocal/instrumental group

16 Jul 64	IT'S ALL OVER NOW	Decca F 11934	1 wk
3 Dec 64	LITTLE RED ROOSTER	Decca F 12014	1 wk

18 Mar 65	THE LAST TIME	Decca F 12104	3 wks
9 Sep 65	(I CAN'T GET NO) SATISFACTION		
		Decca F 12220	2 wks
4 Nov 65	GET OFF OF MY CLOUD	Decca F 12263	3 wks
26 May 66	PAINT IT BLACK	Decca F 12395	1 wk
19 Jun 68	JUMPING JACK FLASH	Decca F 12782	4 wks
23 Jul 69	HONKY TONK WOMEN	Decca F 12952	5 wks

See also David BOWIE and Mick JAGGER

Diana ROSS *US, female vocalist*

21 Aug 71	I'M STILL WAITING	Tamla Motown TMG 781	4 wks
8 Mar 86	CHAIN REACTION	Capitol CL 386	3 wks

See also SUPREMES

Demis ROUSSOS *Greece, male vocalist*

17 Jul 76	THE ROUSSOS PHENOMENON (EP)		
		Philips DEMIS 001	1 wk

Tracks on EP: Forever And Ever, Sing An Ode To Love,
So Dreamy, My Friend The Wind

ROXY MUSIC *UK, male vocal/instrumental group*

14 Mar 81	JEALOUS GUY	Polydor ROXY 2	2 wks

The Pipes and Drums and Military Band of the ROYAL SCOTS DRAGOON GUARDS *UK, military band*

15 Apr 72	AMAZING GRACE	RCA 2191	5 wks

Lita ROZA *UK, female vocalist*

17 Apr 53	(HOW MUCH IS) THAT DOGGIE IN THE WINDOW?	Decca 10070	1 wk

RUBETTES *UK, male vocal/instrumental group*

18 May 74	SUGAR BABY LOVE	Polydor 2058 442	4 wks

Jennifer RUSH *US, female vocalist*

12 Oct 85	THE POWER OF LOVE	CBS A 5003	5 wks

— S —

ST. WINIFRED'S SCHOOL CHOIR *UK, girls' school choir*

27 Dec 80	THERE'S NO-ONE QUITE LIKE GRANDMA		
		MFP FP 900	2 wks

Mike SARNE with Wendy RICHARD *UK, male vocalist with female vocalist*

28 Jun 62	COME OUTSIDE	Parlophone R 4902	2 wks

Peter SARSTEDT *UK, male vocalist*

26 Feb 69	WHERE DO YOU GO TO, MY LOVELY?		
		United Artists UP 2262	4 wks

Telly SAVALAS *US, male vocalist*

8 Mar 75	IF	MCA 174	2 wks

Leo SAYER *UK, male vocalist*

19 Feb 77	WHEN I NEED YOU	Chrysalis CHS 2127	3 wks

SCAFFOLD *UK, male vocal trio*

11 Dec 68	LILY THE PINK	Parlophone R 5734	3 wks
8 Jan 69	LILY THE PINK	Parlophone R 5734	1 wk

SEARCHERS *UK, male vocal/instrumental group*

8 Aug 63	SWEETS FOR MY SWEET	Pye 7N 15533	2 wks
30 Jan 64	NEEDLES AND PINS	Pye 7N 15594	3 wks
7 May 64	DON'T THROW YOUR LOVE AWAY		
		Pye 7N 15630	2 wks

SEEKERS *Australia/Sri Lanka, male/female vocal group*

25 Feb 65	I'LL NEVER FIND ANOTHER YOU		
		Columbia DB 7431	2 wks
25 Nov 65	THE CARNIVAL IS OVER	Columbia DB 7711	3 wks

SHADOWS *UK, male instrumental group*

25 Aug 60	APACHE	Columbia DB 4484	5 wks
5 Oct 61	KON-TIKI	Columbia DB 4698	1 wk
22 Mar 62	WONDERFUL LAND	Columbia DB 4790	8 wks
24 Jan 63	DANCE ON!	Columbia DB 4948	1 wk
28 Mar 63	FOOT TAPPER	Columbia DB 4984	1 wk

See also Cliff RICHARD, JET HARRIS and TONY MEEHAN

Del SHANNON *US, male vocalist*

29 Jun 61	RUNAWAY	London HLX 9317	3 wks

Helen SHAPIRO *UK, female vocalist*

10 Aug 61	YOU DON'T KNOW	Columbia DB 4670	3 wks
19 Oct 61	WALKIN' BACK TO HAPPINESS		
		Columbia DB 4715	3 wks

Feargal SHARKEY *UK, male vocalist*

16 Nov 85	A GOOD HEART	Virgin VS 808	2 wks

Sandie SHAW *UK, female vocalist*

22 Oct 64	(THERE'S) ALWAYS SOMETHING THERE TO REMIND ME	Pye 7B 15704	3 wks
27 May 65	LONG LIVE LOVE	Pye 7N 15841	3 wks
27 Apr 67	PUPPET ON A STRING	Pye 7N 17272	3 wks

Anne SHELTON *UK, female vocalist*

21 Sep 56	LAY DOWN YOUR ARMS	Philips PB 616	4 wks

SHONDELLS – *see* Tommy JAMES and the SHONDELLS

SHOWADDYWADDY *UK, male vocal/instrumental group*

4 Dec 76	UNDER THE MOON OF LOVE	Bell 1495	3 wks

SIMON and GARFUNKEL *US, male vocal duo*

28 Mar 70	BRIDGE OVER TROUBLED WATER	CBS 4790	3 wks

See also Art GARFUNKEL

Frank SINATRA *US, male vocalist*

17 Feb 54	THREE COINS IN THE FOUNTAIN		
		Capitol CL 14120	3 wks
2 Jun 66	STRANGERS IN THE NIGHT	Reprise RS 23052	3 wks

See also Nancy SINATRA and Frank SINATRA

Nancy SINATRA *US, female vocalist*

17 Feb 66	THESE BOOTS ARE MADE FOR WALKIN'		
		Reprise RS 20432	4 wks

See also Nancy SINATRA and Frank SINATRA

Nancy SINATRA and Frank SINATRA *US, female/male vocal duo*
13 Apr 67   SOMETHING STUPID.................. Reprise RS 23166   2 wks
See also Nancy SINATRA, Frank SINATRA

SISTER SLEDGE *US, female vocal group*
29 Jun 85   FRANKIE.............................. Atlantic A 9547   4 wks

SLADE *UK, male vocal/instrumental group*
13 Nov 71   COZ I LUV YOU.................. Polydor 2058 155   4 wks
1 Jul 72   TAKE ME BACK 'OME................................
Polydor 2058 231   1 wk
9 Sep 72   MAMA WEER ALL CRAZEE NOW.......................
Polydor 2058 274   3 wks
3 Mar 73   CUM ON FEEL THE NOIZE........ Polydor 2058 339   4 wks
30 Jun 73   SKWEEZE ME PLEEZE ME........ Polydor 2058 377   3 wks
15 Dec 73   MERRY XMAS EVERYBODY...... Polydor 2058 422   5 wks

SLIK *UK, male vocal/instrumental group*
14 Feb 76   FOREVER AND EVER................ Bell 1464   1 wk
See also Midge URE

SMALL FACES *UK, male vocal/instrumental group*
15 Sep 66   ALL OR NOTHING............... Decca F 12470   1 wk

SOFT CELL *UK, male vocal/instrumental duo*
5 Sep 81   TAINTED LOVE................ Some Bizzare BZS 2   2 wks

SONNY and CHER *US, male/female vocal duo*
26 Aug 65   I GOT YOU BABE............... Atlantic AT 4035   2 wks

David SOUL *US, male vocalist*
15 Jan 77   DON'T GIVE UP ON US.......... Private Stock PVT 84   4 wks
8 Oct 77   SILVER LADY................ Private Stock PVT 115   3 wks

SPANDAU BALLET *UK, male vocal/instrumental group*
30 Apr 85   TRUE................ Reformation/Chrysalis SPAN 1   4 wks

SPECIALS *UK, male vocal/instrumental group*
2 Feb 80   THE SPECIAL A.K.A. LIVE (EP).2 Tone CHS TT 7   2 wks
11 Jul 81   GHOST TOWN.............. 2 Tone CHS TT 17   3 wks
Tracks on EP: Too Much Too Young, Guns Of Navarone, Long Shot Kick De Bucket, The Liquidator, Skinhead Moonstomp

SPINNERS   *– see DETROIT SPINNERS*

SPITTING IMAGE *UK, male/female puppets*
17 May 86   THE CHICKEN SONG........ Virgin SPIT 1   3 wks

Dusty SPRINGFIELD *UK, female vocalist*
28 Apr 66   YOU DON'T HAVE TO SAY YOU LOVE ME..............
Philips BF 1482   1 wk

Jo STAFFORD *US, female vocalist*
16 Jan 53   YOU BELONG TO ME.......... Columbia DB 3152   1 wk

Alvin STARDUST *UK, male vocalist*
9 Mar 74   JEALOUS MIND.................. Magnet MAG 5   1 wk

STARGAZERS *UK, male/female vocal group*
10 Apr 53   BROKEN WINGS............ Decca F 10047   1 wk
12 Mar 54   I SEE THE MOON............ Decca F 10213   5 wks

23 Apr 54   I SEE THE MOON................ Decca F 10213   1 wk

Kay STARR *US, female vocalist*
23 Jan 53   COMES A-LONG A-LOVE...... Capitol CL 13876   1 wk
30 Mar 56   ROCK AND ROLL WALTZ......... HMV POP 168   1 wk

STARSHIP *US, male/female vocal/instrumental group*
9 May 87   NOTHING'S GONNA STOP US NOW.....................
Grunt FB 49757   4 wks

STATUS QUO *UK, male vocal/instrumental group*
18 Jan 75   DOWN DOWN.............. Vertigo 6059 114   1 wk

Tommy STEELE *UK, male vocalist*
11 Jan 57   SINGING THE BLUES........... Decca F 10819   1 wk

Ray STEVENS *US, male vocalist*
15 Jul 74   THE STREAK.............. Janus 6146 201   1 wk

Shakin' STEVENS *UK, male vocalist*
28 Mar 81   THIS OLE HOUSE.......... Epic EPC 9555   3 wks
1 Aug 81   GREEN DOOR.............. Epic A 1354   4 wks
30 Jan 82   OH JULIE............... Epic A 1742   1 wk
28 Dec 85   MERRY CHRISTMAS EVERYONE.... Epic A 6769   2 wks

Dave STEWART with Barbara GASKIN *UK, male instrumentalist (keyboards) with female vocalist*
17 Oct 81   IT'S MY PARTY........ Stiff/Broken BROKEN 2   4 wks

Rod STEWART *UK, male vocalist*
9 Oct 71   MAGGIE MAY.............. Mercury 6052 097   5 wks
2 Sep 72   YOU WEAR IT WELL......... Mercury 6052 171   1 wk
6 Sep 75   SAILING.............. Warner Bros K 16600   4 wks
21 May 77   I DON'T WANT TO TALK ABOUT IT/FIRST CUT IS THE DEEPEST.......... Riva 7   4 wks
2 Dec 78   DA YA THINK I'M SEXY........... Riva 17   1 wk
2 Jul 83   BABY JANE........... Warner Bros W 9608   3 wks

STINGERS   *– see B.BUMBLE and the STINGERS*

Barbra STREISAND *US, female vocalist*
25 Oct 80   WOMAN IN LOVE.............. CBS 8966   3 wks

STYLISTICS *US, male vocal group*
16 Aug 75   CAN'T GIVE YOU ANYTHING (BUT MY LOVE)..........
Avco 6105 039   3 wks

Donna SUMMER *US, female vocalist*
23 Jul 77   I FEEL LOVE............ GTO GT 100   4 wks

SUNSHINE BAND   *– see K.C. and the SUNSHINE BAND*

SUPREMES *US, female vocal group*
19 Nov 64   BABY LOVE............ Stateside SS 350   2 wks
See also Diana ROSS

SURVIVOR *US, male vocal/instrumental group*
4 Sep 82   EYE OF THE TIGER........ Scotti Bros SCT A 2411   4 wks

SWEET *UK, male vocal/instrumental group*
27 Jan 73   BLOCKBUSTER.............. RCA 2305   5 wks

SWEET SENSATION *UK, male vocal group*
19 Oct 74   SAD SWEET DREAMER....... Pye 7N 45385   1 wk

——— T ———

T REX *UK, male vocal/instrumental duo*
20 Mar 71   HOT LOVE.................................... Fly BUG 6   6 wks
24 Jul 71   GET IT ON..................................... Fly BUG 10   4 wks
5 Feb 72   TELEGRAM SAM........................T Rex 101   2 wks
20 May 72   METAL GURU.....................EMI MARC 1   4 wks

TAMS *US, male vocal group*
18 Sep 71   HEY GIRL DON'T BOTHER ME.... Probe PRO 532   3 wks

TEENAGERS featuring Frankie LYMON *US, male vocal group*
20 Jul 56   WHY DO FOOLS FALL IN LOVE......................................
Columbia DB 3772   3 wks

TEMPERANCE SEVEN *UK, male vocal/instrumental jazz band*
25 May 61   YOU'RE DRIVING ME CRAZY.... Parlophone R 4757   1 wk

10 C.C. *UK, male vocal/instrumental group*
23 Jun 73   RUBBER BULLETS.............................UK 36   1 wk
28 Jun 75   I'M NOT IN LOVE........................ Mercury 6008 014   2 wks
23 Sep 78   DREADLOCK HOLIDAY................Mercury 6008 035   1 wk
On Dreadlock Holiday, 10 CC were a vocal/instrumental duo

THREE DEGREES *US, female vocal group*
17 Aug 74   WHEN WILL I SEE YOU AGAIN......................................
Philadelphia International PIR 2155   2 wks

THUNDERBIRDS *– see Chris FARLOWE and the THUNDERBIRDS*

THUNDERCLAP NEWMAN *UK, male vocal/instrumental group*
2 Jul 69   SOMETHING IN THE AIR............... Track 604-031   3 wks

TICH *– see Dave DEE, DOZY, BEAKY, MICK and TICH*

TIGHT FIT *UK, male/female vocal group*
6 Mar 82   THE LION SLEEPS TONIGHT............. Jive JIVE 9   3 wks

Johnny TILLOTSON *US, male vocalist*
12 Jan 61   POETRY IN MOTION................... London HLA 9231   2 wks

TORNADOS *UK, male instrumental group*
4 Oct 62   TELSTAR.. Decca F 11494   5 wks

T'PAU *UK, male/female vocal/instrumental group*
14 Nov 87   CHINA IN YOUR HAND..................... Siren SRN 64   5 wks

John TRAVOLTA and Olivia NEWTON-JOHN *US/UK, male/female vocal duo*
17 Jun 78   YOU'RE THE ONE THAT I WANT........ RSO 006   9 wks
30 Sep 78   SUMMER NIGHTS................................RSO 18   7 wks
See also Olivia NEWTON-JOHN and ELECTRIC LIGHT ORCHESTRA

TREMELOES *UK, male vocal/instrumental group*
18 May 67   SILENCE IS GOLDEN............................ CBS 2723   3 wks
See also Brian POOLE and the TREMELOES

Jackie TRENT *UK, female vocalist*
20 May 65   WHERE ARE YOU NOW (MY LOVE)... Pye 15776   1 wk

TROGGS *UK, male vocal/instrumental group*
4 Aug 66   WITH A GIRL LIKE YOU................ Fontana TF 717   2 wks

TUBEWAY ARMY *– see Gary NUMAN*

Conway TWITTY *US, male vocalist*
19 Dec 58   IT'S ONLY MAKE BELIEVE................... MGM 992   5 wks

Bonnie TYLER *UK, female vocalist*
12 Mar 83   TOTAL ECLIPSE OF THE HEART..CBS TYLER 1   2 wks

TYMES *US, male vocal group*
25 Jan 75   MS. GRACE... RCA 2493   1 wk

TYPICALLY TROPICAL *UK, male vocal/instrumental duo*
9 Aug 75   BARBADOS............................... Gull GULS 14   1 wk

——— U ———

UB40 *UK, male vocal/instrumental group*
3 Sep 83   RED RED WINE.................DEP International 7 DEP 7   3 wks
31 Aug 85   I GOT YOU BABE.................DEP International DEP 20   1 wk
I Got You Babe featured guest vocals by Chrissie HYNDE. See also PRETENDERS

UNION GAP featuring Gary PUCKETT *US, male vocal/instrumental group*
30 May 68   YOUNG GIRL..................................CBS 3365   4 wks

UNIT FOUR PLUS TWO *UK, male vocal/instrumental group*
8 Apr 65   CONCRETE AND CLAY   Decca F 12071   1 wk

Midge URE *UK, male vocalist*
5 Oct 85   IF I WAS...........................Chrysalis URE 1   1 wk
See also SLIK

USA FOR AFRICA *US/Ireland, male/female charity group*
20 Apr 85   WE ARE THE WORLD.....................CBS USAID 1   2 wks

——— V ———

Ricky VALANCE *UK, male vocalist*
29 Sep 60   TELL LAURA I LOVE HER........ Columbia DB 4493   3 wks

Dickie VALENTINE *UK, male vocalist*
7 Jan 55   FINGER OF SUSPICION....................Decca F 10394   1 wk
21 Jan 55   FINGER OF SUSPICION................... Decca F 10394   2 wks
16 Dec 55   CHRISTMAS ALPHABET................Decca F 10628   3 wks

Frankie VAUGHAN *UK, male vocalist*
25 Jan 57   GARDEN OF EDEN......................... Philips PB 660   4 wks
7 Dec 61   TOWER OF STRENGTH....................Philips PB 1195   3 wks

VILLAGE PEOPLE *US, male vocal instrumental group*
6 Jan 79   Y.M.C.A.................................... Mercury 6007 192   3 wks

W

WALKER BROTHERS *US, male vocal/instrumental group*
23 Sep 65   MAKE IT EASY ON YOURSELF.......Philips BF 1428   1 wk
17 Mar 66   THE SUN AIN'T GONNA SHINE ANYMORE.................
Philips BF 1473   4 wks

Anita WARD *US, female vocalist*
16 Jun 79   RING MY BELL..................TK TKR 7543   2 wks

WHAM! *UK, male vocal duo*
2 Jun 84   WAKE ME UP BEFORE YOU GO GO..........................
Epic A 4440   2 wks
20 Oct 84   FREEDOM...........................Epic A 4743   3 wks
30 Nov 85   I'M YOUR MAN......................Epic A 6716   2 wks
28 Jun 86   THE EDGE OF HEAVEN.................Epic FIN 1   2 wks
See also George MICHAEL, George MICHAEL and Aretha
FRANKLIN

Barry WHITE *US, male vocalist*
7 Dec 74   YOU'RE THE FIRST THE LAST MY EVERYTHING......
20th Century BTC 2133   2 wks

David WHITFIELD *UK, male vocalist*
6 Nov 53   ANSWER ME...................Decca F 10192   1 wk
11 Dec 53   ANSWER ME...................Decca F 10192   1 wk
2 Jul 54   CARA MIA.....................Decca F 10327   10 wks
Cara Mia credited David WHITFIELD with the MANTOVANI
ORCHESTRA. See also MANTOVANI

Slim WHITMAN *US, male vocalist*
28 Jul 55   ROSE MARIE....................London HL 8061   11 wks

Andy WILLIAMS *US, male vocalist*
24 May 57   BUTTERFLY.................London HLA 8399   2 wks

Danny WILLIAMS *UK, male vocalist*
28 Dec 61   MOON RIVER....................HMV POP 932   2 wks

Deniece WILLIAMS *US, female vocalist*
7 May 77   FREE.........................CBS 4978   2 wks

Jackie WILSON *US, male vocalist*
27 Dec 86   REET PETITE...................SMP SKM 3   4 wks

WINGS *UK/US, male/female vocal/instrumental group*
3 Dec 77   MULL OF KINTYRE/GIRLS' SCHOOL...........................
Capitol R 6018   9 wks
See also Paul McCARTNEY, Paul McCARTNEY with Stevie
WONDER, BEATLES

WIZZARD *UK, male vocal/instrumental group*
19 May 73   SEE MY BABY JIVE.......................Harvest HAR 5070   4 wks
22 Sep 73   ANGEL FINGERS...........................Harvest HAR 5076   1 wk

Stevie WONDER *US, male vocalist/multi-instrumentalist*
8 Sep 84   I JUST CALLED TO SAY I LOVE YOU...........................
Motown TMG 1349   6 wks
See also Paul McCARTNEY with Stevie WONDER

WURZELS *UK, male vocal/instrumental group*
12 Jun 76   COMBINE HARVESTER (BRAND NEW KEY)...............
EMI 2450   2 wks

Tammy WYNETTE *US, female vocalist*
17 May 75   STAND BY YOUR MAN....................Epic EPC 7137   3 wks

Y

Jimmy YOUNG *UK, male vocalist*
24 Jun 55   UNCHAINED MELODY....................Decca F 10502   3 wks
14 Oct 55   THE MAN FROM LARAMIE..........Decca F 10597   4 wks

Paul YOUNG *UK, male vocalist*
23 Jul 83   WHEREVER I LAY MY HAT (THAT'S MY HOME)......
CBS A 3371   3 wks

Z

ZAGER and EVANS *US, male vocal duo*
30 Aug 69   IN THE YEAR 2525 (EXORDIUM AND TERMINUS)....
RCA 1860   3 wks

PART
3

The Six Hundred Number Ones
Listed Alphabetically By Title

Different songs with the same title (e.g. *The Power Of Love*, which has been a number one title for both Frankie Goes To Hollywood and Jennifer Rush) are differentiated (A) and (B). Where there is no letter in brackets after the titles, all recordings are of the same song (e.g. *Young Love* by Tab Hunter and by Donny Osmond). Individual titles of songs or tunes on the two EPs which reached number one are also included, as are the titles of the EPs. Both sides of double-sided number ones are listed separately.

NUMBER ONES: ALPHABETICALLY BY TITLE

Zager and Evans. *No number one title began with a 'Z' but the* In The Year 2525 *hit makers'
name does.*

PART

4

THE STATISTICS

This section of the book should not be used as proof that Abba are a greater group than the Rolling Stones, nor that Burt Bacharach writes better songs than Carl Sigman. Statistics and information given in this part are sub-divided as follows: The Hits (page 252); The Producers (page 266); The Writers (page 267); The Record Labels (page 270).

MOST NUMBER ONE HITS

Double-sided hits count as only one hit. A disc which returns to the number one slot counts as only one hit.

17 BEATLES
17 ELVIS PRESLEY
10 CLIFF RICHARD
    (+1 with the Young Ones)
 9 ABBA
 8 ROLLING STONES
 6 SLADE
 6 ROD STEWART
 5 BEE GEES
 5 BLONDIE
 5 MADONNA
 5 POLICE
 5 SHADOWS
    (+7 with Cliff Richard)
 4 EVERLY BROTHERS
 4 FRANK IFIELD
 4 JAM
 4 FRANKIE LAINE
 4 GUY MITCHELL
 4 SHAKIN' STEVENS
 4 T REX
 4 WHAM!

3 ADAM & THE ANTS/ADAM ANT
3 DAVID BOWIE
   (+1 with Queen and 1 with Mick Jagger)
3 BROTHERHOOD OF MAN
3 BUCKS FIZZ
3 LONNIE DONEGAN
3 GEORGIE FAME
3 FRANKIE GOES TO HOLLYWOOD
3 GERRY AND THE PACEMAKERS
   (Gerry Marsden 1 more with the Crowd)
3 GARY GLITTER
3 MICHAEL JACKSON
   (1 with Siedah Garrett + 1 with the Jacksons and 1 with USA For Africa)
3 KINKS
3 JOHN LENNON
   (+17 as a Beatle)
3 MANFRED MANN
3 MUD
3 ROY ORBISON
3 DONNY OSMOND
   (+1 with the Osmonds)
3 JOHNNIE RAY
3 SANDIE SHAW

3 SEARCHERS
3 10 C.C.

Boy George has hit the top twice as lead singer of Culture Club and once as a soloist. Art Garfunkel has had two solo number ones and one with Paul Simon. Apart from his participation in 17 Beatles' chart-toppers, Paul McCartney has had one solo number one, one in duet with Stevie Wonder and one with Wings. He was also involved with Band Aid, Ferry Aid and the Crowd.

As well as writing and performing on four Wham! number ones, George Michael has had two solo number ones and one more in partnership with Aretha Franklin. Olivia Newton-John has had two number ones with John Travolta and one with Electric Light Orchestra. Diana Ross has topped the charts twice as a soloist and once more as the lead singer of the Supremes. Frank Sinatra has had two solo number ones and one in duet with his daughter Nancy. Midge Ure has had one solo number one, one with Slik and one more as a prime mover of Band Aid.

The Beatles *breaking all the records.*

MOST WEEKS AT NUMBER ONE

BY ARTIST

73 ELVIS PRESLEY
69 BEATLES
(Paul McCartney 9 more with Wings, 3 more with Stevie Wonder and 2 more solo, total 83 weeks. John Lennon 7 more solo, total 76 weeks. George Harrison 5 more solo, total 74 weeks)
35 CLIFF RICHARD
(+ 3 more with the Young Ones)
32 FRANKIE LAINE
(1 week top equal)
31 ABBA
20 SLADE
19 EVERLY BROTHERS
(1 week top equal)
18 ROLLING STONES
(Mick Jagger 4 more with David Bowie, total 22 weeks)
18 ROD STEWART
17 FRANK IFIELD
16 SHADOWS
(+28 weeks backing Cliff Richard, total 44 weeks. Hank Marvin 3 more weeks with Cliff And The Young Ones, total 47 weeks)
16 T REX
16 JOHN TRAVOLTA & OLIVIA NEWTON-JOHN
(Olivia Newton John 2 more weeks with Electric Light Orchestra, total 18 weeks)
15 DORIS DAY
16 FRANKIE GOES TO HOLLYWOOD
14 GUY MITCHELL
(1 week top equal)
13 BEE GEES
13 EDDIE CALVERT
13 PERRY COMO
13 POLICE
12 BLONDIE
12 CONNIE FRANCIS
12 DAVID WHITFIELD
(1 week top equal)
11 ADAM & THE ANTS/ADAM ANT
11 LONNIE DONEGAN
11 TENNESSEE ERNIE FORD
11 GERRY & THE PACEMAKERS
(Gerry Marsden 2 more weeks as lead vocalist with The Crowd, total 13 weeks)
11 ENGELBERT HUMPERDINCK
11 MADONNA
11 JOHNNIE RAY
11 SLIM WHITMAN
10 MUD

10 DONNY OSMOND
(+3 weeks with the Osmonds, total 13 weeks)
10 SHAKIN' STEVENS

George Michael has been on top as part of Wham! for 9 weeks, as a soloist for 6 more weeks and in duet with Aretha Franklin for another two, total 17 weeks. David Bowie has been on top by himself for 7 weeks plus four more with Mick Jagger and 2 with Queen, total 13 weeks. Queen have been number one for 9 weeks plus 2 with David Bowie, total 11 weeks. Art Garfunkel has been number one for 8 weeks plus 3 with Simon and Garfunkel, total 11 weeks. Lionel Richie has had 6 weeks at number one and 5 more as one of the Commodores, total 11 weeks. Boy George has held the top spot for 2 weeks as a soloist and for 9 more as lead singer with Culture Club, total 11 weeks. Mantovani has been top for 1 week plus 10 more backing David Whitfield, total 11 weeks.

The man with the most weeks at number one –
Elvis Presley.

MOST WEEKS AT NUMBER ONE

BY AN ARTIST IN ONE CALENDAR
YEAR

27	FRANKIE LAINE	1953
	(1 week top equal)	
18	ELVIS PRESLEY	1961
16	BEATLES	1963
16	JOHN TRAVOLTA & OLIVIA-NEWTON-JOHN	1978
15	ELVIS PRESLEY	1962
15	FRANKIE GOES TO HOLLYWOOD	1984
12	CONNIE FRANCIS	1958
12	FRANK IFIELD	1962
12	BEATLES	1964
12	ABBA	1976

Abba *are shown in the white outfits they wore on the cover of* Arrival, *which included* Dancing Queen.

MOST WEEKS AT NUMBER ONE

BY ONE DISC – IN TOTAL

18	I BELIEVE/Frankie LAINE	1953
11	ROSE MARIE/Slim WHITMAN	1955
10	CARA MIA/David WHITFIELD	1954
9	HERE IN MY HEART/Al MARTINO	1952-3
9	OH MEIN PAPA/Eddie CALVERT	1954
9	SECRET LOVE/Doris DAY	1954
9	DIANA/Paul ANKA	1957
9	BOHEMIAN RHAPSODY/QUEEN	1975-6
9	MULL OF KINTYRE/GIRLS' SCHOOL/WINGS	1977-8
9	YOU'RE THE ONE THAT I WANT/John TRAVOLTA and Olivia NEWTON-JOHN	1978
9	TWO TRIBES/FRANKIE GOES TO HOLLYWOOD	1984

MOST WEEKS

AT NUMBER ONE

BY ONE DISC – CONSECUTIVE WEEKS

11	ROSE MARIE/Slim WHITMAN	1955
10	CARA MIA/David WHITFIELD	1954
9	HERE IN MY HEART/Al MARTINO	1952-3
9	I BELIEVE/Frankie LAINE	1953
9	OH MEIN PAPA/Eddie CALVERT	1954
9	DIANA/Paul ANKA	1957
9	BOHEMIAN RHAPSODY/QUEEN	1975-6
9	MULL OF KINTYRE/GIRLS' SCHOOL/ WINGS	1977-8
9	YOU'RE THE ONE THAT I WANT/ John TRAVOLTA and Olivia NEWTON-JOHN	1978
9	TWO TRIBES/FRANKIE GOES TO HOLLYWOOD	1984
8	ANSWER ME/ Frankie LAINE (1 week top equal)	1953-4
8	SECRET LOVE/Doris DAY	1954
8	MAGIC MOMENTS/Perry COMO	1958
8	IT'S NOW OR NEVER/Elvis PRESLEY	1960
8	WONDERFUL LAND/SHADOWS	1962
8	SUGAR SUGAR/ARCHIES	1969

Oh Mein Papa *by* **Eddie Calvert** *was the first British instrumental to sell a million.*

Three decades later, **Doris Day** *still has more weeks at number one than any other female soloist.*

MOST CONSECUTIVE NUMBER ONES

11 in a row: BEATLES
(from FROM ME TO YOU through to
YELLOW SUBMARINE/ELEANOR RIGBY,
1963 to 1966)

6 in a row: BEATLES
(from ALL YOU NEED IS LOVE through to
THE BALLAD OF JOHN AND YOKO, 1967
to 1969)

5 in a row: Elvis PRESLEY
(from HIS LATEST FLAME through to
RETURN TO SENDER, 1961 to 1962)

5 in a row: ROLLING STONES
(from IT'S ALL OVER NOW through to
GET OFF OF MY CLOUD, 1964 to 1965)

4 in a row: Elvis PRESLEY
(from IT'S NOW OR NEVER through to
SURRENDER, 1960 to 1961) The first
number one hat-trick.

4 in a row: T REX
(from HOT LOVE through to METAL
GURU, 1971 to 1972)

3 in a row: Frank IFIELD
(I REMEMBER YOU, LOVESICK BLUES
and WAYWARD WIND, 1962 to 1963) The
first number one hat-trick by a British artist

**3 in a row: GERRY AND THE
PACEMAKERS**
(HOW DO YOU DO IT, I LIKE IT and
YOU'LL NEVER WALK ALONE, 1963)

3 in a row: ABBA
(MAMMA MIA, FERNANDO and
DANCING QUEEN, 1975 to 1976)

3 in a row: ABBA
(KNOWING ME KNOWING YOU, THE
NAME OF THE GAME and TAKE A
CHANCE ON ME, 1977 to 1978)

3 in a row: POLICE
(MESSAGE IN A BOTTLE, WALKING ON
THE MOON and DON'T STAND SO
CLOSE TO ME, 1979 to 1980) The only
instance of the third record of a hat-trick
coming on to the chart at number one.

3 in a row: BLONDIE
(ATOMIC, CALL ME and THE TIDE IS
HIGH, 1980)

3 in a row: John LENNON
(IMAGINE, (JUST LIKE) STARTING OVER
and WOMAN, 1980) Both the fastest and
slowest hat-trick depending on whether it
started when IMAGINE first entered the
chart in November 1975, or when (JUST
LIKE) STARTING OVER came in late in
1980)

**3 in a row: FRANKIE GOES TO
HOLLYWOOD**
(RELAX, TWO TRIBES and THE POWER
OF LOVE, 1984)

Successive releases for the purpose of this
table are successive official single releases.
The Beatles' two runs of number ones were
each interrupted by irregular releases. An
old single with Tony Sheridan reached
number 29 in the midst of their 11 number
ones, and their double EP *Magical Mystery
Tour* made number two while *Hello Goodbye* was becoming the second of their six
chart toppers on the trot. An LP track, *Jeepster*, and an old recording, *Debora/One
Inch Rock* were released during T Rex's run
of number ones while the group were

changing labels. An EP by Elvis, *Follow
That Dream*, pottered about the lower
reaches of the charts during Elvis' run of five
consecutive number ones. During Police's
hat-trick, one single on another label, one
old single re-issued and a six-pack of
singles hit the chart in an attempt to distract
the compilers of this table. John Lennon's
Imagine was the first of the three singles of
his hat-trick (his last single for five years) but
the second of the three to reach the top.
During his hat-trick, a flood of old Lennon
hits swarmed back on to the chart.

Manager Brian Epstein and Gerry Marsden of **Gerry and the Pacemakers** *are shown in April, 1964, wondering if the group's newly released* Don't Let The Sun Catch You Crying *can return them to the number one spot. It didn't, but it broke them in America.*

Stevie Wonder *successfully rebuffed a plagiarism suit concerning* I Just Called To Say I Love You.

SLOWEST NUMBER ONE

If an artist is ever going to have a number one hit, it usually happens within a year or two of that artist's first hit. About half of all the nearly 400 acts who have hit the very top did so with their first chart hit.

At the very end of 1986, the late Jackie Wilson set new standards for slow climbs to the top. It was over 29 years since his chart debut when he finally hit number one, and although Ben E King climbed to second place on this all time list just a few months later, we doubt whether Wilson's record will ever be broken. The full list of those acts whose first number one came more than 10 years after their chart debut is:

29 years 42 days	JACKIE WILSON	(15 Nov 57 to 27 Dec 86)
26 years 19 days	BEN E KING	(2 Feb 61 to 21 Feb 87)
18 years 218 days	STEVIE WONDER	(3 Feb 66 to 8 Sep 84)
18 years 217 days	JOHNNY MATHIS	(23 Feb 58 to 25 Dec 76)
16 years 218 days	BORIS GARDINER	(17 Jan 70 to 23 Aug 86)
15 years 157 days	CHUCK BERRY	(21 Jun 57 to 25 Nov 72)
15 years 127 days	LOUIS ARMSTRONG	(19 Dec 52 to 24 Apr 68)
14 years 279 days	BARBRA STREISAND	(20 Jan 66 to 25 Oct 80)
13 years 140 days	FOUR SEASONS	(4 Oct 62 to 21 Feb 76)
12 years 321 days	PAUL McCARTNEY	(27 Feb 71 to 14 Jan 84)
12 years 260 days	PINK FLOYD	(30 Mar 67 to 15 Dec 79)
11 years 164 days	JOHN LENNON	(9 Jul 69 to 20 Dec 80)
10 years 298 days	BENNY HILL	(16 Feb 61 to 11 Dec 71)
10 years 8 days	SISTER SLEDGE	(21 Jun 75 to 29 Jun 85)

Of these acts, Stevie Wonder, Paul McCartney and John Lennon had featured on number ones before their solo successes. John Lennon in the only act on this list to achieve more than one number one. His first number one was the first of a hat-trick. Paul McCartney overtook Pink Floyd in 1984 as the leading British act on this list.

Only seven records have taken longer than 200 days to hit the top after their first appearance on the chart:

29 years 42 days	REET PETITE by Jackie Wilson	
		(15 Nov 57 to 27 Dec 86)
25 years 244 days	STAND BY ME by Ben E King	
		(22 Jun 61 to 21 Feb 87)
6 years 63 days	SPACE ODDITY by David Bowie	
		(6 Sep 69 to 8 Nov 75)
5 years 70 days	IMAGINE by John Lennon	
		(1 Nov 75 to 10 Jan 81)
322 days	ROCK AROUND THE CLOCK by Bill Haley & his Comets	(7 Jan 55 to 25 Nov 55)
308 days	EYE LEVEL by Simon Park Orchestra	
		(25 Nov 72 to 29 Sep 73)
210 days	THE MODEL/COMPUTER LOVE by Kraftwerk	(11 Jul 81 to 6 Feb 82)

All these records dropped off the charts between their original chart entry and their chart-topping reappearances. The slowest climb to number one by any record that stayed on the chart all the time is 16 weeks (112 days) by THE POWER OF LOVE by Jennifer Rush, from 29 Jun 85 to 12 Oct 85. The previous record of 14 weeks (98 days) had been set only seven months earlier by Dead Or Alive's YOU SPIN ME ROUND (LIKE A RECORD), which took from 1 Dec 84 to 9 Mar 85 to climb to number one.

FASTEST NUMBER ONE

At the other end of the scale from Jackie Wilson, these are the acts who moved from chart debut to the number one slot in the shortest time, starting with Al Martino's entry in the very first chart:

0 days   AL MARTINO (14 Nov 52)
7 days   EDISON LIGHTHOUSE (24 to 31 Jan 70)
7 days   MUNGO JERRY (6 to 13 Jun 70)
7 days   DAVE EDMUNDS (21 to 28 Nov 70)
7 days   NICOLE (8 to 15 May 82)
7 days   MUSICAL YOUTH (25 Sep to 3 Oct 82)
7 days   SPITTING IMAGE (10 to 17 May 86)

Other first-time chart acts who consisted entirely or mainly of people who have been in the charts under some other name and have also had rapid climbs top the top:

0 days   BAND AID (1984)
0 days   DAVID BOWIE & MICK JAGGER (1985)
0 days   FERRY AID (1987)
7 days   GEORGE HARRISON (1971)
7 days   QUEEN & DAVID BOWIE (1981)
7 days   CAPTAIN SENSIBLE (1982)
7 days   USA FOR AFRICA (1985)
7 days   CLIFF RICHARD & THE YOUNG ONES (1986)
7 days   GEORGE MICHAEL & ARETHA FRANKLIN (1987)
7 days   BOY GEORGE (1987)

Musical Youth are shocked to hear what a 'dutchie' really is.

Duran Duran. *Left to right: Nick Rhodes, Simon LeBon and Taylors John, Roger and Andy.*

STRAIGHT IN AT NUMBER ONE

A total of 50 records have entered the charts in one of the top three positions, including 19 that have hit the very top in their first week of chart action. They are:

14 Nov 52	HERE IN MY HEART	Al Martino
24 Jan 58	JAILHOUSE ROCK	Elvis Presley
3 Nov 60	IT'S NOW OR NEVER	Elvis Presley
11 Jan 62	THE YOUNG ONES	Cliff Richard
23 Apr 69	GET BACK	Beatles
3 Mar 73	CUM ON FEEL THE NOIZE	Slade
30 Jun 73	SKWEEZE ME PLEEZE ME	Slade
17 Nov 73	I LOVE YOU LOVE ME LOVE	Gary Glitter
15 Dec 73	MERRY XMAS EVERYBODY	Slade
22 Mar 80	GOING UNDERGROUND/DREAMS OF CHILDREN	Jam
27 Sep 80	DON'T STAND SO CLOSE TO ME	Police
9 May 81	STAND AND DELIVER	Adam & the Ants
13 Feb 82	A TOWN CALLED MALICE/PRECIOUS	Jam

4 Dec 82	BEAT SURRENDER..Jam
26 Mar 83	IS THERE SOMETHINC I SHOULD KNOW?...................
	Duran Duran
16 Jun 84	TWO TRIBES......................Frankie Goes To Hollywood
15 Dec 84	DO THEY KNOW IT'S CHRISTMAS?...............Band Aid
7 Sep 85	DANCING IN THE STREET.......................................
	David Bowie & Mick Jagger
4 Apr 87	LET IT BE... Ferry Aid

Slade remain the only act to enter the chart at number one with consecutive releases. Seven acts – Al Martino, Jam, Adam & the Ants, Duran Duran, Band Aid, David Bowie & Mick Jagger and Ferry Aid – went straight to number one with their first chart topper.

BIGGEST JUMP TO NUMBER ONE

There have been 29 records, apart from those that came on to the chart at number one which are listed separately, which have jumped from outside the Top 10 straight to the top spot.

33 to 1	HAPPY TALK Captain Sensible.............................. 3 Jul 82
27 to 1	SURRENDER Elvis Presley.................................. 27 May 61
26 to 1	PASS THE DUTCHIE Musical Youth.................... 2 Oct 82
22 to 1	GREEN DOOR Shakin' Stevens......................... 1 Aug 81
21 to 1	HEY JUDE Beatles.. 11 Sep 68
21 to 1	(JUST LIKE) STARTING OVER John Lennon.20 Dec 80
19 to 1	ARE YOU LONESOME TONICHT? Elvis Presley.............
	21 Jan 61
19 to 1	HALF AS NICE Amen Corner.......................... 12 Feb 69
19 to 1	LOVE ME FOR A REASON Osmonds.............31 Aug 74
19 to 1	STAND BY ME Ben E King.............................21 Feb 87
17 to 1	GET OFF OF MY CLOUD Rolling Stones...........4 Nov 65
16 to 1	I HEAR YOU KNOCKIN' Dave Edmunds.........28 Nov 70
16 to 1	CHIRPY CHIRPY CHEEP CHEEP Middle Of The Road.
	19 Jun 71
16 to 1	YOUNG LOVE Donny Osmond.........................25 Aug 73
16 to 1	DANCING QUEEN Abba...................................4 Sep 76
15 to 1	I DON'T LIKE MONDAYS Boomtown Rats.........28 Jul 79
15 to 1	THE SPECIAL AKA LIVE EP Specials..............2 Feb 80
14 to 1	EYE LEVEL Simon Park Orchestra....................29 Sep 73
13 to 1	IN THE SUMMERTIME Mungo Jerry................. 13 Jun 70
13 to 1	STAR TREKKIN' Firm....................................20 Jun 87
12 to 1	LOVE GROWS Edison Lighthouse.....................31 Jan 70
11 to 1	(THERE'S) ALWAYS SOMETHING THERE TO REMIND
	ME Sandie Shaw..22 Oct 64
11 to 1	TICKET TO RIDE Beatles...................................22 Apr 65
11 to 1	MICHELLE Overlanders..................................27 Jan 66
11 to 1	LADY MADONNA Beatles............................. 20 Mar 68
11 to 1	SUGAR SUGAR Archies.................................25 Oct 69
11 to 1	SHE Charles Aznavour....................................29 Jun 74
11 to 1	SUMMER NIGHTS John Travolta & Olivia Newton-John.
	30 Sep 78
11 to 1	THE CHICKEN SONG Spitting Image............. 17 May 86

The biggest jump within the chart is a leap of 62 places, from 66 to 4 on 11 Oct 86 by Nick Berry's EVERY LOSER WINS. Two other number one hits have climbed over 50 places in one week on their way to the top – the Firm's STAR TREKKIN' which leapt from 74 to 13 to 1, a leap of 61 places followed by a leap of 12 places, and the Flying Pickets' ONLY YOU, which jumped 51 places on 3 Dec 83. The low-est initial chart entry by a record that hit the top is 74 by STAR TREKKIN', beating the previous record holder, Charlene's I'VE NEVER BEEN TO ME by one place. Charlene entered the chart at 73 on 15 May 82.

Captain Sensible launches himself into his historic chart leap.

POSTHUMOUS NUMBER ONE HITS

The full (and rather grisly) list of people who have hit number one after their death is as follows:

	Died	**Reached No. 1**
BUDDY HOLLY	3 Feb 59...24 Apr 59
EDDIE COCHRAN	17 Apr 60...23 Jun 60
JIM REEVES	31 Jul 64..22 Sep 66
JIMI HENDRIX	18 Sep 70 ....21 Nov 70
ELVIS PRESLEY	16 Aug 77...3 Sep 77
JOHN LENNON	8 Dec 80..20 Dec 80
JACKIE WILSON	21 Jan 84...27 Dec 86

The shortest gap between the death of an artist and his record reaching number one is 12 days in the case of John Lennon. He went on to have three number ones in the ten weeks following his murder. The slowest posthumous hit has been Jackie Wilson's *Reet Petite*, which hit the top 2 years and 340 days after his death.

LAST HIT AT NUMBER ONE

Chart history shows that once an act has scored its first number one, it is far more likely to hit the top again than to have no more hits at all. Disappearing without trace, chartwise, after a number one hit is fairly rare, and apart from the one-hit wonders, listed separately, only 8 acts have failed to follow up a number one. They are: Charles Aznavour, the Firm, Rolf Harris, Benny Hill, Tommy James & the Shondells, Kay Starr, Starship, John Travolta and Olivia Newton-John and Wham!

Rolf Harris emerged from his fallow chart period by participating in the Crowd's *You'll Never Walk Alone*, and both John Travolta and Olivia Newton-John have had solo hits since their final chart topper together. As a duo they share with Kay Starr the unlikely distinction of hitting number one with both their first and their last British hit singles.

Kay Starr *got her big break with Glenn Miller deputising for Marion Hutton. Before* Two Little Boys **Rolf Harris** *had two big top ten hits,* Tie Me Kangaroo Down Sport *and* Sun Arise.

The Crowd. *Same song, same lead singer, same peak position, twenty two years after Gerry and the Pacemakers.*

FIRST THREE HITS AT NUMBER ONE

On 13 Oct 63, GERRY & THE PACE-MAKERS' third single release became their third number one hit, thus establishing as record that was for years considered impossible to equal. On 8 Dec 84, 21 years and 38 days later, FRANKIE GOES TO HOLLY-WOOD's third single release became their third number one hit. It is a curious coincidence that both acts come from Liverpool and both acts' third number one was a pseudo-religious song. Frankie's third hit was the Nativity video hit *The Power Of Love*, a title which was later taken back to the top by Jennifer Rush. Gerry's was *You'll Never Walk Alone*, from the musical *Carousel*, and Gerry himself took that song back to the top in 1985 as lead singer of the Crowd. To complete the coincidence, one track on the 12-inch version of *Relax* was Frankie's interpretation of Gerry's seventh hit, *Ferry Cross The Mersey*, and both acts took their fourth hits to number 2.

*This definitive photograph of a **Harry Belafonte** performance was, surprisingly, taken at the Kilburn State Theatre in 1958.*

George Michael, *upset at the fact that limited airplay on* I Want Your Sex *spoiled his chances for three consecutive number ones with his first three solo releases.*

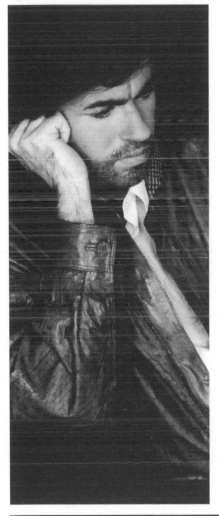

BIGGEST FALLS FROM NUMBER ONE

Only 21 records have ever fallen out of the top five directly from the very top spot, as follows:

1 to 12	MARY'S BOY CHILD	Harry Belafonte	10 Jan 58
1 to 10	ONLY YOU	Flying Pickets	14 Jan 84
1 to 9	YOU'RE DRIVING ME CRAZY	Temperance Seven	1 Jun 61
1 to 9	THESE BOOTS ARE MADE FOR WALKIN'	Nancy Sinatra	17 Mar 66
1 to 8	HELLO GOODBYE	The Beatles	24 Jan 68
1 to 8	LONELY THIS CHRISTMAS	Mud	18 Jan 75
1 to 7	WAYWARD WIND	Frank Ifield	14 Mar 63
1 to 7	YOUNG LOVE	Donny Osmond	22 Sep 73
1 to 7	KNOWING ME KNOWING YOU	Abba	7 May 77
1 to 6	HERE IN MY HEART	Al Martino	16 Jan 53
1 to 6	ROCK AROUND THE CLOCK	Bill Haley & his Comets	20 Jan 56
1 to 6	CATHY'S CLOWN	Everly Brothers	23 Jun 60
1 to 6	SUMMER HOLIDAY	Cliff Richard & the Shadows	11 Apr 63
1 to 6	SUGAR BABY LOVE	Rubettes	15 Jun 74
1 to 6	YOU TO ME ARE EVERYTHING	Real Thing	17 Jul 76
1 to 6	BRIGHT EYES	Art Garfunkel	26 May 79
1 to 6	THERE'S NO ONE QUITE LIKE GRANDMA	St Winifred's School Choir	10 Jan 81
1 to 6	IT'S MY PARTY	Dave Stewart with Barbara Gaskin	14 Nov 81
1 to 6	LET'S DANCE	David Bowie	30 Apr 83
1 to 6	YOU SPIN ME ROUND (LIKE A RECORD)	Dead Or Alive	23 Mar 85
1 to 6	A DIFFERENT CORNER	George Michael	10 May 86

FIRST TWO HITS AT NUMBER ONE

Only 12 acts in the 34 year history of the chart have hit the top with each of their first two chart hits.

EDDIE CALVERT	Oh Mein Papa; Cherry Pink and Apple Blossom White	1954, 55
ADAM FAITH	What Do You Want; Poor Me	1959, 60
TENNESSEE ERNIE FORD	Give Me Your Word; Sixteen Tons	1955, 56
FRANKIE GOES TO HOLLYWOOD	Relax, Two Tribes	1984
ART GARFUNKEL	I Only Have Eyes For You; Bright Eyes	1975, 79
GERRY AND THE PACEMAKERS	How Do You Do It; I Like It	1963
GEORGE MICHAEL	Careless Whisper; A Different Corner	1984, 86

Of these acts only Frankie Goes To Hollywood, Gerry and the Pacemakers, George Michael, Mungo Jerry and John Travolta & Olivia Newton-John hit the top with their first 2 *releases*.

NUMBER ONE HITS AS A SOLOIST AND AS PART OF A GROUP

No fewer than 32 acts have hit the number one spot on the British charts as solo acts and also as an official part of a larger group.

RICK ASTLEY (with Ferry Aid)
HARRY BELAFONTE (with USA For Africa)

DAVID BOWIE (with Queen, Mick Jagger and with Band Aid)
BOY GEORGE (with Culture Club, Ferry Aid and Band Aid)
KATE BUSH (with Ferry Aid)

RAY CHARLES (with USA For Africa)
PHIL COLLINS (in duet with Philip Bailey and with Band Aid)
JIM DIAMOND (with the Crowd)
ART GARFUNKEL (with Simon and Garfunkel)
EDDY GRANT (with the Equals)
ROLF HARRIS (with the Crowd)
GEORGE HARRISON (with the Beatles)
BUDDY HOLLY (with the Crickets)
MICHAEL JACKSON (with the Jacksons and with USA For Africa)
BILLY JOEL (with USA For Africa)
JOHN LENNON (with the Beatles)
JOHNNY LOGAN (with the Crowd)
PAUL McCARTNEY (with the Beatles, Wings, with Stevie Wonder, Band Aid, Ferry Aid and the Crowd!)
GEORGE MICHAEL (with Wham!, Aretha Franklin and Band Aid)
DONNY OSMOND (with the Osmonds)
SUZI QUATRO (with Ferry Aid)
CLIFF RICHARD (with the Young Ones)
LIONEL RICHIE (with the Commodores and USA For Africa)
SMOKEY ROBINSON (with the Miracles and USA For Africa)
DIANA ROSS (with the Supremes and USA For Africa)
FRANK SINATRA (with Nancy Sinatra)
NANCY SINATRA (with Frank Sinatra)
ALVIN STARDUST (with Ferry Aid)
BONNIE TYLER (with Ferry Aid)
MIDGE URE (with Slik and Band Aid)
STEVIE WONDER (with Paul McCartney and USA For Africa)
PAUL YOUNG (with Band Aid)

Five complete chart-topping groups also featured on Ferry Aid, namely BUCKS FIZZ, DR & THE MEDICS, FRANKIE GOES TO HOLLYWOOD, MEL & KIM and NEW SEEKERS. The line up of these groups in 1987 was not necessarily the same as on their number one hits.

The Young Ones *getting up* **Cliff Richard***'s nose.*

ONE HIT WONDERS

Qualification: one number one hit and nothing else ever. 31 immortal acts now make up the list. Only four acts have ever escaped from the list after being on it for more than three years – Art Garfunkel, the England World Cup Squad, Survivor and Johnny Logan.

1954
KITTY KALLEN Little Things Mean A Lot
1956
DREAMWEAVERS It's Almost Tomorrow
1958
KALIN TWINS When
1959
JERRY KELLER Here Comes Summer
1960
RICKY VALANCE Tell Laura I Love Her
1962
B.BUMBLE AND THE STINGERS Nut Rocker
1966
OVERLANDERS Michelle
1968
CRAZY WORLD OF ARTHUR BROWN Fire
1969
ZAGER AND EVANS In The Year 2525 (Exordium and Terminus)
JANE BIRKIN & SERGE GAINSBOURG Je T'Aime . . . Moi Non Plus
ARCHIES Sugar Sugar
1970
LEE MARVIN Wand'rin' Star
NORMAN GREENBAUM Spirit In The Sky
MATTHEWS' SOUTHERN COMFORT Woodstock
1971
CLIVE DUNN Grandad
1973
SIMON PARK ORCHESTRA Eye Level
1975
TYPICALLY TROPICAL Barbados
1976
J J BARRIE No Charge
1977
FLOATERS Float On
1978
ALTHIA AND DONNA Up Town Top Ranking
BRIAN AND MICHAEL Matchstalk Men And Matchstalk Cats And Dogs
1979
ANITA WARD Ring My Bell
LENA MARTELL One Day At A Time
1980
FERN KINNEY Together We Are Beautiful
MASH Theme From M*A*S*H*

Nick Berry arrives at a TV celebrity ball while Every Loser Wins enjoys a number one run.

ST. WINIFRED'S SCHOOL CHOIR There's No-One Quite Like Grandma
1981
JOE DOLCE MUSIC THEATRE Shaddup You Face
CHARLENE I've Never Been To Me
1985
PHYLLIS NELSON Move Closer
1986
NICK BERRY Every Loser Wins
1987
M/A/R/R/S Pump Up The Volume/Anitina

Apart from these acts, 18 other one-hit wonders exist, made up of acts who have had hits in other guises, as follows:

1967
NANCY SINATRA & FRANK SINATRA Something Stupid (both have had solo number one hits)
1974
JOHN DENVER Annie's Song (has also hit with Placido Domingo)

1976
ELTON JOHN & KIKI DEE Don't Go Breaking My Heart (both have had solo hits)
1980
OLIVIA NEWTON-JOHN & ELECTRIC LIGHT ORCHESTRA Xanadu (both have had solo hits)
1981
QUEEN & DAVID BOWIE Under Pressure (both acts have had number one hits)
1982
PAUL McCARTNEY WITH STEVIE WONDER Ebony And Ivory (both acts have had solo number one hits)
1984
BAND AID Do They Know It's Christmas? (a conglomeration of hitmakers)
1985
ELAINE PAIGE & BARBARA DICKSON I Know Him So Well (both have had solo hits)
USA FOR AFRICA We Are The World (another conglomeration of hitmakers)
THE CROWD You'll Never Walk Alone (yet another charity conglomeration)
DAVID BOWIE & MICK JAGGER Dancing In The Street (both have had solo hits)
1986
CLIFF RICHARD & THE YOUNG ONES WITH HANK MARVIN Living Doll (Cliff, Hank and one Young One, neil, have had solo hits)
1987
STEVE 'SILK' HURLEY Jack Your Body (has hit as part of J M Silk)
GEORGE MICHAEL & ARETHA FRANKLIN I Knew You Were Waiting (For Me) (both have had solo hits)
FERRY AID Let It Be (more charity-minded chart regulars)

The backing singers on Brian and Michael's hit were the St. Winifred's School Choir, who for five years held the unique distinction of being one-hit wonders twice, but with the coming of the charity discs, a number of one-hit wonders reappeared under a different guise or two.

The Crowd included Zac Starkey, son of Ringo Starr. Zac and Ringo thus became the first father and son ever to have topped the British charts, either separately or together. Frank and Nancy Sinatra became the first instance of a father and daughter topping the charts, and the Woodwards, Hilda and Rob, both of Lieutenant Pigeon, are the only instance of a mother and son reaching number one. No mother and daughter have yet both hit the very top of the British singles chart.

GAP BETWEEN NUMBER ONE HITS

Of all the acts that have enjoyed two or more number one hits, only five acts have suffered through a gap of more than 7 years between number ones, although one act has, incredibly, done so twice. The Beatles crammed all of their 17 chart toppers into a period of 6 years and 54 days.

14 years 172 days	DIANA ROSS	(17 Sep 71 to 8 Mar 86)
11 years 238 days	FRANK SINATRA	(7 Oct 54 to 2 Jun 66)
11 years 124 days	CLIFF RICHARD	(23 Apr 68 to 25 Aug 79)
9 years 231 days	BEE GEES	(10 Sep 68 to 29 Apr 78)
8 years 215 days	BEE GEES	(16 Mar 79 to 17 Oct 87)
7 years 357 days	DON McLEAN	(30 Jun 72 to 21 Jun 80)

Three of the six 'comeback' chart-toppers were written by Barry, Maurice and Robin Gibb.

There was a gap of 21 years 200 days between 27 November 1963, the last day that Gerry & the Pacemakers' *You'll Never Walk Alone* was at number one, and 15 June 1985, when the same song, with Gerry Marsden again on lead vocals, hit number one, this time by the Crowd.

16 years and 9 days elapsed between the last day of the final Rolling Stones number one, and Mick Jagger's reappearance at the top with David Bowie.

There was a gap of 14 years and 113 days between Eddy Grant's last day at number one as an Equal and his first day at the top as a soloist.

Tears Of A Clown by Smokey Robinson & the Miracles dropped from number one 10 years and 268 days before Smokey's solo hit *Being With You* reached the summit.

LONGEST SPAN OF NUMBER ONE HITS

Only three acts have scored number one hits over a period of more than 20 years. They are:

20 years 87 days	ELVIS PRESLEY	(1957 to 1977)
20 years 52 days	CLIFF RICHARD	(1959 to 1979)
20 years 34 days	BEE GEES	(1967 to 1987)

Cliff Richard was at number one over 26 years after his debut at the top of the chart, but his last chart-topper was in partnership with the Young Ones. Diana Ross first hit number one as lead singer for the Supremes in 1964 and dropped off the top for the final time to date as a soloist in 1986, over 21 years later.

No other acts have been at the top of the charts in three different decades.

Fleetwood Mac *came closest to having the same record reach number one in two separate chart runs.*

MOST WEEKS ON CHART
BY A NUMBER ONE HIT

Surprisingly, chart history shows that the longest running hits in chart terms are often not those that climb all the way to number one. Of the 44 records in history which have so far spent 30 weeks or more on the charts, only 17, listed here, reached number one.

57 wks	ROCK AROUND THE CLOCK	Bill Haley
56 wks	RELEASE ME	Engelbert Humperdinck
52 wks	RELAX!	Frankie Goes To Hollywood
40 wks	RIVERS OF BABYLON	Boney M
40 wks	TIE A YELLOW RIBBON ROUND THE OLD OAK TREE	Dawn
36 wks	I BELIEVE	Frankie Laine
36 wks	I PRETEND	Des O'Connor
36 wks	SHE LOVES YOU	Beatles
36 wks	TAINTED LOVE	Soft Cell
35 wks	ALBATROSS	Fleetwood Mac
34 wks	CHIRPY CHIRPY CHEEP CHEEP	Middle Of The Road
34 wks	THE POWER OF LOVE	Jennifer Rush
34 wks	JE T'AIME . . . MOI NON PLUS	Jane Birkin & Serge Gainsbourg
31 wks	SAILING	Rod Stewart
30 wks	SIDE SADDLE	Russ Conway
30 wks	YOUNG GIRL	Union Gap
30 wks	REET PETITE	Jackie Wilson

Of these records, only *Release Me, Rivers Of Babylon, I Believe, I Pretend, Chirpy Chirpy Cheep Cheep* and *Side Saddle* racked up all their weeks consecutively. *Release Me* still holds the record for the longest continuous chart run of all time.

FEWEST WEEKS ON
CHART BY A NUMBER ONE

At the other end of the record books, these are the records which spent the fewest weeks on the charts, and yet still climbed to the very peak of the lists.

7 wks	CHRISTMAS ALPHABET	Dickie Valentine
7 wks	LET IT BE	Ferry Aid
8 wks	LET'S HAVE ANOTHER PARTY	Winifred Atwell
8 wks	LADY MADONNA	Beatles
8 wks	MARY'S BOY CHILD – OH MY LORD	Boney M
8 wks	MY CAMERA NEVER LIES	Bucks Fizz
8 wks	HAPPY TALK	Captain Sensible
8 wks	START	Jam
8 wks	HEY JOE	Frankie Laine
8 wks	WHAT'S ANOTHER YEAR	Johnny Logan
8 wks	MERRY CHRISTMAS EVERYONE	Shakin' Stevens
9 wks	GIVE A LITTLE LOVE	Bay City Rollers

9 wks	ATOMIC	Blondie
9 wks	CALL ME	Blondie
9 wks	EVERYTHING I OWN	Boy George
9 wks	IS THERE SOMETHING I SHOULD KNOW?	Duran Duran
9 wks	ALWAYS YOURS	Gary Glitter
9 wks	MAKE ME SMILE (COME UP AND SEE ME)	Steve Harley & Cockney Rebel
9 wks	JACK YOUR BODY	Steve 'Silk' Hurley
9 wks	I JUST CAN'T STOP LOVING YOU	Michael Jackson
9 wks	BEAT SURRENDER	Jam

9 wks	A TOWN CALLED MALICE/PRECIOUS	Jam
9 wks	HOUSE OF FUN	Madness
9 wks	I KNEW YOU WERE WAITING (FOR ME)	George Michael & Aretha Franklin
9 wks	OH BOY	Mud
9 wks	A LITTLE PEACE	Nicole
9 wks	LOVE ME FOR A REASON	Osmonds
9 wks	IF	Telly Savalas
9 wks	FOREVER AND EVER	Slik
9 wks	WE ARE THE WORLD	USA For Africa

NUMBER ONE IN TWO DIFFERENT VERSIONS

Eleven songs have been taken to number one in two different versions, as follows:

ANSWER ME
David Whitfield...................6 Nov 53 for 1 wk
11 Dec 53 for 1 wk
Frankie Laine....................13 Nov 53 for 8 wks
(on 11 Dec 53, these two versions were placed top equal)

CHERRY PINK AND APPLE BLOSSOM WHITE
Perez Prado.....................29 Apr 55 for 2 wks
Eddie Calvert....................27 May 55 for 4 wks

EVERYTHING I OWN
Ken Boothe......................26 Oct 74 for 3 wks
Boy George......................14 Mar 87 for 2 wks

I GOT YOU BABE
Sonny and Cher..............26 Aug 65 for 2 wks
UB40 with Chrissie Hynde...........31 Aug 85 for 1 wk

LIVING DOLL
Cliff Richard and the Drifters...........31 Jul 59 for 6 wks
Cliff Richard and the Young Ones....29 Mar 86 for 3 wks

MARY'S BOY CHILD
Harry Belafonte..............22 Nov 57 for 7 wks
Boney M...........................9 Dec 78 for 4 wks

SINGING THE BLUES
Guy Mitchell...........4 Jan 57 for 1 wk, 18 Jan for 1 wk and 1 Feb 57 for 1 wk
Tommy Steele...................11 Jan 57 for 1 wk

SPIRIT IN THE SKY
Norman Greenbaum...........2 May 70 for 2 wks
Dr and the Medics...........7 Jun 86 for 3 wks

THIS OLE HOUSE
Rosemary Clooney...........26 Nov 54 for 1 wk
Shakin' Stevens...............28 Nov 81 for 3 wks

YOU'LL NEVER WALK ALONE
Gerry and the Pacemakers...........31 Oct 63 for 4 wks
The Crowd.......................15 Jun 85 for 2 wks

YOUNG LOVE
Tab Hunter......................22 Feb 57 for 7 wks
Donny Osmond..............25 Aug 73 for 4 wks

*When **Boney M** took Mary's Boy Child to number one, it was the longest gap at the time between a song's two number one versions.*

265

MOST SUCCESSFUL PRODUCERS

Most number one hits produced or co-produced. Double-sided hits count as only one production for each producer.

27	George Martin	4	Stuart Colman	3	Andy Hill
27	Norrie Paramor	4	Don Costa	3	Tony Hiller
17	Mitch Miller	4	Tom Dowd	3	Ray Horricks
15	Steve Sholes	4	Alan Freeman	3	Chris Hughes
11	Chet Atkins	4	Albhy Galuten	3	Quincy Jones
10	Benny Andersson	4	Maurice Gibb	3	Clive Langer
10	Johnny Franz	4	Robin Gibb	3	Mike Leander
10	Bjorn Ulvaeus	4	Graham Gouldman	3	Stewart Levine
9	Mike Chapman	4	Trevor Horn	3	Joe Meek
8	Dick Rowe	4	John Lennon	3	Hugh Mendl
7	Tony Hatch	4	Bunny Lewis	3	Jimmy Miller
7	Norman Newell	4	Tony Macaulay	3	Giorgio Moroder
6	Barry Gibb	4	Paul McCartney	3	Mickie Most
6	Chas Chandler	4	Richard Perry	3	Yoko Ono
6	George Michael	4	Karl Richardson	3	Hugh Padgham
6	Andrew Loog Oldham	4	Mike Stock	3	Marco Pirroni
6	Mike Smith	4	Shel Talmy	3	Nick Rhodes
5	Nicky Chinn	4	Phil Wainman	3	Phil Spector
5	Mike Curb	4	Pete Waterman	3	Eric Stewart
5	Madonna	**3**	Archie Bleyer	3	Rod Stewart
5	Police (Stewart Copeland, Sting, Andy Summers)	3	David Bowie	3	Peter Sullivan
		3	Steve Bray	3	Narada Michael Walden
5	Walter Ridley	3	Larry Butler	3	Alan Winstanley
5	Wesley Rose	3	Denny Cordell	3	Hugo Winterhalter
5	Tony Visconti	3	Phil Coulter		
4	Matt Aitken	3	Milt Gabler		
4	Michael Barclay	3	Lee Gillette		
4	John Burgess	3	Nigel Gray		

Stock (right), **Aitken** (left) and **Waterman** were making faster progression up this list in the late 80s than anyone else on it.

MOST NUMBER ONES WITH DIFFERENT ACTS

This table is designed to distinguish the professional producer from the performer who also produces (e.g. Police or Rod Stewart). Although some of the names in this list have had hits in their own right, like Mitch Miller, Narada Michael Walden and Stock, Aitken, Waterman, the way to be a hit producer is not to worry about being a hit performer as well.

9 Norrie Paramor
8 Johnny Franz
8 Mitch Miller
7 George Martin
6 Norman Newell
6 Mike Smith
5 Tony Hatch
5 Walter Ridley
5 Dick Rowe
4 Matt Aitken
4 Richard Perry

4 Mike Stock
4 Pete Waterman
3 Chet Atkins, Michael Barclay, Archie Bleyer, Mike Chapman, Denny Cordell, Don Costa, Phil Coulter, Mike Curb, Milt Gabler, Albhy Galuten, Barry Gibb, Clive Langer, Bunny Lewis, Tony Macaulay, Paul McCartney, Joe Meek, Hugh Mendl, Giorgio Moroder, Mickie Most, Karl Richardson, Phil Spector, Narada Michael Walden, Phil Wainman, Alan Winstanley

Mike Smith, who produced number one hits for Brian Poole and the Tremeloes, the Tremeloes, Georgie Fame, Love Affair, Marmalade and Christie, has produced the most number one hits without ever producing two for any one act.

Madonna's *first number one, Into The Groove, was released as a 12 inch in the US not as a 7 inch single.*

THE WRITERS

MOST SUCCESSFUL WRITERS

This list shows the writers who have written or co-written the most number one hits. Double-sided number ones count as only one hit for all the writers concerned.

27 John Lennon
26 Paul McCartney
10 Benny Andersson
10 Björn Ulvaeus
7 Burt Bacharach
7 Barry Gibb
7 Robin Gibb
7 Mick Jagger
7 Keith Richard
6 Stig Anderson
6 Hal David
6 Maurice Gibb
6 Oscar Hammerstein II
6 Noddy Holder
6 Jim Lea
6 Tony Macaulay
6 George Michael
6 Richard Rodgers
5 Mike Chapman
5 Nicky Chinn
5 Madonna
5 Roy Orbison
5 Carl Sigman
5 Sting
5 Bruce Welch

4 Marc Bolan
4 David Bowie
4 Phil Coulter
4 Bob Gaudio
4 Wally Gold
4 Bill Martin
4 Bob Merrill
4 Giorgio Moroder
4 Mitch Murray
4 Mort Shuman
4 Rod Stewart
4 George David Weiss
4 Paul Weller

3 Paul Anka, Adam Ant, Jeff Barry, Lionel Bart, Otis Blackwell, Sonny Bono, L Russell Brown, Luigi Creatore, Bob Crewe, Ray Davies, Ray Dorset, Lamont Dozier, Kenny Gamble, David Gates, Bob Geldof, Peter Gill, Gary Glitter, Graham Gouldman, Debbie Harry, Andy Hill, Tony Hiller, Brian Holland, Eddie Holland, Leon Huff, Holly Johnson, Mike Leander, Martin Lee, Jerry Lieber, Jay Livingston, Jerry Lordan, Barry Mason, Mark O'Toole, Hugo Peretti, Marco Pirroni, Doc Pomus, Les Reed, Lionel Richie, Aaron Schroeder, Lee Sheriden, Eddie Snyder, Chris Stein, Mike Stoller, Les Vandyke, Paul Francis Webster, Roy Wood

Stylianos Vlavianos and Robert Constandinos co wrote all four tracks on *The Roussos Phenomenon* EP.

Madonna and Debbie Harry are the only women to have written as many as three number one hits. Jerry Lordan is the only person to have written three instrumental number ones.

The most successful writing partnerships are:

23 Lennon/McCartney
7 Jagger/Richard
6 Andersson/Andersson/Ulvaeus
6 Bacharach/David
6 Barry, Robin and Maurice Gibb
6 Holder/Lea
5 Chapman/Chinn
5 Rodgers/Hammerstein
4 Martin/Coulter
3 Andersson/Ulvaeus
3 Crewe/Gaudio
3 Frankie Goes To Hollywood
3 Gamble/Huff
3 Glitter/Leander
3 Hiller/Lee/Sheriden
3 Holland/Dozier/Holland
3 Lieber/Stoller
3 Pomus/Shuman

MOST VERSATILE WRITERS

The only writers who have co-written number one hits for at least five different acts are:

10 Paul McCartney
9 John Lennon
7 Burt Bacharach
6 Hal David
6 Oscar Hammerstein II
6 Richard Rodgers
5 Tony Macaulay
5 Carl Sigman

Paul McCartney has now performed on 20 number ones as part or all of four acts (Beatles, Wings, Paul McCartney with Stevie Wonder and Paul McCartney). He has written number one hits for all these acts and six other acts who reached the top with his songs. He has produced chart-topping discs by the Beatles and Wings, and another for Mary Hopkin. Nobody else can match his versatility in the making of number one hits.

LONGEST TITLES OF NUMBER ONE HITS

45 letters SAN FRANCISCO (BE SURE TO WEAR SOME FLOWERS IN YOUR HAIR)

37 letters MATCHSTALK MEN AND MATCHSTALK CATS AND DOGS

37 letters WHEN THE GOING GETS TOUGH, THE TOUGH GET GOING

36 letters (THERE'S) ALWAYS SOMETHING THERE TO REMIND ME

36 letters THERE MUST BE AN ANGEL (PLAYING WITH MY HEART)

35 letters WHAT DO YOU WANT TO MAKE THOSE EYES AT ME FOR?

34 letters TIE A YELLOW RIBBON ROUND THE OLD OAK TREE

34 letters WHEN YOU'RE IN LOVE WITH A BEAUTIFUL WOMAN

33 letters I WANNA DANCE WITH SOMEBODY (WHO LOVES ME)

32 letters I LOVE TO LOVE (BUT MY BABY LOVES TO DANCE)

32 letters YOU'RE THE FIRST THE LAST MY EVERYTHING

31 letters ERNIE (THE FASTEST MILKMAN IN THE WEST)

30 letters CHERRY PINK AND APPLE BLOSSOM WHITE

30 letters EVERY LITTLE THING SHE DOES IS MAGIC

30 letters (HOW MUCH) IS THAT DOGGIE IN THE WINDOW

30 letters THEME FROM M*A*S*H* (SUICIDE IS PAINLESS)

SHORTEST TITLES OF NUMBER ONE HITS

2 letters	IF	4 letters	FREE
3 letters	SHE	4 letters	GENO
3 letters	WHY	4 letters	HELP
4 letters	CARS	4 letters	TRUE
4 letters	FAME	4 letters	WHEN
4 letters	FIRE	4 letters	YMCA

CONSECUTIVE NUMBER ONES

Producing three number ones in a row is far more difficult than for a performer to hit the top with three consecutive releases. Apart from the problem of producing a record that will climb to the top, the producer depends on a large slice of luck and must time the release of his productions carefully so that one takes over from another at the top of the charts. The producer's hat-trick has been performed seven times, as follows:

─── Mitch Miller ───

I Believe...Frankie Laine
Look At That Girl...Guy Mitchell
Hey Joe..Frankie Laine
(21 Aug 53 to 5 Nov 53)

─── Mitch Miller ───

A Woman In Love...Frankie Laine
Just Walkin' In The Rain...Johnnie Ray
Singing The Blues..Guy Mitchell
(19 Oct 56 to 10 Jan 57)

─── Norrie Paramor ───

Please Don't Tease...................Cliff Richard & the Shadows
Apache..The Shadows
Tell Laura I Love Her..Ricky Valance
(11 Aug 60 to 19 Oct 60)

─── Norrie Paramor ───

Wayward Wind...Frank Ifield
Summer Holiday.......................Cliff Richard & the Shadows
Foot Tapper..The Shadows
(21 Feb 63 to 10 Apr 63)

─── George Martin ───

How Do You Do It.......................Gerry & the Pacemakers
From Me To You..The Beatles
I Like It.......................................Gerry & the Pacemakers
(11 Apr 63 to 17 Jul 63)

─── George Martin ───

You'll Never Walk Alone...............Gerry & the Pacemakers
She Loves You..The Beatles
I Want To Hold Your Hand.....................................The Beatles
(31 Oct 63 to 15 Jan 64)

─── George Martin ───

Anyone Who Had A Heart..Cilla Black
Little Children.............................Billy J Kramer & the Dakotas
Can't Buy Me Love...The Beatles
(27 Feb 64 to 22 Apr 64)

After Foot Tapper became the third of Norrie Paramor's second hat-trick, *Summer Holiday* climbed back to number one, giving Norrie Paramor a 'fourth' consecutive number one.

Two number ones in a row has now been achieved eleven times, by Dick Rowe (*Broken Wings* and *That Doggie In The Window*), Lee Gillette (*Sixteen Tons* and *Memories Are Made Of This*), Norrie Paramor (*The Next Time/Bachelor Boy* and *Dance On*), George Martin (*Bad To Me* and *She Loves You*), Mike Smith (*The Ballad Of Bonnie and Clyde* and *Everlasting Love*), Nicky Chinn and Mike Chapman (*Tiger Feet* and *Devil Gate Drive*), Alan Parsons (*January* and *Make Me Smile*), Richard Perry (*When I Need You* and *Chanson d'Amour*), John Lennon and Yoko Ono (*Imagine* and *Woman*), Mike Stock, Matt Aitken and Pete Waterman (*Respectable* and *Let It Be*) and Narada Michael Walden (*Nothing's Gonna Stop Us Now* and *I Wanna Dance With Somebody*).

THE RECORD LABELS

MOST NUMBER ONE HITS

50	COLUMBIA	1	AVCO	1	SCOTTI BROTHERS
40	RCA	1	BARCLAY	1	SIREN
38	DECCA	1	BARK	1	SMP
33	CBS	1	BBC	1	SOME BIZZARE
32	EPIC	1	BLUE HORIZON	1	SONET
30	PARLOPHONE	1	BUS STOP	1	SPARTAN
30	PYE/PYE INTERNATIONAL	1	CALIBRE	1	SUN/AID
29	PHILIPS	1	CARRERE	1	SUPREME
20	LONDON/LONDON AMERICAN	1	CHESS	1	TECHNIQUE
18	POLYDOR	1	DERAM	1	TK
16	EMI	1	DJ INTERNATIONAL	1	T REX
15	HMV	1	4AD	1	TROJAN
13	BELL	1	GO! DISCS	1	20TH CENTURY
12	CAPITOL	1	GRUNT	1	U.K.
11	MGM	1	GTO	1	UNI
11	WARNER BROTHERS	1	GULL	1	VERTIGO
10	TAMLA MOTOWN	1	HOLLYWOOD		

TOTAL LABELS: 110

9	A&M	1	ICE
9	MERCURY	1	INVICTUS
8	ATLANTIC/ATLANTIC HANSA	1	IRS
8	CHRYSALIS	1	ISLAND
8	VIRGIN	1	JANUS
6	RAK	1	JAY BOY
5	APPLE	1	JET
5	FONTANA	1	LIBERTY
5	RSO	1	LIGHTNING
5	SIRE	1	MAGNET
4	BRUNSWICK	1	MFP
4	REPRISE	1	PARAMOUNT
4	UNITED ARTISTS	1	PHILADELPHIA INTERNATIONAL
3	HARVEST	1	POWER EXCHANGE
3	MAM	1	PRESIDENT
3	MCA	1	PROBE
3	STIFF	1	PYRAMID
3	TOP RANK	1	REAL
3	TRACK	1	REFORMATION
3	VOGUE CORAL	1	REVUE
3	WEA/GEFFEN	1	REX
3	ZTT	1	ROCKET
2	ARISTA		
2	BEGGARS BANQUET		
2	DAWN		
2	DEP INTERNATIONAL		
2	ENSIGN		
2	FLY		
2	IMMEDIATE		
2	JIVE		
2	MAJOR MINOR		
2	PRIVATE STOCK		
2	REGAL ZONOPHONE		
2	RIVA		
2	STATESIDE		
2	TWO TONE		
1	ABC		
1	ARIOLA/HANSA		

*Multiple number ones for **Parlophone** and **Columbia** were achieved by **Cilla Black** and **Cliff Richard.***

MOST WEEKS AT NUMBER ONE

	weeks		weeks
COLUMBIA	165	EPIC	86
RCA	151	PYE/PYE INTERNATIONAL	77
PHILIPS	109	LONDON	65
DECCA	107	EMI	52
PARLOPHONE	99	POLYDOR	50
CBS	97		

CONSECUTIVE LABEL CATALOGUE NUMBERS AT NUMBER ONE

There have been seven cases of consecutive releases by record companies both hitting the very top of the charts, as follows:

Philips PB 616	LAY DOWN YOUR ARMS	Anne Shelton
Philips PB 617	A WOMAN IN LOVE	Frankie Laine
Philips PB 685	ROCK-A-BILLY	Guy Mitchell
Philips PB 686	YES TONIGHT JOSEPHINE	Johnnie Ray
MGM 974	WHOLE LOTTA WOMAN	Marvin Rainwater
MGM 975	WHO'S SORRY NOW	Connie Francis
RCA 1226	WOODEN HEART	Elvis Presley
RCA 1227	SURRENDER	Elvis Presley
CBS 3124	BALLAD OF BONNIE AND CLYDE	Georgie Fame
CBS 3125	EVERLASTING LOVE	Love Affair
Polydor 2058 421	YOU WON'T FIND ANOTHER FOOL LIKE ME	New Seekers
Polydor 2058 422	MERRY XMAS EVERYBODY	Slade
RAK 166	TIGER FEET	Mud
RAK 167	DEVIL GATE DRIVE	Suzi Quatro

Only three acts have had number one hits on three different labels: T Rex – on Fly, T Rex and EMI; Rod Stewart – on Mercury, Warner Brothers and Riva; Bee Gees – on Polydor, RSO and Warner Brothers.

Paul McCartney has hit the top with the Beatles on Parlophone and Apple, and on Capitol with Wings. All catalogue numbers were, however, in the same sequence (e.g. Parlophone R 5675, Apple R 5722 and Capitol R 6018).

*The **New Seekers'** first three American hits were all covers of Melanie songs.*

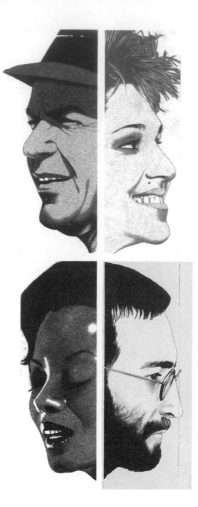

The cover illustrations of Frank Sinatra,
Madonna, Diana Ross and John Lennon are
by Ashley Lloyd.
Cover design: David Roberts